OURSELVES
AMONG OTHERS

*Readings from
Home and Abroad*

OURSELVES AMONG OTHERS

Readings from
Home and Abroad

Fourth Edition

CAROL J. VERBURG

Bedford/St. Martin's   Boston ◆ New York

For Bedford/St. Martin's

Developmental Editor: John E. Sullivan III
Production Editor: Sherri Frank
Production Supervisor: Catherine Hetmansky
Marketing Manager: Karen Melton
Editorial Assistant: Katherine Gilbert
Production Assistant: Helaine Denenberg
Copyeditor: Cynthia Hastings
Text Design: Anna George
Cover Design: Hannus Design Associates
Cover Art: Bill Jacklin, *The Rink,* Washington National Airport Terminal
    Commission (triptych), 1996
Composition: Pine Tree Composition, Inc.
Printing and Binding: Haddon Craftsmen, Inc.

President: Charles H. Christensen
Editorial Director: Joan E. Feinberg
Director of Editing, Design, and Production: Marcia Cohen
Managing Editor: Elizabeth M. Schaaf

Library of Congress Catalog Card Number: 99–65250

Manufactured in the United States of America.

4   3   2   1   0   9
f   e   d   c   b   a

For information, write: Bedford/St. Martin's, 75 Arlington Street, Boston, MA
02116 (617-399-4000)

ISBN: 0–312–20764–6

Acknowledgments

Chinua Achebe, "The Writer and His Community." Copyright © 1984 by Chinua Achebe. From University of California at Los Angeles Regents' Lecture, 1984.

Isabel Allende, "Clarisa," from *The Stories of Eva Luna* by Isabel Allende, translated from Spanish by Margaret Sayers Peden. Copyright © 1989 by Isabel Allende. English translation copyright © 1989 by Isabel Allende. English translation copyright by Macmillan Publishing Company. Reprinted by permission of Scribner, a division of Simon & Schuster, Inc. and Key Porter Books.

Maya Angelou, "Mary," from *I Know Why the Caged Bird Sings* by Maya Angelou. Copyright © 1969 and renewed 1997 by Maya Angelou. Reprinted by permission of Random House, Inc.

PREFACE FOR INSTRUCTORS

Embrace it or deplore it, everybody has noticed it: the cultural shift we might call, tautologically, the globalization of the world. No man is an island — so John Donne observed over three hundred fifty years ago. Today, in the age of laptop computers and cell phones, not even an island is an island.

When Bedford/St. Martin's and I started work on *Ourselves Among Others* in the mid-1980s, we launched the first global reader for college composition courses. Back then, just finding English translations of outstanding writing from other parts of the world was a challenge. The next step was persuading doubtful instructors that their students could appreciate — even enjoy! — an essay from Colombia, France, or Nigeria. Teachers who already believed that world-class writers such as Gabriel García Márquez, Simone de Beauvoir, and Chinua Achebe belong in the composition classroom still faced the uphill battle of selling the idea to their classes and their departments.

The results have been more gratifying than we expected. Teachers wrote to us of lively class discussions, of students reading unassigned selections and continuing through the book even after the course ended. Meanwhile, those exotic names in the table of contents grew more and more familiar. Some of them made the best-seller lists; some made the news. Some won Nobel Prizes. Some saw their books turned into movies. Some were imprisoned in their homelands; some were freed. Some of them died. Many of them appeared on Web pages. Most of them kept on writing.

Should non-U.S. authors be read in composition courses? As we enter the twenty-first century, the very question seems bizarre. A typical American college student's network of family and friends stretches thousands of miles. On the one hand, almost every campus houses nonnative English speakers; on the other, every computer is a virtual multicultural neighborhood. Students can send a message to the far side of the world as easily as they can phone home. They can visit thousands of libraries and databases without leaving their chairs. Even the most parochial are bound either to travel or to meet travelers, and can profit from reading about the diverse pieces that make up the global mosaic.

After all, isn't the United States the home base of the melting pot? — or, as Ishmael Reed calls it, the cultural bouillabaisse?

Information about our global village comes fast and cheap; the challenge is reacting to it. Which events are important? Which speakers are trustworthy? How can students learn to judge their motives, their biases, and the accuracy of their reports? What critical and rhetorical skills will help them first to interpret what they read and then to respond appropriately as citizens and neighbors?

These questions led us to rework *Ourselves Among Others* to meet the demands of our changing world. As you will see, we have added an extensive introduction on active reading and critical thinking to help students comprehend and react to what they read. We also have responded to requests from users of previous editions for more selections from the United States. With a solid base of familiar writers and viewpoints, students and instructors suggested they could better appreciate the unfamiliar ones.

The result is the book in your hands. *Ourselves Among Others: Readings from Home and Abroad* comprises fifty essays and ten stories from inside and outside the United States. These selections are grouped in six thematic parts. The themes are ones that students have found particularly intriguing and teachers have found particularly effective. We begin with the conundrum of "Identifying Ourselves" and progress outward to "Families," "Turning Points," "Opposite Sexes," "Myth and Magic," and "People and Power." Introducing each part are a dozen or so "Observations" — brief comments on the theme from contrasting cultural, political, and social perspectives.

For example, Part One, "Identifying Ourselves," opens with epigraphs on the trick of knowing who you are by Hans Magnus Enzensberger, Bharati Mukherjee, Henry Louis Gates Jr., Adrienne Rich, and others. Readers then are invited to examine their own reflections in mirrors held up by Southern philosopher Walker Percy ("A Short Quiz"), New York journalist Danzy Senna ("The Mulatto Millennium"), and Chinese-American novelist Amy Tan ("Two Kinds"). Susan Orlean's "Quinceañera" looks at self-definition among young Mexican-American women and their families; the Mexican poet Octavio Paz goes behind the scenes with "The Art of the Fiesta." How we express our physical selves is the concern of Australian writer Germaine Greer in "One Man's Mutilation Is Another Man's Beautification." Paul Harrison tracks American and European influence on identity around the globe in "The Westernization of the World." Three close-up views of Western culture's impact are supplied by Es'kia Mphahlele

("African Literature: What Tradition?"); Margaret Atwood ("A View from Canada"); and Salman Rushdie ("Imaginary Homelands").

To introduce each essay or story, biographical and geographical headnotes supply information about the author's background. Questions after each selection help students to think critically about what they have read: "Explorations" probe the author's ideas and rhetorical tactics; "Connections" link one piece with others; "Elaborations" suggest essay topics for students' responses to their reading. A world map at the back of the book locates all the countries treated in the text. A rhetorical index helps to identify writing strategies. A comprehensive instructor's manual provides further background on authors and cultures, guidance for student discussions, a list of writing assignments, and information on multimedia resources, including film, video, and audiocassettes as well as Internet sites and addresses.

The book's greatest asset, of course, is the writing it comprises. The essays, excerpts, and stories included here blend literary excellence with compelling content. Nobel laureates are represented along with a spectrum of writers known and unknown; the variety of countries included shows the diversity of cultural contexts from which good writing emerges. Unlike traditional literary explorations of "foreign lands," *Ourselves Among Others* emphasizes insider accounts. We hear about life in Africa's Kalahari Desert, a Chinese city, or a Turkish village from the women and men who live there. Within the United States, too, people write about what matters to them: Joseph Bruchac involves us in Native American traditions; Eudora Welty guides us back through time in her Mississippi homeland; Toni Morrison dramatizes our national legacy of racial tension.

Acknowledgments

A book this large and complex is built on many people's contributions. I'm grateful to all those who answered questionnaires and reviewed plans to help shape *Ourselves Among Others:* Cathryn Amdahl, Harrisburg Area Community College; Carl J. Arseneault, University of Tennessee; Marlene Baldwin Davis, College of William and Mary; Patrick Baliani, University of Arizona; Natalie S. Daley, Linn-Benton Community College; Gavin Harper, Weber State University; Jeff Henderson, Kalamazoo Valley Community College; Elizabeth Meehan, San Diego City College; Mary O'Connor, South Dakota State University; Brit Osgood, Saddleback College/Fullerton College; W. Prothero,

Weber State University; Jennifer Richardson, Weber State University; Kathleen Ryan, UNC Greensboro; Anthony Samuel, University of Idaho; Cheryl Slobod, California State University — Northridge; Marianne Trale, F.A.S. University of Pittsburgh; and Peter Zollo, Merrimack College, English Department.

Essential contributions to *Ourselves Among Others* also came from the staff at Bedford/St. Martin's. President Chuck Christensen has been a source of ideas for this as for every edition; editorial director Joan Feinberg and editor in chief Karen Henry supplied advice and support throughout. Editor John Sullivan shaped the Introduction and kept the book on course; editorial assistant Katherine Gilbert tracked down elusive selections and authors (with the help of auxiliary sleuths Lisa Whipple and Jessica Foz). Katie also worked with Andrea Kaston, an experienced teacher of composition, on the revised instructor's manual, and with permissions editors Sandy Schechter and Eva Pettersson. Sherri Frank once again gracefully shepherded the book through production.

Thanks most of all to the worldwide writers represented in *Ourselves Among Others*, many of whom make their creative contributions under more difficult conditions than most of us can imagine.

CONTENTS

"We are in the midst of a cultural upheaval in which the body, which for aeons was a holy thing, its excretions and its orifices feared and revered, is becoming . . . a toy, an asset, a commodity, an instrumentality for human will."

"The Third World's obsession with the Western way of life has perverted development and is rapidly destroying good and bad in traditional cultures, flinging the baby out with the bathwater."

"I was brought up on European history and literature and religion and made to identify with European heroes while African heroes were being discredited . . . and African gods were being smoked out."

"Americans and Canadians are not the same; they are the products of two very different histories, two very different situations. Put simply, south of you you have Mexico and south of us we have you."

"The Indian writer, looking back at India, does so through guilt-tinted spectacles. . . . Our identity is at once plural and partial. Sometimes we feel that we straddle two cultures; at other times, that we fall between two stools."

Observations

"When we make love in the darkness of anticipation we are inviting accident and order, the careful lining up of genes. Unlocking the components of another person, we are safecrackers — setting the combinations, unconsciously twirling dials."

"All too often the adult quest for freedom, independence, and choice in family relationships conflicts with a child's developmental needs for stability, constancy, harmony, and permanence in family life."

"Once upon a time I held these beliefs about divorce: that everyone who does it could have chosen not to do it. That it's a lazy way out of marital problems. That it selfishly puts personal happiness ahead of family integrity. Now I tremble for my ignorance."

"The man behind the bar says to Dad, I think now, mister, you've had enough. We're sorry for your troubles but you have to take that child home to his mother that must be heartbroken by the fire. Dad says, One, one more pint, just one, eh?"

"Each one of us, as we grow up, has our own small area of responsibility. This comes from the promises made for the child when he is born, and from the continuity of our customs. . . . From the very first day, the baby belongs to the community."

"Suddenly this sort of light, like a ball of fire, began to glow in the distance. Even while it was still far we kept hearing voices, as if a lot of people around us were grumbling. . . . 'You stubborn, stiff-necked children, we've warned you and warned you but you just won't listen. . . .'"

"[Sally] Hemings and the other Africans held as slaves built Monticello. They made the bricks, planed the lumber, suckled and fed the children. And the white descendants of Jefferson continue to enjoy the wealth and privilege this free labor amassed."

"I was made to understand at a very young age that somewhere, or rather everywhere, an immense silent contest was being fought, that our side was locked in a struggle with another side, and that what was at stake was the very shape of the future."

"The Japanese carried his house around in his mouth and produced it in everyday conversation, using the word *uchi* to mean 'I,' the representative of my house in the world outside."

Observations

"A culture does not need a minister of propaganda issuing proclamations to silence criticism. There are other ways to achieve stupidity, and it appears that, as in so many other things, there is a distinctly American way."

"Everybody said that [the TV series] *Yearning* had brought out the best in them and made them understand better what it meant to be Chinese and how deeply rooted they all were in the Chinese values of family and human relations — and how all this made them yearn for *Yearning* every night."

"People started trickling back almost as soon as they were evacuated" after the nuclear disaster at Chernobyl. "Most of them will tell you they lead futureless lives; tomorrow — the day after radiation — is thousands of years away, which, in human terms, is never."

"Generations before the birth of Hitler, mass murderers already knew that you must first corrupt the words before you can corrupt those who use these words, so that they may be capable of murder in the guise of purification, cleaning, and healing."

"The thinking was that if you left Indian children on reservations, they'd remain 'savages,' so representatives of the Bureau of Indian Affairs virtually kidnapped children from tribes all over the country and bussed them to military-style boarding schools to 'civilize' them."

"Something in the American psyche loves new frontiers. We hanker after wide-open spaces; we like to explore. . . . Lost in the furor over porn on the Net is the exhilarating sense of freedom that this new frontier once promised — and still does in some quarters."

"The causes of poverty within the black community are both structural and behavioral. . . . A household in which its occupants cannot sustain themselves economically cannot possibly harbor hope or optimism, or stimulate eager participation in the full prerogatives of citizenship."

"Why is it that in this courtroom I face a white magistrate, am confronted
by a white prosecutor, and escorted into the dock by a white orderly? . . .
Why is it that no African in this history of this country has ever had the
honor of being tried by his own kith and kin, by his own flesh and
blood?"

"My cellmate was a beautiful young woman, twenty-three-years-old, a
prostitute who'd never been arrested before. She was nervous, but she
had been given the name of an important long-termer. She explained in
a businesslike way that she was beautiful, and would need protection."

"Never, never plead the balance of your mind is disturbed in court: Get a
prison sentence and relax, and wait for time to pass and one day you'll be
free. Once you're in a secure hospital, you may never get out at all."

INTRODUCTION FOR STUDENTS

Crossing Cultures, Reading Actively, and Thinking Critically

What can you gain from using this book?

If you read these selections actively and critically, you will reap two benefits: knowledge of a variety of people and situations you are likely to encounter in and out of college, and the ability to communicate effectively.

Both of these accomplishments hinge on critical thinking. That is, as a reader you play an active role. You attend carefully to what you read, you evaluate it, and you respond to it. You do not take someone else's printed words at face value. Rather, you examine the assumptions and biases behind those statements, the evidence on which assertions are based, the process by which conclusions are drawn, and the rhetorical and stylistic techniques used to make a case.

Becoming an Active Reader and Critical Thinker

In a moment we will look more closely at tactics you can use to become a more active reader and critical thinker. First, two questions: Why should you bother to develop these habits? And, how can *Ourselves Among Others* help you?

Many high schools do not prepare students fully for the challenges they will face in college. Whatever your academic background, age, or educational goals, from now on your success is your responsibility. Although some of your assigned readings will come from textbooks, others will come from primary or secondary sources (journal articles, for example), written by experts in a field for an audience with some background in that field. Most of your reading in college probably will be denser and more demanding than the typical high-school assignment.

In college, if you memorize and repeat course material without really grasping it, you are likely to flounder. Nor can you write an acceptable paper by rephrasing and rearranging information you have read. The facts you glean from other texts are merely a foundation on which to build your own position. The purpose of college, after all, is to introduce you to new ideas and to prepare you to thrive in the working world. The most rewarding jobs in that world require complex skills:

You must be able to identify problems, analyze them accurately, and propose original solutions. That is, you must draw on a broad range of existing knowledge and then interpret it.

To master the challenging texts you will confront in college, you need to become an active reader. What does this mean?

Reading for pleasure often amounts to reading for plot — turning pages to see what happens next, skipping over any new word or passage you don't understand. Like watching TV, this kind of reading is passive, focused on entertainment. It's a perfectly good way to enjoy a mystery novel, for instance, or a magazine article. Most college-level texts, however, call for a different approach: active, reflective, even aggressive reading. Instead of letting the words wash over you, as if you were listening to the radio, your mind is vigorously involved. If something puzzles you, you stop and figure it out — or look it up. You talk back to the writer: respond to ideas, agree or disagree with conclusions.

Once you develop the habit of active reading, you are on your way to becoming a critical thinker. Critical thinking doesn't mean criticizing — finding fault. Rather, it means evaluating what's on the page, weighing it against your own knowledge. Why does the author hold this belief? Is this statement reliable? What unspoken assumptions are behind it? What evidence supports it? By reading critically, you get the most out of the text. You also strengthen the analytical, judgmental, and problem-solving skills that will help you succeed in college and afterward.

Ourselves Among Others has several features designed to hone your ability as an active reader and a critical thinker. First, its contents come from a great range of people and places. The book is organized in six parts, each centered on a theme that has intrigued writers and readers for millennia. From the highly personal topic "Identifying Ourselves," we move outward to "Families," "Turning Points," and "Opposite Sexes," and then on to the more abstract topics of "Myth and Magic," and finally "People and Power." Each part opens with a dozen or so Observations — brief comments on the theme by writers from around the world. Next come essays, excerpts, and stories from the United States and elsewhere.

Some of the writers represented here you will have read before, some you may have heard of, and some probably are strangers to you. Although all of them live on the same planet in the same century, the contrast in their ethnic, religious, political, and personal orientations is striking. Similarly, their viewpoints and beliefs are bound to differ, from each other's and also from yours. To grapple with an unfamiliar piece of writing — to get the most out of a difficult piece — you need to be an active reader and a critical thinker.

Reading and Writing as Dialogue

Think of your interaction with the author as a conversation. Experienced readers ask questions of the author as they read: "What is the point of this paragraph?" "What does this part have to do with what came before?" "What does this word mean?" "Aren't you jumping to conclusions here?" A good writer will provide answers to questions like these, anticipating the reader's part in the conversation. If you own your copy of the book, you can write your questions and comments in the margins. You also can highlight important or controversial points within the text. If you are reading a borrowed book, make your notes on a separate sheet of paper, on post-it notes that you can remove, or in your reading journal.

A good first step when you approach a reading assignment is to skim through it. Pay special attention to its road signs: the title, which may announce your destination; the opening and closing paragraphs, which often contain the author's thesis statements or goals; and any headings, like signposts, in between. Take a look at the biographical and geographical headnotes about the author for clues to his or her biases. Skimming the piece also will give you an idea how long and difficult it is, and how much time you should allot for a first and second reading.

Active Reading: Marking the Text

Experienced readers and writers often read with a pencil in hand, marking the text as they go. Why should you bother to do this? Isn't it enough that you've done your assigned reading? Well, no. Your main reasons for reading are to understand and to learn. The author's main reason for writing, on the other hand, may be to inform, to persuade, or even to mislead. He or she probably spent many hours building a tight, convincing argument. Just as you can't get to know a person in one meeting, you can't appreciate a challenging text in one reading.

Besides, if you mark the text as you read, you create a way to re-enter it later. Without such cues, you may forget what passages you thought were most important, what flaws you spotted in the author's arguments, and what words or ideas you didn't understand. Your notes can be especially valuable when you start to discuss the piece in class several days after reading, or when you have to write about it weeks later. Having marked the text saves you from doing the same work twice. As you sit down to write a paper, you can go straight to the key statements, examples, and quotations you've already identifited. You also can recognize quickly what you weren't sure about, which passages need extra attention. Marking the text makes a written record of the conversation you have with a writer.

When you are ready to read a piece in earnest, bring your tools: a pencil or pen, post-its, a highlighter, your reading journal. There are several ways to mark a text: You can highlight passages, write notes in the margins (called glosses), or underline key words and phrases. Experiment with different methods to see which works best for you. You may want to switch or combine methods depending on what kind of text you are reading and what your goals are.

Highlighting is helpful if there are facts or distinctive observations in the text that you want to be able to find again. Some readers highlight using one color for their initial reading and a new color for their second reading. A highlighter is a useful tool, but it doesn't allow you to respond — by accepting, questioning, or disagreeing — to what a writer says. For that you need to take pen in hand and mark your reactions on the page, on post-its, or in your journal.

Glossing or annotating the text is one of the most important academic skills you can learn. The word *gloss* is related to the more common word *glossary* — a list of specialized or unfamiliar words and their definitions. When you gloss the text you write a note to yourself explaining a key term or phrase or summarizing an important passage: You make an unfamiliar word or phrase familiar. Glossing is a flexible tactic. You can paraphrase what the author has written (to flag a concept or shorten a complicated sentence); you can number the stages of a writer's argument and examples (be on the alert for words like *first, next,* and *finally*); or you can copy a term into the margin (when you need to check it in the dictionary). You also can underline or circle important words within the text. As you progress from paragraph to paragraph, jot down points you agree or disagree with, examples the author treats as especially important, words or ideas you don't understand. Your notes will serve as a road map when you return to the text, helping you to identify the shape of the writer's story or argument, recalling your reactions along the way, and noting your reasons for agreeing or disagreeing.

A word to the wise: Don't try to mark every point that catches your attention. Your purpose in active reading is to select the key passages — usually, the most significant or original ideas — and get into a conversation with the author. Think twice about what is really important in a piece of writing before you wield your pen.

Similarly, you need not grab a dictionary as soon as you spot an unfamiliar word. Some texts contain so many that you won't have time to look up all of them. Often the structure of the piece or the thrust of the argument supplies clues. Try to figure out what the word means by its context — what the author says in the sentences surrounding it. For more clues, take it apart; see if you recognize its roots and any prefix or suffix. When in doubt, though, don't just guess. There's no substitute for a good dictionary.

An Example of Active Reading

Here are the notes one reader made on Deborah Tannen's "How Male and Female Students Use Language Differently" (p. 356), applying these principles of active reading and critical thinking.

A colleague who read my book commented that he had always taken for granted that the best *another teacher's view* way to deal with students' comments is to challenge them; this, he felt it was self-evident, sharpens their minds and helps them develop debating skills. But he had noticed that women *T's colleague changes his style* were relatively silent in his classes, so he decided to try beginning discussion with relatively open- *like what?* ended questions and letting comments go unchallenged. He found, to his amazement and satisfaction, that more women began to speak up.

Though some of the women in his class clearly liked this better, perhaps some of the men liked it *qualifiers* *how students responded* less. One young man in my class wrote in a questionnaire about a history professor who gave students questions to think about and called on *example from student* people to answer them: "He would then play

devil's advocate . . . i.e., he debated us. . . .
That class *really* sharpened me intellectually. . . .
We as students do need to know how to defend
ourselves." This young man valued the experience of being attacked and challenged publicly.   *Yuck!*
Many, (if not) most, women (would) shrink from   *more qualifiers*
such "challenge," experiencing it as public hu-
miliation.

Contrasting perceptions of failure

A professor at Hamilton College told me of a
young man who was upset because he felt his   *another example from a student*
class presentation had been a failure. The profes-
sor was puzzled because he had observed that
class members had listened attentively and
agreed with the student's observations. It turned
out that it was this very agreement that the stu-
dent interpreted as failure: Since no one had en-   *student sees engagement same as argument*
gaged his ideas by arguing with him, he felt they
had found them unworthy of attention.

Notice that in the left margin, the reader has glossed each paragraph
by jotting down a short note that sums up its topic. The right margin
contains comments on key words and phrases underlined and circled in
the text. In the first paragraph, for instance, the reader wonders what
kind of question would be "open-ended," and asks what kind of example Tannen might have used here. When this reader returns to Tannen's essay he will find that he has opened up a number of points he
could pursue in class discussion or in a paper.

Journal Keeping and the Double-Entry Notebook

Even if you aren't required to keep a reading journal, you may find it
a helpful way of making the transition from reading pieces in *Ourselves
Among Others* to writing your own essays. In your journal you can both
collect observations and reflect on them. If you wish, your journal can
be the central file where you keep all your responses to what you read.

Here you can jot down your notes or paste your post-its; you can write your overall or paragraph-by-paragraph summaries of a selection; you can paraphrase ideas that strike you and record where they appeared; and you can keep a log of terms or concepts you don't understand. By gathering all this material in one place, you will find that what you learn in one reading often serves as a frame for interpreting a later one. Finally, a journal can help you identify how much you already know about a subject — sometimes, more than you thought!

There is a particular kind of journal that many writers find useful for recording and considering their observations. Called a "dialectical" or "double-entry" notebook, this journal-keeping system was introduced by an English professor named Ann Berthoff over two decades ago. It is an excellent way to observe your observations and think about your thinking. Here's how it works: Divide a page into two columns by drawing a vertical line down the center. In one column, record important words from your reading and your observations, questions, comments, reactions, glosses, and summaries. In the other column, across from your original entries, record your reflections on what you've written. Writing down your questions helps you to identify what, precisely, you do and don't understand. Using two parallel columns — thinking about your thinking — also can help you spot connections between points that didn't appear to be related. A double-entry notebook allows you to play out on paper the conversation good readers hold in their heads — one side of the page speaks back to the other.

Here is a brief sample from our reader's double-entry notebook. In it he continues thinking about his reading of Deborah Tannen's "How Male and Female Students Use Language Differently."

Tannen 10/6 *"The best way to deal with* *students' comments is to* *challenge them"*	*This guy sounds like Prof. Nicols —* *what a jerk! Teachers can ask* *questions that make students* *think without intimidating them.* *You can't learn if you're* *intimidated.*
"some" women . . . "perhaps" *some . . . men*	*Why qualify these points? Makes* *her sound unsure. Is her class* *different from colleague's? Does* *she know what the other* *students in either class thought?*

(Continued)

A student valued "the experience of being attacked and challenged publicly."	Who would ever think like this? I'd hate to have him for a teacher. Some students do like to argue, though. What benefits are there to public challenge?
Student equates argument with engagement	Big simplification. Definitely could lead to disappointment when others agreed with him. No reward in being right!

From Reading to Writing

Everything you've written down can help you when it comes to producing an essay of your own. By thinking out loud on paper, you've identified the elements of the selection you are reading, and probably some key points for the essay you plan to write. In a sense, your notes are a very rough draft of your essay — bits and pieces you can use to build a finished paper.

Ourselves Among Others also contains some tools to ease your transition from reading to writing. To help sharpen your critical thinking skills, several types of questions encourage you to probe and evaluate what you have read. "Explorations," after the "Observations" that open each part and after each main selection, ask you to scrutinize the writer's arguments, biases, supporting evidence, stylistic techniques, and other tools and tactics. "Connections" relate one selection to others with similar or contrasting elements. For example, how does the Canadian writer Margaret Atwood's concept of "American" compare with the African American writer Ishmael Reed's, or the Colombian writer Gabriel García Márquez's? Looking at the ways different people interpret the same word can increase your appreciation of its meaning not only to them but to you. Even if your instructor does not assign these questions, you may find it helpful to write a response to them in your double-entry notebook. Finally, "Elaborations" take your reactions to your reading a step further by suggesting topics you can write about. These topics, like the questions, also can serve as a springboard for class discussion.

When you are ready to start work on your own essay, you can utilize the material you have read in several ways. First, the facts and interpretations provided by authors in *Ourselves Among Others* can become source material for you. For instance, after reading Kazuo Ishiguro's "A Family Supper," you might want to write an essay on how the family is regarded differently in Japan and the United states. This is where your journal comes in handy. Your notes will steer you to useful information in that selection and elswhere, and also will supply citations for the credit you must give to any author whose ideas or words you use.

Second, you can do your own research to write a response to one (or more) of the selections in this book. Perhaps you think Neil Postman's "Future Shlock" overestimates the problems of the Information Age. With your notes in hand, you can head for the library and find other experts to help you refute his position.

Third, if you are uncertain how to construct your essay, you may want to use a selection in *Ourselves Among Others* as a model. At the back of the book is a rhetorical index that classifies these essays according to their strategy — comparison-contrast, argument, description, and so forth. Looking closely at another writer's methods can help you to refine your own.

The prospect of pushing your mind in all these ways may seem daunting at first — like learning a new language or navigating in a strange city. The rewards are worth the work. Once you master the foreign vocabulary and constructions for Spanish or Japanese, you can converse with a whole new assortment of people. Once you know your way around the Paris Métro or the streets of Johannesburg, you can find restaurants, museums, shops, and parks. Critical thinking, too, is a mental challenge that takes effort at the beginning but opens up a world of new experiences and insights once you develop the habit.

OURSELVES
AMONG OTHERS

Readings from
Home and Abroad

PART ONE

IDENTIFYING
OURSELVES

OBSERVATIONS

Hans Magnus Enzensberger, Bharati Mukherjee,
Henry Louis Gates Jr., Adrienne Rich, Molly Ivins,
Jill Ker Conway, Carlos Fuentes, Richard Rayner,
Ishmael Reed, Anita Desai, Danny Romero, Elaine H. Kim

▼ ▼ ▼

Walker Percy, *A Short Quiz* (UNITED STATES)

Danzy Senna, *The Mulatto Millennium* (UNITED STATES)

Amy Tan, *Two Kinds* (UNITED STATES/CHINA)

Susan Orlean, *Quinceañera* (UNITED STATES/MEXICO)

Octavio Paz, *The Art of the Fiesta* (MEXICO)

Germaine Greer, *One Man's Mutilation Is Another Man's
Beautification* (AUSTRALIA/GREAT BRITAIN)

Paul Harrison, *The Westernization of the World*
(GREAT BRITAIN/WORLD)

Es'kia Mphahlele, *African Literature: What Tradition?*
(SOUTH AFRICA)

Margaret Atwood, *A View from Canada* (CANADA)

Salman Rushdie, *Imaginary Homelands* (INDIA/GREAT BRITAIN)

OBSERVATIONS

In Russian, a German is called *nemets*; this word is derived from *nemoi* which means "dumb" — that is, someone who cannot speak. The Greek word *barbaros* for non-Greeks initially had the meaning "stammering" or "babbling" and often implies "uneducated," "vulgar," "cowardly," "cruel," "uncultured," "violent," "avaricious," and "treacherous."

The Hottentots [of South Africa], a word that in Afrikaans means "stutterer," call themselves *k'oi-n*, "the human beings."

For the Ainu [minority in Japan] too, the group name is identical to the word for human being, whereas the Japanese call them *emishi*, "barbarians."

The same is true of the Kamchatkans [of northeastern Russia], who describe themselves as *itelmen*, "human beings," and [are] outdone only by the Chukchki, who maintain that they are *luorovetlan*, that is, "the true human beings."

Claude Lévi-Strauss has described this universally diffused self-awareness as follows:

> It is well known that the concept "mankind," which includes all life-patterns of the species man, without distinction of race or civilizations, arose very late and is not widespread. . . . Mankind stops at the boundaries of the tribe, the linguistic group, sometimes even of the village, so that a large number of so-called primitive people give themselves a name which means "men" (or sometimes "the good," "the excellent," or "the perfect"), which simultaneously indicates that the other tribes, groups, or villages have no share in the good qualities — or even in the nature — of man but, at most, consist of "the bad," "the evil," "ground apes," or "lice eggs." Sometimes the strangers are even denied this last foothold in reality, and are regarded as "phantoms" or "apparitions."
>
> – HANS MAGNUS ENZENSBERGER
> *Civil Wars: from L.A. to Bosnia*, 1992

▼ ▼ ▼

When I was growing up in Calcutta in the fifties, I heard no talk of "identity crisis" — communal or individual. The concept itself — of a person not knowing who she or he was — was unimaginable in a hierarchical, classification-obsessed society. One's identity was absolutely fixed, derived from religion, caste, patrimony, and mother tongue. A Hindu Indian's last name was designed to announce his or her forefathers' caste and place of origin. A Mukherjee could only be a Brahman from Bengal. Indian tradition forbade intercaste, interlanguage, interethnic marriages. Bengali tradition discouraged even emigration; to remove oneself from Bengal was to "pollute" true culture.

Until the age of eight, I lived in a house crowded with forty or fifty relatives. We lived together because we were "family," bonded by kinship, though kinship was interpreted in flexible enough terms to include, when necessary, men, women, and children who came from the same *desh* — which is the Bengali word for "homeland" — as had my father and grandfather. I was who I was because I was Dr. Sudhir Lal Mukherjee's daughter, because I was a Hindu Brahman, because I was Bengali speaking, and because my *desh* was an East Bengal village called Faridpur. I was encouraged to think of myself as indistinguishable from my dozen girl cousins. Identity was viscerally connected with ancestral soil and family origins. I was first a Mukherjee, then a Bengali Brahman, and only then an Indian.

> — BHARATI MUKHERJEE
> "Beyond Multiculturalism: Surviving the Nineties"
> *MultiAmerica: Essays on Cultural Wars*
> *and Cultural Peace,* 1997

▼ ▼ ▼

My grandfather was colored, my father is Negro, and I am black — so I wrote in my college application essay. Those appellations, of course, did not contain who I was, or even serve to limit who I thought I could be. Yet each successive generation of black folks living in this country has shared certain peculiar psychic and social concerns that come as regularly as dusk in a society where being black was from the start a restrictive covenant that one could run from or live with, but that one could not escape.

> — HENRY LOUIS GATES JR.
> *The Future of the Race* (with Cornel West), 1996

▼ ▼ ▼

My mother is a gentile. In Jewish law I cannot count myself a Jew. If it is true that "we think back through our mothers if we are women" (Virginia Woolf) — and I myself have affirmed this — then even according to lesbian theory, I cannot (or need not?) count myself a Jew. . . . It would be easy to push away and deny the gentile in me — that white southern woman, that social Christian. At different times in my life I have wanted to push away one or the other burden of inheritance, to say merely *I am a woman; I am a lesbian.* If I call myself a Jewish lesbian, do I thereby try to shed some of my southern gentile white woman's

4

culpability? If I call myself only through my mother, is it because I pass more easily through a world where being a lesbian often seems like outsiderhood enough?

> — ADRIENNE RICH
> "Split at the Root: An Essay on Jewish Identity"
> *Blood, Bread, and Poetry:*
> *Selected Prose, 1979–1985*, 1986

▼ ▼ ▼

Of all the odd misperceptions current about homosexuality, perhaps the oddest is that it is a choice, that people choose to be homosexual. That strikes me as so patently silly. Did any of us who are straight choose to be heterosexual? When? Did we wake up one morning when we were fifteen and say, "Gosh, I think I'll be a heterosexual?" For heaven's sakes, how can anyone believe that people choose to be a homosexual? "I think it would be a lot of fun to be called *queer* and *sissy* for the rest of my life, so I think I'll be gay."

> — MOLLY IVINS
> "'Twas a Fine Spring Day to Air Out
> Attitudes"
> *Nothin' But Good Times Ahead*, 1993

▼ ▼ ▼

The red earth, the blazing sun, and the broken hearts of [its] settlers were the recurring subjects of great Australian painting. It had never occurred to me before to wonder why we didn't celebrate the plenty and lyrical beauty of the fertile slopes beyond the mountains. . . . I knew that somehow it had to do with our relationship to nature, and with the way in which the first settlers' encounter with this environment had formed the inner landscape of the mind, the unspoken, unanalyzed relationship to the order of creation which governs our psyches at the deepest level. Australians saw that relationship as cruel and harsh . . . I wished there were a clear way to understand the process by which a people's dominant myths and mental imagery took shape. Now that I had seen England and Europe, these myths seemed more important to me than any study of the politics of Federation, or of the precise details of nineteenth-century land policy.

> — JILL KER CONWAY
> *The Road from Coorain*, 1989

▼ ▼ ▼

The French equate intelligence with rational discourse, the Russians with intense soul-searching. For a Mexican, intelligence is inseparable from maliciousness — in this, as in many other things, we are quite

Italian: *furbería,* rougish slyness, and the cult of appearances, *la bella figura,* are Italianate traits present everywhere in Latin America: Rome, more than Madrid, is our spiritual capital in this sense.

For me, as a child, the United States seemed a world where intelligence was equated with energy, zest, enthusiasm. The North American world blinds us with its energy; we cannot see ourselves, we must see you.

> – CARLOS FUENTES
> "How I Began to Write"
> *Myself with Others,* 1988

▼ ▼ ▼

My wife, from Finland, has a green card; I'm English, in the process of applying for one myself; our son was born an American. When we moved into our house in Venice, California, one of our neighbors, an elderly white woman with whom we're now very friendly, said, "No Americans live on our block anymore."

Maybe she had the jitters about new neighbors, or maybe there was something else at play. I knew that her father had been born in Germany and had journeyed to Detroit, where she was born. I wanted to say that logically, therefore, our son is every bit as American as she is. But in any debate about nationality, I know, logic fades fast.

My own father once traced our family tree back to 1066, when one Baron de Rainier sailed from Normandy to help conquer England. Since then, give or take the occasional Irish excursion, my progenitors were all born within a hundred or so miles of one another in the north of England. So, when I came to America and found that nearly everyone was from somewhere else if they stepped back a generation or two, I found myself thrilled and oddly at ease. It explained America's drive, its generosity and up-for-anything energy. As Melville wrote, "We are not a nation, so much as a world."

> – RICHARD RAYNER
> "What Immigration Crisis?"
> *New York Times Magazine,* 1996

▼ ▼ ▼

[A] blurring of cultural styles occurs in everyday life in the United States to a greater extent than anyone can imagine. The result is what . . . Yale professor Robert Thompson referred to as a "cultural bouillabaisse." Yet members of the nation's present educational and cultural elect still cling to the notion that the United States belongs to some vaguely defined entity they refer to as "Western civilization," by which they mean, presumably, a civilization created by people of Europe, as if Europe can even be viewed in monolithic terms. Is Beethoven's Ninth Symphony, which includes Turkish marches, a part of Western civilization? Or the late-nineteenth- and twentieth-century French paintings, whose creators were influenced by Japanese art? And what of the cubists, through whom the influence of African art changed modern painting? Or the surrealists, who were so impressed with the art of the Pacific Northwest Indians that, in their map of North America, Alaska dwarfs the lower forty-eight states in size?

– Ishmael Reed
"What's American about America?"
Utne Reader, 1989

▼ ▼ ▼

I was born in India, I grew up in India, went to school there, but when one says "India" no Indian really knows what you mean. It's just the opening to a hundred questions. Which region? Which part of India? Which state? Which language? Which religion? What particular background? Because India is a country made up of so many fragments, much smaller than the United States, but each little fragment has a culture which is so distinctly its own — its own language, its own script, its own literature. Which one do I claim as mine? All and none. My parents settled down in a part of India which was home to neither of them. My father came from Bengal, originally from quite a small village in what was then East Bengal, now Bangladesh, probably went to the local village school, belonged to a generation that went to such little local village schools but came out able to quote long passages from Milton's *Paradise Lost* or from Browning with which he used to like to regale us. My mother's home, on the other hand, was in Germany. She left Germany in the late twenties. The Germany she knew was soon after totally destroyed. She never returned to it, and both of them made their home in north India, in Delhi, where I grew up.

It was a home with three languages. Obviously German had to be the very first one because that was the language of infancy, the one my mother spoke to us. With all our neighbors and friends we spoke Hindi, that was the language in Delhi. My parents believed very much in sending us to the local school. I went to the nearest one, the one I could bicycle to, and that happened to be a mission school, run by British missionaries. And so it was a matter of pure chance that the first language I was taught to read and write was English and by that accident it became my literary language. And of course I loved the literature that was given me in the English language, but I very soon became aware that the

7

language did much more than that. It opened up world literature to me in translation. I couldn't have read the Russian literature I did, the French literature I did, the Japanese literature that I did read and love, if it hadn't been for the English language.

– ANITA DESAI
"The Other Voice"
Transition, 1994

▼ ▼ ▼

Before there was a USA, Mexicans lived in the Southwest and California. In 1781, while the American Revolutionary War still raged, the city of Los Angeles was founded in the southern portion of Alta California, as it was then known. Of course, Baja California still exists as present-day Mexico. In fact, the entire Southwest (Texas, Arizona, New Mexico, Utah, Nevada, and Colorado) and California once belonged to Mexico.

Nearly two hundred years later, I grew up in a Mexican neighborhood. . . . My parents baptized me Catholic, like so many Chicanos before me, at La Placita, the mission church of Our Lady Queen of Angels (Nuestra Señora Reina de Los Angeles), across from Olvera Street, right where the city first began.

I am a native son, though many still see me as foreign, in a land and city where the people have spoken Spanish for hundreds of years. But these days some people would have you believe that English is the "official" language.

I call myself Chicano (or Latino) because I was born on this side of the border, though as a young boy I was simply Mexican. And in a real sense I understand that I remain still simply Mexican to the rest of the nation, which has a hard time seeing beyond the notion that only black and white people are born in this country.

So I am Chicano, or Latino, or Mexican, but I am rarely American.

– DANNY ROMERO
"A Chicano in Philadelphia"
*MultiAmerica: Essays on Cultural Wars
and Cultural Peace*, 1997

▼ ▼ ▼

In my view, what has most dramatically separated Asian Americans from other people of color has been manifested in terms of attitudes toward what we call "America." For many Native Americans, America means stolen land. For many Chicanos, it means occupied territory conquered and taken from Mexico 150 years ago. For many African

Americans, it means the country built on slave labor brought here by force. For a large number of Asian Americans, especially of the recent and immigrant generation, America means "promised land" or "dream country." Having immigrated or come as refugees from colonized countries, often escaping from Socialist and Communist governments, many Asian Americans still feel like guests in the house or as a daughter-in-law in her mother-in-law's house. Like a guest or a new bride living with her mother-in-law, she needs to be grateful, obedient, and uncomplaining. She needs to be mindful of the rules and of her host's or mother-in-law's generosity, without which where would she be?

— ELAINE H. KIM
"Asian Americans"
MultiAmerica: Essays on Cultural Wars and Cultural Peace, 1997

EXPLORATIONS

1. Richard Rayner comments on different concepts of "American" (p. 6). Most of the Observations you have just read come from Americans of some kind — or more than one kind. Which of them are North Americans? Which are Central Americans? South Americans? Latin Americans?

2. What criteria besides nationality do these writers use to identify themselves? Which of their criteria do you use most often to identify yourself?

3. How do you think Rayner's elderly neighbor (p. 6) would define an American? How do you think Ishmael Reed (p. 6) would define an American? How would you define an American?

WALKER PERCY

A Short Quiz

Walker Percy was born in Birmingham, Alabama, in 1916. He spent most of his life, and set most of his books, in the South — particularly Louisiana, where he and his bride settled after World War II. Percy's life was as eventful as any Southern novel. His father committed suicide when Walker was thirteen years old; three years later, his mother died in a car accident. In between, Walker was informally adopted by his father's cousin Will in Mississippi. Percy graduated from the University of North Carolina at Chapel Hill and received his medical degree from Columbia University. During his internship, however, Will Percy died of a stroke, and Walker Percy developed tuberculosis. He spent the next three years in a sanitarium, reading intensely, exploring existentialism and other literary and philosophical angles on the cosmos. A year after his marriage, Percy converted to Roman Catholicism, which became a central force in his life and work. He and his wife moved first to New Orleans and then to the nearby small town of Covington. His first novel, *The Moviegoer* (1961), won the National Book Award. Five more novels followed: *The Last Gentleman* (1966), *Love in the Ruins* (1971), *Lancelot* (1977), *The Second Coming* (1980), and *The Thanatos Syndrome* (1987). Percy also published widely in both literary and philosophical journals. "A Short Quiz" comes from *Lost in the Cosmos: The Last Self-Help Book* (1983). Percy died in Covington from cancer in 1990.

Imagine that you are reading a book about the Cosmos. You find it so interesting that you go out and buy a telescope. One fine clear moonless night you set up your telescope and focus on the brightest star in the sky. It is a planet, not a star, with a reddish spot and several moons. Excited, you look up the planets in your book about the Cosmos. You read a description of the planets. You read a sentence about a large yellowish planet with a red spot and several moons. You recognize both the description and the picture. Clearly, you have been looking at Jupiter.

You have no difficulty at all in saying that it is Jupiter, not Mars or Saturn, even though the object you are looking at is something you have never seen before and is hundreds of millions of miles distant.

Now imagine that you are reading the newspaper. You come to the astrology column. You may or may not believe in astrology, but to judge from the popularity of astrology these days, you will probably read your horoscope. According to a recent poll, more Americans set store in astrology than in science or God.

You are an Aries. You open your newspaper to the astrology column and read an analysis of the Aries personality. It says among other things:

> You have the knack of creating an atmosphere of thought and movement, unhampered by petty jealousies. But you have the tendency to scatter your talents to the four winds.

Hm, you say, quite true. I'm like that.

Suddenly you realize you've made a mistake. You've read the Gemini column. So you go back to Aries: 5

> Nothing hurts you more than to be unjustly mistreated or suspected. But you have a way about you, a gift for seeing things through despite all obstacles and distractions. You also have a desperate need to be liked. So you have been wounded more often than you will admit.

Hm, you say, quite true. I'm like that.

The first question is: Why is it that both descriptions seem to fit you — or, for that matter, why do you seem to recognize yourself in the self-analysis of all twelve astrological signs? Or, to put it another way, why is it that you can recognize and identify the planets Jupiter and Venus so readily after reading a bit and taking one look, yet have so much trouble identifying yourself from twelve descriptions when, presumably, you know yourself much better than you know Jupiter and Venus?

(2) Can you explain why it is that there are, at last count, sixteen schools of psychotherapy with sixteen theories of the personality and its disorders and that patients treated in one school seem to do as well or as badly as patients treated in any other — while there is only one generally accepted theory of the cause and cure of pneumococcal pneumonia and only one generally accepted theory of the orbits of the planets and the gravitational attraction of our galaxy and the galaxy M31 in Andromeda? (Hint: If you answer that the human psyche is more complicated than the pneumococcus and the human white-cell response or the galaxies or Einstein's general theory of relativity, keep in mind that the burden of proof is on you. Or if you answer that the study of the

human psyche is in its infancy, remember then this infancy has lasted 2,500 years and, unlike physics, we don't seem to know much more about the psyche than Plato did.)

(3) How do you explain these odd little everyday phenomena with which everyone is familiar:

You have seen yourself a thousand times in the mirror, face to face. No sight is more familiar. Yet why is it that the first time you see yourself in a clothier's triple mirror — from the side, so to speak — it comes as a shock? Or the first time you saw yourself in a home movie: were you embarrassed? What about the first time you heard your recorded voice — did you recognize it? Clearly, you should, since you've been hearing it all your life.

Why is it that, when you are shown a group photograph in which you   10
are present, you always (and probably covertly) seek yourself out? To see what you look like? Don't you know what you look like?

Has this ever happened to you? You are walking along a street of stores. There are other people walking. You catch a glimpse in a store window of a reflection of a person. For a second or so you do not recognize the person. He, she, seems a total stranger. Then you realize it is your own reflection. Then in a kind of transformation, the reflection does in fact become your familiar self.

One of the peculiar ironies of being a human self in the Cosmos: A stranger approaching you in the street will in a second's glance see you whole, size you up, place you in a way in which you cannot and never will, even though you have spent a lifetime with yourself, live in the Century of the Self, and therefore ought to know yourself best of all.

The question is: Why is it that in your entire lifetime you will never be able to size yourself up as you can size up somebody else — or size up Saturn — in a ten-second look?

Why is it that the look of another person looking at you is different from everything else in the Cosmos? That is to say, looking at lions or tigers or Saturn or the Ring Nebula or at an owl or at another person from the side is one thing, but finding yourself looking into the eyes of another person looking at you is something else. And why is it that one can look at a lion or a planet or at someone's finger as long as one pleases, but looking into the eyes of another person is, if prolonged past a second, a perilous affair?

(4) The following experiment was performed on a group of ten sub-   15
jects. See how you would answer the questions.

Think of five acquaintances, not close friends, not lovers, not family members.

Describe each by three adjectives (in the experiment, a "personality characteristic chart" was provided on which one could score an acquaintance on a scale of "good" and "bad" qualities, e.g., more or less trustworthy, attractive, boring, intelligent, selfish, flighty, outgoing, introspective, and so on). Thus, you might describe an acquaintance named Gary McPherson as fairly good company, moderately trustworthy, funny but a little malicious, and so on. Or Linda Ellison: fairly good-looking (a 7 or $7\frac{1}{2}$), more intelligent than she lets on, a good listener. And so on.

Note that most if not all of your adjectives could be placed on a finite scale, say from a plus ten to a minus ten.

Now, having described five acquaintances, do the following. Read these two sentences carefully:

(a) You are extraordinarily generous, ecstatically loving of the right person, supremely knowledgeable about what is wrong with the country, about people, capable of moments of insight unsurpassed by any scientist or artist or writer in the country. You possess an infinite potentiality.

(b) You are of all people in the world probably the most selfish, hateful, envious (e.g., you take pleasure in reading death notices in the newspaper and in hearing of an acquaintance's heart attack), the most treacherous, the most frightened, and above all the phoniest.

Now answer this question as honestly as you can: Which of these two sentences more nearly describes you? CHECK (a), (b), (neither), (both).

If you checked both — 60 percent of respondents did — how can that be?   20

(5) Do you understand sexuality?

That is to say, are you happy with either of the two standard versions of sexuality:

One, the biological — that the sex drive is one among several needs and drives evolved through natural selection as a means of sustaining the life of the organism and ensuring the survival of the species. Thus, sexual desire is one item on a list which includes other such items as hunger, thirst, needs of shelter, nest-building, migration, and so on.

The other, the religious-humanistic — sex is an expression, perhaps the ultimate expression, of love and communication between a man and a woman and is best exemplified in marriage, raising children, the sharing of a life, family, home, and fireside.

Or do you see sexuality as a unique trait of the present-day self   25
(which is the only self we know), occupying an absolutely central locus
in the consciousness particularly as it relates to other sexual beings, of
an order and magnitude of power incommensurate with other "drives"
and also specified by the very structure of the present-day self as its very
core and as its prime avenue of intercourse with others?

If the sexual drive is but one of several biological needs, why are we
living in the most eroticized society in history? Why don't TV, films,
billboards, magazines feature culinary delights, e.g., huge chocolate
cakes, hams, roasts, strawberries, instead of women's bodies?

Or are you more confused about sexuality than any other phenomenon in the Cosmos?

Do you know why it is that men and women exhibit sexual behavior
undreamed of among the other several million species, with every conceivable sexual relation between persons, or with only one person, or
between a male and female, or between two male persons, or two female persons, or two males and one female, or two females and one
male; relationships moreover which can implicate every orifice and ap-
pendage of the human body and which bear no relation to the reproduction and survival of the species?

Is the following statement true or false:

Pornography is not an aberration of a few sexually frustrated middle-   30
aged men in gray raincoats; it is rather a salient and prime property of
modern consciousness, of three hundred years of technology and the
industrial revolution, and is symptomatic of a radical disorder in the relation of the self to other selves which generally manifests itself in the
abstracted state of one self (male) and the degradation of another self
(female) to an abstract object of satisfaction.

(6) Consider the following short descriptions of different kinds of
consciousness of self. Which of the selves, if any, do you identify with?

(a) *The cosmological self.* The self is either unconscious of itself or
only conscious of itself insofar as it is identified with a cosmological
myth or classificatory system, e.g., totemism. Ask a Bororo tribesman:
Who are you? He may reply: I am parakeet. (Ask an L.S.U. fan at a football game: Who are you? He may reply: I am a tiger.)

(b) *The Brahman-Buddhist self.* Who are you? What is your self? My
self in this life is impaled on the wheel of non-being, obscured by the
veil of unreality. But it can realize itself by penetrating the veil of *maya*

and plumbing the depths of self until it achieves *nirvana*, nothingness, or the *Brahman*, God. The *atman* (self) is the *Brahman* (God).

(c) *The Christian self (and, to a degree, the Judaic and Islamic self)*. The self sees itself as a creature, created by God, estranged from God by an aboriginal catastrophe, and now reconciled with him. Before the reconciliation, the self is, as Paul told the Ephesians, a stranger to every covenant, with no promise to hope for, with the world about you and no God. But now the self becomes a son of God, a member of a family of selves, and is conscious of itself as a creature of God embarked upon a pilgrimage in this life and destined for happiness and reunion with God in a later life.

(d) *The role-taking self.* One sociological view of the self is that the self achieves its identity by taking roles and modeling its own role from the roles of others, e.g., one's mother, father, housewife, breadwinner, macho-boy-man, feminine-doll-girl, etc. — and also, as George Mead said, upon how one perceives others' perceptions of oneself.

(e) *The standard American-Jeffersonian high-school-commencement Republican-and-Democratic-platform self.* The self is an individual entity created by God and endowed with certain inalienable rights and the freedom to pursue happiness and fulfill its potential. It achieves itself through work, participation in society, family, the marketplace, the political process, cultural activities, sports, the sciences, and the arts. It follows that in a free and affluent society the self should succeed more often than not in fulfilling itself. Happiness can be pursued and to a degree caught.

(f) *The diverted self.* In a free and affluent society, the self is free to divert itself endlessly from itself. It works in order to enjoy the diversions that the fruit of one's labor can purchase. The pursuit of happiness becomes the pursuit of diversion, and in this society the possibilities of diversion are endless and as readily available as eight hours of television a day: TV, sports, travel, drugs, games, newspapers, magazines, Vegas.

(g) *The lost self.* With the passing of the cosmological myths and the fading of Christianity as a guarantor of the identity of the self, the self becomes dislocated, Jefferson or no Jefferson, is both cut loose and imprisoned by its own freedom, yet imprisoned by a curious and paradoxical bondage like a Chinese handcuff, so that the very attempts to free itself, e.g., by ever more refined techniques for the pursuit of happiness, only tighten the bondage and distance the self ever farther from the very world it wishes to inhabit as its homeland. The rational Jeffersonian pursuit of happiness embarked upon in the American Revolution translates into the flaky euphoria of the late twentieth century. Every advance in an objective understanding of the Cosmos and in its technological control further distances the self from the Cosmos precisely in the degree of the advance — so that in the end the self becomes a spacebound ghost which roams the very Cosmos it understands perfectly.

(h) *The scientific and artistic self.* Or that self which is so totally absorbed in the pursuit of art or science as to be selfless. The modern caricature is the "absentminded professor" or the demonic possessed artist, which is to say that as a self he is "absent" from the usual concerns of the self about itself in the world. E.g., Karl von Frisch and his bees, Schubert in a beer hall writing lieder on the tablecloth, Picasso in a restaurant modeling animals from bread.

(i) *The illusory self.* Or the conviction that one's sense of oneself is a   40 psychological or cultural illusion and that with the advance of science, e.g., behaviorism, Lévi-Strauss's structuralism, the self will disappear.

(j) *The autonomous self.* The self sees itself as a sovereign and individual consciousness, liberated by education from the traditional bonds of religion, by democracy from the strictures of class, by technology from the drudgery of poverty, and by self-knowledge from the tyranny of the unconscious — and therefore free to pursue its own destiny without God.

(k) *The totalitarian self.* The self sees itself as a creature of the state, Fascist or Communist, and understands its need to be specified by the needs of the state.

(CHECK ONE)

EXPLORATIONS

1. How do you think Walker Percy would define the self? How would you summarize Percy's thesis in "A Short Quiz"? (Refer to the title of the book this essay comes from for one clue.)

2. In what ways does Percy's choice of a quiz format suit his material? Specifically, what advantages does he gain by asking questions rather than making

statements? By using the second-person singular ("you") rather than some other pronoun?

3. Reread Question 6 in "A Short Quiz." Which of the selves (6 *a* through *k*) do you identify with, and why?

CONNECTIONS

1. How do you think the "cultural bouillabaisse" described by Ishmael Reed (p. 6) has affected Americans' sense of self? Which of the questions in "A Short Quiz" might not make sense to someone from a culture with only one race, religion, and philosophy?

2. Which of Percy's concepts of self (6 *a* through *k*) are reflected in Adrienne Rich's Observation on page 4? What explanation does Percy suggest for Rich's desire to "push away one or the other burden of inheritance"?

3. In items 6 (*e*) and 6 (*f*), Percy alludes to "a free and affluent society." Which writers of the Observations on pages 3–9 do you think would agree with that phrase as a description of the United States? Which writers do you think would not agree, and why not?

ELABORATIONS

1. Which of the selves described in Question 6 (*a* through *k*) do you see around you most often? Write an essay applying Percy's definitions to contemporary U.S. culture. Support your position with examples.

2. Choose one of Percy's six items in "A Short Quiz" and answer the subquestions in it. Write an essay replying to the item's central question, incorporating and expanding on Percy's discussion and your answers.

DANZY SENNA

The Mulatto Millennium

"It was the contradictions in my own life that most confounded me,"
Danzy Senna has commented, "the experience of looking white
and identifying as black." Senna was born in Boston in 1970 to parents
involved in the civil rights movement. Her mother, a white writer,
and her father, a black scholar, divorced when she and her brother and
sister were small. Senna graduated from Stanford University in 1992
and received her M.F.A. in creative writing from the University of California, Irvine. She has worked as a journalist for several magazines, including *Newsweek* and *Spin*. Her first novel, *Caucasia*, appeared in
1999. The following essay comes from the 1998 collection *Half and
Half*, edited by Claudine O'Hearn. Senna currently lives in Brooklyn,
New York; she teaches at Sarah Lawrence College and is working on her
second novel.

Strange to wake up and realize you're in style. That's what happened
to me just the other morning. It was the first day of the new millennium, and I woke to find that mulattos had taken over. They were
everywhere. Playing golf, running the airwaves, opening restaurants,
modeling clothes, starring in musicals with names like *Show Me the
Miscegenation!* The radio played a steady stream of Lenny Kravitz,
Sade, and Mariah Carey. I thought I'd died and gone to Berkeley. But
then I realized that, according to the racial zodiac, 2000 is the official
Year of the Mulatto. Pure breeds (at least black ones) are out; hybridity
is in. America loves us in all of our half-caste glory. The president announced on Friday that beige will be the official color of the millennium.

Before all of this radical ambiguity, I considered myself a black girl.
Not your ordinary black girl, if such a thing exists. But rather, a black
girl with a WASP mother and black-Mexican father, and a face that
harks back to Andalusia, not Africa. I was born in 1970, when black described a people bonded not by shared complexion or hair texture but
by shared history.

Not only was I black, but I sneered at those by-products of miscegenation who chose to identify as mixed, not black. I thought it wishy-

washy, an act of flagrant assimilation, treason — passing, even. I was an enemy of the mulatto people.

My parents made me this way. In Boston circa 1975, mixed wasn't an option. "A fight, a fight, a nigga and a white!" echoed from schoolyards during recess. You were either white or black. No checking "Other." No halvsies. No in between. Black people, the bottom of Boston's social totem pole, were inevitably the most accepting of difference; they were the only race to come in all colors, and so there I found myself. Sure, I got strange reactions from all quarters when I called myself black. But black people usually got over their initial surprise and welcomed me into the ranks. White folks were the most uncomfortable with the dissonance between the face they saw and the race they didn't. Upon learning who I was, they grew paralyzed with fear that they might have "slipped up" in my presence, that is, said something racist, not knowing there was a Negro in their midst. Often, they had.

Let it be clear — my parents' decision to raise us as black wasn't   5 based on any one-drop-of-blood rule from the days of slavery, and it certainly wasn't based on our appearance, that crude reasoning many black-identified mixed people use: If the world sees me as black, I must be black. If it had been based on appearance, my sister would have been black and my brother Mexican and I Jewish. Instead, my parents' decision arose out of the black power movement, which made identifying as black not a pseudoscientific rule but a conscious choice. Now that we don't have to anymore, we choose to. Because black is beautiful. Because black is not a burden, but a privilege.

Some might say my parents went too far. I remember my father schooling me and my siblings on our racial identity. He would grill us over a greasy linoleum kitchen table, a single bright lightbulb swinging overhead: "Do you have any black friends? How many? Who?" And we, his obedient children, his soldiers in the battle for negritude, would rattle off the names of the black kids we called friends.

Something must have sunk in, because my sister and I grew up with disdain for those who identified as mulatto. A very particular breed got under my skin: the kind who answered, meekly, "Everything" to that incessant question, "What are you?" I veered away from groups of them — children, like myself, who had been born of interracial minglings after dark. Instead, I surrounded myself with bodies darker than my own, hoping the color might rub off on me.

One year, while working as an investigative journalist in Hollywood, I made up a list, evidence I've long since burned. Luckily for my career, it was never published. It was an exposé of who is passing in Hollywood, called "And You Thought It Was Just a Tan?" There were three categories:

Black Folks You May Not Have Known Are Black
Mariah Carey
Jennifer Beals
Tom Hanks
Carly Simon
Slash
Arnold Schwarzenegger
Johnny Depp
Michael Jackson
Kevin Bacon
Robin Quivers
Elizabeth Berkeley
Paula Abdul

Black Folks Who May Not Know They Are Black
Mariah Carey
Jennifer Beals
Tom Hanks
Carly Simon
Slash
Arnold Schwarzenegger
Johnny Depp
Michael Jackson
Kevin Bacon
Robin Quivers
Elizabeth Berkeley
Paula Abdul

Black Folks You Kinda Wish Weren't Black
O. J. Simpson
Michael Jackson
Gary Coleman
Robin Quivers

Needless to say, my list wouldn't have gone over too well with the Mulatto Nation posse (M.N. to those in the know). It was nearly published in a local newsweekly, but the editors balked at the last minute. I bet they're thanking their lucky stars now; in this age of fluidity, it doesn't pay to be blacker than thou.

These days, M.N. folks in Washington have their own census cate-　10
gory — multiracial — but the extremist wing of the Mulatto Nation
finds it inadequate. They want to take things a step further. I guess they
have a point. Why lump us all together? Eskimos have forty different
words for snow. In South Africa, during apartheid, they had fourteen
different types of coloreds. But we've decided on one word, multiracial,
to describe a whole nation of diverse people who have absolutely no relation, cultural or otherwise, to one another. In light of this deficiency, I
propose the following coinages:

Standard Mulatto: White mother, black father. Half-nappy hair, skin
described as "pasty yellow" in winter but turns caramel tan in summer.
Germanic-Afro features. Often raised in isolation from others of its
kind. Does not discover "black identity" till college, when there is usually some change in hair, clothing, or speech, so that the parents don't
recognize the child who arrives home for Christmas vacation ("Honey,
there's a black kid at the door").

African American: The most common form of mulatto in North
America, this breed, seldom described as mixed, is a combination of
African, European, and Native American. May come in any skin tone,
from any cultural background. Often believe themselves to be "pure"
due to historical distance from the original mixture, which was most
often achieved through rape.

Jewlatto: The second most prevalent form, this breed is made in the
commingling of Jews and blacks who met when they were registering
voters down South during Freedom Summer or at a CORE meeting.
Jewlattos often, though not necessarily, have a white father and black
mother (as opposed to the more common black father and white
mother). They are likely to be raised in a diverse setting (New York
City, Berkeley), around others of their kind. Jewlattos are most easily
spotted amid the flora and fauna of Brown University. Famous Jewlattos
include Lenny Kravitz and Lisa Bonet (and we can't forget Zoe, their
love child).

Mestizo: A more complicated mixture: Either the black or the white
parent claims a third race (Native American, Latino) in the parent's
background and thus confuses the child more. The mestizo is likely to
be mistaken for some other, totally distinct ethnicity (Italian, Arab,
Mexican, Jewish, East Indian, Native American, Puerto Rican) and in

fact will be touted by strangers as a perfect representative of that totally new race ("Your face brings me right back to Calcutta").

Cultural Mulatto: Any American born after 1967.   15

Blulatto: A highly rare breed of "blue-blooded" mulattos who can trace their lineage back to the Mayflower. Females are legally entitled to membership in the Daughters of the American Revolution. Blulattos have been spotted in Cambridge and Berkeley but should not be confused with Jewlattos. The Blulatto's mother is almost always the white one, and is either a poet or a painter who disdains her WASP heritage. The father is almost always the black one, is highly educated, and disdains his black heritage.

Cablinasian: An exotic breed found mostly in California, the mother of all mixtures: Asian, American Indian, black, and Caucasian. These show mulattos have great performance skills; they will be whoever the crowd wants them to be, and can switch at the drop of a hat. They do not, however, answer to the name black. If you spot a Cablinasian, contact the Benetton promotions bureau.

Tomatto: A mixed or black person who behaves in an Uncle Tom-ish fashion. The Tomatto may be found in positions of power touted as a symbol of diversity in otherwise all-white settings. Even if the Tomatto has two black parents, his skin is light and his features mixed. If we ever see a first black president, he will most likely be a Tomatto.

Fauxlatto: A person impersonating a mulatto. Can be of white, black, or other heritage, but for inexplicable reasons claims to be of mixed heritage. See Jamiroquai.

The categories could go on and on, and perhaps, indeed, they will.   20
Where do I fit? That's the strange thing. I fit into none and all of the above. I have been each of the above, or at least mistaken for them, at different moments in my life. But somehow, none feels right. Maybe that makes me a Postlatto.
I've learned to flaunt my mixedness at dinner parties, where the guests (most of them white) ooh and aaah about my flavorful background. I've found it's not so bad being a fetishized object, an exotic bird soaring above the racial landscape. And when they start talking about black people, pure breeds, in that way that before the millennium used to make me squirm, I let them know that I'm neutral, nothing to be afraid of. Sometimes I feel it, that remnant of my old self (the angry black girl with the big mouth) creeping out, but most of the time

I don't feel anything at all. Most of the time, I just serve up the asparagus, chimichangas, and fried chicken with a bright, white smile.

EXPLORATIONS

1. In this essay, what aspects of herself does Danzy Senna suggest are central to her identity? What specific facts does she give us about herself? What kinds of identity-related information does she omit? What can you tell about her that she does not explicitly state?
2. How would you summarize this essay's subject? Its thesis? What do you think are Senna's purposes in writing it?
3. What places and people does Senna use symbolically in "The Mulatto Millennium," and what do they symbolize?

CONNECTIONS

1. Like Walker Percy in "A Short Quiz" (p. 10), Senna proposes a system for classifying people. In what ways do these two writers' bases for classification differ? What aspects of a person play the most important role in Percy's system? In Senna's?
2. Which of Percy's selves do you think Senna would identify with, and why?
3. What comments in "The Mulatto Millennium" echo Observations by Henry Louis Gates Jr. on page 4? What conclusions of Senna's (stated or implied) are different from Gates's?

ELABORATIONS

1. Referring to Percy's "A Short Quiz" and Senna's "The Mulatto Millennium," write an essay proposing your own identity classification scheme.
2. In paragraph 4, Senna recalls racism in Boston. Have you ever been classified as part of a group, and treated on that basis? Write an essay describing and analyzing such an experience.

AMY TAN

Two Kinds

Amy Tan's parents emigrated separately from China to Oakland, California, a few years before she was born in 1952. Her Chinese name, An-mei, means "blessing from America." Her mother already had been forced to leave behind three daughters from a previous marriage in China; when Tan was fourteen, her father and older brother both died, and the rest of the family moved to Switzerland. Tan returned to the United States for college and graduated from San Jose State University. She became a language-development consultant for developmentally disabled children, then built a successful career as a business writer. In her mid-thirties she turned to fiction. "Two Kinds" comes from her first novel, *The Joy Luck Club* (1989), which has been translated into seventeen languages and a motion picture. Tan followed it up with two more novels, *The Kitchen God's Wife* (1991) and *The Hundred Secret Senses* (1995), as well as two children's books, *The Moon Lady* (1992) and *The Chinese Siamese Cat* (1994). She and her husband live in San Francisco and New York City.

Like the narrator's mother in "Two Kinds," Amy Tan's mother fled China as Communists led by Mao Zedong were about to take control in 1949. Japan's defeat in World War II had ended its long effort to wrest China away from Nationalist forces led by General Chiang Kai-shek. Civil war followed between Chiang's Kuomintang government, backed by the United States, and Mao's Communist rebels, backed by the Soviet Union. The victorious Maoists forced the Kuomintang into exile on Taiwan and began restructuring China's economy on the Soviet model: Private property was turned over to collectives, and central planning replaced markets. In 1966 the decade-long Cultural Revolution began, glorifying workers, peasants, and soldiers and purging "bourgeois" intellectuals and officials — including Deng Xiaoping, who would become Mao's successor after his death in 1976. Today tight Communist political control continues: In the spring of 1989, students demonstrating in Tiananmen Square for faster-paced and wider-ranging governmental reforms were dispersed by the army, and hundreds — perhaps thousands — of unarmed protesters were killed. Deng's government fended off reprisal from the United States by continuing to loosen economic restrictions on free enterprise and trade with the West.

For more background on China, see page 542.

My mother believed you could be anything you wanted to be in America. You could open a restaurant. You could work for the government and get good retirement. You could buy a house with almost no money down. You could become rich. You could become instantly famous.

"Of course you can be prodigy, too," my mother told me when I was nine. "You can be best anything. What does Auntie Lindo know? Her daughter, she is only best tricky."

America was where all my mother's hopes lay. She had come here in 1949 after losing everything in China: her mother and father, her family home, her first husband, and two daughters, twin baby girls. But she never looked back with regret. There were so many ways for things to get better.

We didn't immediately pick the right kind of prodigy. At first my mother thought I could be a Chinese Shirley Temple. We'd watch Shirley's old movies on TV as though they were training films. My mother would poke my arm and say, "*Ni kan*" — You watch. And I would see Shirley tapping her feet, or singing a sailor song, or pursing her lips into a very round O while saying, "Oh my goodness."

"*Ni kan*," said my mother as Shirley's eyes flooded with tears. "You   5 already know how. Don't need talent for crying!"

Soon after my mother got this idea about Shirley Temple, she took me to a beauty training school in the Mission district and put me in the hands of a student who could barely hold the scissors without shaking. Instead of getting big fat curls, I emerged with an uneven mass of crinkly black fuzz. My mother dragged me off to the bathroom and tried to wet down my hair.

"You look like Negro Chinese," she lamented, as if I had done this on purpose.

The instructor of the beauty training school had to lop off these soggy clumps to make my hair even again. "Peter Pan is very popular these days," the instructor assured my mother. I now had hair the length of a boy's, with straight-across bangs that hung at a slant two inches above my eyebrows. I liked the haircut and it made me actually look forward to my future fame.

In fact, in the beginning, I was just as excited as my mother, maybe even more so. I pictured this prodigy part of me as many different images, trying each one on for size. I was a dainty ballerina girl standing by the curtains, waiting to hear the right music that would send me floating on my tiptoes. I was like the Christ child lifted out of the straw

manger, crying with holy indignity. I was Cinderella stepping from her
pumpkin carriage with sparkly cartoon music filling the air.

In all of my imaginings, I was filled with a sense that I would soon   10
become *perfect*. My mother and father would adore me. I would be beyond reproach. I would never feel the need to sulk for anything.

But sometimes the prodigy in me became impatient. "If you don't
hurry up and get me out of here, I'm disappearing for good," it warned.
"And then you'll always be nothing."

Every night after dinner, my mother and I would sit at the Formica
kitchen table. She would present new tests, taking her examples from
stories of amazing children she had read in *Ripley's Believe It or Not*, or
Good Housekeeping, Reader's Digest, and a dozen other magazines she
kept in a pile in our bathroom. My mother got these magazines from
people whose houses she cleaned. And since she cleaned many houses
each week, we had a great assortment. She would look through them
all, searching for stories about remarkable children.

The first night she brought out a story about a three-year-old boy who
knew the capitals of all the states and even most of the European countries. A teacher was quoted as saying the little boy could also pronounce
the names of the foreign cities correctly.

"What's the capital of Finland?" my mother asked me, looking at the
magazine story.

All I knew was the capital of California, because Sacramento was the   15
name of the street we lived on in Chinatown. "Nairobi!" I guessed, saying the most foreign word I could think of. She checked to see if that
was possibly one way to pronounce "Helsinki" before showing me the
answer.

The tests got harder — multiplying numbers in my head, finding the
queen of hearts in a deck of cards, trying to stand on my head without
using my hands, predicting the daily temperatures in Los Angeles, New
York, and London.

One night I had to look at a page from the Bible for three minutes and
then report everything I could remember. "Now Jehoshaphat had riches
and honor in abundance and . . . that's all I remember, Ma," I said.

And after seeing my mother's disappointed face once again, something inside of me began to die. I hated the tests, the raised hopes and
failed expectations. Before going to bed that night, I looked in the
mirror above the bathroom sink and when I saw only my face staring
back — and that it would always be this ordinary face — I began to cry.
Such a sad, ugly girl! I made high-pitched noises like a crazed animal,
trying to scratch out the face in the mirror.

And then I saw what seemed to be the prodigy side of me — because I had never seen that face before. I looked at my reflection, blinking so I could see more clearly. The girl staring back at me was angry, powerful. This girl and I were the same. I had new thoughts, willful thoughts, or rather thoughts filled with lots of won'ts. I won't let her change me, I promised myself. I won't be what I'm not.

So now on nights when my mother presented her tests, I performed listlessly, my head propped on one arm. I pretended to be bored. And I was. I got so bored I started counting the bellows of the foghorns out on the bay while my mother drilled me in other areas. The sound was comforting and reminded me of the cow jumping over the moon. And the next day, I played a game with myself, seeing if my mother would give up on me before eight bellows. After a while I usually counted only one, maybe two bellows at most. At last she was beginning to give up hope. 20

Two or three months had gone by without any mention of my being a prodigy again. And then one day my mother was watching *The Ed Sullivan Show* on TV. The TV was old and the sound kept shorting out. Every time my mother got halfway up from the sofa to adjust the set, the sound would go back on and Ed would be talking. As soon as she sat down, Ed would go silent again. She got up, the TV broke into loud piano music. She sat down. Silence. Up and down, back and forth, quiet and loud. It was like a stiff embraceless dance between her and the TV set. Finally she stood by the set with her hand on the sound dial.

She seemed entranced by the music, a little frenzied piano piece with this mesmerizing quality, sort of quick passages and then teasing lilting ones before it returned to the quick playful parts.

"*Ni kan*," my mother said, calling me over with hurried hand gestures. "Look here."

I could see why my mother was fascinated by the music. It was being pounded out by a little Chinese girl, about nine years old, with a Peter Pan haircut. The girl had the sauciness of a Shirley Temple. She was proudly modest like a proper Chinese child. And she also did this fancy sweep of a curtsy, so that the fluffy skirt of her white dress cascaded slowly to the floor like the petals of a large carnation.

In spite of these warning signs, I wasn't worried. Our family had no piano and we couldn't afford to buy one, let alone reams of sheet music and piano lessons. So I could be generous in my comments when my mother bad-mouthed the little girl on TV. 25

"Play note right, but doesn't sound good! No singing sound," complained my mother.

"What are you picking on her for?" I said carelessly. "She's pretty good. Maybe she's not the best, but she's trying hard." I knew almost immediately I would be sorry I said that.

"Just like you," she said. "Not the best. Because you not trying." She gave a little huff as she let go of the sound dial and sat down on the sofa.

The little Chinese girl sat down also to play an encore of "Anitra's Dance" by Grieg. I remember the song, because later on I had to learn how to play it.

Three days after watching *The Ed Sullivan Show*, my mother told me   30
what my schedule would be for piano lessons and piano practice. She had talked to Mr. Chong, who lived on the first floor of our apartment building. Mr. Chong was a retired piano teacher and my mother had traded housecleaning services for weekly lessons and a piano for me to practice on every day, two hours a day, from four until six.

When my mother told me this, I felt as though I had been sent to hell. I whined and then kicked my foot a little when I couldn't stand it anymore.

"Why don't you like me the way I am? *I'm* not a genius! I can't play the piano. And even if I could, I wouldn't go on TV if you paid me a million dollars!" I cried.

My mother slapped me. "Who ask you be genius?" she shouted. "Only ask you be your best. For you sake. You think I want you be genius? Hnnh! What for! Who ask you!"

"So ungrateful," I heard her mutter in Chinese. "If she had as much talent as she has temper, she would be famous now."

Mr. Chong, whom I secretly nicknamed Old Chong, was very   35
strange, always tapping his fingers to the silent music of an invisible orchestra. He looked ancient in my eyes. He had lost most of the hair on top of his head and he wore thick glasses and had eyes that always looked tired and sleepy. But he must have been younger than I thought, since he lived with his mother and was not yet married.

I met Old Lady Chong once and that was enough. She had this peculiar smell like a baby that had done something in its pants. And her fingers felt like a dead person's, like an old peach I once found in the back of the refrigerator; the skin just slid off the meat when I picked it up.

I soon found out why Old Chong had retired from teaching piano. He was deaf. "Like Beethoven!" he shouted to me. "We're both listening only in our head!" And he would start to conduct his frantic silent sonatas.

Our lessons went like this. He would open the book and point to different things, explaining their purpose: "Key! Treble! Bass! No sharps or flats! So this is C major! Listen now and play after me!"

And then he would play the C scale a few times, a simple chord, and then, as if inspired by an old, unreachable itch, he gradually added more notes and running trills and a pounding bass until the music was really something quite grand.

I would play after him, the simple scale, the simple chord, and then I   40
just played some nonsense that sounded like a cat running up and down on top of garbage cans. Old Chong smiled and applauded and then said, "Very good! But now you must learn to keep time!"

So that's how I discovered that Old Chong's eyes were too slow to keep up with the wrong notes I was playing. He went through the motions in half-time. To help me keep rhythm, he stood behind me, pushing down on my right shoulder for every beat. He balanced pennies on top of my wrists so I would keep them still as I slowly played scales and arpeggios. He had me curve my hand around an apple and keep that shape when playing chords. He marched stiffly to show me how to make each finger dance up and down, staccato like an obedient little soldier.

He taught me all these things, and that was how I also learned I could be lazy and get away with mistakes, lots of mistakes. If I hit the wrong notes because I hadn't practiced enough, I never corrected myself. I just kept playing in rhythm. And Old Chong kept conducting his own private reverie.

So maybe I never really gave myself a fair chance. I did pick up the basics pretty quickly, and I might have become a good pianist at that young age. But I was so determined not to try, not to be anybody different, that I learned to play only the most ear-splitting preludes, the most discordant hymns.

Over the next year, I practiced like this, dutifully in my own way. And then one day I heard my mother and her friend Lindo Jong both talking in a loud bragging tone of voice so others could hear. It was after church, and I was leaning against the brick wall wearing a dress with stiff white petticoats. Auntie Lindo's daughter, Waverly, who was about my age, was standing farther down the wall about five feet away. We had grown up together and shared all the closeness of two sisters squabbling over crayons and dolls. In other words, for the most part, we hated each other. I thought she was snotty. Waverly Jong had gained a certain amount of fame as "Chinatown's Littlest Chinese Chess Champion."

"She bring home too many trophy," lamented Auntie Lindo that   45
Sunday. "All day she play chess. All day I have no time do nothing but

dust off her winnings." She threw a scolding look at Waverly, who pretended not to see her.

"You lucky you don't have this problem," said Auntie Lindo with a sigh to my mother.

And my mother squared her shoulders and bragged: "Our problem worser than yours. If we ask Jing-mei wash dish, she hear nothing but music. It's like you can't stop this natural talent."

And right then, I was determined to put a stop to her foolish pride.

A few weeks later, Old Chong and my mother conspired to have me play in a talent show which would be held in the church hall. By then, my parents had saved up enough to buy me a secondhand piano, a black Wurlitzer spinet with a scarred bench. It was the showpiece of our living room.

For the talent show, I was to play a piece called "Pleading Child"   50
from Schumann's *Scenes from Childhood*. It was a simple, moody piece that sounded more difficult than it was. I was supposed to memorize the whole thing, playing the repeat parts twice to make the piece sound longer. But I dawdled over it, playing a few bars and then cheating, looking up to see what notes followed. I never really listened to what I was playing. I daydreamed about being somewhere else, about being someone else.

The part I liked to practice best was the fancy curtsy: right foot out, touch the rose on the carpet with a pointed foot, sweep to the side, left leg bends, look up and smile.

My parents invited all the couples from the Joy Luck Club to witness my debut. Auntie Lindo and Uncle Tin were there. Waverly and her two older brothers had also come. The first two rows were filled with children both younger and older than I was. The littlest ones got to go first. They recited simple nursery rhymes, squawked out tunes on miniature violins, twirled Hula-Hoops, pranced in pink ballet tutus, and when they bowed or curtsied, the audience would sigh in unison, "Awww," and then clap enthusiastically.

When my turn came, I was very confident. I remember my childish excitement. It was as if I knew, without a doubt, that the prodigy side of me really did exist. I had no fear whatsoever, no nervousness. I remember thinking to myself, This is it! This is it! I looked out over the audience, at my mother's blank face, my father's yawn, Auntie Lindo's stiff-lipped smile, Waverly's sulky expression. I had on a white dress layered with sheets of lace, and a pink bow in my Peter Pan haircut. As I sat down I envisioned people jumping to their feet and Ed Sullivan rushing up to introduce me to everyone on TV.

And I started to play. It was so beautiful. I was so caught up in how lovely I looked that at first I didn't worry how I would sound. So it was a surprise to me when I hit the first wrong note and I realized something didn't sound quite right. And then I hit another and another followed that. A chill started at the top of my head and began to trickle down. Yet I couldn't stop playing, as though my hands were bewitched. I kept thinking my fingers would adjust themselves back, like a train switching to the right track. I played this strange jumble through two repeats, the sour notes staying with me all the way to the end.

When I stood up, I discovered my legs were shaking. Maybe I had   55 just been nervous and the audience, like Old Chong, had seen me go through the right motions and had not heard anything wrong at all. I swept my right foot out, went down on my knee, looked up and smiled. The room was quiet, except for Old Chong, who was beaming and shouting, "Bravo! Bravo! Well done!" But then I saw my mother's face, her stricken face. The audience clapped weakly, and as I walked back to my chair, with my whole face quivering as I tried not to cry, I heard a little boy whisper loudly to his mother, "That was awful," and the mother whispered back, "Well, she certainly tried."

And now I realized how many people were in the audience, the whole world it seemed. I was aware of eyes burning into my back. I felt the shame of my mother and father as they sat stiffly throughout the rest of the show.

We could have escaped during intermission. Pride and some strange sense of honor must have anchored my parents to their chairs. And so we watched it all: the eighteen-year-old boy with a fake mustache who did a magic show and juggled flaming hoops while riding a unicycle. The breasted girl with white makeup who sang from *Madama Butterfly* and got honorable mention. And the eleven-year-old boy who won first prize playing a tricky violin song that sounded like a busy bee.

After the show, the Hsus, the Jongs, and the St. Clairs from the Joy Luck Club came up to my mother and father.

"Lots of talented kids," Auntie Lindo said vaguely, smiling broadly.

"That was somethin' else," said my father, and I wondered if he was   60 referring to me in a humorous way, or whether he even remembered what I had done.

Waverly looked at me and shrugged her shoulders. "You aren't a genius like me," she said matter-of-factly. And if I hadn't felt so bad, I would have pulled her braids and punched her stomach.

But my mother's expression was what devastated me: a quiet, blank look that said she had lost everything. I felt the same way, and it seemed as if everybody were now coming up, like gawkers at the scene of an accident, to see what parts were actually missing. When we got on the bus to go home, my father was humming the busy-bee tune and my mother was silent. I kept thinking she wanted to wait until we got home before shouting at me. But when my father unlocked the door to our apartment, my mother walked in and then went to the back, into the bedroom. No accusations. No blame. And in a way, I felt disappointed. I had been waiting for her to start shouting, so I could shout back and cry and blame her for all my misery.

I assumed my talent-show fiasco meant I never had to play the piano again. But two days later, after school, my mother came out of the kitchen and saw me watching TV.

"Four clock," she reminded me as if it were any other day. I was stunned, as though she were asking me to go through the talent-show torture again. I wedged myself more tightly in front of the TV.

"Turn off TV," she called from the kitchen five minutes later.   65

I didn't budge. And then I decided. I didn't have to do what my mother said anymore. I wasn't her slave. This wasn't China. I had listened to her before and look what happened. She was the stupid one.

She came out from the kitchen and stood in the arched entryway of the living room. "Four clock," she said once again, louder.

"I'm not going to play anymore," I said nonchalantly. "Why should I? I'm not a genius."

She walked over and stood in front of the TV. I saw her chest was heaving up and down in an angry way.

"No!" I said, and I now felt stronger, as if my true self had finally   70
emerged. So this was what had been inside me all along.

"No! I won't!" I screamed.

She yanked me by the arm, pulled me off the floor, snapped off the TV. She was frighteningly strong, half pulling, half carrying me toward the piano as I kicked the throw rugs under my feet. She lifted me up and onto the hard bench. I was sobbing by now, looking at her bitterly. Her chest was heaving even more and her mouth was open, smiling crazily as if she were pleased I was crying.

"You want me to be someone that I'm not!" I sobbed. "I'll never be the kind of daughter you want me to be!"

"Only two kinds of daughters," she shouted in Chinese. "Those who are obedient and those who follow their own mind! Only one kind of daughter can live in this house. Obedient daughter!"

"Then I wish I wasn't your daughter. I wish you weren't my mother,"   75
I shouted. As I said these things I got scared. I felt like worms and toads

and slimy things were crawling out of my chest, but it also felt good, as if this awful side of me had surfaced, at last.

"Too late change this," said my mother shrilly.

And I could sense her anger rising to its breaking point. I wanted to see it spill over. And that's when I remembered the babies she had lost in China, the ones we never talked about. "Then I wish I'd never been born!" I shouted. "I wish I were dead! Like them."

It was as if I had said the magic words. Alakazam! — and her face went blank, her mouth closed, her arms went slack, and she backed out of the room, stunned, as if she were blowing away like a small brown leaf, thin, brittle, lifeless.

It was not the only disappointment my mother felt in me. In the years that followed, I failed her so many times, each time asserting my own will, my right to fall short of expectations. I didn't get straight As. I didn't become class president. I didn't get into Stanford. I dropped out of college.

For unlike my mother, I did not believe I could be anything I   80
wanted to be. I could only be me.

And for all those years, we never talked about the disaster at the recital or my terrible accusations afterward at the piano bench. All that remained unchecked, like a betrayal that was now unspeakable. So I never found a way to ask her why she had hoped for something so large that failure was inevitable.

And even worse, I never asked her what frightened me the most: Why had she given up hope?

For after our struggle at the piano, she never mentioned my playing again. The lessons stopped. The lid to the piano was closed, shutting out the dust, my misery, and her dreams.

So she surprised me. A few years ago, she offered to give me the piano, for my thirtieth birthday. I had not played in all those years. I saw the offer as a sign of forgiveness, a tremendous burden removed.

"Are you sure?" I asked shyly. "I mean, won't you and Dad miss it?"   85

"No, this your piano," she said firmly. "Always your piano. You only one can play."

"Well, I probably can't play anymore," I said. "It's been years."

"You pick up fast," said my mother, as if she knew this was certain. "You have natural talent. You could been genius if you want to."

"No I couldn't."

"You just not trying," said my mother. And she was neither angry nor   90
sad. She said it as if to announce a fact that could never be disproved. "Take it," she said.

But I didn't at first. It was enough that she had offered it to me. And after that, every time I saw it in my parents' living room, standing in front of the bay windows, it made me feel proud, as if it were a shiny trophy I had won back.

Last week I sent a tuner over to my parents' apartment and had the piano reconditioned, for purely sentimental reasons. My mother had died a few months before and I had been getting things in order for my father, a little bit at a time. I put the jewelry in special silk pouches. The sweaters she had knitted in yellow, pink, bright orange — all the colors I hated — I put those in moth-proof boxes. I found some old Chinese silk dresses, the kind with little slits up the sides. I rubbed the old silk against my skin, then wrapped them in tissue and decided to take them home with me.

After I had the piano tuned, I opened the lid and touched the keys. It sounded even richer than I remembered. Really, it was a very good piano. Inside the bench were the same exercise notes with handwritten scales, the same secondhand music books with their covers held together with yellow tape.

I opened up the Schumann book to the dark little piece I had played at the recital. It was on the left-hand side of the page, "Pleading Child." It looked more difficult than I remembered. I played a few bars, surprised at how easily the notes came back to me.

And for the first time, or so it seemed, I noticed the piece on the right-hand side. It was called "Perfectly Contented." I tried to play this one as well. It had a lighter melody but the same flowing rhythm and turned out to be quite easy. "Pleading Child" was shorter but slower; "Perfectly Contented" was longer but faster. And after I played them both a few times, I realized they were two halves of the same song. 95

EXPLORATIONS

1. How many different meanings for the story's title can you find in "Two Kinds"?

2. What is the primary goal of the narrator's mother in "Two Kinds"? Which of her statements and actions show how important it is to her? What clues in the story's first three paragraphs suggest why she has fixed on this goal?

3. What is the primary goal of the narrator at the beginning of "Two Kinds"? Why has she fixed on this goal? How does her goal change as the story progresses, and why?

CONNECTIONS

1. In both "Two Kinds" and Danzy Senna's "The Mulatto Millennium" (p. 18), the narrator alludes to her parents' ambitions for her. How do parental ambitions differ in these two selections? How do each writer's purposes affect the way she depicts her parents?

2. Which of Walker Percy's definitions of self (pp. 14–16) do you think Amy Tan's narrator would most identify with, and why? Which of these definitions would the narrator's mother prefer that she identify with?

3. James Baldwin writes, "A man is not a man until he is able and willing to accept his own vision of the world, no matter how radically this vision departs from that of others" (p. 263). What comments by Tan's narrator Jing-mei express a similar view? How would you describe Jing-mei's vision of the world?

ELABORATIONS

1. In paragraphs 63–91, Tan's narrator describes a confrontation with her mother and its resolution long afterward. Regarding the years in between, she uses the phrases, "we never talked about," "I never found out," and "I never asked." Is this the same pattern that a conflict in your family might follow? If not, why not? Write an essay either describing and analyzing a similar confrontation between you and a family member, or comparing and contrasting the pattern of conflict and resolution in your family and in Jing-mei's.

2. At some points the narrators in "Two Kinds" and "The Mulatto Millennium" both yield to pressure to play a certain role, and at other points they both fight for the right to choose their own roles. Write an essay comparing and contrasting the roles each narrator accepts and the ones she rejects, or comparing their choices with your own decisions in similar circumstances.

SUSAN ORLEAN

Quinceañera

Susan Orlean was born on Halloween in 1955 in Cleveland, Ohio. After graduating from the University of Michigan she became a writer for *Willamette Week* in Portland, Oregon, then for the *Boston Phoenix*, and then for the *Boston Globe*. Her first book was a collection of essays from the *Globe* entitled *Red Sox and Bluefish: Meditations on What Makes New England New England* (1987); her newest book is *The Orchid Thief* (1999). A widely published commentator on American popular culture, Orlean lives in New York City. She has been a contributing editor for *Rolling Stone* and *Vogue* and in 1992 became a staff writer for *The New Yorker*. "Quinceañera" comes from her 1990 book *Saturday Night*.

Azteca Plaza, the biggest formal-wear shopping center in the world, is on a skinny strip of sandy, cactus-studded Arizona real estate, a few miles east of downtown Phoenix, in a neighborhood that does not yet illustrate the vitality of the Sunbelt economy. . . . Azteca Plaza has the corner on the greater metropolitan Phoenix prom-dress trade. It also does a brisk business in the fancy ball gowns Hispanic girls wear at their *quinceañeras*, the ceremony that takes place when they are fifteen years old — *quinceaños* — to celebrate their passage into womanhood, commitment to Catholicism, and debut into society. In the last decade, the number of Hispanics in Phoenix has grown by 125 percent. The *quinceañera* business at Azteca Plaza has enjoyed a corresponding upswing.

Azteca Plaza is just a few blocks away from Immaculate Heart Church, a boxy stucco-colored structure that serves as a central parish for the Hispanic community in the Phoenix diocese. Immaculate Heart was built in 1928, fourteen years after it was revealed that the priests at the main basilica in Phoenix, St. Mary's, had been obliging their Mexican parishioners to hold their masses and weddings and *quinceañeras* in the basement rather than on the main floor of the church. It used to be common for certain churches to serve an ethnic group rather than a geographical area — in most American cities, there would be French, Hispanic, Polish, Irish, and German Catholic churches. The practice is rare these days, and Immaculate Heart is one of the few such ethnic parishes left in the entire country. Someone in Phoenix, recounting for me the history of Hispanic mistreatment at St. Mary's, credited the continued existence of a national parish in Phoenix to the dry Arizona desert air, which, he claimed, had preserved the unpleasant memory of bargain-basement weddings at the basilica in many Hispanics' minds. Hispanics in Phoenix now regularly attend the churches in their immediate neighborhoods, but for sentimental and historical reasons they continue to think of Immaculate Heart as the mother ship. Not coincidentally, Immaculate Heart was for years the site of most of Phoenix's many *quinceañeras* — that is, the site of the mass when the girl is blessed and is asked to affirm her dedication to the Church. The party in which she is introduced to society and celebrates her birthday is held after the mass at a hotel or hall. For a while, there were so many *quinceañeras* at Immaculate Heart that they outnumbered weddings. For that matter, there were so many *quinceañera* masses and parties that they were a standard Saturday-night social occasion in town.

In early summer I was invited to a large *quinceañera* in Phoenix at which sixteen girls were to be presented. The event was being sponsored by the girls' parents and the Vesta Club, a social organization of Hispanic college graduates. In the Southwest, constituents of this subset are sometimes known as "chubbies" — Chicano urban professionals. Chubbies give Azteca Plaza a lot of business. The girls' fathers and the sixteen young men who were going to be escorts at the *quinceañera* had rented their tuxedos from Azteca Plaza and would be picking them up on Saturday morning. The girls, of course, had gotten their gowns months before.

The traditional Mexican *quinceañera* gown is white or pink, floor length but trainless, snug on top and wide at the bottom, with a skirt shaped like a wedding bell. But like most traditions that migrate a few hundred miles from their point of origin and make it through a couple of generations in this country, *quinceañeras* have yielded somewhat to interpretation, and the gowns that the Vesta Club girls were going to wear demonstrated the effects of Americanization on taste as well as a certain American-style expansiveness in price. All of the gowns were white and full-length, but otherwise they were freestyle — an array of high necks, fluted necklines, sweetheart necklines, leg-o'-mutton sleeves, cap sleeves, cascade collars, gathered bodices, beaded bodices, bustles, and sequins; one had a train and one had a flouncy peplum and a skirt that was narrow from the hip to the floor. Further Americanization has taken place with regards to scheduling. In Mexico, *quinceañeras* traditionally take place on the day the girl actually turns fifteen. In the United States, *quinceañeras* — like many important ceremonies in American life — take place on Saturday nights.

When I first mentioned to a woman I know in Phoenix that I wanted   5
to attend a *quinceañera*, that I thought they seemed like interesting ceremonies and great displays of community feeling and a good example
of how ethnic tradition fits into American Saturday nights, she clucked
sympathetically and said she was very sentimental about her own
quinceañera but had become convinced that they were now going the
way of many other ethnic ceremonies in this country — changed beyond recognition, marketed like theme parks, at the very least irrelevant
to assimilated youngsters who would rather spend Saturday nights at
keg parties than reenacting an old-world ceremony. An inevitable pattern transforms such things: Immigrants gather in their leisure time so
that they can bolster one another and share their imported traditions,
their children tolerate the gatherings occasionally because they have a
likeable familiar ring, and then the children of *those* children deplore
them because they seem corny and pointless, and finally there is a lot of
discussion about how sad it is that the community doesn't get together
anymore.

That is partly what has become of *quinceañeras* in Phoenix, but the
real problem, ironically, is that they have been too popular for their
own good. A few years ago, the bishop of Phoenix, a slight, freckle-faced
man from Indiana named Thomas O'Brien, started hearing complaints
from some priests about *quinceañeras*. According to the bishop, the
chief complaint was that *quinceañera* masses were beginning to dominate church schedules. This would surprise no one with an eye on the
city's demographics: Three-quarters of the Hispanics in Phoenix are
under thirty-five years old and a significant number of them are girls —
all potential subjects of a *quinceañera* mass and party. The priests complained that some girls came to their *quinceañera* mass without the
faintest idea of its religious significance, never came to church otherwise, demanded a mass even if they were pregnant or using drugs or in
some other way drifting outside the categories usually in good stead
with the religious community, and badgered their families — some
chubbies, but many not — into giving them opulent postmass parties.
Some *quinceañera* parties in Phoenix were running into the high four
figures and beyond. Many families could hardly afford this. In response
to these concerns, Father Antonio Sotelo, the bishop's vicar for Hispanic affairs, surveyed the diocese's priests and then wrote a guidebook
for *quinceañeras* similar to ones circulated recently in a few other American parishes with large Hispanic populations, advising that girls take
five classes on Bible study, Hispanic history, *quinceañera* history, and
modern morals, and go on a church-sponsored retreat with their parents
before the event. He also recommended that *quinceañeras* be held for

groups of girls rather than for individuals, in order to offset the queen-
for-a-day quality that many of them had taken on, and so that the cost
could be spread around.

One morning before the Vesta Club *quinceañera*, I stopped by Father Sotelo's office at Immaculate Heart. Besides being vicar for Hispanic affairs, Father Sotelo is the pastor of Immaculate Heart. His small
office in the back of the church is decorated with pictures of his parishioners and dominated by a whale of a desk. Father Sotelo is short and
wiry and has rumpled graying hair, an impish face, and a melodious
voice. His manner of address is direct. He is known for holding and
broadcasting the opinion that anyone who wears shorts and a T-shirt to
church should be escorted out the door, and that the men in his congregation who walk with a sloppy, swinging, barrio-tough gait look like
gorillas. Father Sotelo grew up in San Diego. His heritage is Mexican
and American Indian. He says that he considered the *quinceañera* issue
a simple matter of facing reality, and he doesn't mind that the requirements have discouraged many girls from having *quinceañeras*. "We
knew perfectly well that most girls were only thinking about the party,"
he said. "It was a big dream for them. Everyone wants a fancy *quinceañera* party. Unlike an American debutante ball, *quinceañeras* are
not limited to the upper class. Any girl can celebrate it. But there are
spoiled brats in every class. Many of these girls were demanding that
their parents spend thousands of dollars on them whether they could afford it or not. People at the lower end of the economic scale cling to tradition most fervently, so they were most determined to have a traditional *quinceañera*, and their daughters would have the most expensive
dresses and parties. And when these girls would walk down the aisle
with their parents at the mass, you could tell that quite often the girls
and their parents couldn't stand one another. It was an empty ceremony. For what they were getting out of the church part of the
quinceañera, they could have gone out and done the whole thing in the
desert and had someone sprinkle magic pollen on their heads."

After the guidelines were circulated around the diocese, a few
churches, including Immaculate Heart, set up the *quinceañera* classes
and retreats. But to the enormous displeasure of parishioners who enjoyed spending Saturday nights at their friends' daughters' *quinceañeras*, and who imagined that on some Saturday night in the future
their own daughters would be feted at a mass and nice reception of
their own, many priests in Phoenix announced that they agreed with
Father Sotelo but they lacked the time and facilities to run classes and
retreats. Therefore, they declared, they would no longer perform
quinceañera masses at all.

The one priest who took exception was Frank Peacock, the pastor of a poor church in a scruffy South Phoenix neighborhood. Father Peacock made it known that he thought the guidelines were too strict, and that they inhibited the exercise of a tradition that rightfully belonged to the people, and that as far as he was concerned, anyone in any condition or situation who wanted a *quinceañera* could come to him. "We get calls here all the time from people asking very meekly for Father Peacock's number," Father Sotelo said to me, looking exasperated. "They're not fooling anyone. I know exactly what they want."

A few weeks before I got to Phoenix, a small yucca plant on the corner of Twelfth and Van Buren, about a half mile down the street from Immaculate Heart, sprouted a stem that then shriveled up into an unusual shape and was subsequently noticed by a passerby who thought it bore a striking resemblance to Our Lady of Guadeloupe. The yucca stem was never certified as a genuine miracle by church hierarchy, but for several weeks, until someone shot at it with a small-caliber handgun and then two artists took it upon themselves to cut it down with a chainsaw as the climax of a performance piece, it attracted large crowds of people who came to marvel at it and pray.

Our Lady of Guadeloupe, the vision who appeared to the Mexican-Indian Juan Diego on December 9, 1531, and who was so awe-inspiring a sight that she more or less nailed down the entire country of Mexico for the Catholic Church, has appeared in other places as unlikely as the corner of Twelfth and Van Buren. For instance, Our Lady of Guadeloupe also happens to be spray-painted on the trunk of at least one souped-up low-rider car in Phoenix, which I noticed bouncing down the street one afternoon when I was in town. Father Peacock had seen this same car and says he finds it remarkable. The day before the Vesta Club Ball, he and I had gotten together so he could show me videotapes of some of the outlaw *quinceañera* masses he had presided over at Our Lady of Fatima. Before we started the tapes, I said that Father Sotelo had pointed out that people were perfectly entitled to have *quinceañeras* that cost ten thousand dollars and celebrated fifteen-year-olds with heavy marijuana habits, but that the Church shouldn't necessarily endorse them or hold celebration masses for them. "People have a right to enjoy things that the Church doesn't endorse," Father Peacock said. "We don't endorse low-riders, do we?" He interrupted himself. "Actually, I endorse low-riders. I love them. Have you ever seen one? Oh, they can be gorgeous, really beautiful. Did you ever see the one painted with Our Lady of Guadeloupe?" . . .

Some of the people who come to Father Peacock for a *quinceañera* are poor, or are recent immigrants who are still attached to the traditional Mexican style of the ceremony and resist what they could well consider pointless time-consuming requirements or irritating Americanizations. Quite often, Father Peacock is approached by affluent Hispanics as well, who tell him they want their daughters to have their own celebrations, not *quinceañeras* with a group of other girls, and that they want to go all out with the six-tiered *quinceañera* cake and the rhinestone crown and the catered sit-down dinner for three hundred and the mariachi band and the lavish gifts from the godparents and the fifteen boy escorts and fifteen girl attendants in matching outfits who traditionally accompany the *quinceañera* girl. Father Peacock says he has given *quinceañera* masses for daughters of state senators as well as for girls whose parents are illiterate. Most of the time, he begins his address at the mass by asking for forgiveness for his failures and then says, "You have asked us to take care of a fifteenth-birthday celebration and we say no — this is one of our failures." Sometimes the people at the altar look bored or are wearing dark sunglasses and conspicuous amounts of jewelry and can't even remember the words to the Lord's Prayer when Father Peacock recites it. "That is one of my motivations," he says. "This might be the only chance I have to get that sort of person into church and try to reach them." Some of the families have experienced child abuse, sexual abuse, divorce, separation, or a combination of all four, and Father Peacock says he loves seeing such families together at the occasional happy affair like a *quinceañera*. Some of them take out loans to pay for their daughters' gowns. Father Peacock usually urges the poorer families to hold their parties at South Mountain Park, a city facility with a hall that can be used for free, but he says he can understand if they prefer a fancier place. On this point, he always says something in the homily like, "Through self-sacrifice we get our pleasure," and has said many times that he would rather that people go into hock for a traditional, ethnic, religious occasion — no matter how marginally religious it might turn out to be — than for something like a car or a boat. "A *quinceañera* costs a lot of money," he says. "But it's worth a lot of money. Anyway, I don't try to change people. I like to meet them in their own way." . . .

"Father Peacock will do anything," a young woman named Alice Coronado-Hernandez, this year's chairman of the Vesta Club *Quinceañera* Ball, said to me one afternoon. "Everyone knows that about Father Peacock, so everyone calls him." At the time, I was having lunch at a bad Mexican restaurant in a good part of Phoenix with Alice, her mother, Caroline, and Mary Jo Franco-French, a physician who helped found the Vesta *quinceañera* fifteen years ago. When she was organizing that first *quinceañera*, Mary Jo had just finished medical school and was pregnant with her daughter Laura. This year, Laura was going to be one of the girls up on the stage.

The Vesta Club is not going to be calling on Father Peacock anytime soon. "We're really happy with doing our *quinceañera* the way Father Sotelo has suggested," Caroline said. "We felt the classes and the retreat were really good for the girls. We saw what was going on with the *quinceañeras* — we saw the problem out there. Even if we could afford it, we knew it wasn't good to continue the old way."

Alice said, "It was crazy what people were spending. When I was that age, the girls were really competitive about their *quinceañeras* and about how nice they would be." Caroline nodded. "My *quinceañera* was at the first Vesta Club Ball," Alice went on. "That year, I must have been invited to *quinceañeras* for friends of mine just about every weekend, so it was a pretty regular Saturday-night activity for me. But even then I could see how some people got very extravagant about it."

"They were hocking their souls for the fancy private *quinceañera*," Caroline added. "The diocese could see that it was becoming detrimental to the economy of their parishioners."

The three of them spent some time talking about last-minute details of the Vesta *quinceañera*. After a mass at Immaculate Heart, there was going to be dinner for the four hundred and fifty guests at Camelback Inn, an elegant resort north of the city, and a short ceremony in which each girl would be presented by her father. Then the girls and their escorts would perform a *quinceañera* waltz — a complicated dance to the "Blue Danube" which the kids had practiced once a week for the last three months. "The waltz is such a beautiful tradition," Mary Jo said. "It's what we have that makes the event really special. That, and having them learn about their Hispanic heritage. The kids have worked so hard at that waltz. They've really practiced, and they've really gotten good at it."

"They *have* gotten good at it, haven't they?" Caroline said, nodding. "It's hard to believe that some of them had never danced a step before they started to learn."

The Fifteenth Annual Vesta Club *Quinceañera* Mass began at five o'clock with a procession of the sixteen girls up the center aisle of Immaculate Heart. I sat on the left side of the church, a row behind Mary Jo Franco-French and her husband, Alfred, an eye surgeon of Gallic extraction who has a large practice in Phoenix. Beside me were four cousins of Mary Jo's who had flown in from Juárez, Mexico, for the event. The day had been dry-roasting hot, and at five, the long, dusty southwestern dusk was just beginning and the light was hitting the city at a flat angle and giving everything a yellowy glow. The *quinceañera* girls in their white dresses had been standing on the sidewalk outside the church when I walked in, and each time a car drove down the street in front of the church, the updraft would blow their big skirts around. Immaculate Heart is a bulky, unadorned building with dark wooden pews, a vaulted ceiling, some stained glass, a wide altar with simple lines, and a pail hanging just outside the side door into which parishioners are advised to deposit their chewing gum. After I sat down, I noticed Father Sotelo and Bishop O'Brien seated together at the altar. The Vesta Club *quinceañera* is the only one in Phoenix at which the bishop celebrates the mass. He told me that it is the only one he attends because he liked the seriousness with which the club approached the spiritual content of the ceremony, and also because no one else having a *quinceañera* had ever invited him.

After a few minutes, the organist hit a chord and the procession 20 began. The Vesta Club girls walked in, trailing satin and netting. The gowns were a spectacle: Each one was bright white, with different structural embellishments and complicated effects. I noticed the girl wearing the dress with the little train and the one with the narrow skirt. "Wow," whispered Carmen Gonzalez, one of Mary Jo Franco-French's cousins, who had celebrated her own *quinceañera* a few years ago at a country club in Juárez. "Pretty nice dresses. These girls look so *grown up*."

"The third one down is my niece Maria," the woman behind us said. "Fifteen already, but I still think of her as a baby. I think her mother's praying that Maria keeps her figure so she can wear the dress again when she gets married."

The procession took several minutes. Then the girls sat down in two rows of chairs at the altar, and the bishop made his greetings and began the mass. After a few prayers, he announced that it was time for the parents to bless their daughters individually. He turned and nodded at the dark-haired girl at the end of the row. She stood up cautiously, walked to the center of the apse and down the three steps, turned around and knelt down, partially disappearing in the folds of her dress. Her parents stood up in their pew and walked over to her, leaned down and made the sign of the cross on her forehead, kissed her, whispered something in her ear, and then returned to their seats. The girl rose up and walked back to the altar. Someone in a pew behind me sobbed lightly and then blew loudly into a handkerchief. A faulty key in the church organ stuck and started to squeal. The next girl stood up, smoothed her huge skirt, stepped down, knelt, was blessed by her parents, and returned to her seat. Laura Josefina Franco-French, a tall and elegant-looking fifteen-year-old with long dark hair and a serene expression, came forward and was blessed by Alfred and Mary Jo. Then the girl who was wearing the tight skirt stood up. We all sat forward. She walked in tiny steps across the apse, eased herself down the stairs, turned around, and then, with the agility of a high school cheerleader at the season's big game, she folded her legs beneath her and knelt without straining a seam.

There were still some golfers on the greens at Camelback Inn when the Vesta Club partygoers arrived. The ballroom wasn't ready for us to be seated, so everyone milled around the pool having drinks and talking. I wondered if the golfers were curious about what we were doing — four hundred well-dressed people, mostly adult, and sixteen girls in formal white gowns. It might have looked like a wedding, except there were too many young women in white, and it might have looked like a prom, except no one has parents at her prom. It felt mostly like a community reunion. "It's a big group, but it's a small world," said a woman in a beaded lilac gown standing beside me at the bar.

"Relatives or friends?" I asked.

"Both," she said. "About half of these people were at my daughter's 25 *quinceañera* last year." I must have looked surprised, because she started to laugh and then said, "Some of these families even knew each other in Mexico. You could say that we're just keeping the chain or circle or what have you, intact. I had my *quinceañera* longer ago than I'm happy to say. It's an old-fashioned event but I love it." She took her drink and joined a group of people nearby who were talking about an expensive shopping center just opening in Scottsdale. One of the men in the group kept sweeping his hands out and saying "Boom!" and the woman beside him would then slap his shoulder playfully and say "For godsakes, come on, Adolfo!" Alfred Franco-French III, who was escorting his sister Laura, walked past the bar and muttered that he hoped he would remember the waltz when it came time to waltz. The patio got noisier and noisier. No one was speaking Spanish. One of the girls' fathers started a conversation with me by saying, "There are plenty of bums in the world out there, sad to say," but then he got distracted by someone he hadn't seen in a while and walked away. I had driven out to Camelback with one of Laura Franco-French's school friends, and after a few minutes we ran into each other. She said she was impressed with the *quinceañera* so far. She talked about how there was usually never anything to do on Saturday nights in Phoenix, and then she talked about how favorably Laura's involvement in a formal event, in particular one that required the purchase of a really nice fancy dress, was regarded by other students at their largely non-Hispanic private school. It happened that this girl was not Hispanic and had never been to a *quinceañera* before and had also never before considered what advantages ethnicity might include. She looked across the pool where the debutantes were standing in a cluster and said, "I never thought about it one way or another. But now that I'm at one of these *quinceañeras*, I'm thinking that being Hispanic might be really cool." I walked to the far side of the pool, where I had a long view of all the people at the party, in their fresh tuxes and filmy formals; with their good haircuts and the handsome, relaxed posture common to people whose businesses are doing well and to whom life has been generous; who were standing around the glimmery pool and against the dark, lumpy outline of Camelback Mountain, holding up light-colored drinks in little crystal glasses so that they happened to catch the last bit of daylight. It was a pretty gorgeous sight.

Finally, Alice Coronado-Hernandez and Caroline Coronado sent word that the ballroom was ready. The doors of the Saguaro Room were propped open. The patio emptied as the crowd moved inside. At one end of the ballroom, a mariachi band was ready to play. Around the dance floor were fifty tables set with bunchy flower arrangements and good china. I had been seated with Alice Coronado-Hernandez and her family. At the tables, each place was set with a program printed on stiff, creamy paper; it listed the Vesta Club officers, last year's *quinceañera* debs and escorts, and this year's debs and escorts, and had formal portraits of each of the girls. This was similar in style to the program for the St. Luke's Hospital Visitors' Society Cotillion — Phoenix's premier society event — at which the girls being presented are far more likely to have names like Bickerstaff and Collins than Esparza and Alvarez. I had seen the 1988 St. Luke's program when I had dinner one night with the Franco-Frenches. Laura had been studying the program so energetically that some of the pages were fingerprinted and the binding was broken. In the time since Mexicans in Phoenix were forced to hold their masses in the basement of St. Mary's, a certain amount of social amalgamation has come to pass: Laura Franco-French, half-Mexican in heritage and at least that much in consciousness, will also be presented at St. Luke's in a few years. Similarly, there was a Whitman and a Thornton among the debutantes at the Vesta Ball. . . .

"When do they announce debutante of the year?" Alice's stepdaughter asked her. Alice drummed her fingers on the table and said, "Later."

Just then, the master of ceremonies coughed into the microphone and the room got quiet. The girls lined up around the edge of the dance floor with their fathers. The mothers were stationed near them in chairs, so that they would be readily available for the father-mother waltz, which comes after the father-daughter waltz and after the special *quinceañera* waltz — a complex piece of choreography, in which the girls spin around their escorts and then weave through their arms, form little circles and then big circles and finally waltz in time around the dance floor. After all these waltzes, the mariachi band was going to play — although I had heard that for the sake of the teenagers, who appreciated their heritage but who were, after all, American kids with tastes of their own, the Mexican music was going 'n be alternated throughout the evening with current selections of rock 'n' roll.

The announcer cleared his throat again and said, *"Buenos noches, damas y caballeros."* He had a sonorous, rumbling voice that thundered through the ballroom. *"Buenos noches.* We present to you this year's Vesta Club debutantes."

EXPLORATIONS

1. How does the name of the store with which Susan Orlean opens "Quinceañera" illustrate the dual identity of the culture she is writing about?

2. What purposes was a *quinceañera* originally created to serve (para. 1)? What are the current purposes of a *quinceañera* from the point of view of the Roman Catholic Church? The girl involved? Her parents? What do you think are the main reasons for the ceremony's changes in function since its origin in Mexico?

3. What sources of information does Orlean cite in this essay? What kinds of sources would you expect her to cite that she does not? How does that choice affect "Quinceañera"?

CONNECTIONS

1. Like Amy Tan's "Two Kinds" (p. 24), Orlean's "Quinceañera" depicts American families with roots outside the United States. What factors does Tan mention that foster a sense of community among the Chinese Americans in "Two Kinds"? What factors does Orlean mention that foster a sense of community among the Hispanic Americans in "Quinceañera"?

2. Both "Quinceañera" and "Two Kinds" feature a public performance that

functions as a rite of passage. What does the performance mean to the parents in each selection? How is its meaning similar and different for the children who take part in it?

3. In "A Short Quiz" (p. 10), Walker Percy comments on how much easier it is to size up another person than oneself. Which of Percy's definitions of self (pp. 14–16) do you think Orlean would apply to the subjects of "Quinceañera"? What information in her essay suggests which definitions the subjects would apply to themselves?

ELABORATIONS

1. Orlean observes that all the Vesta Club's *quinceañera* girls wear white gowns. Who benefits from this custom, and why? What are the disadvantages of such uniformity, and how do the girls deal with them? What other situations can you think of in which strict unofficial dress codes play an important role? Write an essay about such a situation, describing the clothes involved and analyzing the ways they enable the wearers to identify themselves and each other.

2. Major social occasions such as proms and weddings often are exciting to look forward to, beautiful or comical to look back on, and miserable to experience. (See, for instance, the talent show in Tan's "Two Kinds.") Has this ever happened to you? Write an essay recalling an event that was supposed to be glorious (for you or a friend or family member) but in fact was either painful or ridiculous.

OCTAVIO PAZ

The Art of the Fiesta

Although Octavio Paz is represented here by an essay, he is also known for his fiction, his art criticism, and his poetry. "Poetic activity is revolutionary by nature," he has written, "a means of interior liberation." Paz was born in Mexico City in 1914. Educated at a Roman Catholic school and the National University of Mexico, he founded an avant-garde literary journal at age seventeen; at nineteen he published his first book of poems. Four years later he went to Europe, where he supported the Republican side in the Spanish Civil War and established himself as part of the international writers' community in Paris. Back in Mexico Paz founded and edited several literary reviews. In 1942 he married the writer Elena Garro; they were later divorced. In 1950 he produced his famous study of Mexican character and culture, *El laberinto de la soledad* (*The Labyrinth of Solitude: Life and Thought in Mexico*, 1961). "The Art of the Fiesta" comes from the chapter "The Day of the Dead"; it was translated from the Spanish by Lysander Kemp. After working for the Mexican embassies in Paris and Japan, Paz served as Mexico's ambassador to India from 1962 to 1968, resigning over Mexico's brutal treatment of student radicals. He also lived in England, France, and the United States, where he taught at Harvard University and at the University of Texas. Following many other awards, Paz won the Nobel Prize for literature in 1990. He died in Mexico City in 1998.

The United States' neighbor to the south has been populated since around 21,000 B.C. The great Olmec, Toltec, Mayan, and Aztec civilizations arose between A.D. 100 and A.D. 900. When Hernán Cortés and other explorers arrived from Spain in the 1500s, they conquered the ruling Aztecs and made Mexico a heavily exploited colony until a series of rebellions achieved independence in 1821. A republic was declared in 1823, followed by two emperors, several dictators, and a series of presidents. Although democracy has persisted, reform has progressed haltingly. "Mexico is a bureaucratic state halfway between capitalism and socialism," Octavio Paz has observed; "it is between democracy and dictatorship with a constitutional transfer of power, but also a president with absolute power and one-party rule." After an oil boom in the 1970s, Mexico's economy declined severely in the mid-1980s. Recently it has been improving, after years of stagnation, as wages, job opportunities, and exports increase; however, most of the rural and much of the urban population remains poor, so many workers seek jobs across the northern border. In the early 1990s, controversy arose over the North American Free Trade Agreement, aimed at lifting economic barriers between Mexico, Canada, and the United States. Meanwhile, Mexico's folk art and fine art have both burgeoned: Writers such as Paz and Carlos Fuentes (see p. 5) are internationally regarded, as are a number of Mexican painters, composers, and other artists.

The solitary Mexican loves fiestas and public gatherings. Any occasion for getting together will serve, any pretext to stop the flow of time and commemorate men and events with festivals and ceremonies. We are a ritual people, and this characteristic enriches both our imaginations and our sensibilities, which are equally sharp and alert. The art of the fiesta has been debased almost everywhere else, but not in Mexico. There are few places in the world where it is possible to take part in a spectacle like our great religious fiestas with their violent primary colors, their bizarre costumes and dances, their fireworks and ceremonies, and their inexhaustible welter of surprises: the fruit, candy, toys, and other objects sold on these days in the plazas and open-air markets.

Our calendar is crowded with fiestas. There are certain days when the whole country, from the most remote villages to the largest cities, prays, shouts, feasts, gets drunk, and kills, in honor of the Virgin of Guadalupe or Benito Juárez. Each year on the fifteenth of September, at eleven o'clock at night, we celebrate the fiesta of the *Grito*[1] in all the plazas of the Republic, and the excited crowds actually shout for a whole hour . . . the better, perhaps, to remain silent for the rest of the year. During the days before and after the twelfth of December,[2] time comes to a full stop, and instead of pushing us toward a deceptive tomorrow that is always beyond our reach, offers us a complete and perfect today of dancing and revelry, of communion with the most ancient and secret Mexico. Time is no longer succession, and becomes what it originally was and is: the present, in which the past and future are reconciled.

But the fiestas which the Church and State provide for the country as a whole are not enough. The life of every city and village is ruled by a patron saint whose blessing is celebrated with devout regularity. Neighborhoods and trades also have their annual fiestas, their ceremonies and fairs. And each one of us — atheist, Catholic, or merely indifferent — has his own saint's day, which he observes every year. It is impossible to calculate how many fiestas we have and how much time and money we

---

[1]Padre Hidalgo's call-to-arms against Spain, 1810. — TRANS.
[2]Fiesta of the Virgin of Guadalupe. — TRANS.

spend on them. I remember asking the mayor of a village near Mitla, several years ago, "What is the income of the village government?" "About 3,000 pesos a year. We are very poor. But the Governor and the Federal Government always help us to meet our expenses." "And how are the 3,000 pesos spent?" "Mostly on fiestas, señor. We are a small village, but we have two patron saints."

This reply is not surprising. Our poverty can be measured by the frequency and luxuriousness of our holidays. Wealthy countries have very few: There is neither the time nor the desire for them, and they are not necessary. The people have other things to do, and when they amuse themselves they do so in small groups. The modern masses are agglomerations of solitary individuals. On great occasions in Paris or New York, when the populace gathers in the squares or stadiums, the absence of people, in the sense of *a* people, is remarkable: There are couples and small groups, but they never form a living community in which the individual is at once dissolved and redeemed. But how could a poor Mexican live without the two or three annual fiestas that make up for his poverty and misery? Fiestas are our only luxury. They replace, and are perhaps better than, the theater and vacations, Anglo-Saxon weekends and cocktail parties, the bourgeois reception, the Mediterranean café.

In all of these ceremonies — national or local, trade or family — the 5 Mexican opens out. They give him a chance to reveal himself and to converse with God, country, friends, or relations. During these days the silent Mexican whistles, shouts, sings, shoots off fireworks, discharges his pistol into the air. He discharges his soul. And his shout, like the rockets we love so much, ascends to the heavens, explodes into green, red, blue, and white lights, and falls dizzily to earth with a trail of golden sparks. This is the night when friends who have not exchanged more than the prescribed courtesies for months get drunk together, trade confidences, weep over the same troubles, discover that they are brothers, and sometimes, to prove it, kill each other. The night is full of songs and loud cries. The lover wakes up his sweetheart with an orchestra. There are jokes and conversations from balcony to balcony, sidewalk to sidewalk. Nobody talks quietly. Hats fly in the air. Laughter and curses ring like silver pesos. Guitars are brought out. Now and then, it is true, the happiness ends badly, in quarrels, insults, pistol shots, stabbings. But these too are part of the fiesta, for the Mexican does not seek amusement: He seeks to escape from himself, to leap over the wall of solitude that confines him during the rest of the year. All are possessed by violence and frenzy. Their souls explode like the colors and voices and emotions. Do they forget themselves and show their true faces? Nobody knows. The important thing is to go out, open a way, get drunk on noise, people, colors. Mexico is celebrating a fiesta. And this fiesta, shot through with lightning and delirium, is the brilliant reverse to our silence and apathy, our reticence and gloom.

According to the interpretation of French sociologists, the fiesta is an excess, an expense. By means of this squandering the community protects itself against the envy of the gods or of men. Sacrifices and offerings placate or buy off the gods and the patron saints. Wasting money and expending energy affirms the community's wealth in both. This luxury is a proof of health, a show of abundance and power. Or a magic trap. For squandering is an effort to attract abundance by contagion. Money calls to money. When life is thrown away it increases; the orgy, which is sexual expenditure, is also a ceremony of regeneration; waste gives strength. New Year celebrations, in every culture, signify something beyond the mere observance of a date on the calendar. The day is a pause: Time is stopped, is actually annihilated. The rites that celebrate its death are intended to provoke its rebirth, because they mark not only the end of an old year but also the beginning of a new. Everything attracts its opposite. The fiesta's function, then, is more utilitarian than we think: waste attracts or promotes wealth, and is an investment like any other, except that the returns on it cannot be measured or counted. What is sought is potency, life, health. In this sense the fiesta, like the gift and the offering, is one of the most ancient of economic forms.

This interpretation has always seemed to me to be incomplete. The fiesta is by nature sacred, literally or figuratively, and above all it is the advent of the unusual. It is governed by its own special rules, that set it apart from other days, and it has a logic, an ethic, and even an economy that are often in conflict with everyday norms. It all occurs in an enchanted world. Time is transformed to a mythical past or a total present; space, the scene of the fiesta, is turned into a gaily decorated world of its own; and the persons taking part cast off all human or social rank and become, for the moment, living images. And everything takes place as if it were not so, as if it were a dream. But whatever happens, our actions have a greater lightness, a different gravity. They take on other meanings and with them we contract new obligations. We throw down our burdens of time and reason.

In certain fiestas the very notion of order disappears. Chaos comes back and license rules. Anything is permitted: The customary hierarchies vanish, along with all social, sex, caste, and trade distinctions. Men disguise themselves as women, gentlemen as slaves, the poor as the rich. The army, the clergy, and the law are ridiculed. Obligatory sacrilege, ritual profanation is committed. Love becomes promiscuity. Sometimes the fiesta becomes a Black Mass. Regulations, habits, and customs are violated. Respectable people put away the dignified expressions and conservative clothes that isolate them, dress up in gaudy colors, hide behind a mask, and escape from themselves.

Therefore the fiesta is not only an excess, a ritual squandering of the goods painfully accumulated during the rest of the year; it is also a revolt, a sudden immersion in the formless, in pure being. By means of the fiesta society frees itself from the norms it has established. It ridicules its gods, its principles, and its laws: It denies its own self.

The fiesta is a revolution in the most literal sense of the word. In the   10 confusion that it generates, society is dissolved, is drowned, insofar as it is an organism ruled according to certain laws and principles. But it drowns in itself, in its own original chaos or liberty. Everything is united: good and evil, day and night, the sacred and the profane. Everything merges, loses shape and individuality and returns to the primordial mass. The fiesta is a cosmic experiment, an experiment in disorder, reuniting contradictory elements and principles in order to bring about a renascence of life. Ritual death promotes a rebirth; vomiting increases the appetite; the orgy, sterile in itself, renews the fertility of the mother or of the earth. The fiesta is a return to a remote and undifferentiated state, prenatal or presocial. It is a return that is also a beginning, in accordance with the dialectic that is inherent in social processes.

The group emerges purified and strengthened from this plunge into chaos. It has immersed itself in its own origins, in the womb from which it came. To express it in another way, the fiesta denies society as an organic system of differentiated forms and principles, but affirms it as a source of creative energy. It is a true "re-creation," the opposite of the "recreation" characterizing modern vacations, which do not entail any rites or ceremonies whatever and are as individualistic and sterile as the world that invented them.

Society communes with itself during the fiesta. Its members return to original chaos and freedom. Social structures break down and new relationships, unexpected rules, capricious hierarchies are created. In the general disorder everybody forgets himself and enters into otherwise forbidden situations and places. The bounds between audience and actors, officials and servants, are erased. Everybody takes part in the fiesta, everybody is caught up in its whirlwind. Whatever its mood, its character, its meaning, the fiesta is participation, and this trait distinguishes it from all other ceremonies and social phenomena. Lay or religious, orgy or saturnalia, the fiesta is a social act based on the full participation of all its celebrants.

Thanks to the fiesta the Mexican opens out, participates, communes with his fellows and with the values that give meaning to his religious or political existence. And it is significant that a country as sorrowful as ours should have so many and such joyous fiestas. Their frequency, their brilliance and excitement, the enthusiasm with which we take part, all suggest that without them we would explode. They free us, if only momentarily, from the thwarted impulses, the inflammable desires that we carry within us. But the Mexican fiesta is not merely a return to an original state of formless and normless liberty: The Mexican is not seeking to return, but to escape from himself, to exceed himself. Our fiestas are explosions. Life and death, joy and sorrow, music and mere noise are united, not to re-create or recognize themselves, but to swallow each other up. There is nothing so joyous as a Mexican fiesta, but there is also nothing so sorrowful. Fiesta night is also a night of mourning.

If we hide within ourselves in our daily lives, we discharge ourselves in the whirlwind of the fiesta. It is more than an opening out: We rend ourselves open. Everything — music, love, friendship — ends in tumult and violence. The frenzy of our festivals shows the extent to which our solitude closes us off from communication with the world. We are familiar with delirium, with songs and shouts, with the monologue . . . but not with the dialogue. Our fiestas, like our confidences, our loves, our attempts to reorder our society, are violent breaks with the old or the established. Each time we try to express ourselves we have to break with ourselves. And the fiesta is only one example, perhaps the most typical, of this violent break. It is not difficult to name others, equally revealing: our games, which are always going to extremes, often mortal; our profligate spending, the reverse of our timid investments and business enterprises; our confessions. The somber Mexican, closed up in himself, suddenly explodes, tears open his breast and reveals himself, though not without a certain complacency, and not without a stopping place in the shameful or terrible mazes of his intimacy. We are not frank, but our sincerity can reach extremes that horrify a European. The explosive, dramatic, sometimes even suicidal manner in which we strip ourselves, surrender ourselves, is evidence that something inhibits and suffocates us. Something impedes us from being. And since we cannot or dare not confront our own selves, we resort to the fiesta. It fires us into the void; it is a drunken rapture that burns itself out, a pistol shot in the air, a skyrocket.

EXPLORATIONS

1. For what kinds of occasions do Mexicans hold fiestas? According to Octavio Paz, how important to a fiesta is the occasion being celebrated? What does Paz suggest are the main reasons why Mexico has so many fiestas?

2. "There is nothing so joyous as a Mexican fiesta, but there is also nothing so sorrowful" (para. 13). What other paradoxes appear in Paz's essay? Why does he think fiestas are so full of them?

3. Have you ever been to a Mardi Gras festival? New Year's Eve in Times Square? Any other mass celebration in the United States? What aspects of such events in this country resemble the Mexican fiestas Paz describes? What aspects are different? To what extent do U.S. "fiestas" play the social role Paz assigns to Mexican fiestas?

CONNECTIONS

1. What common elements appear in the Mexican fiesta described by Paz and the Mexican-American *quinceañera* described by Susan Orlean (p. 36)? What are the most significant differences between these two kinds of celebration?

2. What explanations does Paz offer for the "excess" and "squandering" of the fiesta (para. 6)? Which of these explanations, if any, do you think might apply to the lavish *quinceañeras* mentioned in "Quinceañera" (paras. 6–7, 11–12, 14–16)? What other explanations are offered by the people Orlean interviews?

3. "For a Mexican, intelligence is inseparable from maliciousness," writes Carlos Fuentes (p. 5). What evidence in Paz's essay indicates whether he would agree or disagree?

ELABORATIONS

1. Orlean in "Quinceañera" and Paz in "The Art of the Fiesta" both mention the Virgin of Guadalupe. Using their references as a starting point, find out about Our Lady of Guadeloupe (as she is also called): Who she is, and how and why she became so important to Mexicans.

2. Paz has written: "Mexico is a bureaucratic state halfway between . . . democracy and dictatorship with a constitutional transfer of power, but also a president with absolute power and one-party rule" (p. 48). Investigate the history of Mexico's traditional ruling political party, the Partido Revolucionario Institucional (PRI). Write an essay about the PRI's long-standing monopoly of power or its recent challenges from other parties, or both.

GERMAINE GREER

One Man's Mutilation
Is Another Man's Beautification

Germaine Greer was born in Melbourne, Australia, in 1939. She won scholarships to a convent there and then to Melbourne University, from which she graduated at age twenty. After receiving a First Class Honours master's degree from Sydney University, she taught in a girls' high school and later at the university. Greer went to England in 1964 as a Commonwealth Scholar and received her Ph.D. on Shakespeare from Cambridge University. While working on her thesis she lived in Calabria in southeastern Italy; her observations about the women there feature in her 1985 book *Sex and Destiny*. Greer went on to teach at Warwick University, simultaneously working in television and journalism, and to write her first book, *The Female Eunuch* (1971). This manifesto of the feminist movement made her a celebrity and spokeswoman who continues to travel, lecture, research, and write. Her other books include the feminist interpretation *Shakespeare* (1986), *Slip-shod Sibyls* (1995), and *The Whole Woman* (1999). Greer is currently a Fellow of Newnham College at Cambridge University.

Australia, with an area of almost 3 million square miles, is the world's smallest continent and sixth largest country. It lies south of Indonesia, across the Indian Ocean from southern Africa, and across the Pacific from South America. The native Aborigines may have migrated there from Southeast Asia as long as 40,000 years ago. By 1770, when Captain James Cook claimed Australia for Britain, the Aborigines numbered around 300,000. Among other settlers, the British populated the island with shiploads of transported convicts. The new Australians discovered gold and copper and established sheep ranches, spurring economic growth but displacing the Aborigines. Australia became a commonwealth in 1901 and gained full independence in 1975. Since World War II its ties with Britain have weakened in favor of the United States.

Humans are the only animals which can consciously and deliberately change their appearance according to their own whims. Most animals groom themselves, but humans are tempted to manipulate their appearance in ways much more radical than those open to other animals, not simply because they are able to use tools upon themselves, but also because of some peculiarities in the way in which humans are made. The human body is a curiously ambiguous structure, partaking of almost contradictory attributes. For example, humans are neither furry nor hairless, but variously naked, slightly hairy, and very hirsute. All these variations may be found on the body of a single individual at the same time. Humans are then confronted with a series of managerial problems: among the ways in which they express their cultural identities are the contrasting ways in which they handle these problems.

The Australian Aborigines used to conserve hair; not only did they not eliminate whatever hair was growing on their bodies, they collected extra human hair to work into a thick girdle for men to wear about their hips. We would look askance at anyone who could not bear to discard fallen hair, now that hair shirts are out of fashion, but sophisticated Western people often wear the hair of others as a postiche or toupee. Where the scalp hunter once sought to augment his physical or psychic power by acquiring the hair of others, the literate people of the twentieth century feel that they will acquire youth and beauty through bought hair. They will even pay to have hair stitched into their scalps in a very costly and laborious development of the ancient practice of needle-working living flesh.

Some people identify themselves partly by their refusal to cut hair, as do the Sikhs, who twist the long silky hair of their beards together with what grows on their heads, tie the whole lot up in a chignon, and cover it with a turban. Others insist on the removal of any hair, wherever it is, and they too may choose a turban, this time to hide a bald head. Western conventions of hair management often appeal to younger or recalcitrant members of societies with strict rules for hair management because they find them more convenient; in fact, they are very subtle and difficult, requiring minute calculations of the degree of shagginess which is appropriate to age and economic and social status. The rejection of traditional modes of hair management has less to do with convenience and common sense than with the desire to break out of the confinement of the group. A shaven Sikh might object that he is as much Sikh as ever; he may claim that his elimination of his identifying marks was simply to pour out the bath water while retaining the baby, but in fact he has summarily loosened his ties with his religious group in order to be accepted into another group. If he keeps his steel bracelet, which will be recognized by other Sikhs, it is because he does not wish to lose all the advantages connected with belonging to that group. When a Sikh takes his employer to court for refusing to allow him to wear his turban at work, it is not a mere formality. He is making a serious bid to limit his employer's power over his life.

The impact of technological culture can be measured by the degree of acceptance of Western conventions of body management throughout the world. Fashion, because it is beyond logic, is deeply revealing. Women all over the world have adopted, often in addition to their traditional accoutrements, four Western conventions: high-heeled shoes, lipstick, nail varnish, and the brassiere. The success of all of these fashions, which are not even remotely connected with comfort or common sense, is an indication of the worldwide acceptance of the Western notion that the principal duties of women are sexual attraction and vicarious leisure. The women who have accepted these fashions will justify their decision by saying that all four are more attractive than the alternatives. All that they are really saying is that they themselves were more attracted to alien styles than they were to the styles adopted by their mothers and grandmothers. To give the full answer would be to expose the tensions which are destroying traditional lifestyles all over the world. There is a slight traffic in the opposite direction. Distinguished lady professors of economics may reject high heels, lipstick, nail varnish, and brassiere, and adopt the dress of a Punjabi peasant laborer; Iranian girls may resume the chador. In each case the motive for the change is clearly political; what is not so often realized is that it is equally political when it happens the other way around.

Because what we do with our bodies is so revealing we try to insist that it has no meaning at all. A man whose hair is cut regularly and at great expense, who shaves his face in a careful pattern, will say that he is not concerned with his appearance, while a man with a beard will maintain that he simply cannot be bothered shaving, but the truth is that both have selected an image which they feel best expresses their characters and chosen social roles. The man with a beard probably shaves some part of his face and neck quite regularly, and definitely trims the beard itself. He may frequently be seen grooming it with his hands, patting and stroking it into his preferred shape. Between the shaggy bearded man and the smooth clean-shaven man there lies a vast range of tonsorial modes, all of which have meanings relative to each other. The man who grows his sideburns long is expressing something about his class and his age group. The man who lets his cheek whiskers grow in tufts or shaves his sideburns off is also projecting some part of a chosen self-image. All kinds of curious facial topiary are accepted provided that they have some pedigree within our cultural tradition. The associations of such variations as curled and waxed mustaches, Mexican revolutionary mustaches, pencil mustaches, and toothbrush mustaches are endlessly subtle and constantly being remade.

In the recent past we came to accept long flowing hair as a possible masculine alternative; with the passing of time our initial reactions of outrage have softened into acceptance. Men's long curls are now a sign of nostalgia for the sixties, the last quiver of hippie energy, which was never anything to be feared. By contrast, the man who completely shaves his head still shocks us. It is as if he is flaunting a violence that he has done to himself. Other men, hairless through no choice of their own, may have wigs on the National Health to hide their embarrassing nakedness. Western youths whose heads are shaven in accordance with the practice of oriental monastics will wear wigs when they go to badger people in airports because shaven heads are so alienating to our sensibilities. The man who shaves his head and does not cover it is indulging in a form of indecent exposure, the purpose of which, as usual, is intimidation.

The shaving of women's heads is considered so disfiguring that it seemed adequate punishment for women who collaborated with the Nazis in the Second World War, and yet there are many cultures whose women shave all or part of their heads and would feel dirty or unkempt if they did not. Girls who shave off all the hair except what grows on the crown of their heads are doing no more than the Turkana women of Kenya have always done, but by doing it in a society where such styles have never been seen, they defy the accepted norms and court rejection. The coxcomb and its variants, sometimes called the Mohawk or Mohican hairstyle, imitate the intimidating shapes of the advanced crests of fighting birds. A less daring version, for it can be tamed into smoothness when the wearer is in the haunts of the smooth, is the teased mop. The ferocity mimicked by the hairstyle is further expressed in the studded belts and armlets and earrings in the shape of a skull, but it is clearly a mere affectation. The camp aggressiveness of the display stands in inverse ratio to the social power wielded by the group. Their cultural uniformity is actually competitiveness and does not lead to solidarity.

In most societies which modify the body, the visible changes are outward signs of the fulfilment of the rites of passage. The acceptance of the newborn into the community at a naming ceremony or its equivalent may be marked by a ritual haircut, the shape of which may indicate his or her clan or totem. The approach of puberty may be signalled by circumcision or scarification or the adoption of a new hairstyle. The prelude to marriage may require further scarification or tattooing or fattening or a period of special body painting, while marriage itself may be signified by drastic changes in appearance, especially for women. The birth of children, achievement of elder status, or the death of a spouse bring the last changes. In classless societies where property is either held in common or kept to a minimum, all changes in status must involve changes in physical appearance. Where no one carries an identity card which will, say, permit him to drink in the company of adults, everyone who may must be distinguished by a sign. The achievement of these signs is one of the most important satisfactions of such societies. Before imperialists brought mirrors, such people could not confer the signs upon themselves: The recognition of a transition was given dramatic form by the ceremony of the conferring of signs in which the interested parties all acted as a group.

In Western society the outward signs of social status have withered into mere vestiges. Pubescent boys may live through intense dramas of hair cultivation, struggling for a mustache or bushy sideburns or simply longing to shave every day. Little girls may covet high heels and brassieres and long for the day that they can wear makeup, but the menarche will not be marked in any way: Marriageability will be signified only by the absence of an inconspicuous ring on the fourth finger of the left hand. In Jewish society, circumcision is still a rite of passage, but once the bar mitzvah is over, the initiate cannot be recognized by any other outward sign. Married women used to be expected to dress differently from girls: a pale echo of the sixteenth-century custom which required married women to wear closed bodices and hide their hair under a cap. This persisted into the twentieth century when married women were expected to wear hats on social occasions, but has now died out.

The disappearance of distinguishing marks of social status in industrial societies is not meaningless, nor can it be construed to mean that human beings have outgrown such childish things. It is an accurate reflection of the fact that social relationships, particularly kinship relations, have been and are under intense pressure from economic relationships. The one insignia that is worn, in the United States more than in Europe but the strengthening of the trend is apparent, is the insignia of the employer. The family is no longer the dominant group and human beings are no longer differentiated on the grounds of their status within it. Instead they are differentiated by their consumer behavior, employment status, income, and possessions: The contrasts are so striking that it is considered indiscreet and tasteless to flaunt them by display of wealth. Instead the degrees of difference are signaled, more or less subtly, by grooming and by some carefully chosen attributes; hints to those who know how to take them are conveyed by the watch, the pen, the attaché case, the note case, the cuff links. Along with the indications of success are clues to other allegiances, the college ring, the

lodge pin, the old school tie. Democracy and uniformity in outward appearance are necessitated by the extreme differentiation in economic
circumstances, which might otherwise become a source of tension.

In tribal societies, where economic activity is static, limited as it is to
the repetitive daily functions of survival, there is time to elaborate the
paraphernalia of status considered in all but economic terms and immense satisfaction connected with doing so. The individual who pro-
ceeds through the stages all duly solemnized has conferred an elegance
and order upon the struggle, and within that wider function there is
scope for individual expression and aesthetic concerns.

The motives for Western beautification are very different. . . . People
who are excluded from economic activity . . . cannot compensate by
celebrating other forms of status for these have been eliminated. Un-
happily, as the social roles which evolve out of family relationships
ceased to command respect, the number of older people condemned to
live for many years outside the sphere of economic activity in conditions of mere survival increased and will go on increasing. Among the
displacement activities which this group must now concentrate on in
order to beguile the time between retirement and the grave, there are a
number connected with futile imitation of the group from which they
have been excluded. As there is no prestige or power connected with
being old, it is important to deny the aging process itself. Where once
humans celebrated the achievement of seniority and longevity, they
now invest as much energy or more in trying to resist the inevitable.
Where hair coloring used to be done for fun, it is now done for camou-
flage.

A full head of strawberry blonde curls is only acquired by a sixty-year-
old after regular orgies of dying, setting, and backcombing, all of which
actually speed the degeneration of the scalp and the hair shaft. There is
a good deal of pain involved as the dyes bite into sensitive old skin and
the hot dryers tighten the hair, driving the pins still further into the old
scalp. The ordeal is worth it if the sufferer sees herself rejuvenated by it;
the suffering is an essential part of the prophylaxis, but it must be accompanied by words of tenderness and filial care from the torturers. We
are not surprised to see the hairdresser as a shaman, hung about with
amulets, his face suffused with long-suffering compassion. The payment of money for his services guarantees that the job has been well
done; an old lady with a fifty-dollar hairstyle is still a person to be reck-
oned with. . . .

. . . We are in the midst of a cultural upheaval in which the body,
which for aeons was a holy thing, its excretions and its orifices feared
and revered, is becoming reified. It is becoming a toy, an asset, a com-

modity, an instrumentality for human will, and the pace of the change is much too fast. The intolerability of pictures of stainless steel meticulously carving out faces and breasts, isolating the unwanted and throwing it in the trash, tells us that we are still superstitious. We still suspect that the fantasy which is being imposed upon the body is less potent and less various than the body itself. Yet we cannot ease our anxiety by sneering, for we know the callousness which characterizes our treatment of the old and obese. We can understand why people who have the money will endure pain and risk death rather than go on living inside the bodies which bear the marks of their own history. Cosmetic surgery is the secular version of confession and absolution. It has taken the place of all our lost ceremonies of death and rebirth. It is reincarnation.

Most societies reject the grossly deformed. All societies have notions 15 of beauty and fitness to which they aspire: Relatively non-neurotic societies tend to admire characteristics which are well-distributed among their people, because distance from the culturally recognized norm causes suffering. We are affected by our bodies just as our behavior marks them. Peculiar-looking people tend to behave peculiarly. Criminologists have known for many years that cosmetic surgery may do more for a social delinquent than years of custody and psychiatric care, when it comes to rehabilitation.

Once we begin to sculpt the body to our own aesthetic requirements we enter a realm of shifting values to which there is no guide. In essence, beautification and mutilation are the same activity. The African women who practice genital mutilation do so primarily because they think the result is more attractive; the unreconstructed genitalia are disgusting to them. Very few Westerners really find the female genitalia beautiful, but most of them would be horrified, even nauseated, by the sight of an infibulated vagina. None of them, by contrast, would cry out in disgust at the sight of a mutilated penis, stripped of its foreskin; all of them would be unpleasantly affected by the sight of a sub-incised penis.

Some mutilations have an ulterior purpose; the biting off of little finger joints of the newborn by Aboriginal mothers may be a way of deflecting the attention of evil spirits who would covet a perfect child. The custom of branding sickly infants in India may incidentally eliminate the feebler ones before too much energy has been invested in their care, and even, perhaps, activate sluggish resistance to the pathogens in the environment. In any event, the brands are carefully placed. The endurance of pain, especially in poor communities where pain and discomfort are daily realities, is another important aspect of beautification/

mutilation. Scarification is valued not only because it is symmetrically placed about the body and not only because it implies the achievement of new status, but because it hurts. Where survival is only achieved by constant effort, stoicism and willpower are immensely important. The young woman who lies unflinching while the circumciser grinds her clitoris off between two stones is proving that she will make a good wife, equal to all the anguish of childbearing and daily toil, not only to the witnesses of her bravery, but more importantly, to herself.

Industrialized society is the first in which endurance of physical pain is not a condition of survival. We have identified pain as our enemy and have done our best to eradicate even its most manageable manifestations. Scars have no value for us and their aesthetic appeal has perished alongside their moral value. A few women might confess that they feel strangely drawn to men with scarred faces (or eye patches or limps) but it is generally considered to be an aberrant taste. Yet, augmentation mammoplasty is no more after all than a raised scar. The great difference between ancient and modern beautification/mutilation procedures is that nowadays we must conceal the fact of the procedure itself. The association of sculpted breasts with pain is anaphrodisiac, so much so that a man who guesses that what he is admiring was produced by a knife may lose all interest. Some women may boast of their cosmetic operations, but this is a safety valve against the possibility that they will be found out.

Most mutilations which have been accepted as beautiful are so by consensus; historically the most astonishing distortions have been admired, necks so elongated that they could not hold up the head unless supported by brass rings, teeth filed and knocked out, lips stretched to accommodate large discs, ear-lobes stretched until they hung down in large loops. However *outré* the punks may appear they are the merest beginners in the arts of mutilation. The admiration of certain disfigurements is an important part of the process of self-definition: Contempt for the same practices is one of the ways in which other groups insist upon their separateness. We are not surprised to find the greatest contrasts in groups living side by side. When genetic equipment and economic status are both very similar, contrasting cultural practices become immensely important; they become the expression of the group's introverted altruism. In most tribal societies the attitude is more or less pluralistic; a group of labret wearers, for example, will simply define themselves as labret wearers, without making any attempt to impose labrets on others or to deride them for being without them. Western industrial society, deluded perhaps by its own vastness and uniformity, is not pluralistic, but utterly convinced that its own practices are the product of enlightenment and ought to be followed by all progressive peoples. Thus Western women, fully accoutred with nail polish (which is incompatible with manual work), high-heeled shoes (disastrous for the posture and hence the back, and quite unsuitable for walking long distances over bad roads), and brassieres (which imitate the shape of a pubescent nonlactating breast rather than the useful organs to be found in most of the world) denounce female circumcision, without the shadow of a suspicion that their behavior is absurd.

Yet within this bland but crushing orthodoxy there are spores of   20 something different. Our unemployed young have reverted to tribal practices. They indulge in flamboyant mutilation/beautification which is not understood, let alone appreciated in our common judgment. Teenage daughters come to their parents' dinner parties covered with blue spots, with blue hair standing on end. Deviant groups cemented by shared ritual intoxication or guilt or ordeal or all of these are budding in our rotting inner cities, terrorizing us with raucous music and insulting doggerel. If they had the power to grow like a malignant organism and invade the whole of the body politic we might have reason to be afraid. Like millions of generations of body decorators before them, they have no economic activity beyond survival; they could be toughened by the necessity of existing on the little that society will mete out to them so that they accumulate the collective power to strike at its unprotected underbelly. Or they could fritter away their spare energy in intercommunal war, as gangs have always done. The body art of the urban deviant is unlike any which has appeared on earth before in that it has no socially constructed significance. There is . . . [no] . . . mutual decoration; no young warriors apply magical designs to each other's backs. No priests and witches or mothers and aunts confer new powers upon an initiate. The only human interactions we see are commercial. The manicurists, the cosmetologists, the surgeons, the hairdressers, the tattooists are all professionals. Between the dancer and the dance has been interposed the mirror; the clients have come to the professionals after long and lonely contemplation of the self which dissatisfies them. Individuals do not modify their bodies to please others or to clarify their relationship to others. Rather they inflict changes upon themselves in order to approximate to narcissistic needs which may have been projected on to putative others.

Inside the bodies they have reconstructed, the body builders live incommunicado. The illustrated men disappear behind designs imported from a highly structured alien culture into which they themselves could never be accepted. The body building, the tattooing, the cultivation of cockscombs, the driving of rings, bolts, barbs, and studs through labia, lobes, cartilage, nipples, foreskin are all displacement activities. A caged bird suffering from loneliness and sensory deprivation will turn upon itself and pluck out all its feathers or peck off its own leg. Middle-aged women rejected by their children will turn to surgery, restlessly beautifying/mutilating to no purpose, and a good deal of their activity will be directed against their sexuality. The body builders will proceed until they have become epicene monsters, all body hair shaved off so that the light can catch the slick greased muscles. . . . One of the most potent symbols among all natural symbols is the breast, not only the female breast but by extension the male simulacrum. Only groups doomed to extinction have ever attacked the nipples; cutting, piercing, and distorting them . . . is something hideously strange. . . . Attacks upon the genitalia and the secondary sexual characteristics are attacks upon the continuity of the species; they are only conceivable in lives which are confined to their own duration, on bodies which must be their own gratification, among human contacts which are fleeting and self-centered. . . .

The right to economic activity is no longer a right which our society can guarantee to everyone. We are on the brink of an era in which most people will be condemned to a life of enforced leisure and mere subsistence. It may very well be that these displacement activities will have to evolve into legitimate art forms involving a strong and healthy body decorated with skill, sophistication, and meaning. Perhaps human worker bees will some day be delighted by the displays of squads of human butterflies bred and trained to dance the drab streets as living works of art. It would be a great pity if the dazzling tradition of human body art were to perish in a waste of dreary conformity on the one hand and neurotic self-distortion on the other.

EXPLORATIONS

1. According to Germaine Greer, what are the main reasons why a culture creates a custom of mutilating its members' bodies in a certain way?

2. How would you describe Greer's prose style in this essay? How do her style and tone compare with those of typical contemporary writing about fashion and physical appearance? How does Greer's style contribute to the impact of the points she is making?

3. Find two points where Greer draws her own conclusions about the goal or motive behind a group's (or a group member's) manipulation of physical

appearance. On what kinds of evidence does she base her conclusions? Do you agree with her assessments? Why or why not?

CONNECTIONS

1. According to Greer, how do people use their physical appearance to support their culture's social order, and why? According to Octavio Paz in "The Art of the Fiesta" (p. 48), how do people at a fiesta revolt against the social order, and why?

2. How does Jill Ker Conway describe Australians' "inner landscape of the mind" (p. 5)? What evidence of Conway's view appears in "One Man's Mutilation Is Another Man's Beautification"?

3. Read Gerald Early's short description on page 309 of watching hairdressers at work. Compare Early's comments and questions with Greer's statements in the second half of her paragraph 20. What ideas are expressed by both writers? How would you expect Early to disagree with Greer's analysis?

ELABORATIONS

1. Do you agree with Greer's comments about shaved heads (paras. 6–7)? How have social attitudes toward shaved heads changed since she wrote this essay in 1986? Write your own essay describing and analyzing head shaving in particular, or hair fashions in general, in the contemporary United States.

2. Find several places where Greer describes a current Western fashion. What techniques does she use to make a familiar practice sound like a strange tribal custom? For instance, what kind of vocabulary does she choose? What kind of syntax? Verbs? Pronouns? Does she make value judgments? If so, how are they expressed? Write an essay analyzing Greer's prose style and the effect of her stylistic choices on her essay's impact.

PAUL HARRISON

The Westernization of the World

Paul Harrison is a freelance writer and consultant based in London. He has traveled widely in Asia, Africa, and Latin America and has written extensively about development and the environment. He has done reports for several United Nations agencies, such as the Food and Agriculture Organization, the World Bank, and the UN Fund for Population Activities. Harrison took master's degrees at Cambridge University and the London School of Economics and has a Ph.D. in earth sciences from Cambridge. His interest in the Third World began in 1968 when he was lecturing in French at the University of Ife, Nigeria. Among his recent books are *The Greening of Africa* (1987), *The Third Revolution* (1993), and *Elements of Pantheism* (1999). He is currently president of the World Pantheist Movement.

"The Westernization of the World" comes from the second edition of Harrison's book *Inside the Third World* (1981). He based it on research and travel between 1975 and 1980 in Sri Lanka, Upper Volta and the Ivory Coast, Colombia and Peru, Brazil, Indonesia and Singapore, India, Bangladesh, and Kenya. "In some ways it was a mad enterprise to attempt to cover so much ground," he admits. However, "The underdevelopment of countries and of human beings cannot be compartmentalized if it is to be fully grasped. It is a total situation, in which every element plays a part."

Like many commentators, Harrison refers to underdeveloped countries and their citizens collectively as the *Third World*. The term has more than one definition; typically it is applied to nations in Africa, Asia, and Latin America that are not heavily industrialized and have a low standard of living. Shiva Naipaul has noted ironically: "The exemplary Third World denizen . . . lives a hand-to-mouth existence, he is indifferent to the power struggles of the mighty ones, and he is dark-skinned." Naipaul adds, "To blandly subsume, say, Ethiopia, India, and Brazil under the one banner of Third Worldhood is as absurd and as denigrating as the old assertion that all Chinese look alike." Still, keeping in mind the dangers noted by Simone de Beauvoir of dividing humanity into "us" and "them" (see p. 341), we can use the concept of the Third World to examine, as Harrison does, certain tendencies shared by nations that are otherwise dissimilar.

> The bourgeoisie has, through its exploitation of the world market, given a cosmopolitan character to production and consumption in every country.
>
> – Karl Marx

In Singapore, Peking opera still lives, in the back streets. On Boat Quay, where great barges moor to unload rice from Thailand, raw rubber from Malaysia, or timber from Sumatra, I watched a troupe of traveling actors throw up a canvas-and-wood booth stage, paint on their white faces and lozenge eyes, and don their resplendent vermilion, ultramarine, and gold robes. Then, to raptured audiences of bent old women and little children with perfect circle faces, they enacted tales of feudal princes and magic birds and wars and tragic love affairs, sweeping their sleeves and singing in strange metallic voices.

The performance had been paid for by a local cultural society as part of a religious festival. A purple cloth temple had been erected on the quayside, painted papier-mâché sculptures were burning down like giant joss sticks, and middle-aged men were sharing out gifts to be distributed among members' families: red buckets, roast ducks, candies, and moon cakes. The son of the organizer, a fashionable young man in Italian shirt and gold-rimmed glasses, was looking on with amused benevolence. I asked him why only old people and children were watching the show.

"Young people don't like these operas," he said. "They are too old-fashioned. We would prefer to see a high-quality Western variety show, something like that."

He spoke for a whole generation. Go to almost any village in the Third World and you will find youths who scorn traditional dress and sport denims and T-shirts. Go into any bank and the tellers will be dressed as would their European counterparts; at night the manager will climb into his car and go home to watch TV in a home that would not stick out on a European or North American estate.[1] Every capital city in the world is getting to look like every other; it is Marshall McLuhan's global village, but the style is exclusively Western. And not just in consumer fashions: The mimicry extends to architecture, industrial technology, approaches to health care, education, and housing.

To the ethnocentric Westerner or the Westernized local, that may   5
seem the most natural thing in the world. That is modern life, they might think. That is the way it will all be one day. That is what development and economic growth are all about.

---

[1] Housing development. — ED.

Yet the dispassionate observer can only be puzzled by this growing world uniformity. Surely one should expect more diversity, more indigenous styles and models of development? Why is almost everyone following virtually the same European road? The Third World's obsession with the Western way of life has perverted development and is rapidly destroying good and bad in traditional cultures, flinging the baby out with the bathwater. It is the most totally pervasive example of what historians call cultural diffusion in the history of mankind.

Its origins, of course, lie in the colonial experience. European rule was something quite different from the general run of conquests. Previous invaders more often than not settled down in their new territories, interbred, and assimilated a good deal of local culture. Not so the Europeans. Some, like the Iberians[2] or the Dutch, were not averse to cohabitation with native women: unlike the British, they seemed free of purely racial prejudice. But all the Europeans suffered from the same cultural arrogance. Perhaps it is the peculiar self-righteousness of Pauline[3] Christianity that accounts for this trait. Whatever the cause, never a doubt entered their minds that native cultures could be in any way, materially, morally, or spiritually, superior to their own, and that the supposedly benighted inhabitants of the darker continents needed enlightening.

And so there grew up, alongside political and economic imperialism, that more insidious form of control — cultural imperialism. It conquered not just the bodies but the souls of its victims, turning them into willing accomplices.

Cultural imperialism began its conquest of the Third World with the indoctrination of an elite of local collaborators. The missionary schools sought to produce converts to Christianity who would go out and proselytize among their own people, helping to eradicate traditional culture. Later the government schools aimed to turn out a class of junior bureaucrats and lower military officers who would help to exploit and repress their own people. The British were subtle about this, since they wanted the natives, even the Anglicized among them, to keep their distance. The French, and the Portuguese in Africa, explicitly aimed at the "assimilation" of gifted natives, by which was meant their metamorphosis into model Frenchmen and Lusitanians,[4] distinguishable only by the tint of their skin.

---

[2]Spanish or Portuguese (i.e., from the Iberian peninsula). — ED.
[3]Relating to the writings and teachings of St. Paul. — ED.
[4]Portuguese. Lusitania was the Roman name for the part of the Iberian peninsula that is now Portugal. — ED.

The second channel of transmission was more indirect and volun-   10
tary. It worked by what sociologists call reference-group behavior, found
when someone copies the habits and life-style of a social group he
wishes to belong to, or to be classed with, and abandons those of his
own group. This happened in the West when the new rich of early
commerce and industry aped the nobility they secretly aspired to join.
Not surprisingly, the social climbers in the colonies started to mimic
their conquerors. The returned slaves who carried the first wave of
Westernization in West Africa[5] wore black woolen suits and starched
collars in the heat of the dry season. The new officer corps of India were
molded into what the Indian writer Nirad Chaudhuri has called "imitation, polo-playing English subalterns," complete with waxed mustaches
and peacock chests. The elite of Indians, adding their own caste-
consciousness to the class-consciousness of their rulers, became more
British than the British (and still are).

There was another psychological motive for adopting Western ways,
deriving from the arrogance and haughtiness of the colonialists. As the
Martiniquan political philosopher, Frantz Fanon, remarked, colonial
rule was an experience in racial humiliation. Practically every leader of
a newly independent state could recall some experience such as being
turned out of a club or manhandled on the street by whites, often of low
status. The local elite were made to feel ashamed of their color and of
their culture. "I begin to suffer from not being a white man," Fanon
wrote, "to the degree that the white man imposes discrimination on me,
makes me a colonized native, robs me of all worth, all individuality. . . .
Then I will quite simply try to make myself white: that is, I will compel
the white man to acknowledge that I am human." To this complex
Fanon attributes the colonized natives' constant preoccupation with at-
tracting the attention of the white man, becoming powerful like the
white man, proving at all costs that blacks too can be civilized. Given
the racism and culturism of the whites, this could only be done by suc-
ceeding in their terms, and by adopting their ways.

This desire to prove equality surely helps to explain why Ghana's
Nkrumah built the huge stadium and triumphal arch of Black Star
Square in Accra. Why the tiny native village of Ivory Coast president
Houphouët-Boigny has been graced with a four-lane motorway starting
and ending nowhere, a five-star hotel and ultramodern conference cen-
ter. Why Sukarno transformed Indonesia's capital, Jakarta, into an

---

[5]One of many plans for solving the problem of slavery in the United States was to send
freed slaves to Africa. The Republic of Liberia in West Africa was founded for this purpose
in 1822. — ED.

exercise in gigantism, scarred with six-lane highways and neofascist monuments in the most hideous taste. The aim was not only to show the old imperialists, but to impress other Third World leaders in the only way everyone would recognize: the Western way.

The influence of Western life-styles spread even to those few nations who escaped the colonial yoke. By the end of the nineteenth century, the elites of the entire non-Western world were taking Europe as their reference group. The progress of the virus can be followed visibly in a room of Topkapi, the Ottoman palace in Istanbul, where a sequence of showcases display the costumes worn by each successive sultan. They begin with kaftans and turbans. Slowly elements of Western military uniform creep in, until the last sultans are decked out in brocade, epaulettes, and cocked hats.

The root of the problem with nations that were never colonized, like Turkey, China, and Japan, was probably their consciousness of Western military superiority. The beating of these three powerful nations at the hands of the West was a humiliating, traumatic experience. For China and Japan, the encounter with the advanced military technology of the industrialized nations was as terrifying as an invasion of extraterrestrials. Europe's earlier discovery of the rest of the world had delivered a mild culture shock to her ethnocentric attitudes. The Orient's contact with Europe shook nations to the foundations, calling into question the roots of their civilizations and all the assumptions and institutions on which their lives were based.

In all three nations groups of Young Turks[6] grew up, believing that   15 their countries could successfully take on the West only if they adopted Western culture, institutions, and even clothing, for all these ingredients were somehow involved in the production of Western technology. As early as the 1840s, Chinese intellectuals were beginning to modify the ancient view that China was in all respects the greatest civilization in the world. The administrator Wei Yüan urged his countrymen to "learn the superior technology of the barbarians in order to control them." But the required changes could not be confined to the technical realm. Effectiveness in technology is the outcome of an entire social system. "Since we were knocked out by cannon balls," wrote M. Chiang, "naturally we became interested in them, thinking that by learning to make them we could strike back. From studying cannon balls we came to mechanical inventions which in turn led to political reforms, which led us again to the political philosophies of the West."

---

[6]Members of an aggressive reform group. — ED.

The republican revolution of 1911 attempted to modernize China, but her subjection to the West continued until another Young Turk, Mao Zedong, applied that alternative brand of Westernization: Communism, though in a unique adaptation.

The Japanese were forced to open their border to Western goods in 1853, after a couple of centuries of total isolation. They had to rethink fast in order to survive. From 1867, the Meiji rulers Westernized Japan with astonishing speed, adopting Western science, technology, and even manners: short haircuts became the rule, ballroom dancing caught on, and *moningku* with *haikara* (morning coats and high collars) were worn. The transformation was so successful that by the 1970s the Japanese were trouncing the West at its own game. But they had won their economic independence at the cost of losing their cultural autonomy.

Turkey, defeated in the First World War, her immense empire in fragments, set about transforming herself under that compulsive and ruthless Westernizer, Kemal Atatürk. The Arabic script was abolished and replaced with the Roman alphabet. Kemal's strange exploits as a hatter will probably stand as the symbol of Westernization carried to absurd lengths. His biographer, Lord Kinross, relates that while traveling in the West as a young man, the future president had smarted under Western insults and condescension about the Turkish national hat, the fez. Later, he made the wearing of the fez a criminal offense. "The people of the Turkish republic," he said in a speech launching the new policy, "must prove that they are civilized and advanced persons in their outward respect also. . . . A civilized, international dress is worthy and appropriate for our nation and we will wear it. Boots or shoes on our feet, trousers on our legs, shirt and tie, jacket and waistcoat — and, of course, to complete these, a cover with a brim on our heads. I want to make this clear. This head covering is called a hat."

EXPLORATIONS

1. Early in his essay Paul Harrison asks the central question: "Why is almost everyone following virtually the same European road?" (para. 6). What are the characteristics of this "European road"? What are the origins of the specific examples the author cites?

2. What general cause, and what specific channels, does Harrison cite as responsible for the Third World's Westernization? What differences between Western newcomers and Third World natives seem to have most strongly affected relations between them?

3. "By the end of the nineteenth century," writes Harrison, "the elites of the entire non-Western world were taking Europe as their reference group" (para. 13). How does he explain the initial westward tilt of countries that were never colonized? What explanation does he suggest for their continuing interest in Western ways?

CONNECTIONS

1. In paragraph 10 Harrison discusses "reference-group behavior." What examples of this behavior can you find in Germaine Greer's "One Man's Mutilation Is Another Man's Beautification" (p. 55)?

2. Harrison's subject, the Westernization of the world, leads him to focus on the impact of colonialism. How does his description of Indians at the end of paragraph 10 differ from the ways Salman Rushdie (p. 86) and Anita Desai (p. 7) describe their lives in India? Which of Harrison's ideas also appear in Rushdie's or Desai's recollections? In Bharati Mukherjee's Observation (p. 3)?

3. In paragraph 11, Harrison discusses some racial aspects of Westernization. In what ways does Danzy Senna in "The Mulatto Millennium" (p. 18) suggest that similar processes took place in the United States?

ELABORATIONS

1. Harrison focuses on Westernization in non-Western countries. What explanation (if any) does he offer for the spread of a single cultural trend all over Europe and North America? On the basis of Harrison's theories, plus evidence from other selections you have read, write an essay identifying causes and effects behind the West's homogeneity.

2. It has become fairly common for couples and individuals in the United States to adopt babies from Third World countries. In what ways does cross-cultural adoption benefit the child, the original and adoptive parents, and the child's original and adoptive homelands? What are the drawbacks of this practice? Write an argumentative essay defending or opposing cross-cultural adoption, or a process-analysis essay advising the would-be parent(s) on how to protect the interests of all involved.

ES'KIA MPHAHLELE

African Literature: What Tradition?

Es'kia Mphahlele (pronounced m-fa-lay-lay) was born Ezekiel
Mphahlele in South Africa in 1919. He grew up in the capital city of
Pretoria and received his B.A. with honors from the University of South
Africa. Although he was banned from teaching in 1952 for protesting
the segregationist Bantu Education Act, Mphahlele completed his master's degree and served as fiction editor for a Johannesburg magazine before leaving the country in 1957. In Paris he became director of African
programs for the International Association for Cultural Freedom. Moving to the United States, he received his Ph.D. from the University of
Denver and taught in the English department there; he also has taught
at the University of Pennsylvania and in Kenya, Nigeria, and Zambia.
Mphahlele returned to South Africa in 1977. "There is a force I call the
tyranny of place," he has said; "the kind of unrelenting hold a place has
on a person that gives him the motivation to write and a style." Even
though his books were banned under apartheid, he taught and became
head of African Literature at the University of the Witwatersrand (he is
now a professor emeritus). Mphahlele has published story collections,
works of criticism, novels, a children's book, and the acclaimed autobiography *Down Second Avenue* (1959); his essays have appeared in numerous journals. "African Literature: What Tradition?" comes from a
longer essay by the same title which originally appeared in the *Denver
Quarterly*.

Covering Africa's southern tip, the Republic of South Africa is about
twice the size of Texas. The region's Khoisan tribes — formerly known as
Bushmen and Hottentots — had been joined by Bantus from the north
by the time Dutch settlers arrived in the seventeenth century. Racial
and political conflicts began when the British seized the Cape of Good
Hope in 1806. At that time many Dutch moved north and founded two
new republics, the Transvaal and the Orange Free State, displacing native Khoisan and Bantu tribes. Whites of Dutch descent became known
as Afrikaners and their language as Afrikaans. They and their white com-
patriots kept political control by means of *apartheid*, a policy of racial
separation that severely limited blacks' access to jobs, housing, income,
and influence. Asians (mostly Indians) and Coloureds (those of mixed
descent) also were shut out of power, but less repressively than the majority black population. Conflict intensified when diamonds and gold
were discovered in the late 1800s. The ensuing Anglo-Boer (British versus Dutch) War was won by the British, who created the Union of South
Africa in 1910. In 1948 apartheid became official, legally enforcing

racially separate development and residential areas. In 1961, with only whites allowed to vote, South African voters withdrew their nation from the British Commonwealth; in the late 1980s, Asians and Coloureds received the right to vote (with restrictions), and laws banning interracial marriage were repealed. In 1994, after decades of pressure from Nelson Mandela and other members of the African National Congress (ANC) as well as an international community of allies including writers like Nadine Gordimer (see p. 284), free multiracial elections were held in South Africa for the first time. Mandela became president; for more information on him and his country, see page 600.

It all started when Africa was shanghaied into the history of the West in the late nineteenth century. What were we coming into? — a long line of continuity going back some 9,000 years since the civilizations of the great river valleys of the Nile, the Tigris and Euphrates, the Indus, and the Hwang-ho had launched man on a long intellectual quest. We had been discovered by an aggressive Western culture which was never going to let us be. Nor could we cease following the neon lights — or has it been a will o' the wisp? Time will tell. Perhaps Hegelian historical determinism will have it that it is as it should be: How could Africa be left out of it all indefinitely?

And so here I am, an ambivalent character. But I'm nothing of the oversimplified and sensationalized Hollywood version of a man of two worlds. It is not as if I were pinned on a rock, my legs stretched in opposite directions. Education sets up conflicts but also reconciles them in degrees that depend on the subject's innate personality equipment. It seems to me a writer in an African setting must possess this equipment and must strive toward some workable reconciliation inside himself. It is an agonizing journey. It can also be humiliating to feel that one has continually to be reassessing oneself with reference to the long line of tradition he has entered — the tradition of the West. How else? I have assimilated the only education the West had to offer me. I was brought up on European history and literature and religion and made to identify with European heroes while African heroes were being discredited, except those that became Christians or signed away their land and freedom, and African gods were being smoked out. I later rejected Christianity. And yet I could not return to ancestral worship in any overt way. But this does not invalidate my ancestors for me. Deep down there inside my agnostic self, I feel a reverence for them.

The majority of writers in Africa, I venture to say, are attached in a detached manner to one indigenous religion or another. They are not involved in its ritual, but they look at it with reverence. When, in their full consciousness, they have found themselves Christian — which can often just mean baptized — they have not adopted churchianity. Because our whole education system in Africa has been mission-ridden right from the beginning, and the white minister was supposed by the government or commercial or school-board employer to know the "native," you had always to produce a testimonial signed by a white church minister when you were applying for a job. Not even black ministers could speak for you. If you wanted to go out for further studies, you knew where to find St. Peter. The black minister himself required testimonials from one of his white brethren, never from another black minister. So we called ourselves Christians; we entered "Christian" on the line against an item that asked for it on all the multiplicity of forms, just in order to save ourselves the trouble of explaining and therefore failing to go through the gates. In independent Africa, we are luckily able to trust fellow blacks who vouch for us and others. And you can almost see the Christian veneer peeling off because it has nothing to do with conscience. . . .

By far the larger part of Africa is still traditionally minded in varying degrees. The whole dialogue around tradition is an intellectual one. The parents of people of my generation, although they may be urbanized, are still close to tradition. They worry a great deal about the way in which we break loose at one point and ignore some elements of tradition. Each time an African mother sends a child to high school, it is like giving birth to him all over again. She knows she is yielding something. Dialogue between her and the child decreases and eventually stays on the level of basic essentials: our needs, our family relations, family life, which must continue more or less normally, whatever else around us may progressively be reduced to abstractions or gadgets. It is no less excruciating for the young man who stands in this kind of relationship with his parents. But he can reconcile himself to it — the very educational process that wrenches him from his moorings helps him to arrange a harmonization within himself.

The parent will often moan and complain to him about the awkward distance he has reached away from tradition. But it is never a reprimand; it is an indulgent complaint. Because, I think, the parents are always aware that this whole business of education does not of itself engage you in an activity that expressly subverts the morals of the family, the clan, or of the tribe. They are aware of the many situations around them that require an education to cope with them. The benefits of tradition are abstract, and the parents' own thinking has not been stagnant while the whole landscape around them has been changing, while the white man's government has been impinging on their way of life over several decades. And the benefits of a modern education are tangible, real.

I have always asked myself what it is in one's formal education that leads to the rupture, to the ever-widening gulf between one and one's parents and one's community. You recognize the alphabet, then words, and then you can extract meaning from many sentences in a row. With that shock of recognition, words leap into life in front of you. They set your mind on fire; longings and desires you would never have known are released and seem to whirl around in currents that explode into other currents: something like what you see in a glass flask of water that you have on a naked flame to observe the movement of heat in liquid. From then on, one must not stop. Yet it is not something one can take for granted in an African context, because to start at all is not inevitable: Education is not compulsory, and the financial cost of it is immense.

In your higher education, you assimilate patterns of thought, argument, and so on from an alien culture in an alien language; they become your own. Of course you cannot help using your African setting as your field of reference; you cannot help going out of the queue of Western orientation now and again to consult those of your people who are not physically in it. You try to express their philosophy in a European language whose allegory, metaphor, and so on are alien to the spirit of that philosophy: something that can best be understood in terms of allegory and metaphor that are centered heavily on human relationships and external nature. All the same, you are in the queue, and you belong not only to an African community but also to a worldwide intellectual or worldwide economic community, or both. This is why communication becomes difficult, sometimes impossible, between your people who are still not tuned into Western intellectual systems and yourself. Your mind operates in a foreign language, even while you are actually talking your mother tongue, at the moment you are engaged in your profession. You try hard to find correspondences and you realize there are only a few superficial ones: You have to try to *make* most of them. In the pure sciences, which are universally applicable, the correspondences are numerous; there is no problem.

Indigenous languages that have only recently become literary, that is, only since the church missions established presses in Africa, seem to have relied more and more heavily on the spoken word, so that gesture, facial expression, inflection of voice became vital equipment in communication. Language became almost a ritual in itself, and metaphor and symbol became a matter of art and device. Metaphor became a sacred thing if it had descended from usage in earlier times; when an elder, in a traditional court case, prefaced a proverb or aphorism or metaphor by saying, "Our elders say . . . ," his audience listened with profound reverence. Notice the present tense in "our elders *say.* . . ." Because his elders would be the ancestors, who are still present with us in spirit. You can imagine what confusion prevails in a modern law court when a witness or the accused operate in metaphor and glory in the sensuousness of the spoken word quite irrelevant to the argument at hand. Ask any magistrate or prosecutor or lawyer in a differentiated Western-type society whether they find a court trial a sensuous activity, and hear what they say. Even the rhetoric that a lawyer may indulge in is primarily a thing of the brain rather than of the heart. In African languages, activities overlap a great deal, and there are no sharp dividing lines between various functions.

All that I have said so far has been an attempt to indicate the relative distances between tradition and the present — some shifting, others freezing, some thawing, others again presenting formidable barriers. And we are living in a situation in which the past and the present live side by side, because the past is not just a segment in time to think *back* upon: We can see it in living communities. We need to appreciate these distances if we are to understand what the African writer is about. He is part of the whole pattern.

EXPLORATIONS

1. As an African writer, to what "two worlds" does Es'kia Mphahlele belong? What choices does his dual heritage force him to make?

2. Why does Mphahlele perceive education as so crucial an issue for African writers? What price do they pay for it? What happens if they refuse to pay that price?

3. "The whole dialogue around tradition is an intellectual one," writes Mphahlele (para. 4). Cite three or four passages that show him to be part of the Western intellectual tradition. What passages show that he also belongs to the African tradition, in which speakers "operate in metaphor and glory in the sensuousness of the spoken word" (para. 8)?

CONNECTIONS

1. Reread Paul Harrison's comments on cultural imperialism in "The Westernization of the World" (p. 66, paras. 8–12). What observations by Mphahlele echo Harrison's? How do Mphahlele's views differ from Harrison's?

2. Mphahlele notes, "Africa was shanghaied into the history of the West" (para. 1). In a more literal sense, so were African Americans. What points in "African Literature: What Tradition?" are echoed by Danzy Senna in "The Mulatto Millennium" (p. 18)? What benefits does each writer see in his or her mixed heritage?

3. Mphahlele writes about the rift that develops between parents and their children who are educated in a second language. Which of the changes and problems he mentions also appear in Amy Tan's "Two Kinds" (p. 24)?

ELABORATIONS

1. "I have always asked myself," writes Mphahlele, "what it is in one's formal education that leads to the rupture, to the ever-widening gulf between one and one's parents and one's community" (para. 6). Write a cause-and-effect essay that addresses this question, using "African Literature: What Tradition?" and your own experience as sources.

2. "The benefits of tradition are abstract," writes Mphahlele. "The benefits of a modern education are tangible, real" (para. 5). What does he mean? Looking at your own role in the world as an adult, what have you gained (or do you hope to gain) from your education? From the tradition(s) in which you grew up? Write an essay classifying the abstract and tangible benefits to you of your education and heritage.

MARGARET ATWOOD

A *View from Canada*

Margaret Atwood is one of Canada's most distinguished novelists, poets, and critics. Born in Ottawa, Ontario, in 1939, she began writing as a small child; by age six she had started a novel about an ant. Her father was a forest entomologist, so Atwood had plenty of exposure to both insects and solitude in the Canadian wilderness. Having discovered that writing was "suddenly the only thing I wanted to do," she studied at Victoria College and the University of Toronto in Canada and got her master's degree from Radcliffe College at Harvard University. Atwood has taught at colleges and universities in Canada and the United States and has received more than a dozen literary awards and fellowships. Since her earliest poems and her first novel, *The Edible Woman* (1969), Atwood has published more than twenty-five volumes of poetry, nonfiction, and fiction, as well as occasional plays and children's books. Her virtuosity with language ranges from wildly passionate (*Surfacing*, 1972) to coldly controlled (*Life Before Man*, 1979); her settings span the future (*The Handmaid's Tale*, 1986; motion picture, 1990) and the past (*Alias Grace*, 1996). Atwood currently lives in Toronto with the novelist Graeme Gibson and their daughter. "A View from Canada" comes from a speech given at Harvard University in 1981 and reprinted in *Second Words* (1982).

Canada, the world's second-largest country (after Russia), extends from the Atlantic to the Pacific Ocean and from the North Pole to the U.S. border. The French explorer Jacques Cartier claimed it for France in 1534. Settlers followed, starting in Acadia (now Nova Scotia) and moving into Quebec. As the English colonies to the south became more established, conflicts arose over hunting, trapping, and fishing rights. In the early 1700s the English took over Newfoundland, Hudson Bay, and Acadia. Many of the evicted French speakers migrated south to Louisiana, where *Acadians* became slurred to *Cajuns*. Various British colonies united in 1867 as the Dominion of Canada, which stayed subject to British rule until 1982. Although today Canada's head of government is an elected prime minister, its head of state is still the British monarch. Ottawa, the nation's capital, lies in a narrow section of Ontario between New York State and Quebec, a province where French remains the predominant language. Tension continues between Canadians of English and French heritage, with Quebec periodically threatening to secede. A 1990 vote to give Quebec the protection of distinct constitutional status failed to win national approval; in 1995, Quebec voters narrowly defeated a referendum to create a separate state.

I spent a large part of my childhood in northern Quebec, surrounded by many trees and few people. My attitude toward Americans was formed by this environment. Alas, the Americans we encountered were usually pictures of ineptitude. We once met two of them dragging a heaving metal boat, plus the motor, across a portage from one lake to another because they did not want to paddle. Typically American, we thought, as they ricocheted off yet another tree. Americans hooked other people when they tried to cast, got lost in the woods, and didn't burn their garbage. Of course, many Canadians behaved this way too; but somehow not *as* many. And there were some Americans, friends of my father, who could shoot a rapids without splintering their canoe and who could chop down a tree without taking off a foot in the process. But these were not classed as Americans, not *real* Americans. They were from Upper Michigan State or Maine or places like that, and were classed, I blush to admit, not as Americans but as honorary Canadians. I recognize that particular cross-filing system, that particular way of approving of people you as a rule don't approve of, every time a man tells me I think like a man; a sentence I've always felt had an invisible comma after the word *think*. I've since recognized that it's no compliment to be told you are not who you are, but as children we generalized, cheerfully and shamelessly. The truth, from our limited experience, was clear: Americans were wimps who had a lot of money but did not know what they were doing.

That was the rural part of my experience. The urban part was somewhat different. In the city I went to school, and in the early years at any rate the schools I went to were still bastions of the British Empire. In school we learned the Kings of England and how to draw the Union Jack and sing "Rule Britannia," and poems with refrains like, "Little Indian, Sioux or Cree, Don't you wish that you were me?" Our imaginations were still haunted by the war, a war that we pictured as having been fought between us, that is, the British, and the Germans. There wasn't much room in our minds for the Americans and the Japanese. Winston Churchill was a familiar figure to us; Franklin D. Roosevelt was not.

In public school we did not learn much about Americans, or Canadians either, for that matter. Canadian history was the explorers and was mostly brown and green, for all those trees. British history was kings and queens, and much more exciting, since you could use the silver and gold colored pencils for it.

That era of Canadian colonialism was rapidly disappearing, however. One explanation for the reason it practically vanished during the postwar decade — 1946 to 1957, say, the year I graduated from high school — is an economic one. The Canadians, so the theory goes, overextended themselves so severely through the war effort that they created a capital vacuum in Canada. Nature and entrepreneurs hate a vacuum, so money flowed up from the United States to fill it, and when Canadians woke up in the sixties and started to take stock, they discovered they'd sold their birthright for a mess. This revelation was an even greater shock for me; not only was my country owned, but it was owned by the kind of people who carried tin boats across portages and didn't burn their garbage. One doubted their competence.

Looking back on this decade, I can see that the changeover from British cultural colony to American cultural colony was symbolized by what happened after school as opposed to in it. I know it's hard to believe in view of my youthful appearance, but when I was a child there was no television. There were, however, comic books, and these were monolithically American. We didn't much notice, except when we got to the ads at the back, where Popsicle Pete reigned supreme. Popsicle Pete would give you the earth in exchange for a few sticky wrappers, but his promises always had a little asterisk attached: "Offer good only in the United States." International world cynics may be forgiven for thinking that the same little asterisk is present invisibly in the Constitution and the Declaration of Independence and the Bill of Rights, not to mention the public statements of prominent Americans on such subjects as democracy, human dignity and freedom, and civil liberties. Maybe it all goes back to Popsicle Pete. We may all be in this together, but some of us are asterisked.

Such thoughts did not trouble our heads a great deal. When you were finished with Donald Duck and Mickey Mouse (and Walt Disney was, by the way, a closet Canadian), you could always go on to Superman (whose creator was also one of ours). After that it would be time for Sunday night radio, with Jack Benny and Our Miss Brooks. We knew they talked funny, but we didn't mind. Then of course there were movies, none of which were Canadian, but we didn't mind that either. Everyone knew that was what the world was like. Nobody knew there had once been a Canadian film industry.

After that I went to high school, where people listened to American pop music after school instead of reading comic books. During school hours we studied, among other things, history and literature. Literature was still the British tradition: Shakespeare, Eliot, Austen, Thomas Hardy, Keats and Wordsworth and Shelley and Byron; not experiences anyone should miss, but it did tend to give the impression that all literature was written by dead Englishmen, and — this is important — by dead English*women*. By this time I wanted to be a writer, and you can

5

see it would be a dilemma: Being female was no hindrance, but how could one be a writer and somehow manage to avoid having to become British and dead? . . .

In history it was much the same story. We started with ancient Egypt and worked our way through Greece, Rome, and medieval Europe, then the Renaissance and the birth of the modern era, the invention of the steam engine, the American revolution, the French revolution, the Civil War, and other stirring events, every single one of which had taken place outside Canada.

Finally, in the very last year, by which time many future citizens had dropped out anyway, we got a blue book called *Canada in the World Today*. It was about who grew the wheat, how happy the French were, how well the parliamentary system worked for everybody, and how nice it was that the Indians had given us all their land in exchange for the amenities of civilization. The country we lived in was presented to us in our schools as colorless, dull, and without much historical conflict to speak of, except for a few massacres, and nobody did *that* any more. Even the British war of conquest was a dud, since both of the generals died. It was like a hockey game in which both teams lost.

As for Canada in the World Today, its role, we were assured, was an   10 important one. It was the upper northwest corner of a triangle consisting of Canada, the United States, and Britain, and its position was not one to be sneezed at: Canada, having somehow become an expert at compromise, was the mediator. It was not to be parochial and inward-looking any more but was to be international in outlook. Although in retrospect the role of mediator may shrink somewhat — one cannot quite dispel the image of Canada trotting back and forth across the Atlantic with sealed envelopes, like a glorified errand boy — there's a little truth to be squeezed from this lemon. Canadians, oddly enough, *are* more international in outlook than Americans are; not through any virtue on their part but because they've had to be. If you're a Canadian traveling in the United States, one of the first things you notice is the relative absence of international news coverage. In Canada, one of the most popular news programs ever devised has two radio commentators phoning up just about anyone they can get on the line, anywhere in the world. Canadians live in a small house, which may be why they have their noses so firmly pressed to the windows, looking out.

I remember *Canada in the World Today* with modified loathing — "Canada comes of age," it trumpeted, not bothering to mention that what happened to you when you came of age was that you got pimples or a job or both — and still not a year passes without some politician announcing that Canada has finally grown up. Still, the title is significant. Canada sees itself as part of the world; a small sinking *Titanic* squashed between two icebergs, perhaps, but still inevitably a part. The States, on the other hand, has always had a little trouble with games like chess. Situational strategy is difficult if all you can see is your own borders, and beyond that some wispy brownish fuzz that is barely worth considering. The Canadian experience was a circumference with no center, the American one a center which was mistaken for the whole thing.

A few years ago I was in India and had occasion to visit both the Canadian and American enclaves in New Delhi. The Canadian there lived in a house decorated with Indian things and served us a meal of Indian food and told us all about India. One reason for going into the foreign service, in Canada anyway, is to get out of Canada, and Canadians are good at fitting in, partly because they can't afford to do otherwise. They could not afford, for instance, to have the kind of walled compound the Americans had. We were let in to do some shopping at the supermarket there, and once the gate had closed you were in Syracuse, New York. Hot dogs, hamburgers, Cokes, and rock music surrounded you. Americans enter the outside world the way they landed on the moon, with their own oxygen tanks of American air strapped to their backs and their protective spacesuits firmly in place. If they can't stay in America they take it with them. Not for them the fish-in-the-water techniques of the modern urban guerrilla. Those draft dodgers of the sixties who made it as far as Canada nearly died of culture shock: They thought it was going to be like home.

It's not their fault, though. It's merely that they've been oddly educated. Canadians and Americans may look alike, but the contents of their heads are quite different. Americans experience themselves, individually, as small toads in the biggest and most powerful puddle in the world. Their sense of power comes from identifying with the puddle. Canadians as individuals may have more power within the puddle, since there are fewer toads in it; it's the puddle that's seen as powerless. One of our politicians recently gave a speech entitled, "In the Footsteps of the Giant." The United States of course was the giant and Canada was in its footsteps, though some joker wondered whether Canada was in the footstep just before or just after the foot had descended. One of Canada's problems is that it's always comparing itself to the wrong thing. If you stand beside a giant, of course you tend to feel a little stunted. When we stand beside Australia, say, or the ex-British West Indies, we feel more normal. I had lunch recently with two publishers from Poland. "Do Canadians realize," they said, "that they live in one

of the most peaceful, happy, and prosperous countries on earth?" "No,"
I said. . . .

Americans and Canadians are not the same; they are the products of
two very different histories, two very different situations. Put simply,
south of you you have Mexico and south of us we have you.

But we *are* all in this together, not just as citizens of our respective   15
nation states but more importantly as inhabitants of this quickly shrinking and increasingly threatened earth. There are boundaries and borders, spiritual as well as physical, and good fences make good neighbors. But there are values beyond national ones. Nobody owns the air;
we all breathe it.

EXPLORATIONS

1. How does Margaret Atwood summarize her childhood concept of "typically
   American" (para. 1)? How would you summarize her present concept of
   "typically American"? What qualities does Atwood seem to consider typically Canadian?
2. What aspects of "A View from Canada" show that it was written as a speech,
   to be heard rather than read by its audience? What can you tell about Atwood's intended audience?
3. Find at least three places where Atwood uses humor in "A View from
   Canada." In each case, what purpose(s) does her humor serve?

CONNECTIONS

1. How did Atwood's education in Canada resemble Es'kia Mphahlele's in
   South Africa? (See "African Literature: What Tradition?" on p. 73.) What
   changes does each author seem to be recommending in her or his country's
   approach to educating children?
2. Both Mphahlele's and Atwood's educations showed them they did not fit
   the profile of "writer." What were the main obstacles each one had to overcome to be a writer? What was Atwood's main advantage over Mphahlele?
   What was Mphahlele's main advantage over Atwood?
3. Do you think Richard Rayner (p. 6) and Ishmael Reed (p. 6) would agree
   with Atwood's assessment of Americans? Why or why not?

ELABORATIONS

1. Go through Atwood's essay and note the main points she makes about Canadians and about Americans. Rewrite "A View from Canada" as a shorter, more direct comparison-contrast essay.

2. Did you ever encounter tourists with canoes? The Union Jack? Popsicle Pete? Make a list of observations and events in Atwood's personal history that provoked her to think about being Canadian. Then make a similar list based on your personal history. Use your list as the starting point for an essay about what it means to you to be an American.

SALMAN RUSHDIE

Imaginary Homelands

Ahmed Salman Rushdie was born to a wealthy Muslim family in Bombay, India, in 1947. That same year his homeland won independence from Britain, which partitioned the country into mostly Hindu India and mostly Islamic Pakistan. Rushdie was sent to a British-style private school in Bombay and then to Rugby, an exclusive school in England. He went on to Cambridge University under protest after his family moved to Pakistan, "the unmentionable country across the border" (para. 2). Rushdie published his first novel in 1975; his second, *Midnight's Children*, won the prestigious Booker Prize. The book that made him famous, however, was *The Satanic Verses* (1988). Immediately banned in India, the novel caused a worldwide uproar for allegedly blaspheming Islam. Iran's religious leader, the Ayatollah Khomeini, issued a *fatwa*, or death warrant, and offered a $1 million reward to any Muslim who would assassinate Rushdie. The writer went into hiding, continuing to write but making only a few cautious, usually unannounced public appearances. Rushdie and his wife divorced; in 1990 he declared himself a Muslim, but Khomeini refused to withdraw the *fatwa* and Rushdie recanted. In 1991 the novel's Italian translator was knifed and its Japanese translator was murdered. Despite pressure from the West and from writers and readers around the world, Iran upheld the *fatwa* until 1998. Rushdie's recent books include *East, West* (1994), *The Moor's Last Sigh* (1995), and *The Ground Beneath Her Feet: A Novel* (1999). "Imaginary Homelands," written before the *fatwa*, comes from his 1991 book by the same title.

With a third the area of the United States, India has three times its population. Indian civilization is among the world's oldest, dating back more than 5,000 years. Conquerors around 1500 B.C. laid the foundations of the caste system, a hereditary class structure comprising the Brahman (priests and scholars), the Kshatriya (warriors and rulers), the Vaisya or Bania (farmers and merchants), and the Sudra (peasants and laborers); below these were the now illegal Untouchables, who performed the most menial tasks. A thousand years later, Buddhism originated in India. European traders discovered this South Asian peninsula in the sixteenth century. By 1820, the British had wrested power from the native rajas, ruling in alliance with the Sikhs, a religious minority who controlled the north. After World War I, Mohandas Gandhi (called *Mahatma*, "great soul") led his people in nonviolent resistance and civil disobedience. When the region won independence in 1947, it was partitioned into two nations: India (mostly Hindu) and Pakistan (mostly Muslim). From then until 1989, India's central family was that of its first prime minister, Jawaharlal Nehru, whose daughter Indira Gandhi (no relation to Mohandas) succeeded him and was in turn succeeded by her son Rajiv. The Nehru-Gandhi dynasty ended when Rajiv Gandhi lost the November 1989 election and was assassinated while campaigning two years later. His successors have faced an electorate that is more assertive and more impatient, a new divergence between state and society, increasing clashes between Hindus, Sikhs, and Muslims, and ongoing tensions between India and its neighbors, particularly Pakistan.

For information on Great Britain, see page 617.

An old photograph in a cheap frame hangs on a wall of the room where I work. It's a picture dating from 1946 of a house into which, at the time of its taking, I had not yet been born. The house is rather peculiar — a three-storied gabled affair with tiled roofs and round towers in two corners, each wearing a pointy tiled hat. "The past is a foreign country," goes the famous opening sentence of L. P. Hartley's novel *The Go-Between*, "they do things differently there." But the photograph tells me to invert this idea; it reminds me that it's my present that is foreign, and that the past is home, albeit a lost home in a lost city in the mists of lost time.

A few years ago I revisited Bombay, which is my lost city, after an absence of something like half my life. Shortly after arriving, acting on an impulse, I opened the telephone directory and looked for my father's name. And, amazingly, there it was; his name, our old address, the unchanged telephone number, as if we had never gone away to the unmentionable country across the border. It was an eerie discovery. I felt as if I were being claimed, or informed that the facts of my faraway life were illusions, and that this continuity was the reality. Then I went to visit the house in the photograph and stood outside it, neither daring nor wishing to announce myself to its new owners. (I didn't want to see how they'd ruined the interior.) I was overwhelmed. The photograph had naturally been taken in black and white; and my memory, feeding on such images as this, had begun to see my childhood in the same way, monochromatically. The colors of my history had seeped out of my mind's eye; now my other two eyes were assaulted by colors, by the vividness of the red tiles, the yellow-edged green of cactus-leaves, the brilliance of bougainvillea creeper. It is probably not too romantic to say that that was when my novel *Midnight's Children* was really born; when I realized how much I wanted to restore the past to myself, not in the faded grays of old family-album snapshots, but whole, in Cinema-Scope and glorious Technicolor.

Bombay is a city built by foreigners upon reclaimed land; I, who had been away so long that I almost qualified for the title, was gripped by the conviction that I, too, had a city and a history to reclaim.

It may be that writers in my position, exiles or emigrants or expatriates, are haunted by some sense of loss, some urge to reclaim, to look back, even at the risk of being mutated into pillars of salt.[1] But if we do look back, we must also do so in the knowledge — which gives rise to profound uncertainties — that our physical alienation from India almost inevitably means that we will not be capable of reclaiming precisely the thing that was lost; that we will, in short, create fictions, not actual cities or villages, but invisible ones, imaginary homelands, Indias of the mind.

Writing my book in North London, looking out through my window   5 onto a city scene totally unlike the ones I was imagining onto paper, I was constantly plagued by this problem, until I felt obliged to face it in the text, to make clear that (in spite of my original and I suppose somewhat Proustian ambition to unlock the gates of lost time so that the past reappeared as it actually had been, unaffected by the distortions of memory) what I was actually doing was a novel of memory and about memory, so that my India was just that: "my" India, a version and no more than one version of all the hundreds of millions of possible versions. I tried to make it as imaginatively true as I could, but imaginative truth is simultaneously honorable and suspect, and I knew that my India may only have been one to which I (who am no longer what I was, and who by quitting Bombay never became what perhaps I was meant to be) was, let us say, willing to admit I belonged.

This is why I made my narrator, Saleem, suspect in his narration; his mistakes are the mistakes of a fallible memory compounded by quirks of character and of circumstance, and his vision is fragmentary. It may be that when the Indian writer who writes from outside India tries to reflect that world, he is obliged to deal in broken mirrors, some of whose fragments have been irretrievably lost.

But there is a paradox here. The broken mirror may actually be as valuable as the one which is supposedly unflawed. Let me again try and

---

[1]Rushdie refers to the biblical story of Lot, whose wife was turned into a pillar of salt when she disobeyed God's order not to look back as the couple fled their homeland. — ED.

explain this from my own experience. Before beginning *Midnight's Children,* I spent many months trying simply to recall as much of the Bombay of the 1950s and 1960s as I could; and not only Bombay — Kashmir, too, and Delhi and Aligarh, which, in my book, I've moved to Agra to heighten a certain joke about the Taj Mahal. I was genuinely amazed by how much came back to me. I found myself remembering what clothes people had worn on certain days, and school scenes, and whole passages of Bombay dialogue verbatim, or so it seemed; I even re-membered advertisements, film posters, the neon Jeep sign on Marine Drive, toothpaste ads for Binaca and for Kolynos, and a footbridge over the local railway line which bore, on one side, the legend "Esso puts a tiger in your tank" and, on the other, the curiously contradictory admo-nition: "Drive like Hell and you will get there." Old songs came back to me from nowhere. . . .

I knew that I had tapped a rich seam; but the point I want to make is that of course I'm not gifted with total recall, and it was precisely the partial nature of these memories, their fragmentation, that made them so evocative for me. The shards of memory acquired greater status, greater resonance, because they were *remains*; fragmentation made triv-ial things seem like symbols, and the mundane acquired numinous qualities. There is an obvious parallel here with archaeology. The bro-ken pots of antiquity, from which the past can sometimes, but always provisionally, be reconstructed, are exciting to discover, even if they are pieces of the most quotidian objects.

It may be argued that the past is a country from which we have all emigrated, that its loss is part of our common humanity. Which seems to me self evidently true; but I suggest that the writer who is out-of-country and even out-of-language may experience this loss in an inten-sified form. It is made more concrete for him by the physical fact of dis-continuity, of his present being in a different place from his past, of his being "elsewhere." This may enable him to speak properly and con-cretely on a subject of universal significance and appeal.

But let me go further. The broken glass is not merely a mirror of nos- 10 talgia. It is also, I believe, a useful tool with which to work in the present.

John Fowles begins *Daniel Martin* with the words: "Whole sight: or all the rest is desolation." But human beings do not perceive things whole; we are not gods but wounded creatures, cracked lenses, capable only of fractured perceptions. Partial beings, in all the senses of that phrase. Meaning is a shaky edifice we build out of scraps, dogmas, childhood injuries, newspaper articles, chance remarks, old films, small victories, people hated, people loved; perhaps it is because our sense of what is the case is constructed from such inadequate materials that we defend it so fiercely, even to the death. The Fowles position seems to me a way of succumbing to the guru-illusion. Writers are no longer sages, dispensing the wisdom of the centuries. And those of us who have been forced by cultural displacement to accept the provisional nature of all truths, all certainties, have perhaps had modernism forced upon us. We can't lay claim to Olympus, and are thus released to describe our world in the way in which all of us, whether writers or not, perceive it from day to day. . . .

The Indian writer, looking back at India, does so through guilt-tinted spectacles. (I am of course, once more, talking about myself.) I am speaking now of those of us who emigrated . . . and I suspect that there are times when the move seems wrong to us all, when we seem, to ourselves, post-lapsarian[2] men and women. We are Hindus who have crossed the black water; we are Muslims who eat pork. And as a result — as my use of the Christian notion of the Fall indicates — we are now partly of the West. Our identity is at once plural and partial. Sometimes we feel that we straddle two cultures; at other times, that we fall between two stools. But however ambiguous and shifting this ground may be, it is not an infertile territory for a writer to occupy. If literature is in part the business of finding new angles at which to enter reality, then once again our distance, our long geographical perspective, may provide us with such angles.

EXPLORATIONS

1. What does the mirror represent in Salman Rushdie's essay? What does the broken mirror represent?

2. "We are now partly of the West" (para. 12), says Rushdie of writers who have emigrated from India. What references in "Imaginary Homelands" show that this statement is true of him?

3. What does Rushdie seem to value most about the Western part of his identity? What does he seem to value most about the Indian part?

---

[2]After the Fall; that is, after Adam and Eve's expulsion from Paradise. — ED.

CONNECTIONS

1. India, Canada, and South Africa all are former British colonies. What comments by Margaret Atwood in "A View from Canada" (p. 79) and Es'kia Mphahlele in "African Literature: What Tradition?" (p. 73) suggest that they share Rushdie's mixed feelings about straddling two cultures (see para. 12)?

2. What observations in "Imaginary Homelands" echo comments by Walker Percy in "A Short Quiz" (p. 10)? Do Rushdie and Percy give the same explanation for the ambiguity of the self? If so, what is that explanation? If not, how do their explanations differ?

3. Anita Desai (p. 7), Bharati Mukherjee (p. 3), and Rushdie are Indian emigrants writing in English. What ideas do they share? Do you think Desai or Mukherjee or both would agree with Rushdie's statement, "The Indian writer, looking back at India, does so through guilt-tinted spectacles" (para. 12)? Why or why not?

ELABORATIONS

1. "Our identity is at once plural and partial," writes Rushdie (para. 12). "Sometimes we feel that we straddle two cultures; at other times, that we fall between two stools." How do these comments apply to your perception of your own identity? Write an essay examining ways in which your sense of yourself seems fragmented or changeable. (You may want to draw on ideas from Mphahlele's "African Literature: What Tradition?," Percy's "A Short Quiz," or other selections in this chapter.)

2. Reread Rushdie's essay, particularly paragraph 7. Then think back to a bygone place and time in your own life, and write a description of everything you remember about it: clothes, conversations, signs, songs, and whatever else you can recall. What do you notice is missing? What do you suspect is distorted?

PART TWO

·

FAMILIES

OBSERVATIONS

Naguib Mahfouz, Francine du Plessix Gray, Chang-Rae Lee,
Andrew Mason and Naohiro Ogawa, Frances Rose Besmer,
Angela Davis, Philip Roth, Paula Fomby, James Coogan,
Robert Bly, Julia Alvarez

▼ ▼ ▼

Louise Erdrich, *Making Babies* (UNITED STATES)

Barbara Dafoe Whitehead, *From Death to Divorce*
(UNITED STATES)

Barbara Kingsolver, *Stone Soup* (UNITED STATES)

Frank McCourt, *Limerick Homecoming* (IRELAND)

Rigoberta Menchú, *Birth Ceremonies* (GUATEMALA)

Wole Soyinka, *Nigerian Childhood* (NIGERIA)

Lisa Jones, *Grave Matters at Monticello* (UNITED STATES)

Nicholas Bromell, *Family Secrets* (UNITED STATES)

John David Morley, *Acquiring a Japanese Family* (JAPAN)

Kazuo Ishiguro, *A Family Supper* (JAPAN)

OBSERVATIONS

O housewife, wake up, say your prayers, then spread out your hands in supplication. Get the breakfast ready and call your husband and children to the table.

Help the young ones to wash and frown at those who are too lazy to get up.

Sweep your house and put it in order and amuse yourself by singing a song.

If fate permits, good luck will bring them together around the dinner table.

The children stay on to do their homework and the man goes off to the café for his evening chat.

Wash and comb your hair, change your clothes, and perfume the bedroom with incense.

Today has witnessed something that deserves thanks and praise to God.

Remember that, when the day comes on which all are scattered, each to his own home, and the day on which these memories find no one to remember them.

> — NAGUIB MAHFOUZ
> "The Housewife," translated by Denys Johnson-Davies
> *Echoes of an Autobiography*, 1994

▼ ▼ ▼

What happened to the American family — the fraying effect of harassed working parents, the stranglehold of the media, the pressures of peer culture — is a theme much ranted about. Yet one aspect of what has happened has been overlooked: Kids . . . never seem to sit down to a proper meal at home anymore. This is not another pious harangue on "spiritual starvation"; this is about the fact that we may be witnessing the first generation in history that has not been required to participate in that primal rite of socialization, the family meal. The family meal is not only the core curriculum in the school of civilized discourse; it is also a set of protocols that curb our natural savagery and our animal greed, and cultivate a capacity for sharing and thoughtfulness.

> — FRANCINE DU PLESSIX GRAY
> *The New Yorker*, 1995

▼ ▼ ▼

My mother could whip up most anything, but during our first years of living in this country we ate only Korean foods. At my haranguelike behest, my mother set herself to learning how to cook exotic American dishes. . . . I was an insistent child, and, being my mother's firstborn, much too prized. . . . She reminded me daily that I was her sole son, her reason for living, and that if she were to lose me, either in body or spirit, she wished that God would mercifully smite her, strike her down like a weak branch.

In the traditional fashion, she was the house accountant, the maid, the launderer, the disciplinarian, the driver, the secretary, and, of course, the cook. She was also my first basketball coach. In South Korea, where girls' high-school basketball is a popular spectator sport, she had been a star, the point guard for the national high-school team that once won the all-Asia championships. . . .

It puzzled me how much she considered her own history to be immaterial, and if she never patently diminished herself, she was able to finesse a kind of self-removal by speaking of my father whenever she could.

— CHANG-RAE LEE
"Coming Home Again"
The New Yorker, 1995

▼ ▼ ▼

When a young Japanese woman decides to marry she is undertaking commitments and obligations that are very different from those a young American woman might expect. These differences fall into three roles: wife, mother, and daughter-in-law.

First, her role as wife to her future husband is likely to reflect a different kind of relationship from that found in American marriages. In Japan, there is less emphasis on marital companionship and sharing, and Japanese women depend less on their relationship with their husbands for emotional satisfaction. Arranged marriages are no longer common in Japan, but romantic love plays a less important role in courtship and marriage.

In part, the relationship between husbands and wives is a product of specialization. The typical Japanese husband is the quintessential breadwinner. He works long hours, stays out late, and is rarely involved in child rearing and housekeeping activities. . . .

For most Japanese women, the most essential relationship is between herself and her children. Childless marriages are less common in Japan than in the United States. A high percentage of Japanese women begin

96

childbearing shortly after marriage, have two children, and then stop. Unlike in the United States, births outside marriage are rare. For Japanese women, being married and rearing children are more synonymous than for American women.

Third, when a Japanese woman marries, she takes on important responsibilities as a daughter-in-law. Japan is a patrilineal society. When a woman marries, she becomes part of her husband's family. If she marries an eldest son, she and her husband, by tradition, live with his parents and she assists her mother-in-law in running the household. She also becomes the primary caregiver if and when her husband's parents reach old age.

— Andrew Mason and Naohiro Ogawa
"Why Avoid the Altar?"
Japan: Why It Works, Why It Doesn't, 1997

▼ ▼ ▼

Foster parenting, like parenting one's own children, offers many valuable rewards, but monetary gain is not among them. . . . Providing room and board — three hots and a cot — is just for starters. Medical treatment for infections, lice, or delinquent immunizations plus shopping trips for clothes, a few toys, and favorite foods are immediate needs. Intangible requirements of patience and encouragement are just as important to help a child adjust to eating meals together at a table and sleeping alone in a bed. Food hoarding, biting, temper tantrums, and bed-wetting are common behaviors in dislocated children; depression is recognizable even in tiny babies. A place where the parents are neither drunk nor drugged, where a child is relieved of a surrogate parenting role, and where words rather than fists are used to satisfy wants and vent anger may indeed be safe and warm, but it may not feel at all like home. Once a child's initial anxieties are put to rest, other qualities — a sense of humor, freedom to talk and be listened to, interests in music, sports, or appropriate TV programs — can be nourished. . . .

Single parenthood, abandonment, sexual abuse, substance abuse, and violent behavior occur in all classes of our society; money, or lack of it, determines how these issues are handled. All parents whose children are placed in foster care have at least two things in common: poverty and failure. Among the poor, whatever genuine love and attachments may exist, they are often overwhelmed by the stigma of failure, notwithstanding the millions of dollars being spent on programs for "family reunification." . . . In our experience, few of the foster children who return to their own parents actually remain with them.

– FRANCES ROSE BESMER
"Foster Parenting: Something
to Remember with Affection"
Mount Holyoke Alumnae Quarterly, 1996

▼ ▼ ▼

Much of the public debate in recent years about the breakdown of the African American family has failed to acknowledge that the traditional nuclear family has never been the typical model of the black family. First of all, from the days of slavery to the present, both husband and wife have been compelled to work outside the home. Secondly, the predominant model in the African American community has been the extended family, which has conferred important roles on grandmothers, grandfathers, aunts, uncles, and cousins. This expansive domestic environment has often been much healthier for the child and has functioned as a child-care system available to working parents.

The African American family structure evolved out of the fusion of African extended-family traditions with the conditions imposed by slavery. During this era, the father was relegated to the negligible role of providing the "seed." In most cases, the name of the father was not even acknowledged but was subordinated to the mother's name. If, for example, the father's name was John, and the woman who bore his child was Mary, he would be called "Mary's John" — and his name would not even appear in the birth records. The slave family, as viewed by the slave owners, consisted solely of the mother and her children. This practice succeeded in annihilating the "family space" within which resistance to slavery could develop.

The slave community attempted to challenge this assault on the family by creating surrogate family members and by establishing naming practices which affirmed the place of the father, even though he was often sold away. The creativity with which African American people improvised family connections is a cultural trait that has spanned the centuries.

– ANGELA DAVIS
"Child Care or Workfare"
New Perspectives Quarterly, 1990

▼ ▼ ▼

I knew only two boys in our neighborhood whose families were fatherless, and thought of them as no less blighted than the blind girl who attended our school for a while and had to be read to and shepherded everywhere. . . .

I knew no child whose family was divided by divorce. Outside of the movie magazines and the tabloid headlines, it didn't exist, certainly not among Jews like us. Jews didn't get divorced — not because divorce was forbidden by Jewish law but because that was the way they were. If Jewish fathers didn't come home drunk and beat their wives — and in our neighborhood, which was Jewry to me, I'd never heard of any who did — that too was because of the way they were. In our lore, the Jewish family was an inviolate haven against every form of menace, from personal isolation to gentile hostility. Regardless of internal friction and strife, it was assumed to be an indissoluble consolidation. *Hear, O Israel, the family is God, the family is One.*

Family indivisibility, the first commandment.

— PHILIP ROTH
The Facts, 1988

▼ ▼ ▼

The hardest part of having a gay mother was accepting homosexuality and all its consequences before I even knew what that involved. . . . I'm lucky to have been raised by people I genuinely like, and being a woman raised by women, I've not had the problems in relating to my parents that a man might have had. However, I've heard enough jokes and insults to know that people don't really believe the gay family exists in large numbers and turns out healthy, well-balanced children. It is time for society to expand the definition of family. While everyone can agree that the usual sit-com family is increasingly atypical, there is no description of what has evolved to replace it.

— PAULA FOMBY
"Why I'm Glad I Grew Up in a Gay Family"
Mother Jones, 1991

▼ ▼ ▼

Education rests on what I would call, for the sake of simplicity, a three-legged stool. The school system is the institution that holds up one side. Any weakness there and the stool is naturally going to be unsteady.

The second leg is represented by the students themselves. Some are gifted and some are not. The student who lacks some of the qualities that God may have intended will always have an uphill struggle to become educated.

This is where the third leg of education comes in and that is the institution of the family.

The role of the parents in the education of children may well be the most important part of the support system for the stool. Flawed families reduce the chance that students will be successful. Remove part of the family structure and the job of educating students becomes even more difficult.

When I read stories where students in the Boston school system declare that they won't do homework and it is tolerated, I wonder where the parents are. When the high number of truancies associated with some communities is aired on the evening news, I wonder where the parents are. When my local newspaper features stories of students working almost forty hours a week, much of it on school nights, I wonder where the parents are.

. . . School systems have to play with the cards that are dealt. The chances of a winning hand are, without question, improved by the stability of the community and the families in them.

Unless parents encourage good academic habits at home, no amount of taxpayer dollars or good teachers will make a difference.

> – JAMES COOGAN
> "MCAS: Who's Really Failing?"
> *Cape Cod Times*, 1999

▼ ▼ ▼

Among the Hopis and other native Americans of the Southwest, the old men take the boy away at the age of twelve and bring him *down* into the all-male area of the kiva. He stays *down* there for six weeks, and does not see his mother again for a year and a half.

The fault of the nuclear family today isn't so much that it's crazy and full of double binds (that's true in communes and corporate offices too — in fact, in any group). The fault is that the old men outside the nuclear family no longer offer an effective way for the son to break his link with his parents without doing harm to himself.

The ancient societies believed that a boy becomes a man only through ritual and effort — only through the "active intervention of the older men" . . . [who] welcome the younger man into the ancient, mythologized, instinctive male world.

> – ROBERT BLY
> *Iron John*, 1990

▼ ▼ ▼

For me, with my childhood history set in the Dominican Republic, family was the only neighborhood and country of origin I knew, and so it matters in a way that nothing else has since, except the writing.

I am talking now primarily about my extended *familia* in the Dominican Republic, complete with uncles and aunts and cousins and great-aunts and godmothers and political uncles and aunts of affection and nannies who wiped my bottom when I was a baby and so can tell me what to do even if I am a married woman with graying hair and six books.

Part of the reason I've always felt at home in rural American settings, especially in the South, is that in these places, family — in the extended and historical sense — still operates as the basic social unit. Not office staffs, health clubs, therapy groups, women's groups, play groups, or even nuclear family groups; not AA or Masonic clubs or where you went to college or even the United States of America, but FAMILY in the big, everlastingly messy and complicated way of my Dominican family.

– JULIA ALVAREZ
"Customs"
Something to Declare, 1998

EXPLORATIONS

1. Some of the Observations you have just read mention "the breakdown of the family." What does this phrase mean? What causes do these commentators blame for the family's breakdown? How dangerous a problem do they think it is, and why?

2. According to these commentators, why are families valuable? What ingredients do they suggest are important for strong, healthy families?

3. Which families in these Observations do you think would be the most rewarding for the children in them, and why? Which families do you think would be the least rewarding for children, and why? Which families would be the most rewarding for the parent or parents in them, and why? Which families would be the least rewarding for parents, and why?

LOUISE ERDRICH

Making Babies

The poet and novelist Karen Louise Erdrich (pronounced er-drick) was born in 1954 in Little Falls, Minnesota, the oldest of seven children. Part German, part French, and part Turtle Mountain Chippewa, she grew up near a Sioux Indian reservation in Wahpeton, North Dakota. Erdrich entered Dartmouth College in 1972 as a member of the first class to include women. After graduation she worked on a television documentary about the Northern Plains Indians, earned her master's degree at Johns Hopkins University, worked for the Boston Indian Council, waited tables, taught, wrote, and edited. In 1981 she came back to Dartmouth as a writer in residence, married the writer and teacher Michael Dorris, and became the mother of his three adopted children. Erdrich and Dorris had three more children together. They developed an equally collaborative approach to writing; he was the agent for her first novel, *Love Medicine* (1984), which won the National Book Critics Circle Award and has been translated into over eighteen languages. Other awards for her twelve books include the Pushcart and O. Henry Prizes and fellowships from the National Endowment for the Arts and the Guggenheim Foundation. Erdrich's and Dorris's oldest son, Abel, a victim of Fetal Alcohol Syndrome, died at age 23. The couple later split up, and in 1997 Dorris committed suicide. Erdrich lives in Minneapolis with her three youngest children. "Making Babies" comes from *The Blue Jay's Dance: A Birth Year* (1995).

We conceive our children in deepest night, in blazing sun, outdoors, in barns and alleys and minivans. We have no rules, no ceremonies, we don't even need a driver's license. Conception is often something of a by-product of sex, a candle in a one-room studio, pure brute chance, a wonder. To make love with the desire for a child is to move the act out of its singularity, to make the need of the moment an eternal wish. But of all passing notions, that of a human being for a child is perhaps the purest in the abstract, and the most complicated in reality. Growing, bearing, mothering or fathering, supporting, and at last letting go of an infant is a powerful and mundane creative act that rapturously sucks up whole chunks of life.

Other parents — among them, the first female judge appointed in New Hampshire, my own midwife, a perpetually overwhelmed movie researcher and television producer, and our neighbor, who baby-sits to make a difficult living — seem surprised at their own helplessness in the face of the passion they feel for their children. We live and work with a divided consciousness. It is a beautiful enough shock to fall in love with another adult, to feel the possibility of unbearable sorrow at the loss of that other, essential, personality, expressed just so, that particular touch. But love of an infant is of a different order. It is twinned love, all absorbing, a blur of boundaries and messages. It is uncomfortably close to self-erasure, and in the face of it one's fat ambitions, desperations, private icons, and urges fall away into a dreamlike *before* that haunts and forces itself into the present with tough persistence.

The self will not be forced under, nor will the baby's needs gracefully retreat. The world tips away when we look into our children's faces. The days flood by. Time with children runs through our fingers like water as we lift our hands, try to hold, to capture, to fix moments in a lens, a magic circle of images or words. We snap photos, videotape, memorialize while we experience a fast-forward in which there is no re-play of even a single instant.

We have a baby. Our sixth child, our third birth. During that year, our older, adopted children hit adolescence like runaway trucks. Dear grandparents weaken and die. Michael rises at four in the morning, hardly seems to sleep at all. To keep the door to the other self — the writing self — open, I scratch messages on the envelopes of letters I can't answer, in the margins of books I'm too tired to review. On pharmacy prescription bags, dime-store notebooks, children's construction paper, I keep writing. . . .

December. Deep Snow and Middle Trimester. Where I Work.

The small gray house where I work was built in the hope of feeding 5 snowmobilers. Twenty years ago, a rough trail was carved out of New Hampshire timberland a hundred yards from the door. . . .

I come here every day to work, starting while invisibly pregnant. I imagine myself somewhere else, into another skin, another person, another time. Yet simultaneously my body is constructing its own character. It requires no thought at all for me to form and fix a whole other person. First she is nothing, then she is growing and dividing at such a rate I think I'll drop. I come in eager hope and afraid of labor, all at once, for this is the heart of the matter. Whatever else I do, when it comes to pregnancy I am my physical self first, as are all of us women. We can pump gas, lift weights, head a corporation, lead nations, and tune pianos. Still, our bodies are rounded vases of skin and bones and blood that seem impossibly engineered for birth. I look down onto my smooth, huge lap, feel my baby twist, and I can't figure out how I'll ever stretch wide enough. I fear I've made a ship inside a bottle. I'll have to break. I'm not me. I feel myself becoming less a person than a place, inhabited, a foreign land. I will experience pain, lose physical control, or know the uncertainty of anesthetic. I fear these things, but vaguely, for my brain buzzes in the merciful wash of endorphins that preclude any thought from occupying it too long. Most of all, I worry over what I hold. I want perfection. Each day I pray another perfect cell to form. A million of them. I fear that my tears, my moods, my wrenched weeping will imprint on the baby's psyche. I fear repression, a stoic face shown to the world, will cause our child to hide emotions. I make too much of myself, expect too many favors, or not enough. I rock and rock and stare out the window into my life. . . .

Advice

Most of the instruction given to pregnant women is as chirpy and condescending as the usual run of maternity clothes — the wide tops with droopy bows slung beneath the neck, the T-shirts with arrows pointing to what can't be missed, the childish sailor collars, puffed sleeves, and pastels. It is cute advice — what to pack in the hospital bag (don't forget a toothbrush, deodorant, a comb or hair dryer) — or it's worse: pseudospiritual, misleading, silly, and even cruel. In giving birth to three daughters, I have found it impossible to eliminate pain through breathing, by focusing on a soothing photograph. It is true *pain* one is attempting to endure in drugless labor, not "discomfort," and the way to deal with pain is not to call it something else but to increase in strength, to prepare the will. Women are strong, strong, terribly strong. We don't know how strong we are until we're pushing out our babies. We are too often treated like babies having babies when we should be in training, like acolytes, novices to high priestesshood, like serious applicants for the space program.

January. Sweet Hopes and Poker Hands.

The blueprint for all our inherited characteristics is provided by the DNA molecules in the nuclei of our cells. The entire structure is composed of roughly three billion such pairs, together making up 100,000 genes. It is thrilling, dizzying, to consider the order of these pairs in the human genome, the total genetic message. Staring into my lap, I imagine genes shuffling together like poker hands and my thoughts swim toward stacked, incalculable numbers.

When we make love in the darkness of anticipation we are inviting accident and order, the careful lining up of genes. Unlocking the components of another person, we are safecrackers — setting the combinations, unconsciously twirling dials. Shadow brothers, sisters, potential unfused others, cease. Our children grow into existence particularized, yet random.

Eating

It isn't just eating, of course, and there's the joy. Now it's even better,   10
for I never know which bite is destined for the heart, the muscles, hair, the bones forming like the stalks of flowers, or the lovely eyes. Michael makes Jell-O for me so that the baby will have perfect fingernails. He attempts, in his cooking, to get every part of the baby right. Of course, the real challenge in the beginning of pregnancy is how to find exactly what food is bearable in the clutch of morning sickness.

Sleep is the only truly palatable food at first. I sleep hungrily, angry, needy for sleep, jealous for sleep, devouring it and yet resentful of the time it takes away from conscious life. I dream crazily, powerfully. I catch touchdown passes for the Vikings, incite the jealousy of Princess Di, talk earnestly and intimately with a huge male Kodiak brown bear, fly headlong over these low northeastern mountains. Morning comes. I throw up quickly, efficiently, miserably, and eat a cracker. It does no good at all to fight the feeling. For garden-variety morning sickness, which is all I've ever had, not the serious kind that requires hospitalization, very little can be done except to endure. I am not an advice giver, but I will offer these helpful strategies. When very sick, plain saltines are the best. They are an everyday cracker, though, and one should watch for sales on expensive English water biscuits — something special for the weekends. Plain low-salt wheat thins, Stoned Wheat Thins, mild Cheddar Goldfish crackers, Bremner Wafers, and an occasional cardboard Finland toast make you feel ascetic, balanced. I eat matzos in great tiles and sheets. A meal of croissant crackers and ginger ale drunk from Michael's grandmother's wineglass is both mournful and restorative. The perfect love-gift for this delicate time? A box of Carr's assorted crackers, all of which come in complex toasted shapes, so that you can pretend you are actually eating a variety of foods.

Around month four, if you are fortunate, when you can eat any food and have a roaring appetite, try something intense — say, a food

associated with a first love affair, provided you regard it now with nostalgic joy and are glad it's finished. A jar of bittersweet chocolate syrup,
perhaps, only to be licked from a bare finger. These next few months
are the most sensuous and sexual of your life — you're not too big and
your baby's not in the way and your breasts are stunning creatures right
from the Song of Solomon. . . .

Licorice and Metaphysics

I lumber up and down these roads hoping to engage my baby's head,
hoping she will "drop." With our due date in sight, that is all we talk
about — dropping and engaging — so that I picture her as a rocket
aimed straight out of me. The last months and weeks of pregnancy are
an endless string of hours, the most difficult weeks in which to stay balanced. Time stops and tension builds with every breath. Fear presses its
paws on my chest. I am so heavy that just to mention my suffering is not
enough — I buy a fifty-pound sack of potatoes. Anyone who doubts my
daily effort can lift this sack and understand why I'm not in a good
mood. Fifty extra pounds is what I carry with me at all times.

I suppose, to be accurate, it should be fifty pounds of licorice. To
quit smoking I took the old family remedy, passed down from my
Ojibwa grandfather, Pat Gourneau — black licorice. He gave up snuff
for all forms of licorice, the root itself, delicious, splintery, as well as
ropes, wheels, pipes, twists. My body is now an awkward old-fashioned
fifties-movie diving suit, huge on me, pressurized, made of black
licorice. I'm on the bottom of the ocean taking deep, slow breaths that
rise over me in visible bubbles.

I walk out onto the trails every day, no matter how grim the weather.   15
After a deep snow, I plow calmly through thigh-high powder. My body's
padded, warm and down-packed. I can sit anywhere, for hours. I lounge
in the snow to think as the sun drops a feeble and indifferent light. The
cold does not penetrate. I roll over, a whale in snow dunes, and lie quietly on my back, wishing I could bear this baby quickly, fervently, right
out here in this field, alone.

Hour of the Wolf

Part of a writer's task is to put her failings at the service of her pen.
Just so with insomnia, this habit of waking at the most inconvenient,
still hour of what is technically morning — three or four A.M. — the
hour of the wolf. My eyes flip open. All the lights are on in my head,

thoughts alert and humming. In past times, I could think of the fictional question or problem I was facing, and my brain would snap right off as though confronted by a paralyzing koan. No more. Pregnancy increases my tendency to wakefulness and makes any sleeping medication dangerous, since it passes into the baby affecting god-knows-what developmental moment. As a matter of practicality, knowing I'll be burnt-out and drowsy the next day if I lie stewing and planning in the dark, I get up. I make myself a cup of herbal tea and start writing poetry. The house is bleak and cold, the windows painted with ostrich ferns of frost. I stir the tea, quietly, then swaddle myself in afghans on the living room couch and write until my words lull me back to sleep. Often, satisfactorily weary at four-thirty or five, I pass Michael on the stairs as he rises to stoke the wood fire, make coffee, begin his day.

I write poems during the late nights up until the week of birth, and fiction by day. I suppose one could say, pulling in the obvious metaphors, that my work is hormone driven, inscribed in mother's milk, pregnant with itself. I do begin to think that I am in touch with something larger than me, one of the few things. I feel that I am transcribing verbatim from a flow of language running through the room, an ink current into which I dip the pen. It is a dark stream, swift running, a twisting flow that never doubles back. The amazement is that I need only to enter the room at those strange hours to be drawn back into the language. The frustration is that I cannot be there all the time.

Wintergardens

One evening, our three- and four-year-old daughters are playing and I am working halfheartedly at my usual piles of unanswered correspondence. Suddenly, I overhear them.

"God is made out of sky and wind," says the older in a voice of absolute assurance.

"No," the other is equally firm. "A flower. God is a flower."   20

Outrage ensues. Panic. One threat flies, another. They come to me and I stumble, caught up short and unprepared. I am very much surprised that our daughters, at such young ages, are wrestling with big questions about the foundations of existence. To solve two mysteries at once, they link God and death. One insists to the other that the reason we must die is so that God can stay alive. If we die, then God must die, the other is certain. They look at me, glaring, questioning. I open my mouth, close it, clear my throat. I have never lied to them. I sort quickly through my beliefs, but I don't have a sound set of reassuring answers. Every organized religion seems to me as much political as spiritual, even my grandfather's caretaking traditional Ojibwa worldview, which is closest to my heart. I can't confirm their hopes about an afterlife, describe God's looks, picture a reliable heaven. Their expressions lower in disapproval. They want certainty, not more metaphysical confusion. At last in a burst of stentorian authority the younger gathers herself and bellows out, "*God's in the garden!*"

Her sister narrows her eyes but then, to my relief, slowly nods. "Church is in the woods," she commands in a low voice, and then, rebellious, "I *have* to believe in heaven." They turn to building a block house together. Maybe, as I'm told at bedtime in a whisper, *God is a white rose that blooms in winter.* I fill my thoughts after they are sleeping with that extraordinary image. From there, next summer's season of flowers catches hold. I become obsessive. Having failed to solve my own religious questions, I feel I must help our daughters solve theirs. As post-Christmas seed catalogues flood the mail, I pile them around my reading chair already awash with religious gropings — everything from *The Interior Castle* to birchbark scrolls, the *Tao Te Ching* to A *Treatise on Angel Magic.* Perhaps proving my daughter right about God's whereabouts, however, I find the seed catalogues most comforting. At last I decide there is no better way to spend these last slow suspenseful evenings than plotting out something spiritually definitive, of the earth, an imaginary garden. . . .

Famous Labors

Still, it seems unfair that because I am a mammal I am condemned to give birth through the lower part of my body while flowers, though brainless, have the wisdom to shoot straight upward in a pure green rush from unpromising seeds. I don't like needles, the smell of hospital disinfectants, or anything made of stainless steel that looks even faintly surgical. I once fainted as my hair was being cut. Blood tests dismay me and I don't want anyone, even my dear midwife and friend, to approach the most vulnerable part of me with anything sharp. Birth involves basins and syringes and episiotomies. I mention these hatreds of mine in order to assure other women that I am a coward, physically timid, and yet we are all stronger than we think we are when put to a task.

Yet, why is no woman's labor as famous as the death of Socrates? Over all of the millennia that women have endured and suffered and died during childbirth, we have no one story that comes down to us with attendant reverence, or that exists in pictures — a cultural icon, like that of Socrates holding forth to his companions as he raises the cup of hemlock. In our Western and Westernized culture, women's labor is devalorized beginning with Genesis. Eve's natural intelligence, curiosity, desire, and perhaps sense of justice cause her to taste the fruit of good and evil, the apple of knowledge. Thereafter, goes the story, all women are condemned to bring forth children in pain. Thus are women culturally stripped of any moral claim to strength or virtue in labor. I have no problem with stoicism, I just think it should be acknowledged. War heroes routinely receive medals for killing and defending. Why don't women routinely receive medals for giving birth?

Or for not giving birth — a decision . . . just as profound and inarguably more sensible as our world population burgeons.   25

My mother bore me in Minnesota on a day of high winds, and although she labored for one whole day and part of another she did not make a sound, so all there was, I imagine, in those spaces between contractions, was the moaning and booming of air. She bore seven children, naturally, refusing drugs at a time they were unsafe for infants, and nursing at a time when the prevailing opinion favored bottle-feeding. She trusted herself to a remarkable degree, and because she did so, she also did the work of deciding for me whether to breast-feed, whether I could get through labor, whether I could trust my own instincts to mother a child.

I relied on her in other ways as well. It was no accident that I looked for a midwife instead of an obstetrician and no wonder that Michael and I met our midwife with a feeling of trust at first sight. Complicated, intelligent, with beautiful dark eyes and a quick, warm laugh, Charlotte Houde, our nurse-midwife, is a professional unafraid to make emotional connections. Over the course of delivering our three daughters, the relationship that we develop becomes both medical and loving. In most Western obstetrical relationships there is little sense of spiritual concern, but Charlotte tends to the entire existence of her patients. With every checkup, through every pregnancy, with every baby, I am able to tell her when I'm thrilled, demoralized, afraid, in a state of anguish I can't articulate. Eventually, she gives me a metaphor that I find helpful during the blackest of moments. She compares the deepest wells of depression to gestation, to a time enclosed, a secluded lightlessness in which, unknown and unforced, we grow. . . .

Women's Work

Rocking, breathing, groaning, mouthing circles of distress, laughing, whistling, pounding, wavering, digging, pulling, pushing — labor is the most involuntary work we do. My body gallops to these rhythms. I'm along for the ride, at times in some control and at others dragged along as if foot-caught in a stirrup. I don't have much to do at first but breathe, accept ice chips, make jokes — in fear and pain my family makes jokes, that's how we deal with what we can't change, how we show our courage.

Even though I am a writer and have practiced my craft for years, and have experienced two natural childbirths and an epidural-assisted childbirth, I find women's labor extremely difficult to describe. In the first place, there are all sorts of labor and no "correct" way to do it. I bow to the power and grandeur of those who insist on natural childbirth, but I find the pieties that often attend the process irritating. I am all for pain relief or cesareans when women want and need these procedures. Enduring pain in itself doesn't make one a better person, though if your mind is prepared, pain of this sort — a meaningful and determined pain based on ardor and potential joy — can be deeply instructive, can change your life.

Perhaps there is no adequate description for something that happens   30
with such full-on physical force, but the problem inherent to birth narratives is also historical — women haven't had a voice or education, or have been overwhelmed, unconscious, stifled, just plain worn out or worse, ill to the death. Although every birth is a story, there are only so many outcomes possible. Birth is dictated to the consciousness by the conscious body. There are certain frustrations in approaching such an event, a drama in which the body stars and not the fiction-making mind. In a certain way, I'm jealous. I want to control the tale. I can't — therein lies the conflict that drives this plot in the first place. I have to trust this body — a thing inherently bound to betray me, an unreliable conveyance, a passion-driven cab that tries its best to let me off in bad neighborhoods, an adolescent that rebels against my better self, that eats erratically and sleeps too much, that grows another human with my grudging admiration, a sensation grabber, unpenitent, remorseless, amoral.

Birth is intensely spiritual and physical all at once. The contractions do not stop. There is no giving up this physical prayer. The person who experiences birth with the closest degree of awareness is the mother — but not only am I physically programmed to forget the experience to some degree (our brains "extinct" fear, we are all programmed to forget pain over time, and hormones seem to assist), I am overwhelmed by what is happening to me. I certainly can't take notes, jot down my sensations, or even have them with any perspective after a while. And then, once our baby is actually born, the experience of labor, even at its most intense, is eclipsed by the presence of an infant.

The problem of narrative involves, too, more than just embarrassment about a physical process. We're taught to suppress its importance over time, to devalue and belittle an experience in which we are bound up in the circular drama of human fate, in a state of heightened awareness and receptivity, at a crux where we intuit connections and, for a moment, unlock time's hold like a brace, even step from our bodies. Labor often becomes both paradigm and parable. The story of the body becomes a touchstone, a predictor. A mother or a father, in describing their labor, relates the personality of the child to some piece of the event, makes the story into a frame, an introduction, a prelude to the child's life, molds the labor into the story that is no longer a woman's story or a man's story, but the story of a child.

The first part of labor feels, to me anyway, like dance exercises — slow stretches that become only slightly painful as a muscle is pulled to its limit. After each contraction, the feeling subsides. The contractions move in longer waves, one after another, closer and closer together until a sea of physical sensation washes and then crashes over. In the beginning I breathe in concentration, watching Michael's eyes. I feel myself slip beneath the waves as they roar over, cresting just above my head. I duck every time the contraction peaks. As the hours pass and one wave builds on another there are times the undertow grabs me. I struggle, slammed to the bottom, unable to gather the force of nerve for the next. Thrown down, I rely on animal fierceness, swim back, surface, breathe, and try to stay open, willing. Staying *open and willing* is difficult. Very often in labor one must fight the instinct to resist pain and instead embrace it, move toward it, work with what hurts the most.

The waves come faster. Charlotte asks me to keep breathing yes, yes. To say yes instead of shuddering in refusal. Whether I am standing on the earth or not, whether I am moored to the dock, whether I remember who I am, whether I am mentally prepared, whether I am going to float beneath or ride above, the waves pound in. At shorter intervals, crazy now, electric, in storms, they wash. Sometimes I'm gone. I've poured myself into some deeper fissure below the sea only to be dragged forth, hair streaming. During transition, as the baby is ready to be pushed out into life, the waves are no longer made of water, but neons so brilliant I gasp in shock and flourish my arms, letting the colors explode from my fingertips in banners, in ribbons, in iridescent trails — of pain, it is true, unendurable sometimes, and yet we do endure.

Every birth is profoundly original and yet plotted a billion times, too   35 many times. We move into the narrative with medical advice and technological assistance and frail human hopes, and yet we often find ourselves inadequately shaped by culture, by family, by each other for the scope of the work. The task requires mystical tools and helpers. For religions to make sense to women, there should be a birth ritual that flexes and exercises the most powerful aspects of the personality in preparation. Organized Christian religion is more often about denying the body when what we profoundly need are rituals that take into regard the blood, the shock, the heat, the shit, the anguish, the irritation, the glory, the earnestness of the female body.

Some push once, some don't push at all, some push in pleasure, some not, and some, like me, for hours. We wreak havoc, make animal faces, ugly bare-toothed faces, go red, go darker, whiter, stranger, turn to bears. We choke spouses, beat nurses, beg them, beg doctors, weep and focus. It is our work, our body's work that is involved in its own goodness. For, even though it wants at times to lie down and quit, the body is an honest hardworking marvel that gives everything to this one task. . . .

Archery

During a time of grief in my father and mother's house, during a period when their adolescent children seemed lighted with a self-destructive fire beyond their control, I found the quote so often used about children written on a scrap of paper in my father's odd and lovely handwriting.

You are the bows from which your children as living arrows are sent forth. . . . Let your bending in the archer's hand be for gladness.

Because my parents for a time practiced archery, I know what it is to try to bend a bow that was too massive for my strength. In the last stages of labor, gathering into each push and bearing the strange power of transition, a woman bends the great ash bow with an unpossessed power. She struggles until her body finds the proper angle, the force, the calm. The fiberglass, the burnished woods, increase in tension and resilience. Each archer feels the despairing fear it cannot be done. But it will, somehow. Walking in the streets or the trails sometimes, now, looking at the women and their children as they pass, I think of them all as women who have labored, who have bent the bow too great for their strength.

At last, with the birth of each daughter, Michael and I experience a   40
certainty of apprehension, a sensation so profound that I feel foggy

brained attempting to describe how, in the first moment after birth, the *actual being* of a new person appears.

We touch our baby's essential mystery. The three of us are soul to soul.

EXPLORATIONS

1. "To make love with the desire for a child is . . . to make the need of the moment an eternal wish" (para. 1). For Louise Erdrich, parenthood is full of paradoxes and contradictions. What other examples can you find in her essay?

2. "Love of an infant," Erdrich writes, ". . . is uncomfortably close to self-erasure, and in the face of it one's fat ambitions, desperations, private icons, and urges fall away into a dreamlike *before* that haunts and forces itself into the present with tough persistence" (para. 2). What does she mean? In what sense is this statement a warning to would-be parents? In what sense is it an encouragement?

3. "Conception is . . . a candle in a one-room studio" (para. 1). Erdrich uses metaphors and similes throughout "Making Babies." What does she accomplish by relying on these figures of speech instead of direct description? Which metaphors and similes in her essay struck you as particularly effective?

CONNECTIONS

1. "Growing, bearing, mothering or fathering, supporting, and at last letting go of an infant is a powerful and mundane creative act that rapturously sucks up whole chunks of life" (para. 1). What examples can you find of this statement in the Observations on pages 95–101?

2. Reread the quotation Erdrich cites in paragraph 38. What advice for parents is contained here? Which of the parents who appear in pages 95–101, or whom you have read about elsewhere in this book, follow this advice? Which parents do not?

3. "Today has witnessed something that deserves thanks and praise to God," Naguib Mahfouz writes in his Observation on page 95. "Remember that, when the day comes on which all are scattered, each to his own home, and the day on which these memories find no one to remember them." Compare Erdrich's comments in paragraph 3. What common ideas are both writers expressing?

ELABORATIONS

1. In Erdrich's opinion, the heroism of giving birth never has gotten the credit it deserves. What other landmarks in family life tend to be more difficult or painful or frightening than we anticipated? Choose one or more examples from your own past and write an essay about the experience.

2. Pregnant women, according to Erdrich, "should be in training, like acolytes, novices to high priestesshood, like serious applicants for the space program" (para. 7). What kinds of training are available now for parents-to-be? If you were designing a training or apprenticeship program for mothers (or fathers) along the lines Erdrich recommends, what would you include? Write an essay classifying or describing suitable goals, timing, location, and content of an appropriate preparation for becoming a mother (or father).

BARBARA DAFOE WHITEHEAD

From Death to Divorce

"From Death to Divorce" comes from Barbara Dafoe Whitehead's notorious 1993 *Atlantic Monthly* article "Dan Quayle Was Right." As four of her seven sisters and brothers (who include the actor Willem Dafoe) divorced in the 1970s and 1980s, Whitehead became fascinated by the rising divorce rate and its effect on families. Her title alludes to U.S. Vice President Dan Quayle's 1992 attack on the television series *Murphy Brown*, when the unmarried Murphy decided to become a mother. Whitehead later published the book *The Divorce Culture* (1997); her articles have appeared in the *Wall Street Journal*, the *New York Times*, and other publications. A registered Democrat, she has served as vice president of the Institute for American Values and as co-director of the National Marriage Project. She was born in Rochester, Minnesota, in 1944, graduated from the University of Wisconsin, and holds an M.A. and a Ph.D. from the University of Chicago. Married since 1967, she has three children and lives in Amherst, Massachusetts.

Across time and across cultures, family disruption has been regarded as an event that threatens a child's well-being and even survival. This view is rooted in a fundamental biological fact: unlike the young of almost any other species, the human child is born in an abjectly helpless and immature state. Years of nurture and protection are needed before the child can achieve physical independence. Similarly, it takes years of interaction with at least one but ideally two or more adults for a child to develop into a socially competent adult. Children raised in virtual isolation from human beings, though physically intact, display few recognizably human behaviors. The social arrangement that has proved most successful in ensuring the physical survival and promoting the social development of the child is the family unit of the biological mother and father. Consequently, any event that permanently denies a child the presence and protection of a parent jeopardizes the life of the child.

The classic form of family disruption is the death of a parent. Throughout history this has been one of the risks of childhood. Mothers frequently died in childbirth, and it was not unusual for both parents to die before the child was grown. As recently as the early decades of this century children commonly suffered the death of at least one parent.

Almost a quarter of the children born in this country in 1900 lost one parent by the time they were fifteen years old. Many of these children lived with their widowed parent, often in a household with other close relatives. Others grew up in orphanages and foster homes.

The meaning of parental death, as it has been transmitted over time and faithfully recorded in world literature and lore, is unambiguous and essentially unchanging. It is universally regarded as an untimely and tragic event. Death permanently severs the parent-child bond, disrupting forever one of the child's earliest and deepest human attachments. It also deprives a child of the presence and protection of an adult who has a biological stake in, as well as an emotional commitment to, the child's survival and well-being. In short, the death of a parent is the most extreme and severe loss a child can suffer.

Because a child is so vulnerable in a parent's absence, there has been a common cultural response to the death of a parent: an outpouring of support from family, friends, and strangers alike. The surviving parent and child are united in their grief as well as their loss. Relatives and friends share in the loss and provide valuable emotional and financial assistance to the bereaved family. Other members of the community show sympathy for the child, and public assistance is available for those who need it. This cultural understanding of parental death has formed the basis for a tradition of public support to widows and their children. Indeed, as recently as the beginning of this century widows were the only mothers eligible for pensions in many states, and today widows with children receive more generous welfare benefits from Survivors Insurance than do other single mothers with children who depend on Aid to Families with Dependent Children.

It has taken thousands upon thousands of years to reduce the threat 5 of parental death. Not until the middle of the twentieth century did parental death cease to be a commonplace event for children in the United States. By then advances in medicine had dramatically reduced mortality rates for men and women.

At the same time, other forms of family disruption — separation, divorce, out-of-wedlock birth — were held in check by powerful religious, social, and legal sanctions. Divorce was widely regarded both as a deviant behavior, especially threatening to mothers and children, and as a personal lapse: "Divorce is the public acknowledgment of failure," a 1940s sociology textbook noted. Out-of-wedlock birth was stigmatized, and stigmatization is a powerful means of regulating behavior, as any smoker or overeater will testify. Sanctions against nonmarital childbirth discouraged behavior that hurt children and exacted compensatory behavior that helped them. Shotgun marriages and adoption, two common responses to nonmarital birth, carried a strong message about the risks of premarital sex and created an intact family for the child.

Consequently, children did not have to worry much about losing a parent through divorce or never having had one because of nonmarital birth. After a surge in divorces following the Second World War, the rate leveled off. Only 11 percent of children born in the 1950s would by the time they turned eighteen see their parents separate or divorce. Out-of-wedlock childbirth barely figured as a cause of family disruption. In the 1950s and early 1960s, 5 percent of the nation's births were out of wedlock. Blacks were more likely than whites to bear children outside marriage, but the majority of black children born in the twenty years after the Second World War were born to married couples. The rate of family disruption reached a historic low point during those years.

A new standard of family security and stability was established in postwar America. For the first time in history the vast majority of the nation's children could expect to live with married biological parents throughout childhood. Children might still suffer other forms of adversity — poverty, racial discrimination, lack of educational opportunity — but only a few would be deprived of the nurture and protection of a mother and a father. No longer did children have to be haunted by the classic fears vividly dramatized in folklore and fable — that their parents would die, that they would have to live with a stepparent and stepsiblings, or that they would be abandoned. These were the years when the nation confidently boarded up orphanages and closed foundling hospitals, certain that such institutions would never again be needed. In movie theaters across the country parents and children could watch the drama of parental separation and death in the great Disney classics, secure in the knowledge that such nightmare visions as the death of Bambi's mother and the wrenching separation of Dumbo from his mother were only make-believe.

In the 1960s the rate of family disruption suddenly began to rise. After inching up over the course of a century, the divorce rate soared. Throughout the 1950s and early 1960s the divorce rate held steady at fewer than ten divorces a year per 1,000 married couples. Then, beginning in about 1965, the rate increased sharply, peaking at twenty-three divorces per 1,000 marriages by 1979. (In 1974 divorce passed death as the leading cause of family breakup.) The rate has leveled off at about twenty-one divorces per 1,000 marriages — the figure for 1991. The out-of-wedlock birth rate also jumped. It went from 5 percent in 1960 to 27 percent in 1990. In 1990 close to 57 percent of births among black mothers were nonmarital, and about 17 percent among white mothers. Altogether, about one out of every four women who had a child in 1990 was not married. With rates of divorce and nonmarital birth so high, family disruption is at its peak. Never before have so many children experienced family breakup caused by events other than death. Each year a million children go through divorce or separation and almost as many more are born out of wedlock.

Half of all marriages now end in divorce. Following divorce, many 10 people enter new relationships. Some begin living together. Nearly half of all cohabiting couples have children in the household. Fifteen percent have new children together. Many cohabiting couples eventually get married. However, both cohabiting and remarried couples are more likely to break up than couples in first marriages. Even social scientists find it hard to keep pace with the complexity and velocity of such patterns. In the revised edition (1992) of his book *Marriage, Divorce, Remarriage*, the sociologist Andrew Cherlin ruefully comments: "If there were a truth-in-labeling law for books, the title of this edition should be something long and unwieldy like *Cohabitation, Marriage, Divorce, More Cohabitation, and Probably Remarriage.*"

Under such conditions growing up can be a turbulent experience. In many single-parent families children must come to terms with the parent's love life and romantic partners. Some children live with cohabiting couples, either their own unmarried parents or a biological parent and a live-in partner. Some children born to cohabiting parents see their parents break up. Others see their parents marry, but 56 percent of them (as compared with 31 percent of the children born to married parents) later see their parents' marriages fall apart. All told, about three-quarters of children born to cohabiting couples will live in a single-parent home at least briefly. One of every four children growing up in the 1990s will eventually enter a stepfamily. According to one survey, nearly half of all children in stepparent families will see their parents divorce again by the time they reach their late teens. Since 80 percent of divorced fathers remarry, things get even more complicated when the romantic or marital history of the noncustodial parent, usually the father, is taken into account. Consequently, as it affects a significant number of children, family disruption is best understood not as a single event but as a string of disruptive events: separation, divorce, life in a single-parent family, life with a parent and live-in lover, the remarriage of one or both parents, life in one stepparent family combined with visits to another stepparent family; the breakup of one or both stepparent families. And so on. This is one reason why public schools have a hard time knowing whom to call in an emergency.

Given its dramatic impact on children's lives, one might reasonably expect that this historic level of family disruption would be viewed with alarm, even regarded as a national crisis. Yet this has not been the case. In recent years some people have argued that these trends pose a serious threat to children and to the nation as a whole, but they are dismissed as declinists, pessimists, or nostalgists, unwilling or unable to accept the new facts of life. The dominant view is that the changes in family structure are, on balance, positive.

A Shift in the Social Metric

There are several reasons why this is so, but the fundamental reason is that at some point in the 1970s Americans changed their minds about the meaning of these disruptive behaviors. What had once been regarded as hostile to children's best interests was now considered essential to adults' happiness. In the 1950s most Americans believed that parents should stay in an unhappy marriage for the sake of the children. The assumption was that a divorce would damage the children, and the prospect of such damage gave divorce its meaning. By the mid-1970s a majority of Americans rejected that view. Popular advice literature reflected the shift. A book on divorce published in the mid-1940s tersely asserted: "Children are entitled to the affection and association of two parents, not one." Thirty years later another popular divorce book proclaimed just the opposite: "A two-parent home is not the only emotional structure within which a child can be happy and healthy. . . . The parents who take care of themselves will be best able to take care of their children." At about the same time, the long-standing taboo against out-of-wedlock childbirth also collapsed. By the mid-1970s three-fourths of Americans said that it was not morally wrong for a woman to have a child outside marriage.

Once the social metric shifts from child well-being to adult well-being, it is hard to see divorce and nonmarital birth in anything but a positive light. However distressing and difficult they may be, both of these behaviors can hold out the promise of greater adult choice, freedom, and happiness. For unhappy spouses, divorce offers a way to escape a troubled or even abusive relationship and make a fresh start. For single parents, remarriage is a second try at marital happiness as well as a chance for relief from the stress, loneliness, and economic hardship of raising a child alone. For some unmarried women, nonmarital birth is a way to beat the biological clock, avoid marrying the wrong man, and experience the pleasures of motherhood. Moreover, divorce and out-of-wedlock birth involve a measure of agency and choice; they are man- and woman-made events. To be sure, not everyone exercises choice in divorce or nonmarital birth. Men leave wives for younger women, teenage girls get pregnant accidentally — yet even these unhappy events reflected the expansion of the boundaries of freedom and choice.

This cultural shift helps explain what otherwise would be inexpli-   15 cable: the failure to see the rise in family disruption as a severe and troubling national problem. It explains why there is virtually no widespread public sentiment for restigmatizing either of these classically disruptive behaviors and no sense — no public consensus — that they can or should be avoided in the future. On the contrary, the prevailing opinion is that we should accept the changes in family structure as inevitable and devise new forms of public and private support for single-parent families.

The View from Hollywood

With its affirmation of the liberating effects of divorce and nonmarital childbirth, this opinion is a fixture of American popular culture today. Madison Avenue and Hollywood did not invent these behaviors, as their highly paid publicists are quick to point out, but they have played an influential role in defending and even celebrating divorce and unwed motherhood. More precisely, they have taken the raw material of demography and fashioned it into a powerful fantasy of individual renewal and rebirth. Consider, for example, the teaser for *People* magazine's cover story on Joan Lunden's divorce: "After the painful end of her 13-year marriage, the *Good Morning America* cohost is discovering a new life as a single mother — and as her own woman." *People* does not dwell on the anguish Lunden and her children might have experienced over the breakup of their family, or the difficulties of single motherhood, even for celebrity mothers. Instead, it celebrates Joan Lunden's steps toward independence and a better life. *People*, characteristically, focuses on her shopping: In the first weeks after her breakup Lunden leased "a brand-new six-bedroom, 8,000-square-foot" house and then went to Bloomingdale's, where she scooped up sheets, pillows, a toaster, dishes, seven televisions, and roomfuls of fun furniture that was "totally unlike the serious traditional pieces she was giving up."

This is not just the view taken in supermarket magazines. Even the conservative bastion of the greeting-card industry, Hallmark, offers a line of cards commemorating divorce as liberation. "Think of your former marriage as a record album," says one Contemporary card. "It was full of music — both happy and sad. But what's important now is . . . YOU! the recently released HOT NEW SINGLE! You're going to be at the

TOP OF THE CHARTS!" Another card reads: "Getting divorced can be very healthy! Watch how it improves your circulation! Best of luck! . . ." Hallmark's hip Shoebox Greetings division depicts two female praying mantises. Mantis One: "It's tough being a single parent." Mantis Two: "Yeah . . . Maybe we shouldn't have eaten our husbands."

Divorce is a tired convention in Hollywood, but unwed parenthood is very much in fashion: In the past year or so babies were born to Warren Beatty and Annette Bening, Jack Nicholson and Rebecca Broussard, and Eddie Murphy and Nicole Mitchell. *Vanity Fair* celebrated Jack Nicholson's fatherhood with a cover story (April 1992) called "Happy Jack." What made Jack happy, it turned out, was no-fault fatherhood. He and Broussard, the twenty-nine-year-old mother of his children, lived in separate houses. Nicholson said, "It's an unusual arrangement, but the last twenty-five years or so have shown me that I'm not good at cohabitation. . . . I see Rebecca as much as any other person who is cohabiting. And she prefers it. I think most people would in a more honest and truthful world." As for more permanent commitments, the man who is not good at cohabitation said: "I don't discuss marriage much with Rebecca. Those discussions are the very thing I'm trying to avoid. I'm after this immediate real thing. That's all I believe in." (Perhaps Nicholson should have had the discussion. Not long after the story appeared, Broussard broke off the relationship.)

As this story shows, unwed parenthood is thought of not only as a way to find happiness but also as a way to exhibit such virtues as honesty and courage. A similar argument was offered in defense of Murphy Brown's unwed motherhood. Many of Murphy's fans were quick to point out that Murphy suffered over her decision to bear a child out of wedlock. Faced with an accidental pregnancy and a faithless lover, she agonized over her plight and, after much mental anguish, bravely decided to go ahead. In short, having a baby without a husband represented a higher level of maternal devotion and sacrifice than having a baby with a husband. Murphy was not just exercising her rights as a woman; she was exhibiting true moral heroism.

On the night Murphy Brown became an unwed mother, 34 million Americans tuned in, and CBS posted a 35 percent share of the audience. The show did not stir significant protest at the grass roots and lost none of its advertisers. The actress Candice Bergen subsequently appeared on the cover of nearly every women's and news magazine in the country and received an honorary degree at the University of Pennsylvania as well as an Emmy award. The show's creator, Diane English, popped up in Hanes stocking ads. Judged by conventional measures of approval, Murphy Brown's motherhood was a hit at the box office.

Increasingly, the media depicts the married two-parent family as a source of pathology. According to a spate of celebrity memoirs and interviews, the married-parent family harbors terrible secrets of abuse, violence, and incest. A bumper sticker I saw in Amherst, Massachusetts, read Unspoken Traditional Family Values: Abuse, Alcoholism, Incest. The pop therapist John Bradshaw explains away this generation's problems with the dictum that 96 percent of families are dysfunctional, made that way by the addicted society we live in. David Lynch creates a new aesthetic of creepiness by juxtaposing scenes of traditional family life with images of seduction and perversion. A Boston-area museum puts on an exhibit called "Good-bye to Apple Pie," featuring several artists' visions of child abuse, including one mixed-media piece with knives poking through a little girl's skirt. The piece is titled "Father Knows Best."

No one would claim that two-parent families are free from conflict, violence, or abuse. However, the attempt to discredit the two-parent family can be understood as part of what Daniel Patrick Moynihan has described as a larger effort to accommodate higher levels of social deviance. "The amount of deviant behavior in American society has increased beyond the levels the community can 'afford to recognize,'" Moynihan argues. One response has been to normalize what was once considered deviant behavior, such as out-of-wedlock birth. An accompanying response has been to detect deviance in what once stood as a social norm, such as the married-couple family. Together these responses reduce the acknowledged levels of deviance by eroding earlier distinctions between the normal and the deviant.

Several recent studies describe family life in its postwar heyday as the seedbed of alcoholism and abuse. According to Stephanie Coontz, the author of the book *The Way We Never Were: American Families and the Nostalgia Trap*, family life for married mothers in the 1950s consisted of "booze, bowling, bridge, and boredom." Coontz writes: "Few would have guessed that radiant Marilyn Van Derbur, crowned Miss America in 1958, had been sexually violated by her wealthy, respectable father from the time she was five until she was eighteen, when she moved away to college." Even the budget-stretching casserole comes under attack as a sign of culinary dysfunction. According to one food writer, this homely staple of postwar family life brings back images of "the good mother of the 50s . . . locked in Ozzie and Harriet land, unable to move past the canvas of a Corning Ware dish, the palette of a can of Campbell's soup, the mushy dominion of which she was queen."

Nevertheless, the popular portrait of family life does not simply reflect the views of a cultural elite, as some have argued. There is strong support at the grass roots for much of this view of family change. Survey after survey shows that Americans are less inclined than they were a generation ago to value sexual fidelity, lifelong marriage, and parenthood as worthwhile personal goals. Motherhood no longer defines adult womanhood, as everyone knows; equally important is the fact that fatherhood has declined as a norm for men. In 1976 less than half as many fathers as in 1957 said that providing for children was a life goal. The proportion of working men who found marriage and children burdensome and restrictive more than doubled in the same period. Fewer than half of all adult Americans today regard the idea of sacrifice for others as a positive moral virtue.

Dinosaurs Divorce

It is true that many adults benefit from divorce or remarriage. According to one study, nearly 80 percent of divorced women and 50 percent of divorced men say they are better off out of the marriage. Half of divorced adults in the same study report greater happiness. A competent self-help book called *Divorce and New Beginnings* notes the advantages of single parenthood: single parents can "develop their own interests, fulfill their own needs, choose their own friends, and engage in social activities of their choice. Money, even if limited, can be spent as they see fit." Apparently, some women appreciate the opportunity to have children out of wedlock. "The real world, however, does not always allow women who are dedicated to their careers to devote the time and energy it takes to find — or be found by — the perfect husband and father wanna-be," one woman said in a letter to the *Washington Post*. A mother and chiropractor from Avon, Connecticut, explained her unwed maternity to an interviewer this way: "It is selfish, but this was something I needed to do for me."

There is very little in contemporary popular culture to contradict this optimistic view. But in a few small places another perspective may be found. Several racks down from its divorce cards, Hallmark offers a line of cards for children — To Kids With Love. These cards come six to a pack. Each card in the pack has a slightly different message. According to the package, the "thinking of you" messages will let a special kid "know how much you care." Though Hallmark doesn't quite say so, it's clear these cards are aimed at divorced parents. "I'm sorry I'm not always there when you need me but I hope you know I'm always just a phone call away." Another card reads: "Even though your dad and I don't live together anymore, I know he's still a very special part of your

25

life. And as much as I miss you when you're not with me, I'm still happy that you two can spend time together."

Hallmark's messages are grounded in a substantial body of well-funded market research. Therefore it is worth reflecting on the divergence in sentiment between the divorce cards for adults and the divorce cards for kids. For grown-ups, divorce heralds new beginnings (A HOT NEW SINGLE). For children, divorce brings separation and loss ("I'm sorry I'm not always there when you need me").

An even more telling glimpse into the meaning of family disruption can be found in the growing children's literature on family dissolution. Take, for example, the popular children's book *Dinosaurs Divorce: A Guide for Changing Families* (1986), by Laurene Krasny Brown and Marc Brown. This is a picture book, written for very young children. The book begins with a short glossary of "divorce words" and encourages children to "see if you can find them" in the story. The words include "family counselor," "separation agreement," "alimony," and "child custody." The book is illustrated with cartoonish drawings of green dinosaur parents who fight, drink too much, and break up. One panel shows the father dinosaur, suitcase in hand, getting into a yellow car.

The dinosaur children are offered simple, straightforward advice on what to do about the divorce. On custody decisions: "When parents can't agree, lawyers and judges decide. Try to be honest if they ask you questions; it will help them make better decisions." On selling the house: "If you move, you may have to say good-bye to friends and familiar places. But soon your new home will feel like the place you really belong." On the economic impact of divorce: "Living with one parent almost always means there will be less money. Be prepared to give up some things." On holidays: "Divorce may mean twice as much celebrating at holiday times, but you may feel pulled apart." On parents' new lovers: "You may sometimes feel jealous and want your parent to yourself. Be polite to your parents' new friends, even if you don't like them at first." On parents' remarriage: "Not everyone loves his or her stepparents, but showing them respect is important."

These cards and books point to an uncomfortable and generally un- 30
acknowledged fact: What contributes to a parent's happiness may detract from a child's happiness. All too often the adult quest for freedom, independence, and choice in family relationships conflicts with a child's developmental needs for stability, constancy, harmony, and permanence in family life. In short, family disruption creates a deep division between parents' interests and the interests of children.

One of the worst consequences of these divided interests is a withdrawal of parental investment in children's well-being. As the Stanford economist Victor Fuchs has pointed out, the main source of social investment in children is private. The investment comes from the children's parents. But parents in disrupted families have less time, attention, and money to devote to their children. The single most important source of disinvestment has been the widespread withdrawal of financial support and involvement by fathers. Maternal investment, too, has declined, as women try to raise families on their own and work outside the home. Moreover, both mothers and fathers commonly respond to family breakup by investing more heavily in themselves and in their own personal and romantic lives.

Sometimes the tables are completely turned. Children are called upon to invest in the emotional well-being of their parents. Indeed, this seems to be the larger message of many of the children's books on divorce and remarriage. *Dinosaurs Divorce* asks children to be sympathetic, understanding, respectful, and polite to confused, unhappy parents. The sacrifice comes from the children: "Be prepared to give up some things." In the world of divorcing dinosaurs, the children rather than the grown-ups are the exemplars of patience, restraint, and good sense.

EXPLORATIONS

1. According to Barbara Dafoe Whitehead, which has been historically a more common experience for children: growing up with two parents, or losing one or both parents? What does she mean by "From Death to Divorce"?

2. What attitude change does Whitehead blame for the rising divorce rate during the past few decades? What is her opinion of this change, and why?

3. Where in her essay does Whitehead use research data as evidence for her conclusions? Where does she use popular culture as evidence?

CONNECTIONS

1. Whitehead describes "the social metric shift[ing] from child well-being to adult well-being" (para. 14). In what ways does Louise Erdrich in "Making Babies" (p. 102) emphasize child well-being? In what ways does she emphasize adult well-being? Do you think Whitehead would approve of Erdrich as a mother? Why or why not?

2. Does the family described in Ved Mehta's Observation on page 312 focus more on child well-being or adult well-being? On what evidence do you base your answer? What role does happiness appear to play in this family?

3. Does the family described in Paula Fomby's Observation on page 99 focus more on child well-being or adult well-being? On what evidence do you base your answer? What role does happiness appear to play in this family?

ELABORATIONS

1. "Madison Avenue and Hollywood did not invent these behaviors . . . but they have played an influential role in defending and even celebrating divorce and unwed motherhood" (para. 16). Do you agree? Find examples of advertising or television or motion pictures, or all three, that support or contradict Whitehead's statement. Write an essay arguing in favor of her statement or against it, illustrated with your examples.

2. Choose two families you know that have been affected by parental death or divorce. What has been the impact on the children? Using Whitehead's essay as a resource, compare and contrast the experiences and outcomes in those families.

BARBARA KINGSOLVER

Stone Soup

Barbara Kingsolver grew up in eastern Kentucky, where she was born in 1955. "The options were limited — grow up to be a farmer or a farmer's wife." Instead she left home for DePauw University, majored in biology, took a creative writing course, and protested against the Vietnam war. During school and two years living in Greece and France, Kingsolver worked as an archaeologist, copyeditor, X-ray technician, housecleaner, biological researcher, and translator of medical documents. She got her master's degree in biology and ecology from the University of Arizona and began writing science, then journalism. By night she worked on her first novel, *The Bean Trees* (1988). Her second book was the nonfictional *Women in the Great Arizona Mine Strike of 1983* (1989/1996). Since then she has published three more novels (*Animal Dreams*, 1990; *Pigs in Heaven*, 1993; and *The Poisonwood Bible*, 1999) as well as poetry (*Another America: Otra America*, 1992) and stories (*Homeland and Other Stories*, 1989). "Stone Soup" comes from her nonfiction collection *High Tide in Tucson: Essays from Now and Never* (1995). Kingsolver lives outside Tucson with her second husband and two daughters.

In the catalog of family values, where do we rank an occasion like this? A curly-haired boy who wanted to run before he walked, age seven now, a soccer player scoring a winning goal. He turns to the bleachers with his fists in the air and a smile wide as a gap-toothed galaxy. His own cheering section of grown-ups and kids all leap to their feet and hug each other, delirious with love for this boy. He's Andy, my best friend's son. The cheering section includes his mother and her friends, his brother, his father and stepmother, a stepbrother and stepsister, and a grandparent. Lucky is the child with this many relatives on hand to hail a proud accomplishment. I'm there too, witnessing a family fortune. But in spite of myself, defensive words take shape in my head. I am thinking: I dare *anybody* to call this a broken home.

Families change, and remain the same. Why are our names for home so slow to catch up to the truth of where we live?

When I was a child, I had two parents who loved me without cease. One of them attended every excuse for attention I ever contrived, and the other made it to the ones with higher production values, like piano recitals and appendicitis. So I was a lucky child too. I played with a set of paper dolls called "The Family of Dolls," four in number, who came with the factory-assigned names of Dad, Mom, Sis, and Junior. I think you know what they looked like, at least before I loved them to death and their heads fell off.

Now I've replaced the dolls with a life. I knit my days around my daughter's survival and happiness, and am proud to say her head is still on. But we aren't the Family of Dolls. Maybe you're not, either. And if not, even though you are statistically no oddity, it's probably been suggested to you in a hundred ways that yours isn't exactly a real family, but an impostor family, a harbinger of cultural ruin, a slapdash substitute — something like counterfeit money. Here at the tail end of our century, most of us are up to our ears in the noisy business of trying to support and love a thing called family. But there's a current in the air with ferocious moral force that finds its way even into political campaigns, claiming there is only one right way to do it, the Way It Has Always Been.

In the face of a thriving, particolored world, this narrow view is so   5 pickled and absurd I'm astonished that it gets airplay. And I'm astonished that it still stings.

Every parent has endured the arrogance of a child-unfriendly grump sitting in judgment, explaining what those kids of ours really need (for example, "a good licking"). If we're polite, we move our crew to another bench in the park. If we're forthright (as I am in my mind, only, for the rest of the day), we fix them with a sweet imperious stare and say, "Come back and let's talk about it after you've changed a thousand diapers."

But it's harder somehow to shrug off the Family-of-Dolls Family Values crew when they judge (from their safe distance) that divorced people, blended families, gay families, and single parents are failures. That our children are at risk, and the whole arrangement is messy and embarrassing. A marriage that ends is not called "finished," it's called *failed*. The children of this family may have been born to a happy union, but now they are called *the children of divorce*.

I had no idea how thoroughly these assumptions overlaid my culture until I went through divorce myself. I wrote to a friend: "This might be worse than being widowed. Overnight I've suffered the same losses — companionship, financial and practical support, my identity as a wife and partner, the future I'd taken for granted. I am lonely, grieving, and hard-pressed to take care of my household alone. But instead of bringing casseroles, people are acting like I had a fit and broke up the family china."

Once upon a time I held these beliefs about divorce: that everyone who does it could have chosen not to do it. That it's a lazy way out of marital problems. That it selfishly puts personal happiness ahead of family integrity. Now I tremble for my ignorance. It's easy, in fortunate times, to forget about the ambush that could leave your head reeling: serious mental or physical illness, death in the family, abandonment, financial calamity, humiliation, violence, despair.

I started out like any child, intent on being the Family of Dolls. I set   10 upon young womanhood believing in most of the doctrines of my generation: I wore my skirts four inches above the knee. I had the Barbie with her zebra-striped swimsuit and a figure unlike anything found in nature. And I understood the Prince Charming Theory of Marriage, a quest for Mr. Right that ends smack dab where you find him. I did not completely understand that another whole story *begins* there, and no fairy tale prepared me for the combination of bad luck and persistent hope that would interrupt my dream and lead me to other arrangements. Like a cancer diagnosis, a dying marriage is a thing to fight, to deny, and finally, when there's no choice left, to dig in and survive. Casseroles would help. Likewise, I imagine it must be a painful reckoning in adolescence (or later on) to realize one's own true love will never look like the soft-focus fragrance ads because Prince Charming (surprise!) is a princess. Or vice versa. Or has skin the color your parents didn't want you messing with, except in the Crayola box.

It's awfully easy to hold in contempt the straw broken home, and that mythical category of persons who toss away nuclear family for the sheer fun of it. Even the legal terms we use have a suggestion of caprice. I resent the phrase "irreconcilable differences," which suggests a stubborn refusal to accept a spouse's little quirks. This is specious. Every happily married couple I know has loads of irreconcilable differences. Negotiating where to set the thermostat is not the point. A nonfunctioning marriage is a slow asphyxiation. It is waking up despised each morning, listening to the pulse of your own loneliness before the radio begins to blare its raucous gospel that you're nothing if you aren't loved. It is sharing your airless house with the threat of suicide or other kinds of violence, while the ghost that whispers, "Leave here and destroy your children," has passed over every door and nailed it shut. Disassembling a marriage in these circumstances is as much *fun* as amputating your own gangrenous leg. You do it, if you can, to save a life — or two, or more.

I know of no one who really went looking to hoe the harder row, especially the daunting one of single parenthood. Yet it seems to be the most American of customs to blame the burdened for their destiny.

We'd like so desperately to believe in freedom and justice for all, we can hardly name that rogue bad luck, even when he's a close enough snake to bite us. In the wake of my divorce, some friends (even a few close ones) chose to vanish, rather than linger within striking distance of misfortune.

But most stuck around, bless their hearts, and if I'm any the wiser for my trials, it's from having learned the worth of steadfast friendship. And also, what not to say. That least helpful question is: "Did you want the divorce, or didn't you?" Did I want to keep that gangrenous leg, or not? How to explain, in a culture that venerates choice: two terrifying options are much worse than none at all. Give me any day the quick hand of cruel fate that will leave me scarred but blameless. As it was, I kept thinking of that wicked third-grade joke in which some boy comes up behind you and grabs your ear, starts in with a prolonged tug, and asks, "Do you want this ear any longer?"

Still, the friend who holds your hand and says the wrong thing is made of dearer stuff than the one who stays away. And generally, through all of it, you live. My favorite fictional character, Kate Vaiden (in the novel by Reynolds Price), advises: "Strength just comes in one brand — you stand up at sunrise and meet what they send you and keep your hair combed."

Once you've weathered the straits, you get to cross the tricky juncture from casualty to survivor. If you're on your feet at the end of a year or two, and have begun putting together a happy new existence, those friends who were kind enough to feel sorry for you when you needed it must now accept you back to the ranks of the living. If you're truly blessed, they will dance at your second wedding. Everybody else, for heaven's sake, should stop throwing stones.

Arguing about whether nontraditional families deserve pity or tolerance is a little like the medieval debate about left-handedness as a mark of the devil. Divorce, remarriage, single parenthood, gay parents, and blended families simply are. They're facts of our time. Some of the reasons listed by sociologists for these family reconstructions are: the idea of marriage as a romantic partnership rather than a pragmatic one; a shift in women's expectations, from servility to self-respect and independence; and longevity (prior to antibiotics no marriage was expected to last many decades — in Colonial days the average couple lived to be married less than twelve years). Add to all this our growing sense of entitlement to happiness and safety from abuse. Most would agree these are all good things. Yet their result — a culture in which serial

monogamy and the consequent reshaping of families are the norm —
gets diagnosed as "failing."

For many of us, once we have put ourselves Humpty-Dumpty-wise
back together again, the main problem with our reorganized family is
that other people think we have a problem. My daughter tells me the
only time she's uncomfortable about being the child of divorced parents is when her friends say they feel sorry for her. It's a bizarre sympathy, given that half the kids in her school and nation are in the same
boat, pursuing childish happiness with the same energy as their
married-parent peers. When anyone asks how *she* feels about it, she
spontaneously lists the benefits: our home is in the country and we have
a dog, but she can go to her dad's neighborhood for the urban thrills of
a pool and sidewalks for roller-skating. What's more, she has three sets
of grandparents!

Why is it surprising that a child would revel in a widened family and
the right to feel at home in more than one house? Isn't it the opposite
that should worry us — a child with no home at all, or too few resources
to feel safe? The child at risk is the one whose parents are too immature
themselves to guide wisely; too diminished by poverty to nurture; too far
from opportunity to offer hope. The number of children in the United
States living in poverty at this moment is almost unfathomably large: 20
percent. There are families among us that need help all right, and by
no means are they new on the landscape. The rate at which teenage
girls had babies in 1957 (ninety-six per thousand) was twice what it is
now. That remarkable statistic is ignored by the religious right — probably because the teen birthrate was cut in half mainly by legalized
abortion. In fact, the policy gatekeepers who coined the phrase "family
values" have steadfastly ignored the desperation of too-small families,
and since 1979 have steadily reduced the amount of financial support
available to a single parent. But, this camp's most outspoken attacks
seem aimed at the notion of families getting too complex, with add-ons
and extras such as a gay parent's partner, or a remarried mother's new
husband and his children.

To judge a family's value by its tidy symmetry is to purchase a book
for its cover. There's no moral authority there. The famous family comprised of Dad, Mom, Sis, and Junior living as an isolated economic unit
is not built on historical bedrock. In *The Way We Never Were*,
Stephanie Coontz writes, "Whenever people propose that we go back to
the traditional family, I always suggest that they pick a ballpark date for
the family they have in mind." Colonial families were tidily disciplined,
but their members (meaning everyone but infants) labored incessantly

and died young. Then the Victorian family adopted a new division of labor, in which women's role was domestic and children were allowed time for study and play, but this was an upper-class construct supported by myriad slaves. Coontz writes, "For every nineteenth-century middle-class family that protected its wife and child within the family circle, there was an Irish or German girl scrubbing floors . . . a Welsh boy mining coal to keep the home-baked goodies warm, a black girl doing the family laundry, a black mother and child picking cotton to be made into clothes for the family, and a Jewish or an Italian daughter in a sweatshop making 'ladies' dresses or artificial flowers for the family to purchase."

The abolition of slavery brought slightly more democratic arrange-   20
ments, in which extended families were harnessed together in cottage industries; at the turn of the century came a steep rise in child labor in mines and sweatshops. Twenty percent of American children lived in orphanages at the time; their parents were not necessarily dead, but couldn't afford to keep them.

During the Depression and up to the end of World War II, many millions of U.S. households were more multigenerational than nuclear. Women my grandmother's age were likely to live with a fluid assortment of elderly relatives, in-laws, siblings, and children. In many cases they spent virtually every waking hour working in the company of other women — a companionable scenario in which it would be easier, I imagine, to tolerate an estranged or difficult spouse. I'm reluctant to idealize a life of so much hard work and so little spousal intimacy, but its advantage may have been resilience. A family so large and varied would not easily be brought down by a single blow: it could absorb a death, long illness, an abandonment here or there, and any number of irreconcilable differences.

The Family of Dolls came along midcentury as a great American experiment. A booming economy required a mobile labor force and demanded that women surrender jobs to returning soldiers. Families came to be defined by a single breadwinner. They struck out for single-family homes at an earlier age than ever before, and in unprecedented numbers they raised children in suburban isolation. The nuclear family was launched to sink or swim.

More than a few sank. Social historians corroborate that the suburban family of the postwar economic boom, which we have recently selected as our definition of "traditional," was no panacea. Twenty-five percent of Americans were poor in the mid-1950s, and as yet there were no food stamps. Sixty percent of the elderly lived on less than $1,000 a year, and most had no medical insurance. In the sequestered suburbs, alcoholism and sexual abuse of children were far more widespread than anyone imagined.

Expectations soared, and the economy sagged. It's hard to depend on one other adult for everything, come what may. In the last three decades, that amorphous, adaptable structure we call "family" has been reshaped once more by economic tides. Compared with fifties families, mothers are far more likely now to be employed. We are statistically more likely to divorce, and to live in blended families or other extranuclear arrangements. We are also more likely to plan and space our children, and to rate our marriages as "happy." We are less likely to suffer abuse without recourse, or to stare out at our lives through a glaze of prescription tranquilizers. Our aged parents are less likely to be destitute, and we're half as likely to have a teenage daughter turn up a mother herself. All in all, I would say that if "intact" in modern family-values jargon means living quietly desperate in the bell jar, then hip-hip-hooray for "broken." A neat family model constructed to service the Baby Boom economy seems to be returning gradually to a grand, lumpy shape that human families apparently have tended toward since they first took root in the Olduvai Gorge. We're social animals, deeply fond of companionship, and children love best to run in packs. If there is a *normal* for humans, at all, I expect it looks like two or three Families of Dolls, connected variously by kinship and passion, shuffled like cards and strewn over several shoeboxes.

The sooner we can let go the fairy tale of families functioning perfectly in isolation, the better we might embrace the relief of community. Even the admirable parents who've stayed married through thick and thin are very likely, at present, to incorporate other adults into their families — household help and baby-sitters if they can afford them, or neighbors and grandparents if they can't. For single parents, this support is the rock-bottom definition of family. And most parents who have split apart, however painfully, still manage to maintain family continuity for their children, creating in many cases a boisterous phenomenon that Constance Ahrons in her book *The Good Divorce* calls the "binuclear family." Call it what you will — when ex-spouses beat swords into plowshares and jump up and down at a soccer game together, it makes for happy kids.

Cinderella, look, who needs her? All those evil stepsisters? That story always seemed like too much cotton-picking fuss over clothes. A childhood tale that fascinated me more was the one called "Stone Soup," and the gist of it is this: Once upon a time, a pair of beleaguered soldiers straggled home to a village empty-handed, in a land ruined by war. They were famished, but the villagers had so little they shouted evil words and slammed their doors. So the soldiers dragged out a big kettle, filled it with water, and put it on a fire to boil. They rolled a clean round stone into the pot, while the villagers peered through their curtains in amazement.

"What kind of soup is that?" they hooted.

"Stone soup," the soldiers replied. "Everybody can have some when it's done."

"Well, thanks," one matron grumbled, coming out with a shriveled carrot. "But it'd be better if you threw this in."

And so on, of course, a vegetable at a time, until the whole suspi-   30
cious village managed to feed itself grandly.

Any family is a big empty pot, save for what gets thrown in. Each stew turns out different. Generosity, a resolve to turn bad luck into good, and respect for variety — these things will nourish a nation of children. Name-calling and suspicion will not. My soup contains a rock or two of hard times, and maybe yours does too. I expect it's a heck of a bouillabaisse.

EXPLORATIONS

1. What is the impact of Barbara Kingsolver's choice to explain her essay's title at the end rather than the beginning? What points made over the course of her essay are summed up by its closing "childhood tale"?

2. What does Kingsolver cite as the greatest dangers to the children in a family? What does she cite as the greatest dangers to the adults in a family? How does each affect the other?

3. At what points in "Stone Soup" does Kingsolver use data to support her arguments? At what points does she use metaphor or analogy? Which kind of support does she depend on more heavily? How would her essay change if the balance tipped in the other direction?

CONNECTIONS

1. "Why is it surprising that a child would revel in a widened family and the right to feel at home in more than one house?" asks Kingsolver in paragraph 18. How do you think Barbara Dafoe Whitehead ("From Death to Divorce," p. 115) would reply to this question?

2. On what points does Kingsolver disagree with Whitehead? On what points do these two writers agree?

3. Which of the writers represented in the Observations on pages 95–101 do you think would side with Whitehead regarding families and divorce? Which writers do you think would side with Kingsolver? On what clues did you base your answers?

ELABORATIONS

1. Choose an argument on which Kingsolver and Whitehead differ. Write an essay comparing and contrasting their views and making a case for the position you agree with.

2. What kind of family do you live in, or did you grow up in? What are its biggest pros and cons? Write an essay responding to Kingsolver or Whitehead or both, using your own experience as a resource.

FRANK McCOURT

Limerick Homecoming

Francis McCourt was born in Brooklyn, New York, in 1930 after his poverty-stricken parents moved there from Ireland. When he was four years old, his family — still poor but now including four young sons — returned in desperation to the mother's hometown of Limerick. The following essay about that homecoming comes from McCourt's book *Angela's Ashes* (1996). McCourt returned to the United States at age nineteen and was drafted into the army. Although he never finished high school, he attended New York University on the GI Bill. After graduating in 1957 he began teaching in and around New York City, and in 1970 became an English teacher at the renowned Stuyvesant High School. In 1988 he retired to travel around the world with his brother Malachy and perform an autobiographical cabaret show they had developed, *A Couple of Blaguards*. He was in his mid-sixties when he wrote *Angela's Ashes*, which won the Pulitzer Prize, sold more than two million copies worldwide, and became a motion picture. McCourt, who recently finished his second autobiographical book, *'Tis: A Memoir* (1999), now lives and writes in New York City.

Eire, or the Republic of Ireland, occupies all of the island of Ireland except for six northern counties known as Ulster, which are part of the United Kingdom of Great Britain and Northern Ireland (U.K.). Ireland has been inhabited since the Stone Age. Around the fourth century B.C., Celts from the European mainland established a Gaelic civilization. St. Patrick brought Christianity in A.D. 432, and monasteries became learning centers comparable to universities. In the twelfth century the Pope gave Ireland to Henry II of England. In the 1600s, after Henry VIII quit the Roman Catholic Church, Protestants from Scotland began immigrating to Ulster and displacing Gaelic-speaking Catholics. In 1801 the Act of Union formally united England, Scotland, and Ireland. Nationalist uprisings led to the proclamation of an Irish republic in 1919 and its recognition as the Irish Free State, a dominion of Great Britain. (Ulster voted to stay with the U.K. Although the rest of Ireland is mostly Catholic, the North was by then mostly Protestant.) In 1949 the Republic of Ireland became official and left the British Commonwealth. Catholic resentment in Northern Ireland flared in 1968–1969 into demonstrations against housing, voting, and unemployment discrimination. As the outlawed Irish Republican Army (IRA) emerged as a militant force, Protestant paramilitary groups formed to oppose it. Turmoil continued until Britain agreed over Loyalist protests to give the

Republic of Ireland a voice in governing Northern Ireland. In 1994 the
IRA declared a cease-fire, and peace negotiations began between representatives of Britain, Ireland, Ulster, and the IRA.

There she was on the platform at Limerick — Grandma, white hair,
sour eyes, a black shawl, and no smile for my mother or any of us, even
my brother Malachy, with his big smile and sweet white teeth. Mam
pointed to Dad. This is my husband, she said, and Grandma nodded
and looked away. She called two boys who were hanging around the
railway station and paid them to carry the trunk. The boys had shaved
heads, snotty noses, and no shoes and we followed them through the
streets of Limerick. I asked Mam why they had no hair and she said
their heads were shaved so that the lice would have no place to hide.
Malachy said, What's a lice? and Mam said, Not lice. One of them is a
louse. Grandma said, Will ye stop it! What kind o' talk is this? The boys
whistled and laughed and trotted along as if they had shoes and
Grandma told them, Stop that laughin' or 'tis droppin' an' breakin' that
trunk ye'll be. They stopped the whistling and laughing and we followed them into a park with grass so green it dazzled you.

Dad carried the twins, Mam carried a bag in one hand and held
Malachy's hand with the other. When she stopped every few minutes to
catch her breath, Grandma said, Are you still smokin' them fags? Them
fags will be the death of you. There's enough consumption in Limerick
without people smokin' fags on top of it an' 'tis a rich man's foolishness.

Along the path through the park there were hundreds of flowers of
different colors that excited the twins. Dad stopped and put Eugene and
Oliver down. He said, Flowers, and the twins ran back and forth, pointing, trying to say "flowers." One of the boys with the trunk said, God,
are they Americans? and Mam said, They are. They were born in New
York. The boy said to the other boy, God, they're Americans. They put
the trunk down and stared at us and we stared back at them till
Grandma said, Are ye goin' to stand here all day lookin' at flowers an'
gawkin' at each other? And we all moved on again, out of the park,
down a narrow lane, and into another lane to Grandma's house.

There is a row of small houses on each side of the lane and Grandma
lives in one of the small houses. Her kitchen has a shiny polished black
iron range with a fire glowing in the grate. There is a picture on the
wall by the range of a man with long brown hair and sad eyes. He is
pointing to his chest, where there is a big heart with flames coming out

of it. Mam tells us, That's the Sacred Heart of Jesus, and I want to know
why the man's heart is on fire and why doesn't He throw water on it?
Grandma says, Don't these children know anything about their religion? and Mam tells her it's different in America. Grandma says the Sacred Heart is everywhere and there's no excuse for that kind of ignorance.

There aren't enough chairs for everyone so I sit on the stairs with my   5
brothers to have some bread and tea. Dad and Mam sit at the table and
Grandma sits under the Sacred Heart. She says, I don't know under
God what I'm goin' to do with ye. There is no room in this house.
There isn't room for even one of ye.

Malachy says, Ye, ye, and starts to giggle and I say, Ye, ye, and the twins
say, Ye, ye, and we're laughing so hard we can hardly eat our bread.

Grandma glares at us. What are ye laughin' at? There's nothin' to
laugh at in this house. Ye better behave yeerselves before I go over to ye.

She won't stop saying Ye, and now Malachy is helpless with laughter,
spewing out his bread and tea, his face turning red.

That night Mam's sister, Aunt Aggie, came home from her job in the
clothing factory. She was big and she had flaming-red hair. She was living at Grandma's because she had had a fight with her husband, Pa
Keating, who told her, when he had taken drink, You're a great fat cow,
go home to your mother. That's what Grandma told Mam and that's
why there was no room for us in Grandma's house. She had herself,
Aunt Aggie, and her son Pat, who was my uncle and who was out selling newspapers.

Grandma spread coats and rags on the floor of the little back room   10
and we slept there and in the morning Aunt Aggie came for her bicycle
telling us, Will ye mind yeerselves, will ye. Will ye get out of my way?

When she left, Malachy kept saying, Will ye mind yeerselves, will
ye? Will ye get out of the way, will ye? and I could hear Dad laughing
out in the kitchen till Grandma came down the stairs and he had to tell
Malachy be quiet.

That day Grandma and Mam went out and found a furnished room
on Windmill Street. Grandma paid the rent, ten shillings for two weeks.
She gave Mam money for food, loaned us a kettle, a pot, a frying pan,
knives and spoons, jam jars to be used for mugs, a blanket and a pillow.
She said that was all she could afford, that Dad would have to get up off
his arse, get a job, go on the dole, go for the charity at the St. Vincent
de Paul Society, or go on the relief.

The room had a fireplace where we could boil water for our tea or
for an egg in case we ever came into money. We had a table and three

chairs and a bed that Mam said was the biggest she had ever seen. It didn't matter that there were six of us in the bed, we were together, away from grandmothers, Malachy could say Ye, ye, ye, and we could laugh as much as we liked.

Dad and Mam lay at the head of the bed, Malachy and I at the bottom, the twins wherever they could find comfort. In the moonlight I could look up the length of the bed and see Dad still awake and when Oliver cried in his sleep Dad reached for him and held him. Whisht, he said. Whisht.

Then Eugene sat up, screaming, tearing at himself. Ah, ah, Mommy, Mommy. Dad sat up. What? What's up, son? Eugene went on crying and when Dad leaped from the bed and turned on the gaslight we saw the fleas, leaping, jumping, fastened to our flesh. We slapped at them and slapped but they hopped from body to body, hopping, biting. We jumped from the bed, the twins crying, Mam moaning, Oh, Jesus, will we have no rest! Dad poured water and salt into a jam jar and dabbed at our bites. The salt burned, but he said we'd feel better soon.

Mam sat by the fireplace with the twins on her lap. Dad pulled on his trousers and dragged the mattress off the bed and out to the street. He filled the kettle and the pot with water, stood the mattress against the wall, pounded it with a shoe, told me to keep pouring water on the ground to drown the fleas dropping there. The Limerick moon was so bright I could see bits of it shimmering in the water and I wanted to scoop up moon bits, but how could I with the fleas leaping on my legs?

A man on a bicycle stopped and wanted to know why Dad was beating that mattress. Mother o' God, he said, I never heard such a cure for fleas. Do you know that if a man could jump like a flea one leap would take him halfway to the moon? The thing to do is this, When you go back inside with that mattress stick it on the bed upside down and that will confuse the little buggers. They won't know where they are and they'll be biting the mattress or each other, which is the best cure of all. They're a right bloody torment an' I should know for didn't I grow up in Limerick, down in the Irish Town, an' the fleas there were so plentiful an' forward they'd sit on the toe of your boot an' discuss Ireland's woeful history with you. It is said there were no fleas in ancient Ireland, that they were brought in by the English to drive us out of our wits entirely, an' I wouldn't put it past the English.

Dad said, You wouldn't by any chance have a cigarette, would you?

A cigarette? Oh, sure, of course. Here you are. Aren't I nearly destroyed from the fags myself. The oul' hacking cough, you know. So

powerful it nearly knocks me off the bicycle. I can feel that cough stirring in me solar plexus an' workin' its way up through me entrails till
the next thing it takes off the top o' me head.

He wobbled away on his bicycle, a cigarette dangling from his   20
mouth, the cough racking his body. Dad said, Limerickmen talk too
much. Come on, we'll put this mattress back and see if there's any sleep
in this night.

Eugene is sleeping under a coat on the bed. Dad sits by the fireplace
with Oliver on his lap. Oliver's cheeks are bright red and he's staring
into the dead fire. Mam puts her hand on his forehead. I think he has a
fever, she says. I wish I had an onion and I'd boil it in milk and pepper.
That's good for the fever. But even if I had what would I boil the milk
on? We need coal for that fire.

She gives Dad the docket for the coal down the Dock Road. He takes
me with him, but it's dark and all the coalyards are closed.

What are we going to do now, Dad?

I don't know, son.

Ahead of us, women in shawls and small children are picking up   25
coal along the road.

There, Dad, there's coal.

Och, no, son. We won't pick coal off the road. We're not beggars.

He tells Mam the coalyards are closed and we'll have to drink milk
and eat bread tonight, but when I tell her about the women on the road
she passes Eugene to him.

If you're too grand to pick coal off the road I'll put on my coat and go
down the Dock Road.

She gets a bag and takes Malachy and me with her. Beyond the   30
Dock Road there is something wide and dark with lights glinting in it.
Mam says that's the River Shannon. She says that's what she missed
most of all in America, the River Shannon. The Hudson was lovely but
the Shannon sings. I can't hear the song, but my mother does and that
makes her happy. The other women are gone from the Dock Road and
we search for the bits of coal that drop from lorries. Mam tells us gather
anything that burns, coal, wood, cardboard, paper. She says, There are
them that burn the horse droppings but we're not gone that low yet.
When her bag is nearly full she says, Now we have to find an onion for
Oliver. Malachy says he'll find one but she tells him, No, you don't find
onions on the road, you get them in shops.

The minute he sees a shop he cries out, There's a shop, and runs in.

Oonyen, he says. Oonyen for Oliver.

Mam runs into the shop and tells the woman behind the counter, I'm sorry. The woman says, Lord, he's a dote. Is he an American or what?

Mam says he is. The woman smiles and shows two teeth, one on each side of her upper gum. A dote, she says, and look at them gorgeous goldy curls. And what is it he wants now? A sweet?

Ah, no, says Mam. An onion. I wanted to get an onion for my other 35 child that's sick.

True for you, missus. You can't beat the onion boiled in milk. And look, little boy, here's a sweet for yourself and one for the other little boy, the brother, I suppose. And here's a nice onion for the sick child, missus.

Mam says, God bless you, ma'am, and her eyes are watery.

Dad is walking back and forth with Oliver in his arms and Eugene is playing on the floor with a pot and a spoon. Dad says, Did you get the onion?

I did, says Mam, and more. I got coal and the way of lighting it.

I knew you would. I said a prayer to St. Jude. He's my favorite saint, 40 patron of desperate cases.

I got the coal. I got the onion, no help from St. Jude.

Dad says, You shouldn't be picking up coal off the road like a common beggar. It isn't right. Bad example for the boys.

Then you should have sent St. Jude down the Dock Road.

Mam gets the fire going, cuts the onion in half, and drops it in boiling milk. She takes Oliver on her lap and tries to feed him, but he turns away and looks into the fire.

Ah, come on, love, she says. Good for you. Make you big and strong. 45

He tightens his mouth against the spoon. She puts the pot down, rocks him till he's asleep, lays him on the bed, and tells the rest of us to be quiet or she'll demolish us. She slices the other half of the onion and fries it in butter with slices of bread. She lets us sit on the floor around the fire where we eat the fried bread and sip at scalding sweet tea in jam jars.

The fire makes the room warm and with the flames dancing in the coal you can see faces and mountains and valleys and animals leaping. Eugene falls asleep on the floor and Dad lifts him to the bed beside Oliver. Mam puts the boiled-onion pot up on the mantelpiece for fear a mouse or a rat might be at it.

Soon we're all in bed and if there's the odd flea I don't mind because it's warm in the bed with the six of us and I love the glow of the fire the way it dances on the walls and ceiling and makes the room go red and

black, red and black, till it dims to white and black and all you can hear
is a little cry from Oliver turning in my mother's arms.

Dad is touching my shoulder. Come on, Francis, you have to take
care of your little brothers.

Mam is slumped on the edge of the bed, making small crying sounds   50
like a bird. Grandma is pulling on her shawl. She says, I'll go down to
Thompson the undertaker about the coffin and the carriage. The St.
Vincent de Paul Society will surely pay for that, God knows.

Dad stands facing the wall over the fire, beating on his thighs with
his fists, sighing, Och, och, och.

Dad frightens me with his Och, och, och, and Mam frightens
me with her small bird sounds, and I don't know what to do, though
I wonder if anyone will light the fire in the grate so that we can have
tea and bread. If Dad would move away from the fireplace I could light
the fire myself. All you need is paper, a few bits of coal or turf, and
a match. He won't move so I try to go around his legs while he's beating on his thighs, but he notices me and wants to know why I'm
trying to light the fire. I tell him we're all hungry and he lets out a
crazy laugh. Hungry? he says. Och, Francis, your wee brother Oliver is
dead.

He picks me up and hugs me so hard I cry out. Then Malachy cries,
my mother cries, Dad cries, I cry, but Eugene stays quiet. Then Dad
sniffles, We'll have a feast. Come on, Francis.

He carries me through the streets of Limerick and we go from shop
to shop with him asking for food or anything they can give to a family
that has two children dead in a year, one in America, one in Limerick,
and in danger of losing three more for the want of food and drink. Most
shopkeepers shake their heads.

Dad says he's glad to see the spirit of Christ alive in Limerick and   55
they tell him they don't need the likes of him with his Northern accent
to be telling them about Christ and he should be ashamed of himself
dragging a child around like that, like a common beggar, a tinker, a
knacker.

A few shopkeepers give bread, potatoes, tins of beans and Dad says,
We'll go home now and you boys can eat something, but we meet
Uncle Pa Keating and he tells Dad he's very sorry for his troubles and
would Dad like to have a pint in this pub here?

There are men sitting in this pub with great glasses of black stuff before them. They lift their glasses carefully and slowly drink. There is
creamy white stuff on their lips which they lick with little sighs.

Uncle Pa says, Frankie, this is the pint. This is the staff of life. This is the best thing for nursing mothers and for those who are long weaned.

He laughs and Dad smiles and I laugh because I think that's what you're supposed to do when Uncle Pa says something. He doesn't laugh when he tells the other men about Oliver dying. The other men tip their hats to Dad. Sorry for your troubles, mister, and surely you'll have a pint.

Dad says yes to the pints and soon he's singing "Roddy McCorley" and "Kevin Barry" and song after song I never heard before and crying over his lovely little girl, Margaret, that died in America and his little boy Oliver. It frightens me the way he yells and cries and sings and I wish I could be at home with my three brothers, no, my two brothers, and my mother.

The man behind the bar says to Dad, I think now, mister, you've had enough. We're sorry for your troubles but you have to take that child home to his mother that must be heartbroken by the fire.

Dad says, One, one more pint, just one, eh? and the man says no. Dad shakes his fist. I did me bit for Ireland, and when the man comes out and takes Dad's arm Dad tries to push him away.

Uncle Pa says, Come on now, stop the blackguarding. You have to go home to Angela. You have a funeral tomorrow and the lovely children waiting for you.

Dad wants to go to another place for a pint but Uncle Pa says he has no more money. Dad says he'll tell everyone his sorrows and they'll give him pints. Uncle Pa says that's a disgraceful thing to do and Dad cries on his shoulder. You're a good friend, he tells Uncle Pa. It's terrible, terrible, says Uncle Pa, but you'll get over this in time.

Dad straightens up and looks at him. Never, he says. Never.

Next day we rode to the hospital in a carriage with a horse. They put Oliver into a white box that came with us in the carriage and we took him to the graveyard. I did not like the jackdaws that perched on the trees and gravestones and I did not want to leave Oliver with them. I threw a rock at a jackdaw that waddled over toward Oliver's grave. Dad says I shouldn't throw rocks at jackdaws, they might be somebodies' souls. I didn't know what a soul was but I didn't ask him, because I didn't care. Oliver was dead and I hated jackdaws. I'd be a man someday and I'd come back with a bag of rocks and I'd leave the graveyard littered with dead jackdaws.

The morning after Oliver's burial Dad went to the Labour Exchange to sign and collect the week's dole, nineteen shillings and sixpence. He said he'd be home by noon, that he'd get coal and make a fire, that we'd have rashers and eggs and tea in honor of Oliver, that we might even have a sweet or two.

He wasn't home by noon, or one, or two, and we boiled and ate the few potatoes the shopkeepers had given us. He wasn't home anytime before the sun went down that day in May. There was no sign of him till we heard him, long after the pubs closed, rolling along Windmill Street, singing.

He stumbled into the room, hanging on to the wall. A snot oozed from his nose and he wiped it away with the back of his hand. He tried to speak. Zeeze shildren should be in bed. Lishen to me. Shildren go to bed.

Mam faced him. These children are hungry. Where's the dole   70
money?

She tried to stick her hands into his pockets but he pushed her away. Have reshpeck, he said. Reshpeck in front of shildren.

She struggled to get at his pockets. Where's the money? The children are hungry. You mad oul' bastard, did you drink all the money again? Just what you did in Brooklyn.

He blubbered, Och, poor Angela. And poor wee Margaret and poor wee Oliver.

He staggered to me and hugged me and I smelled the drink I used to smell in America. My face was wet from his tears and his spit and his snot and I was hungry and I didn't know what to say when he cried all over my head.

EXPLORATIONS

1. Who are the living members of Frank McCourt's family when they arrive in Ireland? When and how do we find out that there was another child in the family? How does the way this information is revealed affect its impact?

2. How do the readers of this essay learn that the narrator came to Limerick from America? How do other characters in the narrative learn where the McCourts came from?

3. At what points in "Limerick Homecoming" does McCourt write in the present tense? In the past tense? How does the essay's effect change when he changes tense?

CONNECTIONS

1. In "Stone Soup" (p. 127), Barbara Kingsolver argues that we should worry less about the impact of divorce on children and more about other threats: "The child at risk is the one whose parents are too immature themselves to guide wisely; too diminished by poverty to nurture; too far from opportunity to offer hope" (para. 18). What support does "Limerick Homecoming" supply for each part of Kingsolver's statement?

2. The McCourt family moved from New York City to Limerick in 1934. According to Barbara Dafoe Whitehead ("From Death to Divorce," p. 115), what was the prevailing social attitude toward the nuclear family at that time? Judging from the information in Whitehead's essay and McCourt's reminiscences, what factors do you think kept his family together? What were the advantages to this choice, and what were the disadvantages?

3. In her Observation on page 97, Frances Rose Besmer writes about the impact of poverty and failure on families. Which of her comments apply to the McCourt family, and in what way? What advantages do the McCourts have over the families Besmer describes?

ELABORATIONS

1. What are the strengths and weaknesses of the parents and other adults in "Limerick Homecoming"? What choices do they make that save the day or that lead to disaster? Pick at least one good choice and one bad one. Write an essay showing how each decision affected the family and projecting how things could have gone differently if the decision maker had chosen differently

2. What rhetorical strategies does McCourt use in "Limerick Homecoming" to narrate events convincingly from a child's point of view? Write an essay identifying his tactics and describing their effects.

RIGOBERTA MENCHÚ

Birth Ceremonies

The week that marked the 500th anniversary of Christopher Columbus's arrival in the New World also saw the Nobel Peace Prize awarded to a thirty-three-year-old Central American Indian. Rigoberta Menchú Tum is a Mayan of Guatemala's Quiché group. Her book *Me llamo Rigoberta Menchú y asi me nacio la conciencia* ("I am named Rigoberta Menchú and so my conscience was born") describes her remarkable life. Menchú grew up poor and uneducated in the village of Chimel with her parents and ten brothers and sisters. A migrant farm worker from the age of eight, she later became a live-in maid in Guatemala City, where she taught herself to read and write Spanish. Her father, an organizing member of the Peasant Unity Committee, fought for property rights. In 1979 her sixteen-year-old brother was kidnaped by Guatemalan soldiers, tortured for two weeks, flayed, and burned alive with several other prisoners in front of their families. The next year her father was killed when police stormed the Spanish embassy his group was occupying and burned it. Soon afterward, Menchú's mother was abducted, raped, and tortured to death by soldiers. Menchú fled to Mexico City. There the Venezuelan writer Elisabeth Burgos-Debray helped her create her book. Although some autobiographical details have been found to be inaccurate, Menchú's account of life among the Quiché Indians remains unique and valuable. "Birth Ceremonies" comes from the English translation by Ann Wright, *I, Rigoberta Menchú: An Indian Woman in Guatemala* (1984). Menchú continues to work for peace and reform through her own foundation.

The Mayan empire flourished in Mexico and Guatemala for a thousand years before Spanish conquistadors colonized the region. Famed for their advances in medicine, mathematics, and astronomy, the Maya left behind the great ruin of Tikal, still a source of pride to Guatemalans. Although Indians remain a majority of the country's 10 million population, *ladinos* (Spanish speakers of mixed descent) are politically and economically dominant. The Central American states declared independence from Spain in 1821; the Republic of Guatemala was established in 1839. Following the CIA-assisted overthrow of an elected leftist government in 1954, a series of military governments gave the country one of the hemisphere's worst human-rights records as well as one of its longest-running civil wars: In thirty-six years, well over 100,000 people died. In 1996, newly elected President Alvaro Arzu Irigoyen ordered a purge of the military and police forces which provoked a wave of murder, kidnapping, theft, and death threats, but also made possible a long-awaited peace accord between the government and rebels.

> Whoever may ask where we are, tell them what you know of us and nothing more.
>
> Learn to protect yourselves, by keeping our secret.
>
> – Popol Vuh[1]

In our community there is an elected representative, someone who is highly respected. He's not a king but someone whom the community looks up to like a father. In our village, my father and mother were the representatives. Well, then the whole community becomes the children of the woman who's elected. So a mother, on her first day of pregnancy, goes with her husband to tell these elected leaders that she's going to have a child, because the child will not only belong to them but to the whole community and must follow as far as he can our ancestors' traditions. The leaders then pledge the support of the community and say: "We will help you, we will be the child's second parents." They are known as *abuelos*, "grandparents" or "forefathers." The parents then ask the "grandparents" to help them find the child some godparents, so that if he's orphaned, he shouldn't be tempted by any of the bad habits our people sometimes fall into. So the "grandparents" and the parents choose the godparents together. It's also the custom for the pregnant mother's neighbors to visit her every day and take her little things, no matter how simple. They stay and talk to her, and she'll tell them all her problems.

Later, when she's in her seventh month, the mother introduces her baby to the natural world, as our customs tell her to. She goes out in the fields or walks over the hills. She also has to show her baby the kind of life she leads, so that if she gets up at three in the morning, does her chores and tends the animals, she does it all the more so when she's pregnant, conscious that the child is taking all this in. She talks to the child continuously from the first moment he's in her stomach, telling him how hard his life will be. It's as if the mother were a guide explaining things to a tourist. She'll say, for instance, "You must never abuse nature and you must live your life as honestly as I do." As she works in the fields, she tells her child all the little things about her work. It's a duty to her child that a mother must fulfill. And then, she also has to think of a way of hiding the baby's birth from her other children.

---

[1]Sacred book of the Quiché Indian tribe.

When her baby is born, the mother mustn't have her other children around her. The people present should be the husband, the village leaders, and the couple's parents. Three couples. The parents are often away in other places, so if they can't be there, the husband's father and the wife's mother can perhaps make up one pair. If one of the village leaders can't come, one of them should be there to make up a couple with one of the parents. If none of the parents can come, some aunts and uncles should come to represent the family on both sides, because the child is to be part of the community. The birth of a new member is very significant for the community, as it belongs to the community, not just to the parents, and that's why three couples (but not just anybody) must be there to receive it. They explain that this child is the fruit of communal love. If the village leader is not a midwife as well, another midwife is called (it might be a grandmother) to receive the child. Our customs don't allow single women to see a birth. But it does happen in times of need. For instance, I was with my sister when she went into labor. Nobody else was at home. This was when we were being heavily persecuted. Well, I didn't exactly see, but I was there when the baby was born.

My mother was a midwife from when she was sixteen right up to her death at forty-three. She used to say that a woman hadn't the strength to push the baby out when she's lying down. So what she did with my sister was to hang a rope from the roof and pull her up, because my brother wasn't there to lift her up. My mother helped the baby out with my sister in that position. It's a scandal if an Indian woman goes to the hospital and gives birth there. None of our women would agree to that. Our ancestors would be shocked at many of the things which go on today. Family planning, for example. It's an insult to our culture and a way of swindling the people, to get money out of them.

This is part of the reserve that we've maintained to defend our customs and our culture. Indians have been very careful not to disclose any details of their communities, and the community does not allow them to talk about Indian things. I too must abide by this. This is because many religious people have come among us and drawn a false impression of the Indian world. We also find a *ladino* using Indian clothes very offensive. All this has meant that we keep a lot of things to ourselves and the community doesn't like us telling its secrets. This applies to all our customs. When the Catholic Action[2] arrived, for instance, everyone started going to mass and praying, but it's not their only reli-

---

[2]Association created in 1945 by Monsignor Rafael Gonzalez, to try and control the Indian fraternities of the *Altiplano*.

gion, not the only way they have of expressing themselves. Anyway, when a baby is born, he's always baptized within the community before he's taken to church. Our people have taken Catholicism as just another channel of expression, not our one and only belief. Our people do the same with other religions. The priests, monks, and nuns haven't gained the people's confidence because so many of their things contradict our own customs. For instance, they say, "You have too much trust in your elected leaders." But the village elects them *because* they trust them, don't they? The priests say, "The trouble is you follow those sorcerers," and speak badly of them. But for our people this is like speaking ill of their own fathers, and they lose faith in the priests. They say, "Well, they're not from here, they can't understand our world." So there's not much hope of winning our people's hearts.

To come back to the children, they aren't to know how the baby is born. He's born somewhere hidden away and only the parents know about it. They are told that a baby has arrived and that they can't see their mother for eight days. Later on, the baby's companion, the placenta, that is, has to be burned at a special time. If the baby is born at night, the placenta is burned at eight in the morning, and if he's born in the afternoon, it'll be burned at five o'clock. This is out of respect for both the baby and his companion. The placenta is not buried, because the earth is the mother and the father of the child and mustn't be abused by having the placenta buried in it. All these reasons are very important for us. Either the placenta is burned on a log and the ashes left there, or else it is put in the *temascal.* This is a stove which our people use to make vapor baths. It's a small hut made of adobe and inside this hut is another one made of stone, and when we want to have a bath, we light a fire to heat the stones, close the door, and throw water on the stones to produce steam. Well, when the woman is about four months pregnant, she starts taking these baths infused with evergreens, pure natural aromas. There are many plants the community uses for pregnant women, colds, headaches, and things like that. So the pregnant mother takes baths with plants prescribed for her by the midwife or the village leader. The fields are full of plants whose names I don't know in Spanish. Pregnant women use orange and peach leaves a lot for bathing and there's another one we call Saint Mary's leaf which they use. The mother needs these leaves and herbs to relax because she won't be able to rest while she's pregnant since our women go on working just as hard in the fields. So after work, she takes this calming bath so that she can sleep well, and the baby won't be harmed by her working hard. She's given medicines to take as well. And leaves to feed the child. I believe that in practice (even if this isn't a scientific recommendation) these leaves work very well, because many of them contain vitamins. How else would women who endure hunger and hard work give birth to healthy babies? I think that these plants have helped our people survive.

The purity with which the child comes into the world is protected for eight days. Our customs say that the newborn baby should be alone with his mother in a special place for eight days, without any of her other children. Her only visitors are the people who bring her food. This is the baby's period of integration into the family; he very slowly becomes a member of it. When the child is born, they kill a sheep and there's a little fiesta just for the family. Then the neighbors start coming to visit and bring presents. They either bring food for the mother or something for the baby. The mother has to taste all the food her neighbors bring to show her appreciation for their kindness. After the eight days are over, the family counts up how many visitors the mother had and how many presents were received; things like eggs or food apart from what was brought for the mother, or clothing, small animals, and wood for the fire, or services like carrying water and chopping wood. If, during the eight days, most of the community has called, this is very important, because it means that this child will have a lot of responsibility toward his community when he grows up. The community takes over all the household expenses for these eight days and the family spends nothing.

After eight days, everything has been received, and another animal is killed as recognition that the child's right to be alone with his mother is over. All the mother's clothes, bedclothes, and everything she used during the birth are taken away by our elected leader and washed. She can't wash them in the well, so no matter how far away the river is, they must be carried and washed there. The baby's purity is washed away and he's ready to learn the ways of humanity. The mother's bed is moved to a part of the house which has first been washed with water and lime. Lime is sacred. It strengthens the child's bones. I believe this really is true. It gives a child strength to face the world. The mother has a bath in the *temascal* and puts on clean clothes. Then the whole house is cleaned. The child is also washed and dressed and put into the new bed. Four candles are placed on the corners of the bed to represent the four corners of the house and show him that this will be his home. They symbolize the respect the child must have for his community, and the responsibility he must feel toward it as a member of a household. The candles are lit and give off an incense which incorporates the child into the world he must live in. When the baby is born, his hands and feet are bound to show him that they are sacred and must only be used to work or do whatever nature meant them to do. They must never steal or abuse the natural world, or show disrespect for any living thing.

After the eight days, his hands and feet are untied and he's now with his mother in the new bed. This means he opens the doors to the other members of the community, because neither the family or the community know him yet. Or rather, they weren't shown the baby when he was born. Now they can all come and kiss him. The neighbors bring another animal, and there's a big lunch in the new baby's house for all the community. This is to celebrate his integration "in the universe," as our parents used to say. Candles will be lit for him, and his candle becomes part of the candle of the whole community, which now has one more person, one more member. The whole community is at the ceremony, or at least, if not all of it, then some of it. Candles are lit to represent all the things which belong to the universe — earth, water, sun, and man — and the child's candle is put with them, together with incense (what we call *pom*) and lime — our sacred lime. Then the parents tell the baby of the suffering of the family he will be joining. With great feeling, they express their sorrow at bringing a child into the world to suffer. To us, suffering is our fate, and the child must be introduced to the sorrows and hardship, but he must learn that despite his suffering, he will be respectful and live through his pain. The child is then entrusted with the responsibility for his community and told to abide by its rules. After the ceremony comes the lunch, and then the neighbors go home. Now there is only the baptism to come.

When the baby is born, he's given a little bag with a garlic, a bit of   10
lime, salt, and tobacco in it to hang round his neck. Tobacco is important because it is a sacred plant for Indians. This all means that the child can ward off all the evil things in life. For us, bad things are like spirits, which exist only in our imagination. Something bad, for instance, would be if the child were to turn out to be a gossip — not sincere, truthful, and respectful, as a child should be. It also helps him collect together and preserve all our ancestors' things. That's more or less the idea of the bag — to keep him pure. The bag is put inside the four candles as well, and this represents the promise of the child when he grows up.

When the child is forty days old, there are more speeches, more promises on his behalf, and he becomes a full member of the community. This is his baptism. All the important people of the village are invited and they speak. The parents make a commitment. They promise to teach the child to keep the secrets of our people, so that our culture and customs will be preserved. The village leaders come and offer their experience, their example, and their knowledge of our ancestors. They explain how to preserve our traditions. Then, they promise to be responsible for the child, teach him as he grows up, and see that he follows in their ways. It's also something of a criticism of humanity, and of the many people who have forsaken their traditions. They say almost a prayer, asking that our traditions again enter the spirits of those who have forsaken them. Then, they evoke the names of our ancestors, like Tecun Umán and others who form part of the ceremony, as a kind of chant. They must be remembered as heroes of the Indian peoples. And then they say, . . . "Let no landowner extinguish all this, nor any rich man wipe out our customs. Let our children, be they workers or servants, respect and keep their secrets." The child is present for all of this, although he's all wrapped up and can scarcely be seen. He is told that he will eat maize,[3] and that, naturally, he is already made of maize because his mother ate it while he was forming in her stomach. He must respect the maize; even the grain of maize which has been thrown away, he must pick up. The child will multiply our race, he will replace all those who have died. From this moment, he takes on this responsibility, and is told to live as his "grandparents" have lived. The parents then reply that their child promises to accomplish all this. So, the village leaders and the parents both make promises on behalf of the child. It's his initiation into the community.

The ceremony is very important. It is also when the child is considered a child of God, our one father. We don't actually have the word God but that is what it is, because the one father is the only one we have. To reach this one father, the child must love beans, maize, the earth. The one father is the heart of the sky, that is, the sun. The sun is the father and our mother is the moon. She is a gentle mother. And she lights our way. Our people have many notions about the moon, and about the sun. They are the pillars of the universe.

When children reach ten years old, that's the moment when their parents and the village leaders talk to them again. They tell them that they will be young men and women and that one day they will be fathers and mothers. This is actually when they tell the child that he must never abuse his dignity, in the same way his ancestors never abused their dignity. It's also when they remind them that our ancestors were dishonored by the White Man, by colonization. But they don't tell them the way that it's written down in books, because the majority of Indians can't read or write, and don't even know that they have their own texts. No, they learn it through oral recommendations, the way it

---

[3]Corn. — ED.

has been handed down through the generations. They are told that the Spaniards dishonored our ancestors' finest sons, and the most humble of them. And it is to honor these humble people that we must keep our secrets. And no one except we Indians must know. They talk a lot about our ancestors. And the ten-years ceremony is also when our children are reminded that they must respect their elders, even though this is something their parents have been telling them ever since they were little. For example, if an old person is walking along the street, children should cross over to allow him to pass by. If any of us sees an elderly person, we are obliged to bow and greet him. Everyone does this, even the very youngest. We also show respect to pregnant women. Whenever we make food, we always keep some for any of our neighbors who are pregnant.

When little girls are born, the midwives pierce their ears at the same time as they tie their umbilical cords. The little bags around their necks and the thread used to tie their umbilical cord are both red. Red is very significant for us. It means heat, strength, all living things. It's linked to the sun, which for us is the channel to the one God, the heart of everything, of the universe. So red gives off heat and fire, and red things are supposed to give life to the child. At the same time, it asks him to respect living things too. There are no special clothes for the baby. We don't buy anything special beforehand but just use pieces of *corte*[4] to wrap him in.

When a male child is born, there are special celebrations, not because he's male but because of all the hard work and responsibility he'll have as a man. It's not that *machismo* doesn't exist among our people, but it doesn't present a problem for the community because it's so much part of our way of life. The male child is given an extra day alone with his mother. The usual custom is to celebrate a male child by killing a sheep or some chickens. Boys are given more, they get more food because their work is harder and they have more responsibility. At the same time, he is head of the household, not in the bad sense of the word, but because he is responsible for so many things. This doesn't mean girls aren't valued. Their work is hard too and there are other things that are due to them as mothers. Girls are valued because they are part of the earth, which gives us maize, beans, plants, and everything we live on. The earth is like a mother which multiplies life. So the girl child will multiply the life of our generation and of our

15

---

[4]Multicolored material that Guatemalan women use as a skirt. It is part of their traditional costume.

ancestors whom we must respect. The girl and the boy are both integrated into the community in equally important ways; the two are interrelated and compatible. Nevertheless, the community is always happier when a male child is born and the men feel much prouder. The customs, like the tying of the hands and feet, apply to both boys and girls.

Babies are breast-fed. It's much better than any other sort of food. But the important thing is the sense of community. It's something we all share. From the very first day, the baby belongs to the community, not only to the parents, and the baby must learn from all of us. . . . In fact, we behave just like bourgeois families in that, as soon as the baby is born, we're thinking of his education, of his well-being. But our people feel that the baby's school must be the community itself, that he must learn to live like all the rest of us. The tying of the hands at birth also symbolizes this; that no one should accumulate things the rest of the community does not have and he must know how to share, to have open hands. The mother must teach the baby to be generous. This way of thinking comes from poverty and suffering. Each child is taught to live like the fellow members of his community.

We never eat in front of pregnant women. You can only eat in front of a pregnant woman if you can offer something as well. The fear is that, otherwise, she might abort the baby or that the baby could suffer if she didn't have enough to eat. It doesn't matter whether you know her or not. The important thing is sharing. You have to treat a pregnant woman differently from other women because she is two people. You must treat her with respect so that she recognizes it and conveys this to the baby inside her. You instinctively think she's the image of the baby about to be born. So you love her. Another reason why you must stop and talk to a pregnant woman is because she doesn't have much chance to rest or enjoy herself. She's always worried and depressed. So when she stops and chats a bit, she can relax and feel some relief.

When the baby joins the community, with him in the circle of candles — together with his little red bag — he will have his hoe, his machete, his axe, and all the tools he will need in life. These will be his playthings. A little girl will have her washing board and all the things she will need when she grows up. She must learn the things of the house, to clean, to wash, and to sew her brothers' trousers, for example. The little boy must begin to live like a man, to be responsible and learn to love the work in the fields. The learning is done as a kind of game. When the parents do anything they always explain what it means. This includes learning prayers. This is very important to our people. The mother may say a prayer at any time. Before getting up in the morning, for instance, she thanks the day which is dawning because it might be a very important one for the family. Before lighting the fire, she blesses the wood because that fire is going to cook food for the whole family. Since it's the little girl who is closest to her mother, she learns all of this. Before washing the *nixtamal*,[5] the woman blows on her hands and puts them in the *nixtamal*. She takes everything out and washes it well. She blows on her hands so that her work will bear fruit. She does it before she does the wash as well. She explains all these little details to her daughter, who learns by copying her. With the men it's the same. Before they start work every day, whatever hour of the morning it is, they greet the sun. They remove their hats and talk to the sun before starting work. Their sons learn to do it too, taking off their little hats to talk to the sun. Naturally, each ethnic group has its own forms of expression. Other groups have different customs from ours. The meaning of their weaving patterns, for example. We realize the others are different in some things, but the one thing we have in common is our culture. Our people are mainly peasants, but there are some people who buy and sell as well. They go into this after they've worked on the land. Sometimes when they come back from working in the *finca*,[6] instead of tending a little plot of land, they'll start a shop and look for a different sort of life. But if they're used to greeting the sun every morning, they still go on doing it. And they keep all their old customs. Every part of our culture comes from the earth. Our religion comes from the maize and bean harvests which are so vital to our community. So even if a man goes to try and make some money, he never forgets his culture springs from the earth.

As we grow up we have a series of obligations. Our parents teach us to be responsible, just as they have been responsible. The eldest son is responsible for the house. Whatever the father cannot correct is up to the eldest son to correct. He is like a second father to us all and is responsible for our upbringing. The mother is the one who is responsible for keeping an account of what the family eats and what she has to buy. When a child is ill, she has to get medicine. But the father has to solve a lot of problems too. And each one of us, as we grow up, has our own small area of responsibility. This comes from the promises made for the child when he is born, and from the continuity of our customs. The child can make the promise for himself when his parents have taught him to do it. The mother, who is closest to the children, does this, or sometimes the father. They talk to their children explaining what they have to do and what our ancestors used to do. They don't impose it as a law, but just give the example of what our ancestors have always done. This is how we all learn our own small responsibilities. For example,

---

[5]Cauldron where the maize is cooked.
[6]Plantation, estate.

the little girl begins by carrying water, and the little boy begins by tying up the dogs when the animals are brought into the yard at night, or by fetching a horse which has wandered off. Both girls and boys have their tasks and are told the reasons for doing them. They learn responsibility because if they don't do their little jobs well, their father has the right to scold them, or even beat them. So, they are very careful about learning to do their jobs well, but the parents are also very careful to explain exactly why the jobs have to be done. The little girl understands the reasons for everything her mother does. For example, when she puts a new earthenware pot on the fire for the first time, she hits it five times with a branch, so that it knows its job is to cook and so that it lasts. When the little girl asks, "Why did you do that?" her mother says, "So that it knows what its job is and does it well." When it's her turn to cook, the little girl does as her mother does. Again this is all bound up with our commitment to maintain our customs and pass on the secrets of our ancestors. The elected fathers of the community explain to us that all these things come down to us from our grandfathers and we must conserve them. Nearly everything we do today is based on what our ancestors did. This is the main purpose of our elected leader — to embody all the values handed down from our ancestors. He is the leader of the community, a father to all our children, and he must lead an exemplary life. Above all, he has a commitment to the whole community. Everything that is done today is done in memory of those who have passed on.

EXPLORATIONS

1. Besides recognizing biological parenthood, in what other ways do the Quiché Indians apply the concepts of mother and father?

2. What ceremonies mark the landmarks in a Quiché child's life, both before and after birth? What are the main purposes of these ceremonies?

3. What specific steps are taken by a Quiché baby's parents, and what steps are taken by others in the community, to make sure the child learns his or her responsibilities?

CONNECTIONS

1. What ideas about community and family appear in both "Birth Ceremonies" and Frank McCourt's "Limerick Homecoming" (p. 136)? How do these ideas operate differently in practice in the Quiché families described by Menchú and the Irish family described by McCourt? What reasons can you identify for the differences?

2. Compare Menchú's depiction of the mother-infant relationship with Louise Erdrich's in "Making Babies" (p. 102) and Barbara Kingsolver's in "Stone Soup" (p. 127). How have cultural pressures and opportunities encouraged these contrasting arrangements?

3. What ideals proposed by Barbara Dafoe Whitehead in "From Death to Divorce" (p. 115) are carried out by the Quiché families Menchú describes? Where on Whitehead's time line of family development (see paras. 2–10) do the Quiché appear to fall?

ELABORATIONS

1. In Quiché society, talismans are given to a child to "ward off all the evil things in life" (para. 10). What evil things are warded off in this way? What tactics are used in the United States to ward off similar (or different) evils? Write an essay classifying the dangers from which our culture tries to protect children, and the methods we use to do this.

2. How are Quiché children taught to regard their ancestors? Write a narrative or descriptive essay about the role of ancestors in your life or in your culture.

WOLE SOYINKA

Nigerian Childhood

Playwright, poet, novelist, and critic Wole Soyinka (pronounced *woh*-leh shoy-*yin*-ka) won the 1986 Nobel Prize for literature. He was born Akinwande Oluwole Soyinka near Abeokuta, Nigeria, in 1934. Educated in Ibadan, Nigeria, and at Leeds University in England, he studied theater in London and had a number of plays produced there. Returning to Ibadan, Soyinka became co-editor of the literary journal *Black Orpheus* and was instrumental in the development of a Nigerian theater. His career was interrupted by two years in prison for allegedly supporting Biafra's secession from Nigeria (see p. 489). Soyinka has taught drama and comparative literature at the universities of Ibadan, Lagos, and Ife in Nigeria, and at Cambridge, Cornell, and Emory universities. He holds the French title of Commander of the Legion of Honor, the traditional Yoruba chieftaincy title Akogun (Warlord) of Isara, and several honorary degrees. His award-winning plays have appeared in theaters around the world, including Ife, London, Stratford, New York, and Chicago. Soyinka chairs the editorial board of the influential international journal *Transition*. A vocal opponent of the brutal regime of General Sani Abacha, he fled from Nigeria to Paris in 1994 when "we learned that plans to turn me into the next high-profile hostage had reached the stage of execution." In 1998, after Abacha's death, Soyinka returned at the invitation of interim ruler General Abdulsalami Abubakar. Soyinka's most recent books are *Art, Dialogue, and Outrage: Essays on Literature and Culture* (1994) and *The Open Sorrow of a Continent: A Personal Narrative of the Nigerian Crisis* (1996). "Nigerian Childhood" comes from his 1981 autobiography *Aké: The Years of Childhood*. It takes place about twenty years before the end of British rule. At that time Soyinka lived with his father, here called Essay, the headmaster of the Anglican Girls' School in the town of Aké; his mother, called Wild Christian; and his sister Tinu. "Bishop Ajayi Crowther" is Samuel Ajayi Crowther: Enslaved in 1821, freed and educated by the British, he became the first black African bishop of the Anglican church.

Rich in oil and other natural resources, Nigeria lies in the large curve of Africa's western coast. Portuguese and British slavers began arriving in the fifteenth century. In 1861 Britain seized the capital city of Lagos during an antislavery campaign and gradually extended its control over the country. Nigeria regained its independence a century later and is now a republic within the British Commonwealth. For most of the thirty years since independence, the nation's governments have been military. General Ibrahim Babangida, who became president in a 1985 coup, pledged to return the country to civilian rule in 1992, but declared the democratic election invalid when it was won by Soyinka's fellow Yoruba, Chief Moshood Abiola. Babangida was then overthrown by General Abacha, who imprisoned Abiola and dozens of other supporters of democracy. After executing many of his perceived enemies, including the poet and novelist Ken Saro-Wiwa, Abacha died suddenly in 1998. A month later, so did Abiola. Although Abacha was succeeded by one of his generals, Nigeria held elections in 1999 and chose Olusegun Obasanjo as the nation's first civilian president in fifteen years.

If I lay across the lawn before our house, face upwards to the sky, my head towards BishopsCourt, each spread-out leg would point to the inner compounds of Lower Parsonage. Half of the Anglican Girls' School occupied one of these lower spaces, the other half had taken over BishopsCourt. The lower area contained the school's junior classrooms, a dormitory, a small fruit garden of pawpaws, guava, some bamboo, and wild undergrowth. There were always snails to be found in the rainy season. In the other lower compound was the mission bookseller, a shriveled man with a serene wife on whose ample back we all, at one time or the other, slept or reviewed the world. His compound became a shortcut to the road that led to Ibarà, Lafenwá, or Igbèin and its Grammar School over which Ransome-Kuti presided and lived with his family. The bookseller's compound contained the only well in the parsonage; in the dry season, his place was never empty. And his soil appeared to produce the only coconut trees.

BishopsCourt, of Upper Parsonage, is no more. Bishop Ajayi Crowther would sometimes emerge from the cluster of hydrangea and bougainvillea, a gnomic face with popping eyes whose formal photograph had first stared at us from the frontispiece of his life history. He had lived, the teacher said, in BishopsCourt and from that moment, he peered out from among the creeping plants whenever I passed by the house on an errand to our Great Aunt, Mrs. Lijadu. BishopsCourt had become a boarding house for the girls' school and an extra playground for us during the holidays. The Bishop sat, silently, on the bench beneath the wooden porch over the entrance, his robes twined through and through with the lengthening tendrils of the bougainvillea. I moved closer when his eyes turned to sockets. My mind wandered then to another photograph in which he wore a clerical suit with waistcoat and I wondered what he really kept at the end of the silver chain that vanished into the pocket. He grinned and said, Come nearer, I'll show you. As I moved towards the porch he drew on the chain until he had lifted out a wholly round pocket watch that gleamed of solid silver. He pressed a button and the lid opened, revealing, not the glass and the face dial but a deep cloudfilled space. Then, he winked one eye, and it fell from his face into the bowl of the watch. He snapped back the lid, nodded again and his head went bald, his teeth disappeared, and the skin pulled backward till the whitened cheekbones were exposed. Then he stood up and, tucking the watch back into the waistcoat pocket, moved a step towards me. I fled homewards.

BishopsCourt appeared sometimes to want to rival the Canon's house. It looked like a houseboat despite its guard of whitewashed stones and luxuriant flowers, its wooden fretwork frontage almost wholly immersed in bougainvillea. And it was shadowed also by those omnipresent rocks from whose clefts tall, stout-boled trees miraculously grew. Clouds gathered and the rocks merged into their accustomed gray turbulence, then the trees were carried to and fro until they stayed suspended over BishopsCourt. This happened only in heavy storms. BishopsCourt, unlike the Canon's house, did not actually border the rocks or the woods. The girls' playing fields separated them and we knew that this buffer had always been there. Obviously bishops were not inclined to challenge the spirits. Only the vicars could. That Bishop Ajayi Crowther frightened me out of that compound by his strange transformations only confirmed that the Bishops, once they were dead, joined the world of spirits and ghosts. I could not see the Canon decaying like that in front of my eyes, nor the Rev. J. J. who had once occupied that house, many years before, when my mother was still like us. J. J. Ransome-Kuti had actually ordered back several ghommids[1] in his lifetime; my mother confirmed it. She was his grandniece and, before she came to live at our house, she had lived in the Rev. J. J.'s household. Her brother Sanya also lived there and he was acknowledged by all to be an òrò,[2] which made him at home in the woods, even at night. On one occasion, however, he must have gone too far.

"They had visited us before," she said, "to complain. Mind you, they wouldn't actually come into the compound, they stood far off at the edge, where the woods ended. Their leader, the one who spoke, emitted wild sparks from a head that seemed to be an entire ball of embers — no, I'm mixing up two occasions — that was the second time when he chased us home. The first time, they had merely sent an emis-

---

[1] Wood spirits. — ED.
[2] A kind of tree demon.

sary. He was quite dark, short and swarthy. He came right to the backyard and stood there while he ordered us to call the Reverend.

"It was as if Uncle had been expecting the visit. He came out of the   5
house and asked him what he wanted. We all huddled in the kitchen,
peeping out."

"What was his voice like? Did he speak like an *egúngún?*"[3]

"I'm coming to it. This man, well, I suppose one should call him a
man. He wasn't quite human, we could see that. Much too large a
head, and he kept his eyes on the ground. So, he said he had come to
report us. They didn't mind our coming to the woods, even at night, but
we were to stay off any area beyond the rocks and that clump of bamboo
by the stream."

"Well, what did Uncle say? And you haven't said what his voice was
like."

Tinu turned her elder sister's eye on me. "Let Mama finish the
story."

"You want to know everything. All right, he spoke just like your fa-   10
ther. Are you satisfied?"

I did not believe that but I let it pass. "Go on. What did Grand Uncle
do?"

"He called everyone together and wanted us to keep away from the
place."

"And yet you went back!"

"Well, you know your Uncle Sanya. He was angry. For one thing the
best snails are on the other side of that stream. So he continued to complain that those *òrò* were just being selfish, and he was going to show
them who he was. Well, he did. About a week later he led us back. And
he was right you know. We gathered a full basket and a half of the
biggest snails you ever saw. Well, by this time we had all forgotten
about the warning, there was plenty of moonlight and anyway, I've told
you Sanya is an *òrò* himself. . . ."

"But why? He looks normal like you and us."   15

"You won't understand yet. Anyway, he is *òrò*. So with him we felt
quite safe. Until suddenly this sort of light, like a ball of fire, began to
glow in the distance. Even while it was still far we kept hearing voices,
as if a lot of people around us were grumbling the same words together.
They were saying something like, 'You stubborn, stiff-necked children,
we've warned you and warned you but you just won't listen. . . .'"

Wild Christian looked above our heads, frowning to recollect the
better. "One can't even say 'they.' It was only this figure of fire that I saw

---

[3]Spirit of a dead ancestor. — ED.

and he was still very distant. Yet I heard him distinctly, as if he had many mouths which were pressed against my ears. Every moment, the fireball loomed larger and larger."

"What did Uncle Sanya do? Did he fight him?"

"*Sanya wo ni yen*? He was the first to break and run. *Bo o ló o yă mi, o di kítìpà kítìpà!*[4] No one remembered all those fat snails. That *iwin*[5] followed us all the way to the house. Our screams had arrived long before us and the whole household was — well, you can imagine the turmoil. Uncle had already dashed down the stairs and was in the backyard. We ran past him while he went out to meet the creature. This time that *iwin* actually passed the line of the woods, he continued as if he meant to chase us right into the house, you know, he wasn't running, just pursuing us steadily." We waited. This was it! Wild Christian mused while we remained in suspense. Then she breathed deeply and shook her head with a strange sadness.

"The period of faith is gone. There was faith among our early Christians, real faith, not just church-going and hymn-singing. Faith. *Igbàgbó*. And it is out of that faith that real power comes. Uncle stood there like a rock, he held out his Bible and ordered, 'Go back! Go back to that forest which is your home. Back, I said, in the name of God.' Hm. And that was it. The creature simply turned and fled, those sparks falling off faster and faster until there was just a faint glow receding into the woods." She sighed. "Of course, after prayers that evening, there was the price to be paid. Six of the best on every one's back. Sanya got twelve. And we all cut grass every day for the next week."

I could not help feeling that the fright should have sufficed as punishment. Her eyes gazing in the direction of the square house, Wild Christian nonetheless appeared to sense what was going on in my mind. She added, "Faith and — Discipline. That is what made those early believers. Psheeaw! God doesn't make them like that any more. When I think of that one who now occupies that house . . ."

Then she appeared to recall herself to our presence. "What are you both still sitting here for? Isn't it time for your evening bath? Lawanle!"

"Auntie" Lawanle replied "Ma" from a distant part of the house. Before she appeared I reminded Wild Christian, "But you haven't told us why Uncle Sanya is *òrò*."

She shrugged, "He is. I saw it with my own eyes."

We both clamored, "When? When?"

---

[4]If you aren't moving, get out of my way!
[5]A ghommid; a wood sprite which is also believed to live in the ground.

She smiled. "You won't understand. But I'll tell you about it some   25
other time. Or let him tell you himself next time he is here."

"You mean you saw him turn into an *òrò*?"

Lawanle came in just then and she prepared to hand us over. "Isn't it
time for these children's bath?"

I pleaded, "No, wait Auntie Lawanle," knowing it was a waste of
time. She had already gripped us both, one arm each. I shouted back,
"Was Bishop Crowther an *òrò*?"

Wild Christian laughed. "What next are you going to ask? Oh I see.
They have taught you about him in Sunday school have they?"

"I saw him." I pulled back at the door, forcing Lawanle to stop. "I see   30
him all the time. He comes and sits under the porch of the Girls'
School. I've seen him when crossing the compound to Auntie Mrs. Lijadu."

"All right," sighed Wild Christian. "Go and have your bath."

"He hides among the bougainvillea. . . ." Lawanle dragged me out of
hearing.

Later that evening, she told us the rest of the story. On that occasion,
Rev. J. J. was away on one of his many mission tours. He traveled a lot,
on foot and on bicycle, keeping in touch with all the branches of his
diocese and spreading the Word of God. There was frequent opposition
but nothing deterred him. One frightening experience occurred in one
of the villages in Ijebu. He had been warned not to preach on a particular day, which was the day for an *egúngún* outing, but he persisted and
held a service. The *egúngún* procession passed while the service was in
progress and, using his ancestral voice, called on the preacher to stop at
once, disperse his people, and come out to pay obeisance. Rev. J. J. ignored him. The *egúngún* then left, taking his followers with him but,
on passing the main door, he tapped on it with his wand, three times.
Hardly had the last member of his procession left the church premises
than the building collapsed. The walls simply fell down and the roof
disintegrated. Miraculously however, the walls fell outwards while the
roof supports fell among the aisles or flew outwards — anywhere but on
the congregation itself. Rev. J. J. calmed the worshipers, paused in his
preaching to render a thanksgiving prayer, then continued his sermon.

Perhaps this was what Wild Christian meant by Faith. And this
tended to confuse things because, after all, the *egúngún* did make the
church building collapse. Wild Christian made no attempt to explain
how that happened, so the feat tended to be of the same order of Faith
which moved mountains or enabled Wild Christian to pour ground-nut
oil from a broad-rimmed bowl into an empty bottle without spilling
a drop. She had the strange habit of sighing with a kind of rapture,

crediting her steadiness of hand to Faith and thanking God. If however the basin slipped and she lost a drop or two, she murmured that her sins had become heavy and that she needed to pray more.

If Rev. J. J. had Faith, however, he also appeared to have Stubborn-   35
ness in common with our Uncle Sanya. Stubbornness was one of the earliest sins we easily recognized, and no matter how much Wild Christian tried to explain the Rev. J. J. preaching on the *egúngún's* outing day, despite warnings, it sounded much like stubbornness. As for Uncle Sanya there was no doubt about his own case; hardly did the Rev. J. J. pedal out of sight on his pastoral duties than he was off into the woods on one pretext or the other, and making for the very areas which the *òrò* had declared out of bounds. Mushrooms and snails were the real goals, with the gathering of firewood used as the dutiful excuse.

Even Sanya had however stopped venturing into the woods at night, accepting the fact that it was far too risky; daytime and early dusk carried little danger as most wood spirits only came out at night. Mother told us that on this occasion she and Sanya had been picking mushrooms, separated by only a few clumps of bushes. She could hear his movements quite clearly, indeed, they took the precaution of staying very close together.

Suddenly, she said, she heard Sanya's voice talking animatedly with someone. After listening for some time she called out his name but he did not respond. There was no voice apart from his, yet he appeared to be chatting in friendly, excited tones with some other person. So she peeped through the bushes and there was Uncle Sanya seated on the ground chattering away to no one that she could see. She tried to penetrate the surrounding bushes with her gaze but the woods remained empty except for the two of them. And then her eyes came to rest on his basket.

It was something she had observed before, she said. It was the same, no matter how many of the children in the household went to gather snails, berries, or whatever, Sanya would spend most of the time playing and climbing rocks and trees. He would wander off by himself, leaving his basket anywhere. And yet, whenever they prepared to return home, his basket was always fuller than the others'. This time was no different. She came closer, startling our Uncle, who snapped off his chatter and pretended to be hunting snails in the undergrowth.

Mother said that she was frightened. The basket was filled to the brim, impossibly bursting. She was also discouraged, so she picked up her near empty basket and insisted that they return home at once. She led the way but after some distance, when she looked back, Sanya appeared to be trying to follow her but was being prevented, as if he was being pulled back by invisible hands. From time to time he would snatch forward his arm and snap,

"Leave me alone. Can't you see I have to go home? I said I have   40 to go."

She broke into a run and Sanya did the same. They ran all the way home.

That evening, Sanya took ill. He broke into a sweat, tossed on his mat all night, and muttered to himself. By the following day the household was thoroughly frightened. His forehead was burning to the touch and no one could get a coherent word out of him. Finally, an elderly woman, one of J. J.'s converts, turned up at the house on a routine visit. When she learnt of Sanya's condition, she nodded wisely and acted like one who knew exactly what to do. Having first found out what things he last did before his illness, she summoned my mother and questioned her. She told her everything while the old woman kept on nodding with understanding. Then she gave instructions:

"I want a basket of àgìdi, containing fifty wraps. Then prepare some èkuru in a large bowl. Make sure the èkuru stew is prepared with plenty of locust bean and crayfish. It must smell as appetizing as possible."

The children were dispersed in various directions, some to the market to obtain the àgìdi, others to begin grinding the beans for the amount of èkuru which was needed to accompany fifty wraps of àgìdi. The children's mouths watered, assuming at once that this was to be an appeasement feast, a sàarà[6] for some offended spirits.

When all was prepared, however, the old woman took everything to   45 Sanya's sickroom, plus a pot of cold water and cups, locked the door on him, and ordered everybody away

"Just go about your normal business and don't go anywhere near the room. If you want your brother to recover, do as I say. Don't attempt to speak to him and don't peep through the keyhole."

She locked the windows too and went herself to a distant end of the courtyard where she could monitor the movements of the children. She dozed off soon after, however, so that mother and the other children were able to glue their ears to the door and windows, even if they could not see the invalid himself. Uncle Sanya sounded as if he was no longer alone. They heard him saying things like:

"Behave yourself, there is enough for everybody. All right you take this, have an extra wrap . . . Open your mouth . . . here . . . you don't have to fight over that bit, here's another piece of crayfish . . . behave, I said . . ."

---

[6]An offering, food shared out as offering.

And they would hear what sounded like the slapping of wrists, a scrape of dishes on the ground, or water slopping into a cup.

When the woman judged it was time, which was well after dusk, 50 nearly six hours after Sanya was first locked up, she went and opened the door. There was Sanya fast asleep but, this time, very peacefully. She touched his forehead and appeared to be satisfied by the change. The household who had crowded in with her had no interest in Sanya however. All they could see, with astonished faces, were the scattered leaves of fifty wraps of *àgìdi*, with the contents gone, a large empty dish which was earlier filled with *èkuru*, and a water pot nearly empty.

No, there was no question about it, our Uncle Sanya was an *òrò*; Wild Christian had seen and heard proofs of it many times over. His companions were obviously the more benevolent type or he would have come to serious harm on more than one occasion, J. J.'s protecting Faith notwithstanding.

EXPLORATIONS

1. What is the relationship in Wole Soyinka's family between Anglican religious beliefs and traditional African magic? At what points in "Nigerian Childhood" do parents use each of these belief systems to control or teach children? At what points do the children's beliefs guide them toward "good" behavior?

2. "Stubbornness was one of the earliest sins we easily recognized," writes Soyinka in paragraph 35. What other virtues, failings, and rules of behavior have these children evidently been taught? Cite specific evidence for your conclusions.

3. What aspects of Soyinka's narrative make it clear that he was an adult when he wrote "Nigerian Childhood"? What passages indicate that he is telling his story from a child's rather than an adult's point of view?

CONNECTIONS

1. How have Soyinka's Yoruba community and Rigoberta Menchú's Quiché Indian community ("Birth Ceremonies," p. 146) responded similarly to Christianity? What are the reasons for each group's reaction? What role does religion appear to play for the Yoruba villagers? The Quiché? The outsiders who introduced Christianity into these communities?

2. In her Observation on page 98, Angela Davis refers to "African extended-family traditions." In what specific ways does Soyinka's family in "Nigerian Childhood" show what Davis means?

3. Es'kia Mphahlele mentions in "African Literature: What Tradition?" (p. 73) the reverence given to someone in a traditional law court who quotes a saying handed down from the elders: "Because his elders would be the ancestors, who are still present with us in spirit" (para. 8). What evidence of this statement appears in Soyinka's memoir?

ELABORATIONS

1. In "African Literature: What Tradition?" (p. 73), Mphahlele talks of embodying two distinct cultural histories. How has Soyinka made use of a similar dual heritage? Is Soyinka writing as "an ambivalent character . . . a man of two worlds" (Mphahlele's self-description) or as someone who has reconciled his histories? Write a comparison-contrast essay using Mphahlele and Soyinka as examples of Mphahlele's theses.

2. When you were a child, were you afraid of imaginary monsters? Have you or a friend ever had an encounter with a ghost? Write a narrative essay about an experience that most American adults would respond to with skepticism, depicting it (as Soyinka does) as a real event.

LISA JONES

Grave Matters at Monticello

Playwright, journalist, and author Lisa Jones described herself in
Essence magazine as "a writer whose work is dedicated to exploring the
hybridity of African American culture and of American culture in gen-
eral." She also notes, "My mother is White. I am Black. This is how I
choose to define myself, and this is how America chooses to define me."
Jones's mother, Hettie, was disowned by her first-generation American
Jewish parents for marrying the legendary black writer LeRoi Jones (who
later changed his name to Amiri Baraka). After the couple separated,
Hettie Jones brought up their two daughters in the black community.
Lisa Jones currently lives in Brooklyn. A staff writer for *The Village
Voice*, she also contributes to *Essence* and *Vibe*. Her essay collection
Bulletproof Diva: Tales of Race, Sex, and Hair appeared in 1994. Jones
has created three works for New American Radio: "Aunt Aida's Hand"
(with Alva Rogers, 1989); "Stained" (with Alva Rogers, 1991); and "Ethnic Cleansing" (1993). She won a Bessie Award for the stage adaptation
of *Stained*. Her play *Combination Skin*, which premiered at the Company One Theater in Hartford, Connecticut, in 1992, has been staged
around the country. "Grave Matters at Monticello" comes from the
12/30/98–1/5/99 issue of *The Village Voice* (online).

We cruise the aisles at Wal-Mart and eat chicken-fried steak at
Shoney's. This routine alone is enough to keep me coming back, but
really why I go is to hear the same family stories told year after year. A
favorite involves my great-great-grandfather, Jack Johns, an African
American, and my great-great-grandmother, Anna, his Jewish wife; they
fell in love while working as domestics at a plantation near Bishopsville,
South Carolina, shortly after the Civil War. Who said interracial cou-
pling first blossomed in the Age of Aquarius?

My holidays are synonymous with a trip to Hartsville, South Carolina (about an hour upstate from Columbia, the capital), for my annual family reunion, which brings together relatives from around the
country. On the topics of race, sex, and hair, there's always plenty to report. This year, I noticed what an openly multiculti family we've become. Our mixed ancestry, like that of most blacks, is not news. The
news is the family's sense of comfort with it. In the future, I see our

gathering evolving from a black family reunion into what one might call a historically black reunion of Americans.

In June, another cousin of my generation will marry, as folks used to say, "outside the race." And a highlight of this year's reunion was the wedding video of yet another interracial couple. The family sat around eating Cheez Doodles and enjoying the obvious devotion between two middle-class kids from Palo Alto. "Love, we are standing here in the fullness of your presence," said the minister, and no one in front of the VCR batted an eye. A far cry, I imagined, from when my white mother and black father tied the knot in 1958, their union still illegal in most Southern states.

It's no sweet irony that despite the current state of my family, the state of South Carolina exists in an entirely different stratosphere. In November, South Carolinians voted on whether to abolish a 103-year-old ban on interracial marriage. This Jim Crow managed to remain part of the state constitution despite Loving v. Virginia, the Supreme Court case that struck down miscegenation laws in 1967. (Alabama is the only other state that still has such a law; there is currently a campaign to remove it.)

South Carolina voters ended up siding against the ban, but only by a two-thirds margin. Several state representatives wanted to keep it. Said Representative Lanny Littlejohn, Republican from Spartanburg, just before the vote, "I think God has a perfect plan, and man has screwed it up." Here's to the new millennium. Whose American future will prevail — Mr. Littlejohn's or my family's?

One family reunion in particular has made headlines of late, though in this case the parties were brought together by means of a test tube. Last month, DNA tests confirmed that Thomas Jefferson fathered a child with one of his slaves, Sally Hemings. The Jefferson-Hemings link has been a hotbed of contention for 200 years. And the DNA "bombshell," as some saw it, reignited the debate about our third president's character and legacy. Was he the architect of American equality struggling with the question of slavery, or a slave owner who warned against race mixing while feasting on taboo sex across the color line? Or just another human specimen of contradictions?

Before DNA sent mainstream scholars scrambling to revise their canons, they happily bypassed stacks of circumstantial evidence and oral history from black families attesting to the relationship. The most damning clue all along, to my mind, is that Hemings herself was the half-sister of Jefferson's wife, née Martha Wayles, who died young. Martha's father had six children by Sally's mother. (Historians have long accepted oral history accounts of the black Wayles children, but not of the black Jeffersons.) Jefferson romantics like to claim the president was immune to the ethos of slave owner as sultan, but he was surely surrounded by it, and not just philosophically.

African Americans didn't need DNA to give credence to the Hemings-Jefferson story; we just look at our rainbow of skin tones and our family trees full of European and Indian ancestors. Without question, the concubinage of black females was central to American slavery. And given that nine out of our first twelve presidents owned slaves, one can only imagine how many other colored descendants of note are among our ranks.

The only scoop from Monticello was no scoop at all. The real issue, as talk-radio host Earl Ofari Hutchinson told Don Terry at the *New York Times*, is "why there was such denial for so long among historians and so many whites."

Indeed, the presumed crime of race mixing looms large here. (More   10
attention was paid to Hemings's race than to the fact that she was three decades Jefferson's junior, Lolita's age when accounts say their relationship began.) Jefferson's sex with Hemings suddenly became a "crime more heinous than the crime of his legal ownership of her," to quote Annette Gordon-Reed, whose *Thomas Jefferson and Sally Hemings: An American Controversy* examines the racial protectionism that litters Jefferson scholarship. And while we're on the subject, one of the least-explored crimes of American slavery was that whites didn't just own and rape their African property, but committed the offspring of these unions, their own flesh and blood, to bondage as well.

Many commentators label the Jefferson-Hemings chronicle a presidential sex scandal with convenient parallels to the Clinton era. The heart of the matter is not sex at all, but family and American identity. This country is a "family not just in democratic theory, but in blood," as writer and Jefferson descendant Lucian K. Truscott IV quoted Gordon-Reed in the *New York Times*, and we've been so since our Colonial beginnings. According to Frank Shuffleton, editor of *A Mixed Race: Ethnicity in Early America*, Americans have been a creole people, culturally and genetically, since the mid-1800s. Yet the reality of our shared blood is constantly denied, particularly by whites. So are the lines between races carefully drawn — manufactured is a better word (witness the "one-drop rule" in determining race) — because they limit the pool of those entitled to the privileges of whiteness.

Truscott's fiery op-eds about the upcoming showdown at Monticello caught my eye. An army brat who grew up in the integrated armed services, Truscott says he's been writing for thirty-two years, but never had the desire to weigh in about his lineage until he heard his relatives spout off like "rednecks" when faced with the DNA findings.

The Monticello Association, the official society of white descendants of Jefferson, will vote this spring whether to accept black descendants. Membership gets you into the annual reunion at Monticello, and allows you to rest in peace in the president's graveyard. Truscott has invited all the Hemings kin to attend this May, and challenged the whites to "look our slave descendants in the face when you vote to exclude them from our family." Some members are threatening to quit if blacks are voted in; others will quit, and sue, if they aren't.

Last month Truscott took part in a made-for-Oprah reunion with his Hemings cousins, including the descendants of Thomas Woodson, reportedly the first son of Hemings and Jefferson, conceived during their time in Paris. No DNA match for the descendants of Woodson has yet been found. Truscott thinks DNA is "horseshit." No one's asking the white descendants for their DNA. Obviously blacks are being held to a higher standard of proof for family membership than whites.

White scientists published the DNA findings, and a white historian, 15 Joseph J. Ellis, introduced them, trumping the decades-long battle for acknowledgment of the Hemings-Jefferson family line waged by African Americans. Truscott put me in touch with Michele Cooley-Quille, whom he calls one of his "Hemings cousins," though she's a sixth-generation Woodson. Cooley-Quille, thirty-three, an assistant professor at Johns Hopkins School of Hygiene and Public Health, is a daughter of the late Robert H. Cooley III, considered by many to be the catalyst behind recognition for the black descendants.

Cooley, a retired federal magistrate and lieutenant colonel in the army, had been waging a campaign since the early '90s, appearing on TV to declare his ancestry and talk about the Woodson Family Association, which claims 1,400 known descendants. The Woodsons, a distinguished African American family of college presidents and federal prosecutors, have criticized the DNA study, and stand by their 200-year-old oral history.

In the early '90s, Cooley was asked by the Thomas Jefferson Memorial Foundation (which runs Monticello and is guardian of the historical legacy) to take part in the 250th anniversary celebration of the president's birth. He requested permission to stage the semiannual Woodson Family Reunion at Monticello for the first time, which he did in 1992. Judge Cooley was the impetus for the foundation to begin oral history documentation of the descendants of Monticello's slaves, abstracts of which can be found on their Web site (www.monticello.org).

Cooley died suddenly in July, just months before the DNA results were published. Two weeks before his death, he'd appeared on an ABC news show and said one thing he wanted from his crusade was to be buried at Monticello. Cooley-Quille contacted the Monticello Association immediately after her father passed and requested permission.

But the Monticello Association, the more conservative body, turned down Cooley-Quille's request to bury her father. Robert Gillespie, president of the association, says the decision was based on lack of space in the yard. Gillespie acknowledges that the association has never asked to review the Woodson family records.

A magazine editor I know finds the whole question of who gets to be buried at Monticello a vapid symbol, nothing more than blacks coveting all things white. To Cooley-Quille, the graveyard is no symbol, but part of the "equity in rights and privileges" that she feels are due black families. (Jefferson descendants attend the University of Virginia, which the president founded, for free. Cooley-Quille and her two siblings all went to UVA, but the judge paid their way.)

Truscott calls the graveyard tussle serious business: "This is about blood, race, and land, the same things *Gone with the Wind* is about . . . the biggest unexamined subjects we have in this country. And the most explosive. The slaves worked the land, and what did they get for it? Nothing."

I can't think of a more potent metaphor of American race relations at the millennium than the battle over graveyard space at Monticello. There seems to be only one mature choice for the Monticello Association. If it welcomes African American descendants of Jefferson, the association will embrace the future. If it says no, it replays our segregated past. (Truscott says Gillespie once called for the creation of a separate graveyard for Hemings descendants — a Jim Crow solution if ever there was one.)

Even if Hemings kin weren't Jefferson's blood relatives, the Monticello Association courts shame by keeping them out of the graveyard. Hemings and the other Africans held as slaves built Monticello. They made the bricks, planed the lumber, suckled and fed the children. And the white descendants of Jefferson continue to enjoy the wealth and privilege this free labor amassed. Ancestral labor, as much as common blood, demands that kin of former slaves share Monticello. The Monticello Association must know they owe the black descendants a lot more than a place in the family plot.

EXPLORATIONS

1. What clues in paragraphs 1–3 of "Grave Matters at Monticello" suggest why Lisa Jones takes a personal interest in the relationship between Thomas Jefferson and Sally Hemings? In what ways would her essay's impact change without these opening paragraphs about her own family?

2. From the information in this essay, how do you think Thomas Jefferson would have defined *family*? What criteria determined who counted as a member of his family, and who did not? What criteria determined who counted as a member of Sally Hemings's family and who did not? How have the criteria of family membership changed since their day?

3. How does Jones make the segue from her family to Thomas Jefferson's? What ideas does she establish in her essay's opening section that continue through, or reappear in, its longer main section? What additional ideas does she introduce in the short section between the two that help her to make the transition?

CONNECTIONS

1. What is the role of oral history in "Grave Matters at Monticello"? What is the role of oral history in "Nigerian Childhood" (p. 158)? Do you think Wole Soyinka's family would agree with the families in Jones's essay who place more faith in oral history than in DNA? Why or why not?

2. In African American families during the era of slavery, Angela Davis notes on page 98, "the father was relegated to the negligible role of providing the 'seed.'" According to Davis, what advantages did the slave owner gain by this policy? After reading Jones's essay, what other advantages can you identify?

3. What background and attitudes do Danzy Senna ("The Mulatto Millennium," p. 18) and Jones have in common? In what respects do these two writers disagree? Which of Senna's categories do you think she would apply to Jones, and why?

ELABORATIONS

1. Compare the views of family described in the Observations by Bharati Mukherjee on page 3 and Philip Roth on page 98 with the views of family Jones presents in "Grave Matters at Monticello." Which is closest to your family's view of itself and of what *family* means or should be? Write an essay defining *family* as you have experienced it, or comparing your family's self-definition with that of one (or more) of these writers.

2. Find out more about Thomas Jefferson, Sally Hemings, and their families, and write your own essay about an aspect of them that interests you.

NICHOLAS BROMELL

Family Secrets

Nicholas Bromell describes his unorthodox childhood in this essay, which appeared in the 1993 collection *Turning Toward Home: Reflections on the Family*. Bromell graduated magna cum laude from Amherst College in 1972. After completing the Radcliffe Publishing Procedures Course in Cambridge, Massachusetts, he worked for Harvard University Press and later became editor in chief of the *Boston Review*. Bromell was awarded a teaching fellowship at Stanford University and received his Ph.D. there in English and American literature. Winning a Massachusetts Artists Foundation Fellowship in nonfiction writing in 1987, he taught at Brandeis University, served as a preceptor in the Public Policy Communications Program at Harvard's Kennedy School of Government, and continued to publish essays, feature stories, and journal articles in a variety of publications. He is now an associate professor and associate director of graduate studies at the University of Massachusetts, Amherst.

In *The Teachings of Don Juan*, Carlos Castaneda learns from his Yaqui shaman that each person has his "spot" in the world, a place where the strength of the earth wells up and protects him from the demons of the psyche. But because of the work my father used to do, I come from nowhere and have no spot. Often I feel I've built my life atop an emptiness that could implode at any moment. It is, moreover, an emptiness held firm by silence, by the untellable oddity of my childhood. My wife, who rolls her eyes when my most mundane childhood stories play out in places such as Baghdad, Piraeus, Petra, or Shiraz, doesn't believe that I am awed by her childhood in a small Catholic parish on the South Side of Chicago. She can't understand that I envy her because she is a *real* American — because she experienced a childhood other Americans recognize. We all try to make sense of our lives by having stories to tell, and, like all narratives, these stories are subject to conventions. The chief of these, in this country at least, is a prohibition against the exotic. A Southern boyhood, or a prep-school boyhood, or an only-child boyhood might be interesting, but to be told, they must be grounded in the ordinary. If the prep school is in Bogotá, or if the father is a Rockefeller, the story becomes unreal and untellable. And if

the father is a spy — or, as he prefers to call himself, an intelligence officer — the story becomes untellable twice over. You grow up swearing
an oath of silence without knowing it and owing allegiance to an institution you will never see or know.

But now, after the demise of the Soviet Union and the war against
Iraq, I have come to realize that my childhood had a certain historical
specificity. It was, with more intensity than most, a Cold War childhood. Born precisely at midcentury, I was made to understand at a very
young age that somewhere, or rather everywhere, an immense silent
contest was being fought, that our side was locked in a struggle with another side, and that what was at stake was the very shape of the future.
Of course, every American child of my generation was born into a
world structured by this Manichaean paradigm — us against them, good
against evil — but when your father's daily work actually contributes to
this struggle, it has a different, more intimate, meaning. Not that my father was vocal about the Cold War. I never heard him say a word
against the Russians. But somehow we knew (I think probably from our
grandmother, his doting mother) that he did not work for money, and
that his work mattered in some deeper, stronger way that could never be
discussed.

When we were "home" in the United States, Dad left the house for
"work" in some unspecified "office" we never saw. Overseas, however,
his work was more visible, no matter how painstakingly he tried to conceal it. To me and my two brothers, the fact of what my father did was
the very ground we walked on, and the élan with which he and his colleagues conducted themselves was the air we breathed. For them,
World War II had never ended. They slipped out of flight jackets and
fatigues and into gray suits, but their new anonymity was even more lus-
trous than their celebrated role as soldiers. They were an elite. They
were a team. They knew one another, but no one knew them. On
spring weekends we took picnics to ancient ruins in the desert; while
the mothers scratched in the sand for shards and the men relaxed with
cold martinis poured from my parents' thermos, my brothers and I
scouted the hillocks and ravines, finally sneaking up behind the men,
listening to their deep laughter, their sudden moments of seriousness,
and unconsciously reproducing in our games of creeping and spying
the work a number of them performed out of their embassy offices.
Hearing their laughter in memory now, I feel that it perfectly expressed
the double life most of them led: one day, a relaxed picnic with the
family; the next, a trek in dusty Land Rovers deep into the wastes where
the oil pipelines ran; where a solitary coffeehouse marked the borders of
Iraq, Syria, and Jordan; where Arab armies engaged in maneuvers;

where bedouin chieftains beckoned them into black-cloth tents for hot, sugary tea drunk from little glasses with gold rims.

My brothers and I came to accept certain announcements as plain matters of fact. Mother: "Your father won't be home tonight." Father: "I'm expecting visitors this afternoon; I want you all to stay outside the house until after five." One morning my older brother sprang from behind a door to scare our father, who instantly spun around, fists raised to strike, and then, ashen, explained that we were never, ever to jump out and scare him. And in order to make his prohibition convincing, he had to drop a corner of the curtain he kept between us and his profession. "In my job I have to worry that someone might want to sneak up behind me like that, and I have to be ready to defend myself," he explained gently. "I might hurt you before I could stop myself." Many years later, in another country, a team of men from the embassy came to our house with suitcases of electronics equipment, tripod-mounted antennas, headphones, and other gear, and my brothers and I were old enough to realize what they were doing — debugging our house. But we were hardly surprised. Without ever knowing that we knew, we had understood for some time that our father was a spy.

The silence of this acknowledged fact was the silence that legiti-   5 mated many other silences within our family. "There are certain things we don't talk about," we were told. "It would be better if you didn't mention to your friends where we went this weekend." I realize now how often we must have been part of my father's cover. When we went as a family to visit a man somewhere, and to drink sickly sweet rose water ("Drink a little to be polite!") on the terrace while he and my father conversed inside, we made quite a different impression on the neighbors than my father would have made arriving and entering the house alone. We were a family of conspirators. One afternoon my best friend saw all of us piling into an army helicopter that had landed in the fields near our house. The next day he confronted me with what he had seen, and I blithely denied it. Us? Piling into a helicopter? What on earth for? And because he had no one to corroborate the outrageous thing he had seen, my friend shook his head and soon disbelieved it himself. More than most other children, I think, I grew up seeing the world double. I saw not just the doubleness of adults pretending things to children but the doubleness of adults pretending things to one another. And knowing no other world, this seemed normal to me.

The Cold War, which was not a war, or not the war it pretended to be — a war of doubleness — was thus the architecture of my family and childhood. For middle-class Americans back home, and for children my age growing up in suburban neighborhoods of bikes and lawns and newspaper routes — things I knew about only from movies and old tele-vision shows — the Cold War was at most the sound of distant thunder. It came home to them only at moments — when Francis Gary Powers was shot down, when Nikita Khrushchev famously banged his shoe on a table at the United Nations. I found, when I entered college in 1968, that my new friends were shocked by revelations about American du-plicity at home and abroad. My father and his colleagues had done their work too well. All their efforts at the front lines, keeping the enemy at bay, had preserved the American delusion that the world could be seen in terms of right and wrong, communism and democ-racy. That the United States had actually undermined democracies (in, for example, Iran) was incredible to my classmates. They had to rethink everything they knew, or thought they had known, about the world, about power, about history. I joined them in their expressions of out-rage, I marched with them on Washington, but though I shared their disapproval of American policies I could not quite share their disgust and disappointment. I had been prepared, having known for as long as I could remember that things are seldom what they seem.

In 1957 we went overseas for the first time, sailing from New York on the S.S. *Excambian* and bound for Beirut. There we stayed briefly at the Hotel St. Georges, at that time the city's only luxury hotel, a faded, *fin de siècle* symbol of an era about to pass, and which my memory con-flates with the "large, proud, rose-colored hotel" of F. Scott Fitzgerald's *Tender Is the Night*. The St. Georges, however, had no "bright tan prayer rug of a beach." The green Mediterranean thundered onto the rocks surrounding the great railed veranda that jutted into the sea. In the morning we ate in the shade of the hotel, spearing with tiny forks the scalloped butter pats nestled in their dewy serving dish and drinking dark hot chocolate from a pewter urn. In the evening, as the sky flushed to apricot over the water, children and their nannies were given license to run, skip, hide, play over the veranda. Then night fell and waiters cir-culated busily, setting out tables, lighting small lanterns. Long after our bedtime we boys crouched on our balcony, peering down at the grown-ups eating their dinner, listening to the murmur of their conversation mingling with the murmur of waves in the darkness beyond the lights.

My senses — the senses of a seven-year-old — absorbed everything. I was a roll of film stretched open beneath the summer sun. Every pho-ton that hit me sank and stayed. Even today, when I happen to get a starched white napkin at a restaurant, the smell of fresh bread issuing miraculously from the fabric strips away the years and drops me, a boy, into the morning shade of the veranda of the St. Georges. But these memories are now more than ever evanescent sensations. Whether we know it or not, in Brattleboro as much as in Beirut, history flows through childhood the way light passes through the curtains of a bedroom. I see now that the rolls and butter I consumed on the veranda of the St. Georges were not ahistorical fragments tumbling through the empty space of time but precise embodiments of French colonialism, which at that very moment was giving way to an American "presence." The St. Georges itself is just such history writ large. It was named, of course, for the warrior-saint whose lance speared the serpent of heathenism and whose emblem accompanied thousands of Christian soldiers during the Crusades. Since the time we stayed there, it metamorphosed gradually into a modern but charmless hotel in the American style. Later still, seized now by one and now by another militant faction, it crumbled under twenty years of internecine warfare to a ghostly, but miraculously functioning, ruin — like the city itself.

We flew from Beirut to Baghdad, where my father had been posted to the embassy, and stepped out of the airplane into a heat so white and thick that I gasped. Driving to what would be our house, I gazed stupidly at the tall palm trees — I had never seen palms before — beneath whose leaves hung clusters of what looked like enormous cockroaches (dates, my mother explained). The car stopped at a pair of gates set in a high mud wall. Twenty feet away, on a pile of refuse bulkier than the car, two emaciated dogs lolled motionless, not even panting. The gates swung open. This was "our" garden and that was "our" house. Inside, we found the shutters closed, the hall dark as a cave. Huge fans turned beneath immensely high ceilings. The American couple who had met us at the airport introduced us to our cook, our houseboy, our nanny, and our gardener. In low tones the American woman spoke reassuringly to our mother. Then the grown-ups moved into the "library," where the man mixed them drinks, and we boys were left alone to explore.

Looking back, I realize how young my parents were (in their early   10 thirties) and how innocent. All of this was as new to them as it was to us. Still, I am astonished that they did not explain more to us. They had just transported their children to a place that was as different as another planet, and they simply let us loose in it. We were on our own, instructed only not to drink the water from the faucets and never to ask the servants for anything. We ambled around the shadowy house, touching, smelling, examining. In the library brown veins ran down the walls, and the books we opened had tiny sand tunnels running through them. Termites, my father explained. The kitchen cupboards were stocked with foods we had never heard of: squash (not sodas), biscuits (not crackers), sweets (not candies). Down in the basement we found

the belongings, awaiting shipment, of the family we had replaced; sur-
reptitiously, we pried into the boxes and lifted out treasures — chief
among them a magnificent set of albums filled with huge, colorful
stamps, most of them, if I remember correctly, from the Belgian Congo,
my father's predecessor's former post.

One evening a light rain fell. We stood at an open upstairs window
and looked down over the garden wall at the street. Traffic had halted
and Baghdadis ran out of the shops, hands uplifted, to touch and greet
the spattering drops. Soon thereafter the days grew cooler at last; we
began to play in the garden. Arranging our soldiers (all of them British
lead soldiers with red uniforms and black beaver hats — the only kind
available in the local stores) on fortifications we had built alongside the
irrigation ditches, we stayed for hours in our smaller world that we
could control and understand. Like all colonial children, we discovered
the mysteries of servants' quarters — a small building behind the
kitchen, occupied by our cook and houseboy. We learned enough Arabic to communicate brokenly, but more often we played our spying
games on them, climbing into the trees near their door and watching
them move back and forth from the kitchen to their quarters, understanding almost nothing of what they said but delighting in the mere
fact of being unseen, unheard, and watching.

We had just begun to explore the world beyond our garden walls —
riding our bikes to the British Council library one afternoon, where we
watched Laurence Olivier in the film version of *Richard III* — when the
mood of the city palpably changed. Winter dust storms blew out of the
desert, and coated trees and streets and cars in a fine yellow dust that
penetrated doors and shutters and blurred the glossy surface of the
dining-room table. But more than the weather changed. One day our
cook invited us to go with him to a hanging, and when my older brother
went to ask our mother for permission, she slapped him before she
could think or speak. When we drove down Al-Raschid Street, we
began to notice more crowds, more speeches, more banners, more soldiers. The city seemed to turn in upon itself. Then we learned the word
"curfew" when the government imposed one. At dusk merchants pulled
down the metal grates in front of their shops and went home. Even the
tiny corner store where we bought Mars bars and firecrackers closed before dark. Because we had diplomatic plates on our car, we were allowed to drive after dusk, and the city we passed through seemed to eye
us through a thousand shuttered windows.

Then it happened. The army revolted. The young king whose face
was familiar to us from the stamps we collected was shot in his palace.
We heard rumors that a mob chased two Americans into the Hilton

Hotel, caught them in the lobby, dragged them outside, and tore them limb from limb. Tanks and armored cars squatted at the end of our street. My mother came into our room and told us to pick one book and one toy each. We were packing. We were leaving that night on a special plane. We learned two more words that day: "revolution" and "evacuation."

While my father remained with a small delegation in Iraq, we flew to Rome, where we stayed for three days at the luxurious Hassler Hotel before moving to a tiny pensione in a street of perpetual shadows. Through the open bedroom window there came the sounds and smells of that great city, waking us in the morning and lulling us to sleep at night. I was eight years old — listless, restless, perhaps irked by my father's double absence. One day at lunch I watched my mother open a fresh pack of cigarettes, then I covertly pocketed the slender strip of red cellophane she discarded in the ashtray. That afternoon, during siesta, in obedience to some inarticulate inner prompting, I walked down the hall to the pensione's only bathroom, tied one end of the red strip to the bolt of the lock, closed the door, and carefully pulled the strip back through, thereby locking the door from the outside. With a swift jerk I yanked most of the strip free, leaving nothing visible. Then I returned to our bedroom and told my incredulous brothers what I had done.

We waited. At four o'clock the pensione began to stir. Pans clattered in the kitchen. The telephone rang in the vestibule. Footsteps padded by as people woke up and made their way to the bathroom. Gradually a murmur arose in the hall, and we drifted out to see what was the matter. A small crowd milled in front of the bathroom. Someone knocked, then thumped, then banged. Angry voices shouted in Italian. The proprietress emerged from the kitchen, straightened her apron, and knocked. No answer. She shouted. Finally they sent for a man who put a ladder against the wall of the building, climbed two stories, entered through the bathroom window, and opened the bathroom door to the angry, mystified crowd.

"*Ma chi è?*" cried the landlady, pouncing on the red strip dangling from the lock. At that point we thought it best to retire to our room, grateful that our father was not there to catch us in the act of imitating him.

We spent eight months in Rome without my father. Mother moved us into and out of a series of apartments with dysfunctional central heating. She found us a pretty English nanny named Nina whom I loved but who had an Italian boyfriend who was a pilot for a mercenary army fighting somewhere in Africa. Mother bought us matching flannel shorts and V-necked blue sweaters and took us out for dinner to small restaurants where the men made much of us and more of her — a beautiful young woman alone in Rome with her three boys. After the inevitable violinist had played the inevitable song that brought the inevitable tears to Mother's dark eyes, we walked home through the cobblestone streets, banging our heels on the manhole covers embossed with the letters *S.P.Q.R.*

S.P.Q.R.: *Senatus Populusque Romanus.* An empire once, a city now. Who can account for the influence that the vestiges of empire had on the historical consciousness of an eight-year-old American boy? At the time I understood nothing. But I absorbed, in the yellow Roman light, the knowledge that history is more than an aggregate of moments, of names of generals and dates of battles learned in school. History turns suddenly on a pivot. Whole orders of being pass away. No one tried to answer because I never asked the question that shadowed every monument and ruin we saw: What happened? But I felt that no gradual process of change could possibly connect the Arch of Constantine with the Fiats and Vespas swirling noisily beneath it. History must be dramatic, swift, inexplicable. And it is; the Cold War ended in three months, without a shot fired.

We were living in Maadi, a suburb of Cairo, when the Six-Day War between Israel and Egypt broke out in June of 1967. Egypt immediately severed diplomatic relations with the United States, and for the second time in my life I was evacuated, this time to Athens. Once again my father stayed behind to perform the invisible work that sustained us.

None of us really knows what he did for the next six months: He wrote one postcard, telling us that he went out a lot at night wearing the soft-soled shoes he jokingly called his "brothel creepers." Many years later, however, and after much wine, he uncharacteristically dropped the veil and let one story slip. On the night President Gamal Abdel Nasser announced he would resign, my father had needed to go out and visit certain "people" in various quarters of Cairo. The city was in upheaval. Distraught crowds roamed the streets, carrying placards of Nasser and crying out for vengeance against Israel and its chief ally, the United States. Around midnight, in a dark street of one of the city's poorer sections, my father turned a corner and found himself twenty yards away from just such a crowd. (He is recognizably American and speaks no Arabic.) Almost before he could move, he was surrounded. A young man seized him by the arms, and instead of resisting, my father took the young man's hand and guided his fingers to the skin under his own glasses. The man paused, stepped back, then turned and quieted the crowd. When he had finished, he put his arm around my father and guided him through the mass, which parted like the waters of the Red Sea. My father continued quietly on his way.

What had happened? On seeing the crowd, my father spat on his hands and rubbed them beneath his eyes. The moisture there convinced the young man that my father, like so many Egyptians, had been weeping with sorrow at the news that Nasser planned to resign. This is what the man had explained to the crowd and why they had let my father through.

An example of quick thinking, no doubt. But more than that. My father, I know, truly was saddened by Nasser's announcement; if he were a man capable of crying easily, he might have cried that night. He wasn't just tricking the crowd; he was feeling with them. But at the same time, this moment of communion with the people of Egypt was forced to be an act of duplicity. There will always be a need for subterfuge in foreign relations and in the gathering of intelligence, but during the Cold War these necessities became enshrined as virtues. And not just overseas. For many American men of my father's generation, the Cold War paradigm of interminable struggle against an implacable foe was just the most focused articulation of a general state of being. Unlike Vietnam veterans later, many men of my father's generation who returned home from war may not have had to deal with the shock of peace. There was no peace. A new war was nurtured into being, providing them a field in which to go on fighting — not just abroad but at home, where the ethos of conflict made the pursuit of success a cause, not just a fate. While the idea of capitalism had to be protected by cold warriors like my father, its actual triumph could be assured only by the unremitting and self-sacrificing struggle of corporate cadres back home — a struggle that has, they claim, paid off at last.

But now what? Thirty years ago, on a spring night in Washington, a man who was an intelligence officer stood with a martini in hand beside a charcoal grill, watching the coals glow. That afternoon, he had left a large office building, driven home anonymously, had doffed tie and jacket and rolled up his shirtsleeves. Now his sneakers rested lightly on the brick patio of a Georgetown garden, and his gaze, when he looked up at the pale spring sky, was at once vague and vigilant. We played at his feet, and he protected us. Inside the house his wife, our mother, made potato salad and placed plastic forks and paper plates on a tray to carry out to us.

Today my own young children take root and flourish in a small town in New England. Outside, sprawled on a chaise lounge and sipping wine as hamburgers cook, I protect them from nothing. Their horizon does not end at a wall topped with barbed wire but expands indefinitely. I realize now that I have tried to make my work the exact opposite of my father's. Against his commitment to silence I oppose my claims to speech — as a teacher and a writer. At the same time, though, I inevitably reproduce him — in manner, in temperament, and even in work. Closeted in my study, demanding a household of silence while I write, I may be as mysterious to my sons as my father was to his.

Constantine Cavafy's poem "Waiting for the Barbarians" asks: "And 25 now, without the Barbarians, what is to become of us?/After all, those people were a kind of solution." The premise of the Cold War was a bipolar world, every nation allied with us or with our "enemies." For more than forty years the Cold War made this particular construction of reality more real than others. For many Americans — and I hope for my sons, whose shouts float up from the bottom of the garden — a choice has emerged: to view the world as a more complicated place, requiring subtler thinking and more varied partnerships; or to retrench behind a new polarity, peering over the battlements at the numerous, angry poor. Not, unfortunately, that these options necessarily exclude each other.

I rise to prod the hamburgers. The world is no longer two; it is many. But the boys have armed themselves anyway, I see. Hefting sticks, since we don't allow them toy guns, they stalk each other through the dusk. At their age, my brothers and I mowed down legions of Nazis and Commies. Watching my sons join the ancient hunt, I wonder: Who will be designated as their enemies?

EXPLORATIONS

1. According to Nicholas Bromell, what criteria define a real American childhood (para. 1)? Which of these criteria does his own childhood fail to meet? Do you agree with his definition? Why or why not?

2. At what points does Bromell's family seem most ordinary to other people? At what points does his family seem most ordinary to its members? What qualities create the impression of normality in each case?

3. What proper names does Bromell mention? How does he identify his family members? How does his use of names affect his essay?

CONNECTIONS

1. Among what kinds of people does Bromell feel like an outsider, and why? Is Lisa Jones ("Grave Matters at Monticello," p. 168) part of the group that excludes him? Among what kinds of people does Jones suggest that she feels like an outsider and an insider? For each of these writers, what role does family play in his or her sense of belonging and identification?

2. What elements does Bromell's childhood in "Family Secrets" have in common with Wole Soyinka's ("Nigerian Childhood," p. 158)? What vision of himself does each writer give us before he shows us his family?

3. In what ways is the role of Bromell's family in his life similar to the role of Julia Alvarez's family in her life (p. 101)? What are the important differences between Bromell's family and Alvarez's?

ELABORATIONS

1. "History flows through childhood the way light passes through the curtains of a bedroom" (para. 8). What does Bromell mean by this? Think of some national or world event that occurred when you were younger, and recall the personal incidents and sensations you experienced in your own smaller world at the same time. Using Bromell's essay (or part of it) as a model, write your own essay about history flowing through childhood.

2. In his last four paragraphs, Bromell describes two parallel "real American childhood" scenes. Did your childhood include summer evenings of charcoal-grilled hamburgers and homemade potato salad? What family activities do you recall as most classic or typical? Write an essay describing your memories.

JOHN DAVID MORLEY

Acquiring a Japanese Family

John David Morley, the son of a British foreign officer, was born in Singapore in 1948 and grew up speaking Malay. After a year in Ghana (then the Gold Coast), he went to Britain for school in 1955. Morley took a first-class honors degree from Oxford University in 1969 and moved to Munich. His first job, however, was in Mexico, as tutor to the children of Elizabeth Taylor and Richard Burton. Working in the theatre in Germany had led him to develop an interest in the drama — and later the general culture — of Japan. He taught himself Japanese and went to Japan on a Japanese government scholarship, to study at the Language Research Institute of Waseda University, Tokyo. "Acquiring a Japanese Family" comes from his autobiographical novel *Pictures from the Water Trade: Adventures of a Westerner in Japan* (1985). Morley moved back to Germany (then West Germany) in time for the fall of the Berlin Wall in 1989, which he covered from East Germany for the *London Sunday Times*. Material gathered then appears in his 1996 novel *Destiny, or the Attraction of Affinities*. Morley worked as European coordinator for the Japanese Broadcasting Corporation from the late 1970s to the 1980s. He has continued to write both fiction and nonfiction, including novels, film scripts, and articles for newspapers including the *London Times* and the *New York Times* as well as German publications. "From a professional point of view, living as an English writer in a non–English-speaking country has been problematic," he writes; but "At some time or other in my life I have been most places."

Japan is a 2,360-mile archipelago off Asia's east coast consisting of four main islands and more than three thousand smaller ones. Most of the country is hills and mountains, many of them dormant or active volcanoes. Japan has intrigued Westerners since its self-imposed isolation was ended in 1854 by U.S. Commodore Matthew C. Perry, who forced the opening of trade. Japan was then ruled by the shoguns, a series of military governors who had held power since 1192. Before the shogunate came the empire, which supposedly began in 660 B.C., and which reestablished itself in 1868 (the Meiji Restoration). Soon afterward Japan began an aggressive campaign of expansion, clashing with China, then Russia, Korea, Germany, and finally the United States. At the outset of World War II, Japan allied with Germany and the other Axis powers. Its attack on Pearl Harbor in Hawaii in 1941 led to its defeat four years later after the United States dropped the world's first nuclear bombs on Hiroshima and Nagasaki. In its postwar constitution Japan renounced the right to wage war and shifted law-making authority to the

Diet, or parliament. Today Emperor Akihito is Japan's head of state in a parliamentary democracy led by a prime minister. In 1993, a series of scandals and widespread corruption ended thirty-eight years of one-party rule by the Liberal Democrats. Since then, both its government and its economy — once the envy of the world — have undergone repeated upheavals.

Boon did not like the Foreign Students Hall where it had been arranged for him to live, and on the same evening he moved in he decided he would move out. . . . But the decision that he did not want to live there was one thing, finding somewhere else to stay was quite another, and this in turn would have been impossible or at least very difficult if he had not happened to meet Sugama a few days after arriving in the country.

The introduction was arranged through a mutual acquaintance, Yoshida, at the private university where Boon was taking language courses and where Sugama was employed on the administrative staff. They met one afternoon in the office of their acquaintance and inspected each other warily for ten minutes.

"Nice weather," said Boon facetiously as he shook hands with Sugama. Outside it was pouring with rain.

"Nice weather?" repeated Sugama doubtfully, glancing out of the window. "But it's raining."

It was not a good start.   5

Sugama had just moved into a new apartment. It was large enough for two, he said, and he was looking for someone to share the expenses. This straightforward information arrived laboriously, in bits and pieces, sandwiched between snippets of Sugama's personal history and vague professions of friendship, irritating to Boon, because at the time he felt they sounded merely sententious. All this passed back and forth between Sugama and Boon through the mouth of their mutual friend, as Boon understood almost no Japanese and Sugama's English, though well-intentioned, was for the most part impenetrable.

It made no odds to Boon where he lived or with whom. All he wanted was a Japanese-speaking environment in order to absorb the language as quickly as possible. He had asked for a family, but none was available.

One windy afternoon in mid-October the three of them met outside the gates of the university and set off to have a look at Sugama's new apartment. It was explained to Boon that cheap apartments in Tokyo were very hard to come by, the only reasonable accommodation available being confined to housing estates subsidized by the government. Boon wondered how a relatively prosperous bachelor like Sugama managed to qualify for government-subsidized housing. Sugama admitted that this was in fact only possible because his grandfather would also be living there. It was the first Boon had heard of the matter and he was rather taken aback.

It turned out, however, that the grandfather would "very seldom" be there — in fact, that he wouldn't live there at all. He would only be there on paper, he and his grandson constituting a "family." That was the point. "You must *say* he is there," said Sugama emphatically.

The grandfather lived a couple of hundred miles away, and although he never once during the next two years set foot in the apartment he still managed to be the bane of Boon's life. A constant stream of representatives from charities, government agencies, and old people's clubs, on average one or two a month, came knocking on the door, asking to speak to grandfather. At first grandfather was simply "not in" or had "gone for a walk," but as time passed and the flow of visitors never faltered, Boon found himself having to resort to more drastic measures. Grandfather began to make long visits to his home in the country; he had not yet returned because he didn't feel up to making the journey; his health gradually deteriorated. Finally Boon decided to have him invalided, and for a long time his condition remained "grave." On grandfather's behalf Boon received the condolences of all these visitors, and occasionally even presents.

Two years later grandfather did in fact die. Boon was thus exonerated, but in the meantime he had got to know grandfather well and had become rather fond of him. He attended his funeral with mixed feelings.

Sugama had acquired tenure of his government-subsidized apartment by a stroke of luck. He had won a ticket in a lottery. These apartments were much sought after, and in true Japanese style their distribution among hundreds of thousands of applicants was discreetly left to fate. The typical tenant was a young couple with one or two children, who would occupy the apartment for ten or fifteen years, often under conditions of bleak frugality, in order to save money to buy a house. Although the rent was not immoderate, prices generally in Tokyo were high, and it was a mystery to Boon how such people managed to live at all. Among the lottery winners there were inevitably also those people for whom the acquisition of an apartment was just a prize, an unexpected bonus, to be exploited as a financial investment. It was no problem for these nominal tenants to sublet their apartments at prices well above the going rate.

Boon had never lived on a housing estate and his first view of the tall concrete compound where over fifty thousand people lived did little to reassure him. Thousands of winner families were accommodated in about a dozen rectangular blocks, each between ten and fifteen stories high, apparently in no way different (which disappointed Boon most of all) from similar housing compounds in Birmingham or Berlin. He had naively expected Japanese concrete to be different, to have a different color, perhaps, or a more exotic shape.

But when Sugama let them into the apartment and Boon saw the interior he immediately took heart: this was unmistakably Japanese. Taking off their shoes in the tiny boxlike hall, the three of them padded reverently through the kitchen into the *tatami* rooms.

"Smell of fresh *tatami*," pronounced Sugama, wrinkling his nose.   15

Boon was ecstatic. Over the close-woven pale gold straw matting lay a very faint greenish shimmer, sometimes perceptible and sometimes not, apparently in response to infinitesimal shifts in the texture of the falling light. The *tatami* was quite unlike a carpet or any other form of floor covering he had ever seen. It seemed to be alive, humming with colors he could sense rather than see, like a greening tree in the brief interval between winter and spring. He stepped onto it and felt the fibers recoil, sinking under the weight of his feet, slowly and softly.

"You can see green?" asked Sugama, squatting down.

"Yes indeed."

"Fresh *tatami*. Smell of grass, green color. But not for long, few weeks only."

"What exactly is it?"   20

"Yes."

Boon turned to Yoshida and repeated the question, who in turn asked Sugama and conferred with him at great length.

"*Tatami* comes from *oritatamu*, which means to fold up. So it's a kind of matting you can fold up."

"Made of straw."

"Yes."   25

"How long does it last?"

Long consultation.

"He says this is not so good quality. Last maybe four, five years."

"And then what?"

"New *tatami*. Quite expensive, you see. But very practical."   30

The three *tatami* rooms were divided by a series of *fusuma*, sliding screens made of paper and light wood. These screens were decorated at the base with simple grass and flower motifs; a natural extension, it occurred to Boon, of the grasslike *tatami* laid out in between. Sugama explained that the *fusuma* were usually kept closed in winter, and in summer, in order to have "nice breeze," they could be removed altogether. He also showed Boon the *shoji*, a type of sliding screen similar to the *fusuma* but more simple: an open wooden grid covered on one side with semitransparent paper, primitive but rather beautiful. There was only one small section of *shoji* in the whole apartment; almost as a token, thought Boon, and he wondered why.

With the exception of a few one- and two-room apartments, every house that Boon ever visited in Japan was designed to incorporate these three common elements: *tatami*, *fusuma*, and *shoji*. In the houses of rich people the *tatami* might last longer, the *fusuma* decorations might be more costly, but the basic concept was the same. The interior design of all houses being much the same, it was not surprising to find certain similarities in the behavior and attitudes of the people who lived in them.

The most striking feature of the Japanese house was lack of privacy; the lack of individual, inviolable space. In winter, when the *fusuma* were kept closed, any sound above a whisper was clearly audible on the other side, and of course in summer they were usually removed altogether. It is impossible to live under such conditions for very long without a common household identity emerging which naturally takes precedence over individual wishes. This enforced family unity was still held up to Boon as an ideal, but in practice it was ambivalent, as much a yoke as a bond.

There was no such thing as the individual's private room, no bedroom, dining- or sitting-room as such, since in the traditional Japanese house there was no furniture determining that a room should be reserved for any particular function. A person slept in a room, for example, without thinking of it as a bedroom or as his room. In the morning his bedding would be rolled up and stored away in a cupboard; a small table known as the *kotatsu*, which could also be plugged into the mains to provide heating, was moved back into the center of the room and here the family ate, drank, worked, and relaxed for the rest of the day. Although it was becoming standard practice in modern Japan for children to have their own rooms, many middle-aged and nearly all older Japanese still lived in this way. They regarded themselves as "one flesh," their property as common to all; the *uchi* (household, home) was constituted according to a principle of indivisibility. The system of movable screens meant that the rooms could be used by all the family and for all purposes: walls were built round the *uchi*, not inside it.

Boon later discovered analogies between this concept of house and the Japanese concept of self. The Japanese carried his house around in   35 his mouth and produced it in everyday conversation, using the word *uchi* to mean "I," the representative of my house in the world outside. His self-awareness was naturally expressed as corporate individuality, hazy about quite what that included, very clear about what it did not. . . .

The almost wearying sameness about all the homes which Boon visited, despite differences in the wealth and status of their owners, prompted a rather unexpected conclusion: the classlessness of the Japanese house. The widespread use of traditional materials, the preservation of traditional structures, even if in such contracted forms as to have become merely symbolic, suggested a consensus about the basic requirements of daily life which was very remarkable, and which presumably held implications for Japanese society as a whole. Boon's insight into that society was acquired very slowly, after he had spent a great deal of time sitting on the *tatami* mats and looking through the sliding *fusuma* doors which had struck him as no more than pleasing curiosities on his first visit to a Japanese-style home.

Sugama, Yoshida, and Boon celebrated the new partnership at a restaurant in Shinjuku, and a week later Boon moved in.

The moment he entered the apartment a woman who was unexpectedly standing in the kitchen dropped down on her knees and prostrated herself in a deep bow, her forehead almost touching the floorboards, introducing herself with the words *"Irrashaimase. Sugama de gozaimasu . . ."*

Boon was extremely startled. He wondered whether he should do the same thing and decided not, compromising with a halfhearted bow which unfortunately the woman couldn't even see, because she had her face to the ground. She explained that she was *o-kaasan*, Sugama's mother.

Sugama had a way of springing surprises — or rather, he indicated   40
his intentions so obtusely that Boon usually failed to realize what would happen until it was already in progress — and so for quite a while Boon assumed that there must have been a change in plan, that the mother had perhaps joined the household as a stand-in for the grandfather. He greeted her in fluent Japanese (he had been studying introductions for the past week) and promptly fell into unbroken silence, mitigated by the occasional appreciative nod. Boon for his part hardly understood a word of what Sugama's mother was saying but she, encouraged by the intelligible sounds he had initially produced, talked constantly for the best part of an hour, and by the time Sugama eventually arrived Boon

had become resigned to the idea that his talkative mother was going to be a permanent resident.

The misunderstanding was swiftly ironed out. No, *o-kaasan* had only come up to Tokyo for a few days (from whatever angle of the compass one approached Tokyo the journey to the capital was described as an elevation) in order to help with the move.

Sugama's mother was a small, wiry woman in her late fifties. Her teeth protruded slightly; like most Japanese women, even those who had very good teeth, she covered her mouth with her hand whenever she laughed. She was a vivacious woman and laughed frequently, so one way and another, with all the cooking, cleaning, and sewing she also did during the next four days, her hands were kept continually busy. She was of slight build but very sound in lung, with the effect that when she laughed it resounded throughout her whole body, as if the laugh were more than the body could accommodate. Perhaps this laughter drew Boon's attention to a girlish quality she had about her, despite her age and a rather plain appearance. He often watched her working, and in the spare, effortless movements of a woman who has performed the same tasks so many times that not even the tiniest gesture is superfluous there was also something unexpectedly graceful.

On the far side of the *fusuma* Boon often heard them talking late into the night. Night after night she sawed away at him with her flinty, abrasive voice. In the mornings Sugama was moody, the atmosphere in the house increasingly tense. Boon was left guessing. Gradually, in the course of weeks and months, Sugama began to take him into his confidence, and in retrospect he learned what must have been the subject of those nightly conversations.

O-kaasan's most pressing concern was that her son, at the advanced age of twenty-eight, was still unmarried. Boon couldn't see what the fuss was about, but Sugama was slowly coming round to his mother's view, who was quite sure it was a disaster. "The wind blows hard," he announced mysteriously, apparently by way of explanation — Boon himself had to blow pretty hard to keep up with conversations on this level. He said it was up to Sugama to decide when and whether he wanted to get married. It wasn't anybody else's business. Sugama would clearly have liked to be able to agree with this facile advice and just as clearly he could not, entangled in a web of sentiment and duty of which Boon was wholly ignorant.

The promptings of filial duty which caused Sugama such heartache   45
and which to Boon were so alien demanded of Sugama a second, even more painful decision. He was the *chonan*, the eldest son, thereby

inheriting the obligation not merely to provide for his aging parents but to live with them in the same house. There were two alternatives open to him. He could either bring his parents to live with him in Tokyo or he could return home to his province in the north. A house in Tokyo large enough to provide room for grandfather, parents, Sugama, and — sooner or later — a fourth-generation family was out of the question; on his present salary he would have to work for several lifetimes in order to pay for it. A one-way ticket home came a great deal cheaper, which was just as well, since the only job awaiting him at the other end would be poorly paid and with even poorer prospects. Such was the path of righteousness. . . .

O-kaasan had only just packed her bags and gone home when — as usual without any forewarning — Sugama turned up late one evening accompanied by an old man, his wife, and an enormous cardboard box. Boon was sitting in his pajamas eating noodles out of a saucepan when these unexpected visitors arrived. Consternation. The old lady caught sight of him and dropped her bag (very probably she had not been forewarned either), immediately prostrating herself on the floor in the deepest of deep bows, old-style obeisance with the added advantage of concealing momentary shock and embarrassment. The old man was no slouch either. Palms on the floor and fingers turned inwards he bobbed his head up and down several times in Boon's direction, apologizing profusely every time he came up for air. All this happened so quickly that the astonished Boon didn't even have the presence of mind to put down the saucepan he was holding, and he sat there in his pajamas uneasily aware that he was the most unworthy object of the visitors' attentions.

Sugama came forward rather sheepishly, stepping in cavalier fashion between the prone bodies on the kitchen floor, and explained who they were.

"My grandfather's brother — younger brother — and wife."

"Not your grandfather?" asked Boon doubtfully, always alert to the possibility of misunderstandings when Sugama ventured into English.

"No, no *not* my grandfather."   50

"Your *great*-uncle, then."

"Ah! Great-uncle? *Great* uncle?"

Sugama paused to digest this new word, mustering his ancient relative with pursed lips. It was clear what was passing through his mind.

Boon was still not reassured. He kept an eye on the ominous cardboard box, quite large enough to accommodate a third, perhaps enfeebled relative, and wondered what else was in store for him.

"What are they doing here?"   55

"Earthquake," said Sugama simply. Boon fetched his dictionary and Sugama, reverting to Japanese, sat down to explain the situation.

At about nine o'clock that evening his great-uncle had called him in his office (Sugama worked a late shift) with the startling news that a major earthquake was imminent. How did he know? His wife had told him so. How did she know? A fortune-teller she regularly visited and in whom she placed absolute confidence had seen it in his cards and crystal ball. She was terrified, and having personally experienced the Great Kanto Earthquake of 1923 in which over a hundred thousand people had died she was not taking any chances. Her fortune-teller couldn't predict exactly when the earthquake would occur, but it might be at any time within the next three days; the greatest likelihood of its occurrence was forecast for midnight on the following day. The two old people ran a little shop in the downtown area of Tokyo where many of the houses were flimsy wooden structures which tended to slump and collapse very easily, even without the encouragement of an earthquake. But their great-nephew, they heard, had just moved into a marvelous modern building that was supposed to be *earthquake-proof*. Could they come and stay for a few days? Of course, said Sugama. So without more ado they bundled their worldly goods into the largest available box and Sugama brought them over in a neighbor's truck.

As a matter of fact there had been a slight tremor the previous evening. It was Boon's first. He had been standing in the kitchen helping himself to another glass of whiskey when the floor unaccountably began to sway and a set of irreproachable stainless steel ladles, which until then had given him no cause for complaint, started rattling menacingly on the kitchen wall. Boon had replaced the whiskey and made himself a cup of tea instead.

Great-uncle and his wife knelt on the *tatami* listening to Sugama's recital, wagging their heads and smiling from time to time, as if allowing that there was something rather droll about the situation, but also wanting to be taken absolutely seriously. However, with every moment they spent in the apartment this became increasingly hard to do, for the eccentric old couple seemed to be guided by a mischievous genius — they belonged to nature's blunderers, everything they touched turned to farce. Their great-nephew had just finished his dramatic account when there was a shrill call of *ohayo!* (Good morning) from the kitchen, and all eyes turned to the neglected cardboard box.

"Oh dear! The poor thing!" crowed the old lady, getting up at once   60
and pattering over to the box. She pulled open the flap and gently lifted

out a bright yellow parrot. The indignant bird rapped her knuckles a couple of times with the side of his beak and settled frostily on the tip of her finger.

Sugama, Boon, the elderly couple, and the yellow parrot housed together for the next three days. Once he had provided his relatives with a roof over their heads Sugama took no further interest in them and was unaccountably busy for as long as they stayed there, leaving the house earlier and returning later than usual. His prodigiously long working hours impressed great-uncle and worried his wife, who took to preparing nutritious cold snacks for the laboring hero before retiring for the night. Sugama did justice to these snacks with the same appetite he applied himself to his work, warding off their anxieties with careless equanimity.

"You've got to hand it to him — he certainly works hard," said great-uncle at breakfast one morning, just after Sugama had left the house.

"Ah," replied Boon noncommittally. He knew perfectly well that Sugama's overtime was not spent at the office but at mah-jongg parlors in Nakano and Takadanobaba.

In the meantime Boon was left to study the evacuees and the evacuees Boon with mutual curiosity. On the whole he had the impression that they were rather disappointed in him. At first they looked at him as if he had descended from another planet, but when it became obvious that he was not going to live up to these expectations their interest declined into an attitude of gently reproachful familiarity. For Boon did not sleep on a bed, he dispensed with bacon and egg, he knew nothing about baseball, ate rice and drank green tea with relish, and was unpardonably fond of dried cuttlefish and raw squid, foods which foreigners were commonly supposed to regard with horror and loathing. Altogether Boon was not as Boon should be, and they were rather disconcerted.

This attitude — a national prejudice, really — that foreigners and the   65 Japanese way of life must almost as a matter of principle be wholly incompatible was something Boon encountered time and again. Under the cover of courtesy, of polite considerations for differences in tastes and customs, many Japanese would gleefully reveal their own select cabinet of horrors, confronting their guest with fermented bean curd or prawns drowned in sake not as something he might care to sample but as a kind of ethnological litmus test: If he found it indigestible and swiftly turned green this would be taken by them as confirmation of their own cultural and racial singularity. With barely concealed triumph the host would commiserate with his victim, invariably remarking *Yappari, nihonjin ja nai to* . . . (Ah well, unless one is Japanese . . .) . . .

On the fateful morning great-uncle took cover under the *kotatsu* earlier than usual and sat tight for the rest of the day. His wife went about her household tasks as briskly as ever, but when there was nothing left for her to do and at last she knelt down beside great-uncle at the little table it became evident how restless she really was. From time to time she laid down her sewing, listened intently, sighed, and picked it up again. As the evening wore on and the tension began to mount, Boon couldn't resist cracking a few jokes, which great-uncle good-humoredly deflected at his wife. It was only to set her mind at rest that they had come to stay, he assured Boon. Women couldn't resist fortune-tellers, but it was just a lot of nonsense after all; and for good measure he made a few jokes himself at her expense. Boon was not deceived. Throughout the evening great-uncle helped himself to the bottle of fine old malt whiskey, originally intended as Sugama's present, much more liberally than he otherwise did and by midnight he was in true fighting spirit, his face shining with such particular splendor that his wife's attention was diverted from the impending destruction of Tokyo to the threat of great-uncle's imminent collapse.

There was no earthquake that night, but the old lady couldn't quite believe this and for two more days she sat it out in her nephew's apartment waiting for the dust to clear. Sugama was dispatched, like a kind of dove from Noah's Ark, to report on the state of the world, and it was only after he had personally confirmed that the house in downtown Tokyo was still in perfect order that she consented to their departure. Boon particularly regretted the loss of the parrot, which spoke few words of Japanese but those very frequently, thus improving his pronunciation of the language.

EXPLORATIONS

1. According to John David Morley, what are the two meanings of the Japanese term *uchi* (paras. 34–35)?

2. How are Sugama's obligations to the older members of his family different from those of most twenty-eight-year-olds in the United States?

3. Morley describes his experiences in Japan through the eyes of the fictional character Boon. What advantages do you think Morley gains from writing in the third person rather than the first person?

CONNECTIONS

1. In paragraph 33, Morley writes about "a common household identity emerging which naturally takes precedence over individual wishes." What factors create such an identity? What factors create such an identity for the Bromell family in "Family Secrets" (p. 174)? In what specific ways does the Bromells' household unity take precedence over individual wishes?

2. "Acquiring a Japanese Family," like Wole Soyinka's "Nigerian Childhood" (p. 158), depicts characters with beliefs that most people in the United States would regard as superstitious. What similarity do you notice between Morley's and Soyinka's ways of handling these beliefs? How does the author's approach affect your response to his characters' superstitions?

3. What ideas about the role of family and the obligations of family members are shared by the Japanese family as Morley describes it and the Indian family as Bharati Mukherjee and Ved Mehta describe it (pp. 3 and 312), but not by most families in the United States?

ELABORATIONS

1. Much of the information Morley gives his readers about the Japanese family is indirect: for example, his discussion of the interior of Japanese homes and the concept of *uchi*. After carefully rereading "Acquiring a Japanese Family," write an essay describing Japanese attitudes toward the family: its social role, its influence on the individual, and the responsibilities and privileges of family members.

2. Morley writes: "The most striking feature of the Japanese house was lack of privacy; the lack of individual, inviolable space. . . . It is impossible to live under such conditions for very long without a common household identity emerging which naturally takes precedence over individual wishes. This enforced family unity was still held up to Boon as an ideal, but in practice it was ambivalent, as much a yoke as a bond" (para. 33). In your own family, in what ways did a common household identity develop as a result of living together? For instance, what habits did you pick up from other members of your family or in response to their needs? (Examples might include getting up, going to bed, eating, bathing, or watching television at certain times; preparing foods or folding laundry in certain ways; buying certain products.) Write an essay about your own *uchi*.

KAZUO ISHIGURO

A Family Supper

Kazuo Ishiguro was born in Nagasaki, Japan, in 1954, less than a decade after the United States dropped an atomic bomb on the city to end World War II. When he was six years old his family moved to England, where he has lived ever since. Ishiguro studied at the University of Kent in Canterbury and the University of East Anglia. At the age of twenty-five he won recognition for some early writing anthologized in a collection of stories by promising young authors. His first novel, *A Pale View of Hills* (1982), won the Royal Society of Literature's Winifred Holtby Prize; his second novel, *An Artist of the Floating World* (1986), was named Whitbread Book of the Year. His third novel, *The Remains of the Day* (1989), won Britain's highest literary award, the Booker Prize, and was subsequently made into a film starring Anthony Hopkins and Emma Thompson. Ishiguro visited the United States on the publication of *The Unconsoled* (1995); he lives in London. His story "A Family Supper" first appeared in 1990.

Fugu is a fish caught off the Pacific shores of Japan. The fish has held a special significance for me ever since my mother died after eating one. The poison resides in the sex glands of the fish, inside two fragile bags. These bags must be removed with caution when preparing the fish, for any clumsiness will result in the poison leaking into the veins. Regrettably, it is not easy to tell whether or not this operation has been carried out successfully. The proof is, as it were, in the eating.

Fugu poisoning is hideously painful and almost always fatal. If the fish has been eaten during the evening, the victim is usually overtaken by pain during his sleep. He rolls about in agony for a few hours and is dead by morning. The fish became extremely popular in Japan after the war. Until stricter regulations were imposed, it was all the rage to perform the hazardous gutting operation in one's own kitchen, then to invite neighbors and friends round for the feast.

At the time of my mother's death, I was living in California. My relationship with my parents had become somewhat strained around that period and consequently I did not learn of the circumstances of her death until I returned to Tokyo two years later. Apparently, my mother had always refused to eat fugu, but on this particular occasion she had made an exception, having been invited by an old school friend whom she was anxious not to offend. It was my father who supplied me with the details as we drove from the airport to his house in the Kamakura district. When we finally arrived, it was nearing the end of a sunny autumn day.

"Did you eat on the plane?" my father asked. We were sitting on the tatami floor of his tearoom.

"They gave me a light snack."   5

"You must be hungry. We'll eat as soon as Kikuko arrives."

My father was a formidable-looking man with a large stony jaw and furious black eyebrows. I think now, in retrospect, that he much resembled [Chinese Communist leader] Chou En-lai, although he would not have cherished such a comparison, being particularly proud of the pure samurai blood that ran in the family. His general presence was not one that encouraged relaxed conversation; neither were things helped much by his odd way of stating each remark as if it were the concluding one. In fact, as I sat opposite him that afternoon, a boyhood memory came back to me of the time he had struck me several times around the head for "chattering like an old woman." Inevitably, our conversation since my arrival at the airport had been punctuated by long pauses.

"I'm sorry to hear about the firm," I said when neither of us had spoken for some time. He nodded gravely.

"In fact, the story didn't end there," he said. "After the firm's collapse, Watanabe killed himself. He didn't wish to live with the disgrace."

"I see."   10

"We were partners for seventeen years. A man of principle and honor. I respected him very much."

"Will you go into business again?" I asked.

"I am . . . in retirement. I'm too old to involve myself in new ventures now. Business these days has become so different. Dealing with foreigners. Doing things their way. I don't understand how we've come to this. Neither did Watanabe." He sighed. "A fine man. A man of principle."

The tearoom looked out over the garden. From where I sat I could make out the ancient well that as a child I had believed to be haunted. It was just visible now through the thick foliage. The sun had sunk low and much of the garden had fallen into shadow.

"I'm glad in any case that you've decided to come back," my father   15
said. "More than a short visit, I hope."

"I'm not sure what my plans will be."

"I, for one, am prepared to forget the past. Your mother, too, was always ready to welcome you back — upset as she was by your behavior."

"I appreciate your sympathy. As I say, I'm not sure what my plans are."

"I've come to believe now that there were no evil intentions in your mind," my father continued. "You were swayed by certain . . . influences. Like so many others."

"Perhaps we should forget it, as you suggest."   20

"As you will. More tea?"

Just then a girl's voice came echoing through the house.

"At last." My father rose to his feet. "Kikuko has arrived."

Despite our difference in years, my sister and I had always been close. Seeing me again seemed to make her excessively excited, and for a while she did nothing but giggle nervously. But she calmed down somewhat when my father started to question her about Osaka and her university. She answered him with short, formal replies. She in turn asked me a few questions, but she seemed inhibited by the fear that her questions might lead to awkward topics. After a while, the conversation had become even sparser than prior to Kikuko's arrival. Then my father stood up, saying: "I must attend to the supper. Please excuse me for being burdened by such matters. Kikuko will look after you."

My sister relaxed quite visibly once he had left the room. Within a   25
few minutes, she was chatting freely about her friends in Osaka and about her classes at university. Then quite suddenly she decided we should walk in the garden and went striding out onto the veranda. We put on some straw sandals that had been left along the veranda rail and stepped out into the garden. The light in the garden had grown very dim.

"I've been dying for a smoke for the last half hour," she said, lighting a cigarette.

"Then why didn't you smoke?"

She made a furtive gesture back toward the house, then grinned mischievously.

"Oh, I see," I said.

"Guess what? I've got a boyfriend now."   30

"Oh, yes?"

"Except I'm wondering what to do. I haven't made up my mind yet."

"Quite understandable."

"You see, he's making plans to go to America. He wants me to go with him as soon as I finish studying."

"I see. And you want to go to America?"   35

"If we go, we're going to hitchhike." Kikuko waved a thumb in front of my face. "People say it's dangerous, but I've done it in Osaka and it's fine."

"I see. So what is it you're unsure about?"

We were following a narrow path that wound through the shrubs and finished by the old well. As we walked, Kikuko persisted in taking unnecessarily theatrical puffs on her cigarette.

"Well, I've got lots of friends now in Osaka. I like it there. I'm not sure I want to leave them all behind just yet. And Suichi . . . I like him, but I'm not sure I want to spend so much time with him. Do you understand?"

"Oh, perfectly."   40

She grinned again, then skipped on ahead of me until she had reached the well. "Do you remember," she said as I came walking up to her, "how you used to say this well was haunted?"

"Yes, I remember."

We both peered over the side.

"Mother always told me it was the old woman from the vegetable store you'd seen that night," she said. "But I never believed her and never came out here alone."

"Mother used to tell me that too. She even told me once the old   45
woman had confessed to being the ghost. Apparently, she'd been taking a shortcut through our garden. I imagine she had some trouble clambering over these walls."

Kikuko gave a giggle. She then turned her back to the well, casting her gaze about the garden.

"Mother never really blamed you, you know," she said, in a new voice. I remained silent. "She always used to say to me how it was their fault, hers and Father's, for not bringing you up correctly. She used to tell me how much more careful they'd been with me, and that's why I was so good." She looked up and the mischievous grin had returned to her face. "Poor Mother," she said.

"Yes. Poor Mother."

"Are you going back to California?"

"I don't know. I'll have to see."   50

"What happened to . . . to her? To Vicki?"

"That's all finished with," I said. "There's nothing much left for me now in California."

"Do you think I ought to go there?"

"Why not? I don't know. You'll probably like it." I glanced toward the house. "Perhaps we'd better go in soon. Father might need a hand with the supper."

But my sister was once more peering down into the well. "I can't see   55
any ghosts," she said. Her voice echoed a little.

"Is Father very upset about his firm collapsing?"

"Don't know. You never can tell with Father." Then suddenly she
straightened up and turned to me. "Did he tell you about old Watanabe? What he did?"

"I heard he committed suicide."

"Well, that wasn't all. He took his whole family with him. His wife
and his two little girls."

"Oh, yes?"   60

"Those two beautiful little girls. He turned on the gas while they
were all asleep. Then he cut his stomach with a meat knife."

"Yes, Father was just telling me how Watanabe was a man of principle."

"Sick." My sister turned back to the well.

"Careful. You'll fall right in."

"I can't see any ghost," she said. "You were lying to me all that time."   65

"But I never said it lived down the well."

"Where is it then?"

We both looked around at the trees and shrubs. The daylight had almost gone. Eventually I pointed to a small clearing some ten yards
away.

"Just there I saw it. Just there."

We stared at the spot.   70

"What did it look like?"

"I couldn't see very well. It was dark."

"But you must have seen something."

"It was an old woman. She was just standing there, watching me."

We kept staring at the spot as if mesmerized.   75

"She was wearing a white kimono," I said. "Some of her hair came
undone. It was blowing around a little."

Kikuko pushed her elbow against my arm. "Oh, be quiet. You're trying to frighten me all over again." She trod on the remains of her cigarette, then for a brief moment stood regarding it with a perplexed
expression. She kicked some pine needles over it, then once more
displayed her grin. "Let's see if supper's ready," she said.

We found my father in the kitchen. He gave us a quick glance, then
carried on with what he was doing.

"Father's become quite a chef since he's had to manage on his own,"
Kikuko said with a laugh.

He turned and looked at my sister coldly. "Hardly a skill I'm proud   80
of," he said. "Kikuko, come here and help."

For some moments my sister did not move. Then she stepped forward and took an apron hanging from a drawer.

"Just these vegetables need cooking now," he said to her. "The rest just needs watching." Then he looked up and regarded me strangely for some seconds. "I expect you want to look around the house," he said eventually. He put down the chopsticks he had been holding. "It's a long time since you've seen it."

As we left the kitchen I glanced toward Kikuko, but her back was turned.

"She's a good girl," my father said.

I followed my father from room to room. I had forgotten how large   85
the house was. A panel would slide open and another room would appear. But the rooms were all startlingly empty. In one of the rooms the lights did not come on, and we stared at the stark walls and tatami in the pale light that came from the windows.

"This house is too large for a man to live in alone," my father said. "I don't have much use for most of these rooms now."

But eventually my father opened the door to a room packed full of books and papers. There were flowers in vases and pictures on the walls. Then I noticed something on a low table in the corner of the room. I came nearer and saw it was a plastic model of a battleship, the kind constructed by children. It had been placed on some newspaper; scattered around it were assorted pieces of gray plastic.

My father gave a laugh. He came up to the table and picked up the model.

"Since the firm folded," he said, "I have a little more time on my hands." He laughed again, rather strangely. For a moment his face looked almost gentle. "A little more time."

"That seems odd," I said. "You were always so busy."   90

"Too busy, perhaps." He looked at me with a small smile. "Perhaps I should have been a more attentive father."

I laughed. He went on contemplating his battleship. Then he looked up. "I hadn't meant to tell you this, but perhaps it's best that I do. It's my belief that your mother's death was no accident. She had many worries. And some disappointments."

We both gazed at the plastic battleship.

"Surely," I said eventually, "my mother didn't expect me to live here forever."

"Obviously you don't see. You don't see how it is for some parents.   95
Not only must they lose their children, they must lose them to things they don't understand." He spun the battleship in his fingers. "These little gunboats here could have been better glued, don't you think?"

"Perhaps. I think it looks fine."

"During the war I spent some time on a ship rather like this. But my ambition was always the air force. I figured it like this: If your ship was struck by the enemy, all you could do was struggle in the water hoping for a lifeline. But in an airplane — well, there was always the final weapon." He put the model back onto the table. "I don't suppose you believe in war."

"Not particularly."

He cast an eye around the room. "Supper should be ready by now," he said. "You must be hungry."

Supper was waiting in a dimly lit room next to the kitchen. The only source of light was a big lantern that hung over the table, casting the rest of the room in shadow. We bowed to each other before starting the meal.

There was little conversation. When I made some polite comment about the food, Kikuko giggled a little. Her earlier nervousness seemed to have returned to her. My father did not speak for several minutes. Finally he said:

"It must feel strange for you, being back in Japan."

"Yes, it is a little strange."

"Already, perhaps, you regret leaving America."

"A little. Not so much. I didn't leave behind much. Just some empty rooms."

"I see."

I glanced across the table. My father's face looked stony and forbidding in the half-light. We ate on in silence.

Then my eye caught something at the back of the room. At first I continued eating, then my hands became still. The others noticed and looked at me. I went on gazing into the darkness past my father's shoulder.

"Who is that? In that photograph there?"

"Which photograph?" My father turned slightly, trying to follow my gaze.

"The lowest one. The old woman in the white kimono."

My father put down his chopsticks. He looked first at the photograph, then at me.

"Your mother." His voice had become very hard. "Can't you recognize your own mother?"

"My mother. You see, it's dark. I can't see it very well."

No one spoke for a few seconds, then Kikuko rose to her feet. She took the photograph down from the wall, came back to the table, and gave it to me.

"She looks a lot older," I said.

"It was taken shortly before her death," said my father.

"It was dark. I couldn't see very well."

I looked up and noticed my father holding out a hand. I gave him the photograph. He looked at it intently, then held it toward Kikuko. Obediently, my sister rose to her feet once more and returned the picture to the wall.

There was a large pot left unopened at the center of the table. When   120 Kikuko had seated herself again, my father reached forward and lifted the lid. A cloud of steam rose up and curled toward the lantern. He pushed the pot a little toward me.

"You must be hungry," he said. One side of his face had fallen into shadow.

"Thank you." I reached forward with my chopsticks. The steam was almost scalding. "What is it?"

"Fish."

"It smells very good."

In the soup were strips of fish that had curled almost into balls. I   125 picked one out and brought it to my bowl.

"Help yourself. There's plenty."

"Thank you." I took a little more, then pushed the pot toward my father. I watched him take several pieces to his bowl. Then we both watched as Kikuko served herself.

My father bowed slightly. "You must be hungry," he said again. He took some fish to his mouth and started to eat. Then I, too, chose a piece and put it in my mouth. It felt soft, quite fleshy against my tongue.

The three of us ate in silence. Several minutes went by. My father lifted the lid and once more steam rose up. We all reached forward and helped ourselves.

"Here," I said to my father, "you have this last piece."   130

"Thank you."

When we had finished the meal, my father stretched out his arms and yawned with an air of satisfaction. "Kikuko," he said, "prepare a pot of tea, please."

My sister looked at him, then left the room without comment. My father stood up.

"Let's retire to the other room. It's rather warm in here."

I got to my feet and followed him into the tearoom. The large sliding   135 windows had been left open, bringing in a breeze from the garden. For a while we sat in silence.

"Father," I said, finally.

"Yes?"

"Kikuko tells me Watanabe-san took his whole family with him."

My father lowered his eyes and nodded. For some moments he seemed deep in thought. "Watanabe was very devoted to his work," he said at last. "The collapse of the firm was a great blow to him. I fear it must have weakened his judgment."

"You think what he did . . . it was a mistake?"   140

"Why, of course. Do you see it otherwise?"

"No, no. Of course not."

"There are other things besides work," my father said.

"Yes."

We fell silent again. The sound of locusts came in from the garden. I 145 looked out into the darkness. The well was no longer visible.

"What do you think you will do now?" my father asked. "Will you stay in Japan for a while?"

"To be honest, I hadn't thought that far ahead."

"If you wish to stay here, I mean here in this house, you would be very welcome. That is, if you don't mind living with an old man."

"Thank you. I'll have to think about it."

I gazed out once more into the darkness.   150

"But of course," said my father, "this house is so dreary now. You'll no doubt return to America before long."

"Perhaps. I don't know yet."

"No doubt you will."

For some time my father seemed to be studying the back of his hands. Then he looked up and sighed.

"Kikuko is due to complete her studies next spring," he said. "Per- 155 haps she will want to come home then. She's a good girl."

"Perhaps she will."

"Things will improve then."

"Yes, I'm sure they will."

We fell silent once more, waiting for Kikuko to bring the tea.

EXPLORATIONS

1. How would the impact of "A Family Supper" change without the opening section (paras. 1–3) on fugu? How would it change without the father's comments about his business partner (paras. 9–13 and 139–142)?

2. In what ways does Kazuo Ishiguro supply information about the relationships between the various members of the narrator's family in "A Family

Supper"? Which sources of this information do you find most and least believable, and why?

3. What are the effects of Ishiguro's telling this story from the first-person viewpoint of a participant instead of the third-person viewpoint of an outside observer? How would you interpret the story's outcome differently if it were told in the third person?

CONNECTIONS

1. What descriptions does Ishiguro supply of the house in which the story takes place? Having read John David Morley's "Acquiring a Japanese Family" (p. 185), what more do you know about the house than Ishiguro tells us?

2. "You don't see how it is for some parents," says the father in Ishiguro's story. "Not only must they lose their children, they must lose them to things they don't understand" (para. 95). Recall the information given by Morley and by Andrew Mason and Naohiro Ogawa on page 96 about Japanese parents' expectations of their children. What hopes do you think the narrator's parents in "A Family Supper" had for their son and daughter that they have failed to meet?

3. What point is Egyptian writer Naguib Mahfouz making in the Observation on page 95? In what sense might his remarks be addressed to one (or more) of the characters in "A Family Supper"? Which character in Ishiguro's story do you think would be most receptive to what Mahfouz is saying, and why?

ELABORATIONS

1. The Nobel Prize–winning Japanese writer Kenzaburo Oe has observed: "Contemporary Japan is split between two opposite poles of ambiguity. . . . The modernization of Japan was oriented toward learning from and imitating the West, yet the country is situated in Asia and has firmly maintained its traditional culture." Using "Acquiring a Japanese Family" as an additional resource, write an essay analyzing the "poles of ambiguity" Ishiguro's characters feel and represent in "A Family Supper."

2. Much of the key information in "A Family Supper" is not stated explicitly. Imagine you are a journalist assigned to go to this family's home the day after the well-known retiree's supper with his children and write an article about their reunion. In your news story, state the important facts that Ishiguro has revealed indirectly.

PART THREE

TURNING POINTS

OBSERVATIONS

Clive Barker, Bob Seger, Gail Sheehy, Michael Dorris,
Gloria Anzaldúa, Malcolm X with Alex Halcy,
Sven Birkerts, Günter Grass,
Joseph Brodsky, Aleksandr Solzhenitsyn, Kit R. Roane

▼ ▼ ▼

Maya Angelou, *Mary* (UNITED STATES)

Liliana Heker, *The Stolen Party* (ARGENTINA)

Sophronia Liu, *So Tsi-fai* (HONG KONG)

Andre Dubus, *Imperiled Men* (UNITED STATES)

T. Coraghessan Boyle, *Achates McNeil* (UNITED STATES)

James Baldwin, *The New Lost Generation*
(UNITED STATES/FRANCE)

Richard Rodriguez, *Europe Once Gripped
America's Imagination — Now It's the Other Way Around*
(UNITED STATES/EUROPE)

Alessandra Stanley, *The New Europeans: Multilingual,
Cosmopolitan, Borderless* (EUROPE)

Nadine Gordimer, *Where Do Whites Fit In?* (SOUTH AFRICA)

Robert Reich, *The Three Jobs of the Future* (UNITED STATES)

OBSERVATIONS

As a child you are given dream time as part of your fictional life. Into your hands go the books of dream travel, Dorothy's dream travel, the Darling family's dream travel in *Peter Pan*, the children of Narnia. You're given books in which children with whom you identify take journeys which are essentially dream journeys. They are to places in which the fantastical not only happens, but is commonplace. Alice falls down a hole, the Darling children take flight, the tornado picks up Dorothy's house. These children are removed and taken to a place which is essentially a place of dreams.

And then, at the age of five or something like that, they start to teach you the gross national product of Chile. And you're left thinking, Wait! What happened to Oz and Never-Never Land and Narnia? Are they no longer relevant? One of the things you're taught is No! they are no longer relevant. They are, as it were, a sweet introduction to the business of living. And now comes the real stuff — so get on with it.

> — CLIVE BARKER
> *Writers Dreaming*
> (Naomi Epel, ed.), 1993

▼ ▼ ▼

I wish I didn't know now what I didn't know then.

> — BOB SEGER
> "Against the Wind"
> *Against the Wind*, 1980

▼ ▼ ▼

After eighteen, we begin Pulling Up Roots in earnest. College, military service, and short-term travels are all customary vehicles our society provides for the first round trips between family and a base of one's own. In the attempt to separate our view of the world from our family's view, despite vigorous protestations to the contrary — "I know exactly what I want!" — we cast about for any beliefs we can call our own. And in the process of testing those beliefs we are often drawn to fads, preferably those most mysterious and inaccessible to our parents. . . .

A stormy passage through the Pulling Up Roots years will probably facilitate the normal progression of the adult life cycle. If one doesn't have an identity crisis at this point, it will erupt during a later transition, when the penalties may be harder to bear.

> — GAIL SHEEHY
> *Passages*, 1974

▼ ▼ ▼

In most cultures, adulthood is equated with self-reliance and responsibility, yet often Americans do not achieve this status until we are in our late twenties or early thirties — virtually the entire average lifespan of a person in a traditional non-Western society. We tend to treat prolonged adolescence as a warm-up for real life, as a wobbly suspension bridge between childhood and legal maturity. Whereas a nineteenth-century Cheyenne or Lakota teenager was expected to alter self-conception in a split-second vision, we often meander through an analogous rite of passage for more than a decade — through high school, college, graduate school.

Though he had never before traveled alone outside his village, the Plains Indian male was expected at puberty to venture solo into the wilderness. There he had to fend for and sustain himself while avoiding the menace of unknown dangers, and there he had absolutely to remain until something happened that would transform him. Every human being, these tribes believed, was entitled to at least one moment of personal, enabling insight.

Anthropology proposes feasible psychological explanations for why this flash was eventually triggered: Fear, fatigue, reliance on strange foods, the anguish of loneliness, stress, and the expectation of ultimate success all contributed to a state of receptivity. Every sense was quickened, altered to perceive deep meaning, until at last the interpretation of an unusual event — a dream, a chance encounter, or an unexpected vista — reverberated with metaphor. Through this unique prism, abstractly preserved in a vivid memory or song, a boy caught foresight of both his adult persona and of his vocation, the two inextricably entwined.

– Michael Dorris
"Life Stories"
Antaeus, 1989

▼ ▼ ▼

Coyolxhauqui was the Aztec moon goddess; her brother Huitzilopochtli dismembered her. He started human sacrifice and she was the first. In taking the risk to make a work, to write that poem or story or theoretical piece, you may feel like the moon goddess — like you are jumping off the temple steps or off a cliff. You land at the bottom and you're broken in pieces. At this stage your work is shit, it doesn't say anything. But the next step in the creative process is picking up the pieces and moving them around — restructuring that broken body of Coyolxhauqui. You don't put her together in the same way; you end up with something new, and something has changed in you because of going

210

through this struggle. You end up not quite the same person that you were. And the viewer or reader of your piece also undergoes a change of consciousness, moving from a before to an after. That traversal I call the *nepantla* stage — between the worlds.

I see what's happening to our country in the same way; we're going through a stage of being pulled apart. We're trying to recompose the nation — recreate it. A person who is undergoing therapy for a trauma like incest or assault is doing the same thing, and so is a mathematician or a scientist trying to figure out new theories.

— GLORIA ANZALDÚA
"Afterthoughts"
Utne Reader, 1996

▼ ▼ ▼

I had come to the Norfolk Prison Colony still going through only book-reading motions. Pretty soon, I would have quit even these motions, unless I had received the motivation that I did.

I saw that the best thing I could do was get hold of a dictionary — to study, to learn some words. I was lucky enough to reason also that I should try to improve my penmanship. It was sad. I couldn't even write in a straight line. It was both ideas together that moved me to request a dictionary along with some tablets and pencils from the Norfolk Prison Colony school.

. . . I started copying what eventually became the entire dictionary. It went a lot faster after so much practice helped me to pick up handwriting speed. Between what I wrote in my tablet, and writing letters, during the rest of my time in prison I would guess I wrote a million words.

I suppose it was inevitable that as my word base broadened, I could for the first time pick up a book and read and now begin to understand what the book was saying. Anyone who has read a great deal can imagine the new world that opened. Let me tell you something: From then until I left that prison, in every free moment I had, if I was not reading in the library, I was reading on my bunk. You couldn't have gotten me out of books with a wedge. . . . Months passed without my even thinking about being imprisoned. In fact, up to then, I never had been so truly free in my life. . . .

I have often reflected upon the new vistas that reading opened to me. I knew right there in prison that reading had changed forever the course of my life. As I see it today, the ability to read awoke inside me some long dormant craving to be mentally alive. I certainly wasn't seeking any degree, the way a college confers a status symbol upon its students. My homemade education gave me, with every additional book that I

211

read, a little bit more sensitivity to the deafness, dumbness, and blindness that was afflicting the black race in America. Not long ago, an English writer telephoned me from London, asking questions. One was, "What's your alma mater?" I told him, "Books." You will never catch me with a free fifteen minutes in which I'm not studying something I feel might be able to help the black man.

– Malcolm X with Alex Haley
"Learning to Read"
The Autobiography of Malcolm X, 1964

▼ ▼ ▼

When we look at the large-scale shift to an electronic culture, looking as if at a time-lapse motion study, we can see not only how our situation has come about but also how it is in our nature that it should have. At every step — this is clear — we trade for ease. And ease is what quickly swallows up the initial strangeness of a new medium or tool. Moreover, each accommodation paves the way for the next. The telegraph must have seemed to its first users a surpassingly strange device, but its newfangledness was overridden by its usefulness. Once we had accepted the idea of mechanical transmission over distances, the path was clear for the telephone. Again, a monumental transformation: turn select digits on a dial and hear the voice of another human being. And on it goes, the inventions coming gradually, one by one, allowing society to adapt. We mastered the telephone, the television with its few networks running black-and-white programs. And although no law required citizens to own or use either, these technologies did in a remarkably short time achieve near total saturation.

We are, then, accustomed to the process; we take the step that will enlarge our reach, simplify our communication, and abbreviate our physical involvement in some task or chore. The difference between the epoch of early modernity and the present is — to simplify drastically — that formerly the body had time to accept the graft, the new organ, whereas now we are hurtling forward willy-nilly, assuming that if a technology is connected with communications or information processing it must be good, we must need it. I never cease to be astonished at what a mere two decades have brought us. Consider the evidence. Since the early 1970s we have seen the arrival of — we have accepted, deemed all but indispensable — personal computers, laptops, telephone-answering machines, calling cards, fax machines, cellular phones, VCRs, modems, Nintendo games, E-mail, voice mail, camcorders, and CD players. Very quickly, with almost no pause between increments, these circuit-driven tools and entertainments have moved into our lives, and with a minimum rippling of the waters, really — which, of course, makes them seem natural, even inevitable. Which perhaps they are. Marshall McLuhan called improvements of this sort "extensions of man," and this is their secret. We embrace them because they seem a part of us, an enhancement. They don't seem to challenge our power so much as add to it.

I am startled, though, by how little we are debating the deeper philosophical ramifications. We talk up a storm when it comes to policy issues — who should have jurisdiction, what rates may be charged — and there is great fascination in some quarters with the practical minutiae of functioning, compatibility, and so on. But why do we hear so few people asking whether we might not *ourselves* be changing, and whether the changes are necessarily for the good?

– SVEN BIRKERTS
"The Electronic Hive"
Harper's, May 1994

▼ ▼ ▼

In May 1945, when I was seventeen years of age, living with a hundred thousand others in an American prison camp out under the open sky, in a foxhole, I was famished, and because of this I focused, with a cunning born of hunger, exclusively on survival — otherwise I had not a clear notion in my head. Rendered stupid by dogma and accordingly fixated on lofty goals: This was the state in which the Third Reich released me and many of my generation from our oaths of loyalty. "The flag is superior to death" was one of its life-denying certainties.

All this stupidity resulted not only from a schooling knocked full of holes by the war — when I reached fifteen, my time as Luftwaffe helper began, which I mistakenly welcomed as liberation from school — it was, rather, an overarching stupidity, one that transcended difference of class and religion, one that was nourished by German complacency. Its ideological slogans usually began with "We Germans are . . . ," "To be German means . . . ," and, finally, "A German would never . . ."

This last-quoted rule lasted even beyond the capitulation of the Greater German Reich and took on the stubborn force of incorrigibility. For when I, with many of my generation — leaving aside our fathers and mothers for now — was confronted with the results of the crimes for which Germans were responsible, crimes that would be summed up in the image of *Auschwitz*, I said: Impossible. I said to myself and to others, and others said to themselves and to me: "Germans would never do a thing like that."

– GÜNTER GRASS
"Writing After Auschwitz"
Two States — One Nation, 1990

▼ ▼ ▼

Ambivalence, I think, is the chief characteristic of my nation. There isn't a Russian executioner who isn't scared of turning victim one day, nor is there the sorriest victim who would [not] acknowledge (if only to himself) a mental ability to become an executioner. Our immediate history has provided well for both. There is some wisdom in this. One might even think that this ambivalence *is* wisdom, that life itself is neither good nor bad, but arbitrary.

– JOSEPH BRODSKY
Less than One: Selected Essays, 1986

▼ ▼ ▼

Man has from the beginning been so constituted that his view of the world (if it is not induced by hypnosis), his motivations and scale of values, his actions and his intentions, are all defined by his experience as an individual and as a member of a group. In the words of the Russian proverb: "Your brother, he might lie; trust instead your own bad eye." This is the soundest of bases for understanding one's environment and for acting in it. And for many long centuries, while our world was completely and mysteriously dispersed — before it was interlaced by unbroken lines of communication and turned into a single feverishly throbbing mass — people were unfailingly guided by their own experience within their community, within their society, and finally within their national territory. At that time it was possible for the individual human eye to see and accept a certain common scale of values: what was considered average, what unbelievable; what was cruel, what was beyond villainy; what constituted honesty, and what deceit. And even though the scattered nations lived quite differently, and the scales of their social values could diverge as strikingly as their systems of measurement, these discrepancies astonished only the infrequent wayfarer or turned up as curiosities in magazines. They held no danger for humanity, which was not yet united.

But in the course of the last few decades, humanity has imperceptibly and suddenly become united — a unity fraught with hope and with danger — so that shocks or inflammations in one part are instantly passed on to the other portions — some of which may well lack the appropriate immunity. Humanity has become one, but it is not the stable undividedness of a former community or even that of a nation. It is a unity achieved not by means of gradually acquired experience, not from the eye, affably referred to as "bad" in the proverb, not even through a common native language; but rather — surmounting all barriers — this unity brought about by international radio and the press. Onrushing waves of events bear down upon us: Half the world learns in one minute of what is splashed ashore. But lacking are the scales or yardsticks to measure these events and to evaluate them according to the laws of the parts of the world unfamiliar to us.

— ALEKSANDR SOLZHENITSYN
"The Nobel Lecture on Literature," 1972

▼ ▼ ▼

Amina Brka, fourteen, returned this week to a world she had only seen on television and read about in letters from home. This was her country, but it bore little resemblance to the one she had left nearly four years ago. Much of its beauty had been burned or mangled under the barrage of war, and when she rode into Sarajevo, she was surprised that anything was left at all.

"It's not as bad as I had pictured it," Amina said as she tussled with new school books on her first day of class here. "My visions were much worse. And from the pictures I saw on television, with all the grenades thrown from the mountains, I thought Sarajevo had been flattened."

Amina, who is Muslim, is one of more than 300 pupils returning after a long hiatus; peace is expected to bring many more. They enter a situation both familiar and strange to them. They are forced to pick up survival skills from others and cull the reality from the stories they hear on the streets. . . .

There is much to cull from the ruins. In her class, children described famine. Their teachers recalled months when shelling was so heavy that children never left their basements, and the false moments of calm that always ended in massacre. On some of these days, teachers said, children watched their parents blown apart, then went out to play without shedding a tear in public.

"The shocking thing is their understanding of death," said Casar Jadranka, a general studies teacher. "Normal people are shocked by death. These kids take it lightly."

"It's just no big deal anymore," said Spaho Sanin, fourteen, as he lounged in the back of a chilly chemistry class. "A girl in our class found a gun and blew her head off last week and an old woman hanged herself in her closet just a while ago.

"There have been a lot of people killed during the war and I believe there has been a suicide in every building in the city," he added. "People are just not normal anymore."

– KIT R. ROANE
"For Bosnian Schoolgirl
an Uneasy Homecoming"
New York Times, 1995

EXPLORATIONS

1. Which other Observations for this chapter contain the same idea as the lines from Bob Seger's song "Against the Wind" (p. 209)? Which Observations contain a contrasting idea about knowledge, and what is it?

2. Compare Kit R. Roane's description of postwar Sarajevo with the Observations by Günter Grass (p. 213) and Joseph Brodsky (p. 213). What do you think are the reasons why "these kids take [death] lightly" and "there has been a suicide in every building in the city" (Roane, p. 215)?

3. What similar ideas about technological change are expressed by Aleksandr Solzhenitsyn (p. 214) and Sven Birkerts (p. 212)? Which writer focuses more on the causes of change, and which one on its effects? How do you think Solzhenitsyn would answer Birkerts's final question?

MAYA ANGELOU

Mary

Maya Angelou came to nationwide attention in 1993 when President Clinton asked her to compose an original poem ("On the Pulse of Morning"), which she delivered at his inauguration. In 1995 Angelou starred in the film *How to Make an American Quilt*; in 1998 she directed *Down in the Delta*. She was already known to television audiences for her performance in Alex Haley's serial *Roots*, for which she received an Emmy Award nomination.

At the time "Mary" took place, Angelou was still going by her birth name, Marguerite Johnson. Born in St. Louis, Missouri, in 1928, by the age of sixteen she had survived rape, the breakup of her family, and unwed motherhood. (The rapist was her mother's friend Mr. Freeman, who was tried, convicted, and later found beaten to death — the sequence of events Angelou refers to in paragraph 21.) Support from her mother and her brother, Bailey, helped to keep her going through five years in which she never spoke. She later became a dancer, appeared in several plays (including a twenty-two-nation tour of *Porgy and Bess*), worked with the Harlem Writers' Guild, lived in Ghana, and produced a series on Africa for the Public Broadcasting System. Angelou has been awarded numerous honorary doctorates and, at the request of Martin Luther King Jr., served as a coordinator for the Southern Christian Leadership Conference. President Ford appointed her to the Bicentennial Commission and President Carter to the Commission of International Woman's Year. The author of many books of poetry, songs and musical scores, plays, and screenplays, Angelou is best known for her five-volume autobiography. "Mary" comes from the first volume, *I Know Why the Caged Bird Sings* (1970), which recounts her childhood in Stamps, Arkansas. She currently lives in North Carolina, where she holds a lifetime chair in American Studies at Wake Forest University.

Recently a white woman from Texas, who would quickly describe herself as a liberal, asked me about my hometown. When I told her that in Stamps my grandmother had owned the only Negro general merchandise store since the turn of the century, she exclaimed, "Why, you were a debutante." Ridiculous and even ludicrous. But Negro girls in small Southern towns, whether poverty-stricken or just munching along on a few of life's necessities, were given as extensive and irrelevant preparations for adulthood as rich white girls shown in magazines. Admittedly the training was not the same. While white girls learned to waltz and sit gracefully with a tea cup balanced on their knees, we were lagging behind, learning the mid-Victorian values with very little money to indulge them. (Come and see Edna Lomax spending the money she made picking cotton on five balls of ecru tatting thread. Her fingers are bound to snag the work and she'll have to repeat the stitches time and time again. But she knows that when she buys the thread.)

We were required to embroider and I had trunkfuls of colorful dish-towels, pillowcases, runners, and handkerchiefs to my credit. I mastered the art of crocheting and tatting, and there was a lifetime's supply of dainty doilies that would never be used in sacheted dresser drawers. It went without saying that all girls could iron and wash, but the finer touches around the home, like setting a table with real silver, baking roasts, and cooking vegetables without meat, had to be learned elsewhere. Usually at the source of those habits. During my tenth year, a white woman's kitchen became my finishing school.

Mrs. Viola Cullinan was a plump woman who lived in a three-bedroom house somewhere behind the post office. She was singularly unattractive until she smiled, and then the lines around her eyes and mouth which made her look perpetually dirty disappeared, and her face looked like the mask of an impish elf. She usually rested her smile until late afternoon when her women friends dropped in and Miss Glory, the cook, served them cold drinks on the closed-in porch.

The exactness of her house was inhuman. This glass went here and only here. That cup had its place and it was an act of impudent rebellion to place it anywhere else. At twelve o'clock the table was set. At 12:15 Mrs. Cullinan sat down to dinner (whether her husband had arrived or not). At 12:16 Miss Glory brought out the food.

It took me a week to learn the difference between a salad plate, a bread plate, and a dessert plate.   5

Mrs. Cullinan kept up the tradition of her wealthy parents. She was from Virginia. Miss Glory, who was a descendant of slaves that had worked for the Cullinans, told me her history. She had married beneath her (according to Miss Glory). Her husband's family hadn't had their money very long and what they had "didn't 'mount to much."

As ugly as she was, I thought privately, she was lucky to get a husband above or beneath her station. But Miss Glory wouldn't let me say a thing against her mistress. She was very patient with me, however, over the housework. She explained the dishware, silverware, and servants' bells.

The large round bowl in which soup was served wasn't a soup bowl, it was a tureen. There were goblets, sherbet glasses, ice-cream glasses, wine glasses, green glass coffee cups with matching saucers, and water glasses. I had a glass to drink from, and it sat with Miss Glory's on a separate shelf from the others. Soup spoons, gravy boat, butter knives, salad forks, and carving platter were additions to my vocabulary and in fact almost represented a new language. I was fascinated with the novelty, with the fluttering Mrs. Cullinan and her Alice-in-Wonderland house.

Her husband remains, in my memory, undefined. I lumped him with all the other white men that I had ever seen and tried not to see.

On our way home one evening, Miss Glory told me that Mrs. Culli-   10 nan couldn't have children. She said that she was too delicate-boned. It was hard to imagine bones at all under those layers of fat. Miss Glory went on to say that the doctor had taken out all her lady organs. I reasoned that a pig's organs included the lungs, heart, and liver, so if Mrs. Cullinan was walking around without those essentials, it explained why she drank alcohol out of unmarked bottles. She was keeping herself embalmed.

When I spoke to Bailey about it, he agreed that I was right, but he also informed me that Mr. Cullinan had two daughters by a colored lady and that I knew them very well. He added that the girls were the spitting image of their father. I was unable to remember what he looked like, although I had just left him a few hours before, but I thought of the Coleman girls. They were very light-skinned and certainly didn't look very much like their mother (no one ever mentioned Mr. Coleman).

My pity for Mrs. Cullinan preceded me the next morning like the Cheshire cat's smile. Those girls, who could have been her daughters, were beautiful. They didn't have to straighten their hair. Even when they were caught in the rain, their braids still hung down straight like tamed snakes. Their mouths were pouty little cupid's bows. Mrs. Cullinan didn't know what she missed. Or maybe she did. Poor Mrs. Cullinan.

For weeks after, I arrived early, left late, and tried very hard to make up for her barrenness. If she had had her own children, she wouldn't have had to ask me to run a thousand errands from her back door to the back door of her friends. Poor old Mrs. Cullinan.

Then one evening Miss Glory told me to serve the ladies on the porch. After I set the tray down and turned toward the kitchen, one of the women asked, "What's your name, girl?" It was the speckled-faced one. Mrs. Cullinan said, "She doesn't talk much. Her name's Margaret."

"Is she dumb?"   15

"No. As I understand it, she can talk when she wants to but she's usually quiet as a little mouse. Aren't you, Margaret?"

I smiled at her. Poor thing. No organs and couldn't even pronounce my name correctly.

"She's a sweet little thing, though."

"Well, that may be, but the name's too long. I'd never bother myself. I'd call her Mary if I was you."

I fumed into the kitchen. That horrible woman would never have   20
the chance to call me Mary because if I was starving I'd never work for her. I decided I wouldn't pee on her if her heart was on fire. Giggles drifted in off the porch and into Miss Glory's pots. I wondered what they could be laughing about.

Whitefolks were so strange. Could they be talking about me? Everybody knew that they stuck together better than the Negroes did. It was possible that Mrs. Cullinan had friends in St. Louis who heard about a girl from Stamps being in court and wrote to tell her. Maybe she knew about Mr. Freeman.

My lunch was in my mouth a second time and I went outside and relieved myself on the bed of four-o'clocks. Miss Glory thought I might be coming down with something and told me to go on home, that Momma would give me some herb tea, and she'd explain to her mistress.

I realized how foolish I was being before I reached the pond. Of course Mrs. Cullinan didn't know. Otherwise she wouldn't have given me the two nice dresses that Momma cut down, and she certainly wouldn't have called me a "sweet little thing." My stomach felt fine, and I didn't mention anything to Momma.

That evening I decided to write a poem on being white, fat, old, and without children. It was going to be a tragic ballad. I would have to watch her carefully to capture the essence of her loneliness and pain.

The very next day, she called me by the wrong name. Miss Glory   25
and I were washing up the lunch dishes when Mrs. Cullinan came to the doorway. "Mary?"

Miss Glory asked, "Who?"

Mrs. Cullinan, sagging a little, knew and I knew. "I want Mary to go down to Mrs. Randall's and take her some soup. She's not been feeling well for a few days."

Miss Glory's face was a wonder to see. "You mean Margaret, ma'am. Her name's Margaret."

"That's too long. She's Mary from now on. Heat that soup from last night and put it in the china tureen and, Mary, I want you to carry it carefully."

Every person I knew had a hellish horror of being "called out of his   30
name." It was a dangerous practice to call a Negro anything that could
be loosely construed as insulting because of the centuries of their
having been called niggers, jigs, dinges, blackbirds, crows, boots, and
spooks.

Miss Glory had a fleeting second of feeling sorry for me. Then as she
handed me the hot tureen she said, "Don't mind, don't pay that no
mind. Sticks and stones may break your bones, but words . . . You
know, I been working for her for twenty years."

She held the back door open for me. "Twenty years. I wasn't much
older than you. My name used to be Hallelujah. That's what Ma named
me, but my mistress give me 'Glory,' and it stuck. I likes it better too."

I was in the little path that ran behind the houses when Miss Glory
shouted, "It's shorter too."

For a few seconds it was a tossup over whether I would laugh (imagine being named Hallelujah) or cry (imagine letting some white
woman rename you for her convenience). My anger saved me from either outburst. I had to quit the job, but the problem was going to be
how to do it. Momma wouldn't allow me to quit for just any reason.

"She's a peach. That woman is a real peach." Mrs. Randall's maid   35
was talking as she took the soup from me, and I wondered what her
name used to be and what she answered to now.

For a week I looked into Mrs. Cullinan's face as she called me Mary.
She ignored my coming late and leaving early. Miss Glory was a little
annoyed because I had begun to leave egg yolk on the dishes and wasn't
putting much heart in polishing the silver. I hoped that she would complain to our boss, but she didn't.

Then Bailey solved my dilemma. He had me describe the contents
of the cupboard and the particular plates she liked best. Her favorite
piece was a casserole shaped like a fish and the green glass coffee cups.
I kept his instructions in mind, so on the next day when Miss Glory was
hanging out clothes and I had again been told to serve the old biddies
on the porch, I dropped the empty serving tray. When I heard Mrs.
Cullinan scream, "Mary!" I picked up the casserole and two of the
green glass cups in readiness. As she rounded the kitchen door I let
them fall on the tiled floor.

I could never absolutely describe to Bailey what happened next, because each time I got to the part where she fell on the floor and screwed
up her ugly face to cry, we burst out laughing. She actually wobbled
around on the floor and picked up shards of the cups and cried, "Oh,
Momma. Oh, dear Gawd. It's Momma's china from Virginia. Oh,
Momma, I sorry."

Miss Glory came running in from the yard and the women from the porch crowded around. Miss Glory was almost as broken up as her mistress. "You mean to say she broke our Virginia dishes? What we gone do?"

Mrs. Cullinan cried louder, "That clumsy nigger. Clumsy little black   40 nigger."

Old speckled-face leaned down and asked, "Who did it, Viola? Was it Mary? Who did it?"

Everything was happening so fast I can't remember whether her action preceded her words, but I know that Mrs. Cullinan said, "Her name's Margaret, goddamn it, her name's Margaret!" And she threw a wedge of the broken plate at me. It could have been the hysteria which put her aim off, but the flying crockery caught Miss Glory right over her ear and she started screaming.

I left the front door wide open so all the neighbors could hear.

Mrs. Cullinan was right about one thing. My name wasn't Mary.

EXPLORATIONS

1. When Maya Angelou first goes to work for Mrs. Cullinan, what is her attitude toward her employer? At what points does her attitude change, in what ways, and for what reasons?

2. What reason does Angelou give for a black person's horror of being "called out of his name" (para. 30)? Why does she find her change of name so offensive?

3. In paragraph 24, young Marguerite decides "to write a poem on being white, fat, old, and without children." Why do you think she wanted to do this? What personal goals does Angelou seem to have achieved by writing about Mrs. Cullinan in her autobiography?

CONNECTIONS

1. How does Angelou's reaction to being renamed by Mrs. Cullinan illustrate the creative process Gloria Anzaldúa describes on page 210? What specific comments by Anzaldúa apply to the events (internal as well as overt) in "Mary"?

2. In what ways does Angelou's account exemplify the points made by Henry Louis Gates Jr. (p. 4)? Which of Gates's "appellations" best fit the era and consciousness Angelou describes?

3. In paragraphs 1–2 Angelou compares the "extensive and irrelevant prepara-

tions for adulthood" of Negro and white girls in her hometown. How do these two sets of preparations compare with the preparations described by Susan Orlean in "Quinceañera" (p. 36)? In each case, what kind of adulthood are the girls being prepared for? What aspects of their training are especially relevant and irrelevant to the futures they face?

ELABORATIONS

1. How old were you when you first worked for money? What do you remember of your reactions to the job, the people involved, and having an income? What were the sources of conflict? Using "Mary" as a model, write an essay about your recollections.

2. In paragraph 4 Angelou describes the "inhuman" exactness of Mrs. Cullinan's house: glasses precisely placed, meals precisely scheduled. Do you know anyone who is so demanding? Is there any aspect of your life — the way you arrange your desk, a recipe you prepare, specialized clothing you put on for some activity — that is so exact? Write a descriptive or process analysis essay about your experience with exactness.

LILIANA HEKER

The Stolen Party

Argentine journalist and fiction writer Liliana Heker was born in 1943 in Buenos Aires, where she still lives. She published her highly regarded first volume of short stories, *Those Who Beheld the Burning Bush*, while still in her teens. As editor in chief of the literary magazine *El Ornitorrinco* ("The platypus") from 1977 to 1986, Heker kept open a national forum for writers throughout Argentina's chaotic and bloody military dictatorships. Rather than flee the country, she took a position similar to Nadine Gordimer's in South Africa (see p. 284): "To be heard, we must shout from within." Heker's second novel, *Zona de Clivage*, was published in 1988 and won the Buenos Aires Municipal Prize. In 1997 she was awarded a fellowship at the Civitella Ranieri Center for artists near Perugia, Italy. "The Stolen Party," first published in 1982, was translated from the Spanish by Alberto Manguel for his anthology *Other Fires* (1985). It later became the title story of Heker's 1994 short-story collection in English.

Four times the size of Texas, Argentina occupies most of South America's southern tip. When the first Spanish settlers appeared in the early 1500s, nomadic Indians roamed the pampas. By the late 1800s nearly all of them had been killed, making room for the influx of Europeans who today are 97 percent of the population. Argentina had won independence from Spain in 1819; by the century's end it was the most prosperous, educated, and industrialized Latin American nation. Military dictatorships and coups have dominated this century, however. Aside from General Juan Perón, elected president from 1946 to 1955 and again in 1973, most regimes have been nasty, brutish, and short-lived. Argentina's failed attempt to take the Islas Malvinas (Falkland Islands) from Great Britain in 1982 led to the first general election since Perón's, which established a democratic government in this economically beleaguered nation. Political and military jockeying for power continued throughout the 1980s. Despite opposition from former military officers and some of his fellow Peronists, President Carlos Menem's aggressive economic policies slowed inflation and the budget deficit; however, the trade deficit, foreign debt, and the gap between rich and poor kept widening, provoking political shifts and continuing economic turmoil throughout the nineties.

As soon as she arrived she went straight to the kitchen to see if the monkey was there. It was: What a relief! She wouldn't have liked to admit that her mother had been right. *Monkeys at a birthday?* her mother had sneered. *Get away with you, believing any nonsense you're told!* She was cross, but not because of the monkey, the girl thought; it's just because of the party.

"I don't like you going," she told her. "It's a rich people's party."

"Rich people go to Heaven too," said the girl, who studied religion at school.

"Get away with Heaven," said the mother. "The problem with you, young lady, is that you like to fart higher than your ass."

The girl didn't approve of the way her mother spoke. She was barely   5
nine, and one of the best in her class.

"I'm going because I've been invited," she said. "And I've been invited because Luciana is my friend. So there."

"Ah yes, your friend," her mother grumbled. She paused. "Listen, Rosaura," she said at last. "That one's not your friend. You know what you are to them? The maid's daughter, that's what."

Rosaura blinked hard: She wasn't going to cry. Then she yelled: "Shut up! You know nothing about being friends!"

Every afternoon she used to go to Luciana's house and they would both finish their homework while Rosaura's mother did the cleaning. They had their tea in the kitchen and they told each other secrets. Rosaura loved everything in the big house, and she also loved the people who lived there.

"I'm going because it will be the most lovely party in the whole   10
world, Luciana told me it would. There will be a magician, and he will bring a monkey and everything."

The mother swung around to take a good look at her child, and pompously put her hands on her hips.

"Monkeys at a birthday?" she said. "Get away with you, believing any nonsense you're told!"

Rosaura was deeply offended. She thought it unfair of her mother to accuse other people of being liars simply because they were rich. Rosaura too wanted to be rich, of course. If one day she managed to live in a beautiful palace, would her mother stop loving her? She felt very sad. She wanted to go to that party more than anything else in the world.

"I'll die if I don't go," she whispered, almost without moving her lips.

And she wasn't sure whether she had been heard, but on the morn-   15
ing of the party she discovered that her mother had starched her Christmas dress. And in the afternoon, after washing her hair, her mother

rinsed it in apple vinegar so that it would be all nice and shiny. Before going out, Rosaura admired herself in the mirror, with her white dress and glossy hair, and thought she looked terribly pretty.

Señora Ines also seemed to notice. As soon as she saw her, she said: "How lovely you look today, Rosaura."

Rosaura gave her starched skirt a slight toss with her hands and walked into the party with a firm step. She said hello to Luciana and asked about the monkey. Luciana put on a secretive look and whispered into Rosaura's ear: "He's in the kitchen. But don't tell anyone, because it's a surprise."

Rosaura wanted to make sure. Carefully she entered the kitchen and there she saw it: deep in thought, inside its cage. It looked so funny that the girl stood there for a while, watching it, and later, every so often, she would slip out of the party unseen and go and admire it. Rosaura was the only one allowed into the kitchen. Señora Ines had said: "You yes, but not the others, they're much too boisterous, they might break something." Rosaura had never broken anything. She even managed the jug of orange juice, carrying it from the kitchen into the dining room. She held it carefully and didn't spill a single drop. And Señora Ines had said: "Are you sure you can manage a jug as big as that?" Of course she could manage. She wasn't a butterfingers, like the others. Like that blonde girl with the bow in her hair. As soon as she saw Rosaura, the girl with the bow had said:

"And you? Who are you?"   20

"I'm a friend of Luciana," said Rosaura.

"No," said the girl with the bow, "you are not a friend of Luciana because I'm her cousin and I know all her friends. And I don't know you."

"So what," said Rosaura. "I come here every afternoon with my mother and we do our homework together."

"You and your mother do your homework together?" asked the girl, laughing.

"I and Luciana do our homework together," said Rosaura, very seri-   25
ously.

The girl with the bow shrugged her shoulders.

"That's not being friends," she said. "Do you go to school together?"

"No."

"So where do you know her from?" said the girl, getting impatient.

Rosaura remembered her mother's words perfectly. She took a deep   30
breath.

"I'm the daughter of the employee," she said.

Her mother had said very clearly: "If someone asks, you say you're the daughter of the employee; that's all." She also told her to add: "And proud of it." But Rosaura thought that never in her life would she dare say something of the sort.

"What employee?" said the girl with the bow. "Employee in a shop?"

"No," said Rosaura angrily. "My mother doesn't sell anything in any shop, so there."

"So how come she's an employee?" said the girl with the bow.   35

Just then Señora Ines arrived saying *shh shh*, and asked Rosaura if she wouldn't mind helping serve out the hotdogs, as she knew the house so much better than the others.

"See?" said Rosaura to the girl with the bow, and when no one was looking she kicked her in the shin.

Apart from the girl with the bow, all the others were delightful. The one she liked best was Luciana, with her golden birthday crown; and then the boys. Rosaura won the sack race, and nobody managed to catch her when they played tag. When they split into two teams to play charades, all the boys wanted her for their side. Rosaura felt she had never been so happy in all her life.

But the best was still to come. The best came after Luciana blew out the candles. First the cake. Señora Ines had asked her to help pass the cake around, and Rosaura had enjoyed the task immensely, because everyone called out to her, shouting "Me, me!" Rosaura remembered a story in which there was a queen who had the power of life or death over her subjects. She had always loved that, having the power of life or death. To Luciana and the boys she gave the largest pieces, and to the girl with the bow she gave a slice so thin one could see through it.

After the cake came the magician, tall and bony, with a fine red   40 cape. A true magician: He could untie handkerchiefs by blowing on them and make a chain with links that had no openings. He could guess what cards were pulled out from a pack, and the monkey was his assistant. He called the monkey "partner." "Let's see here, partner," he would say, "turn over a card." And, "Don't run away, partner: Time to work now."

The final trick was wonderful. One of the children had to hold the monkey in his arms and the magician said he would make him disappear.

"What, the boy?" they all shouted.

"No, the monkey!" shouted back the magician.

Rosaura thought that this was truly the most amusing party in the whole world.

The magician asked a small fat boy to come and help, but the small   45 fat boy got frightened almost at once and dropped the monkey on the floor. The magician picked him up carefully, whispered something in his ear, and the monkey nodded almost as if he understood.

"You mustn't be so unmanly, my friend," the magician said to the fat boy.

"What's unmanly?" said the fat boy.

The magician turned around as if to look for spies.

"A sissy," said the magician. "Go sit down."

Then he stared at all the faces, one by one. Rosaura felt her heart   50
tremble.

"You, with the Spanish eyes," said the magician. And everyone saw that he was pointing at her.

She wasn't afraid. Neither holding the monkey, nor when the magician made him vanish; not even when, at the end, the magician flung his red cape over Rosaura's head and uttered a few magic words . . . and the monkey reappeared, chattering happily, in her arms. The children clapped furiously. And before Rosaura returned to her seat, the magician said:

"Thank you very much, my little countess."

She was so pleased with the compliment that a while later, when her mother came to fetch her, that was the first thing she told her.

"I helped the magician and he said to me, 'Thank you very much,   55
my little countess.'"

It was strange because up to then Rosaura had thought that she was angry with her mother. All along Rosaura had imagined that she would say to her: "See that the monkey wasn't a lie?" But instead she was so thrilled that she told her mother all about the wonderful magician.

Her mother tapped her on the head and said: "So now we're a countess!"

But one could see that she was beaming.

And now they both stood in the entrance, because a moment ago Señora Ines, smiling, had said: "Please wait here a second."

Her mother suddenly seemed worried.   60

"What is it?" she asked Rosaura.

"What is what?" said Rosaura. "It's nothing; she just wants to get the presents for those who are leaving, see?"

She pointed at the fat boy and at a girl with pigtails who were also waiting there, next to their mothers. And she explained about the presents. She knew, because she had been watching those who left before her. When one of the girls was about to leave, Señora Ines would give her a bracelet. When a boy left, Señora Ines gave him a yo-yo. Rosaura preferred the yo-yo because it sparkled, but she didn't mention that to her mother. Her mother might have said: "So why don't you ask for one, you blockhead?" That's what her mother was like. Rosaura didn't feel like explaining that she'd be horribly ashamed to be the odd one out. Instead she said:

"I was the best-behaved at the party."

And she said no more because Señora Ines came out into the hall 65 with two bags, one pink and one blue.

First she went up to the fat boy, gave him a yo-yo out of the blue bag, and the fat boy left with his mother. Then she went up to the girl and gave her a bracelet out of the pink bag, and the girl with the pigtails left as well.

Finally she came up to Rosaura and her mother. She had a big smile on her face and Rosaura liked that. Señora Ines looked down at her, then looked up at her mother, and then said something that made Rosaura proud:

"What a marvelous daughter you have, Herminia."

For an instant, Rosaura thought that she'd give her two presents: the bracelet and the yo-yo. Señora Ines bent down as if about to look for something. Rosaura also leaned forward, stretching out her arm. But she never completed the movement.

Señora Ines didn't look in the pink bag. Nor did she look in the blue 70 bag. Instead she rummaged in her purse. In her hand appeared two bills.

"You really and truly earned this," she said handing them over. "Thank you for all your help, my pet."

Rosaura felt her arms stiffen, stick close to her body, and then she noticed her mother's hand on her shoulder. Instinctively she pressed herself against her mother's body. That was all. Except her eyes. Rosaura's eyes had a cold, clear look that fixed itself on Señora Ines's face.

Señora Ines, motionless, stood there with her hand outstretched. As if she didn't dare draw it back. As if the slightest change might shatter an infinitely delicate balance.

EXPLORATIONS

1. In what senses is Luciana's birthday party a stolen party?

2. At the end of "The Stolen Party," what is the intended message of Señora Ines's gift to Rosaura? What message does Rosaura draw from the gift? What changes occur in the characters' perceptions of each other, and of themselves, in the story's last two paragraphs?

3. Rosaura has a number of standards for judging people — more specifically, for measuring herself against others. For example, in paragraph 5: "The girl

didn't approve of the way her mother spoke. She was barely nine, and one of the best in her class." Find at least four other points in the story when Rosaura makes a comparative judgment. How well does she fare in her own estimation? What do you learn about Rosaura as a character from these judgments?

CONNECTIONS

1. What similarities do you notice between Rosaura's situation and that of Maya Angelou in "Mary" (p. 217)? How are these two girls' problems, and the solutions they choose, different?

2. What seem to be the goals of Luciana's mother for her daughter's birthday party? How do her goals differ from Luciana's? What seem to be the goals of the mothers in charge of the *quinceañera* in Susan Orlean's "Quinceañera" (p. 36)? How would you guess their goals differ from their daughters'?

3. In paragraphs 4–7 of "African Literature: What Tradition?" (p. 73), Es'kia Mphahlele discusses "the ever-widening gulf between one and one's parents and one's community" that comes with education (para. 6). Why does Luciana's birthday party open a gulf between Rosaura and her mother? What factors mentioned by Mphahlele are likely to widen this gulf further? Which problems (and remedies) mentioned by Mphahlele are not relevant for Rosaura?

ELABORATIONS

1. The characters in "The Stolen Party" — particularly the two mother-daughter pairs — all have different concepts of the extent to which they control their own destinies. Write an essay classifying these concepts: Describe each mother's and daughter's sense of herself as a social actor; identify the factors she views as conferring or limiting her power, such as age, intelligence, and social class; and cite the evidence in the story that supports your conclusions.

2. Several writers in this book, including Liliana Heker in "The Stolen Party," Maya Angelou in "Mary," Amy Tan in "Two Kinds" (p. 24), and Frank Mc-Court in "Limerick Homecoming" (p. 136), are concerned with the suffering that comes when youthful innocence ends. In what ways is this suffering due to the young person's ignorance? In what ways is it due to ignorance on the part of the more powerful adults whose world the young person is entering? Write an essay discussing whether and how parents can protect their children from suffering as they enter adulthood. Use evidence from selections such as Heker's, Angelou's, Tan's, and McCourt's to support your ideas.

SOPHRONIA LIU

So Tsi-fai

Born in Hong Kong in 1953, Sophronia Liu came to the United States to study at age twenty. After receiving her bachelor's and master's degrees from the University of South Dakota, she taught composition at the University of Minnesota while pursuing her Ph.D. in English. She still lives in the Twin Cities, where she has worked as an educational consultant for Asian-American Literature Designs; run teacher-training workshops for the Minnesota Center for Arts Education; done freelance translating for a Hong Kong company; and served as a medical interpreter for new Chinese immigrants. Liu also writes, directs, and performs in theater productions and is a founding member of the community-based arts group Asian-American Renaissance. Her work helping to organize the 1992 Asian-American Renaissance Conference, the largest Asian-American arts festival in the Upper Midwest, won her the 1993 Governor's Award for Leadership and Contribution to the State of Minnesota. In the fall of 1990 Liu returned to Hong Kong on a research trip; a 1996 travel and study grant from the Jerome Foundation enabled her to go back several times over the next two years. "I was there for most of 1997 during the Handover" (see her article "Hong Kong Diary," *Colors Magazine*, November 1997). "I stayed in my ancestral village, Sheung Shui, for part of that time . . . just across the river from the Chinese border. My clan settled there over 700 years ago; my parents — and all of my ancestors — are buried there, and some of my brothers still live there." Liu is also a professional interpreter and translator and a trained T'ai Chi instructor. "So Tsi-fai" was written in response to a class assignment and originally appeared in the Minnesota feminist publication *Hurricane Alice*.

Hong Kong, where Liu attended the Little Flower's School with So Tsi-fai, lies at the mouth of the Pearl River on the South China Sea. A British Crown colony at that time, its nucleus is Hong Kong Island, which Britain acquired from China in 1841. Most of the colony's 409 square miles consisted of other Chinese territory held by Britain on a ninety-nine-year lease. Hong Kong's population of over five million included fewer than 20,000 British, however; the colony absorbed more than a million Chinese refugees after Mao Zedong's Communists took over the mainland in 1949 (see page 24). In 1985 Britain yielded to pressure from Mao's successors to return this thriving capitalist port to Chinese control in 1997, when the lease expired. The agreement stipulated that Hong Kong would keep its own social, economic, and legal system for fifty years after that. As the Handover approached, the British governor strengthened the colony's democratic institutions (over China's objections), while many pessimistic residents emigrated. China quickly began imposing its own policies and government (over residents' and Britain's objections); friction continues over Hong Kong's status.

Voices, images, scenes from the past — twenty-three years ago, when I was in sixth grade:

"Let us bow our heads in silent prayer for the soul of So Tsi-fai. Let us pray for God's forgiveness for this boy's rash taking of his own life . . ." Sister Marie (Mung Gu-liang). My sixth-grade English teacher. Missionary nun from Paris. Principal of The Little Flower's School. Disciplinarian, perfectionist, authority figure: awesome and awful in my ten-year-old eyes.

"I don't need any supper. I have drunk enough insecticide." So Tsi-fai. My fourteen-year-old classmate. Daredevil; good-for-nothing lazy-bones (according to Mung Gu-liang). Bright black eyes, disheveled hair, defiant sneer, creased and greasy uniform, dirty hands, careless walk, shuffling feet. Standing in the corner for being late, for forgetting his homework, for talking in class, for using foul language. ("Shame on you! Go wash your mouth with soap!" Mung Gu-liang's sharp command. He did, and came back with a grin.) So Tsi-fai: Sticking his tongue out behind Mung Gu-liang's back, passing secret notes to his friends, kept behind after school, sent to the Principal's office for repeated offense. So Tsi-fai: incorrigible, hopeless, and without hope.

It was a Monday in late November when we heard of his death, returning to school after the weekend with our parents' signatures on our midterm reports. So Tsi-fai also showed his report to his father, we were told later. He flunked three out of the fourteen subjects: English Grammar, Arithmetic, and Chinese Dictation. He missed each one by one to three marks. That wasn't so bad. But he was a hopeless case. Overaged, stubborn, and uncooperative; a repeated offender of school rules, scourge of all teachers; who was going to give him a lenient passing grade? Besides, being a few months over the maximum age — fourteen — for sixth graders, he wasn't even allowed to sit for the Secondary School Entrance Exam.

All sixth graders in Hong Kong had to pass the SSE before they   5 could obtain a seat in secondary school. In 1964 when I took the exam, there were more than 20,000 candidates. About 7,000 of us passed: 4,000 were sent to government and subsidized schools, the other 3,000 to private and grant-in-aid schools. I came in around number 2,000; I was lucky. Without the public exam, there would be no secondary school for So Tsi-fai. His future was sealed.

Looking at the report card with three red marks on it, his father was furious. So Tsi-fai was the oldest son. There were three younger children. His father was a vegetable farmer with a few plots of land in Wong Juk-hang, by the sea. His mother worked in a local factory. So Tsi-fai helped in the fields, cooked for the family, and washed his own clothes. ("Filthy, dirty boy!" gasped Mung Gu-liang. "Grime behind the ears, black rims on the fingernails, dirty collar, crumpled shirt. Why doesn't your mother iron your shirt?") Both his parents were illiterate. So Tsi-fai was their biggest hope: He made it to the sixth grade.

Who woke him up for school every morning and had breakfast waiting for him? Nobody. ("Time for school! Get up! Eat your rice!" Ah Ma nagged and screamed. The aroma of steamed rice and Chinese sausages spread all over the house. "Drink your tea! Eat your oranges! Wash your face! And remember to wash behind your ears!") And who helped So Tsi-fai do his homework? Nobody. Did he have older brothers like mine who knew all about the arithmetic of rowing a boat against the currents or with the currents, how to count the feet of chickens and rabbits in the same cage, the present perfect continuous tense of "to live" and the future perfect tense of "to succeed"? None. Nil. So Tsi-fai was a lost cause.

I came first in both terms that year, the star pupil. So Tsi-fai was one of the last in the class: He was lazy; he didn't care. Or did he?

When his father scolded him, So Tsi-fai left the house. When he showed up again, late for supper, he announced, "I don't need any supper. I have drunk enough insecticide." Just like another one of his practical jokes. The insecticide was stored in the field for his father's vegetables. He was rushed to the hospital; dead upon arrival.

"He gulped for a last breath and was gone," an uncle told us at the   10 funeral. "But his eyes wouldn't shut. So I said in his ear, 'You go now and rest in peace.' And I smoothed my hand over his eyelids. His face was all purple."

His face was still purple when we saw him in his coffin. Eyes shut tight, nostrils dilated and white as if fire and anger might shoot out, any minute.

In class that Monday morning, Sister Marie led us in prayer. "Let us pray that God will forgive him for his sins." We said the Lord's Prayer and the Hail Mary. We bowed our heads. I sat in my chair, frozen and dazed, thinking of the deadly chill in the morgue, the smell of disinfectant, ether, and dead flesh.

"Bang!" went a gust of wind, forcing open a leaf of the double door leading to the back balcony. "Flap, flap, flap." The door swung in the wind. We could see the treetops by the hillside rustling to and fro against a pale blue sky. An imperceptible presence had drifted in with the wind. The same careless walk and shuffling feet, the same daredevil air — except that the eyes were lusterless, dripping blood; the tongue hanging out, gasping for air. As usual, he was late. But he had come back to claim his place.

"I died a tragic death," his voice said. "I have as much right as you to be here. This is my seat." We heard him; we knew he was back.

... So Tsi-fai: Standing in the corner for being late, for forgetting his   15
homework, for talking in class, for using foul language. So Tsi-fai: palm outstretched, chest sticking out, holding his breath: "Tat. Tat. Tat." Down came the teacher's wooden ruler, twenty times on each hand. Never batting an eyelash: then back to facing the wall in the corner by the door. So Tsi-fai: grimy shirt, disheveled hair, defiant sneer. So Tsi-fai. Incorrigible, hopeless, and without hope.

The girls in front gasped and shrank back in their chairs. Mung Gu-liang went to the door, held the doorknob in one hand, poked her head out, and peered into the empty balcony. Then, with a determined jerk, she pulled the door shut. Quickly crossing herself, she returned to the teacher's desk. Her black cross swung upon the front of her gray habit as she hurried across the room. "Don't be silly!" she scolded the frightened girls in the front row.

What really happened? After all these years, my mind is still haunted by this scene. What happened to So Tsi-fai? What happened to me? What happened to all of us that year in sixth grade, when we were green and young and ready to fling our arms out for the world? All of a sudden, death claimed one of us and he was gone.

Who arbitrates between life and death? Who decides which life is worth preserving and prospering, and which to nip in its bud? How did it happen that I, at ten, turned out to be the star pupil, the lucky one, while my friend, a peasant's son, was shoveled under the heap and lost forever? How could it happen that this world would close off a young boy's life at fourteen just because he was poor, undisciplined, and lacked the training and support to pass his exams? What really happened?

Today, twenty-three years later, So Tsi-fai's ghost still haunts me. "I died a tragic death. I have as much right as you to be here. This is my seat." The voice I heard twenty-three years ago in my sixth-grade classroom follows me in my dreams. Is there anything I can do to lay it to rest?

EXPLORATIONS

1. How do you think Sophronia Liu regarded So Tsi-fai before his death? How did her view change after his suicide? How can you tell? What other attitudes did Liu evidently reexamine and alter at that point?

2. Whom and what does Liu blame for So Tsi-fai's suicide? What preventive measures does her story suggest to protect other students from a similar fate? Judging from Liu's narrative, what changes in Hong Kong's social and educational institutions do you think would help students like So Tsi-fai?

3. Liu's first three paragraphs consist almost entirely of incomplete sentences. How does she use these sentence fragments to establish her essay's central conflict? At what points does she use complete sentences? What is their effect?

CONNECTIONS

1. Both Liu's "So Tsi-fai" and Liliana Heker's "The Stolen Party" (p. 224) focus on young people who represent, to themselves or their families or both, ambitions higher than their present circumstances. What disadvantages do So Tsi-fai and Rosaura share? Why does Rosaura appear likely to succeed where So Tsi-fai fails?

2. Like So Tsi-fai, Sugama in John David Morley's "Acquiring a Japanese Family" (p. 185) is his parents' oldest son. What dilemma does this status create for Sugama? What dilemma does it create for So Tsi-fai?

3. Look back at Wole Soyinka's "Nigerian Childhood" (p. 158). Both Soyinka and Liu describe encounters with ghosts. What role does each ghost play in the narrative? How are their dramatic functions different? What cultural similarities do they suggest between Nigeria and Hong Kong?

ELABORATIONS

1. What is the role of Mung Gu-liang/Sister Marie in "So Tsi-fai"? Do you think the nun would agree with Liu's assessment of what happened? How might her memory and interpretation of these events differ from Liu's? Write a narrative or argumentative version of So Tsi-fai's story from Mung Gu-liang's point of view.

2. When you were in elementary school, who were the outcasts in your class and why? If you recall one student in particular who was regarded as "different," write an essay describing him or her and narrating some of the incidents that set him or her apart. If your class consisted of two or more distinct groups, write an essay classifying these groups according to their special characteristics and their behavior toward each other. In either case, how has your attitude toward the "outcasts" changed?

ANDRE DUBUS

Imperiled Men

Andre Dubus (pronounced de-*buse*) was born in 1936 in Lake Charles, Louisiana. After graduating from McNeese State University in 1958, he became a lieutenant in the U.S. Marine Corps. Experiences such as the one he describes in "Imperiled Men" provoked him into becoming a writer; he left the Marines as a captain in 1964 to study for his M.F.A. at the University of Iowa's legendary Writers' Workshop. Dubus's first novel, *The Lieutenant*, appeared in 1967. He is best known for his short stories, however, which have appeared in numerous periodicals and in more than half a dozen collected volumes. His last story collection was *Dancing After Hours* (1996); his last essay collection was *Meditations from a Movable Chair* (1998). Dubus taught fiction and writing at Bradford College in Massachusetts from 1966–1984, won a writing fellowship from the National Endowment for the Arts in 1985, and continued to publish fiction and nonfiction in the *Sewanee Review*, *The New Yorker*, *Ploughshares*, and elsewhere. Among other events, his life was altered by a 1986 auto accident in which he lost a leg, and by a 1988 five-year MacArthur Fellowship. He lived in northeastern Massachusetts until his death from a heart attack in 1999. "Imperiled Men" first appeared in *Harper's* in June 1993, shortly after President Clinton drew heated opposition for trying to lift the ban on gay men and lesbians in the military.

He was a navy pilot in World War II and in Korea, and when I knew him in 1961 for a few months before he killed himself he was the Commander of the Air Group aboard the USS *Ranger*, an aircraft carrier, and we called him by the acronym CAG. He shot himself with his .38 revolver because two investigators from the Office of Naval Intelligence came aboard ship while we were anchored off Iwakuni in Japan and gave the ship's captain a written report of their investigation of CAG's erotic life. CAG was a much-decorated combat pilot, and his duty as a commander was one of great responsibility. The ship's executive officer, also a commander, summoned CAG to his office, where the two investigators were, and told him that his choices were to face a general court-martial or to resign from the navy. Less than half an hour later CAG was dead in his stateroom. His body was flown to the United States; we were told that he did not have a family, and I do not know where he was buried. There was a memorial service aboard ship, but I do not remember it; I only remember a general sadness like mist in the passageways.

I did not really know him. I was a first lieutenant then, a career marine; two years later I would resign and become a teacher. On the *Ranger* I was with the marine detachment; we guarded the planes' nuclear weapons stored below decks, ran the brig, and manned one of the antiaircraft gun mounts. We were fifty or so enlisted men and two officers among a ship's crew of about 3,000 officers and men. The Air Group was not included in the ship's company. They came aboard with their planes for our seven-month deployment in the western Pacific. I do not remember the numbers of pilots and bombardier-navigators, mechanics and flight controllers, and men who worked on the flight deck, but there were plenty of all, and day and night you could hear planes catapulting off the front of the deck and landing on its rear.

The flight deck was 1,052 feet long, the ship weighed 81,000 tons fully loaded, and I rarely felt its motion. I came aboard in May for a year of duty, and in August we left our port in San Francisco Bay and headed for Japan. I had driven my wife and three young children home to Louisiana, where they would stay during the seven months I was at sea, and every day I longed for them. One night on the voyage across the Pacific I sat in the wardroom drinking coffee with a lieutenant commander at one of the long tables covered with white linen. The wardroom was open all night because men were always working. The lieutenant commander told me that Soviet submarines tracked us, they recorded the sound of our propellers and could not be fooled by the sound of a decoy ship's propellers, and that they even came into San Francisco Bay to do this; our submarines did the same with Soviet carriers. He said that every time we tried in training exercises to evade even our own submarines we could not do it, and our destroyers could not track and stop them. He said, "So if the whistle blows we'll get a nuclear fist up our ass in the first thirty minutes. Our job is to get the birds in the air before that. They're going to Moscow."

"Where will they land afterward?"

"They won't. They know that."   5

The voyage to Japan was five or six weeks long because we did not go directly to Japan; the pilots flew air operations. Combat units are always trained for war, but these men who flew planes, and the men in orange suits and ear protectors who worked on the flight deck during landings and takeoffs, were engaging in something not at all as playful as marine field exercises generally were. They were imperiled. One pilot told me that from his fighter-bomber in the sky the flight deck looked like an aspirin tablet. On the passage to Japan I became friendly with some pilots drinking coffee in the wardroom, and I knew what CAG looked like because he was CAG. He had dark skin and alert eyes, and he walked proudly. Then in Japan I sometimes drank with young pilots. I was a robust twenty-five-year-old, one of two marine officers aboard ship, and I did not want to be outdone at anything by anyone. But I could not stay with the pilots; I had to leave them in the bar, drinking and talking and laughing, and make my way back to the ship to sleep and wake with a hangover. Next day the pilots flew; if we did not go to sea, they flew from a base on land. Once I asked one of them how he did it.

"The pure oxygen. Soon as you put on the mask, your head clears."

It was not simply the oxygen, and I did not understand any of these wild, brave, and very efficient men until years later when I read Tom Wolfe's *The Right Stuff.*

It was on that same tour that I saw another pilot die. I worked below decks with the marine detachment, but that warm gray afternoon the entire ship was in a simulated condition of war, and my part was to stand four hours of watch in a small turret high above the ship. I could move the turret in a circular way by pressing a button, and I looked through binoculars for planes or ships in the 180-degree arc of our port side. On the flight deck planes were taking off; four could do this in quick sequence. Two catapults launched planes straight off the front of the ship, and quickly they rose and climbed. The third and fourth catapults were on the port side where the flight deck angled sharply out to the left, short of the bow. From my turret I looked down at the ship's bridge and the flight deck. A helicopter flew low near the ship, and planes were taking off. On the deck were men in orange suits and ear protectors; on both sides of the ship, just beneath the flight deck, were nets for these men to jump into, to save themselves from being killed by a landing plane that veered or skidded or crashed. One night I'd inspected a marine guarding a plane on the flight deck; we had a sentry there because the plane carried a nuclear bomb. I stepped from a hatch into the absolute darkness of a night at sea and into a strong wind that lifted my body with each step. I was afraid it would lift me off the deck and hurl me into the sea, where I would tread water in that great expanse and depth while the ship went on its way; tomorrow they would learn that I was missing. I found the plane and the marine; he stood with one arm around that cable that held the wing to the deck.

In the turret I was facing aft when it happened: Men in orange were   10
at the rear of the flight deck, then they sprinted forward, and I rotated my turret toward the bow and saw a plane in the gray sea and an orange-suited pilot lying facedown in the water, his parachute floating beyond his head, moving toward the rear of the ship. The plane had dropped

off the port deck and now water covered its wing, then its cockpit, and it sank. The pilot was behind the ship; his limbs did not move, his face was in the sea, and his parachute was filling with water and starting to sink. The helicopter hovered low and a sailor on a rope descended from it; he wore orange, and I watched him coming down and the pilot floating and the parachute sinking beneath the waves. There was still some length of parachute line remaining when the sailor reached the pilot; he grabbed him; then the parachute lines tightened their pull and drew the pilot down. There was only the sea now beneath the sailor on the rope. Then he ascended.

I shared a stateroom with a navy lieutenant, an officer of medical administration, a very tall and strong man from Oklahoma. He had been an enlisted man, had once been a corpsman aboard a submarine operating off the coast of the Soviet Union, and one night their periscope was spotted, destroyers came after them, and they dived and sat at the bottom and listened by sonar to the destroyers' sonar trying to find them. He told me about the sailor who had tried to save the pilot. In the dispensary they gave him brandy, and the sailor wept and said he was trained to do that job, and this was his first time, and he had failed. Of course he had not failed. No man could lift another man attached to a parachute filled with water. Some people said the helicopter had not stayed close enough to the ship while the planes were taking off. Some said the pilot was probably already dead; his plane dropped from the ship, and he ejected himself high into the air, but not high enough for his parachute to ease his fall. This was all talk about the mathematics of violent death; the pilot was killed because he flew airplanes from a ship at sea.

He was a lieutenant commander, and I knew his face and name. As he was being catapulted, his landing gear on the left side broke off and his plane skidded into the sea. He was married; his widow had been married before, also to a pilot who was killed in a crash. I wondered if it were her bad luck to meet only men who flew; years later I believed that whatever in their spirits made these men fly also drew her to them.

I first spoke to CAG at the officers' club at the navy base in Yokosuka. The officers of the Air Group hosted a party for the officers of the ship's company. We wore civilian suits and ties, and gathered at the club to drink. There were no women. The party was a matter of protocol, probably a tradition among pilots and the officers of carriers; for us young officers it meant getting happily drunk. I was doing this with pilots at the bar when one of them said, "Let's throw CAG into the pond."

He grinned at me, as I looked to my left at the small shallow pond with pretty fish in it; then I looked past the pond at CAG, sitting on a soft leather chair, a drink in his hand, talking quietly with two or three other commanders sitting in soft leather chairs. All the pilots with me were grinning and saying yes, and the image of us lifting CAG from his chair and dropping him into the water gave me joy, and I put my drink on the bar and said, "Let's go."

I ran across the room to the CAG, grabbed the lapels of his coat, 15 jerked him up from his chair, and saw his drink spill onto his suit; then I fell backward to the floor, still holding his lapels, and pulled him down on top of me. There was no one else with me. He was not angry yet, but I was a frightened fool. I released his lapels and turned my head and looked back at the laughing pilots. Out of my vision the party was loud, hundreds of drinking officers who had not seen this, and CAG sounded only puzzled when he said, "What's going on?"

He stood and brushed at the drink on his suit, watching me get up from the floor. I stood not quite at attention but not at ease either. I said, "Sir, I'm Marine Lieutenant Dubus. Your pilots fooled me." I nodded toward them at the bar, and CAG smiled. "They said, 'Let's throw CAG into the pond.' But, sir, the joke was on me."

He was still smiling.

"I'm very sorry, sir."

"That's all right, Lieutenant."

"Can I get the Commander another drink, sir?" 20

"Sure," he said, and told me what he was drinking, and I got it from the bar, where the pilots were red-faced and happy, and brought it to CAG, who was sitting in his chair again with the other commanders. He smiled and thanked me, and the commanders smiled; then I returned to the young pilots and we all laughed.

Until a few months later, on the day when he killed himself, the only words I spoke to CAG after the party were greetings. One night I saw him sitting with a woman in the officers' club, and I wished him good evening. A few times I saw him in the ship's passageways; I recognized him seconds before the features of his face were clear: He had a graceful, athletic stride that dipped his shoulders. I saluted and said, "Good morning, sir" or "Good afternoon, sir." He smiled as he returned my salute and greeting, his eyes and voice mirthful, and I knew that he was seeing me again pulling him out of his chair and down to the floor, then standing to explain myself and apologize. I liked being a memory that gave him sudden and passing amusement.

On a warm sunlit day we were anchored off Iwakuni, and I planned to go with other crew members on a bus to Hiroshima. I put on civilian clothes and went down the ladder to the boat that would take us ashore. I was not happily going to Hiroshima; I was going because I was an American, and I felt that I should look at it and be in it. I found a seat on the rocking boat, then saw CAG in civilian clothes coming down the ladder. There were a few seats remaining, and he chose the one next to me. He asked me where I was going, then said he was going to Hiroshima, too. I was relieved and grateful; while CAG was flying planes in World War II, I was a boy buying savings stamps and bringing scrap metal to school. On the bus he would talk to me about war, and in Hiroshima I would walk with him and look with him, and his sea-soned steps and eyes would steady mine. Then from the ship above us the officer of the deck called down, "CAG?"

CAG turned and looked up at him, a lieutenant junior grade in white cap and short-sleeved shirt and trousers.

"Sir, the executive officer would like to see you."   25

I do not remember what CAG said to me. I only remember my dis-appointment when he told the boat's officer to go ashore without him. All I saw in CAG's face was the look of a man called from rest back to his job. He climbed the ladder, and soon the boat pulled away.

Perhaps when I reached Hiroshima CAG was already dead; I do not remember the ruins at ground zero or what I saw in the museum. I walked and looked, and stood for a long time at a low arch with an open space at the ground, and in that space was a stone box that held the names of all who died on the day of the bombing and all who had died since because of the bomb. That night I ate dinner alone, then rode the boat back to the ship, went to my empty room, climbed to my upper bunk, and slept for only a while, till the quiet voice of my roommate woke me: "The body will be flown to Okinawa."

I looked at him standing at his desk and speaking into the telephone.

"Yes. A .38 in the temple. Yes."

I turned on my reading lamp and watched him put the phone down.   30
He was sad, and he looked at me. I said, "Did someone commit sui-cide?"

"CAG."

"CAG?"

I sat up.

"The ONI investigated him."

Then I knew what I had not known I knew, and I said, "Was he a ho-   35
mosexual?"

"Yes."

My roommate told me the executive officer had summoned CAG to his office, shown him the report, and told him that he could either resign or face a general court-martial. Then CAG went to his room. Fifteen minutes later the executive officer phoned him; when he did not answer, the executive officer and the investigators ran to his room. He was on his bunk, shot in the right temple, his pilot's .38 revolver in his hand. His eyelids fluttered; he was unconscious but still alive, and he died from bleeding.

"They *ran?*" I said. "They *ran* to his room?"

Ten years later one of my shipmates came to visit me in Massachusetts; we had been civilians for a long time. In my kitchen we were drinking beer, and he said, "I couldn't tell you this aboard ship, because I worked in the legal office. They called CAG back from that boat you were on because he knew the ONI was aboard. His plane was on the ground at the base of Iwakuni. They were afraid he was going to fly it and crash into the sea and they'd lose the plane."

All 3,000 of the ship's crew did not mourn. Not every one of the hundreds of men in the Air Group mourned. But the shock was general and hundreds of men did mourn, and each morning we woke to it, and it was in our talk in the wardroom and in the passageways. In the closed air of the ship it touched us, and it lived above us on the flight deck and in the sky. One night at sea a young pilot came to my room; his face was sunburned and sad. We sat in desk chairs, and he said, "The morale is very bad now. The whole Group. It's just shot." 40

"Did y'all know about him?"

"We all knew. We didn't care. We would have followed him into hell."

Yes, they would have followed him; they were ready every day and every night to fly with him from a doomed ship and follow him to Moscow, to perish in their brilliant passion.

EXPLORATIONS

1. What meaning does Andre Dubus specify in his essay for its title, "Imperiled Men"? What other meanings for this title does the essay imply?

2. What is the effect of Dubus's choice not to name any of the characters in his essay but himself? What kinds of information does he give us about CAG and the other people aboard the Ranger? What is his opinion of CAG? How can you tell?

3. What point is Dubus making with his repeated question (para. 38), "'They *ran?*' I said. 'They *ran* to his room?'" What is the impact of giving this

question a paragraph to itself? How does the next paragraph amplify Dubus's point?

CONNECTIONS

1. Why do you think CAG shot himself? Why do you think So Tsi-fai poisoned himself (p. 231)? What important similarities and differences can you identify in the reasons for their deaths?

2. Like Sophronia Liu and Maya Angelou (p. 217), Dubus gives us advance warning of the central event in his narrative. How do you think the impact of "Imperiled Men" would change if we did not know about CAG's suicide until it happens?

3. Compare Dubus's recollections of military service with the American Indian rites of passage Michael Dorris describes on page 210. How do these two kinds of experience play a similar role for young men? What are the advantages and disadvantages of each in the process Gail Sheehy calls "Pulling Up Roots" (p. 209)?

ELABORATIONS

1. "Imperiled Men" appeared in *Harper's* shortly after President Clinton tried unsuccessfully to lift the ban on gay men and women serving in the U.S. armed forces. What is the nation's current policy on gays in the military? What do you think our policy should be, and why? Write an essay explaining and supporting your decision.

2. Dubus's drunken attempt to throw CAG into the pond (paras. 13–22), although embarrassing at the time, had unexpected positive effects. Have you ever played a trick on someone that backfired? What were the results? Have you ever done something unkind (or been the victim of unkindness) that ultimately produced a better understanding between you and the other person involved? Recall such an experience and write an essay about it.

T. CORAGHESSAN BOYLE

Achates McNeil

T. Coraghessan Boyle (pronounced co-*rag*-a-san) was born Thomas
John Boyle in Peekskill, New York, in 1948. He changed his middle
name at age seventeen but is still known as Tom. A music student at the
State University of New York (SUNY) at Potsdam, he graduated in 1970
and became a high school teacher. In the meantime he had discovered
a flair for writing. After his first story was published, Boyle applied to
the University of Iowa's Writers' Workshop. He received his Ph.D. in
1977 and went to teach at the University of Southern California, where
he is now a professor of creative writing. He lives outside Santa Barbara
with his wife and three children. Boyle's first collection, *The Descent of
Man* — titled for a story about a woman in love with a brilliant chim-
panzee — appeared in 1979; his first novel, *Water Music*, which follows
an explorer and a con man across Africa, came two years later. Other
books include *The Road to Wellville* (1993), about an eccentric cereal
magnate's sanitarium, which later became a movie, and his most recent
novel, *Riven Rock* (1998). "Achates McNeil" appeared in the July 3,
1995, issue of *The New Yorker*.

My father is a writer. A pretty well-known one, too. You'd recognize
the name if I mentioned it, but I won't mention it, I'm tired of mention-
ing it — every time I mention it I feel as if I'm suffocating, as if I'm in a
burrow deep in the ground and all these fine grains of dirt are raining
down on me. We studied him in school, in the tenth grade, a story of
his in one of those all-purpose anthologies that dislocate your wrists and
throw out your back just to lift it from the table, and then again this
year, my freshman year, in college. I had to take an American Lit class
second semester, and they were doing two of his novels, along with a
three-page list of novels and collections by his contemporaries, and I
knew some of them, too — or at least I'd seen them at the house. I kept
my mouth shut, though, especially after the professor, this blond poet in
her thirties who once wrote a novel about a nymphomaniac pastry-
maker, made a joke the first day when she came to my name in the
register.

"Achates McNeil," she called out.

245

"Here," I said, feeling hot and cold all over, as if I'd gone from a sauna into a snowbank and back again. I knew what was coming; I'd been through it before.

She paused, looking up from her list to gaze out the window on the frozen wastes of the campus in the frozen skullcap of New York state, and then came back to me and held my eyes a minute. "You wouldn't happen by any chance to be a relation of anybody on our reading list, would you?"

I sat cramped in the hard wooden seat, thinking about the faceless le- 5 gions who'd sat there before me, people who'd squirmed over exams and unfeeling professorial remarks and then gone on to become plastic surgeons, gas-station attendants, insurance salesmen, bums, and corpses. "No," I said. "I don't think so."

She gave me a mysterious little smile. "I was thinking of Theresa Golub or maybe Irving Thalamus?" It was a joke. One or two of the literary cretins in back gave it a nervous snort and chuckle and I began to wonder, not for the first time, if I was really cut out for academic life. This got me thinking about the various careers available to me as a college dropout — rock-and-roller, chairman of the board, center for the New York Knicks — and I missed the next couple of names, coming back to the world as the name "Victoria Roethke" descended on the room and hung in the air like the aftershock of a detonation in the upper atmosphere.

She was sitting two rows up from me, and all I could see was her hair, a Medusan snarl of wild demi-dreadlocks draped over everything within a three-foot radius. Her hair was red — red as in pink rather than carrottop — and it tended to be darker on the ends but ran to the color of the stuff they line Easter baskets with up close to her scalp. She didn't say "here" or "present" or "yes" or even nod her amazing head. She just cleared her throat and announced, "He was my grandfather."

I stopped her in the hallway after class and saw that she had all the usual equipment as well as a nose ring, and two eyes the color of the cardboard stiffeners you get as a consolation prize when you have to buy a new shirt. "Are you really — " I began, thinking we had a lot in common, thinking we could commiserate, drown our sorrows together, have sex, whatever, but before I could finish the question she said, "No, not really."

"You mean you — "

"That's right."   10

I gave her a look of naked admiration. And she was looking at me, sly and composed, looking right into my eyes. "But aren't you afraid you're going to be on Professor What's-Her-Face's shit list when she finds out?" I said finally.

Victoria was still looking right into me. She fiddled with her hair, touched her nose ring, and gave it a quick squeeze with a nervous flutter of her fingers. Her fingernails, I saw, were painted black. "Who's going to tell her?" she said.

We were complicitous. Instantly. Half a beat later, she asked me if I wanted to buy her a cup of ramen noodles in the Student Union, and I said yeah, I did, as if it was something I had any choice about.

We ran through a crust of dead snow in a stiff wind and temperature that hadn't risen above minus ten in the past two weeks, and there were a lot of people running with us, a whole thundering herd — up here everybody ran everywhere; it was a question of survival.

In the Union she shook out her hair, and five minutes after we'd found a table in the corner and poured the hot water into the plastic-foam containers of dehydrated mystery food I could still smell the cold her hair had trapped. I also smelled the multilayered, festering odors of the place, generic to college cafeterias nationwide: coffee, twice-worn underwear, cream-of-tomato soup. If they enclosed the place in plastic and sealed it like a tomb it'd smell the same way two thousand years from now. I'd never been in the kitchen, but I remembered the kitchen from elementary school, with its big aluminum pots and microwave ovens and all the rest, and pictured the cafeteria ladies back there now, with their dyed hair and their miserable small-town loutish-husband lives, boiling up big cauldrons of cream-of-tomato soup. Victoria's nose was white from the cold, but right where the nose ring plunged in over the flange of her left nostril there was a spot of flesh as pink as the ends of her hair.

"What happens when you get a cold?" I said. "I mean I've always wondered."

She was blowing into her noodles and she looked up to shoot me a quick glance out of her cardboard eyes. Her mouth was small, her teeth the size of individual kernels of niblet corn. When she smiled, as she did now, she showed acres of gum. "It's a pain in the ass." Half a beat: that was her method. "I suffer it all for beauty."

And, of course, this is where I got all gallant and silver-tongued and told her how striking it was, she was, her hair and her eyes and — but she cut me off. "You really are his son, aren't you?" she said.

There was a sudden eruption of jocklike noises from the far end of the room — some athletes with shaved heads making sure everybody knew they were there — and it gave me a minute to compose myself,

15.

aside from blowing into my noodles and adjusting my black watch cap with the Yankees logo for the fourteenth time, that is. I shrugged. Looked into her eyes and away again. "I really don't want to talk about it."

But she was on her feet suddenly and people were staring at her and   20 there was a look on her face like she'd just won the lottery or the trip for two to the luxurious Spermata Inn on the beach at Waikiki. "I don't believe it," she said, and her voice was as deep as mine, strange really, but with a just detectable breathiness or hollowness to it that made it recognizably feminine.

I was holding onto my plastic-foam container of hot noodles as if somebody was trying to snatch it away from me. A quick glance from side to side reassured me that the people around us had lost interest, absorbed once again in their newspapers, cherry Cokes, and plates of reheated stir fry. I gave her a weak smile.

"You mean you're like really Tom McNeil's son, no bullshit?"

"Yes," I said, and though I liked the look of her, of her breasts clamped in the neat interwoven grid of a blue thermal undershirt and her little mouth and the menagerie of her hair, and I liked what she'd done in class, too, my voice was cold. "And I have a whole other life, too."

But she wasn't listening. "Oh, my God!" she squealed, ignoring the sarcasm and all it was meant to imply. She did something with her hands, her face; her hair helicoptered around her head. "I can't believe it. He's my hero, he's my god. I want to have his baby!"

The noodles congealed in my mouth like wet confetti. I didn't have   25 the heart to point out that I *was* his baby, for better or worse.

It wasn't that I hated him, exactly — it was far more complicated than that, and I guess it got pretty Freudian, too, considering the way he treated my mother and the fact that I was thirteen and having problems of my own when he went out the door like a big cliché and my mother collapsed into herself as if her bones had suddenly melted. I'd seen him maybe three or four times since and always with some woman or other and a fistful of money and a face that looked like he'd just got done licking a pile of dogshit off the sidewalk. What did he want from me? What did he expect? At least he'd waited till my sister and brother were in college, at least they were out of the house when the cleaver fell, but what about me? I was the one who had to go into that classroom in the tenth grade and read that shitty story and have the teacher look at me like I had something to share, some intimate little anecdote I could relate about what it was like living with a genius — or having lived with a genius. And I was the one who had to see his face all over the newspapers and magazines when he published *Blood Ties*, his postmodernist take on the breakdown of the family, a comedy no less, and then read in the interviews about how his wife and children had held him back and stifled him — as if we were his jailers or something. As if I'd ever bothered him or dared to approach the sanctum of his upstairs office when his genius was percolating, or asked him to go to a Little League game and sit on the stands and yabber along with the rest of the parents. Not me. No, I was the dutiful son of the big celebrity, and the funny thing was, I wouldn't have even known he was a celebrity if he hadn't packed up and left.

He was my father. A skinny man in his late forties with kinky hair and a goatee who dressed like he was twenty-five and had a dead-black morbid outlook on life and twisted everything into the kind of joke that made you squirm. I was proud of him. I loved him. But then I saw what a monster of ego he was, as if anybody could give two shits for literature anymore, as if he were the center of the universe while the real universe went on in the streets, on the Internet, on TV, and in the movie theaters. Who the hell was he to reject me?

So: Victoria Roethke.

I told her I'd never licked anybody's nose ring before, and she asked me if I wanted to go over to her apartment and listen to music and have sex, and though I felt like shit, like my father's son, like the negative image of something I didn't want to be, I went. Oh, yes: I went.

Victoria lived in a cramped, drafty, ancient wreck of a nondescript 30 house from the wood-burning era, about five blocks from campus. We ran all the way, of course — it was either that or freeze to the pavement — and the shared effort, the wheezing lungs and burning nostrils, got us over any initial awkwardness. We stood a minute in the superheated entryway that featured a row of tarnished brass coat hooks, a dim hallway lined with doors coated in drab, shiny paint, and a smell of cat litter and old clothes. I followed her hair up a narrow stairway and into a one-room apartment not much bigger than a prison cell. It was dominated by a queen-size mattress laid out on the floor and a pair of speakers big enough to double as end tables, which they did. Bricks and boards for the bookcases that lined the walls and pinched them in like one of those shrinking rooms in a sci-fi flick, posters to cover up the faded nineteenth-century wallpaper, a greenish-looking aquarium with one pale bloated fish suspended like a mobile in the middle of it. The solitary window looked out on everything that was dead in the world. Bathroom down the hall.

And what did her room smell like? Like an animal's den, like a burrow or a hive. And female. Intensely female. I glanced at the pile of
brassieres, panties, body stockings, and sweat socks in the corner, and
she lit a joss stick, pulled the curtains, and put on a CD by a band I
don't want to name here, but which I like — there was no problem with
her taste or anything like that. Or so I thought.

She straightened up from bending over the CD player and turned to
me in the half-light of the curtained room and said, "You like this
band?"

We were standing there like strangers amidst the intensely personal
detritus of her room, awkward and insecure. I didn't know her. I'd never
been here before. And I must have seemed like some weird growth
sprung up on the unsuspecting flank of her personal space. "Yeah," I
said, "they're hot," and I was going to expand on that with some technical praise, just to let her see how hip and knowing I was, when she
threw out a sigh and let her arms fall to her sides. "I don't know," she
said, "what I really like is soul and gospel — especially gospel. I put this
on for you."

I felt deflated suddenly, unhip and uncool. There she was, joss stick
sweetening the air, her hair a world of its own, my father's fan — my absent, famous, self-absorbed son of a bitch of a father actually pimping
for me — and I didn't know what to say. After an awkward pause, the familiar band slamming down their chords and yowling out their shop-
worn angst, I said, "Let's hear some of your stuff, then."

She looked pleased, her too-small mouth pushed up into something 35
resembling a smile, and then she stepped forward and enveloped me in
her hair. We kissed. She kissed me, actually, and I responded, and then
she bounced the two steps to the CD player and put on Berna Berne
and the Angeline Sisters, a slow thump of tinny drums and an organ
that sounded like something fresh out of the muffler shop, followed by a
high-pitched blur of semi-hysterical voices. "Like it?" she said.

What could I say? "It's different," I said.

She assured me it would grow on me, like anything else, if I gave it
half a chance, ran down the other band for their pedestrian posturing,
and invited me to get into her bed. "But don't take off your clothes," she
said, "not yet."

I had a three-o'clock class in psychology, the first meeting of the semester, and I suspected I was going to miss it. I was right. Victoria made
a real ritual of the whole thing, clothes coming off with the masturba-
tory dalliance of a strip show, the covers rolling back periodically to
show this patch of flesh or that strategically revealed. I discovered her
breasts one by one, admired the tattoo on her ankle (a backward S that

signified, according to her, that she was a reincarnated Norse skald), and saw that she really was a redhead in the conventional sense. Her lips were dry, her tongue unstoppable, her hair a primal encounter. When we were done, she sat up, and I saw that her breasts pointed in two different directions, and that was human in a way I can't really express, a very personal thing, as if she was letting me in on a secret that was more intimate than the sex itself. I was touched. I admit it. I looked at those mismatched breasts, and they meant more to me than her lips and her eyes and the deep thrumming instrument of her voice, if you know what I mean.

"So," she said, sipping from a mug of water she produced from somewhere among the books and papers scattered beside the mattress, "what do I call you? I mean, Achates — right? — that's a real mouthful."

"That's my father," I said. "One of his bullshit affectations — how 40 could the Great One have a kid called Joe or Evan or Jim-Bob or Dickie?" My head was on the pillow, my eyes on the ceiling. "You know what my name means? It means 'faithful companion.' Can you believe that?"

She was silent a moment, her gray eyes locked on me over the lip of the cup, her breasts dimpling with the cold. "Yeah," she said, "I can see what you mean," and she pulled the covers up to her throat. "But what do people call you?"

I stared bleakly across the room, fastening on nothing, and when I exhaled I could see my breath. Berna Berne and the Angeline Sisters were still at it, punishing the rhythm section and charging after the vocals till you'd think somebody had set their dresses on fire. "My father calls me Ake," I said finally, "or at least he used to when I used to know him. And in case you're wondering how you spell that, that's Ake with a 'k.'"

Victoria dropped out of the blond poet-novelist's lit class, but I knew where she lived, and you couldn't miss her hair jogging across the tundra. I saw her maybe two or three times a week, especially on weekends. When things began to get to me — life, exams, too many shooters of Jack or tequila, my mother's zombielike voice on the telephone — I would sink into the den of Victoria's room with its animal funk and shrinking walls as if I'd never climb back out, and it was nothing like the cold, dry burrow I thought of when I thought of my father. Just the opposite: Victoria's room, with Victoria in it, was positively tropical, whether you could see your breath or not. I even began to develop a tolerance for the Angeline Sisters.

I avoided class the day we dissected the McNeil canon, but I was there for Delmore Schwartz and his amazing re-creation of a young man watching his parents' courtship unfolding on a movie screen in his head. "In dreams begin responsibilities" — yes, sure, but whose responsibility was I? And how long would I have to wait before we got to the sequel and *my* dreams? I'd looked through the photo albums, my mother an open-faced hippie in cutoffs and serape with her seamless blond hair and Slavic cheekbones and my father cocky and staring into the lens out of the shining halo of his hair, everything a performance, even a simple photograph, even then. The sperm and the egg, that was a biological concept, that was something I could envision up there on the big screen, the wriggling clot of life, the wet glowing ball of the egg; but picturing them coming together, with his coldness, his arrogance, his total absorption in himself — that was beyond me. Chalk it up to reticence. To DNA. To the grandiosity of the patriarchal cock. But then, he was me and I was him, and how else could you account for it?

It was Victoria who called my attention to the poster. The posters, 45 that is — about six million of them, plastered all over every stationary object within a two-mile orbit of the campus as if he were a rock star or something, as if he really counted for anything, as if anybody could even read anymore, let alone give half a shit about a balding, leather-jacketed, ex-hippie wordmeister who worried about his image first, his groin second, and nothing else after that. How did I miss it? A near-sighted dwarf couldn't have missed it — in fact, all the nearsighted dwarves on campus had already seen it and were lining up with everybody even vaguely ambulatory for their $2.50 Student Activities Board–sponsored tickets:

TOM MCNEIL
READING FROM
ELECTRONIC ORPHANS
&
BLOOD TIES
FEB. 28, 8:00 P.M.
DUBOFSKY HALL

Victoria was right there with me, in front of the Student Union, the poster with his mug shot of a photo staring out at me from behind the double-insulated glass panel that reflected the whole dead arctic world and me in the middle of it, and we had to dance on our toes and do aerobics for a full two minutes there to stave off hypothermia while I let the full meaning of it sink in. My first response was outrage, and so was my second. I bundled Victoria through the door and out of the blast of the cold, intimately involved in the revolution of her hair, the smell of her gray, bristling, fake-fur coat that looked like half a dozen opossums dropped on her from on high, even the feel of her breasts beneath all that wintry armament, and I howled in protest.

"How in Christ's name could he do this to me?" I shouted across the echoing entranceway, pink-nosed idiots in their hooded parkas coming and going, giving me their eat-shit-and-die looks. I was furious, out of control. Victoria snatched at my arm to calm me, but I tore away from her.

"He planned this, you know. He had to. He couldn't leave well enough alone, couldn't let me get away from him and be just plain nobody up here amongst the cow flops in this podunk excuse for a university — no, it's not Harvard, it's not Stanford, but at least I didn't take a nickel of his money for it. You think he'd ever even consider reading here otherwise, even if the Board of Regents got down and licked his armpits and bought him a new Porsche and promised him all the coeds in Burge to fuck one by one till they dropped dead from the sheer joy of it?"

Victoria just stood there looking at me out of her flat gray eyes, rocking back and forth on the heels of her red leather boots with the cowgirl filigree. We were blocking the doors, and people were tramping in and out, passing between us, a trail of yellow slush dribbling behind them in either direction. "I don't know," Victoria said over the heads of two Asian girls wrapped up like corpses, "I think it's kind of cool."

A day later, the letter came. Personalized stationery, California address. I tore it open in the hallway outside the door of my overheated, overlit, third-floor room in the sad-smelling old dorm: 50

QUERIDO AKE:

I know it's been a while but my crazy life just gets crazier what with the European tour for "Orphans" and Judy and Josh, but I want to make it up to you however I can. I asked Jules to get me the gig at Arcadia purposely to give me an excuse to see how you're getting along. Let's do dinner or something afterward — bring one of your girlfriends along. We'll do it up. We will.

Mucho,

DAD

This hit me like a body blow in the late rounds of a prizefight. I was already staggering, bloodied from a hundred hooks and jabs, ten to one against making it to the bell, and now this. Boom. I sat down on my institutional bed and read the thing over twice. Judy was his new wife, and Josh, six months old and still shitting in his pants, was my new brother. Half brother. DNA rules. Shit, it would have been funny if he were dead and I were dead and the whole world a burned-out cinder floating in the dead-black hole of the universe. But I wasn't dead, and didn't want to be, not yet, at least. The next best thing was being drunk, and that was easy to accomplish. Three Happy Hours and a good lip-splitting, sideburn-thumping altercation with some mountainous ass-hole in a pair of Revo shades later, and I was ready for him.

You probably expect me to report that my father, the genius, blew in to town and fucked my lit professor, Victoria, the cafeteria ladies, and two or three dogs he stumbled across on the way to the reading, but that's not the way it fell out. Not at all. In fact, he was kind of sorry and subdued and old-looking. Real old-looking, though by my count he must have been fifty-three or maybe fifty-four. It was as if his whole head had collapsed like a rotten jack-o'-lantern, his eyes sucking down these volcanoes of wrinkles, his hair standing straight up on his head like a used toilet brush. But I'm getting ahead of myself. According to my roommate, he'd called about a hundred times the day before and fi-nally left a message saying he was coming in early and wanted to have lunch, too, if that was O.K. with me. It wasn't O.K. I stayed away from the telephone and I stayed away from my room. In fact, I didn't even go near the campus for fear of running into him as he long-legged his way across the quad, entourage in tow. I blew off my classes and sank into Victoria's nest as if it were an opium den, sleep and forgetfulness, Berna Berne and the Angeline Sisters keeping me company, along with a bottle of Don Q that Victoria's dad had brought back from Puerto Rico for her. What was my plan? To crash and burn. To get so fucked up I'd be in a demi-coma till the lunch was eaten, the reading read, and din-ner forgotten. I mean, fuck him. Really.

The fatal flaw in my plan was Victoria.

She didn't stay there to comfort me with her hair, her neat little zip-per of a mouth, and her mismatched breasts. No, she went to class — very big day, exams and papers and quizzes. So she said. But do I have to tell you where she really was? Can't you picture it? Somebody who supposedly cared about me, and there she was, the fan, the diehard, camped outside his hotel in the arctic wind with the snot crusted around her nose ring. They wouldn't tell her what room he was in, and when she took exception to the attitude of the girl behind the desk they told her she'd have to wait outside — on the public sidewalk. While she was waiting and freezing and I was attempting to drink myself co-matose, he was making phone calls. Another hundred to my room, and

then to the registrar and the dean and anybody else who might have a
glimmer of my whereabouts, and of course they all fell over dead and
contacted my professors, the local police — Christ, probably even the
FBI, the CIA, and TRW.

And then it was lunchtime, and all the honchos and cheeses from   55
the English Department wanted to break bread with him, so out the
door he went, not with Judy on his arm, or some more casual acquaintance who might have been last night's groin massager or the flight attendant who'd served him his breakfast, but his biographer. His biographer. Arm in arm with this bald guy half his height with a face depleted
by a pair of glasses the size of the ones Elton John used to wear onstage,
trailing dignitaries and toadies, and who does he run into?

Ten minutes later he's coming up the stairs at Victoria's place, and
beneath the wailing of the Sisters and the thump of the organ I can
hear his footsteps, his and nobody else's, and I know this: after all these
years, my father has come for me.

Lunch was at the Bistro, one of the few places in town that aspired to
anything more than pizza, burgers, and burritos. My father sat at the
head of the table, of course, and I, three-quarters drunk on white rum,
sat at his right hand. Victoria was next to me, her expression rapt, her
hair snaking out behind me in the direction of the great man like the
tendrils of some unkillable plant, and the biographer, sunk behind his
glasses, hunched beside her with a little black notepad. The rest of the
table, from my father's other side down, was occupied by various members of the English Department whom I vaguely recognized and older
lawyer types who must have been deans or whatever. There was a tense
moment when Dr. Delson, my American Lit professor, came in, but
her eyes, after registering initial surprise and recalculating our entire relationship from the first day's roll call on, showed nothing but a sort of
fawning, shimmering awe. And how did I feel about that? Sick. Just
plain sick.

I drank desperate cups of black coffee and tried to detoxify myself
with something called coquilles St. Jacques, which amounted to an in-
definable rubbery substance sealed in an impenetrable layer of baked
cheese. My father held forth, witty, charming, as pleased with himself
as anybody alive. He said things like "I'm glad you're asking me to speak
on the only subject I'm an authority on — me," and with every other
breath he dropped the names of the big impressive actors who'd starred
in the big impressive movie version of his last book. "Well," he'd say,
"as far as that goes, Meryl once told me . . ." or "When we were on location in Barbados, Brad and Geena and I used to go snorkeling practically

every afternoon, and then it was conch *ceviche* and this rum drink they
call Mata-Mata, after the turtle, and believe me, kill you it does."

Add to this the fact that he kept throwing his arm around the back of
my chair (and so, my shoulders) as if I'd been there with him through
every scintillating tête-à-tête and sexual and literary score, and you
might begin to appreciate how I felt. But what could I do? He was playing a role that would have put to shame any of the big-gun actors he
named, and I was playing my role, too, and though I was seething inside, though I felt betrayed by Victoria and him and all the stupid nosh-
ing doglike faces fawning round the table, I played the dutiful and
proud son to Academy Award proportions. Or maybe I wasn't so great.
At least I didn't jump up and flip the table over and call him a fraud, a
cheat, and a philanderer who had no right to call anybody his son, let
alone me. But oh, how those deans and professors sidled up to me afterward to thoroughly kiss my ass, while Dr. Delson glowed over our little
secret and tried to shoulder Victoria out of the way. And Victoria. That
was another thing. Victoria didn't seem to recall that I was still alive, so
enthralled was she by the overblown spectacle of my father the genius.

He took me aside just before we stepped back out into the blast of   60
the wind, confidential and fatherly, the others peeling back momentarily in deference to the ties of the blood, and asked me if I was all
right. "Are you all right?" he said.

Everything was in a stir, crescendoing voices, the merry ritual of the
zippers, the gloves, the scarves and parkas, a string quartet keening
through the speakers in some weird key that made the hair stand up on
the back of my neck. "What do you mean?" I said.

I looked into his face then, and the oldness dropped away from him:
he was my pal, my dad, the quick-blooded figure I remembered from
the kitchen, den, and bedroom of my childhood. "I don't know," he
said, shrugging. "Victoria said — that's her name, right? Victoria?"

I nodded.

"She said you were feeling sick, the flu or something," and he let it
trail off. Somebody shouted, "You should have seen it in December!"
and the quartet choked off in an insectlike murmur of busy strings and
nervous fingers. "Cute kid, Victoria," he said. "She's something." And
then a stab at a joke: "Guess you inherited my taste, huh?"

But the dutiful son didn't smile, let alone laugh. He was feeling less   65
like Achates than Oedipus.

"You need any money?" my father said, and he was reaching into the
pocket of his jeans, an automatic gesture, when the rest of the group
converged on us and the question fell dead. He threw an arm around
me suddenly and managed to snag Victoria and the proud flag of her

hair in the other. He gave a two-way squeeze with his skinny arms and said, "See you at the reading tonight, right?"

Everyone was watching, right on down to the busboys, not to mention the biographer, Dr. Delson, and all the by now stunned, awed, and grinning strangers squinting up from their coquilles and *fritures*. It was a real biographical moment. "Yeah," I said, and I thought for a minute they were going to break into applause. "Sure."

The hall was packed, standing room only, hot and stifling with the crush of bodies and the coats and scarves and other paraphernalia that were like a second, shadowy crowd gathered at the edges of the living and breathing one — students, faculty, and townspeople wedged into every available space. Some of them had come from as far away as Vermont and Montreal, I heard, and when we came through the big main double doors, scalpers were selling the $2.50 Student Activities Board–sponsored tickets for three and four times that. I sat in the front row with my father's vacant seat between me and the biographer (whose name was Mal, as in Malcolm) while my father made the rounds, pumping hands and signing books, napkins, sheets of notebook paper, and whatever else the adoring crowd thrust at him. Victoria, the mass of her hair enlarged to even more stupendous proportions thanks to some mysterious chemical treatment she'd undergone in the bathroom down the hall from her room, sat sprouting beside me.

I was plunging in and out of the jungle of Victoria to make small talk, trying not to watch my father, unconcerned, unflappable, no problem at all, when Mal leaned across the vacant seat and poked my arm with the butt of his always handy Scripto pen. I turned to him, Victoria's hand clutched tightly in mine — she hadn't let go, not even to unwrap her scarf, since we'd climbed out of the car — and stared into the reflected blaze of his glasses. They were amazing, those glasses, like picture windows, like a scuba mask grafted to his hairless skull. "Nineteen eighty-nine," he said, "when he wrecked the car? The BMW, I mean?" I sat there frozen, waiting for the rest of it, the man's voice snaking into my consciousness till it felt like the voice of my innermost self. "Do you remember if he was still living at home then? Or was that after . . . after he, uh, moved out?"

Moved out. Wrecked the car.   70

"Do you remember what he was like then? Were there any obvious changes? Did he seem depressed?"

He must have seen from my face how I felt about the situation because his glasses suddenly flashed light, he tugged twice at his lower lip, and murmured, "I know this isn't the time or place, I was just curious, that's all. But I wonder, would you mind — maybe we could set up a time to talk?"

What could I say? Victoria clutched my hand like a trophy hunter, my fellow-students rumbled and chattered and stretched in their bolted-down seats, and my father squatted here, sprang up there, lifted his eyebrows and laid down a layer of witty banter about half a mile thick. I shrugged. Looked away. "Sure," I said.

Then the lights dimmed once, twice, and went all the way down, and the chairman of the English Department took the podium while my father scuttled into the seat beside me and the audience hushed. I won't bother describing the chairman — he was generic, and he talked for a mercifully short five minutes or so about how my father needed no introduction et cetera, et cetera, before giving the podium over to Mal-as-in-Malcolm, the official hagiographer. Mal bounced up onto the stage like a trained seal, and if the chairman was selfless and brief, Mal was windy, verbose, a man who really craved an audience. He softened them up with half a dozen anecdotes about the great man's hyperinflated past, with carefully selected references to drug abuse, womanizing, unhinged driving, and of course movies and movie stars. By the time he was done, he'd made my father sound like a combination of James Dean, Tolstoy, and Enzo Ferrari. They were thrilled, every last man, woman, and drooling freshman. And me, the only one in the audience who really knew him? I wanted to puke, puke till the auditorium was filled with it. But I couldn't. I was trapped, just like in some nightmare. Right there in the middle of the front row.

When Mal finally ducked his denuded head and announced my father, the applause was seismic, as if the whole auditorium had been tipped on end, and the great man, in one of his own tour T-shirts and the omnipresent leather jacket, took the stage and engaged in a little high-fiving with the departing biographer while the thunder gradually subsided and the faces around me went slack with wonder. For the next fifteen minutes, he pranced and strutted across the stage, ignoring the podium and delivering a pre-programmed monologue that was the equal of anything you'd see on late-night TV. At least, all the morons around me thought so. He charmed them, out-hipped them, and they laughed, snorted, sniggered, and howled. Some of them, no doubt my fellow-freshmen, even stamped their feet in thunderous unison, as if they were at a pep rally or something. And the jokes — the sort of thing he'd come on with at lunch — were all so self-effacing, at least on the surface, but deep down each phrase and buttressed pause was calculated to remind us we were in the presence of one of the heroes of literature. There was the drinking-with-Bukowski story, which had been reproduced in every interview he'd done in the last twenty years, the traveling-through-Russia-with-nothing-but-a-pair-of-jeans-two-socks-and-a-leather-jacket-after-his-luggage-was-stolen story, the obligatory movie-star story and three or four don't-ask-me-now references to his wild past. I sat there like a condemned man awaiting the lethal injection, a rigid smile frozen to my face. My scalp itched, both nostrils, even the crotch of my underwear. I fought for control.

And then the final blow fell, as swift and sudden as a meteor shrieking down from outer space and against all odds blasting through the roof of the auditorium and drilling right into the back of my reeling head. My father raised a hand to indicate that the jokes were over, and the audience choked off as if he'd tightened a noose around each and every throat. Suddenly, he was more professorial than the professors — there wasn't a murmur in the house, not even a cough. He held up a book, produced a pair of wire-rim glasses — a prop if ever I saw one — and glanced down at me. "The piece I want to read tonight, from *Blood Ties*, is something I've wanted to read in public for a long time. It's a deeply personal piece, and painful, too, but I read it tonight as an act of contrition. I read it for my son."

He spread open the book with a slow, sad deliberation I'm sure they all found very affecting, but to me he was like a terrorist opening a suitcase full of explosives, and I shrank into my seat, as miserable as I've ever been in my life. He can't be doing this, I thought, he can't. But he was. It was his show, after all.

And then he began to read. At first, I didn't hear the words, didn't want to — I was in a daze, mesmerized by the intense weirdness of his voice, which had gone high-pitched and nasal all of a sudden, with a kind of fractured rhythm that made it seem as if he were translating from another language. It took me a moment, and then I understood: this was his reading voice, another affectation. Once I got past that, there were the words themselves, each one a little missile aimed at me, the hapless son, the victim who only wanted to be left lying in the wreckage where he'd fallen. He was reading a passage in which the guilt-wracked but lusty father takes the thirteen-year-old son out to the best restaurant in town for a heart-to-heart talk about those lusts, about dreams, responsibilities, and the domestic life that was dragging him down. I tried to close myself off, but I couldn't. My eyes were burning. Nobody in the auditorium was watching him anymore — how could they be? No, they were watching me. Watching the back of my head. Watching the fiction come to life.

When he got to the part where the son, tears streaming into his chocolate mousse, asks him Why, why dad, why, I stood up, right there, right in the middle of the front row, all those eyes drilling into me. I tore my hand away from Victoria's, stared down the biographer and Dr. Delson and all the rest of them, and stalked straight out the nearest exit, even as my father's amplified voice wavered, faltered, and then came back strong again, nothing wrong, nothing the matter, nothing a little literature wouldn't cure.

I don't know what happened between him and Victoria at the muted   80
and minimally celebratory dinner later that night, but I don't suspect it was much, if anything. That wasn't the problem, and both of us — she and I, that is — knew it. I spent the night hiding out in the twenty-four-hour laundromat wedged between Brewskies Pub and Taco Bell, and in the morning I ate breakfast in a greasy spoon only the townies frequented, and then I caught up on some of Hollywood's distinguished products at the local cineplex for as long as I could stand it. By then, I was sure the great man would have gone on to his many other great appointments, all his public posturing aside. And that was just what happened — he canceled his first flight and hung around till he could hang around no longer, flying out at 4:15 with his biographer and all the sympathy of the deeply yearning and heartbroken campus. And me? I was nobody again. Or so I thought.

I, too, dropped out of Dr. Delson's class — I couldn't stand the thought of that glazed-blue look of accusation in her eyes — and though I occasionally spotted Victoria's hair riding the currents around campus, I avoided her. She knew where to find me if she wanted me, but all that was over, I could see that; I wasn't his son, after all. A few weeks later I noticed her in the company of this senior who played keyboards in one of the local bands, and I felt something — I don't know what it was, but it wasn't jealousy. And then, at the end of a lonely semester in a lonely town in the lonely hind end of nowhere, the air began to soften, and a few blades of yellow grass poked up through the rotting snow, and my roommate took me downtown to Brewskies to celebrate.

The girl's name was Marlena, but she didn't pronounce it like the old German actress who was practically dead before she was born, she said Mar-*lenna*, the second syllable banged out so it sounded as if she were calling herself Lenny. I liked the way her smile showed off the gold caps on her molars. The band I didn't want to mention earlier was playing through the big speakers over the bar and there was a whole undercurrent of noise and excitement mixed with the smells of tap beer, Polish sausage, and salt-and-vinegar chips. "I know you," she said. "You're, um, Tom McNeil's son, right?"

I never looked away from her, never blinked. All that was old news now, dead and buried, like some battle in the Civil War.

"That's right," I said. "How did you guess?"

EXPLORATIONS

1. What part of "Achates McNeil" is written in the past tense? What part is written in the present tense? What does the story's use of tenses reveal about the ultimate impact of its events on its narrator?

2. ". . . All that was over, I could see that; I wasn't his son, after all" (para. 81; compare para. 18). What is the narrator saying about his relationship with Victoria Roethke? His relationship with his father? His sense of himself?

3. Find at least three descriptions of Victoria's hair and her nose ring. How does T. Coraghessan Boyle use these descriptions to show developments in the story and its narrator?

CONNECTIONS

1. "You'd recognize the name if I mentioned it, but I won't mention it," declares Boyle's narrator in paragraph 1. How long into the story does it take him to mention his father's name and his own? What is the effect of Boyle's making so much of his characters' names? Compare the way Andre Dubus identifies his essay's central character in paragraph 1 of "Imperiled Men" (p. 237), and its other characters after that. What is the effect of Dubus's making so little of his characters' names?

2. In what ways is the narrator's evolution in "Achates McNeil" similar to Rosaura's evolution in Liliana Heker's "The Stolen Party" (p. 224)? Who warns each character (and the reader) about impending danger when the story starts? How do Boyle and Heker arrange for danger to strike their characters (and us) unexpectedly in spite of this warning? How would these two stories affect us differently if the characters (and we) were not warned?

3. Francine du Plessix Gray writes: "The family meal is not only the core curriculum in the school of civilized discourse; it is also a set of protocols that curb our natural savagery and our animal greed, and cultivate a capacity for sharing and thoughtfulness" (p. 95). Reread the two meal scenes in "Achates McNeil" (paras. 15–25 and 57–59). Do you think Boyle agrees with Gray? On what evidence do you base your answer?

ELABORATIONS

1. What roles does literature play in "Achates McNeil"? Look through the story for references to literary characters and to the writing and the study of literature. How important is this theme, and why? How would the story's impact change if the opening sentence were, for instance, "My father is a banker"? Write an essay classifying the ways Boyle uses the cornerstones of his own occupation to construct (and deconstruct) this powerful, difficult father-son relationship.

2. During what month or months does "Achates McNeil" take place? How do you know? How would the story's impact change if the location or time of year or both were warm instead of cold? Write an essay about the role of winter in this story, citing specific examples.

JAMES BALDWIN

The New Lost Generation

As the following essay describes, James Baldwin decided in his twenties to leave the United States for France. Born in New York City's
Harlem in 1924, he grew up in a family of ten step- and half-siblings.
His father, a rigid disciplinarian, worked in a bottling plant and
preached in a local church; his mother worked as a maid, often leaving
James to baby-sit. At Frederick Douglass Junior High School, one of his
teachers was the poet Countee Cullen, who introduced him to other
writers of the Harlem Renaissance and encouraged his obvious talent.
Baldwin graduated from a Bronx high school in 1942, having concealed
from his literary-minded friends (most of them white, many of them
Jewish) that he also preached at the Fire Side Pentecostal Assembly.
After his father's funeral, which coincided with a massive riot in
Harlem, Baldwin moved downtown to Greenwich Village. There he
met Richard Wright, who helped the younger author to win one of
many literary prizes that would support his writing. Baldwin published
his first novel, the autobiographical *Go Tell It on the Mountain*, in
1953. The essay collection *Notes of a Native Son* — its title a homage to
Wright's novel *Native Son* — followed two years later. A self-described
transatlantic commuter, Baldwin continued to produce influential novels, essays, and plays (including *Blues for Mr. Charlie*, 1964) until his
death from cancer in 1987.

This is an extremely difficult record to assess. Perhaps it begins for
me in 1946, when my best friend took his life. He was an incandescent
Negro boy of twenty-four, whose future, it had seemed to all of us,
would unfailingly be glorious. He and I were Socialists, as were most of
our friends, and we dreamed of this utopia, and worked toward it. We
may have evinced more conviction than intelligence or skill, and more
youthful arrogance than either, but we, nevertheless, had carried petitions about together, fought landlords together, worked as laborers together, been fired together, and starved together.

But for some time before his death, troubles graver than these had
laid hold of my friend. Not only did the world stubbornly refuse his vision; it despised him for his vision, and scourged him for his color. Of
course, it despised and scourged me, too, but I was different from my
friend in that it took me nearly no time to despise the world right back

and decide that I would accomplish, in time, with patience and cunning and by becoming indestructible, what I might not, in the moment, achieve by force or persuasion. My friend did not despise anyone. He really thought that people were good, and that one had only to point out to them the right path in order to have them, at once, come flocking to it in loudly rejoicing droves.

Before his death, we had quarreled very bitterly over this. I had lost my faith in politics, in right paths; if there *were* a right path, one might be sure (I informed him with great venom) that whoever was on it was simply asking to be stoned to death — by all the world's good people. I didn't give a damn, besides, *what* happened to the miserable, the unspeakably petty world. There was probably not a handful of decent people in it. My friend looked very saddened by these original reflections. He said that it seemed to him that I had taken the road which ended in fascism, tyranny, and blood.

So, I told him, have you. One fine day, you'll realize that people don't *want* to be better. So you'll have to make them better. And how do you think you'll go about it?

He said nothing to this. He was sitting opposite me, in a booth, in a   5
Greenwich Village diner.

What about love? he asked me.

His question threw me off guard, and frightened me. With the indescribable authority of twenty-two, I snarled: Love! You'd better forget about that, my friend. That train has *gone*.

The moment I said this, I regretted it, for I remembered that he *was* in love: with a young white girl, also a Socialist, whose family was threatening to have him put in prison. And the week before, a handful of sailors had come across them in the subway and beaten him very badly.

He looked at me and I wanted to unsay what I had said, to say something else. But I could not think of anything which would not sound, simply, like unmanly consolation, which would not sound as though I were humoring him.

You're a poet, he said, and you don't believe in love.   10

And he put his head down on the table and began to cry.

We had come through some grueling things together, and I had never seen him cry. In fact, he went into and came out of battles laughing. We were in a hostile, public place. New York was fearfully hostile in those days, as it still is. He was my best friend, and for the first time in our lives I could do nothing for him; and it had been my ill-considered rage which had hurt him. I wanted to take it back, but I did not know how. I *would* have known how if I had been being insincere. But, though I know now that I was wrong, I did not know it then. I had meant what I had said, and my unexamined life would not allow me to speak otherwise. I really did not, then, as far as I knew, believe that love existed, except as useless pain; and the time was far from me when I would begin to see the contradiction implicit in the fact that I was bending all my forces, or imagined I was, to protect myself against it.

He wept; I sat there; no one, for a wonder, bothered us. By and by we paid, and walked out into the streets. This was the last time, but one, that I ever saw him; it was the very last time that we really spoke. A very short time after this, his body was found in the Hudson River. He had jumped from the George Washington Bridge.

Why do I begin my sketch of Americans abroad with this memory? I suppose that there must be many reasons. I certainly cannot hope to tell or, for that matter, to face them all. One reason, of course, is that I thought for a very long time that I had hastened him to his death. *You're a poet, and you don't believe in love.* But, leaving aside now this hideous and useless speculation, it is from the time of my friend's death that I resolved to leave America. There were two reasons for this. One was that I was absolutely certain, from the moment I learned of his death, that I, too, if I stayed here, would come to a similar end. I felt then, and, to tell the truth, I feel now, that he would not have died in such a way and certainly not so soon, if he had not been black. (Legally speaking. Physically, he was almost, but not quite, light enough to pass.) And this meant that he was the grimmest, until then, of a series of losses for which I most bitterly blamed the American republic. From the time of his death, I began to be afraid of enduring any more. I was afraid that hatred, and the desire for revenge, would reach unmanageable proportions in me, and that my end, even if I should not physically die, would be infinitely more horrible than my friend's suicide.

He was not the only casualty of those days. There were others, white,   15 friends of mine, who, at just about the time his indescribably colored body was recovered from the river, were returning from the world's most hideous war. Some were boys with whom I had been to high school. One boy, Jewish, sat with me all night in my apartment on Orchard Street, telling me about the camps he had seen in Germany and the Germans he had blasted off the face of the earth. I will never forget his face. I had once known it very well — shortly before, when we had been children. It was not a child's face now. He had *seen* what people would do to him — because he was a Jew he knew what he had done to Germans; and not only could nothing be undone, it might very well be that this was all that the world could ever be, over and over again, forever. All political hopes and systems, then, seemed morally bankrupt:

for, if Buchenwald was wrong, what, then, *really* made Hiroshima right? He shook his head, an old Jew already, an old man. If all visions of human nature are to be distrusted, and all hopes, what about love?

The people I knew found the most extraordinary ways of dealing with this question, but it was a real question. Girls who had been virgins when they married their husbands — and there were some, I knew them — sometimes had to have abortions before their husbands returned from overseas. The marriages almost never survived the returning pressures, and, very often, the mental equilibrium of the partners — or ex-partners — was lost, never to be regained. Men who had had homosexual adventures in CO camps, or in the service, could not accept what had happened to them, could not forget it, dared not discover if they desired to repeat it, and lapsed into a paralysis from which neither men nor women could rouse them. It was a time of the most terrifying personal anarchy. If one gave a party, it was virtually certain that someone, quite possibly oneself, would have a crying jag or have to be restrained from murder or suicide. It was a time of experimentation, with sex, with marijuana, and minor infringements of the law, such as "boosting" from the A & P and stealing electricity from Con Edison. I knew some people who had a stolen refrigerator for which they had no room and no use, and which they could not sell; it was finally shipped, I believe, of all places, to Cuba. But, finally, it seems to me that life was beginning to tell us who we are, and what life was — news no one has ever wanted to hear: and we fought back by clinging to our vision of ourselves as innocent, of love perhaps imperfect but reciprocal and enduring. And we did not know that the price of this was experience. We had been raised to believe in formulas.

In retrospect, the discovery of the orgasm — or, rather, of the orgone box — seems the least mad of the formulas that came to mind. It seemed to me — though I was, perhaps, already too bitterly inoculated against groups or panaceas — that people turned from the idea of the world being made better through politics to the idea of the world being made better through psychic and sexual health like sinners coming down the aisle at a revival meeting. And I doubted that their conversion was any more to be trusted than that. The converts, indeed, moved in a certain euphoric aura of well-being, which could not last. They had not become more generous, but less, not more open, but more closed. They ceased, totally, to listen and could only proselytize; nor did their private lives become discernibly less tangled. There are no formulas for the improvement of the private, or any other life — certainly not the formula of more and better orgasms. (Who decides?) The people I had been raised among had orgasms all the time, and still chopped each other up with razors on Saturday nights.

By this wild process, then, of failure, elimination, and rejection, I, certainly, and most of the people whom I knew got to Europe, and, roughly speaking, "settled there." Many of us have returned, but not all: It is important to remember that many expatriates vanish into the lives of their adopted country, to be flushed out only, and not always then, by grave international emergency. This applies especially, of course, to women, who, given the pressures of raising a family, rarely have time to be homesick, or guilty about "escaping" the problems of American life. Their first loyalties, thank heaven, are to the men they married and the children they must raise. But I know American couples, too, who have made their homes in Europe quite happily, and who have no intention of returning to this country. It is worth observing, too, that these people are nearly always marked by a lack of spite or uneasiness concerning this country which quite fails to characterize what I tend to think of as the "displaced" or "visible" expatriate. That is, remarkable as this may sound, it is not necessary to hate this country in order to have a good time somewhere else. In fact, the people who hate this country never manage, except physically, to leave it, and have a wretched life wherever they go.

And, of course, many of us have become, in effect, commuters; which is a less improbable state now than it was a decade ago. Many have neither returned nor stayed, but can be found in Village bars, talking about Europe, or in European bars, talking about America.

Apart from GIs who remained in Europe, thoughtfully using up all   20
the cheap studios, and nearly all, as it turned out, of the available good will, we, who have been described (not very usefully) as the "new" expatriates, began arriving in Paris around '45, '46, '47, and '48. The character of the influx began to change very radically after that, if only because the newcomers had had the foresight to arm themselves with jobs: American government jobs, which also meant that they had housing allowances and didn't care how much rent they paid. Neither, of course, did the French landlords, with the result that rents rose astronomically and we who had considered ourselves forever installed in the Latin Quarter found ourselves living all over Paris. But this, at least for some of us, turned out to be very healthy and valuable. We were in Paris, after all, because we had presumably put down all formulas and all safety in favor of the chilling unpredictability of experience.

Voyagers discover that the world can never be larger than the person that is in the world; but it is impossible to foresee this, it is impossible to be warned. It is only when time has begun spilling through his fingers like water or sand — carrying away with it, forever, dreams, possibilities, challenges, and hopes — that the young man realizes that he will not be young forever. If he wishes to paint a picture, raise a family, write a book, design a building, start a war — well, he does not have forever in which to do it. He has only a certain amount of time, and half of that time is probably gone already. As long as his aspirations are in the realm of the dream, he is safe; when he must bring them back into the world, he is in danger.

Precisely for this reason, Paris was a devastating shock. It was easily recognizable as Paris from across the ocean: that was what the letters on the map spelled out. This was not the same thing as finding oneself in a large, inconvenient, indifferent city. Paris, from across the ocean, looked like a refuge from the American madness; now it was a city four thousand miles from home. It contained — in those days — no dough-nuts, no milk shakes, no Coca-Cola, no dry martinis; nothing resem-bling, for people on our economic level, an American toilet; as for toilet paper, it was yesterday's newspaper. The concierge of the hotel did not appear to find your presence in France a reason for rejoicing; rather, she found your presence, and in particular your ability to pay the rent, a matter for the profoundest suspicion. The policemen, with their re-volvers, clubs, and (as it turned out) weighted capes, appeared to be convinced of your legality only after the most vindictive scrutiny of your passport; and it became clear very soon that they were not kidding about the three-month period during which every foreigner had to buy a new visa or leave the country. Not a few astounded Americans, unable to call their embassy, spent the night in jail, and steady offenders were escorted to the border. After the first street riot, or its aftermath, one wit-nessed in Paris, one took a new attitude toward the Paris paving stones, and toward the café tables and chairs, and toward the Parisians, indeed, who showed no signs, at such moments, of being among the earth's most cerebral or civilized people. Paris hotels had never heard of cen-tral heating or hot baths or showers or clean towels and sheets or ham and eggs; their attitude toward electricity was demonic — once one had seen what they thought of as wiring one wondered why the city had not, long ago, vanished in flame; and it soon became clear that Paris hospi-tals had never heard of Pasteur. Once, in short, one found oneself di-vested of all the things that one had fled from, one wondered how people, meaning, above all, oneself, could possibly do without them.

And yet one did, of course, and in the beginning, and sporadically, thereafter, found these privations a subject for mirth. One soon ceased expecting to be warm in one's hotel room, and read and worked in the cafés. The French, at least insofar as student hotels are concerned, do not appear to understand the idea of a social visit. They expect one's callers to be vastly more intimate, if not utilitarian, than that, and much prefer that they register and spend the night. This aspect of Parisian life would seem vastly to simplify matters, but this, alas, is not the case. It merely makes it all but impossible to invite anyone to your hotel room. Americans do not cease to be Puritans when they have crossed the ocean; French girls, on the other hand, contrary to legend, tend, preponderantly, to be the marrying kind; thus, it was not long before we brave voyagers rather felt that we had been turned loose in a fair in which there was not a damn thing we could buy, and still less that we could sell.

And I think that when we began to be frightened in Paris, to feel baffled and betrayed, it was because we had failed, after all, somehow, and once again, to make the longed-for, magical human contact. It was on this connection with another human being that we had felt that our lives and our work depended. It had failed at home. We had thought we knew why. Everyone at home was too dry and too frightened, mercilessly pinned beneath the thumb of the Puritan God. Yet, here we were, surrounded by quite beautiful and sensual people, who did not, however, appear to find us beautiful or sensual. They said so. By the time we had been abroad two years, each of us, in one way or another, had received this message. It was one of the things that was meant when we were referred to as children. We had been perfectly willing to refer to all the other Americans as children — in the beginning; we had not known what it meant; we had not known that we were included.

By 1950 some of us had already left Paris for more promising ports of 25 call. Tangiers for some, or Italy, or Spain; Sweden or Denmark or Germany for others. Some girls had got married and vanished; some had got married and vanished and reappeared — minus their husbands. Some people got jobs with the ECA and began a slow retreat back into the cocoon from which they had never quite succeeded in emerging. Some of us were going to pieces — spectacularly, as in my own case, quietly, in others. One boy, for example, had embarked on the career which I believe still engages him, that of laboriously writing extremely literary plays in English, translating them — laboriously — into French and Spanish, reading the trilingual results to a coterie of friends who were, even then, beginning to diminish, and then locking them in his trunk. Magazines were popping up like toadstools and vanishing like fog. Painters and poets of thin talent and no industry began to feel abused by the lack of attention their efforts elicited from the French, and made outrageously obvious — and successful — bids for

the attention of visiting literary figures from the States, of whose industry, in any case, there could be no doubt. And a certain real malice now
began to make itself felt in our attitudes toward the French, as well as a
certain defensiveness concerning whatever it was we had come to Paris
to do and clearly were not doing. We were edgy with each other, too.
Going, going, going, gone — were the days when we walked through
Les Halles, singing, loving every inch of France, and loving each other;
gone were the jam sessions in Pigalle, and our stories about the whores
there; gone were the nights spent smoking hashish in Arab cafés; gone
were the mornings which found us telling dirty stories, true stories, sad
and earnest stories, in gray, workingmen's cafés. It was all gone. We
were secretive with each other. I no longer talked about my novel. We
no longer talked about our love affairs, for either they had failed, were
failing, or were serious. Above all, they were private — how can love be
talked about? It is probably the most awful of all the revelations this
little life affords. We no longer walked about, as a friend of mine once
put it, in a not dissimilar context, in "friendly groups of five thousand."
We were splitting up, and each of us was going for himself. Or, if not
precisely for himself, his own way; some of us took to the needle, some
returned to the family business, some made loveless marriages, some
ceased fleeing and turned to face the demons that had been on the trail
so long. The luckiest among us were these last, for they managed to go
to pieces and then put themselves back together with whatever was left.
This may take away one's dreams, but it delivers one to oneself. Without this coming together, the longed-for love is never possible, for the
confused personality can neither give nor take.

In my case, I think my exile saved my life, for it inexorably confirmed something which Americans appear to have great difficulty accepting. Which is, simply, this: A man is not a man until he is able and
willing to accept his own vision of the world, no matter how radically
this vision departs from that of others. (When I say "vision," I do not
mean "dream.") There are long moments when this country resembles
nothing so much as the grimmest of popularity contests. The best thing
that happened to the "new" expatriates was their liberation, finally,
from any need to be smothered by what is really nothing more (though
it may be something less) than mother love. It need scarcely, I hope, be
said that I have no interest in hurling gratuitous insults at American
mothers; they are certainly helpless, if not entirely blameless; and my
point has nothing to do with them. My point is involved with the great
emphasis placed on public approval here, and the resulting and quite
insane system of penalties and rewards. It puts a premium on medioc-

rity and has all but slaughtered any concept of excellence. This corruption begins in the private life and unfailingly flowers in the public life. Europeans refer to Americans as children in the same way that American Negroes refer to them as children, and for the same reason: They mean that Americans have so little experience — experience referring not to *what* happens, but to *who* — that they have no key to the experience of others. Our current relations with the world forcibly suggest that there is more than a little truth to this. What Europe still gives an American — or gave us — is the sanction, if one can accept it, to become oneself. No artist can survive without this acceptance. But rare indeed is the American artist who achieved this without first becoming a wanderer, and then, upon his return to his own country, the loneliest and most blackly distrusted of men.

EXPLORATIONS

1. How did James Baldwin change his life after his best friend's suicide, and why? How do you think Baldwin's life would have been different if his friend had not died the way he did?

2. What aspects of the United States made Baldwin leave it? What did he hope to find in Europe? In what ways did the life of an expatriate match his expectations, and in what ways did it surprise him?

3. At what points does Baldwin use the pronouns "you" and "one" in writing about his own experience? What are the effects of this choice?

CONNECTIONS

1. "I really did not . . . believe that love existed, except as useless pain; [nor] see the contradiction implicit in the fact that I was bending all my forces, or imagined I was, to protect myself against it" (para. 12). How does this statement apply to Achates McNeil's attitude and actions in T. Coraghessan Boyle's story by that name (p. 245)?

2. Are the reasons for Baldwin's friend's suicide more like those of CAG in Andre Dubus's "Imperiled Men" (p. 237) or of So Tsi-fai in Sophronia Liu's "So Tsi-fai" (p. 231)? What factors does each writer blame for the untimely death of his or her friend?

3. What comments about U.S. expatriates in "The New Lost Generation" correspond to elements in Walker Percy's definition of "the lost self" (p. 10)? How do you think Percy would explain Baldwin's emigration to Paris?

ELABORATIONS

1. What was "the lost generation"? Why was it so called? What is the meaning of Baldwin's title "The New Lost Generation"? Write an essay defining the term as it was originally used and comparing the meaning Baldwin gives to it.

2. "Voyagers discover that the world can never be larger than the person that is in the world" (para. 21). What does Baldwin mean by this? Do you agree with him? Write an essay explaining and exploring his statement.

RICHARD RODRIGUEZ

Europe Once Gripped America's Imagination — Now It's the Other Way Around

Much of Richard Rodriguez's writing centers on the contrasts and contradictions of growing up in California as the son of Mexican immigrants. Born in San Francisco in 1944, he was called Ricardo and spoke only Spanish until he entered school. His parents were committed to his education despite the distance it put between him and them. With their support, Rodriguez went from private Roman Catholic schools in Sacramento to Stanford University, graduating in 1967; he received his M.A. from Columbia University, did graduate work at the University of California at Berkeley, and won a Fulbright Fellowship to the Warburg Institute in London for 1972 to 1973. He turned down several teaching offers and held assorted jobs before settling into writing as a full-time occupation. Personal experience has made him skeptical of bilingual education and affirmative action policies, two of the many subjects he has addressed in his magazine features, his essays for *The NewsHour* on PBS, and his two memoirs, *Hunger of Memory: The Education of Richard Rodriguez* (1982) and *Days of Obligation: An Argument with My Mexican Father* (1992). Rodriguez is also an editor with the Pacific News Service and a contributing editor for *Harper's* and the *Los Angeles Times*. He lives in San Francisco. The following essay comes from the April 1998 on-line magazine *Cronica*.

For information on Europe, see page 277.

It used to be that Americans — bohemians and millionaires, intellectuals and socialites — needed to go to Europe to learn about life. Europe the old country, Europe the American obsession, Europe the fatherland.

You do not have to be of European ancestry to feel its hold on the American imagination. All my life, for example, my literary imagination has been focused on Europe. Only lately have I bothered to notice that the best books in English about Mexico have been written by British writers. American writers did not write about Mexico or Canada or Australia.

Traditionally, if an American writer ventured beyond our borders, he ventured to Europe — inevitably so, oddly so. Inevitably, because for most of our history, we have thought of ourselves as being a country derived from Europe. But oddly so, because the United States was founded in rebellion against an overbearing British crown and the old aristocratic order.

By the late nineteenth century, immigrants from Germany and Italy and Sweden fled to Ellis Island, escaping European poverty. But if Europe was the old country, America the new, immigrants found themselves in a place that seemed to have no history, no memory, therefore no knowledge of life. We Americans judged ourselves inexperienced.

When Mark Twain, our most self-conscious American writer, trans- 5 ported his literary persona to Europe, he portrayed himself as an "innocent abroad." Henry James wrote novels about young heroines, with names as fresh as Daisy Miller, who got ensnared in cynical European drawing rooms.

But still Americans went. The newly rich from Pittsburgh and Chicago took "the grand tour," hoping to buy experience, to learn sophistication. To this day, Americans grow flustered by haughty French waiters, and Cary Grant's middle-class British accent sounds mighty grand to our American ears.

Recently, when the story of Monica Lewinsky broke, I'd hear people criticizing their fellow Americans for a lack of sophistication. People said, after all, in Europe sexual matters are of little concern. Just look at what happened when the French president died. His wife and his mistress were both at his funeral.

Europe, the sophisticate. America, the yokel.

In truth, the twentieth century has not been a good one for European moral superiority. Twice within forty years, Europe devoured itself. Europe gave the world Hitler and Stalin, Mussolini and Franco.

In the aftermath of World War II, one sensed a decline of Europe in 10 the American imagination, until today we easily recognize that America is a global society, not just Europe's invention. With that confidence, American pop culture has grown dominant in the world.

At the other end of this century, the American writer Gertrude Stein, living in Paris, described the city of Oakland, California, as having "no there there." Today, I do not know of any young Americans who dream of going to Paris to become writers. But I know young Africans in Paris who take their cues from Afro-American Oakland.

In the last fifty years, we have come to be seen by people all over the world as too powerful to be able to pass ourselves off as innocents. Curiously enough, as the century ends, Europeans are inclined to play the innocent, and they regard us as the contaminating other.

A few months ago, on British radio, an interviewer kept badgering me, blaming America — our music, our movies — for the rising crime rate in London (gangs, guns, graffiti).

Roles have changed. As the century ends, young and not-so-young Europeans head for New York and Los Angeles, especially L.A., to become screen writers and directors. German and Italian tourists — sometimes called "Euro-trash" by jaded Americans — head for decadent San Francisco or Miami.

In truth, there isn't much moral difference between San Francisco   15 and Berlin. "The only difference," a German friend of mine says, "is that sin has a sharper tang in San Francisco, because you Americans still like to imagine yourselves morally innocent."

EXPLORATIONS

1. Where does Richard Rodriguez first introduce his essay's thesis? At what other points and in what other words does he state it? How would you state the thesis of this essay?

2. What definition of Europe is Rodriguez using in this essay? What definition is he using of America? How does he let us know what his definitions are? How would his essay's impact change if it included explicit definitions of these two key terms?

3. In the historical "before and after" Rodriguez sets up, what is his dividing line? What kinds of evidence does he use to support the "before"? The "after"? Which kinds of evidence do you find most and least convincing?

CONNECTIONS

1. In "The New Lost Generation," James Baldwin writes: "We were in Paris, after all, because we had presumably put down all formulas and all safety in favor of the chilling unpredictability of experience" (p. 263, para. 20). On what points do Baldwin and Rodriguez agree regarding the reasons for Americans' emigration to Europe? On what points don't these two writers agree?

2. Which of Rodriguez's observations are echoed by Margaret Atwood in "A View from Canada" (p. 79)? What observations by Atwood suggest that she would agree or disagree with Rodriguez's paragraph 3?

3. Does Rodriguez's comparison apply only to America and Europe? What contrasts in his essay also appear in Amy Tan's "Two Kinds" (p. 24)? In Salman Rushdie's "Imaginary Homelands" (p. 86)? How do you think each of these writers might restate Rodriguez's thesis to fit her or his own bicultural experience?

ELABORATIONS

1. What caused the "decline of Europe in the American imagination" (para. 10) that Rodriguez is writing about? Using this essay, Baldwin's "The New Lost Generation," and Paul Harrison's "The Westernization of the World" (p. 66) as sources, write an essay investigating when and why American and European attitudes toward each other changed.

2. Have you ever been to Europe? If so, where did you go, and why? If not, do you want to go? If so, where and why? If not, why not? Write an essay analyzing your attitude toward going to Europe, or comparing and contrasting your attitude with that of your parents.

ALESSANDRA STANLEY

The New Europeans: Multilingual, Cosmopolitan, Borderless

Alessandra Stanley became chief of the *New York Times*'s Rome bureau in 1998. Born in Boston in 1955, she grew up in Washington, D.C., and Europe. She graduated from Harvard with a major in comparative literature in 1977; she speaks Russian, French, and Italian. Stanley worked for *Time* magazine in Nicaragua and El Salvador, traveling on special assignment for the magazine to Afghanistan, Burma, Mozambique, and Northern Ireland. After serving as a *Time* stringer in Paris, she became a correspondent at their Los Angeles bureau in 1981, then a senior correspondent in their Washington bureau, writing on politics and national affairs. Stanley has been a guest on numerous television and radio shows and has written articles and profiles for publications including *The New Republic*, *GQ*, and *Vogue* magazines. In 1990 she joined the *New York Times* as a metropolitan reporter. Four years later she moved to Moscow as a foreign correspondent for the *Times*, writing extensively about life in Russia after Communism as well as covering the war in Chechnya and the 1996 Russian presidential elections. In September 1996 she became the newspaper's co–bureau chief in Moscow. The following essay appeared in the *New York Times* on December 24, 1998.

The European Union (EU) is a rapidly evolving community that currently consists of fifteen member nations. It grew out of the older European Economic Community (Common Market), European Coal and Steel Community, and European Atomic Energy Community. The EU comprises Austria, Belgium, Denmark, Finland, France, Germany, Greece, Ireland, Italy, Luxembourg, the Netherlands, Portugal, Spain, Sweden, and the United Kingdom. Begun as a regional economic alliance, the EU now represents a long-range plan for member nations to move toward economic and political unity. Acting cooperatively has decreased friction and red tape within Europe, allowing people, goods, capital, and services to circulate freely; it also has increased members' economic and political clout in relation to other nations and alliances. To gain these advantages, member countries have had to yield some individual sovereignty and in several cases ally themselves with ancient rivals.

The EU (although not its individual member nations) is currently governed by its own democratic institutions. A commission proposes policies and legislation and monitors compliance with EU decisions. A council of ministers from each member country enacts legislation. The 518-member European Parliament works cooperatively with these two groups. The Court of Justice adjudicates disputes. An economic and social committee supplies proposals and policy advice. A court of auditors reviews spending, while the European Investment Bank is the world's largest international financing institution.

Palm Pilot in one hand, cellular phone in the other, Jean-Marc Routiers, twenty-six, was juggling business calls halfway between London and Paris. When his phone went dead as the high-speed Eurostar train pulled into the underwater tunnel that links England to the Continent, the London-based French banker loosened his Italian silk tie and introduced himself.

"I definitely describe myself as a European," he said in the fluent English he perfected working at an Australian bank. "I may get sentimental when they play the Marseillaise,[1] but for all the practical things, I see myself as a citizen of Europe. I like the lifestyle in France, but I don't make my living there."

The year 1999 is the official start-up date of the euro, the common European currency that will unite eleven countries monetarily. But throughout Europe, a different kind of integration has already taken root.

Mr. Routiers, who was spending a day in Paris to meet with his bank's French clients, is at the vanguard of a new generation of Europeans who do not have to brace themselves for a shock in the new year. Mobile, fluent in several languages, and aggressively non-nationalistic, they are already living the kind of borderless, cosmopolitan existence that the single European currency is supposed to advance.

They do not share their parents' memories of World War II or their   5
parents' sense of national identity.

"People worry when they hear talk of a common European defense policy because it suggests that at the end of the day, we have one government," said Kleon Papadopoulos, a Greek banker based in London. "Countries are afraid to lose their sovereignty, but I don't see it as a bad thing. If a government is good, stable, and efficient, who cares if it is based in Berlin or Athens?"

Mr. Papadopoulos, thirty-six, who studied business in the United States and Britain, could serve as a model for the new Europeans. He works for a Swiss bank in London, speaks Greek, English, and French,

---

[1]*The Marseillaise:* French national anthem. — ED.

and in the past year has traveled, among other places, to Belgium, the United States, Cuba, Switzerland, and Italy.

Like hundreds of thousands of other Europeans, he chose London — and its busy financial markets — as the best place to work.

He said he does not feel as if he lives in England. He lives in London, the clubhouse of financial Europe. And membership has its privileges. Mr. Papadopoulos lives in the fashionable Knightsbridge area, drives a Porsche he bought in Brussels, and works out at the fashionable gym of the Carleton Towers.

"I went to the London School of Economics in 1984, and the only other 'foreigners' I met were from the Middle East," he says. "Now friends and co-workers are Italian, French, Greek, Spanish, German, even Russian. You feel it everywhere. The streets are jammed with foreigners. Not tourists — people who live and work here."

Baby-boomers in Europe often describe themselves as the 1968 generation, weaned on the protest and social turmoil that convulsed European societies thirty years ago. Less dramatic but equally significant was a 1968 law guaranteeing freedom of movement within what were then the six countries of the Common Market. A Frenchman could work in Holland, an Italian could work in Germany without a permit.

Back then some economists dourly predicted huge migrations, particularly of unskilled laborers moving from southern countries to the more prosperous north. Actually, as huge industries like steel shrank in the 1970s and 1980s, so did the job opportunities for working-class Europeans.

There are fifteen countries within what is now the European Union, but only a small percentage of their citizens have moved to other countries, according to estimates prepared by Eurostat. Those who do mostly find jobs in the service industry as waiters, maids, or garbage collectors. There are still legal barriers preventing most doctors, lawyers, and academics from finding work in other countries.

So far the European Union has been most profitably put to use by white-collar business executives who eagerly followed career opportunities across national borders, time zones, and language barriers.

Twenty-five years ago that kind of mobility was the preserve of a far smaller elite, the top executives of major companies or multinational corporations. Technology, from high-speed trains to the ever-evolving apparatus of business — lap-top computers, cell phones, fax machines — has made European mobility accessible to midlevel managers, young entrepreneurs, and even students. Cable television, which allows Germans to watch Italian game shows or Swedes to watch French news programs, has spread the Zeitgeist to the masses.

This year Superga, an Italian brand of sports clothes and shoes, opened a major advertising campaign with a series of magazine ads that show fashionable young people saucily cavorting with European leaders — a leggy young woman pushes her bicycle up the steps of the Elysée Palace to greet [French] President Jacques Chirac, a young man playfully sticks his tongue out the window of the plane of the former German chancellor, Helmut Kohl.

"This kind of ad would not have been possible five or ten years ago," said Aldo Cernuto, executive creative director of the Milan office of Pirella Gottsche Lowe, an international advertising agency. "Now European unification is on the TV all the time; it has seeped into people's unconscious. Even people who do not care about politics recognize the faces of a Tony Blair or Jacques Chirac. Ten years ago, very few people did."

According to the European Union, Britain has twice as many EU citizens as France, but it is not the country with the highest concentration of residents from other European countries. According to estimates based on surveys prepared by Eurostat, nearly a third of the residents of tiny Luxembourg, which has low unemployment and a high standard of living, are from other European countries. Belgium, which has the European Commission and NATO [North Atlantic Treaty Organization] headquarters, is second, with 5.4 percent.

Paradoxically, perhaps, Britain, the one major European nation that has held off from joining the euro, is widely viewed as the nerve center of the new cosmopolitanism, headquarters for the New Europeans — bankers and business executives drawn by London's financial district, a more flexible bureaucracy, and the universality of the English language.

Perhaps just as surprisingly, London also serves as an example of another less obvious aspect of European cosmopolitanism — the breakdown of certain social barriers.   20

Studying abroad was once a privilege reserved to the sons and daughters of Europe's elite. Now the European Union has a twelve-year-old scholarship program, called Socrates-Erasmus, that this year allowed 200,000 European university students — 5 percent of the EU's entire university population — to study in other countries within the Union for up to a year, free.

In the last twenty years, business schools in Europe have multiplied, and most offer U.S.-style MBA programs that teach an American approach to business. This too has allowed a measure of meritocracy to creep into European business.

"Juergen Schrempp, the head of Daimler, started as a car mechanic," noted Stephen Szabo, a professor of European Affairs at the Johns Hopkins University School for International Studies in Washington. "That would have been unthinkable in Germany twenty years ago."

Social mobility, moreover, is fueled by movement. When people transfer to another country, they find it easier to shed the psychological or cultural trappings of home.

"I could never have the kind of job I have had I stayed in Paris," Mr.   25
Routier explained. "France is still very hierarchical. Bosses want to know where you went to school, what your father does. In London, none of that matters as long as you make money."

Many Britons still view their country as weighed down by heavy class distinctions.

For example, Tony Smith, thirty-six, editor of several Portuguese magazines in Lisbon, seized an opportunity to study in Vienna fourteen years ago, and never looked back. He has lived all over Europe, and is fluent in Portuguese, Spanish, German, French, and Serbo-Croatian. His father, a car mechanic, had not traveled out of Britain until 1992. Mr. Smith said he could never have succeeded as well had he stayed home. "I didn't go to public schools or Oxbridge,"[2] he explained. "I'm not saying it's impossible, but it would have been much more difficult in England."

Yet Continental Europeans who flock to London find themselves bypassing English society and joining a cosmopolitan world where birth and breeding do not matter as much.

Ildiko Iliffe, thirty, chose to work in London to escape the sexism she encountered on the Continent. Mrs. Iliffe, who is Hungarian, speaks fluent English, German, French, and Italian, and met her Canadian husband, Roger Iliffe, thirty, while both were attending the University of Bocconi business school, in Milan, in 1995. Like his wife, Mr. Iliffe speaks four languages and has lived and traveled all over the world. She works on the Eastern European desk of a British bank; he works for a major international consulting firm. Originally they planned to work in Italy, but Mrs. Iliffe said the prevailing attitude toward working women there made it impossible for her to find as good a job.

"I went to job interviews at Italian banks and they only asked me about   30
my husband's job," she said with a grimace. "And they made it clear that they were afraid I would get pregnant and ask for maternity leave."

Philippe Haspeslagh, forty-eight, a professor at Insead, the prestigious international business school in Fontainebleau, outside Paris, called Mrs. Iliffe's choices cherry-picking — choosing the best deal for herself. As he put it, "If they cannot find what they want in one country, they can pick up and seek it elsewhere."

Twenty-five years ago, Mr. Haspeslagh was a pioneer when he did the same thing. A Belgian who studied business at Harvard, he lives and teaches in France and does consulting work all over Europe, from Swe-

---

[2] *Oxbridge* refers to England's exclusive Oxford and Cambridge Universities. — ED.

den to the Czech Republic. The message on his cell phone is in three languages — French, Flemish, and English. His students, a generation behind him, see nothing exceptional in his transnationalism.

These Europeans form an advance guard that is still relatively small in numbers, but experts say they carry a disproportionate influence on their societies.

"In Germany, for example, it is the businesspeople who are pushing ahead with change and pulling politicians along behind them kicking and screaming," Mr. Szabo said. "They are looking at a larger market and feel the competitive pressures of globalization. Politicians are responding to a domestic constituency. They are answering to an international one."

EXPLORATIONS

1. Judging from this essay, what are the advantages of being a "new European"? What are the drawbacks?

2. What are the requirements to become a "new European"? In what ways are they more rigorous than the requirements to be a traditional European? In what ways are they less rigorous?

3. What sources of information does Alessandra Stanley use for her essay? What roles does the author's own experience play? How would the essay's impact change if it were written in the first person?

CONNECTIONS

1. How does the portrait of Europe painted by Stanley in "The New Europeans: Multilingual, Cosmopolitan, Borderless" differ from the portrait of Europe painted by Richard Rodriguez in "Europe Once Gripped America's Imagination — Now It's the Other Way Around" (p. 273)? What seems to be the attitude toward America of the Europeans whom Stanley interviews?

2. In comparing America and Europe, both Rodriguez and James Baldwin ("The New Lost Generation," p. 263) allude to the contrast between innocence and experience. What role, if any, does that contrast play in Stanley's essay, and why?

3. Paul Harrison, writing about nonwestern countries in "The Westernization of the World" (p. 66), asks: "Why is almost everyone following virtually the same European road?" (para. 6). What is Harrison's answer to this question? How do you think the people in his essay would respond to the European banker's question quoted by Stanley: "If a government is good, stable, and efficient, who cares if it is based in Berlin or Athens?" (para. 6)?

ELABORATIONS

1. When Italians evaluate Germany, or Europeans evaluate America, what criteria do they use? For instance, in Rodriguez's "Europe Once Gripped America's Imagination — Now It's the Other Way Around" (p. 273), what is the role of geography? History? Ethnicity? Morality? Socioeconomic status? What other factors are significant in each group's view of the other's native land? In "The New Europeans: Multilingual, Cosmopolitan, Borderless," are the criteria the same or different? Write an essay responding to Rodriguez's essay or Stanley's or both, classifying the aspects of life in a place that shape outsiders' attitudes toward it.

2. Are you a cherry-picker? Based on the kind of work you do, or plan to do after you complete your education, where is the best place for you to live? How do you expect to decide where you (and your family, if any) will settle? Reread the comments of the Europeans quoted in paragraphs 20 and following. Then write an essay describing how the factors that influenced their choices are likely to influence yours.

NADINE GORDIMER

Where Do Whites Fit In?

Born in a small gold-mining town in South Africa in 1923, Nadine Gordimer is an outspoken civil libertarian who has always believed that change in her country's policies is best spurred from within. Much of her writing has focused on the impact of apartheid—institutionalized racial segregation—on South Africans. Gordimer started writing in childhood; she was educated at a convent school and Witwatersrand University but gives most credit to her local library. Her novels, short stories, and essays have won her numerous awards and honorary degrees. She has contributed to many American magazines, including *The New Yorker, Harper's, The Atlantic Monthly*, and *The New York Review of Books*, as well as taught creative writing at Columbia University's Graduate School of the Arts. In 1978 she was elected an honorary member of the American Academy and Institute of Arts and Letters. In 1991 she became the first South African to win the Nobel Prize for literature. Gordimer currently lives with her family in Johannesburg. Her novels include *The Conservationist* (1974), *July's People* (1981), *A Sport of Nature* (1987), and *The House Gun* (1998). In her 1995 book *Writing and Being*, drawn from a lecture series at Harvard University, she considers not only her fellow South African writers but Naguib Mahfouz of Egypt (see p. 95), Chinua Achebe of Nigeria (see p. 489), and Amos Oz of Israel (see p. 569). The book's final sentences make a fitting postscript for "Where Do Whites Fit In?" (which first appeared in 1959 in *Twentieth Century*): "My country is the world, whole, a synthesis. I am no longer a colonial. I may now speak of 'my people.'"

For information on South Africa, see pages 73 and 600.

Where do whites fit in in the New Africa? *Nowhere,* I'm inclined to say, in my gloomier and least courageous moods; and I do believe that it is true that even the gentlest and most westernized Africans would like the emotional idea of the continent entirely without the complication of the presence of the white man for a generation or two. But *nowhere,* as an answer for us whites, is in the same category as remarks like *What's the use of living?* in the face of threat of atomic radiation. We are living; we are in Africa. *Nowhere* is the desire to avoid painful processes and accept an ultimate and final solution (which doesn't exist in the continuous process that is life itself); the desire to have over and done with; the death wish, if not of the body, at least of the spirit.

For if we're going to fit in at all in the new Africa, it's going to be sideways, where-we-can, wherever-they'll-shift-up-for-us. This will not be comfortable; indeed, it will be hardest of all for those of us (I am one myself) who want to belong in the new Africa as we never could in the old, where our skin color labeled us as oppressors to the blacks and our views labeled us as traitors to the whites. We want merely to be ordinary members of a multicolored, any-colored society, freed both of the privileges and the guilt of the white sins of our fathers. This seems to us perfectly reasonable and possible and, in terms of reason, it is. But belonging to a society implies two factors which are outside reason: the desire to belong, on the one part, and acceptance, on the other part. The new Africa may, with luck, grant us our legal rights, full citizenship, and the vote, but I don't think it will accept us in the way we're hankering after. If ever, it will take the confidence of several generations of jealous independence before Africa will feel that she can let us belong.

There is nothing so damaging to the ego as an emotional rebuff of this kind. (More bearable by far the hate-engendered hate that the apartheiders must expect.) And you don't have to be particularly thin-skinned in order to feel this rebuff coming in Africa. Africans are prickling with the desire to be off on their own; the very fact that you welcome the new Africa almost as fervently as they do seems an intrusion in itself. They have had so much of us — let's not go through the whole list again, from tear gas and taxes to brotherly advice — that all they crave is to have no part of us.

You'll understand that I'm not speaking in economic or even political, but purely in human or, if you prefer it, psychological terms. For the purposes of what I have to say it may be true that in South Africa, for example, foreign capital and skills would have to be retained, in order to keep the mines and industry going, by wide concessions given by any black independent government with its head screwed on the right way. But the fact that we might go on living in our comfortable houses in the suburbs of Johannesburg under a black republic just as we do under a white near-republic, does not mean that we should feel ourselves accepted as part of the homogeneous society of the new Africa. For a long time to come any white South African must expect to find any black man, from any African territory, considered by the black South African as more of a brother than the white South African himself. No personal bonds of loyalty, friendship, or even love will change this; it is a nationalism of the heart that has been brought about by suffering. There is no share in it we can hope to have. I for one can read this already in the faces, voices, and eloquently regretful but firm handclasps of my own African friends.

Make no mistake, those moderate African political leaders who offer   5
us whites — with sincerity, I believe — full participation in the new life
of Africa offer us only the tangibles of existence. The intangibles that
make up emotional participation and the sense of belonging cannot be
legislated for.

What are we to do? Shall we go? Shall we leave Africa? For those
small white communities who are truly foreign to the African territories
in which they live, "sent out" from a homeland in Europe for a spell of
duty on administrative jobs or as representatives of commercial firms,
there can't be much question of staying on. But in those territories,
such as South Africa and the Rhodesias, where there is a sizable and
settled white population whose *home* is Africa, there is no easy answer;
sometimes, it seems no answer at all. I do not attempt to speak, of
course, for the stubborn mass that will continue, like a Napoleon in a
madhouse, to see itself as the undisputed master and make no attempt
to consider the reality of living another role. I do not even try to guess
what will happen to them; what *can* happen to them in a situation that
they find unthinkable. I can only fear that events will deal with them
grimly, as events usually do with people who refuse to think. I speak for
people like myself, who think almost too much about the whole business and hope to arrive at an honest answer, without self-pity for the
whites or sentiment about the blacks.

Some of us in South Africa want to leave; a few of us have gone already. And certainly, when one comes to Europe on a visit, one becomes a little uneasy at the number of friends (well-informed friends
with a good perspective on the swerves and lurches of the way the world
is going) who take one aside and ask whether one isn't planning to leave
Africa? Which brings me to the reasons why some people have left and
why these friends in Europe think one should pack up, too. A few have
left because they cannot bear the guilt and ugliness of the white man's
easy lot here; a few have left because they are afraid of the black man;
and most, I should say, have left because of a combination of the two. I
doubt if any consciously have left for the long-term reason I have elabo-
rated here — the growing unwelcomeness of the white man in Africa.
Yet I feel that if the white man's lot were to become no better and no
worse than anyone else's tomorrow and the fear of violence at the hands
of the black man (which we all have) were to have been brought to the
test and disproved, unwelcomeness might still remain as the factor that
would, in the end, decide many of us to give up our home and quit
Africa.

I myself fluctuate between the desire to be gone — to find a society
for myself where my white skin will have no bearing on my place in the

community — and a terrible, obstinate, and fearful desire to stay. I feel the one desire with my head and the other with my guts. I know that there must be many others who feel as I do, and who realize that generally the head is the more sensible guide of the two. Those of us who stay will need to have the use of our heads in order to sustain the emotional decision that home is not necessarily where you belong ethnogenically, but rather the place you were born to, the faces you first saw around you, and the elements of the situation among your fellow men in which you found yourself and with which you have been struggling, politically, personally, or artistically, all your life.

The white man who wants to fit in in the new Africa must learn a number of hard things. He'd do well to regard himself as an immigrant to a new country; somewhere he has never lived before, but to whose life he has committed himself. He'll have to forget the old impulses to leadership, and the temptation to give advice backed by the experience and culture of Western civilization — Africa is going through a stage when it passionately prefers its own mistakes to successes (or mistakes) that are not its own. This is an absolutely necessary stage in all political, sociological, and spiritual growth, but it is an uncomfortable and disillusioning one to live through. And giving up the impulse to advise and interfere and offer to resume responsibility may not be as easy as we whites think. Even those of us who don't want to be boss (or *baas*, rather) have become used to being bossy. We've been used to assuming leadership or at least tutorship, even if it's only been in liberal campaigns to secure the rights of the Africans to vote and speak for themselves. Out of our very concern to see Africans make a go of the new Africa, we may — indeed, I know we shall — be tempted to offer guidance when we haven't been consulted. The facts that we'll be well-meaning and that the advice may be good and badly-needed do not count; the sooner we drum that into our egos the better. What counts is the need of Africa to acquire confidence through the experience of picking itself up, dusting itself down, and starting all over again; and the quickening marvel of often getting things right into the bargain.

It's hard to sit quiet when you think you can tell how a problem may   10 be solved or a goal accomplished, but it may be even harder to give help without recriminations or, worse, smugness when it is sought. If we want to fit in anywhere in Africa, that is what we'll have to teach ourselves to do; answer up, cheerfully and willingly, when we're called upon and shut up when we're not. Already I notice that the only really happy whites I know in Africa — the only ones who are at peace with themselves over their place in the community — are some South African friends of mine who have gone to live in Ghana, and who have an educational job to do on contract from the government. They are living as equals among the Africans, they have no say in the affairs of the country for the Africans to resent, and they are contributing something useful and welcome to the development of Africa. In other words, they are in the position of foreign experts, employed at the government's pleasure. I can positively feel my fellow whites in Africa swelling with indignance at this extreme picture of the white man's future life on the continent; and it makes me feel rather indignant myself. But I think we've got to accept the home truth of the picture, whether we like it or not, and whether or not what we see there seems fair. All that the new Africa will really want from us will be what we can give as "foreign experts" — the technical, scientific, and cultural knowledge that white civilization has acquired many hundreds of years before black civilization, and on which, whether the Africans like it or not, their own aspirations are based.

I suppose we may get over being a minority minority instead of the majority minority we've been used to being all these past years, but I don't know whether that valuable change of attitude will actually bring us much nearer the integration we seek. Will intermarriage help us? It would, of course, on a large scale, but personally I don't believe that it will happen on a large scale in Africa. Intermarriage has always been regarded as a social stigma by whites, even in those territories where, unlike South Africa, it is not actually a crime, but I have never been able to find out whether, among blacks, it is regarded as a stigma or a step up in the world. (Most whites assume it is regarded as a deeply desired privilege, of course.) I know that, for example, in South Africa many Africans who are not Bechuanas, and have nothing whatever to do with the people of Bechuanaland, have on their walls a picture of Ruth and Seretse Khama.[1] It is difficult to say whether this means that they take pride in the fact that a white woman chose to marry an important African, or whether the picture simply gives them a chance to identify themselves with the ex-chief's successful defiance of white taboo and authority.

Once the social stigma is removed — in the new Africa marriage with an African will be marrying into the ruling class, remember, and no one can measure how much of color-prejudice is purely class-prejudice, in a country where there has been a great gap between the living standards

---

[1]Seretse Khama, who became president of Botswana (formerly Bechuanaland) after it gained independence from Britain (see p. 363) married Englishwoman Ruth Williams. — ED.

of black and white — and once (in the case of South Africa) there are no legal disabilities in mixed marriages, I think that intermarriage will increase at two extreme levels of the social scale, but scarcely at all in between. Intellectuals will intermarry because they feel closer to intellectuals, whatever their race or color, than to the mass, and the humbler and poorly adjusted fringes of both the black and white masses, who have not found acceptance in their own societies, will intermarry in order to find a home somewhere — if not within the confines of their own background, then in someone else's. But I don't think we can hope for intermarriage on an effective scale between ordinary people, and I shouldn't be surprised if independent black Africa frowned upon it, in an unofficial but firm way. Especially in a country like South Africa, where there might remain whites in sufficiently large numbers to create an unease at the possibility that they might try to close their hands once again on those possessions of power from which their fingers had been prised back one by one. It is quite likely that there will be a social stigma, among ordinary people whose sense of nationalism is well stoked up, attached to marrying whites; it may be considered un-African. (Nkrumah[2] has set the official precedent already, by choosing not a Ruth Williams, but a girl who "belongs" to the continent — a bride from Nasser's Egypt.) If white numbers do not dwindle in those areas of the continent which are heavily white-populated, and there is integration in schools and universities and no discrimination against white children, the picture will change in a few generations, of course. I do not see those young people as likely to regard parental race prejudice on either side as anything but fuddy-duddy. But will the whites remain, stick it out anywhere in Africa in sufficient numbers for this to come about? Isn't it much more likely that they will dwindle to small, socially isolated communities, whites in the diaspora?

If one will always have to feel white first, and African second, it would be better not to stay on in Africa. It would not be worth it for this. Yet, although I claim no mystique about Africa, I fear that like one of those oxen I sometimes read about in the Sunday papers, I might, dumped somewhere else and kindly treated, continually plod blindly back to where I came from.

---

[2]Kwame Nkrumah was the first president of independent Ghana. — ED.

EXPLORATIONS

1. What is Nadine Gordimer's first answer to the question "Where Do Whites Fit In?" How would you summarize her real answer to this question? What are the effects of her starting with a more extreme answer than she ends up with?

2. For Gordimer, what is the critical factor in deciding whether to stay in South Africa or leave? What evidence in her essay suggests that she sees the same factor as critical to South Africa's future success under black rule?

3. What is Gordimer's definition of "African" in this essay? What term or terms does she use for people in her own racial and national group? How does her usage bolster her essay's thesis?

CONNECTIONS

1. ". . . Home is not necessarily where you belong ethnogenically, but rather the place you were born to, the faces you first saw around you, and the elements of the situation among your fellow men in which you found yourself and with which you have been struggling, politically, personally, or artistically, all your life" (para. 8). What are these "faces" and "elements" for Gordimer? What are they for the "new Europeans" described by Alessandra Stanley (p. 277)? What are the most important contrasts in the concept of home between Gordimer's Africans and Stanley's Europeans?

2. In paragraph 9 Gordimer discusses the need in the new Africa for the former ruling class to resist the temptation "to offer guidance when we haven't been consulted." How do her observations here apply to Rosaura's mother in Liliana Heker's "The Stolen Party" (p. 224)? Does Rosaura's mother follow Gordimer's advice? What are the results?

3. Compare Gordimer's arguments for and against leaving Africa with James Baldwin's arguments for and against emigrating from the United States to Europe (p. 263). What points do both writers make? What points does Baldwin make about the problems that follow emigration that probably would affect Gordimer and other white ex-Africans?

ELABORATIONS

1. Which of the racial challenges Gordimer describes in South Africa also are faced by us in the United States? How do our country's location, history, and population make our problems different? Write an essay comparing and contrasting the two countries' racial dilemmas. Or, write your own local version of "Where Do Whites Fit In?"

2. Many of Gordimer's observations in "Where Do Whites Fit In?" could be applied to other groups besides white South Africans: mothers of newly married sons, for instance, or officers at a formerly all-male military academy. Choose some group that has lost its former exclusivity or dominance and write an essay redirecting Gordimer's ideas and recommendations to that group.

ROBERT REICH

The Three Jobs of the Future

Robert Reich (pronounced rysh) served as secretary of labor for the Clinton administration from 1993 to 1997. A contemporary of President Clinton's, he graduated from Dartmouth College, earned his master's degree as a Rhodes scholar at Oxford University, and received his J.D. from Yale Law School. His interest in public service started early: Reich worked as a summer intern for Senator Robert Kennedy and was coordinator of Senator Eugene McCarthy's 1968 presidential campaign. He also advised presidential candidates Walter Mondale and Michael Dukakis. "I have dedicated my life to ensuring that the economy works for everyone," he has stated. His jobs in public service include assistant to the solicitor general and policy planning director for the Federal Trade Commission. Meanwhile, he wrote: The best known of his five books, *The Work of Nations: Preparing Ourselves for 21st-Century Capitalism* (1991), has been translated into fourteen languages. The following essay is taken from it. Reich lectured for twelve years at Harvard University's Kennedy School of Government before becoming the Clinton administration's first secretary of labor. He is now a university professor at Brandeis University, where he established the Center on Jobs, the Economy, and Society at the Heller Graduate School for Advanced Studies in Social Welfare. Reich lives in Cambridge, Massachusetts, with his wife, a law professor, and their two sons.

The usual discussion about the future of the American economy focuses on topics like the competitiveness of General Motors, or of the American automobile industry, or, more broadly, of American manufacturing, or, more broadly still, of the American economy. But, as has been observed, these categories are becoming irrelevant. They assume the continued existence of an American economy in which jobs associated with a particular firm, industry, or sector are somehow connected within the borders of the nation, so that American workers face a common fate; and a common enemy as well: The battlefields of world trade pit our corporations and our workers unambiguously against theirs.

No longer. In the emerging international economy, few American companies and American industries compete against foreign companies and industries — if by *American* we mean where the work is done and the value is added. Becoming more typical is the global web, perhaps headquartered in and receiving much of its financial capital from the United States, but with research, design, and production facilities spread over Japan, Europe, and North America; additional production facilities in Southeast Asia and Latin America; marketing and distribution centers on every continent; and lenders and investors in Taiwan, Japan, and West Germany as well as the United States. This ecumenical company competes with similarly ecumenical companies headquartered in other nations. Battle lines no longer correspond with national borders.

So, when an "American" company like General Motors shows healthy profits, this is good news for its strategic brokers in Detroit and its American investors. It is also good news for other GM executives worldwide and for GM's global employees, subcontractors, and investors. But it is not necessarily good news for a lot of routine assembly-line workers in Detroit, because there are not likely to be many of them left in Detroit, or anywhere else in America. Nor is it necessarily good news for the few Americans who are still working on assembly lines in the United States, who increasingly receive their paychecks from corporations based in Tokyo or Bonn.

The point is that Americans are becoming part of an international labor market, encompassing Asia, Africa, Latin America, Western Europe, and, increasingly, Eastern Europe and the Soviet Union. The competitiveness of Americans in this global market is coming to depend, not on the fortunes of any American corporation or on American industry, but on the functions that Americans perform — the value they add — within the global economy. Other nations are undergoing precisely the same transformation, some more slowly than the United States, but all participating in essentially the same transnational trend. Barriers to cross-border flows of knowledge, money, and tangible products are crumbling; groups of people in every nation are joining global webs. In a very few years, there will be virtually no way to distinguish one national economy from another except by the exchange rates of their currencies — and even this distinction may be on the wane.

Americans thus confront global competition ever more directly, un-   5
mediated by national institutions. As we discard vestigial notions of the competitiveness of American corporations, American industry, and the American economy, and recast them in terms of the competitiveness of the American workforce, it becomes apparent that successes or failures will not be shared equally by all our citizens.

Some Americans, whose contributions to the global economy are more highly valued in world markets, will succeed, while others, whose contributions are deemed far less valuable, fail. GM's American execu-

tives may become more competitive even as GM's American production workers become less so, because the functions performed by the
former group are more highly valued in the world market than those of
the latter. So when we speak of the "competitiveness" of Americans in
general, we are talking only about how much the world is prepared to
spend, *on average,* for services performed by Americans. Some Americans may command much higher rewards; others, far lower. No longer
are Americans rising or falling together, as if in one large national boat.
We are, increasingly, in different, smaller boats.

In order to see in greater detail what is happening to American jobs
and to understand why the economic fates of Americans are beginning
to diverge, it is first necessary to view the work that Americans do in
terms of categories that reflect their real competitive positions in the
global economy.

Official data about American jobs are organized by categories that are
not very helpful in this regard. The U.S. Bureau of the Census began in-
quiring about American jobs in 1820, and developed a systematic way of
categorizing them in 1870. Beginning in 1943, the Census came up with
a way of dividing these categories into different levels of "social-
economic status," depending upon, among other things, the prestige and
income associated with each job. In order to determine the appropriate
groupings, the Census first divided all American jobs into either business
class or working class . . . and then divided each of these, in turn, into
subcategories. In 1950, the Census added the category of "service workers" and called the resulting scheme America's "Major Occupational
Groups," which it has remained ever since. All subsequent surveys have
been based on this same set of categories. Thus, even by 1990, in the eyes
of the Census, you were either in a "managerial and professional specialty," in a "technical, sales, and administrative support" role, in a "service occupation," an "operator, fabricator, and laborer," or in a "trans-
portation and material moving" occupation.

This set of classifications made sense when the economy was focused
on high-volume, standardized production, in which almost every job fit
into, or around, the core American corporation, and when status and
income depended on one's ranking in the standard corporate bureaucracy. But these categories have little bearing upon the competitive positions of Americans worldwide, now that America's core corporations
are transforming into finely spun global webs. Someone whose job falls
officially into a "technical" or "sales" subcategory may, in fact, be
among the best-paid and most influential people in such a web. To un-

derstand the real competitive positions of Americans in the global economy, it is necessary to devise new categories.

Essentially, three broad categories of work are emerging, correspond-   10
ing to the three different competitive positions in which Americans
find themselves. The same three categories are taking shape in other
nations. Call them *routine production services, in-person services,* and
symbolic-analytic services.

Routine production services entail the kinds of repetitive tasks performed by the old foot soldiers of American capitalism in the high-
volume enterprise. They are done over and over — one step in a sequence of steps for producing finished products tradeable in world
commerce. Although often thought of as traditional blue-collar jobs,
they also include routine supervisory jobs performed by low- and midlevel managers — foremen, line managers, clerical supervisors, and section chiefs — involving repetitive checks on subordinates' work and the
enforcement of standard operating procedures.

Routine production services are found in many places within a mod
ern economy apart from older, heavy industries (which, like elderly citizens, have been given the more delicate, and less terminal, appellation:
"mature"). They are found even amid the glitter and glitz of high technology. Few tasks are more tedious and repetitive, for example, than
stuffing computer circuit boards or devising routine coding for computer software programs.

Indeed, contrary to prophets of the "information age" who buoyantly
predicted an abundance of high-paying jobs even for people with
the most basic of skills, the sobering truth is that many information-
processing jobs fit easily into this category. The foot soldiers of the information economy are hordes of data processors stationed in "back offices" at computer terminals linked to worldwide information banks.
They routinely enter data into computers or take it out again — records
of credit card purchases and payments, credit reports, checks that have
cleared, customer accounts, customer correspondence, payroll, hospital
billings, patient records, medical claims, court decisions, subscriber
lists, personnel, library catalogues, and so forth. The "information revolution" may have rendered some of us more productive, but it has also
produced huge piles of raw data which must be processed in much the
same monotonous way that assembly-line workers and, before them,
textile workers processed piles of other raw materials.

Routine producers typically work in the company of many other
people who do the same thing, usually within large enclosed spaces.
They are guided on the job by standard procedures and codified rules,
and even their overseers are overseen, in turn, by people who routinely

monitor — often with the aid of computers — how much they do and how accurately they do it. Their wages are based either on the amount of time they put in or on the amount of work they do.

Routine producers usually must be able to read and to perform   15 simple computations. But their cardinal virtues are reliability, loyalty, and the capacity to take direction. Thus does a standard American education, based on the traditional premises of American education, normally suffice.

By 1990, routine production work comprised about one-quarter of the jobs performed by Americans, and the number was declining. Those who dealt with metal were mostly white and male; those who dealt with fabrics, circuit boards, or information were mostly black or Hispanic, and female; their supervisors, white males.

In-person services, the second kind of work that Americans do, also entail simple and repetitive tasks. And like routine production services, the pay of in-person servers is a function of hours worked or amount of work performed; they are closely supervised (as are their supervisors), and they need not have acquired much education (at most, a high school diploma, or its equivalent, and some vocational training).

The big difference between in-person servers and routine producers is that *these* services must be provided person-to-person, and thus are not sold worldwide. (In-person servers might, of course, work for global corporations. Two examples: In 1988, Britain's Blue Arrow PLC acquired Manpower Inc., which provides custodial services throughout the United States. Meanwhile, Denmark's ISS-AS already employed over 16,000 Americans to clean office buildings in most major American cities.) In-person servers are in direct contact with the ultimate beneficiaries of their work; their immediate objects are specific customers rather than streams of metal, fabric, or data. In-person servers work alone or in small teams. Included in this category are retail sales workers, waiters and waitresses, hotel workers, janitors, cashiers, hospital attendants and orderlies, nursing-home aides, child-care workers, house cleaners, home health-care aides, taxi drivers, secretaries, hairdressers, auto mechanics, sellers of residential real estate, flight attendants, physical therapists, and — among the fastest-growing of all — security guards.

In-person servers are supposed to be as punctual, reliable, and tractable as routine production workers. But many in-person servers share one additional requirement: They must also have a pleasant demeanor. They must smile and exude confidence and good cheer, even when they feel morose. They must be courteous and helpful, even to the most obnoxious of patrons. Above all, they must make others feel happy and at ease. It should come as no surprise that, traditionally, most in-person servers have been women. The cultural stereotype of women as nurturers — as mommies — has opened countless in-person service jobs to them.

By 1990, in-person services accounted for about 30 percent of the   20
jobs performed by Americans, and their numbers were growing rapidly. For example, Beverly Enterprises, a single nursing-home chain operating throughout the United States, employed about the same number of Americans as the entire Chrysler Corporation (115,174 and 116,250, respectively) — although most Americans were far more knowledgeable about the latter, including the opinions of its chairman. In the United States during the 1980s, well over 3 million *new* in-person service jobs were created in fast-food outlets, bars, and restaurants. This was more than the *total* number of routine production jobs still existing in America by the end of the decade in the automobile, steelmaking, and textile industries combined.

Symbolic-analytic services, the third job category, include . . . problem-solving, problem-identifying, and strategic-brokering activities. . . . Like routine production services (but *unlike* in-person services), symbolic-analytic services can be traded worldwide and thus must compete with foreign providers even in the American market. But they do not enter world commerce as standardized things. Traded instead are the manipulations of symbols — data, words, oral and visual representations.

Included in this category are the problem-solving, -identifying, and -brokering of many people who call themselves research scientists, design engineers, software engineers, civil engineers, biotechnology engineers, sound engineers, public relations executives, investment bankers, lawyers, real estate developers, and even a few creative accountants. Also included is much of the work done by management consultants, financial consultants, tax consultants, energy consultants, agricultural consultants, armaments consultants, architectural consultants, management information specialists, organization development specialists, strategic planners, corporate headhunters, and systems analysts. Also: advertising executives and marketing strategists, art directors, architects, cinematographers, film editors, production designers, publishers, writers and editors, journalists, musicians, television and film producers, and even university professors.

Symbolic analysts solve, identify, and broker problems by manipulating symbols. They simplify reality into abstract images that can be rearranged, juggled, experimented with, communicated to other specialists, and then, eventually, transformed back into reality. The manipulations are done with analytic tools, sharpened by experience.

The tools may be mathematical algorithms, legal arguments, financial gimmicks, scientific principles, psychological insights about how to persuade or to amuse, systems of induction or deduction, or any other set of techniques for doing conceptual puzzles.

Some of these manipulations reveal how to more efficiently deploy resources or shift financial assets, or otherwise save time and energy. Other manipulations yield new inventions — technological marvels, innovative legal arguments, new advertising ploys for convincing people that certain amusements have become life necessities. Still other manipulations — of sounds, words, pictures — serve to entertain their recipients, or cause them to reflect more deeply on their lives or on the human condition. Others grab money from people too slow or naive to protect themselves by manipulating in response.

Like routine producers, symbolic analysts rarely come into direct 25 contact with the ultimate beneficiaries of their work. But other aspects of their work life are quite different from that experienced by routine producers. Symbolic analysts often have partners or associates rather than bosses or supervisors. Their incomes may vary from time to time, but are not directly related to how much time they put in or the quantity of work they put out. Income depends, rather, on the quality, originality, cleverness, and, occasionally, speed with which they solve, identify, or broker new problems. Their careers are not linear or hierarchical; they rarely proceed along well-defined paths to progressively higher levels of responsibility and income. In fact, symbolic analysts may take on vast responsibilities and command inordinate wealth at rather young ages. Correspondingly, they may lose authority and income if they are no longer able to innovate by building on their cumulative experience, even if they are quite senior.

Symbolic analysts often work alone or in small teams, which may be connected to larger organizations, including worldwide webs. Teamwork is often critical. Since neither problems nor solutions can be defined in advance, frequent and informal conversations help ensure that insights and discoveries are put to their best uses and subjected to quick, critical evaluation.[1]

When not conversing with their teammates, symbolic analysts sit before computer terminals — examining words and numbers, moving

---

[1]The physical environments in which symbolic analysts work are substantially different from those in which routine producers or in-person servers work. Symbolic analysts usually labor within spaces that are quiet and tastefully decorated. Soft lights, wall-to-wall carpeting, beige and puce colors are preferred. Such calm surroundings typically are encased within tall steel-and-glass buildings or within long, low, postmodernist structures carved into hillsides and encircled by expanses of well-manicured lawn. — Reich's note. All other notes have been deleted. — ED.

them, altering them, trying out new words and numbers, formulating and testing hypotheses, designing or strategizing. They also spend long hours in meetings or on the telephone, and even longer hours in jet planes and hotels — advising, making presentations, giving briefings, doing deals. Periodically, they issue reports, plans, designs, drafts, memoranda, layouts, renderings, scripts, or projections — which, in turn, precipitate more meetings to clarify what has been proposed and to get agreement on how it will be implemented, by whom, and for how much money. Final production is often the easiest part. The bulk of the time and cost (and, thus, real value) comes in conceptualizing the problem, devising a solution, and planning its execution.

Most symbolic analysts have graduated from four-year colleges or universities; many have graduate degrees as well. The vast majority are white males, but the proportion of white females is growing, and there is a small, but slowly increasing, number of blacks and Hispanics among them. All told, symbolic analysis currently accounts for no more than 20 percent of American jobs. The proportion of American workers who fit this category has increased substantially since the 1950s (by my calculation, no more than 8 percent of American workers could be classified as symbolic analysts at midcentury), but the pace slowed considerably in the 1980s — even though certain symbolic-analytic jobs, like law and investment banking, mushroomed.

These three functional categories cover more than three out of four American jobs. Among the remainder are farmers, miners, and other extractors of natural resources, who together comprise less than 5 percent of American workers. The rest are mainly government employees (including public school teachers), employees in regulated industries (like utility workers), and government-financed workers (American engineers working on defense weapons systems and physicians working off Medicaid and Medicare), almost all of whom are also sheltered from global competition.

Some traditional job categories — managerial, secretarial, sales, and 30 so on — overlap with more than one of these functional categories. The traditional categories, it should be emphasized, date from an era in which most jobs were as standardized as the products they helped create. Such categories are no longer very helpful for determining what a person actually does on the job and how much that person is likely to earn for doing it. Only some of the people who are classified as "secretaries," for example, perform strictly routine production work, such as entering and retrieving data from computers. Other "secretaries" provide in-person services, like making appointments and fetching coffee.

A third group of "secretaries" perform symbolic-analytic work closely al-lied to what their bosses do. To classify them all as "secretaries" glosses over their very different functions in the economy. Similarly, "sales" jobs can fall within any one of the three functional groups: some sales-people simply fill quotas and orders; others spend much of their time performing in-person services, like maintaining machinery; and some are sophisticated problem-identifiers no different from high-priced management consultants. "Computer programmers" (one of the more recent additions to the standard list of occupations) are as varied: They might be doing routine coding, in-person troubleshooting for particular clients, or translating complex functional specifications into software.

That a job category is officially classified "professional" or "mana-gerial" likewise has little bearing upon the function its occupant ac-tually performs in the world economy. Not all professionals, that is, are symbolic analysts. Some lawyers spend their entire working lives doing things that normal people would find unbearably monotonous — cranking out the same old wills, contracts, and divorces, over and over, with only the names changed. Some accountants do routine audits with-out the active involvement of their cerebral cortices. Some managers take no more responsibility than noting who shows up for work in the morning, making sure they stay put, and locking the place up at night. (I have even heard tell of university professors who deliver the same lec-tures for thirty years, long after their brains have atrophied, but I do not believe such stories.) None of these professionals is a symbolic analyst.

Nor are all symbolic analysts professionals. In the older, high-volume economy, a "professional" was one who had mastered a particular do-main of knowledge. The knowledge existed in advance, ready to be mastered. It had been recorded in dusty tomes or codified in precise rules and formulae. Once the novitiate had dutifully absorbed the knowledge and had passed an examination attesting to its absorption, professional status was automatically conferred — usually through a cer-emony of appropriately medieval pageantry and costume. The profes-sional was then authorized to place a few extra letters after his or her name, mount a diploma on the office wall, join the professional associa-tion and attend its yearly tax-deductible meeting in Palm Springs, and pursue clients with a minimum of overt avarice.

But in the new economy — replete with unidentified problems, un-known solutions, and untried means of putting them together — mastery of old domains of knowledge isn't nearly enough to guarantee a good income. Nor, importantly, is it even necessary. Symbolic analysts often can draw upon established bodies of knowledge with the flick of a computer key. Facts, codes, formulae, and rules are easily accessible.

What is much more valuable is the capacity to effectively and creatively *use* the knowledge. Possessing a professional credential is no guarantee of such capacity. Indeed, a professional education which has emphasized the rote acquisition of such knowledge over original thought may retard such capacity in later life.

How, then, do symbolic analysts describe what they do? With difficulty. Because a symbolic analyst's status, influence, and income have little to do with formal rank or title, the job may seem mysterious to people working outside the enterprise web, who are unfamiliar with the symbolic analyst's actual function within it. And because symbolic analysis involves processes of thought and communication, rather than tangible production, the content of the job may be difficult to convey simply. In answering the question "What did you do today, Mommy (or Daddy)?" it is not always instructive, or particularly edifying, to say that one spent three hours on the telephone, four hours in meetings, and the remainder of the time gazing at a computer screen trying to work out a puzzle.

Some symbolic analysts have taken refuge in job titles that communicate no more clearly than this, but at least sound as if they confer independent authority nonetheless. The old hierarchies are breaking down, but new linguistic idioms have arisen to perpetuate the time-honored custom of title-as-status. 35

Herewith a sample. Add any term from the first column to any from the second, and then add both terms to any from the third column, and you will have a job that is likely (but not necessarily) to be inhabited by a symbolic analyst.

Communications	Management	Engineer
Systems	Planning	Director
Financial	Process	Designer
Creative	Development	Coordinator
Project	Strategy	Consultant
Business	Policy	Manager
Resource	Applications	Adviser
Product	Research	Planner

The "flat" organization of high-value enterprise notwithstanding, there are subtle distinctions of symbolic-analytic rank. Real status is inversely related to length of job title. Two terms signify a degree of authority. (The first or second column's appellation is dropped, leaving a simpler and more elegant combination, such as "Project Engineer" or "Creative Director.") Upon the most valued of symbolic analysts, who have moved beyond mere technical proficiency to exert substantial influence on their peers within the web, is bestowed the highest honor — a title comprising a term from the last column preceded by a dignified adjective like Senior, Managing, Chief, or Principal. One becomes a "Senior Producer" or a "Principal Designer" not because of time loyally served or routines impeccably followed, but because of special deftness in solving, identifying, or brokering new problems.

Years ago, fortunate and ambitious young people ascended career ladders with comfortable predictability. If they entered a core corporation, they began as, say, a second assistant vice president for marketing. After five years or so they rose to the rank of first assistant vice president, and thence onward and upward. Had they joined a law firm, consulting group, or investment bank, they would have started as an associate, after five to eight years ascended to junior partner, and thence to senior partner, managing partner, and finally heaven.

None of these predictable steps necessitated original thought. Indeed, a particularly creative or critical imagination might even be hazardous to career development, especially if it elicited questions of a subversive sort, like "Aren't we working on the wrong problem?" or "Why are we doing this?" or, most dangerous of all, "Why does this organization exist?" The safest career path was the surest career path, and the surest path was sufficiently well worn by previous travelers so that it could not be missed.

Of course, there still exist organizational backwaters in which career   40
advancement is sequential and predictable. But fewer fortunate and ambitious young people dive into them, or even enter upon careers marked by well-worn paths. They dare not. In the emerging global economy, even the most impressive of positions in the most prestigious of organizations is vulnerable to worldwide competition if it entails easily replicated routines. The only true competitive advantage lies in skill in solving, identifying, and brokering new problems.

EXPLORATIONS

1. According to Robert Reich, what are the three categories of American jobs? In which of these categories have you worked? Do you agree with Reich's classification? Why or why not?

2. What reasons does Reich give for the transformation of the American job force? When does he believe the change took place?

3. What sources of information does Reich rely on? How would his essay's impact change if he based more of his conclusions on personal experience or interviews?

CONNECTIONS

1. "No longer are Americans rising or falling together, as if in one large national boat. We are, increasingly, in different, smaller boats" (para. 6). How do you think the economic changes Reich describes will affect the political and social changes in South Africa that Nadine Gordimer outlines in "Where Do Whites Fit In?" (p. 284).

2. What ideas proposed by Reich also appear in Alessandra Stanley's "The New Europeans: Multilingual, Cosmopolitan, Borderless" (p. 277)? Do you think Stanley perceives the same workforce transformation affecting Europeans that Reich sees among Americans? Why or why not?

3. James Baldwin and Richard Rodriguez (pp. 263 and 273) write about various reasons why Americans have moved to Europe in the past. Judging from Reich's essay, are those reasons still valid in the present? What new reasons are likely to prompt Americans to move to Europe (or vice versa) in the future?

ELABORATIONS

1. According to Reich, "No longer are Americans rising or falling together, as if in one large national boat. We are, increasingly, in different, smaller boats" (para. 6). According to Gordimer, ". . . Any white South African must expect to find any black man, from any African territory, considered by the black South African as more of a brother than the white South African himself" (p. 284, para. 4). As economic, technological, and political developments change the function of national boundaries, how are human beings reacting? In the twenty-first century, who will be in the same boat with whom? Will we identify ourselves by nationality, or job category, or employer, or what? Based on your reading in this chapter, write an essay responding to these questions.

2. How has the workforce transformation Reich describes affected your life? Among your family and friends, how have job choices been shaped by the expanding "global web" (para. 2)? What kind or kinds of work have you done in the past, and why? In which of Reich's categories do you hope to work in the future, and why? What kind of work will you encourage your children to do, and why? Write an essay relating Reich's ideas to your own experience.

PART FOUR

OPPOSITE SEXES

OBSERVATIONS

Paula Gunn Allen, David Friedman, Naomi Wolf,
Gerald Early, Andrew Sullivan, Population
Communications International, Lawrence Wright,
Caryl Rivers, Violeta Chamorro, Dympna Ugwu-Oju, Ved Mehta

▼ ▼ ▼

John Updike, *The Disposable Rocket* (UNITED STATES)

Curtis Sittenfeld, *Your Life as a Girl* (UNITED STATES)

Camille Paglia, *Woman and Nature* (UNITED STATES)

Sam Keen, *Man and WOMAN* (UNITED STATES)

Simone de Beauvoir, *Woman as Other* (FRANCE)

Alberto Moravia, *The Chase* (ITALY)

Deborah Tannen, *How Male and Female Students Use Language
Differently* (UNITED STATES)

Marjorie Shostak, *Nisa's Marriage* (BOTSWANA)

Jan Goodwin, *Muslims, the First Feminists* (ARABIA)

Yashar Kemal, *A Dirty Story* (TURKEY)

OBSERVATIONS

An American Indian woman is primarily defined by her tribal iden-tity. In her eyes, her destiny is necessarily that of her people, and her sense of herself as a woman is first and foremost prescribed by her tribe. The definitions of woman's roles are as diverse as tribal cultures in the Americas. In some she is devalued, in others she wields considerable power. In some she is a familial/clan adjunct, in some she is as close to autonomous as her economic circumstances and psychological traits permit. But in no tribal definitions is she perceived in the same way as are women in Western industrial and postindustrial cultures.

In the West, few images of women form part of the cultural mythos, and these are largely sexually charged. Among Christians, the Madonna is the female prototype, and she is portrayed as essentially passive: Her contribution is simply that of birthing. Little else is attributed to her, and she certainly possesses few of the characteristics that are attributed to mythic figures among the Indian tribes. This image is countered (rather than balanced) by the witch-goddess/whore characteristics de-signed to reinforce cultural beliefs about women, as well as Western ad-versarial and dualistic perceptions of reality.

The tribes see women variously, but they do not question the power of femininity. Sometimes they see women as fearful, sometimes peace-ful, sometimes omnipotent and omniscient, but they never portray women as mindless, helpless, simple, or oppressed. And while the women in a given tribe, clan, or band may be all these things, the indi-vidual woman is provided with a variety of images of women from the interconnected supernatural, natural, and social worlds she lives in.

> – Paula Gunn Allen
> "Where I Come from Is Like This"
> *The Sacred Hoop*, 1986

▼ ▼ ▼

The Sioux have a name for the rite of passage the rest of us call be-coming a man.

They call it "The Big Impossible."

And the rest of us are only now learning how right they are.

A century after the death of Sitting Bull, today's male finds himself perplexed, confused, and frustrated by the requirements of masculinity. This befuddlement is so great, in fact, that many men have dropped out of the process completely. If becoming a man really is as dubious a proposition as the Sioux believe, these dropouts wonder what's the point in trying. Instead of failing to be a man, why not succeed at something equally rewarding (at least to males), definitely easier, and — why deny it — a lot more fun?

The heck with being a man. The '90s male would rather be a guy.

Unlike a man, a guy is far less interested in the serious ramifications of manhood, such as becoming a parent or sustaining a meaningful career. He is, in fact, far less interested in the serious ramifications of anything. And that certainly includes finding his lost manhood in the woods while banging on a drum.

According to Dave Barry, the Robert Bly of the Guy Movement and author of the best-seller *Dave Barry's Complete Guide to Guys*, guys share certain primal characteristics:

• They like neat stuff, especially if it's expensive and more powerful than necessary.

• They like to scratch, even in public. Especially in public.

• They like pointless challenges.

• They do not have a rigid, well-defined moral code — least of all about sex.

• They have a Noogie Gene.

• They are not great at communicating intimate feelings — assuming they have any, which is not a smart assumption.

• And, most of all, they like hanging out with other guys.

In fact, there's probably a guy inside all men just waiting to burst out — the more inopportune the moment, the better.

– David Friedman
"The 'Guy' Thing"
Newsday, 1995

▼ ▼ ▼

When women talk about politics, culture, science, and the law in relation to female experience — i.e., rape statutes, fertility drugs, misogyny in film, or abortion rights — they are perceived as talking about their feelings and bodies. Whereas when men talk about their feelings and bodies — i.e., free speech in relation to their interest in pornography, gun ownership in relation to their fear of criminal assault, the drive for prostate cancer research in relation to their fears of impotence, new sexual harassment guidelines in relation to their irritation at having their desire intercepted in the workplace — they are read as if they are talking about politics, culture, science, and the law.

– Naomi Wolf
"Are Opinions Male?"
The New Republic, 1993

▼ ▼ ▼

What did I see as a boy when I passed the large black beauty shop on Broad and South Streets in Philadelphia where the name of its owner, Adele Reese, commanded such respect or provoked such jealousy? What did I see there but a long row of black women dressed immaculately in white tunics, washing and styling the hair of other black women. That was a sign of what culture, of what set of politics? The sheen of those straightened heads, the entire enterprise of the making of black feminine beauty: Was it an enactment of a degradation inspirited by a bitter inferiority or was it a womanly laying on of hands where black women were, in their way, helping themselves to live through and transcend their degradation?

> – GERALD EARLY
> "Life With Daughters: Watching
> the Miss America Pageant"
> *Kenyon Review,* 1992

▼ ▼ ▼

Race is always visible; sexuality can be hidden. Race is in no way behavioral; sexuality, though distinct from sexual activity, is profoundly linked to a settled pattern of behavior.

For lesbians and gay men, the option of self-concealment has always existed and still exists, an option that means that in a profound way, discrimination against them is linked to their own involvement, even acquiescence.

> – ANDREW SULLIVAN
> "The Politics of Homosexuality"
> *The New Republic,* 1993

▼ ▼ ▼

In addition to more "traditional" abuses of women, domestic violence in developing countries is often rooted in deeply entrenched cultural attitudes and practices. In India, "bride burning" by family members or in-laws is a well-known practice; official police records show that 4,835 women were killed in 1990 because of their families' failure to meet demands for money and goods. In greater Bombay, one of every five deaths among women aged fifteen to forty-four was listed as a case of "accidental burning." Female infanticide is an old and widely practiced form of family violence in Asia, where girls are often killed within a few days of birth. In South Asia, according to one survey, 58 percent of known female infanticide was committed by feeding babies the poisonous sap of a plant or by choking them by lodging rice hulls soaked in milk in their throats. The culturally dictated practice of genital mutilation of young girls, obligatory in much of the Middle East and Africa and in some Asian countries, has been carried to the United States and Canada by immigrants. Globally, at least 2 million girls a year experience the violence demanded by their societies and approved by their families. And every day, there are 6,000 new cases — or five girls genitally mutilated every minute. As for "traditional" family violence against women, in Costa Rica 95 percent of pregnant hospital clients under fifteen were found to be incest victims. At a police station in São Paulo, Brazil, 70 percent of all reported cases of violence against women took place in the home. Similarly, in Santiago, Chile, some 75 percent of all assault-related injuries of women were caused by family members. In a hospital in Peru, researchers found 90 percent of young mothers twelve to sixteen years old were victims of rape, often by a father, stepfather, or other close relative. Violence during pregnancy is a major reason for miscarriage. A Mexico City sampling found 20 percent of battered women reported blows to the stomach by their partners.

– POPULATION COMMUNICATIONS INTERNATIONAL
Focus on Women: Violence Against Women, 1995

▼ ▼ ▼

Is it possible that of the two genders nature created, one is nearly perfect and the other is badly flawed? Well, yes, say the psychobiologists. Unlike women, who carry two X chromosomes, men have an X and a Y. The latter has relatively little genetic information except for the gene that makes us men. A woman who has a recessive gene on one X chromosome might have a countering dominant gene on the other. That's not true for men, who are therefore more vulnerable to biological and environmental insults, as well as more prone to certain behavioral tendencies that may be genetically predetermined. Although male hormones (called androgens) don't cause violent criminal or sexual behavior, they apparently create an inclination in that direction.... Androgens are associated with a number of other male traits (in humans as well as animals), including assertive sexual behavior, status-related aggression, spatial reasoning, territoriality, pain tolerance, tenacity, transient bonding, sensation seeking, and predatory behavior. Obviously, this list posts many of the most common female complaints about men, and yet androgens make a man a man; one can't separate maleness from characteristic male traits.

. . . Anyone looking at men today should be able to see that they are confused and full of despair. It's not just our place in society or the family that we are struggling for; we're fighting against our own natures. We

310

didn't create the instincts that make us aggressive, that make us value action over consensus, that make us more inclined toward strength than sympathy. Nature and human history have rewarded those qualities and in turn have created the kind of people men are. Moreover, these competitive qualities have been necessary for the survival of the species, and despite the debate over masculinity, they are still valued today.

– LAWRENCE WRIGHT
Texas Monthly, 1992

▼ ▼ ▼

For centuries, *Homo sapiens* was a fragile, embattled species, beset by predators and struggling for survival. Having large numbers of offspring was an important survival strategy; woman's most important quality often was her fecundity. Women couldn't be spared for combat, even though some women were taller, stronger, and more aggressive than some men. A few males, after all, could repopulate a tribe if many men were killed, but one woman could bear and raise only a few children.

Today, the situation is very different. *Homo sapiens* is not a fragile species but the undisputed master of the planet. Modern medicine has reduced infant mortality to the point where parents can expect most of their children to survive. Today, in fact, the survival of the species and the planet itself depends on curbing population growth.

If there were, indeed, a new reproductive paradigm, we would expect to see women having fewer children and the easing of taboos on risky work behavior for women. That's exactly what's happening. Not only are women moving increasingly into military roles, including combat, but they are also engaging in other kinds of risky behavior. They are driving more aggressively and getting into more accidents, taking part in risky sports such as mountain climbing and boxing. And around the world, female involvement in violent crime is rising rapidly.

– CARYL RIVERS
Cape Cod Times, 1997

▼ ▼ ▼

As you know, certain studies show that women traditionally lead by means of reconciliation, interrelations, and persuasion, considering the fact that society has traditionally counted on the women to keep the family together, while men usually lead through control and intimidation. When women entered the fields of politics and business, they brought with them the moral values they had learned from home. These values have shown good results; I dare say they have even shown

311

better results than did the traditional model created by men. . . . I think it is time that male leaders look to women leaders as role models. They will find that persuasion brings better results than confrontation. And, finally, they will realize that, when dealing with the nations of the world, reconciliation unites people and allows them to work together for the benefit of all.

— VIOLETA CHAMORRO
Women World Leaders
(Laura A. Lizwood), 1995

▼ ▼ ▼

An Ibo woman has very little personal identity, even if she lives in the United States and has success in her career. Our culture takes very little pride in a woman's accomplishment. At an Ibo gathering a woman is more likely to be asked whose wife or mother she is before she is asked her name or what she does for a living. If the woman is accomplished but unmarried, people will say, "But where is she going with all that success?" Ibos cling to the adage that a woman is worth nothing unless she's married and has children.

I am as guilty as any other Ibo woman living in the United States in perpetuating this. Professionally, I am more successful than the majority of Ibo men I've met in this country, yet when we gather for a party, usually to celebrate a marriage or a birth, I join the women in the kitchen to prepare food and serve the men. I remember to curtsy just so before the older men, looking away to avoid meeting their eyes. I glow with pride when other men tease my husband about his "good wife." . . .

Hundreds of thousands of women from the Third World and other traditional societies share my experience. We straddle two cultures, cultures that are often in opposition. Mainstream America, the culture we embrace in our professional lives, dictates that we be assertive and independent — like men. Our traditional culture, dictated by religion and years of socialization, demands that we be docile and content in our roles as mothers and wives — careers or not.

— DYMPNA UGWU-OJU
New York Times Magazine, 1993

▼ ▼ ▼

Before we moved to Lahore, Daddyji had gone to Mussoorie, a hill station in the United Provinces, without telling us why he was going out of the Punjab. Now, several months after he made that trip, he gathered us around him in the drawing room at 11 Temple Road while Mamaji mysteriously hurried Sister Pom upstairs. He started talking as if we

312

were all very small and he were conducting one of our "dinner-table-school" discussions. He said that by right and tradition the oldest daughter had to be given in marriage first, and that the ripe age for marriage was nineteen. He said that when a girl approached that age her parents, who had to take the initiative, made many inquiries and followed many leads. They investigated each young man and his family background, his relatives, his friends, his classmates, because it was important to know what kind of family the girl would be marrying into, what kind of company she would be expected to keep. . . . "That's why I said nothing to you children when I went to Mussoorie," he concluded. "I went to see a young man for Pom. She's already nineteen."

We were stunned. We have never really faced the idea that Sister Pom might get married and suddenly leave, I thought.

"We won't lose Pom, we'll get a new family member," Daddyji said, as if reading my thoughts.

Then all of us started talking at once. We wanted to know if Sister Pom had been told; if she'd agreed; whom she'd be marrying.

"Your mother has just taken Pom up to tell her," Daddyji said. "But she's a good girl. She will agree."

– VED MEHTA
The Ledge Between the Streams, 1982

EXPLORATIONS

1. Which of the Observations you have just read depict men as having a privileged status, and in what ways? Which Observations depict women as having a privileged status, and in what ways?

2. Which of these writers comment on what men are like? What points do some or all of them agree on? What points do they disagree on? In what respects do you agree and disagree with them?

3. Which of these writers comment on what women are like? What points do some or all of them agree on? What points do they disagree on? In what respects do you agree and disagree with them?

JOHN UPDIKE

The Disposable Rocket

John Updike credits his mother for encouraging him early to write. Today he is one of the most prolific and respected authors in the United States, having published more than a dozen each of novels, short story collections, and volumes of poetry, as well as several plays and children's books. Also a noted critic, Updike has won most of this country's major literary prizes, including the National Book Award, American Book Award, and Pulitzer Prize. He was born in Shillington, Pennsylvania, in 1932. After graduating summa cum laude from Harvard University, he studied in Oxford, England, at the Ruskin School of Drawing and Fine Arts. Among Updike's best-known works are *Rabbit, Run* (1960), the first of four novels about a small-town Pennsylvania car salesman; *Couples* (1968), a chronicle of suburban infidelities; and *The Witches of Eastwick* (1984), which became the basis for a motion picture. His most recent novels are *Toward the End of Time* (1997) and *Bech at Bay* (1998). Updike is highly regarded for, among other things, his sharp observation of manners and mores, his vivid descriptions, and his grapplings with the Christian dilemmas of faith, passion, and evil (see p. 411). A member of the American Academy, he lives with his wife Martha north of Boston. "The Disposable Rocket" originally appeared in the *Michigan Quarterly Review* (1994).

Inhabiting a male body is like having a bank account; as long as it's healthy, you don't think much about it. Compared to the female body, it is a low-maintenance proposition: a shower now and then, trim the fingernails every ten days, a haircut once a month. Oh yes, shaving — scraping or buzzing away at your face every morning. Byron, in *Don Juan*, thought the repeated nuisance of shaving balanced out the periodic agony, for females, of childbirth. Woman are, his lines tell us,

> Condemn'd to child-bed, as men for their sins
> Have shaving too entail'd upon their chins, —
>
> A daily plague, which in the aggregate
>   May average on the whole with parturition.

From the standpoint of reproduction, the male body is a delivery system, as the female is a mazy device for retention. Once the delivery is

made, men feel a faint but distinct falling-off of interest. Yet against the
enduring female heroics of birth and nurture should be set the male's
superhuman frenzy to deliver his goods: He vaults walls, skips sleep,
risks wallet, health, and his political future all to ram home his seed
into the gut of the chosen woman. The sense of the chase lives in him
as the key to life. His body is, like a delivery rocket that falls away in
space, a disposable means. Men put their bodies at risk to experience
the release from gravity.

When my tenancy of a male body was fairly new — of six or so years'
duration — I used to jump and fall just for the joy of it. Falling — back-
wards, or down stairs — became a specialty of mine, an attention-getting
stunt I was still practicing into my thirties, at suburban parties. Falling
is, after all, a kind of flying, though of briefer duration than would be
ideal. My impulse to hurl myself from high windows and the edges of
cliffs belongs to my body, not my mind, which resists the siren call of
the chasm with all its might; the interior struggle knocks the wind from
my lungs and tightens my scrotum and gives any trip to Europe, with its
Alps, castle parapets, and gargoyled cathedral lookouts, a flavor of nightmare. Falling, strangely, no longer figures in my dreams, as it often did
when I was a boy and my subconscious was more honest with me. An
airplane, that necessary evil, turns the earth into a map so quickly the
brain turns aloof and calm; still, I marvel that there is no end of young
men willing to become jet pilots.

Any accounting of male-female differences must include the male's
superior recklessness, a drive not, I think, toward death, as the darker
feminist cosmogonies would have it, but to test the limits, to see what
the traffic will bear — a kind of mechanic's curiosity. The number of
men who do lasting damage to their young bodies is striking; war and
car accidents aside, secondary-school sports, with the approval of parents and the encouragement of brutish coaches, take a fearful toll of
skulls and knees. We were made for combat, back in the postsimian,
East-African days, and the bumping, the whacking, the breathlessness,
the pain-smothering adrenaline rush form a cumbersome and unfash-
ionable bliss, but bliss nevertheless. Take your body to the edge, and see
if it flies.

The male sense of space must differ from that of the female, who has
such interesting, active, and significant inner space. The space that interests men is outer. The fly ball high against the sky, the long pass spi-
raling overhead, the jet fighter like a scarcely visible pinpoint nozzle
laying down its vapor trail at forty thousand feet, the gazelle haunch
flickering just beyond arrow-reach, the uncountable stars sprinkled on
their great black wheel, the horizon, the mountaintop, the quasar —

these bring portents with them and awaken a sense of relation with the invisible, with the empty. The ideal male body is taut with lines of potential force, a diagram extending outward; the ideal female body curves around centers of repose. Of course, no one is ideal, and the sexes are somewhat androgynous subdivisions of a species: Diana the huntress is a more trendy body type nowadays than languid, overweight Venus, and polymorphous Dionysus poses for more underwear ads than Mars. Relatively, though, men's bodies, however elegant, are designed for covering territory, for moving on.

An erection, too, defies gravity, flirts with it precariously. It extends 5 the diagram of outward direction into downright detachability — objective in the case of the sperm, subjective in the case of the testicles and penis. Men's bodies, at this juncture, feel only partly theirs; a demon of sorts has been attached to their lower torsos, whose performance is erratic and whose errands seem, at times, ridiculous. It is like having a (much) smaller brother toward whom you feel both fond and impatient; if he is you, it is you in curiously simplified and ignoble form. This sense, of the male body being two of them, is acknowledged in verbal love play and erotic writing, where the penis is playfully given a pet name, an individuation not even the rarest rapture grants a vagina. Here, where maleness gathers to a quintessence of itself, there can be no insincerity, there can be no hiding; for sheer nakedness, there is nothing like a hopeful phallus; its aggressive shape is indivisible from its tender-skinned vulnerability. The act of intercourse, from the point of view of a consenting female, has an element of mothering, of enwrapment, of merciful concealment, even. The male body, for this interval, is tucked out of harm's way.

To inhabit a male body, then, is to feel somewhat detached from it. It is not an enemy, but not entirely a friend. Our being seems to lie not in cells and muscles but in the traces that our thoughts and actions inscribe on the air. The male body skims the surface of nature's deeps wherein the blood and pain and mysterious cravings of women perpetuate the species. Participating less in nature's processes than the female body, the male body gives the impression — false — of being exempt from time. Its powers of strength and reach descend in early adolescence, along with acne and sweaty feet, and depart, in imperceptible increments, after thirty or so. It surprises me to discover, when I remove my shoes and socks, the same paper-white, hairless ankles that struck me as pathetic when I observed them on my father. I felt betrayed when, in some tumble of touch football twenty years ago, I heard my tibia snap; and when, between two reading engagements in Cleveland, my appendix tried to burst; and when, the other day, not for the first time, there arose to my nostrils out of my own body the musty attic smell my grandfather's body had.

A man's body does not betray its tenant as rapidly as a woman's. Never as fine and lovely, it has less distance to fall; what rugged beauty it has is wrinkleproof. It keeps its capability of procreation indecently long. Unless intense athletic demands are made upon it, the thing serves well enough to sixty, which is my age now. From here on, it's chancy. There are no breasts or ovaries to admit cancer to the male body, but the prostate, that awkwardly located little source of seminal fluid, shows the strain of sexual function with fits of hysterical cell replication, and all that male-bonding beer and potato chips add up in the coronary arteries. A writer, whose physical equipment can be minimal as long as it gets him to the desk, the lectern, and New York City once in a while, cannot but be grateful to his body, especially to his eyes, those tender and intricate sites where the brain extrudes from the skull, and to his hands, which hold the pen or tap the keyboard. His body has been, not himself exactly, but a close pal, potbellied and balding like most of his other pals now. A man and his body are like a boy and the buddy who has a driver's license and the use of his father's car for the evening; one goes along, gratefully, for the ride.

EXPLORATIONS

1. Where in "The Disposable Rocket" does John Updike use the analogy of his title, and in what ways does he apply it? In what additional way is the analogy implied in his essay's last paragraphs?

2. What is the central comparison-contrast in this essay? Where and how does Updike introduce it? How does he change the terms of the comparison in his opening paragraph?

3. What additional comparisons and analogies appear in "The Disposable Rocket"? Find at least six. In this essay, what advantages does Updike gain by leaning more heavily on comparison than on other techniques such as description and abstract explanation?

CONNECTIONS

1. What similar ideas appear in Updike's essay and Caryl Rivers's Observation (p. 311)? How do Updike and Rivers approach these ideas differently?

2. In his first paragraph on page 310, Lawrence Wright lists some male traits associated with androgens. Which of the same traits does Updike refer or allude to? Which ones does Updike treat more positively than Wright, and in what ways?

3. What does Updike say about flying? Which of his comments are echoed or implied by the pilots in Andre Dubus's "Imperiled Men" (p. 237)?

ELABORATIONS

1. What does it mean to you to be whichever gender you are? How has your concept of maleness or femaleness changed over the course of your life? What gender-related traits do you enjoy most and least? What traits do you mind the most and envy the most in the opposite sex? Keeping in mind John Updike's use of comparison and contrast, write your own essay addressing some or all of these questions.

2. Updike mentions dreams of falling, akin to dreams of flying. What dreams have you had that involve these or similar physical sensations? How did such dreams relate to your waking life? Write an essay either describing your dreams and your reaction to them, or explaining how your dreams helped you to understand real events.

CURTIS SITTENFELD

Your Life as a Girl

Curtis Sittenfeld was born in 1975 and grew up in Cincinnati, Ohio. She wrote "Your Life as a Girl" when she was a seventeen-year-old senior at Groton School in Massachusetts. It was published in *Ms.* magazine and the collection *Listen Up: Voices from the Next Feminist Generation*, edited by Barbara Findlen (1995). Sittenfeld's stories won first place in *Seventeen* magazine's 1992 fiction contest and third place in *Sassy*'s 1993 fiction contest; her writing also has appeared in the *Washington Post*. She attended Vassar College and received her B.A. from Stanford University in 1997. She now lives in Boston and works for *FastCompany*, a business magazine. As we go to press, she is planning to attend the Iowa Writers' Workshop in the fall of 1999.

In fifth grade, you can run faster than any other girl in your class. One day in the spring, the gym teacher has all of you do a timed mile, and by the third lap, half the girls are walking. You come in seventh, and the boys who are already finished stick up their hands, and you high-five them. When you play kickball you're the first girl to be picked, and when you play capture the flag you're the one who races across the other team's side to free the prisoners. At recess, you're the foursquare queen. You slam the red rubber ball onto your three opponents' patches of pavement, and you gloat when they get disqualified. Sometimes your teacher supervises, standing in a raincoat by the door to the school building. Once, after she's rung the bell to call you inside, you pass her, your body still tense and excited, your face flushed. She says in a low voice, a voice that sounds more like the one she uses with adults and not with the other children in your class, "Anna, aren't you being just a bit vicious?" The next time you're playing, you fumble and let the ball slide beyond the thin white lines that serve as boundaries.

By sixth grade, your friends no longer like foursquare. Neither, really, do you, though you teach the game to your younger sister and sometimes play it with her in your driveway, in the evenings. At school, you sit with the other girls on top of the jungle gym by the swing set, and you argue about how often you're supposed to shave your legs. Your friend Nell says every two days. You probably talk about other things, but later, you can't remember what they are.

When Nell spends a Saturday night at your house, her boyfriend Steve calls seven times. At eleven o'clock, you grab the phone from Nell and say: "Steve, we have to go. My parents will be home soon, and they'll be mad if we're still talking to you." He protests but then relents and asks to say good-bye to Nell. You pass her the phone. After she's hung up, she says that he told her to tell you that you're a bitch.

You can't learn how to play football. Early in the winter of seventh grade, you stand with your junior high gym class on the field behind the cafeteria. The gym teacher, whose name is Ted and who has a mustache, goes over various kinds of passes. They all seem alike to you though, and mid-game, when someone tosses you the ball, you just stand there with no idea what to do. "Throw it," bellow the boys on your team, so you do, but you don't want to watch where it lands or who catches it. After that, for the remaining weeks of football and even on into basketball and volleyball season, you're careful to station yourself in the back, or at the edges, wherever you're least likely to be accountable.

In the spring, you get moved from the higher to the lower math class, because you have a C-plus average. At first, you don't mind because in lower math you have the best grade in your class. Your teacher, Mr. Willet, asks for the answers to problems he's working out on the chalkboard, and he's pleased when you respond. But sometimes he doesn't call on you, even when you're the only one raising your hand, and he says in a humorless voice: "Well, we all know Anna has the answer. Let's see if anyone else does." On the comments sent home to your parents, Mr. Willet writes that though he appreciates your hard work, he wishes you'd give other students a chance to speak. He says that you're intimidating them.

At the Halloween dance in eighth grade, when you and Nell are standing by the buffet table, Jimmy Wrightson appears from nowhere and says, "Hey, Anna, can I suck your tits?" At first you don't understand what he's said, but he's coming closer, and Nell is giggling, and then Jimmy is pawing you. You press your fists into his stomach, pushing him away. He smirks at you before he saunters back to where his friends are waiting. You still don't know what he's said, and you have to ask Nell.

You don't tell any teachers, of course. You're not a snitch, and besides, you can take care of yourself. In social studies class the following Monday, you're sitting next to Nate, one of Jimmy's friends. You ask why Jimmy tried to feel you up, and Nate shrugs and says, "Probably

5

someone dared him to." You say, "Yeah, well it was kind of obnoxious." Nate gives you a scornful expression. "It was a joke," he says. "Take it easy."

You hear that Jimmy got ten dollars.

In the summers, you swim for the team at the country club near your house. Before your races you wander around in a huge T-shirt, and you never eat. You and your friends go on a thousand diets, and you don't say anything else as often as you say that you're fat. In June, your father keeps the air-conditioning blasting through your house. You always wear sweatpants, even though it's ninety degrees outside. You spend the mornings making elaborate desserts: lemon tarts, puddings, pies. You allow yourself to eat the batter but not the finished product. You jog in place, or you do jumping jacks, leaping around your kitchen like a crazy lady. Two or three years later, you find photographs of yourself from that summer when you were fourteen. The girl you see looks grim, pale, and so thin her collarbone sticks out like a rod.

In ninth grade, you go away to boarding school, where you begin to   10 practice making ashamed facial expressions in the mirror. You embarrass yourself on a daily basis, so you want to make sure you're acting appropriately. Everything about you is horrifying: your voice, body, hair, inability to be witty, and panicky desires for approval and companionship. In classes you speak as infrequently as possible and walk around with your head lowered. You play on the soccer team, but if boys ever watch, you make only halfhearted attempts to kick the ball.

To your mother's dismay, you begin reading romance novels. The covers show chesty, lusty heroines in torn clothing and men with long hair and fierce stares. The premises of the stories are identical, though the specifics change: The man and woman are attracted to each other, they quarrel, they end up alone together, they have wild sex. The women always say they don't want it, but they really do. The characters live in eighteenth-century France or on the Scottish moors or in Hawaii. You start to think that you were born at the wrong time. You would have done better a hundred years ago, when a girl knew that she'd be protected, that she wouldn't have to find a man because one would come to claim her.

When you're in tenth grade the students who write for your high school yearbook compile a list of people's nicknames and what they're known for. You hear that for your roommate they're going to write "doesn't like cherries." This is supposed to be a subtly amusing reference to the fact that at a party in the fall, she had sex with a guy she barely knew. You go to the yearbook editor and say, looking at the floor, that you think your roommate would be very upset if that particular line were printed. Afterward you blush, which is something you've just begun to do. You're glad that you got the hang of it because there certainly is a lot for you to be ashamed of. When you walk away from the editor, you hear him murmur, "What a weirdo."

On your grandmother's bed, she has a small pillow that says in needlepoint, "Women are such expensive things." When you and your sister go to your grandmother's house for brunch, your grandmother gives the two of you advice about men. First off, she says, learn to dance. And be a good conversationalist. Read book reviews, and even read the newspaper from time to time, in case he's an intellectual. Never turn down a date, because he might have a handsome brother. Once when your mother cannot open a jam jar, she passes it to your father, and your grandmother says chirpily, "The women admit their natural inferiority." "I think I'm going to throw up," says your sister. You laugh as if you agree, but for a minute you're not even sure what she's referring to.

Every day during the summer after your junior year in high school, you run two miles to the country club, then you climb 250 flights on the StairMaster. You wear spandex shorts that make you feel like your legs are pieces of sausage, and you pant the whole time. Men stick their heads out the windows of their cars and hoot at you as you run past. At first you take their yells as compliments, but you realize how hideous you look, and then you realize that they aren't seeing you, not as a person. They are seeing you as long hair and bare legs, and you are frightened. Recently, you have found yourself wishing that you'd get raped now, and then it would be done with. It will happen sooner or later; you've read the news reports, and you'd rather just get it out of the way.

Senior year, you develop a schedule: Sunday mornings you burn   15 your skin. Not in glory, though, not you: What you do is rub hot wax onto your calves, and then for half a day, your legs are as smooth as pebbles. Or you use rotating silver coils that rip out hair from the root, or you use bleaching cream. You stand in front of the mirror, bleeding and stinging and knowing full well that the boys in your class will never think you're beautiful anyway.

Sometimes the boys are just so rich and handsome and indifferent. They get drunk on Saturday nights, and after they've seen a movie with an attractive woman in it, they say, "Hell yeah, I'd do her." It is hard to explain how your insides collapse when they say those words, how far apart from them you start to feel. Maybe they don't know that you want terribly to like them, or maybe they know that you'll like them anyway, however they act. When you protest, even mildly, the boys have words for you: cunt, ho, bitch. They say feminist like it's a nasty insult.

You've changed a little. You've read magazine articles that discuss other teenage girls who get eating disorders and flunk math, and now you know that you're a statistic, not a freak. Somewhere inside, you start to feel a little pissed off. You think of the fairy tales your mother read to you when you were small: Cinderella and Snow White and Rapunzel and the rest of their dippy, flaxen-haired sisters. You think of the songs you chanted with the neighborhood kids, tapping each other to see who had to be "it" when you were playing tag or hide-and-seek: "Inka-binka-bottle-of-ink/The cork falls off and you stink/Not because you're dirty/Not because you're clean/Just because you kissed the boy behind the magazine." Or, "My mother and your mother were hanging up clothes/My mother punched your mother in the nose/What color blood came out?" The world has given you two options: You can be a slut or a matron.

Late at night a kind of sadness descends and grips the girls in your dorm. You watch television shows about men and women who go to work in the morning, who experience amusing mishaps like getting stuck in elevators with their bosses or having their mother's parakeet die, and then they go on, to sleep or home or to more places where equally witty encounters are had by the handful. The characters' lives unfold in front of you, brisk and brightly colored, and you are sitting on the common room floor or on lumpy, worn couches, you're eating pork-flavored noodles and raw cookie dough, and you have four papers to write before Tuesday. You're waiting for your life to start.

And maybe the boys can save you. Maybe if you do sit-ups before you go to bed at night your stomach will be flat, and they'll love you well. Not that you actually believe that, not that you haven't been told a million times about just waiting until college where dozens of guys will treat you nicely. But you want love now, you want to have a boy standing there after you've failed a French test or fought with your roommate. The boy can hold you up with his strong arms and his common sense. You'll start to cry, and he'll get embarrassed and shuffle around and say, "Come on, Anna, don't worry like this." You'll worship his incoherence. You'll wish that you could stay up all night like he does. At two in the morning, guys watch the *Home Shopping Network* with the younger kids in the dorm, or they set up hockey games with bottles of ketchup, or they play complex tricks involving vacuum cleaners on each other, and the next morning they snore through math class.

Friday night the boy next to you is feeling playful. No one has more than three classes the following morning, so you stay at dinner an hour and a half. The boy keeps saying he's in love with you. He rubs your shoulders and says, "Your hair is magnificently soft," and everyone at the table cracks up. You say, "I forgot to wish you Happy Birthday   20 yesterday," so he says, "Do it now," and he sticks out his cheek for you to kiss. You say, "No way!" You're grinning ferociously, you're practically hyper from the attention, and you think that if he offers you the option of kissing him, you couldn't be that gross after all. And then on Saturday morning, when you pass in the hall, he looks at you exhaustedly and says not a word.

Girls like you are well-fed and well-clothed and are loved by parents who send checks and say that you don't call home enough. Alumni return to tell you that when God was creating the world, He smiled just a little longer on your campus. On sunny days you believe this. But in the middle of the term, when the sky is gray and your notebooks are shabby and your skin is dry, it gets harder. The weather grows so cold it reminds you of cruelty.

You and your friends get sick with fevers, and you are hungry for something immense. You say, "Let's buy hamburgers, let's order pizza," and you walk to town blowing your noses on your parkas. At the grocery store you are so overwhelmed by the variety of food that you don't buy anything but Pepsi.

In the morning, after the heater has roared all night, your skin is so dehydrated you tell your roommate you're starting the Roasted Nostrils Club, only boarding school students need apply. You find yourself deliciously witty over toothpaste and Ivory soap, and then at breakfast you start slipping. It's the boys' tiredness. They kill you with their tiredness. You just wish they were more interested. You wish you knew the thing to say to make them stop shoveling oatmeal in their mouths. You want to shout, "Look at me! Dammit!" But you murmur, "I'm worried about the physics quiz/I heard it's supposed to rain tomorrow."

Once when it snows, you and your friends go to the lower fields and make angels. Other eighteen-year-olds are enlisting in the army or getting married, but at boarding school, you still open Advent calendars. When a group of boys in your class comes over the hill and down toward where you are standing, you pack the snow into balls and throw them. The boys fly forward, retaliating, smothering you. The air is filled with powdery flakes and everyone is yelling and laughing. One of the boys grabs you around the waist and knocks you down, and he's on top of you, stuffing snow in your mouth. At first you are giggling, and then you are choking and spitting, and you say, "Stop, come on." Your hat has fallen off, and the boy is pressing his arm on your hair so that your head is pulled backward. "Please," you gasp. "Come on." For an instant, your eyes meet his. Your faces are only about three inches apart, and his stare is like a robot's. You think he is breaking your neck, you're going to die or be paralyzed. But then the other boys are wanting to leave, and the boy pulls away and towers over you.

"What the hell is wrong with you?" you ask. You're still lying on the ground shaking, but you're furious, which is something you haven't been for a long time. Your fury gives you power. "Why did you just do that?"

The boy grins sickeningly and says, "Suck it up, Anna." Then he turns and walks away.

You never tell your friends because you yourself can hardly believe it happened. Later, it seems like a nightmare — rapid, violent, vague. When you were a first-year student, there was a beautiful senior girl in your dorm, and her boyfriend was president of the student council. You heard that they'd go for walks off campus and get in fights. He'd beat her and leave her there, and later, bearing roses or pieces of jewelry, he'd apologize tearfully. It sounded glamorous to you, at the time.

When the sun is out, the boys tease you again. From across the quadrangle, they shout your name in an enthusiastic voice, then they walk over, thrilled to see you, and the golden sky shines down, lighting their hair from behind, and they are wonderfully good-looking and clever, and you think how absolutely happy they sometimes make you.

After class, you are feeling so good that you boldly announce they'd better do their parts of the lab that's due on Monday, and they give you a phony smile and turn away. They are walking with a boy you know less well than the other boys, and they gesture toward you and mutter something to him. You cannot hear everything they say, but you make out your name and the word "nagging." You have overstepped your boundaries, and they have put you in your place.

You've had trouble sleeping lately. You can fall asleep easily enough, but you awaken during the night as many as nine times. Often, your heart is pounding, and you have the sensation that you've narrowly missed something disastrous, but you never can identify what it was. The dark hours pass slowly, and when it's finally light outside, you start to relax. Your bones loosen, your head feels large and soft. You fall asleep again around dawn, and dreams from a long time ago come to you: across all the distance of your life so far, you go back to elementary school, to the afternoon when you ran a timed mile. The air was warm and green, your lungs were burning, and clear, pure lines of sweat fell down the sides of your face. You crossed the finish line, and your eyes met the eyes of the six boys who were already cooling down. For a minute, in the sunlight, they smiled at you, and you smiled back as if you all had something in common.

EXPLORATIONS

1. When "Your Life as a Girl" opens, how does Anna feel about herself? What are the sources of her self-esteem in this phase of her life? When does her attitude change, in what ways, and for what reasons?

2. At what points in "Your Life as a Girl" does Anna feel betrayed? Who betrays her and why? Over the course of the story, what actions does Anna take to avoid being betrayed? Which of her tactics are most and least successful?

3. What are the effects of Curtis Sittenfeld's writing this story in the second person? How would its impact change if it were written in the third person? The first person?

CONNECTIONS

1. "Inhabiting a male body is like having a bank account; as long as it's healthy, you don't think much about it," writes John Updike in "The Disposable Rocket" (p. 314). How do you think Anna in "Your Life as a Girl" would summarize inhabiting a female body? What similar ideas about physicality appear in both selections? According to these two writers, what are the sharpest contrasts in having a male or a female body?

2. Judging from the comments by Updike and by David Friedman (p. 307), do you think the boys in "Your Life as a Girl" are as self-confident as they appear to Anna? As hostile? At what points in Sittenfeld's story does boys' behavior match the list of "primal guy characteristics" cited by Friedman? What reasons do Friedman and Updike suggest for these behaviors?

3. At what point does Anna confront the same choices described by Dympna Ugwu-Oju (p. 312)? After reading "Your Life as a Girl," why do you think Ugwu-Oju makes the choices that she does?

ELABORATIONS

1. Choose a scene from "Your Life as a Girl" involving a conflict between Anna and a boy. Rewrite that scene from the boy's point of view. If you wish, use Updike's or Friedman's selection or both as resources.

2. Choose an episode in "Your Life as a Girl" that resembles an incident in your own life. Write a true or fictional version of your experience in the second person, using Sittenfeld's story as a model. Or, write an expository or cause-and-effect essay analyzing how incidents like this figure in the process of growing up.

CAMILLE PAGLIA

Woman and Nature

Camille Paglia thrives on controversy. As a child growing up in Endicott, New York, where she was born in 1947, she was immersed in academia and the arts by her father's job as a professor of romance languages. She graduated from the State University of New York at Binghamton in 1968 and received her Ph.D. from Yale University in 1974. By then she was already teaching in the Literature and Languages Division at Bennington College; she now is a professor of humanities at the University of the Arts in Philadelphia. Paglia's unorthodox views on the role of sexuality in Western civilization stirred up debate from the publication of her first book, *Sexual Personae: Art and Decadence from Nefertiti to Emily Dickinson* (1990). The following essay is excerpted from that book's chapter "Sex and Violence, or Nature and Art," which appeared originally in *Western Humanities Review* (1988). Fascinated by popular as well as classical culture, Paglia has lived as colorfully as she writes. Her essay collection *Sex, Art, and American Culture* (1992) includes enthusiastic commentaries on Madonna and the Rolling Stones, among others. Her most recent book is *The Birds* (1998).

The identification of woman with nature was universal in prehistory. In hunting or agrarian societies dependent upon nature, femaleness was honored as an immanent principle of fertility. As culture progressed, crafts and commerce supplied a concentration of resources freeing men from the caprices of weather or the handicap of geography. With nature at one remove, femaleness receded in importance.

Buddhist cultures retained the ancient meanings of femaleness long after the West renounced them. Male and female, the Chinese yang and yin, are balanced and interpenetrating powers in man and nature, to which society is subordinate. This code of passive acceptance has its roots in India, a land of sudden extremes where a monsoon can wipe out 50,000 people overnight. The femaleness of fertility religions is always double-edged. The Indian nature-goddess Kali is creator *and* destroyer, granting boons with one set of arms while cutting throats with the other. She is the lady ringed with skulls. The moral ambivalence of the great mother goddesses has been conveniently forgotten by those

American feminists who have resurrected them. We cannot grasp nature's bare blade without shedding our own blood.

Western culture from the start has swerved from femaleness. The last
major Western society to worship female powers was Minoan Crete.
And significantly, that fell and did not rise again. The immediate cause
of its collapse — quake, plague, or invasion — is beside the point. The
lesson is that cultic femaleness is no guarantee of cultural strength or vi-
ability. What did survive, what did vanquish circumstance and stamp its
mind-set on Europe was Mycenaean warrior culture, descending to us
through Homer. The male will-to-power: Mycenaeans from the south
and Dorians from the north would fuse to form Apollonian Athens,
from which came the Greco-Roman line of Western history.

Both the Apollonian and Judeo-Christian traditions are transcendental. That is, they seek to surmount or transcend nature. Despite Greek
culture's contrary Dionysian element, which I will discuss, high classi-
cism was an Apollonian achievement. Judaism, Christianity's parent
sect, is the most powerful of protests against nature. The Old Testament
asserts that a father god made nature and that differentiation into objects and gender was after the fact of his maleness. Judeo-Christianity,
like Greek worship of the Olympian gods, is a sky-cult. It is an advanced
stage in the history of religion, which everywhere began as earth-cult,
veneration of fruitful nature.

The evolution from earth-cult to sky-cult shifts woman into the   5
nether realm. Her mysterious procreative powers and the resemblance
of her rounded breasts, belly, and hips to earth's contours put her at the
center of early symbolism. She was the model for the Great Mother figures who crowded the birth of religion worldwide. But the mother cults
did not mean social freedom for women. On the contrary, as I will show
in a discussion of Hollywood in the sequel to this book, cult-objects are
prisoners of their own symbolic inflation. Every totem lives in taboo.

Woman was an idol of belly-magic. She seemed to swell and give
birth by her own law. From the beginning of time, woman has seemed
an uncanny being. Man honored but feared her. She was the black
maw that had spat him forth and would devour him anew. Men, bonding together, invented culture as a defense against female nature. Sky-
cult was the most sophisticated step in this process, for its switch of the
creative locus from earth to sky is a shift from belly-magic to head-
magic. And from this defensive head-magic has come the spectacular
glory of male civilization, which has lifted woman with it. The very language and logic modern woman uses to assail patriarchal culture were
the invention of men.

Hence the sexes are caught in a comedy of historical indebtedness. Man, repelled by his debt to a physical mother, created an alternate reality, a heterocosm to give him the illusion of freedom. Woman, at first content to accept man's protections but now inflamed with desire for her own illusory freedom, invades man's systems and suppresses her indebtedness to him as she steals them. By head-magic she will deny there ever was a problem of sex and nature. She has inherited the anxiety of influence.

The identification of woman with nature is the most troubled and troubling term in this historical argument. Was it ever true? Can it still be true? Most feminist readers will disagree, but I think this identification not myth but reality. All the genres of philosophy, science, high art, athletics, and politics were invented by men. But by the Promethean law of conflict and capture, woman has a right to seize what she will and to vie with man on his own terms. Yet there is a limit to what she can alter in herself and in man's relation to her. Every human being must wrestle with nature. But nature's burden falls more heavily on one sex. With luck, this will not limit woman's achievement, that is, her action in male-created social space. But it must limit eroticism, that is, our imaginative lives in sexual space, which may overlap social space but is not identical with it.

Nature's cycles are woman's cycles. Biologic femaleness is a sequence of circular returns, beginning and ending at the same point. Woman's centrality gives her a stability of identity. She does not have to become but only to be. Her centrality is a great obstacle to man, whose quest for identity she blocks. He must transform himself into an independent being, that is, a being free of her. If he does not, he will simply fall back into her. Reunion with the mother is a siren call haunting our imagination. Once there was bliss, and now there is struggle. Dim memories of life before the traumatic separation of birth may be the source of Arcadian fantasies of a lost golden age. The Western idea of history as a propulsive movement into the future, a progressive or Providential design climaxing in the revelation of a Second Coming, is a male formulation. No woman, I submit, could have coined such an idea, since it is a strategy of evasion of woman's own cyclic nature, in which man dreads being caught. Evolutionary or apocalyptic history is a male wish list with a happy ending, a phallic peak.

Woman does not dream of transcendental or historical escape from   10 natural cycle, since she *is* that cycle. Her sexual maturity means marriage to the moon, waxing and waning in lunar phases. Moon, month, menses: same word, same world. The ancients knew that woman is bound to nature's calendar, an appointment she cannot refuse. The Greek pattern of free will to hybris to tragedy is a male drama, since woman has never been deluded (until recently) by the mirage of free will. She knows there is no free will, since she is not free. She has no choice but acceptance. Whether she desires motherhood or not, nature yokes her into the brute inflexible rhythm of procreative law. Menstrual cycle is an alarming clock that cannot be stopped until nature wills it.

Woman's reproductive apparatus is vastly more complicated than man's, and still ill-understood. All kinds of things can go wrong or cause distress in going right. Western woman is in an agonistic[1] relation to her own body: for her, biologic normalcy is suffering, and health an illness. Dysmenorrhea,[2] it is argued, is a disease of civilization, since women in tribal cultures have few menstrual complaints. But in tribal life, woman has an extended or collective identity; tribal religion honors nature and subordinates itself to it. It is precisely in advanced Western society, which attempts to improve or surpass nature and which holds up individualism and self-realization as a model, that the stark facts of woman's condition emerge with painful clarity. The more woman aims for personal identity and autonomy, the more she develops her imagination, the fiercer will be her struggle with nature — that is, with the intractable physical laws of her own body. And the more nature will punish her: do not dare to be free! for your body does not belong to you.

The female body is a chthonian[3] machine, indifferent to the spirit who inhabits it. Organically, it has one mission, pregnancy, which we may spend a lifetime staving off. Nature cares only for species, never individuals: the humiliating dimensions of this biologic fact are most directly experienced by women, who probably have a greater realism and wisdom than men because of it. Woman's body is a sea acted upon by the month's lunar wave-motion. Sluggish and dormant, her fatty tissues are gorged with water, then suddenly cleansed at hormonal high tide. Edema is our mammalian relapse into the vegetable. Pregnancy demonstrates the deterministic character of woman's sexuality. Every pregnant woman has body and self taken over by a chthonian force beyond her control. In the welcome pregnancy, this is a happy sacrifice. But in the unwanted one, initiated by rape or misadventure, it is a horror. Such unfortunate women look directly into nature's heart of darkness. For a fetus is a benign tumor, a vampire who steals in order to live. The so-called miracle of birth is nature getting her own way.

---

[1]*agonistic:* Combative, in struggle. — ED.
[2]*dysmenorrhea:* Painful menstruation. — ED.
[3]*chthonian:* Relating to deities and spirits dwelling under the earth (classical). — ED.

EXPLORATIONS

1. According to Camille Paglia, why was "the identification of woman with nature . . . universal in prehistory" (para. 1)? How does she believe this identification did and does affect the way women are regarded and treated?

2. "Western culture from the start has swerved from femaleness" (para. 3). What does Paglia mean by this? What impact does she suggest this shift has had on Western culture? On the opportunities available to men and women in Western culture?

3. What does Paglia mean by her statement that "cult-objects are prisoners of their own symbolic inflation" (para. 5)? Give two examples of this phenomenon.

CONNECTIONS

1. "Every human being must wrestle with nature. But nature's burden falls more heavily on one sex" (para. 8). What support for these declarations appears in Curtis Sittenfeld's "Your Life as a Girl" (p. 319)? In John Updike's "The Disposable Rocket" (p. 314)?

2. "The Western idea of history as a propulsive movement into the future, a progressive or Providential design climaxing in the revelation of a Second Coming, is a male formulation" (para. 9). How does Paglia's choice of words reflect her reasons for believing this? What points in Updike's "The Disposable Rocket" might she cite as evidence for her assertion?

3. "A fetus is a benign tumor, a vampire who steals in order to live" (para. 12). What observations in Louise Erdrich's "Making Babies" (p. 102) make a similar point? How does the contrast between Paglia's and Erdrich's language affect your response to what they are saying?

ELABORATIONS

1. Choose a paragraph in "Woman and Nature" and expand it into an argumentative essay, explaining what Paglia means and supplying details, evidence, and examples. You may use your essay to prove her either right or wrong.

2. How has your life been limited or expanded, or both, by the physical constraints of being female or male? Pick an idea on this topic in Paglia's essay, and write a cause-and-effect or definition essay applying it to your own experience.

SAM KEEN

Man and WOMAN

Sam Keen graduated from Ursinus College in 1953 and holds advanced degrees from Harvard Divinity School and Princeton University. After completing his Ph.D. at Princeton he taught philosophy of religion at Louisville Presbyterian Theological Seminary from 1962 to 1968 before becoming a contributing editor for *Psychology Today* magazine. His writing and teaching have explored religion, philosophy, and psychology at the grass-roots level; his first book to attract significant attention was *Apology for Wonder* (1969), in which he looks at the role of wonder in the approach of children and ancient societies to the world. Over the next two decades Keen continued to lecture, consult, and lead groups at colleges, corporations, and a variety of other institutions all over the United States, as well as to write books and magazine features. In 1987 he collaborated on a public-television documentary based on his book *Faces of the Enemy* (1986). Keen's best-known book is *Fire in the Belly: On Being a Man* (1991), which gave him the status of a leader (along with Robert Bly; see p. 100) of the men's movement. "Man and WOMAN" comes from the introduction to *Fire in the Belly*. Keen's latest book is *Learning to Fly: Trapeze — Reflections on Fear, Trust, and the Joy of Letting Go* (1999). He lives in Sonoma, California, with his wife and daughters.

One of the major tasks of manhood is to explore the unconscious feelings that surround our various images of WOMAN, to dispel false mystification, to dissolve the vague sense of threat and fear, and finally to learn to respect and love the strangeness of womankind. It may be useful to think about sexual-spiritual maturation — the journey of manhood — as a process of changing WOMAN into women into Jane (or one certain woman), of learning to see members of the opposite sex not as archetypes or members of a class but as individuals. It is the WOMAN in our heads, more than the women in our beds or boardrooms, who causes most of our problems. And these archetypical creatures — goddesses, bitches, angels, Madonnas, castrators, witches, Gypsy maidens, earth mothers — must be exorcised from our minds and hearts before we can learn to love women. So long as our house is haunted by the ghost of WOMAN we can never live gracefully with any woman. If we continue to deny that she lives in the shadows she will continue to have power over us.

A man's journey in relationship to WOMAN involves three stages. In the beginning he is sunk deep in an unconscious relationship with a falsely mystified figure who is composed of unreal opposites: virgin-whore, nurturer-devouring mother, goddess-demon. To grow from man-child into man, in the second stage, he must take leave of WOMAN and wander for a long time in the wild and sweet world of men. Finally, when he has learned to love his own manhood, he may return to the everyday world to love an ordinary woman.

In the first stage of his journey, or so long as he remains unconscious, the trinity that secretly controls man is: WOMAN as goddess and creatrix, WOMAN as mother and matrix, and WOMAN as erotic-spiritual power.

WOMAN *as Goddess and Creatrix*

Woman was, is, and always will be goddess and creatrix. She is the womb from which we sprang, the ground of our being. Feminists who argue that goddess-worship historically preceded the notion of God as father are certainly correct. What they fail to see is that the goddess, since her historical dethronement, has remained alive and well, and continues to exert power from deep in the hidden recesses of the male psyche. Granted, she has been sentenced to remain in a kind of internal exile, under house arrest, but her power is obvious from the efforts spent to keep her imprisoned.

As our source, the goddess is both historically and psychologically   5 primary. She has been an inevitable symbol of divinity since the beginning of time and remains a sacred presence in the timeless dimension of every psyche. The earliest images we have of WOMAN and divinity are one and the same, stone figurines such as the so-called Venus of Willendorph — women without faces or feet, with ponderous breasts and prominent vulvas. When we look at these early icons of mother-goddesses it doesn't require much empathy to imagine the overwhelming sense of awe men experienced at woman's capacity to give birth. She was at once the revelation and the incarnation of creativity. Her womb was of the same substance as the fruitful earth. She was Mother Nature.

In explaining the continuing power of WOMAN as creatrix over men, psychologists have often reduced the mystery of gender to a matter of "penis envy" or "womb envy." But to name the awe we feel in the presence of the opposite sex "envy" is mean and mistaken. Call it "womb awe" or even "womb worship," but it is not simple envy.

I don't remember ever wanting to be a woman. But each of the three times I have been present at the birth of one of my children I have been overwhelmed by a sense of reverence. As the event of birth approached, the delivery room was bathed in a transcendent light and transformed into a stage for a cosmic drama. It was, quite suddenly, the first day of creation; the Goddess was giving birth to a world. When Jessamyn, my last child, was born, the doctors had to attend to Jananne, my wife. I took off my shirt, put the baby next to my body, and walked and sang her welcome into the world. In that hour all my accomplishments — books I had written, works of will and imagination, small monuments to my immortality — shrank into insignificance. Like men since the beginning of time I wondered: What can I ever create that will equal the magnificence of this new life?

As creatrix, WOMAN addresses an inescapable challenge to a man to justify his existence. She gives birth to meaning out of her body. Biology alone assures her of a destiny, of making a significant contribution to the ongoing drama of life. A man responds to her challenge by simulating creation, by making, fabricating, and inventing artifacts. But while she creates naturally and literally, he creates only artificially and metaphorically. She creates from her corpus; he invents a "corporation," a fictitious legal body with endowed rights of a natural person. Her creation sustains the eternal cycle of nature. Each of his artifacts contributes to making history a series of unrepeatable events. (Sometimes I imagine that the hidden intent of technology is to create a perfect mechanical baby — an automobile, a machine that moves by itself, is capable of perpetual motion, is fed its daily bottle of petroleum, and has its pollution diapered.) In response to the power of the goddess, man creates himself in the image of a god he imagines has fabricated the world like a craftsman working with a blueprint to shape matter into meaningful objects. Much of the meaning men attribute to their work is a response to the question posed to us by WOMAN'S capacity to give life.

WOMAN *as Mother and Matrix*

WOMAN, in her second aspect as mother and matrix, is food, everlasting arms, teacher of language and philosophy, the horizon within which we live and move and have our being. To paraphrase an old hymn, She is "so high you can't get over her, so low you can't get under her, so wide you can't get around her." She exists; therefore I am. Within the warp of her womb our bodies are woven — flesh of her flesh. Within the woof of her arms our minds, spirits, and visions of the world are braided together. She is teacher of the categories by which we will understand ourselves. Her face was our first mirror. A newborn is programmed for immediate face recognition and will spend 90 percent of its waking time focused on the mother. The changing pattern of her face — her smile, her frown, the joy or sadness in her eyes — is the infant's barometer of reality. If she smiles I am good. If she is angry I am bad. There was terror in her disapproving glance, and bliss when her face shone upon us.

Consider the fundamental categories of our emotional and intellec-   10
tual life that we learn before we are weaned. At the breast we learn: desire, satisfaction, disappointment, anger, fear, authority, expectation, judgment. Little wonder that Hindu philosophers identify WOMAN with Maya — illusion — as well as nurturance. Her body is our first information system. If she is warm and sensuous and loves to hold us, we learn that the world is supported by trustworthy and everlasting arms. If she is tense and unhappy we learn the world is fearful and filled with nameless dangers.

WOMAN, as the mother, continues to have enormous power over our adult lives because her most important lessons are taught wordlessly. She shapes us before we understand language, and therefore her influence is hidden from our adult consciousness. Her instructions remain within us like posthypnotic suggestion. Imagine that long ago your mother wrote and inserted the software disk that preprogrammed your life. She etched the script for your life, inserted a philosophy-of-life program, on the blank pages of your mind. This set of instructions remains in the archaic layers of your psyche and continues to shape your perceptions and feelings well into adulthood. The language in which she wrote is as cryptic and difficult to decipher as ancient hieroglyphics, and yet to break the spell she has woven you must learn to decipher these early messages and bring the wordless information and misinformation into the light of consciousness.

In the degree that Mother remains a shadow presence in the life of a man, he will see himself and all women as if reflected in Mother's eyes. He will perform for them as he performed for her, fearing displeasure, courting approval. The size of his ego and the size of his cock will be determined by what he sees in the mirror she holds. And all the while he will imagine that her judgments are those of the flesh-and-blood women in his life. Just like the song says, he will "marry a girl just like the girl that married dear old Dad," and will love and hate her accordingly. Almost inevitably, men marry Mother unless they have undertaken the long struggle to recognize and exorcise WOMAN from their psyches.

Modern men bear a special burden in relationship to Mother; our task of separation is more difficult than that of traditional men. For most modern sons, Mother is a problem that needs to be solved and we find it difficult to break the symbiotic bond.

Freud said that the first major crisis in a boy's life was severing his attachment to his mother and identifying with his father. In the gospel according to Freud, every boy wants to possess and sleep with his mother and displace his powerful father. But he fears being castrated or killed by the father (a fear substantiated by his observation that women and little girls lack, and therefore must have lost, the penis). About the age of six the son learns to live by the ancient adage, "If you can't beat them, join them." He renounces his desire to be his mother's lover and makes common cause with his enemy — the father. This successful resolution of the Oedipus complex, like ancient initiation rites, involves identification with power, authority, and the values of the father and the male establishment.

If this classical drama of separation from Mother and the initiation of   15
the son by the father sounds strange to our ears it is because the world has changed. Since the industrial revolution, the son is more likely to have remained mama's boy than to have identified with any powerful male authority. The powerful father has been all but replaced by the powerful mother.

Dad is no longer present to teach his sons how to be men. More than any other single factor, this absence of the father from the modern family is what presently disturbs the relationship between mothers and their sons and therefore between men and women, husbands and wives. Where once there was a father, there is now a vacuum. Dad belongs more to the world of work than to the family. He is, or was until recently, the provider, but he is gone from the home most of the time. Someone, using what I call SWAG statistics (Scientific Wild-Ass Guess) has estimated that prior to World War I men spent four hours a day with their children, between World War I and World War II two hours, and since World War II twenty minutes.

There are many variations on the modern mother-son theme, but in some degree most sons were forced to step into the role of husband and lover to their mother. As a friend told me: "Mother made me into the husband my father never was. I was the listener, the helper, the ally in hard times. In a sense I became the man of the house. I was super-responsible, so I never really got a chance to be a kid." While the love between mother and son seldom becomes literally incestuous, it becomes too close for comfort. Rollo May, in a conversation with me, characterized the problem of the son who is too close to his mother as the opposite of that which Freud presented. "The dilemma of the modern son is that he *wins* the Oedipal battle against the father and gets Mother. And then he doesn't know what to do with her because she overwhelms him."

Ambivalence is the consequence of the modern mother-son relationship. The son experiences the mother as nearly omnipotent. She works outside the home, manages the household, and provides for his daily needs. But he learns from the rhetoric and values of the surrounding society that women are less important than men, that child rearing is an inferior task, that men have real power and authority, and that what counts is success in the public arena of business and politics. So the son is faced with a tragic, schizophrenic choice. If he is to become a man and play a role in the "real" world, he must deny his visceral knowledge of the goodness of Mother's caring power and join the male conspiracy to "keep women in their place," in the missionary position, beneath men.

Meanwhile the son must develop various strategies to deal with the power of Mother. He may surrender, becoming mama's boy, and devote his life to pleasing her, and later his wife or lover. If he takes this tack his relationships with women will be dominated by the desire to perform well, to gain approval, and to avoid female anger or rejection. Or he may take an opposite course and reduce females to either servants or sex objects. The Don Juan male constantly tries to prove his potency by seduction and conquest. The more violent man who is obsessed with pornography or rape is compelled to demean and take revenge on woman in order to deny her power over him.

To be free from and for women, to discover the unique ground of 20 manhood, a man must take leave of Motherland.

WOMAN *as Erotic-Spiritual Power*

The third aspect of WOMAN is as an irresistible erotic-spiritual force. She is the magnet, and men the iron filings that lie within her field.

It is difficult to give this aspect of WOMAN a familiar name because Western mythology, philosophy, and psychology have never acknowledged its reality. Once, men and women assumed that the goddess controlled all things that flow and ebb — the waxing and waning moon, the rise and fall of tide and phallus. But ever since God became Father, and men have considered themselves the lords over nature (and women), we have defined man as active and WOMAN as reactive. Consequently, we have never developed a language that does justice to WOMAN'S erotic-spiritual power.

In Eastern mythology, notions of gender are reversed. The female principle is seen as active and the male as responsive. Among human beings, lions, and other members of the animal kingdom, the female of the species sends out her invitations on the wind and commands the male's response. He may think he initiates, but her sexual perfumes (pheromones) and inspiring image influence him to action. She is the prime mover, the divine eros, whose power draws him to her. As Joseph Campbell points out,[1] the term *Shakti* in Hindu mythology names the energy or active power of a male divinity that is embodied in his spouse. "Every wife is her husband's Shakti and every beloved woman her lover's. Beatrice was Dante's. Carried further still: The word connotes female spiritual power in general, as manifest, for instance, in the radiance of beauty, or on the elemental level in the sheer power of the female sex to work effects on the male."

To detect this important aspect of men's experience of WOMAN that our language or philosophy of gender does not name or honor, we have to look at the angelic and demonic extremes of men's sexuality — the ways in which WOMAN figures in the imaginations of artists and rapists.

For many creative men WOMAN is the muse and inspiration for their work. She possesses a semidivine power to call forth their creativity. Without her inspiration they cannot paint, write, or manage. She is the anima, the spirit and soul of a man. Without her a man is only will and intellect and blind force.

At the opposite end of the spectrum the rapist confesses the same experience of the irresistible erotic power of WOMAN. His defense is inevitably: "She tempted me. She wanted it. She seduced me." For a moment, put aside the correct response to such deluded excuses, which is that it is *not* the victim's fault, and consider the raw unconscious experience of WOMAN that underlies rape no less than the inspiration of the artist. In both cases, she is experienced as the active, initiatory power.

When we consider how most "civilized" men have repressed their experience of the power of WOMAN as goddess, mother, and erotic-

---

[1]Joseph Campbell and M. J. Abadie, *The Mythic Image* (Princeton, N.J.: Princeton University Press, 1981).

spiritual motivator, it is easy to understand the reasons that lie in back of the history of men's cruelty to women. We fear, therefore deny, therefore demean, therefore (try to) control the power of WOMAN. There is no need here to rehearse the routine insults and gynocidal hatreds of men toward women. Mary Daly, Susan Griffin, and other feminist thinkers have traced this painful history in brilliant and convincing fashion.

As men we need to recollect our experience, reown our repressed knowledge of the power of WOMAN, and cease establishing our manhood in reactionary ways. If we do not, we will continue to be workers desperately trying to produce trinkets that will equal WOMAN'S creativity, macho men who confuse swagger with independence, studs who anxiously perform for Mother's eyes hoping to win enough applause to satisfy a fragile ego, warriors and rapists who do violence to a feminine power they cannot control and therefore fear.

So long as we define ourselves by our reactions to unconscious images of WOMAN we remain in exile from the true mystery and power of manhood.

EXPLORATIONS

1. What point of view does author Sam Keen use in "Man and WOMAN"? What is his intended audience? How can you tell? Where in this selection does Keen's personal experience play a role, and what role does it play?

2. What does Keen mean by WOMAN? What does he believe is the usual relationship between men and women before "sexual-spiritual maturation — the journey of manhood" (para. 1)? What does he believe is the ideal relationship between men and women after this maturation journey?

3. On what kinds of information does Keen base his statements about WOMAN? What sources does he cite? On what basis do you think Keen expects readers to accept his statements?

CONNECTIONS

1. What ideas about woman appear in both "Man and WOMAN" and Camille Paglia's "Woman and Nature" (p. 327)? Which of these ideas do Keen and Paglia interpret differently?

2. According to Keen, what three aspects of WOMAN comprise "the trinity that secretly controls man" (para. 3)? How do you think Keen would classify

John Updike's depiction of women in "The Disposable Rocket" (p. 314)? How do you think Updike would respond to Keen's trinity?

3. How does Paula Gunn Allen summarize Western images of women (p. 307)? In what ways does Keen's description of WOMAN match Allen's summary? How would you expect Allen's recommendations to men regarding women to be like and unlike Keen's?

ELABORATIONS

1. Choose one of the historic or religious references in "Man and WOMAN" that interests you, such as the ancient tradition of goddess-worship (paras. 4–5) or the psychoanalytic theory of penis envy (para. 6), and find out enough about it to write an essay.

2. Write an essay about either WOMAN or MAN from your own sex's point of view. You may want to use "Man and WOMAN" as a structural or stylistic model, or you may want to write an argument critiquing or rebutting Keen's ideas.

SIMONE DE BEAUVOIR

Woman as Other

Simone de Beauvoir was born in Paris in 1908 and lived there most of her life, though her interests and influence were worldwide. Having a devout Catholic mother and an agnostic father who practiced law and was involved in amateur theater encouraged her to think for herself. She vowed early to be a writer rather than a wife. True to her plan, Beauvoir is best known for her feminist fiction and nonfiction and for her lifelong relationship with the existentialist philosopher and writer Jean-Paul Sartre. She was twenty when she met Sartre while studying at the Sorbonne. The two never married, lived together, or viewed their liaison as exclusive, but they worked closely together and kept apartments in the same building until Sartre's death in 1980. Beauvoir's several memoirs chronicle her social and political development; her novels examine existentialist ideas and sometimes their proponents as well. *The Mandarins* (1954), based on her affair with American novelist Nelson Algren, won the prestigious Prix Goncourt. Beauvoir's most famous work is the international best-seller *The Second Sex* (1952; *Le deuxième sexe*, 1949), translated from the French by H. M. Parshley, from which "Woman as Other" is taken. A vigorous and compassionate champion of antiestablishment causes, Beauvoir died in Paris in 1986.

Although France was settled by the Parisii in the third century B.C., the French celebrated their bicentennial in 1989. Bastille Day, July 14, marks the date in 1789 when outraged citizens stormed Paris's notorious Bastille prison and launched the Revolution, which ended nearly a thousand years of monarchy. King Louis XVI was beheaded by the guillotine in 1793, followed by his queen, the extravagant and unpopular Marie Antoinette. After a two-year orgy of executions and a short-lived republic, Napoleon Bonaparte ruled as emperor from 1804 to 1815. After him came a series of republics and the brief Second Empire, culminating in the Fifth Republic, which holds power today. During World War II, France was occupied by Germany. Having accumulated worldwide colonies during the centuries of European expansion, France withdrew in the 1950s from Indochina, Morocco, and Tunisia, and subsequently from most of its other African territories. France also withdrew most of its troops in 1966 from the North Atlantic Treaty Organization (NATO), although it remains a member. A founding member of the European Union (see p. 277), France continues to play a significant political, economic, and cultural role in Europe and the world.

What is a woman?

To state the question is, to me, to suggest, at once, a preliminary answer. The fact that I ask it is in itself significant. A man would never get the notion of writing a book on the peculiar situation of the human male. But if I wish to define myself, I must first of all say: "I am a woman"; on this truth must be based all further discussion. A man never begins by presenting himself as an individual of a certain sex; it goes without saying that he is a man. The terms *masculine* and *feminine* are used symmetrically only as a matter of form, as on legal papers. In actuality the relation of the two sexes is not quite like that of two electrical poles, for man represents both the positive and the neutral, as is indicated by the common use of *man* to designate human beings in general; whereas woman represents only the negative, defined by limiting criteria, without reciprocity. In the midst of an abstract discussion it is vexing to hear a man say: "You think thus and so because you are a woman"; but I know that my only defense is to reply: "I think thus and so because it is true," thereby removing my subjective self from the argument. It would be out of the question to reply: "And you think the contrary because you are a man," for it is understood that the fact of being a man is no peculiarity. A man is in the right in being a man; it is the woman who is in the wrong. It amounts to this: Just as for the ancients there was an absolute vertical with reference to which the oblique was defined, so there is an absolute human type, the masculine. Woman has ovaries, a uterus; these peculiarities imprison her in her subjectivity, circumscribe her within the limits of her own nature. It is often said that she thinks with her glands. Man superbly ignores the fact that his anatomy also includes glands, such as the testicles, and that they secrete hormones. He thinks of his body as a direct and normal connection with the world, which he believes he apprehends objectively, whereas he regards the body of woman as a hindrance, a prison, weighed down by everything peculiar to it. "The female is a female by virtue of a certain *lack* of qualities," said Aristotle; "we should regard the female nature as afflicted with a natural defectiveness." And St. Thomas for his part pronounced woman to be an "imperfect man," an "incidental" being. This is symbolized in Genesis where Eve is depicted as made from what Bossuet called "a supernumerary bone" of Adam.

Thus humanity is male and man defines woman not in herself but as relative to him; she is not regarded as an autonomous being. Michelet writes: "Woman, the relative being. . . ." And Benda is most positive in his *Rapport d'Uriel:* "The body of man makes sense in itself quite apart from that of woman, whereas the latter seems wanting in significance by itself. . . . Man can think of himself without woman. She cannot think of herself without man." And she is simply what man decrees; thus she is called "the sex," by which is meant that she appears essentially to the male as a sexual being. For him she is sex — absolute sex, no less. She is defined and differentiated with reference to man and not he with reference to her; she is the incidental, the inessential as opposed to the essential. He is the Subject, he is the Absolute — she is the Other.

The category of the *Other* is as primordial as consciousness itself. In the most primitive societies, in the most ancient mythologies, one finds the expression of a duality — that of the Self and the Other. This duality was not originally attached to the division of the sexes; it was not dependent upon any empirical facts. It is revealed in such works as that of Granet on Chinese thought and those of Dumézil on the East Indies and Rome. The feminine element was at first no more involved in such pairs as Varuna-Mitra, Uranus-Zeus, Sun-Moon, and Day-Night than it was in the contrasts between Good and Evil, lucky and unlucky auspices, right and left, God and Lucifer. Otherness is a fundamental category of human thought.

Thus it is that no group ever sets itself up as the One without at once 5 setting up the Other over against itself. If three travelers chance to occupy the same compartment, that is enough to make vaguely hostile "others" out of all the rest of the passengers on the train. In small-town eyes all persons not belonging to the village are "strangers" and suspect; to the native of a country all who inhabit other countries are "foreigners"; Jews are "different" for the anti-Semite, Negroes are "inferior" for American racists, aborigines are "natives" for colonists, proletarians are the "lower class" for the privileged.

Lévi-Strauss, at the end of a profound work on the various forms of primitive societies, reaches the following conclusion: "Passage from the state of Nature to the state of Culture is marked by man's ability to view biological relations as a series of contrasts; duality, alternation, opposition, and symmetry, whether under definite or vague forms, constitute not so much phenomena to be explained as fundamental and immediately given data of social reality." These phenomena would be incomprehensible if in fact human society were simply a *Mitsein* or fellowship based on solidarity and friendliness. Things become clear, on the contrary, if, following Hegel, we find in consciousness itself a fundamental hostility toward every other consciousness; the subject can be posed only in being opposed — he sets himself up as the essential, as opposed to the other, the inessential, the object.

But the other consciousness, the other ego, sets up a reciprocal claim. The native traveling abroad is shocked to find himself in turn regarded as a "stranger" by the natives of neighboring countries. As a matter of fact, wars, festivals, trading, treaties, and contests among tribes, nations, and classes tend to deprive the concept *Other* of its absolute sense and to make manifest its relativity; willy-nilly, individuals and groups are forced to realize the reciprocity of their relations. How is it, then, that this reciprocity has not been recognized between the sexes, that one of the contrasting terms is set up as the sole essential, denying any relativity in regard to its correlative and defining the latter as pure otherness? Why is it that women do not dispute male sovereignty? No subject will readily volunteer to become the object, the inessential; it is not the Other who, in defining himself as the Other, establishes the One. The Other is posed as such by the One in defining himself as the One. But if the Other is not to regain the status of being the One, he must be submissive enough to accept this alien point of view. Whence comes this submission in the case of woman?

There are, to be sure, other cases in which a certain category has been able to dominate another completely for a time. Very often this privilege depends upon inequality of numbers — the majority imposes its rule upon the minority or persecutes it. But women are not a minority, like the American Negroes or the Jews; there are as many women as men on earth. Again, the two groups concerned have often been originally independent; they may have been formerly unaware of each other's existence, or perhaps they recognized each other's autonomy. But a historical event has resulted in the subjugation of the weaker by the stronger. The scattering of the Jews, the introduction of slavery into America, the conquests of imperialism are examples in point. In these cases the oppressed retained at least the memory of former days; they possessed in common a past, a tradition, sometimes a religion or a culture.

The parallel drawn by Bebel between women and the proletariat is valid in that neither ever formed a minority or a separate collective unit of mankind. And instead of a single historical event it is in both cases a historical development that explains their status as a class and accounts for the membership of *particular individuals* in that class. But proletarians have not always existed, whereas there have always been women. They are women in virtue of their anatomy and physiology. Throughout history they have always been subordinated to men, and hence their dependency is not the result of a historical event or a social change — it was not something that *occurred*. The reason why otherness in this case seems to be an absolute is in part that it lacks the contingent or incidental nature of historical facts. A condition brought about at a certain time can be abolished at some other time, as the Negroes of Haiti and others have proved; but it might seem that a natural condition is beyond the possibility of change. In truth, however, the nature of things is no more immutably given, once for all, than is historical reality. If woman seems to be the inessential which never becomes the essential, it is because she herself fails to bring about this change. Proletarians say "We"; Negroes also. Regarding themselves as subjects, they transform the bourgeois, the whites, into "others." But women do not say "We," except at some congress of feminists or similar formal demonstration; men say "women," and women use the same word in referring to themselves. They do not authentically assume a subjective attitude. The proletarians have accomplished the revolution in Russia, the Negroes in Haiti, the Indochinese are battling for it in Indochina; but the women's effort has never been anything more than a symbolic agitation. They have gained only what men have been willing to grant; they have taken nothing, they have only received.

The reason for this is that women lack concrete means for organizing   10
themselves into a unit which can stand face to face with the correlative unit. They have no past, no history, no religion of their own; and they have no such solidarity of work and interest as that of the proletariat. They are not even promiscuously herded together in the way that creates community feeling among the American Negroes, the ghetto Jews, the workers of Saint-Denis, or the factory hands of Renault. They live dispersed among the males, attached through residence, housework, economic condition, and social standing to certain men — fathers or husbands — more firmly than they are to other women. If they belong to the bourgeoisie, they feel solidarity with men of that class, not with proletarian women; if they are white, their allegiance is to white men, not to Negro women. The proletariat can propose to massacre the ruling class, and a sufficiently fanatical Jew or Negro might dream of getting sole possession of the atomic bomb and making humanity wholly Jewish or black; but woman cannot even dream of exterminating the males. The bond that unites her to her oppressors is not comparable to any other. The division of the sexes is a biological fact, not an event in human history. Male and female stand opposed within a primordial *Mitsein*, and woman has not broken it. The couple is a fundamental unity with its two halves riveted together, and the cleavage of society along the line of sex is impossible. Here is to be found the basic trait of woman: She is the Other in a totality of which the two components are necessary to one another.

One could suppose that this reciprocity might have facilitated the liberation of woman. When Hercules sat at the feet of Omphale and helped with her spinning, his desire for her held him captive; but why did she fail to gain a lasting power? To revenge herself on Jason, Medea killed their children; and this grim legend would seem to suggest that she might have obtained a formidable influence over him through his love for his offspring. In *Lysistrata* Aristophanes gaily depicts a band of women who joined forces to gain social ends through the sexual needs of their men; but this is only a play. In the legend of the Sabine women, the latter soon abandoned their plan of remaining sterile to punish their ravishers. In truth woman has not been socially emancipated through man's need — sexual desire and the desire for offspring — which makes the male dependent for satisfaction upon the female.

Master and slave, also, are united by a reciprocal need, in this case economic, which does not liberate the slave. In the relation of master to slave the master does not make a point of the need that he has for the other; he has in his grasp the power of satisfying this need through his own action; whereas the slave, in his dependent condition, his hope and fear, is quite conscious of the need he has for his master. Even if the need is at bottom equally urgent for both, it always works in favor of the oppressor and against the oppressed. That is why the liberation of the working class, for example, has been slow.

Now, woman has always been man's dependent, if not his slave; the two sexes have never shared the world in equality. And even today woman is heavily handicapped, though her situation is beginning to change. Almost nowhere is her legal status the same as man's, and frequently it is much to her disadvantage. Even when her rights are legally recognized in the abstract, long-standing custom prevents their full expression in the mores. In the economic sphere men and women can almost be said to make up two castes; other things being equal, the former hold the better jobs, get higher wages, and have more opportunity for success than their new competitors. In industry and politics men have a great many more positions and they monopolize the most important posts. In addition to all this, they enjoy a traditional prestige that the education of children tends in every way to support, for the present enshrines the past — and in the past all history has been made by men. At the present time, when women are beginning to take part in the affairs of the world, it is still a world that belongs to men — they have no doubt of it at all and women have scarcely any. To decline to be the Other, to refuse to be a party to the deal — this would be for women to renounce all the advantages conferred upon them by their alliance with the superior caste. Man-the-sovereign will provide woman-the-liege with material protection and will undertake the moral justification of her existence; thus she can evade at once both economic risk and the metaphysical risk of a liberty in which ends and aims must be contrived without assistance. Indeed, along with the ethical urge of each individual to affirm his subjective existence, there is also the temptation to forgo liberty and become a thing. This is an inauspicious road, for he who takes it — passive, lost, ruined — becomes henceforth the creature of another's will, frustrated in his transcendence and deprived of every value. But it is an easy road; on it one avoids the strain involved in undertaking an authentic existence. When man makes of woman the *Other*, he may, then, expect her to manifest deep-seated tendencies toward complicity. Thus, woman may fail to lay claim to the status of subject because she lacks definite resources, because she feels the necessary bond that ties her to man regardless of reciprocity, and because she is often very well pleased with her role as the *Other*.

EXPLORATIONS

1. "Woman as Other" was originally published as part of *The Second Sex* in 1949. Which, if any, of Simone de Beauvoir's observations about women's status have been invalidated since then by political and social changes? Which of the problems she mentions are live issues in our society today?

2. What emotionally loaded words, phrases, and sentences indicate that Beauvoir is presenting an argument in "Woman as Other"? Who is her intended audience? To what extent, and for what reasons, do you think she expects part or all of her audience to resist the case she is making?

3. What kinds of sources does Beauvoir cite? In what ways would her essay gain or lose impact if she included quotations from interviews with individual women and men? In what ways would it gain or lose impact if she cut all references to outside sources?

CONNECTIONS

1. Which comments in Sam Keen's "Man and WOMAN" (p. 332) show men viewing women as "Other"? Which comments recommend ways to overcome the problems Beauvoir describes?

2. In paragraph 2, Beauvoir describes the traditional view of woman as imprisoned and limited by her biological differences from men. What is Beauvoir's opinion of this view? What opinion of this view does Camille Paglia express in "Woman and Nature" (p. 327)?

3. What evidence in Curtis Sittenfeld's "Your Life as a Girl" (p. 319) shows Anna, the narrator, perceiving herself as defined by or dependent on males

in the ways Beauvoir describes? How do you think Beauvoir would explain to Anna why boys often seem hostile to her?

ELABORATIONS

1. Beauvoir notes that male glands affect men's thinking as much as female glands affect women's thinking. How do the writers of the Observations on pages 307–13 apply this idea? On the basis of their comments, Beauvoir's, Keen's, Paglia's, Sittenfeld's, and John Updike's in "The Disposable Rocket" (p. 314), write a cause-and-effect essay about the relationship (or absence of a relationship) between gender and attitudes.

2. "What is a woman?" asks Beauvoir in her opening paragraph. She goes on: "If I wish to define myself, I must first of all say: 'I am a woman.'" Already she is letting her readers know that her choice of *definition* as the form for her inquiry has a political as well as a rhetorical basis. That is, she is not simply defining woman, as her opening question implies; she is examining a definition of woman imposed by men. The same tactic can be applied to any issue in which a preexisting definition is crucial to the argument. Choose such an issue that interests you — for instance, What is a drug? or What is military defense? Write a definition essay exploring the issue by examining the tacit definitions that underlie it.

ALBERTO MORAVIA

The Chase

Alberto Moravia has been called the first existentialist novelist in Italy — a forerunner of Jean-Paul Sartre and Albert Camus in France. Moravia is best known in the United States for the films that have been based on his work: Michelangelo Antonioni's *L'Avventura* (1961), Jean-Luc Godard's *Le Mépris* (*Contempt*, 1965), and Bernardo Bertolucci's *The Conformist* (1970). The film of *Conjugal Love* (1949) was directed by Moravia's wife, Dacia Maraini. Born Alberto Pincherle in Rome in 1907, Moravia had little formal schooling but was taught to read English, French, and German by governesses and earned a high school diploma. He began his first novel at age sixteen while in a sanatorium for the tuberculosis he had contracted when he was nine; he considered his long illness a major influence on his career. Moravia's novels, stories, and scripts are too numerous to list. Many of them, including his 1987 novel *The Voyeur*, are available in English. "The Chase," translated from the Italian in 1969 by Angus Davidson, is from the story collection *Command, and I Will Obey You*. Moravia also represented Italy in the European Parliament as of 1984. He died in 1990.

Italy, a boot-shaped peninsula across the Mediterranean Sea from Libya, has been occupied since the Stone Age. Its political heyday was the Roman Empire, which by A.D. 180 ruled from Britain to Africa to Persia (now Iran). The Roman civilization fell to barbarian invaders in the fourth and fifth centuries but left as a legacy its capital city, alphabet, roads, laws, and arts. The United Nations Educational, Scientific, and Cultural Organization (UNESCO) estimates that half of the world's cultural heritage has come from Italy, which still houses much of the finest architecture, sculpture, painting, and other visual arts in Europe.

Italy remained politically fragmented until the 1860s, when it united under a parliament and king. In 1922 Fascist dictator Benito Mussolini took over the government, proclaiming Victor Emmanuel III emperor and subsequently joining Germany in World War II. After Fascism was overthrown in 1943, Italy declared war on Germany and Japan. Mussolini was killed in 1946, and the monarchy was voted out. Democratic postwar governments have tended to be short-lived. However, Italy was a founding member of the European Union (see p. 277) and continues to have a thriving market economy.

I have never been a sportsman — or, rather, I have been a sportsman only once, and that was the first and last time. I was a child, and one day, for some reason or other, I found myself together with my father, who was holding a gun in his hand, behind a bush, watching a bird that had perched on a branch not very far away. It was a large, gray bird — or perhaps it was brown — with a long — or perhaps a short — beak; I don't remember. I only remember what I felt at that moment as I looked at it. It was like watching an animal whose vitality was rendered more intense by the very fact of my watching it and of the animal's not knowing that I was watching it.

At that moment, I say, the notion of wildness entered my mind, never again to leave it: Everything is wild which is autonomous and unpredictable and does not depend upon us. Then all of a sudden there was an explosion; I could no longer see the bird and I thought it had flown away. But my father was leading the way, walking in front of me through the undergrowth. Finally he stooped down, picked up something, and put it in my hand. I was aware of something warm and soft and I lowered my eyes: There was the bird in the palm of my hand, its dangling, shattered head crowned with a plume of already-thickening blood. I burst into tears and dropped the corpse on the ground, and that was the end of my shooting experience.

I thought again of this remote episode in my life this very day after watching my wife, for the first and also the last time, as she was walking through the streets of the city. But let us take things in order.

What had my wife been like; what was she like now? She once had been, to put it briefly, "wild" — that is, entirely autonomous and unpredictable; latterly she had become "tame" — that is, predictable and dependent. For a long time she had been like the bird that, on that far-off morning in my childhood, I had seen perching on the bough; latterly, I am sorry to say, she had become like a hen about which one knows everything in advance — how it moves, how it eats, how it lays eggs, how it sleeps, and so on.

Nevertheless I would not wish anyone to think that my wife's wildness consisted of an uncouth, rough, rebellious character. Apart from being extremely beautiful, she is the gentlest, politest, most discreet person in the world. Rather her wildness consisted of the air of charming unpredictability, of independence in her way of living, with which during the first years of our marriage she acted in my presence, both at home and abroad. Wildness signified intimacy, privacy, secrecy. Yes, my wife as she sat in front of her dressing table, her eyes fixed on the looking glass, passing the hairbrush with a repeated motion over her long, loose hair, was just as wild as the solitary quail hopping forward along a sun-filled furrow or the furtive fox coming out into a clearing and stopping to look around before running on. She was wild because I, as I looked at her, could never manage to foresee when she would give a last stroke with the hairbrush and rise and come toward me; wild to such a degree that sometimes when I went into our bedroom the smell of her, floating in the air, would have something of the acrid quality of a wild beast's lair.

Gradually she became less wild, tamer. I had had a fox, a quail, in the house, as I have said; then one day I realized that I had a hen. What effect does a hen have on someone who watches it? It has the effect of being, so to speak, an automaton in the form of a bird; automatic are the brief, rapid steps with which it moves about; automatic its hard, terse pecking; automatic the glance of the round eyes in its head that nods and turns; automatic its ready crouching down under the cock; automatic the dropping of the egg wherever it may be and the cry with which it announces that the egg has been laid. Good-bye to the fox; good-bye to the quail. And her smell — this no longer brought to my mind, in any way, the innocent odor of a wild animal; rather I detected in it the chemical suavity of some ordinary French perfume.

Our flat is on the first floor of a big building in a modern quarter of the town; our windows look out on a square in which there is a small public garden, the haunt of nurses and children and dogs. One day I was standing at the window, looking in a melancholy way at the garden. My wife, shortly before, had dressed to go out; and once again, watching her, I had noticed the irrevocable and, so to speak, invisible character of her gestures and personality: something which gave one the feeling of a thing already seen and already done and which therefore evaded even the most determined observation. And now, as I stood looking at the garden and at the same time wondering why the adorable wildness of former times had so completely disappeared, suddenly my wife came into my range of vision as she walked quickly across the garden in the direction of the bus stop. I watched her and then I almost jumped for joy; in a movement she was making to pull down a fold of her narrow skirt and smooth it over her thigh with the tips of her long, sharp nails, in this movement I recognized the wildness that in the past had made me love her. It was only an instant, but in that instant I said to myself: She's become wild again because she's convinced that I am not there and am not watching her. Then I left the window and rushed out.

But I did not join her at the bus stop; I felt that I must not allow myself to be seen. Instead I hurried to my car, which was standing nearby, got in, and waited. A bus came and she got in together with some other people; the bus started off again and I began following it. Then there came back to me the memory of that one shooting expedition in which I had taken part as a child, and I saw that the bus was the undergrowth with its bushes and trees, my wife the bird perching on the bough while I, unseen, watched it living before my eyes. And the whole town, during this pursuit, became, as though by magic, a fact of nature like the countryside: The houses were hills, the streets valleys, the vehicles hedges and woods, and even the passersby on the pavements had something unpredictable and autonomous — that is, wild — about them. And in my mouth, behind my clenched teeth, there was the acrid, metallic taste of gunfire; and my eyes, usually listless and wandering, had become sharp, watchful, attentive.

These eyes were fixed intently upon the exit door when the bus came to the end of its run. A number of people got out, and then I saw my wife getting out. Once again I recognized, in the manner in which she broke free of the crowd and started off toward a neighboring street, the wildness that pleased me so much. I jumped out of the car and started following her.

She was walking in front of me, ignorant of my presence, a tall   10
woman with an elegant figure, long-legged, narrow-hipped, broad-backed, her brown hair falling on her shoulders.

Men turned around as she went past; perhaps they were aware of what I myself was now sensing with an intensity that quickened the beating of my heart and took my breath away: the unrestricted, steadily increasing, irresistible character of her mysterious wildness.

She walked hurriedly, having evidently some purpose in view, and even the fact that she had a purpose of which I was ignorant added to her wildness; I did not know where she was going, just as on that far-off morning I had not known what the bird perching on the bough was about to do. Moreover I thought the gradual, steady increase in this quality of wildness came partly from the fact that as she drew nearer to the object of this mysterious walk there was an increase in her — how shall I express it? — of biological tension, of existential excitement, of vital effervescence. Then, unexpectedly, with the suddenness of a film, her purpose was revealed.

A fair-haired young man in a leather jacket and a pair of corduroy trousers was leaning against the wall of a house in that ancient, narrow street. He was idly smoking as he looked in front of him. But as my wife passed close to him, he threw away his cigarette with a decisive gesture, took a step forward, and seized her arm. I was expecting her to rebuff him, to move away from him, but nothing happened: Evidently obeying the rules of some kind of erotic ritual, she went on walking beside the young man. Then after a few steps, with a movement that confirmed her own complicity, she put her arm around her companion's waist and he put his around her.

I understood then that this unknown man who took such liberties with my wife was also attracted by wildness. And so, instead of making a conventional appointment with her, instead of meeting in a café with a handshake, a falsely friendly and respectful welcome, he had preferred, by agreement with her, to take her by surprise — or, rather, to pretend to do so — while she was apparently taking a walk on her own account. All this I perceived by intuition, noticing that at the very moment when he stepped forward and took her arm her wildness had, so to speak, given an upward bound. It was years since I had seen my wife so alive, but alas, the source of this life could not be traced to me.

They walked on thus entwined and then, without any preliminaries, 15 just like two wild animals, they did an unexpected thing: They went into one of the dark doorways in order to kiss. I stopped and watched them from a distance, peering into the darkness of the entrance. My wife was turned away from me and was bending back with the pressure of his body, her hair hanging free. I looked at that long, thick mane of brown hair, which as she leaned back fell free of her shoulders, and I felt at that moment her vitality reached its diapason, just as happens with wild animals when they couple and their customary wildness is redoubled by the violence of love. I watched for a long time and then, since the kiss went on and on and in fact seemed to be prolonged beyond the limits of my power of endurance, I saw that I would have to intervene.

I would have to go forward, seize my wife by the arm — or actually by that hair, which hung down and conveyed so well the feeling of feminine passivity — then hurl myself with clenched fists upon the blond young man. After this encounter I would carry off my wife, weeping, mortified, ashamed, while I was raging and brokenhearted, upbraiding her and pouring scorn upon her.

But what else would this intervention amount to but the shot my father fired at that free, unknowing bird as it perched on the bough? The disorder and confusion, the mortification, the shame that would follow would irreparably destroy the rare and precious moment of wildness that I was witnessing inside the dark doorway. It was true that this wildness was directed against me; but I had to remember that wildness, always and everywhere, is directed against everything and everybody.

After the scene of my intervention it might be possible for me to regain control of my wife, but I should find her shattered and lifeless in my arms like the bird that my father placed in my hand so that I might throw it into the shooting bag.

The kiss went on and on: Well, it was a kiss of passion — that could not be denied. I waited until they finished, until they came out of the doorway, until they walked on again still linked together. Then I turned back.

EXPLORATIONS

1. What are the functions of the long opening section of "The Chase"? What role does the narrator assign himself here in relation to the adult male world? How would the story's impact change without this section?

2. At what point(s) in "The Chase" does the narrator recall his childhood hunting incident? How is his role different now from the first time he mentioned the incident? How does the narrator vacillate between roles at the end of the story, and what role does he finally choose for himself?

3. Reread Alberto Moravia's last sentence; then look back at his third paragraph. What do you conclude that the narrator has done, and intends to do, after the point when the story ends? In what way is he himself adopting qualities he prizes in his wife? What effects does he apparently expect this behavior to have on his marriage?

CONNECTIONS

1. What evidence in "The Chase" confirms Simone de Beauvoir's contention in "Woman as Other" (p. 341) that men perceive women as Other? What evidence suggests that this perception has hurt the relationship between Moravia's narrator and his wife? What can you deduce from the story about his wife's view of their situation?

2. What are the similarities between Moravia's idea of wildness and Beauvoir's idea of otherness? What are the differences? What advantages does Moravia see in the traditional setup Beauvoir wants to change?

3. Which of the three aspects of WOMAN Sam Keen describes in "Man and WOMAN" (p. 332) is the focus of Moravia's story? How do you think Keen would explain the reactions of Moravia's narrator to his wife's outing?

ELABORATIONS

1. Near the end of "The Chase" the narrator observes, "Wildness, always and everywhere, is directed against everything and everybody" (para. 17). What does he mean? Do you agree? What other aspects of life are affected by wildness as Moravia defines it? Write an essay arguing for or against Moravia's statement, or examining a specific human action (e.g., putting animals in zoos or destroying ancient forests) to which his statement applies.

2. In the first section of "The Chase," Moravia's narrator speaks as if he knows his wife as completely as a farmer knows his hens. In the second section, he discovers that he does not know her so well after all. Think of a situation in which you based your expectations about another person on an image — perhaps an idealized social role, such as mother, grandfather, friend, or fiancé. How did you come to realize that the person was not as predictable as you thought? Write a narrative essay about the incident(s) that changed your attitude.

DEBORAH TANNEN

How Male and Female Students Use Language Differently

The youngest of three daughters, Deborah Tannen was born in Brooklyn, New York, in 1945. She graduated from Harpur College in 1966 and traveled to Europe, where she worked in Crete teaching English as a second language and in Athens as an instructor at the Hellenic-American Union. Returning to the United States, she received her M.A. in English literature from Wayne State University; taught in New Jersey and New York; then returned to school for a Ph.D. in linguistics from the University of California at Berkeley. She joined the faculty at Georgetown University in 1979 and still holds the title of university professor there.

Tannen had published many scholarly articles and two books before winning popular attention with *That's Not What I Meant!: How Conversational Style Makes or Breaks Relationships* (1986). Readers' response led her to follow up with *You Just Don't Understand: Women and Men in Conversation* (1990), which was on the *New York Times* best-seller list for nearly four years and has been translated into twenty-five languages. Ever since, Tannen's teaching and writing have been interspersed with media and lecture appearances. She has served on a variety of editorial boards and advisory panels and won numerous awards while continuing to edit and write books, as well as poetry and plays. Her most recent book is *The Argument Culture: Stopping America's War of Words* (1999). "How Male and Female Students Use Language Differently" first appeared in 1991 in the *Chronicle of Higher Education*. Tannen and her husband live in Washington, D.C., and New York.

When I researched and wrote my book *You Just Don't Understand: Women and Men in Conversation*, the furthest thing from my mind was reevaluating my teaching strategies. But that has been one of the direct benefits of having written the book.

The primary focus of my linguistic research always has been the language of everyday conversation. One facet of this is conversational style:

how different regional, ethnic, and class backgrounds, as well as age and gender, result in different ways of using language to communicate. *You Just Don't Understand* is about the conversational styles of women and men. As I gained more insight into typically male and female ways of using language, I began to suspect some of the causes of the troubling facts that women who go to single-sex schools do better in later life, and that when young women sit next to young men in classrooms, the males talk more. This is not to say that all men talk in class, nor that no women do. It is simply that a greater percentage of discussion time is taken by men's voices.

The research of sociologists and anthropologists such as Janet Lever, Marjorie Harness Goodwin, and Donna Eder has shown that girls and boys learn to use language differently in their sex-separate peer groups. Typically, a girl has a best friend with whom she sits and talks, frequently telling secrets. It's the telling of secrets, the fact and the way that they talk to each other, that makes them best friends. For boys, activities are central: Their best friends are the ones they do things with. Boys also tend to play in larger groups that are hierarchical. High-status boys give orders and push low-status boys around. So boys are expected to use language to seize center stage: by exhibiting their skill, displaying their knowledge, and challenging and resisting challenges.

These patterns have stunning implications for classroom interaction. Most faculty members assume that participating in class discussion is a necessary part of successful performance. Yet speaking in a classroom is more congenial to boys' language experience than to girls', since it entails putting oneself forward in front of a large group of people, many of whom are strangers and at least one of whom is sure to judge speakers' knowledge and intelligence by their verbal display.

Another aspect of many classrooms that makes them more hospitable 5 to most men than to most women is the use of debate-like formats as a learning tool. Our educational system, as Walter Ong argues persuasively in his book *Fighting for Life* (Cornell University Press, 1981), is fundamentally male in that the pursuit of knowledge is believed to be achieved by ritual opposition: public display followed by argument and challenge. Father Ong demonstrates that ritual opposition — what he calls "adversativeness" or "agonism" — is fundamental to the way most males approach almost any activity. (Consider, for example, the little boy who shows he likes a little girl by pulling her braids and shoving her.) But ritual opposition is antithetical to the way most females learn and like to interact. It is not that females don't fight, but that they don't fight for fun. They don't *ritualize* opposition.

Anthropologists working in widely disparate parts of the world have found contrasting verbal rituals for women and men. Women in completely unrelated cultures (for example, Greece and Bali) engage in ritual laments: spontaneously produced rhyming couplets that express their pain, for example, over the loss of loved ones. Men do not take part in laments. They have their own, very different verbal ritual: a contest, a war of words in which they vie with each other to devise clever insults.

When discussing these phenomena with a colleague, I commented that I see these two styles in American conversation: Many women bond by talking about troubles, and many men bond by exchanging playful insults and put-downs, and other sorts of verbal sparring. He exclaimed: "I never thought of this, but that's the way I teach: I have students read an article, and then I invite them to tear it apart. After we've torn it to shreds, we talk about how to build a better model."

This contrasts sharply with the way I teach: I open the discussion of readings by asking, "What did you find useful in this? What can we use in our own theory building and our own methods?" I note what I see as weaknesses in the author's approach, but I also point out that the writer's discipline and purposes might be different from ours. Finally, I offer personal anecdotes illustrating the phenomena under discussion and praise students' anecdotes as well as their critical acumen.

These different teaching styles must make our classrooms wildly different places and hospitable to different students. Male students are more likely to be comfortable attacking the readings and might find the inclusion of personal anecdotes irrelevant and "soft." Women are more likely to resist discussion they perceive as hostile, and, indeed, it is women in my classes who are most likely to offer personal anecdotes.

A colleague who read my book commented that he had always taken   10
for granted that the best way to deal with students' comments is to challenge them; this, he felt it was self-evident, sharpens their minds and helps them develop debating skills. But he had noticed that women were relatively silent in his classes, so he decided to try beginning discussion with relatively open-ended questions and letting comments go unchallenged. He found, to his amazement and satisfaction, that more women began to speak up.

Though some of the women in his class clearly liked this better, perhaps some of the men liked it less. One young man in my class wrote in a questionnaire about a history professor who gave students questions to think about and called on people to answer them: "He would then play devil's advocate . . . i.e., he debated us. . . . That class *really* sharpened me intellectually. . . . We as students do need to know how to defend ourselves." This young man valued the experience of being attacked and challenged publicly. Many, if not most, women would shrink from such "challenge," experiencing it as public humiliation.

A professor at Hamilton College told me of a young man who was upset because he felt his class presentation had been a failure. The professor was puzzled because he had observed that class members had listened attentively and agreed with the student's observations. It turned out that it was this very agreement that the student interpreted as failure: Since no one had engaged his ideas by arguing with him, he felt they had found them unworthy of attention.

So one reason men speak in class more than women is that many of them find the "public" classroom setting more conducive to speaking, whereas most women are more comfortable speaking in private to a small group of people they know well. A second reason is that men are more likely to be comfortable with the debatelike form that discussion may take. Yet another reason is the different attitudes toward speaking in class that typify women and men.

Students who speak frequently in class, many of whom are men, assume that it is their job to think of contributions and try to get the floor to express them. But many women monitor their participation not only to get the floor but to avoid getting it. Women students in my class tell me that if they have spoken up once or twice, they hold back for the rest of the class because they don't want to dominate. If they have spoken a lot one week, they will remain silent the next. These different ethics of participation are, of course, unstated, so those who speak freely assume that those who remain silent have nothing to say, and those who are reining themselves in assume that the big talkers are selfish and hoggish.

When I looked around my classes, I could see these differing ethics 15 and habits at work. For example, my graduate class in analyzing conversation had twenty students, eleven women and nine men. Of the men, four were foreign students: two Japanese, one Chinese, and one Syrian. With the exception of the three Asian men, all the men spoke in class at least occasionally. The biggest talker in the class was a woman, but there were also five women who never spoke at all, only one of whom was Japanese. I decided to try something different.

I broke the class into small groups to discuss the issues raised in the readings and to analyze their own conversational transcripts. I devised three ways of dividing the students into groups: one by the degree program they were in, one by gender, and one by conversational style, as closely as I could guess it. This meant that when the class was grouped according to conversational style, I put Asian students together, fast talkers together, and quiet students together. The class split into groups six times during the semester, so they met in each grouping twice. I told students to regard the groups as examples of interactional data and to note the different ways they participated in the different groups. Toward the end of the term, I gave them a questionnaire asking about their class and group participation.

I could see plainly from my observation of the groups at work that women who never opened their mouths in class were talking away in the small groups. In fact, the Japanese woman commented that she found it particularly hard to contribute to the all-woman group she was in because "I was overwhelmed by how talkative the female students were in the female-only group." This is particularly revealing because it highlights that the same person who can be "oppressed" into silence in one context can become the talkative "oppressor" in another. No one's conversational style is absolute; everyone's style changes in response to the context and others' styles.

Some of the students (seven) said they preferred the same-gender groups; others preferred the same-style groups. In answer to the question "Would you have liked to speak in class more than you did?" six of the seven who said yes were women; the one man was Japanese. Most startlingly, this response did not come only from quiet women; it came from women who had indicated they had spoken in class never, rarely, sometimes, and often. Of the eleven students who said the amount they had spoken was fine, seven were men. Of the four women who checked "fine," two added qualifications indicating it wasn't completely fine: One wrote in "maybe more," and one wrote, "I have an urge to participate but often feel I should have something more interesting/relevant/wonderful/intelligent to say!!"

I counted my experiment a success. Everyone in the class found the small groups interesting, and no one indicated he or she would have preferred that the class not break into groups. Perhaps most instructive, however, was the fact that the experience of breaking into groups, and of talking about participation in class, raised everyone's awareness about classroom participation. After we had talked about it, some of the quietest women in the class made a few voluntary contributions, though sometimes I had to ensure their participation by interrupting the students who were exuberantly speaking out.

Americans are often proud that they discount the significance of cultural differences: "We are all individuals," many people boast. Ignoring such issues as gender and ethnicity becomes a source of pride: "I treat everyone the same." But treating people the same is not equal treatment if they are not the same. 20

The classroom is a different environment for those who feel comfortable putting themselves forward in a group than it is for those who find the prospect of doing so chastening, or even terrifying. When a professor asks, "Are there any questions?" students who can formulate statements the fastest have the greatest opportunity to respond. Those who need significant time to do so have not really been given a chance at all, since by the time they are ready to speak, someone else has the floor.

In a class where some students speak out without raising hands, those who feel they must raise their hands and wait to be recognized do not have equal opportunity to speak. Telling them to feel free to jump in will not make them feel free; one's sense of timing, of one's rights and obligations in a classroom, are automatic, learned over years of interaction. They may be changed over time, with motivation and effort, but they cannot be changed on the spot. And everyone assumes his or her own way is best. When I asked my students how the class could be changed to make it easier for them to speak more, the most talkative woman said she would prefer it if no one had to raise hands, and a foreign student said he wished people would raise their hands and wait to be recognized.

My experience in this class has convinced me that small-group interaction should be part of any class that is not a small seminar. I also am convinced that having the students become observers of their own interaction is a crucial part of their education. Talking about ways of talking in class makes students aware that their ways of talking affect other students, that the motivations they impute to others may not truly reflect others' motives, and that the behaviors they assume to be self-evidently right are not universal norms.

The goal of complete equal opportunity in class may not be attainable, but realizing that one monolithic classroom-participation structure is not equal opportunity is itself a powerful motivation to find more diverse methods to serve diverse students — and every classroom is diverse.

EXPLORATIONS

1. According to Deborah Tannen, what is the main difference between women's and men's use of language in social groups? How does this difference affect their use of language in classrooms?

2. On what sources does Tannen base her statements? Which kinds of evidence in her essay did you find most convincing, and why?

3. According to Tannen, what factors besides students' gender affect who speaks out the most in class? In what ways do your college classes match (or not) Tannen's depiction?

CONNECTIONS

1. Which of the male-female patterns Tannen identifies can you find in Alberto Moravia's "The Chase" (p. 349)? In what sense would the title of Tannen's best-selling book, *You Just Don't Understand*, be an apt title for Moravia's story?

2. What does Tannen say about the ways women and men influence each other's behavior in the classroom? After reading "Man and WOMAN" (p. 332), what do you think Sam Keen would say about male and female students' influence on one another's tendency to speak, argue, or be silent in class? What do you think Camille Paglia (p. 327) might add?

3. What does Dympna Ugwu-Oju's description of being an Ibo woman in the United States (p. 312) have in common with Tannen's description of male and female styles of communication? What explanation would you expect Ugwu-Oju to offer for the ethnic differences in communication style that Tannen noticed in her class?

ELABORATIONS

1. What happens to conversational style when women and men leave the classroom? Choose one or more selections from this book that show members of both sexes interacting in ways Tannen describes, such as Curtis Sittenfeld's "Your Life as a Girl" (p. 319), Frank McCourt's "Limerick Homecoming" (p. 136), or Kazuo Ishiguro's "A Family Supper" (p. 197). Write an essay applying Tannen's ideas to other situations besides the ones she considers. You may use evidence from your chosen selection(s) to support Tannen's conclusions or to dispute them.

2. Which of the factors Tannen mentions have the most effect on your participation in class? What other factors do you find significant that Tannen does not mention? Write an essay describing the ideal class structure. Explain how and why you believe it would be effective, using examples from your own experience.

MARJORIE SHOSTAK

Nisa's Marriage

"Nisa's Marriage" comes from Marjorie Shostak's 1981 book *Nisa: The Life and Words of a !Kung Woman*, based on Shostak's two and a half years among the !Kung San of Botswana. (The ! indicates a clicking sound.) At the time, she was a research assistant on the Harvard Kalahari Desert Project, having previously received a bachelor's degree in English literature from Brooklyn College. Shostak, born in 1945, was newly married when she went to the Kalahari in 1971. She hunted, foraged, ate, and slept with Nisa's tribe, teaching herself their language. In 1989 she returned to Botswana and met up again with Nisa, who was then in her mid-sixties. Shostak was writing a book about their visit and was teaching anthropology at Emory University, in Atlanta, when she died of cancer in 1996.

In her introduction to *Nisa*, Shostak writes: "Nisa is a member of one of the last remaining traditional gatherer-hunter societies, a group calling themselves the *Zhun/twasi*, the 'real people,' who currently live in isolated areas of Botswana, Angola, and Namibia. . . . They are also known as the !Kung Bushmen, the !Kung San, or simply the !Kung. They are short — averaging about five feet in height — lean, muscular, and, for Africa, light-skinned. They have high cheekbones and rather Oriental-looking eyes." Population biologists call these people Khoisan, from *Khoi*, the group previously known as Hottentots, and *San*, the group known as Bushmen, who together were the original inhabitants of South Africa (see pp. 73 and 600). Botswana, Nisa's homeland, gained its name and independence in 1966 after eighty years as the British protectorate of Bechuanaland. The !Kung live on the edges of the Kalahari Desert, which occupies much of Botswana's center and southwest.

Shostak describes meeting Nisa, who was then close to fifty years old: "Nisa wore an old blanket loosely draped over the remnants of a faded, flower-print dress, sizes too big. . . . [She] was all activity: Constantly in motion, her face expressive, she spoke fast and was at once strong and surprisingly coquettish." In the following excerpt, the events Nisa describes took place more than thirty-five years earlier, just as she entered puberty.

The day of the wedding, everyone was there. All of Tashay's friends were sitting around, laughing and laughing. His younger brother said, "Tashay, you're too old. Get out of the way so I can marry her. Give her to me." And his nephew said, "Uncle, you're already old. Now, let *me* marry her." They were all sitting around, talking like that. They all wanted me.

I went to my mother's hut and sat there. I was wearing lots of beads and my hair was completely covered and full with ornaments.

That night there was another dance. We danced, and some people fell asleep and others kept dancing. In the early morning, Tashay and his relatives went back to their camp; we went into our huts to sleep. When morning was late in the sky, they came back. They stayed around and then his parents said, "Because we are only staying a short while — tomorrow, let's start building the marriage hut."

The next day they started. There were lots of people there — Tashay's mother, my mother, and my aunt worked on the hut; everyone else sat around, talking. Late in the day, the young men went and brought Tashay to the finished hut. They set him down beside it and stayed there with him, sitting around the fire.

I was still at my mother's hut. I heard them tell two of my friends to   5 go and bring me to the hut. I thought, "Oohh . . . I'll run away." When they came for me, they couldn't find me. They said, "Where did Nisa go? Did she run away? It's getting dark. Doesn't she know that things may bite and kill her?" My father said, "Go tell Nisa that if this is what she's going to do, I'll hit her and she won't run away again. What made her want to run away, anyway?"

I was already far off in the bush. They came looking for me. I heard them calling, "Nisa . . . Nisa . . ." I sat down at the base of a tree. Then I heard Nukha, "Nisa . . . Nisao . . . my friend . . . a hyena's out there . . . things will bite and kill you . . . come back . . . Nisa . . . Nisao . . ."

When Nukha finally saw me, I started to run. She ran after me, chasing me, and finally caught me. She called out to the others, "Hey! Nisa's here! Everyone, come! Help me! Take Nisa, she's here!"

They came and brought me back. Then they laid me down inside the hut. I cried and cried. People told me, "A man is not something that kills you; he is someone who marries you, who becomes like your father or your older brother. He kills animals and gives you things to eat. Even tomorrow, while you are crying, Tashay may kill an animal. But when he returns, he won't give you any meat; only he will eat. Beads, too. He will get beads but he won't give them to you. Why are you so afraid of your husband and what are you crying about?"

I listened and was quiet. Later, we went to sleep. Tashay lay down beside the opening of the hut, near the fire, and I lay down inside; he thought I might try and run away again. He covered himself with a blanket and slept.

While it was dark, I woke up. I sat up. I thought, "How am I going to   10
jump over him? How can I get out and go to mother's hut to sleep beside her?" I looked at him sleeping. Then came other thoughts, other
thoughts in the middle of the night, "Eh . . . this person has just married me . . ." and I lay down again. But I kept thinking, "Why did
people give me this man in marriage? The older people say he is a good
person, yet . . ."

I lay there and didn't move. The rain came beating down. It fell
steadily and kept falling. Finally, I slept. Much later dawn broke.

In the morning, Tashay got up and sat by the fire. I was so frightened
I just lay there, waiting for him to leave. When he went to urinate, I
went and sat down inside my mother's hut.

That day, all his relatives came to our new hut — his mother, his father, his brothers . . . everyone! They all came. They said, "Go tell Nisa
she should come and her in-laws will put the marriage oil on her. Can
you see her sitting over there? Why isn't she coming so we can put the
oil on her in her new hut?"

I refused to go. They kept calling for me until finally, my older
brother said, "Uhn uhn. Nisa, if you act like this, I'll hit you. Now, get
up and go over there. Sit over there so they can put the oil on you."

I still refused and just sat there. My older brother grabbed a switch   15
from a nearby tree and started coming toward me. I got up. I was afraid.
I followed him to where the others were sitting. Tashay's mother
rubbed the oil on me and my aunt rubbed it on Tashay.

Then they left and it was just Tashay and me. . . .

That Zhun/twa, that Tashay, he really caused me pain.

Soon after we were married, he took me from my parents' village to
live at his parents' village. At first my family came and lived with us, but
then one day they left, left me with Tashay and his parents. That's when
I started to cry. Tashay said, "Before your mother left, you weren't crying. Why didn't you tell me you wanted to go with them? We could
have followed along." I said, "I was afraid of you. That's why I didn't tell
you."

But I still wanted to be with my mother, so later that day, I ran away.
I ran as fast as I could until I finally caught up with them. When my
mother saw me she said, "Someday a hyena is going to kill this child in
the bush. She's followed us. Here she is!" I walked with them back to
their village and lived with them a while.

A long time passed. One day Tashay left and came to us. When I saw   20
him, I started to cry. He said, "Get up. We're going back." I said, "Why
does this person keep following me? Do I own him that he follows me

everywhere?" My father said, "You're crazy. A woman follows her husband when he comes for her. What are you just sitting here for?"

Tashay took me with him and I didn't really refuse. We continued to live at his village and then we all went and lived at another water hole. By then, I knew that I was no longer living with my mother. I had left my family to follow my husband.

We lived and lived and then, one day, my heart started to throb and my head hurt; I was very sick. My father came to visit and went into a medicinal trance to try and cure me. When I was better, he left and I stayed behind.

After Tashay and I had been living together for a long time, we started to like each other with our hearts and began living nicely together. It was really only after we had lived together for a long time that he touched my genitals. By then, my breasts were already big.

We were staying in my parents' village the night he first had sex with me and I didn't really refuse. I agreed, just a little, and he lay with me. But the next morning, I was sore. I took some leaves and wound them around my waist, but I continued to feel pain. I thought, "Ooo . . . what has he done to my insides that they feel this way?"

I went over to my mother and said, "That person, last night . . . I'm   25 only a child, but last night he had sex with me. Move over and let me eat with you. We'll eat and then we'll move away. Mother . . . mother . . ."

My mother turned to my father and said, "Get up, get a switch and hit this child. She's ruining us. Get up and find something to hit her with." I thought, "What? Did I say something wrong?"

My father went to find a switch. I got up and ran to my aunt's hut. I sat there and thought, "What was so bad? How come I talked about something yet . . . is that something so terrible?"

My father said to my aunt, "Tell Nisa to come back here so I can beat her. The things this young girl talks about could crack open the insides of her ears."

My mother said, "This child, her talk is terrible. As I am now, I would stick myself with a poison arrow; but my skin itself fears and that's why I won't do it. But if she continues to talk like that, I will!"

They wanted me to like my husband and not to refuse him. My   30 mother told me that when a man sleeps with his wife, she doesn't tell; it's a private thing.

I got up and walked away from them. I was trembling, "Ehn . . . nn . . . nn . . ." I looked at my genitals and thought, "Oh, this person . . . yesterday he took me and now my genitals are ruined!" I took some water and washed my genitals, washed and washed.

Because, when my genitals first started to develop, I was afraid. I'd look at them and cry and think something was wrong with them. But people told me, "Nothing's wrong. That's what you yourself are like."

I also thought that an older person, an adult like my husband, would tear me apart, that his penis would be so big that he would hurt me. Because I hadn't known older men. I had only played sex play with little boys. Then, when Tashay did sleep with me and it hurt, that's when I refused. That's also when I told. But people didn't yell at him, they only yelled at me, and I was ashamed.

That evening, we lay down again. But this time, before he came in, I took a leather strap, held my leather apron tightly against my legs, tied the strap around my genitals, and then tied it to the hut's frame. I was afraid he'd tear me open and I didn't want him to take me again.

The two of us lay there and after a long time, he touched me. When he touched my stomach, he felt the leather strap. He felt around to see what it was. He said, "What is this woman doing? Last night she lay with me so nicely when I came to her. Why has she tied her genitals up this way? What is she refusing to give me?" 35

He sat me up and said, "Nisa . . . Nisa . . . what happened? Why are you doing this?" I didn't answer. He said, "What are you so afraid of that you had to tie up your genitals?" I said, "Uhn, uhn. I'm not afraid of anything." He said, "No, now tell me. In the name of what you did, I'm asking you."

Then he said, "What do you think you're doing when you do something like this? When you lie down with me, a Zhun/twa like yourself, it's not as though you were lying with another, a stranger. We are both Zhun/twasi, yet you tied yourself up!"

I said, "I refuse to lie down with anyone who wants to take my genitals. Last night you had sex with me and today my insides hurt. That's why I've tied myself up and that's why you won't take me again."

He said, "Untie the strap. Do you see me as someone who kills people? Am I going to eat you? No, I'm not going to kill you, but I have married you and want to make love to you. Do you think I married you thinking I wouldn't make love to you? Did you think we would just live beside each other? Do you know any man who has married a woman and who just lives beside her without having sex with her?"

I said, "I don't care. I don't want sex. Today my insides hurt and I refuse." He said, "Mm, today you will just lie there, but tomorrow, I will take you. If you refuse, I'll pry your legs open and take you by force." 40

He untied the strap and said, "If this is what use you put this to, I'm going to destroy it." He took his knife and cut it into small pieces. Then he put me down beside him. He didn't touch me; he knew I was afraid. Then we went to sleep.

The next day we got up, did things, and ate things. When we returned to our hut that night, we lay down again. That's when he forced himself on me. He held my legs and I struggled against him. But I knew he would have sex with me and I thought, "This isn't helping me at all. This man, if he takes me by force, he'll really hurt me. So I'll just lie here, lie still and let him look for the food he wants. But I still don't know what kind of food I have because even if he eats he won't be full."[1]

So I stopped fighting and just lay there. He did his work and that time it didn't hurt so much. Then he lay down and slept.

After that, we just lived. I began to like him and he didn't bother me again, he didn't try to have sex with me. Many months passed — those of the rainy season, those of the winter season, and those of the hot season. He just left me alone and I grew up and started to understand about things. Because before that, I hadn't really known about men. . . .

We continued to live and it was as if I was already an adult. Because,   45
beginning to menstruate makes you think about things. Only then did I bring myself to understand, only then did I begin to be a woman.

When Tashay wanted to lie with me, I no longer refused. We just had sex together, one day and then another. In the morning, I'd get up and sit beside our hut and I wouldn't tell. I'd think, "My husband is indeed my husband now. What people told me, that my husband is mine, is true."

We lived and lived, the two of us, together, and after a while I started to really like him and then, to love him. I had finally grown up and had learned how to love. I thought, "A man has sex with you. Yes, that's what a man does. I had thought that perhaps he didn't."

We lived on and I loved him and he loved me. I loved him the way a young adult knows how to love; I just *loved* him. Whenever he went away and I stayed behind, I'd miss him. I'd think, "Oh, when is my husband ever coming home? How come he's been gone so long?" I'd miss him and want him. When he'd come back my heart would be happy, "Eh, hey! My husband left and once again has come back."

We lived and when he wanted me, I didn't refuse; he just lay with me. I thought, "Why had I been so concerned about my genitals? They aren't that important, after all. So why was I refusing them?"

---

[1]Food and eating are universally used by the !Kung as metaphors for sex. However, they claim no knowledge or practice of oral-genital contact.

I thought that and gave myself to him, gave and gave. We lay with   50
each other and my breasts were very large. I was becoming a woman.

EXPLORATIONS

1. Judging from "Nisa's Marriage," what specific rituals are part of a Zhun/twasi wedding? What is the practical or symbolic (or both) purpose of each ritual?

2. What facts can you glean about the Zhun/twasi way of life from "Nisa's Marriage"? What appears to be the group's main food source? What dangers do they fear? What images in their speech reflect these basic elements of their existence?

3. When Nisa runs home to her mother after having sex with her husband, her mother says, "As I am now, I would stick myself with a poison arrow; but my skin itself fears and that's why I won't do it. But if she continues to talk like that, I will!" (para. 29). What does she mean? How might an American mother express the same sentiments?

CONNECTIONS

1. What incidents in "Nisa's Marriage" show women and men using language in contrasting ways, and for contrasting purposes, in a pattern similar to the one Deborah Tannen describes (p. 356)? What practical advantages do gender-differentiated verbal styles have for the Zhun/twasi?

2. On what points do you think Nisa would agree with Simone de Beauvoir ("Woman as Other," p. 341), and why? On what points do you think Nisa would agree with Camille Paglia ("Woman and Nature," p. 327), and why?

3. After reading "Nisa's Marriage," look back at John Updike's "The Disposable Rocket" (p. 314). Which of Updike's ideas about the male body seem rooted in contemporary Western culture? Which ideas also appear among the Zhun/twasi?

ELABORATIONS

1. "Nisa's Marriage" illustrates a very different approach to sexuality from that of Western cultures. List all the rules you can identify that govern marriage, sexual intercourse, and gender roles among the Zhun/twasi. What needs of the society shape its sexual rules? Write an essay comparing and contrasting social needs and sexual rules among the Zhun/twasi with those you are familiar with as an American.

2. Nisa's last sentence is: "I was becoming a woman." What does she mean? How does her definition of *woman* compare with others you have encountered in this chapter? Write an essay about the ways different cultures or groups define manhood and womanhood, and the reasons why their definitions differ.

JAN GOODWIN

Muslims, the First Feminists

Jan Goodwin is an award-winning journalist and human rights activist. Her articles on social conflicts around the world have appeared in publications including the *New York Times*, *Utne Reader*, and *On the Issues* (an online magazine), of which she is editor. Her book *Caught in the Crossfire* (1987) examines the conflict in Afghanistan. "Muslims, the First Feminists" is excerpted from the chapter by that name in her 1994 book *Price of Honor*.

> Treat your women well, and be kind to them.
> — Prophet Mohammad

Despite its rapid spread, Islam is not a religion for those who are casual about such things; adhering to its five pillars takes effort and discipline. One must rise before dawn to observe the first of five ritual prayers required daily, none of which can take place without first ritually cleansing oneself. Sleep, work, and recreational activities take second place to prayer. Fasting for the month of Ramadan, undertaking the Hajj pilgrimage to Mecca at least once in a lifetime, paying *Zakat* tax for relief of the Muslim poor, in addition to accepting Islam's creed, which begins, "There is no God but Allah, and Mohammad is his messenger," require a serious and energetic commitment. And the vast majority of Muslims worldwide do observe those tenets.

Every condition and circumstance of life is believed contained within the Koran, the *hadiths* (the reported traditions recording the Prophet Mohammad's behavior and sayings), and the *Shariah*, the Islamic code of law. The most minute details of everyday existence are governed, such as the correct way to style one's hair, or by which foot one should enter a toilet. The Koran's teachings, in their entirety, are meant to be observed in their original purity. Unlike the Bible, for example, the Koran may not be given contemporary interpretation; it is considered incontrovertible, modern mores notwithstanding. It is for that reason that Muslims, no matter their mother tongue, are expected to read their holy book in the original Arabic, not in translation, which may change the meaning originally intended.

So it is ironic that the most outstanding contradiction regarding the inequities suffered by Muslim women is that Mohammad, the founder of Islam, was among the world's greatest reformers on behalf of women. He abolished such sex-discriminating practices as female infanticide, slavery, and levirate (marriage between a man and his brother's widow), while introducing concepts guaranteeing women the right to inherit and bequeath property, and the right to exercise full possession and control over their own wealth. Islam, in fact, may be the only religion that formally specified women's rights and sought ways to protect them. Today's Islamic spokesmen frequently extol the Prophet's revolutionary innovations, but usually fail to note that they are rarely honored in reality.

They fail to observe, for example, that it is not the Koran that compels Islamic women to be enshrouded from head to toe or confined to their homes while men feel free to pester women who do venture out. Mohammad's directives on this issue were addressed to both sexes and could not be clearer:

> Say to the believing men that they should
> lower their gaze and guard their modesty . . .
> And say to believing women that they should
> lower their gaze and guard their modesty . . .

Said Islamic scholar Dr. Zaki Badawi, "This section of the Koran   5
also states that women should not show 'their adornment except what normally appears.' This means it is left to custom. There has never been an Islamic obligation for women to cover at any time. In fact, veiling the face is an innovation that has no foundation whatsoever in Islam. Even in Saudi Arabia the covering of women from head to toe is recent; it was not required before the discovery of oil.

"The *hijab* veil (which covers all of a Muslim woman's hair) is also not obligatory. And in Europe, for example, it should be prohibited because it creates a lot of problems for women. If women are attacked because they are wearing the *hijab*, as happened in France not so long ago, then they should not wear it. I have spoken out on this issue on a number of occasions, and since I began doing so, a lot of Muslim women in Europe have started leaving off the head covering."

The veil originated as a Persian elitist fashion to distinguish aristocracy from the common masses, and has moved in and out of fashion ever since. Early Islamic scholars, for example, tried to enforce veiling by declaring "all of woman is pudendal." Islamic studies specialist Nancy Dupree, of Duke University, explained its more recent use. "At the time of national movements against colonial powers, it became a symbol of resistance against alien policies that were generally viewed as a move to encourage female overpermissiveness. After independence was won and governments embarked on their indigenous Western-oriented paths, the veil was discredited as an emblem of enforced ortho-doxy and suffocating social control, an archaic social institution similar to slavery."

Like Pakistan's first female prime minister, Benazir Bhutto, many Muslim women who grew up in this less-restrictive era wore Western dress. Bhutto took to Islamizing her wardrobe only when she began her election campaign. Throughout her time in office she has had great dif-ficulty keeping her head modestly covered simply because she is un-used to wearing the *chador* intended for that purpose, and it keeps slid-ing off.

As Islamic radicalism rose at the beginning of the last decade, the pen-dulum for Muslim women swung the other way again. Once more they were to be hidden behind veils, a development that now seemed to legit-imize and institutionalize inequality for women. In fact, calls by Islamist organizations in recent years for Muslim women to veil themselves have been followed shortly thereafter by demands that women stop working, stay home, limit their educations, and resign positions of authority. Insists Dr. Badawi, however, "This is not required by Islam. According to our re-ligion, women have a perfect right to take part in society."

Despite the limitations placed on them, Muslim women have   10 achieved amazing gains. In Islamic cultures, where education for women often began only three or four decades ago, women whose mothers are totally illiterate frequently earn advanced degrees. One need only look to the percentage of women teaching in universities in Muslim countries to see how fast change is occurring for women. "In 1981, in Egyptian universities, twenty-five percent of the faculty were women. In American universities at the same time, it was twenty-four percent and in Germany, twenty-five percent," says Fatima Mernissi, a leading Moroccan sociologist. "Even in conservative Saudi Arabia, women have invaded sexually segregated academic space. They are twenty-two percent of university faculty there." It was also in this era that Benazir Bhutto became the first woman to head a modern Muslim state, and many other women succeeded to public office. A number of Arab states, however, had female ministers as early as the fifties, long be-fore most Western countries. These Muslim women are the ones who have been able to balance their culture's traditional customs and de-mands at home — arranged marriages, obedience to their husbands — with the progressiveness their careers demand.

Women who do work in Gulf and Middle Eastern countries often enjoy job benefits their female counterparts in the West would envy. Equal pay with men has existed in a number of the countries since the 1970s, while women in the United States and Britain still earn only slightly more than half a man's salary for the same job. In Iraq, where human rights are scant, a woman's employment benefits are extensive and include free childcare while she is working and the right to retire with a full pension after fifteen years of employment. And in virtually all Arab countries, maternity leave on full pay is substantially longer than it is in the United States.

Dichotomously, as we near the twenty-first century, the majority of Muslim women still find their lives controlled by their closest male relative. They are the daughters whose future marriage partners continue to be determined by their fathers. They are the brides who must be virgins on their wedding nights in a culture where if they are not, honor killings are common and often carried out by the girl's own brothers. To guard against this, a simple surgical procedure — hymen restoration — is equally common in the Muslim world. Fratricide can occur when a young woman refuses to marry a man of her family's choice. Even though Islam states that a woman has the right to refuse a husband selected for her, in reality, familial pressures can be so strong, they may result in her death if she is not acquiescent.

Bride-price still exists in Muslim countries, a convention that only serves to confirm that a woman is a man's property. Once married, every aspect of a woman's life will be dictated by her husband: what she does, who her friends are, where she is permitted to go, how her children are raised, and even whether she may use birth control or be sterilized. She cannot obtain a passport or travel abroad without his written approval.

And if she is not obedient, her husband may take another wife. Polygyny is the specter that haunts every married Muslim woman: husbands are entitled to take four wives. According to Koranic dictates, should a man decide to marry again, he is supposed to obtain his first wife's permission. He is also required to treat each wife exactly the same, in affection, time spent together, material possessions, and status. In practice, if his first wife doesn't agree, he gets married anyway, and human nature being what it is, he invariably favors the newer and younger spouse.

I remember a discussion with a woman whose husband had taken a 15 second wife when she was twenty-six and had borne six children. "He just moved her into our home. He didn't tell me. One day she wasn't there, the next day she was. After that time, I sit in the same room with them and he hardly speaks to me, he has never come into my bed again, and he ignores our children and favors hers. It is difficult to get him even to buy clothes for mine." Now ten years later, she is delighted that her husband is taking a third wife. "Good," she told me. "Now his second wife will know what it was like for me. She can watch, as I did, as he ignores her and spends all his time with the new wife."

Not so long ago, a young woman began a national outcry in Pakistan when she questioned in a letter to a newspaper why, if polygyny was really the Islamic right of men, Islamic law did not grant similar rights of polyandry to women. Outraged religious and political leaders publicly condemned the woman, terming her statement "illegal, immoral, and highly irresponsible." She was ordered to "repent, or she would be declared apostate."

The point the young woman was making that was completely overlooked in the furor is that polygyny was not intended to be an automatic right for Muslim men, a chance to trade in the old model for a sleeker, newer version. The Prophet Mohammad's original intention was to provide protection to widows and orphans. The Koranic verses on polygyny were recorded shortly after a major battle, when many Muslim males were killed, and women would have been left destitute unless the surviving males took additional wives.

Originally, in the pre-Islamic or Jahilliah period of Arabian society, often referred to as an era of ignorance, polygyny and polyandry were recognized institutions. Men *and* women were allowed to have multiple spouses. Islam, however, condemned these practices for both sexes. The Koran permitted polygyny only in exceptional cases, principally for war widows, whom the Prophet feared would become impoverished or "unprotected" once their husbands were dead. Later, when the early Islamic caliphate was replaced by monarchy, wealthy males with the assistance of the then half-educated ulema (religious and legal leaders) again revived the pre-Islamic form of polygyny. Polyandry for women, however, stayed banned. At the same time, men began to ignore the Koranic preconditions for polygyny, and instead of marrying unprotected widows, it became, and remains, the practice for them to take young, unwed women as their subsequent wives.

There is a continuing debate in the Islamic world over whether polygyny is outdated and should be expunged from Islam. Modernists insist it is inappropriate today, anti-woman, and some go as far as to argue that when one man impregnates multiple wives, it only exacerbates the high birthrates in Muslim countries. Traditionalists insist polygyny is a Muslim male's right and that the word of God as recorded in the Koran may not be changed. But despite insistences that Koranic intent not be modified at all, concubinage and slavery — which still stand in the Koran — have been subsequently abrogated.

Tunisia prohibited polygamy in 1957. It cited the Koranic verse in   20 which Mohammad acknowledges that men "have it not in your power to deal equally between wives, however much you may wish it. . . ." Tunisian religious authorities concluded that "unless and until adequate evidence was forthcoming that the wives would be treated impartially, which was virtually impossible, the essential conditions of polygamy could not be met."

In Turkey, Ataturk abolished the veil by decree when he came to power in the twenties, the first Muslim ruler to do so. But today, despite Turkey's now having a woman premier, in small towns and villages in the interior of the country women are rarely seen on the streets without being covered by a black *chador,* and polygamy is still practiced although it is legally forbidden. Feminists say that what Ataturk may have accomplished on paper still has to be accepted in practice by many Turks.

How is it then that Islam, the only religion to outline formally the protection of women's rights, is also the faith most perceived to oppress women? When Islam began fourteen hundred years ago, the women around the Prophet participated in public life, were vocal about social inequities, and often shared decision making with him. In fact, many women displayed traits that a modern-day feminist would recognize.

Theirs was a relationship as contemporary as today.

She was an international trader, forty years old and widowed twice, who headed her own thriving business. A mature, aristocratic beauty of substantial wealth, she moved in the elite circles of her world. And as an intelligent and determined woman, and an excellent judge of character, she was, not surprisingly, influential in her community.

He was a twenty-five-year-old freelance importer-exporter, a slim   25 young man of average height, whose beard, like his hair, was thick, black, and given to curl. The aquiline nose was typical of his ancestors, but it was his eyes that caught one's attention: large and set wide, with long, dark lashes, they had a luminous quality that everyone who met him commented on.

Orphaned as a child, he began work at twelve. Thirteen years later he was still too impecunious to marry. His first marriage proposal was rejected; the girl's father considered him insufficiently established financially. By his twenties, his strongest asset was still only his professional reputation.

Considered honest, reliable, and trustworthy by the traders for whom he had worked, he was well known in his field. She needed someone with those qualities to oversee a large shipment of her merchandise that would be traded in Syria, and so she hired him.

He was a skilled businessman, and the commodities he brought home sold for double the amount of the original investment.

Shortly after, she asked him to marry her, and he accepted.

Fifteen years his senior and his employer, Khadija bint Khuwaylid 30 became the first wife of Mohammad, the man destined to be the Prophet and founder of Islam.

It was a harmonious and monogamous marriage of twenty-five years that ended only when she died, and even after he remarried, he spoke of her constantly and with great affection. She bore him six children, four girls and two boys; both sons died in childhood.

Was Khadija unusual in sixth-century Mecca, in what is now Saudi Arabia? She was, after all, a publicly visible woman who was economically independent due to inherited wealth, and who had initiated her own marriage to a man many years younger than her. Pre-Islamic Arabia is believed to have been a male-dominated society, where women were scarcely more than sales commodities, and girl babies were so little valued they were frequently buried alive. Although many women were treated as slaves, in major cities and trading centers, affluent women like Khadija occasionally had opportunities to enter commerce. And in Khadija's case, according to Professor Leila Ahmed, chair of the women's studies department at the University of Massachusetts, "the wealth she earned from caravan trains freed Mohammad from working and enabled him to become contemplative, the prelude to his prophethood."

Certainly his first wife appears to have contributed to Mohammad's respect and concern for women. During her lifetime, she was his confidante and counselor, his strongest supporter. She shared his ideology, became his first convert to Islam and a leading proselytizer of the new faith. And throughout their marriage, he turned to her for reassurance when he was threatened by his enemies or bewildered by his religious revelations. It was she who held him close and reassured him that he was not insane or sick after he received his first vision.

Mohammad was forty years old in A.D. 610, when Angel Gabriel first appeared to him and commanded him to read, a seemingly odd instruction to a man who, like most of his contemporaries, was illiterate. At that time he was meditating alone, as he did frequently, in a mountainside cave above Mecca, when he heard a voice tell him, "O Mohammad, thou art the apostle of God, I am Gabriel."

Over the next twenty-two years, Mohammad received many revela- 35 tions, the contents of which became the Koran, the divine guide for all

Muslims, who are required to accept every word as the literal word of God.

"Some eighty percent of Koranic rulings are devoted to regulating marital relations and the conduct of women," says Professor Ahmed, an authority on women and Islam. "The area in which Islam introduced the greatest reform was marriage and sexual relations." This is not surprising given the Prophet's statement that "marriage is half the religion."

Many of those rulings, most being of a practical nature and intended to improve and regulate the everyday life of Muslims, often occurred in circumstances when the Prophet had been undergoing some profound experience in his own life. The various domestic dramas that the Prophet experienced with his wives frequently were used as the sources of his own enlightenment.

When Khadija died in A.D. 620, Mohammad, then aged fifty, was bereft, and friends recommended that he marry again. They suggested two potential spouses, Sawdah bint Zam'ah, who was in her thirties and who had been recently widowed, or A'isha, the daughter of his closest friend, Abu Bakr. It depended, the Prophet was told, on whether he wanted to marry a virgin or nonvirgin. The Prophet chose both, marrying Sawdah first. At his marriage to six-year-old A'isha a few months later, the child-bride was not present, and the union was contracted between Mohammad and the girl's father. Because of A'isha's youth, she continued to live at her parents' home, unaware of her new marital state.

Three months later, the Prophet married again, this time to Hafsa, whose husband had just died in a recent battle, and who was the daughter of another of Mohammad's most powerful supporters. It was after the prophet's fourth marriage that the Koranic verses regarding polygyny were revealed to him: "Marry of the women who seem good to you, two or three or four. And if ye fear that ye cannot do justice to so many, then marry only one."

In the twelve years following Khadija's death until his own demise at age sixty-two, Mohammad married between nine and twelve women (the exact figure has been lost in history). He was apparently not subject to the four-wife restriction because of his position. He did, however, endeavor to treat all his wives fairly. After every marriage, a room of identical proportions was added to the Prophet's home to accommodate the new wife. Mohammad did not have quarters built for himself; instead, he shared those of each of his wives in turn.

Of all the world's religions, Islam is closest to Christianity, yet the Christian world has reviled it and its founder from the Crusades until today. A frequent point of attack was the Prophet's multiple marriages, which caused Christian critics to denounce him as "lustful"; Voltaire went so far as to accuse him of being sexually insatiable. Such arguments drew apparent support from the writings of the early Islamic chroniclers of the *hadiths*, who described Mohammad's sexual vigor as being "equal to that of forty men."

There were, however, sound political and social motivations for the Prophet's numerous marriages. At a time when Islam had gained many converts and Mohammad was well established as its Prophet, the new religion continued to meet with enormous resistance. By selecting the wives he chose to marry, the Prophet forged alliances with tribes that had been bitter enemies of Islam and in the forefront of battles against it. His marriage to Safiya bint Huyay, the daughter of an important Jewish chief, for example, diminished Jewish opposition to the Prophet's mission. Important clans suppressed long-standing feuds with Muslims and accepted the new faith.

Even the consummation of his marriage to A'isha when she was ten, an age later critics considered scandalously young, took place at the request of her father, who wanted to strengthen the bonds between the two families. It was A'isha's father, Abu Bakr, an important supporter of Islam, who succeeded Mohammad after his death.

With the exception of A'isha, all of Mohammad's wives were widows, many of whom lost their husbands during wars. By marrying widows in an age when few were permitted to remarry after their husbands died, the Prophet tried to ensure that women who would otherwise have been unprotected were cared for.

Mohammad is described as being tolerant, flexible, affectionate, and good-humored with his wives. But he was unable to live up to his own ideal of treating them equally. That he tried to, they recognized, as he drew lots among them to select a companion to accompany him when traveling, and systematically spent each night with a different wife. And it was he who stated in a *hadith*, "A man who marries more than one woman and then does not deal justly between them will be resurrected with half his faculties paralyzed." 45

The Prophet's downfall was Maryam, a Coptic Christian slave renowned for her beauty, who had been sent to him as a gift by the ruler of Egypt. Mohammad was so enamored of her he began to spend days and nights in her company, ignoring his wives, who became increasingly jealous. Eventually, the Prophet's wives became so resentful that Mohammad retreated from his household to meditate. While he was gone, rumors spread rapidly that he was about to divorce all of his wives. His followers were appalled, recognizing that divorce would destroy the earlier tribal alliances brought about by the Prophet's marriages.

During his long meditation, he received a vision in which he was shown how to bring harmony back to his home and restore peace among the women he loved. A month later, Mohammad returned to his family and told his wives God had given them a choice: either they could accept an ordinary life and be honorably divorced, or, if they "desired Allah and his Messenger and the abode hereafter, then Allah [would] prepare [them] a great reward. . . . " If they chose the latter, however, Allah required that they "stay at home and not display themselves as in the days of ignorance." Influenced by A'isha, his wives all chose to stay with the Prophet.

The Prophet's other wives were equally jealous of the time he spent with A'isha. It was clear he was fondest of her, and those who wanted to please Mohammad would donate their turn with him to her. But when they voiced any feelings of discontent, the Prophet chastised them. It was in A'isha's company, he told them, that he received the most revelations. . . .

But it was an incident with A'isha that not only led to the Koranic punishment for slander but also is believed to have instigated the initial rupture in Islam, which created the religion's Sunni and Shi'a sects.

In the eighth year of A'isha's marriage to the Prophet, she accompanied him on one of his frequent expeditions, and was traveling in an enclosed howdah on a camel. On one of their regular halts to pray, A'isha slipped away from the men to seek privacy to perform the ritual washing required beforehand. Adjusting her veil as she rejoined the party, she realized she had lost her necklace and turned back to find it. The beads had great sentimental value for her, having been a wedding gift from her mother. By the time she located the necklace, the expedition had left, assuming she was inside the howdah. A'isha had no choice but to wait for someone to realize the error and return for her.

As she waited, a young man she had known in the days before she married rode by and recognized her. He offered to help her catch up with Mohammad's party, and, seating her on his camel, he led A'isha back to the city. Gossip traveled faster than they did: people who saw the attractive couple together concluded that Mohammad's favorite wife, then only fourteen, preferred the company of a younger man to that of the now aging Prophet. It was the beginning of a scandal that shook the community. The uproar came at a disturbing time for Mohammad; the Muslim community was showing signs of disunity, and his divine revelations had apparently ceased. He became cold toward

A'isha, and began to question many people about her character and fidelity. All but one of the men with whom he discussed the issue spoke well of her. Only his cousin and son-in-law Ali, who was married to Mohammad's daughter Fatima, did not. "Women are plentiful, you can always change one for another," said Ali, encouraging the Prophet to divorce A'isha. A'isha never forgave him for it. This antipathy between the two would later cause Islam to splinter into two main sects.

The drama was finally brought to a close with another revelation in which the Prophet was told that his wife was not guilty of the accusations against her. The Koranic verse still used today in adultery cases dates from this time: "And those who accuse honorable women but bring not four witnesses, flog them with eighty stripes, and never again accept their evidence. For such men are evil-doers."

Throughout his life, the Prophet's affection and concern for women, and for mothers in particular, was evident. On one occasion when asked by a follower to whom one should show the most respect and kindness, the Prophet responded, "Your mother." "And then who?" insisted the questioner. "Your mother," Mohammad replied again. "And then who?" "Your mother," responded the Prophet for the third time. The questioner persisted: "And after that who?" "Your father," Mohammad replied, positioning men in fourth place. Similarly, on another occasion, when the Prophet was asked whether there was a shortcut to Paradise, he responded, "Paradise lies under the feet of the mother."

And in what turned out to be his final public address to Muslims from Mount Arafat near Mecca, the Prophet exhorted them, "Treat your women well and be kind to them."

Shortly after, Mohammad, now in his sixty-second year, began to complain of debilitating headaches. The pain intensified, and he finally collapsed. He was carried to A'isha's room and was nursed by all his wives. A few days later, on June 11, in the year 632, the man known to Muslims as the final Prophet died in the arms of A'isha, his favorite wife, who was then only eighteen. . . .

55

It begins at birth. The delivery of a baby boy is greeted with felicitations, parties, and, in some Muslim countries, even celebratory bursts of gunfire. The birth of a girl, on the other hand, is invariably a time for mourning. Even in everyday speech in much of the Arab world, when a silence falls at a gathering, the phrase uttered is *Yat Bint*, "a girl is born." And when one is, midwives have been known to abandon a delivery the moment they realize the child they have just helped into the world is of the "wrong" sex. Even before the umbilical cord is cut, more than one mother has had her face slapped for daring to give birth to a girl.

Husbands frequently feel shame, women feel guilt, and their family and friends offer whispered condolences instead of the customary sweets. "It is God's will," they say sadly, using the same expression employed when someone dies. "Next time," the new mother is told, "next time, you'll give him a son."

Modern Muslim physicians recognize the problem. A woman obstetrician at a high-tech Arab hospital in the Gulf told me, "We never inform women of the sex of their baby-to-be after they've had a sonogram. We find they can cope much better and longer with labor pains if they don't know they are giving birth to a girl."

If a Muslim woman doesn't present her husband with a son, chances are high that he will eventually take a second wife. He may even divorce her, which, in much of the Islamic world, can render her a social pariah. In a culture where men, on being asked how many children they have, will reply, for example, "Four children," meaning four sons, and when pushed will reluctantly add, "and three daughters," women are blamed for the birth of girls. Few Muslim males, even educated ones, accept that it is he, not his wife, who determines the gender of their child. "My wife is worthless, she has only given me girls," is a common refrain. And indeed, a woman's place in many Muslim societies can be determined by her sons; without them she is frequently viewed as having lower status than other women. Similarly, the woman is held responsible if the couple is unable to have children.

The low value placed on the average female Muslim child may have 60 its genesis in the title used to describe a girl before marriage: translated, it means "another's wealth." The epithet refers to the fact that any investment made in a girl in her early years will be enjoyed only by her husband's family when she moves in with them permanently upon marriage. Because she is seen as having only "temporary guest membership" in her own family, money, time, and effort spent on her childhood development may be minimal.

In 1985, the president of Pakistan established a commission to investigate the status of women. The report concluded, "The average woman is born into near slavery, leads a life of drudgery, and dies invariably in oblivion. This grim condition is the stark reality of half our population simply because they happen to be female." Not surprisingly, the government suppressed the report.

Few statistics are available in most Muslim countries for the simple reason that all information is tightly controlled by the governing regimes; concerning women, however, they scarcely exist, and when they do, they can be grim. In Pakistan women have a lower life expectancy than men. In fact, the country is listed in *The Guinness Book of World Records* for an unusual reason — the world's lowest female-male ratio: 936 women to every 1,000 men. The world average is the reverse: 1,110 women to 1,000 men. The main reason for this is poor health in women caused by the discrimination they face from the time of birth. A boy infant, for example, is breast-fed for two years as prescribed by the Koran. A female baby is frequently weaned much earlier. In the majority of families, girls and their mothers usually eat only after the males in the family; not surprisingly, therefore, girls have a much higher malnutrition rate than boys. And even in privileged homes, sons are more likely than daughters to be given milk, eggs, meat, and fruit.

Though she eats less than her brothers, a girl in an ordinary household does twice the work. Her fragile nutritional status leads to anemia and other nutritional deficiencies, and exposes her to infection. She is ill more often than her brothers. But even when she is ill, studies show that she is more likely to be treated at home, whereas boys are taken to doctors or hospitals. Women and girls have died when the men in their families have refused permission for them to be examined by male physicians because of Islamic modesty dictates, and female physicians are still rare.

Studies show that in Pakistan, for example, female deaths between the ages of fifteen and forty are fully 75 percent more frequent than male deaths. A significant cause of this is the extremely high rate of maternal mortality — Pakistan has one of the highest in the world — which is caused by one of the highest nutritional anemia rates. A shocking 97.4 percent of all pregnant women in Pakistan are anemic.

Such cause and effect is not confined to Pakistan. Many Muslim countries share depressingly similar practices, except among the minority, the educated elite. And even then, while women's physical needs may be well attended to, frequently their emotional needs are ignored.

From the time a girl is five or six, preparation for the only acceptable role for her — wife and mother — begins. She is groomed to be a good wife: docile, obedient, and self-sacrificing. She will learn that her brothers come first in everything, and that even her younger ones hold sway in her life. I found it unnerving to watch a nine-year-old boy walk into a room and with barely a glance cause his seventeen-year-old sister to give up her chair to him and sit at his feet. I was told by a young woman graduate student whose class was about to go on a perfectly ordinary half-day field trip, "My father gave me permission to go. But my younger brother became very angry and said it was not appropriate for his sister to go out on such a trip. He was so angry, he said he would leave our house if my father permitted it. And so I couldn't go." A more depressing example of male dominance is a seven-year-old who told his mother he would not give her his permission to go out when she wanted to attend a course in mother-and-child health care, and she complied.

As a Muslim girl approaches adolescence, the injunctions to walk, talk, and dress unobtrusively — to be invisible — become more stringent. She is constantly imbued with such values as the following: "A girl should be like water, unresisting. It takes on the shape of the container into which it is poured but has no shape of its own." Even her movements and associations are strictly curtailed. Her place is at home, she is not allowed to play outside, and her friends are limited. If she is fortunate enough to have attended school, which is usually segregated by gender except for the very young, she is often withdrawn as a teenager.

And once she reaches puberty, her world will be severely circumscribed. How much her world is limited depends on where she lives, and to which class she belongs. Only after menopause does she attain any real authority. No longer able to bear children, she is often considered an honorary male. And if she has been totally veiled, it is at this age she may uncover her face, but by then she may no longer want to.

Feminism in the Islamic world, however, has a long history. The first Islamic feminist movement began in Egypt at the end of the last century and quickly spread to Turkey, Syria, and Iran. Women lobbied heavily for changes in polygyny, divorce, inheritance, and child custody laws, but won only minor successes. Then in the twenties in Egypt, women began to shed their veils. In Iran, the veil was formerly abolished in 1936 by Reza Shah, and the king did the same for Afghanistan in 1921. The law there was soon reversed in a conservative whiplash. But in 1959, Afghanistan's President Daoud reversed it again, and most women unveiled.

Between the 1950s and 1970s, women in a number of Muslim countries made great strides. Today, however, the situation is reversing, as Islamic conservative movements such as the Muslim Brotherhood, and Wahabi-backed groups and Rabitat-Islami, both originating in Saudi Arabia, grow and spread.

"For a period of time, Muslim women were able to obtain education, to work, and, in some cases, even join their country's armed forces. A middle class was born in some of these states, and women were an active part in it," says Iranian scholar and professor of Middle Eastern studies Shaul Bakhash. "Things began to reverse for these women at the end of the seventies. If you look at Muslim countries today, across the board the direction is toward Islamist movements. The current situation for women is not at all encouraging; the reverse, in fact: it is regressive.

"In countries like Iran where harsh restrictions have been placed on women, there is a tremendous amount of resistance against them from the new educated female elite. And because of this, Muslim movements back to traditionalism may have to yield on some issues. Conversely, in a number of Muslim countries, women are again being viewed as a potential source of corruption in the society (by their very existence), one that has to be watched most carefully so that such influence can be guarded against."

For Akbar S. Ahmed, an Islamic scholar of international repute, formerly of both Princeton and Harvard, the current change in the Islamic world regarding the situation vis-à-vis women comes down to a simple equation: "The position of women in Muslim society mirrors the destiny of Islam: when Islam is secure and confident so are its women; when Islam is threatened and under pressure so, too, are they."

EXPLORATIONS

1. Why does Jan Goodwin call Muslims "the first feminists"? What Islamic policies are intended to protect women, and what Islamic practices help to assure them a fair place in society and the workforce?

2. Why does Goodwin think it necessary to defend her notion of Muslims as feminists? What Islamic policies and practices undermine women's ability to participate as full partners in society and the workforce?

3. What role has the veil played in determining or reflecting women's status in Islamic societies? When and why did it originate? How is it regarded now?

CONNECTIONS

1. In what ways is Nisa's role as a woman and wife, as presented by Marjorie Shostak in "Nisa's Marriage" (p. 363), similar to that of the women in "Muslims, the First Feminists"? After reading Nisa's account of her tribe's customs, how do you think the Muslim women in Goodwin's essay might see their position differently from the way a Western reader sees it?

2. What statements in "Muslims, the First Feminists" could serve as evidence for arguments made by Simone de Beauvoir in "Woman as Other" (p. 341)? What counterarguments would you expect the men in Goodwin's essay to make in response to Beauvoir?

3. Reread Goodwin's description of a Muslim girl's upbringing in paragraphs 66–67. What similarities do you notice to the female role depicted in "Your Life as a Girl" (p. 319)? Given the geographic, cultural, and religious differences between the young women in Goodwin's essay and in Curtis Sittenfeld's story, what do you think are the reasons for these similarities? How do you think Camille Paglia would explain them?

ELABORATIONS

1. Using the other selections you have read in this chapter as resources, write an essay comparing and contrasting the role of either women or men in Muslim countries and Western countries. Do additional research if you wish.

2. At what point in your life were you made aware that cultural expectations are different for males and females? How did you react to this discovery? How have you adapted to, fought with, taken advantage of, and maneuvered around the demands of your role as a female or male? Write an essay either narrating an incident in your life that involved your gender role, or classifying the ways a person of your sex (or the opposite sex) copes with his or her gender role.

YASHAR KEMAL

A Dirty Story

Yashar Kemal, a perennial Nobel Prize candidate, is widely considered Turkey's greatest living writer. Born in 1923 as Yashar Kemal Gokceli, he grew up among the desperately poor Anatolian peasants, whose plight became a central theme of his writing and his life. At the age of five he saw his father murdered in a mosque; after three years of secondary school he went to work in the Turkish cotton fields and factories. Kemal held a variety of jobs before his arrest in 1950 for alleged Communist propaganda (he was later acquitted). Moving to Istanbul, he dropped his surname, became a journalist, and rose to the post of Anatolian bureau chief of the daily paper *Cumhuriyet*. His 1955 novel *Ince Memed*, translated into more than fifteen languages, reached the English-speaking world in two parts: *Memed, My Hawk* (1961) and *They Burn the Thistles* (1977). Other fiction, nonfiction, and plays have followed, including *The Sea-Crossed Fisherman* (1985) and *The Birds Have Also Gone* (1987). "A Dirty Story" comes from *Anatolian Tales* (*Butun hikayeler*, 1967) and was translated from the Turkish by the author's wife, Thilda Kemal. In the mid-sixties Kemal was a member of the central committee and a political candidate for the Turkish Workers' Party (now banned); in 1971 he was again arrested and briefly imprisoned for Communist propaganda. In 1995 an article he wrote on the oppression of Turkish Kurds led to his trial for violating Turkey's antiterrorism laws; he received a suspended sentence. Kemal lives in Istanbul.

The Islamic nation of Turkey consists of a European section and an Asian section separated by water. European Turkey borders Greece and Bulgaria. Asian Turkey, or Anatolia, is many times larger; it borders Syria, Iraq, Iran, Armenia, and Georgia and includes the capital city of Ankara. Human habitation there dates back to the Stone Age, at least 7000 B.C. Istanbul, perhaps the most strategically sited city in the world, stands mostly in Europe with suburbs in Asia. Founded by Greeks as Byzantium in the seventh century B.C., it was captured after a thousand years by the Roman emperor Constantine, who made it his capital and renamed it Constantinople. In 1453 the Ottoman sultan Mehmed II swept westward from Anatolia and took the city. The Ottoman Empire, which in the sixteenth century ruled much of Europe, the Middle East, and North Africa, lasted through World War I. The Young Turk movement started a revolt in 1908, which culminated in Turkey's becoming a republic under President Kemal Ataturk in 1923. After siding with Germany in World War I, Turkey stayed neutral through most of World

War II and joined the North Atlantic Treaty Organization (NATO) in 1952. As Yashar Kemal's story suggests, the economy remains agrarian, and many of the Turks must eke out a living under unfavorable conditions.

The three of them were sitting on the damp earth, their backs against the dung-daubed brush wall and their knees drawn up to their chests, when another man walked up and crouched beside them.

"Have you heard?" said one of them excitedly. "Broken-Nose Jabbar's done it again! You know Jabbar, the fellow who brings all those women from the mountain villages and sells them in the plain? Well, this time he's come down with a couple of real beauties. The lads of Misdik have got together and bought one of them on the spot, and now they're having fun and making her dance and all that . . . It's unbelievable! Where does the fellow find so many women? How does he get them to come with him? He's the devil's own son, he is . . ."

"Well, that's how he makes a living," commented one of the men. "Ever since I can remember, this Jabbar's been peddling women for the villagers of the Chukurova plain. Allah provides for all and sundry . . ."

"He's still got the other one," said the newcomer, "and he's ready to give her away for a hundred liras."

"He'll find a customer soon enough," put in another man whose   5
head was hunched between his shoulders. "A good woman's worth more than a team of oxen, at least, in the Chukurova plain she is. You can always put her to the plow and, come summer, she'll bind and carry the sheaves, hoe, do anything. What's a hundred liras? Why, a woman brings in that much in one single summer. In the fields, at home, in bed. There's nothing like a woman. What's a hundred liras?"

Just then, Hollow Osman came up mumbling to himself and flopped down beside them without a word of greeting. He was a tall, broad-shouldered man with a rather shapeless potbellied body. His lips drooped foolishly and his eyes had an odd squintlike gaze.

"Hey, Osman," the man who had been talking addressed him. "Broken-Nose Jabbar's got a woman for sale again. Only a hundred liras. Tell Mistress Huru to buy her for you and have done with living alone and sleeping in barns like a dog."

Osman shrugged his shoulders doubtfully.

"Look here, man," pursued the other, "this is a chance in a million. What's a hundred liras? You've been slaving for that Huru since you dropped out of your mother's womb and she's never paid you a lira. She owes you this. And anyway she'll get back her money's worth in just one summer. A woman's good for everything, in the house, in the fields, in bed . . ."

Osman rose abruptly.   10

"I'll ask the Mistress," he said. "How should I know? . . ."

A couple of days later, a short, broad-hipped girl with blue beads strung into her plaited hair was seen at the door of Huru's barn in which Hollow Osman always slept. She was staring out with huge wondering eyes.

A month passed. Two months . . . And passersby grew familiar with the sight of the strange wide-eyed girl at the barn door.

One day, a small dark boy with a face the size of a hand was seen pelting through the village. He rushed up to his mother where she sat on the threshold of her hut gossiping with Seedy Doneh.

"Mother," he screeched, "I've seen them! It's the truth, I swear it is.   15
Uncle Osman's wife with . . . May my eyes drop out right here if I'm telling a lie."

Seedy Doneh turned to him sharply.

"What?" she cried. "Say it again. What's that about Fadik?"

"She was with the Agha's son. I saw them with my own eyes. He went into the barn with her. They couldn't see me where I was hiding. Then he took off his boots, you know the shiny yellow boots he wears . . . And then they lay down and . . . Let my two eyes drop out if . . ."

"I knew it!" crowed Seedy Doneh. "I knew it would turn out this way."

"Hollow Osman never had any manhood in him anyway," said the   20
child's mother. "Always under that viper-tongued Huru's petticoats . . ."

"Didn't I tell you, Ansha, the very first day she came here that this would happen?" said Doneh. "I said this girl's ready to play around. Pretending she was too bashful to speak to anyone. Ah, still waters run deep . . ."

She rose quickly and hurried off to spread the news.

"Have you heard? Just as I foretold . . . Still waters . . . The Agha's son . . . Fadik . . ."

In a trice all the neighboring women had crowded at Ansha's door, trying to squeeze the last drop of information out of the child.

"Come on, tell us," urged one of the women for perhaps the hun-   25
dredth time. "How did you see them?"

"Let my two eyes drop out right here if I'm lying," the child repeated again and again with unabated excitement. "The Agha's son came in,

and then they lay down, both of them, and did things . . . I was
watching through a chink in the wall. Uncle Osman's wife, you know,
was crying. I can't do it, she was saying, and she was sobbing away all
the time. Then the Agha's son pulled off those shiny yellow boots of
his . . . Then I ran right here to tell Mother."

The news spread through the village like wildfire. People could talk
about nothing else. Seedy Doneh, for one, seemed to have made it her
job to leave no man or woman uninformed. As she scoured the village
for new listeners, she chanced upon Osman himself.

"Haven't you heard what's come upon you?" she said, drawing him
aside behind the wall of a hut. "You're disgraced, you jackass. The
Agha's son has got his fingers up your wife's skirt. Try and clear your
good name now if you can!"

Osman did not seem to understand.

"I don't know . . ." he murmured, shrugging his shoulders. "I'll have   30
to ask the Mistress. What would the Agha's son want with my wife?"

Doneh was incensed.

"What would he want with her, blockhead?" she screamed. "Damn
you, your wife's become a whore, that's what! She's turned your home
into a brothel. Anyone can come in and have her." She flounced off
still screaming. "I spit on you! I spit on your manhood . . ."

Osman was upset.

"What are you shouting for, woman?" he called after her. "People
will think something's wrong. I have to ask the Mistress. She knows
everything. How should I know?"

He started walking home, his long arms dangling at his sides as   35
though they had been hitched to his shoulders as an afterthought, his
fingers sticking out wide apart as was his habit. This time he was waylaid by their next-door neighbor, Zeynep, who planted herself before
him and tackled him at the top of her voice.

"Ah Osman! You'd be better off dead! Why don't you go and bury
yourself? The whole village knows about it. Your wife . . . The Agha's
son . . . Ah Osman, how could you have brought such a woman into
your home? Where's your honor now? Disgraced . . . Ah Osman!"

He stared at her in bewilderment.

"How should I know?" he stammered, his huge hands opening out
like pitchforks. "The Mistress knows all about such things. I'll go and
ask her."

Zeynep turned her back on him in exasperation, her large skirt ballooning about her legs.

"Go bury yourself, Osman! I hope I see you dead after this."   40

A group of children were playing tipcat nearby. Suddenly one of them broke into a chant.

"Go bury yourself, Osman . . . See you dead, Osman . . ."

The other children joined in mechanically without interrupting their game.

Osman stared at them and turned away.

"How should I know?" he muttered. "I must go to the Mistress."   45

He found Huru sitting at her spinning wheel. Fadik was there too, squatting near the hearth and listlessly chewing mastic gum.

"Mistress," said Osman, "have you heard what Seedy Donch's saying? She's saying I'm disgraced . . ."

Huru stepped on the pedal forcefully and brought the wheel to a stop.

"What's that?" she said. "What about Seedy Doneh?"

"I don't know . . . She said Fadik . . ."   50

"Look here," said Huru, "you mustn't believe those lying bitches. You've got a good wife. Where would you find such a woman?"

"I don't know. Go bury yourself, they said. The children too . . ."

"Shut up," cried Huru, annoyed. "People always gossip about a beautiful woman. They go looking for the mote in their neighbor's eye without seeing the beam in their own. They'd better hold their peace because I've got a tongue in my head too . . ."

Osman smiled with relief.

"How could I know?" he said.   55

Down in the villages of the Chukurova plain, a sure sign of oncoming spring is when the women are seen with their heads on one another's lap, picking the lice out of one another's hair. So it was, on one of the first warm days of the year. A balmy sun shone caressingly down on the fields and village, and not a leaf stirred. A group of women were sitting before their huts on the dusty ground, busy with the lice and wagging their tongues for all they were worth. An acrid odor of sweat hung about the group. Seedy Doneh was rummaging in the hair of a large woman who was stretched full length on the ground. She decided that she had been silent long enough.

"No," she declared suddenly, "it's not as you say, sister! He didn't force her or any such thing. She simply fell for him the minute she saw those shiny yellow boots. If you're going to believe Huru! . . . She's got to deny it, of course."

"That Huru was born with a silver spoon in her mouth," said white-haired, toothless old Zala, wiping her bloodstained fingers on her ragged skirt. "Hollow Osman's been slaving for her like twenty men ever since she took him in, a kid the size of your hand! And all for a mere pittance of food. And now there's the woman too. Tell me, what's there left for Huru to do?"

"Ah," sighed another woman, "fortune has smiled on Huru, she has indeed! She's got two people serving her now."

"And both for nothing," old Zala reminded her.   60

"What it amounts to," said Seedy Doneh spitefully, "is that Huru used to have one wife and now she's got two. Osman was always a woman, and as for Fadik she's a real woman. He-he!"

"That she is, a real woman!" the others agreed.

"Huru says the Agha's son took her by force," pursued Doneh. "All right, but what about the others? What about those lining up at her door all through the night, eh? She never says no to any one of them, does she? She takes in everyone, young and old."

"The Lady Bountiful, that's what she is," said Elif. "And do you know something? Now that Fadik's here, the young men are leaving Omarja's yellow bitch in peace . . ."

"They've got somewhere better to go!" cackled the others.   65

Omarja's dumpy wife jumped up from where she was sitting on the edge of the group.

"Now look here, Elif!" she cried. "What's all this about our yellow dog? Stop blackening people's characters, will you?"

"Well, it's no lie, is it?" Doneh challenged her. "When was that bitch ever at your door where she should be all night? No, instead, there she came trotting up a-mornings with a rope dangling from her neck!"

"Don't go slandering our dog," protested Omarja's wife. "Why, if Omarja hears this, he'll kill the poor creature. Upon my word he will!"

"Go on!" said Doneh derisively. "Don't you come telling me that   70
Omarja doesn't know his yellow bitch is the paramour of all the village youths! What about that time when Stumpy Veli caught some of them down by the river, all taking it in turns over her? Is there anyone in this village who didn't hear of that? It's no use trying to whitewash your bitch to us!"

Omarja's wife was alarmed.

"Don't, sister," she pleaded. "Omarja'll shoot the dog, that's sure . . ."

"Well, I'm not to blame for that, sister," retorted Doneh tartly. "Anyway, the bitch'll be all right now that Fadik's around. And so will Kurdish Velo's donkey . . ."

Kurdish Velo's wife began to fidget nervously.

"Not our fault," she blurted out in her broken Turkish. "We lock our   75
donkey in, but they come and break the door! Velo furious. Velo say

people round here savage. He say, with an animal deadly sin! He say he kill someone. Then he complain to the Headman. Velo going sell this donkey."

"You know what I think?" interposed Seedy Doneh. "They're going to make it hot for her in this village. Yes, they'll do what they did to Esheh."

"Poor Esheh," sighed old Zala. "What a woman she was before her man got thrown into prison! She would never have come to that, but she had no one to protect her. May they rot in hell, those that forced her into it! But she is dead and gone, poor thing."

"Eh!" said Doneh. "How could she be otherwise after the youths of five villages had done with her?" She straightened up. "Look here, sister," she said to the woman whose head was on her lap, "I couldn't get through your lice in days! They say the Government's invented some medicine for lice which they call Dee-Dee. Ah, if only we had a spoonful of that . . . Do you know, women, that Huru keeps watch over Fadik at night? She tells the youths when to come in and then drives them out with a stick. Ha-ha, and she wants us to believe in Fadik's virtue . . ."

"That's because it suits her. Where will she find people who'll work for nothing like those two?"

"Well, the lads are well provided for this year," snickered Doneh.   80
"Who knows but that Huru may hop in and help Fadik out!"

Just then, Huru loomed up from behind a hut. She was a large woman with a sharp chin and a wrinkled face. Her graying hair was always carefully dyed with henna.

"Whores!" she shouted at the top of her voice, as she bore down upon them with arms akimbo. "City trollops! You get hold of a poor fellow's wife and let your tongues go wagging away. Tell me, are you any better than she? What do you want of this harmless mountain girl?" She pounced on Doneh who cringed back. "As for you, you filthy shitty-assed bitch, you'll shut your mouth or I'll start telling the truth about you and that husband of yours who pretends he's a man. You know me, don't you?"

Doneh blenched.

"Me, sister?" she stammered. "Me? I never . . . Other people's good name . . ."

The women were dispersing hastily. Only Kurdish Velo's wife, un-   85
aware of what was going on, continued picking lice out of her companion's hair.

"Velo says in our country women like this burnt alive. He says there no virtue in this Chukurova. No honor . . ."

The eastern sky had only just begun to pale as, with great hullabaloo and calls and cries, the women and children drove the cattle out to pasture. Before their houses, red-aproned matrons were busy at the churns beating yogurt. The damp air smelled of spring.

Osman had long ago yoked the oxen and was waiting at Huru's door. She appeared in the doorway.

"Osman, my lion," she said, "you're not to come back until you've   90
plowed through the whole field. The girl Aysheh will look after your food and get you some bedding. Mind you do the sowing properly, my child. Husneh's hard pressed this year. And there's your wife to feed too now . . . "

Husneh was Huru's only child, whom in a moment of aberration she had given in marriage to Ali Efendi, a low-salaried tax collector. All the product of her land, everything Huru had, was for this daughter.

Osman did not move or say a word. He stood there in the half-light, a large black shadow near the yoked oxen whose tails were flapping their legs in slow rhythm.

Huru stepped up to him.

"What's the matter with you, Osman, my child?" she said anxiously. "Is anything wrong?"

"Mistress," whispered Osman, "it's what Seedy Doneh's saying. And   95
Zeynep too . . . That my house . . . I don't know . . ."

Huru flared up.

"Shut up, you spineless dolt," she cried. "Don't you come babbling to me about the filthy inventions of those city trollops. I paid that broken-nosed thief a hundred good bank notes for the girl, didn't I? Did I ask you for as much as a lira? You listen to me. You can find fault with pure gold, but not with Fadik. Don't let me hear such nonsense from you again!"

Osman hesitated.

"I don't know . . ." he murmured, as he turned at last and drove the oxen off before him.

It was midmorning. A bright sun glowed over the sparkling fields.   100

Osman was struggling with the lean, emaciated oxen, which after plowing through only one acre had stretched themselves on the ground and simply refused to budge. Flushed and breathless, he let himself drop onto a mound and took his head in his hands. After a while, he rose and tried pulling the animals up by the tail.

"Accursed beasts," he muttered. "The Mistress says Husneh's in need this year. Get up this minute, accursed beasts!"

He pushed and heaved, but to no avail. Suddenly in a burst of fury, he flung himself on the black ox, dug his teeth into its nose, and shook it with all his might. Then he straightened up and looked about him sheepishly.

"If anyone saw me . . ." He swore as he spat out blood. "What can I do? Husneh's in need and there's Fadik to feed too. And now these heathen beasts . . . I don't know."

It was in this state of perplexity that Stumpy Veli found him when he strolled over from a neighboring field.

"So the team's collapsed, eh?" he commented. "Well, it was to be expected. Look at how their ribs are sticking out. You won't be able to get anything out of them."

"I don't know," muttered Osman faintly. "Husneh's in a bad way and I got married . . ."

"And a fine mess that's landed you in," burst out Veli angrily. "You'd have been better off dead!"

"I don't know," said Osman. "The Mistress paid a hundred liras for her . . ."

Stumpy Veli took hold of his arm and made him sit down.

"Look, Osman," he said, "the villagers told me to talk to you. They say you're giving the village a bad name. Ever since the Agha's son took up with your wife, all the other youths have followed suit and your house is just like a brothel now. The villagers say you've got to repudiate her. If you don't, they'll drive you both out. The honor of the whole village is at stake, and you know honor doesn't grow on trees . . ."

Osman, his head hanging down, was as still as a statue. A stray ant had caught his eye.

What's this ant doing around here at this time of day, he wondered to himself. Where can its nest be?

Veli nudged him sharply.

"Damn you, man!" he cried. "Think what'll happen if the police get wind of this. She hasn't got any papers. Why, if the gendarmes once lay their hands on her, you know how it'll be. They'll play around with her for months, poor creature."

Osman started as though an electric current had been sent through his large frame.

"I haven't got any papers either," he whispered.

Veli drew nearer. Their shoulders touched. Osman's were trembling fitfully.

"Papers are the business of the Government," Veli said. "You and me, we can't understand such things. If we did, then what would we need a Government for? Now, listen to me. If the gendarmes get hold of her, we'll be the laughingstock of villages for miles around. We'll never be able to hold up our heads again in the Chukurova. You mustn't trifle with the honor of the whole village. Get rid of her before she drags you into more trouble."

"But where will I be without her?" protested Osman. "I'll die, that's   120
all. Who'll do my washing? Who'll cook bulgur pilaf for me? I'll starve to death if I have to eat gruel again every day. I just can't do without her."

"The villagers will buy you another woman," said Veli. "We'll collect the money among us. A better woman, an honorable one, and beautiful too . . . I'll go up into the mountain villages and pick one for you my-self. Just you pack this one off quickly . . ."

"I don't know," said Osman. "It's the Mistress knows about these things."

Veli was exasperated.

"Damn the Mistress!" he shouted. "It's up to you, you idiot!"

Then he softened. He tried persuasion again. He talked and talked.   125
He talked himself hoarse, but Osman sat there immovable as a rock, his mouth clamped tight. Finally Veli spat in his face and stalked off.

It was well on in the afternoon when it occurred to Osman to unyoke the team. He had not stirred since Veli's departure. As for the oxen, they had just lain there placidly chewing the cud. He managed to get them to their feet and let them wander about the field, while he walked back to the village. He made straight for the Agha's house and waited in the yard, not speaking to anyone, until he saw the Agha's son riding in, the bridle of his horse lathered with sweat.

The Agha's son was taken aback. He dismounted quickly, but Osman waylaid him.

"Listen," he pleaded, "you're the son of our all-powerful Agha. What do you want with my wife?"

The Agha's son became the color of his famous boots. He hastily pulled a five-lira note out of his pocket and thrust it into Osman's hand.

"Take this," he mumbled and hurried away.   130

"But you're a great big Agha's son!" cried Osman after him. "Why do you want to drive her away? What harm has she done you? You're a great big . . ."

He was crushed. He stumbled away toward Huru's house, the five-lira note still in his hand.

At the sight of Osman, Huru blew her top.

"What are you doing here, you feebleminded ass?" she shouted. "Didn't I tell you not to come back until you'd finished all the plowing? Do you want to ruin me, you idiot?"

"Wait, Mistress," stammered Osman. "Listen . . ."   135

"Listen, he says! Damn the fool!"

"Mistress," he pleaded, "let me explain . . ."

Huru glared at him.

"Mistress, you haven't heard. You don't know what the villagers are going to do to me. They're going to throw me out of this village. Stumpy Veli said so. He said the police . . . He said papers . . . We haven't got any papers. Fadik hasn't and I haven't either. He said the gendarmes would carry Fadik away and do things to her. He said I must repudiate her because my house is a brothel. That's what he said. I said the Mistress knows these things . . . She paid the hundred liras . . ."

Huru was dancing with fury. She rushed out into the village square 140 and began howling at the top of her voice.

"Bastards! So she's a thorn in your flesh, this poor fellow's wife! If you want to drive whores out of this village why don't you start with your own wives and daughters? You'd better look for whores in your own homes, pimps that you are, all of you! And tell your sons to leave poor folks' women alone . . ."

Then she turned to Osman and gave him a push.

"Off you go! To the fields! No one's going to do anything to your wife. Not while I'm alive."

The villagers had gathered in the square and had heard Huru out in profound silence. As soon as she was gone, though, they started muttering among themselves.

"Who does that bitch think she is, abusing the whole village like 145 that? . . ."

The Agha, Wolf Mahmut, had heard her too.

"You just wait, Huru," he said grinding his teeth. "If you think you're going to get away with this . . ."

The night was dark, a thick damp darkness that seemed to cling to the face and hands. Huru had been waiting for some time now, concealed in the blackest shadow of the barn, when suddenly she perceived a stirring in the darkness, and a voice was calling softly at the door.

"Fadik! Open up, girl. It's me . . ."

The door creaked open and a shadow glided in. An uncontrollable 150 trembling seized Huru. She gripped her stick and flung herself on the door. It was unbolted and went crashing back against the wall. As she stood there trying to pierce the darkness, a few vague figures hustled by and made their escape. Taken by surprise, she hurled out a vitriolic oath and started groping about until she discovered Fadik crouching in a corner. She seized her by the hair and began to beat her with the stick.

"Bitch!" she hissed. "To think I was standing up for you . . ."

Fadik did not utter a sound as the blows rained down on her. At last Huru, exhausted, let go of her.

"Get up," she ordered, "and light some kindling."

Fadik raked out the dying embers and with much puffing and blowing managed to light a stick of torchwood. A pale honeyed light fell dimly over the stacked hay. There was an old pallet in one corner and a few kitchen utensils, but nothing else to show that the place was lived in.

Huru took Fadik's hand and looked at her sternly.   155

"Didn't you promise me, girl, that you'd never do it again?"

Fadik's head hung low.

"Do you know, you bitch," continued Huru, "what the villagers are going to do? They're going to kick you out of the village. Do you hear me?"

Fadik stirred a little. "Mistress, I swear I didn't go after them! They just came in spite of everything."

"Listen to me, girl," said Huru. "Do you know what happened to   160 Esheh? That's what you'll come to if you're not careful. They're like ravening wolves, these men. If you fall into their clutches, they'll tear you to shreds. To shreds, I tell you!"

"But Mistress, I swear I never did anything to —"

"You must bolt your door because they'll be after you whether you do anything or not, and their pimps of fathers will put the blame on me. It's my hundred liras they can't swallow. They're dying to see it go to pot . . . Just like Esheh you'll be. They had no one in the world, she and her man, and when Ali was thrown into jail she was left all alone. He'd lifted a sheep from the Agha's flock and bought clothes and shoes for their son. A lovely child he was, three years old . . . Ali doted on him. But there he was in jail, and that yellow-booted good-for-nothing was soon after Esheh like the plague. She kept him at arm's length for as long as she could, poor Esheh, but he got what he wanted in the end. Then he turned her over to those ravening wolves . . . They dragged her about from village to village, from mountain to mountain. Twenty, thirty good-for-nothings . . . Her child was left among strangers, the little boy she had loved so. He died . . . Those who saw her said she was like a consumptive, thin and gray, but still they wouldn't let her go, those scoundrels. Then one day the village dogs came in all smeared with blood, and an eagle was circling over the plain. So the men went to look, and they found Esheh, her body half devoured by the dogs . . . They'd made her dance naked for them . . . They'd done all sorts of things to her. Yes, they as good as killed her. That's what the police said when they came up from the town. And when Ali heard of it, he died of grief in jail. Yes, my girl, you've got Esheh's fate before you. It isn't my hundred liras that I care for, it's you. As for Osman, I can always find another woman for him. Now I've warned you. Just call me if they come again. Esheh was all alone in the world. You've got me, at least. Do you swear to do as I'm telling you?"

"I swear it, Mistress," said Fadik.

Huru was suddenly very tired.

"Well, I'm going. You'll call me, won't you?"   165

As soon as she was gone, the youths crept out of the darkness and sneaked into the barn again.

"Hey, Fadik," they whispered. "Huru was lying to you, girl. Esheh just killed herself . . ."

There was a stretch of grass in front of the Agha's house, and on one side of it dung had been heaped to the size of a small hillock. The dung steamed in the early morning sun and not a breath stirred the warm air. A cock climbed to the top of the heap. It scraped the dung, stretched its neck, and crowed triumphantly, flapping its wings.

The group of villagers squatting about on the grass silently eyed the angry Agha. Wolf Mahmut was a huge man whose shadow when he was sitting was as large as that of an average man standing up. He was never seen without a frayed, checked overcoat, the only one in the village, that he had been wearing for years now.

He was toying irritably with his metal-framed glasses when Stumpy   170
Veli, who had been sent for a while ago, made his appearance. The Agha glared at him.

"Is this the way you get things done, you fraud?" he expostulated. "So you'd have Hollow Osman eating out of your hand in no time, eh?"

Stumpy Veli seemed to shrink to half his size.

"Agha," he said, "I tried everything. I talked and talked. I told him the villagers would drive them both out. I warned him of the gendarmes. All right, he said, I'll send her away. And then he didn't . . . If you ask me, Huru's at the bottom of it all."

The others stirred. "That she is!" they agreed.

Mahmut Agha jumped up. "I'll get even with her," he growled.   175

"That, you will, Agha," they assented. "But . . ."

"We've put up with that old whore long enough," continued the Agha, sitting down again.

"Yes, Agha," said Stumpy Veli, "but, you see, she relies on her son-in-law Ali, the tax collector. They'd better stop treading on my toes, she said, or I'll have Ali strip this village bare . . ."

"He can't do anything," said the Agha. "I don't owe the Government a bean."

"But we do, Agha," interposed one of the men. "He can come here 180 and take away our blankets and rugs, whatever we have . . ."

"It's because of Huru that he hasn't fleeced this village up to now," said another. "We owe a lot of money, Agha."

"Well, what are we to do then?" cried Mahmut Agha angrily. "All our youths have left the plow and the fields and are after the woman night and day like rutting bulls. At this rate, the whole village'll starve this year."

An old man spoke up in a tremulous voice. "I'm dead, for one," he wailed. "That woman's ruined my hearth. High morning it is already. Go to the plow, my son, I beg the boy. We'll starve if you don't plow. But he won't listen. He's always after that woman. I've lost my son because of that whore. I'm too old to plow anymore. I'll starve this year. I'll go and throw myself at Huru's feet. There's nothing else to do . . ."

The Agha rose abruptly. "That Huru!" He gritted his teeth. "I'll settle her account."

He strode away.   185

The villagers looked up hopefully. "Mahmut Agha'll settle her account," they muttered. "He'll find a way . . ."

The Agha heard them and swelled with pride. "Yes, Mahmut Agha'll settle her account," he repeated grimly to himself.

He stopped before a hut and called out.

"Hatije Woman! Hatije!"

A middle-aged woman rushed out wiping her hands on her apron.   190

"Mahmut Agha!" she cried. "Welcome to our home. You never visit us these days." Then she whirled back. "Get up, you damned lazybones," she shouted angrily. "It's high morning, and look who's here."

Mahmut Agha followed her inside.

"Look, Agha," she complained, pointing to her son, "it's high morning and Halil still abed!"

Startled at the sight of the Agha, Halil sprang up and drew on his black *shalvar* trousers shamefacedly, while his mother continued with her lamentations.

"Ah, Mahmut Agha, you don't know what's befallen us! You don't 195 know, may I kiss your feet, my Agha, or you wouldn't have us on your land any longer . . . Ah, Mahmut Agha! This accursed son of mine . . . I would have seen him dead and buried, yes, buried in this black earth before . . ."

"What are you cursing the lad for?" Mahmut Agha interrupted her. "Wait, just tell me first."

"Ah, Agha, if you knew! It was full day when he came home this night. And it's the same every night, the same ever since Hollow Osman's woman came to the village. He lies abed all through the live-long day. Who'll do the plowing, I ask you? We'll starve this year. Ah, Mahmut Agha, do something! Please do something . . ."

"You go outside a little, will you, Hatije," said the Agha. Then he turned to Halil, stretching out his long, wrinkled neck which had become as red as a turkey's. "Listen to me, my boy, this has got to end. You must get this whore out of our village and give her to the youths of another village, any village. She's got to go and you'll do it. It's an order. Do you hear me?"

"Why, Agha!" Halil said ingratiatingly. "Is that what's worrying you? I'll get hold of her this very night and turn her over to Jelil from Ortakli village. You can count on me."

The Agha's spirits rose.   200

"Hatije," he called out, "come in here. See how I'm getting you out of this mess? And all the village too . . . Let that Huru know who she's dealing with in the future. They call me Wolf Mahmut and I know how to put her nose out of joint."

Long before dawn, piercing shrieks startled the echoes in the village.

"Bastards! Pimps!" Huru was howling. "You won't get away with this, not on your life you won't. My hundred liras were too much for you to swallow, eh, you fiends? You were jealous of this poor fellow's wife, eh? But you just wait and see, Wolf Mahmut! I'll set the tax collector after you all in no time. I'll get even with you if I have to spend my last penny! I'll bribe the Mudir, the Kaymakam, all the officials. I'll send telegrams to Ankara, to Ismet Pasha, to the head of the Democrats. I'll have you all dragged into court, rotting away in police stations. I'll get my own back on you for Fadik's sake."

She paused to get her breath and was off again even louder than before.

Fadik had disappeared, that was the long and the short of it. Huru   205 soon found out that someone else was missing too. Huseyin's half-witted son, The Tick.

"Impossible," she said. "The Tick ravishing women? Not to save his life, he couldn't! This is just another trick of those good-for-nothings . . ."

"But really, Huru," the villagers tried to persuade her, "he was after her all the time. Don't you know he gathered white snails in the hills, threaded them into a necklace, and offered it to Fadik, and she hung it up on her wall as a keepsake? That's the plain truth, Huru."

"I don't believe it," Huru said stubbornly. "I wouldn't even if I saw them together with my own eyes . . ."

The next day it started raining, that sheer, plumb-line torrent which sets in over the Chukurova for days. The minute the bad news had reached him, Osman had abandoned his plow and had rushed back to the village. He was standing now motionless at Huru's door, the peak of his cap drooping over his eyes. His wet clothes clung to his flesh, glistening darkly, and his rawhide boots were clogged with mud.

"Come in out of the rain, Osman, do!" Huru kept urging him.   210

"I can't. I don't know . . ." was all he could say.

"Now, look here, Osman," said Huru. "She's gone, so what? Let them have that bitch. I'll find you a good woman, my Osman. Never mind the money. I'll spend twice as much on a new wife for you. Just you come in out of the rain."

Osman never moved.

"Listen, Osman. I've sent word to Ali. Come and levy the taxes at once, I said. Have no mercy on these ungrateful wretches. If you don't fleece them to their last rag, I said, you needn't count on me as a mother again. You'll see what I'm going to do to them, my Osman. You just come inside . . ."

The rain poured down straight and thick as the warp in a loom, and   215
Osman still stood there, his chin resting on his staff, like a thick tree whose branches have been lopped off.

Huru appealed to the neighbors. Two men came and pulled and pushed, but he seemed nailed to the ground. It was well in the afternoon when he stirred and began to pace the village from one end to the other, his head sunk between his shoulders and the rain streaming down his body.

"Poor fellow, he's gone mad," opined the villagers.

A few strong men finally carried him home. They undressed him and put him to bed.

Huru sat down beside him. "Look, Osman, I'll get you a new woman even if it costs me a thousand liras. You mustn't distress yourself so. Just for a woman . . ."

The next morning he was more his normal self, but no amount of   220
reasoning or pleading from Huru could induce him to go back to the field. He left the house and resumed his pacing up and down.

The villagers had really begun to feel sorry for him now.

"Alas, poor Osman!" they murmured as he passed between the huts.

Osman heard them and heaved deep, heartrending sighs. And still he roamed aimlessly round and round.

Wolf Mahmut should have known better. Why, the whole village saw with half an eye what a rascal Halil was! How could he be trusted to give up a woman once he had got her into his hands? He had indeed got Fadik out of the way, but what he had done was to shut her up in one of the empty sheep pens in the hills beyond the village, and there he had posted The Tick to guard her.

"Play around with her if you like," he had told him contemptuously.   225
"But if you let her give you the slip —" and he had seized The Tick's wrist and squeezed it until it hurt — "you're as good as dead."

Though twenty years old, The Tick was so scraggy and undersized that at first glance people would take him to be only ten. His arms and legs were as thin as matchsticks and he walked sideways like a crab. He had always had a way of clinging tenaciously to people or objects he took a fancy to, which even as a child had earned him his nickname. No one had ever called him by his real name and it looked as though his own mother had forgotten it too . . .

Halil would come every evening bringing food for Fadik and The Tick, and he would leave again just before dawn. But it was not three days before the village youths found out what was going on. After that there was a long queue every night outside the sheep pen. They would take it in turns, heedless of Fadik's tears and howls, and at daybreak, singing and firing their guns as though in a wedding procession, they would make their way back to the village.

Night was falling and Fadik began to tremble like a leaf. They would not be long now. They would come again and torture her. She was weak with fear and exhaustion. For the past two days, her gorge had risen at the very sight of food, and she lay there on the dirt floor, hardly able to move, her whole body covered with bruises and wounds.

The Tick was dozing away near the door of the pen.

Fadik tried to plead with him. "Let me go, brother," she begged. "I'll   230
die if I have to bear another night of this."

The Tick half-opened his eyes. "I can't," he replied.

"But if I die, it'll be your fault. Before God it will . . . Please let me go."

"Why should it be my fault?" said The Tick. "I didn't bring you here, did I?"

"They'll never know. You'll say you fell asleep. I'll go off and hide somewhere. I'll go back to my mother . . ."

"I can't," said The Tick. "Halil would kill me if I let you go."   235

"But I want to go to my mother," she cried desperately. "You must let me go. Please let me go . . ."

It was dark now and the sound of singing drifted up from the village.

Fadik was seized with a violent fit of trembling. "They're coming," she said. "Let me get away now, brother. Save me! If you save me, I'll be your woman. I'll do anything . . ."

But The Tick had not been nicknamed for nothing.

"They'd kill me," he said. "Why should I die because of you? And   240
Halil's promised to buy me a pair of shoes, too. I'm not going to go without shoes because of you."

Fadik broke into wild sobbing. There was no hope now.

"Oh, God," she wept, "what shall I do now? Oh, Mother, why was I ever born?"

They lined up as usual at the entrance to the pen. The first one went in and a nerve-racking scream rose from Fadik, a scream that would have moved the most hardened of hearts. But the youths were deaf to everything. In they went, one after the other, and soon Fadik's screams died down. Not even a moan came out of her.

There were traces of blood on the ground at the back of the sheep pen. Halil and the Agha's son had had a fight the night before and the Agha's son had split open Halil's head.

"The woman's mine," Halil had insisted. "I've a right to go in first."   245

"No, you haven't," the Agha's son had contended. "I'm going to be the first."

The other youths had taken sides and joined the fray which had lasted most of the night, and it was a bedraggled band that wended back to the village that night.

Bowed down with grief, Hatije Woman came weeping to the Muhtar.

"My son is dying," she cried. "He's at his last gasp, my poor Halil, and it's the Agha's son who did it, all because of that whore of Huru's. Ah, Muhtar, if my son dies what's to become of me? There he lies struggling for life, the only hope of my hearth. But I won't let the Agha get away with this. I'll go to the Government. An old woman's only prop, I'll say . . ."

The Muhtar had great difficulty in talking Hatije out of her purpose.   250

"You go back home, Hatije Woman," he said when she had calmed down a little, "and don't worry. I'll deal with this business."

He summoned the Agha and the elders, and a long discussion ensued. It would not do to hand over the woman to the police station.

These rapacious gendarmes! . . . The honor of the whole village was at stake. And if they passed her on to the youths of another village, Huru was sure to find out and bring her back. She would not rest until she did.

After long deliberation, they came to a decision at last. The woman would be returned to Osman, but on one condition. He would take himself off with her to some distant place and never appear in the village again. They had no doubt that Osman, grateful to have Fadik back to himself, would accept. And that would cook Huru's goose too. She would lose both the woman and Osman. It would teach her to insult a whole village!

A couple of men went to find Osman and brought him back with them to the Muhtar's house.

"Sit down," they urged him, but he just stood there grasping his staff, staring about him with bloodshot eyes. His clothes hung down torn and crumpled and stained yellow from his lying all wet on the hay. His hair was a tangled, clotted mass and bits of straw clung to the stubble on his chin.

Wolf Mahmut took off his glasses and fidgeted with them.

"Osman, my lad," he remonstrated, "what's this state you're in? And all for a woman! Does a man let himself break down like this just for a woman? You'll die if you go on like this . . ."

"I don't know," said Osman. "I'll die . . ."

"See here, Osman," said the Agha. "We're here to help you. We'll get your woman back for you from out of those rascals' hands. Then you'll take her and go. You'll both get away from here, as far as possible. But you're not to tell Huru. She mustn't know where you are."

"You see, Osman," said Stumpy Veli, "how good the Agha's being to you. Your own father wouldn't have done more."

"But you're not to tell Huru," the Agha insisted. "If you do, she'll never let you go away. And then the youths will come and take your woman away from you again. And how will you ever get yourself another woman?"

"And who'll wash your clothes then?" added Stumpy Veli. "Who'll cook your bulgur pilaf for you? You mustn't breathe a word to Huru. Just take Fadik and go off to the villages around Antep. Once there, you'll be sure to get a job on a farm. You'll be much better off than you ever were with Huru, and you'll have your woman with you too . . ."

"But how can I do that?" protested Osman. "The Mistress paid a hundred liras for Fadik."

"We'll collect that much among us," the Agha assured him. "Don't you worry about that. We'll see that Huru gets her money back. You just take the woman and go."

"I don't know," said Osman. His eyes filled with tears and he swal- 265
lowed. "The Mistress has always been so good to me . . . How can I . . .
Just for a woman . . ."

"If you tell Huru, you're lost," said the Agha. "Is Huru the only mistress in the world? Aren't there other villages in this country? Take the
woman and go. You'll never find another woman like Fadik. Listen,
Veli'll tell you where she is and tomorrow you'll take her and go."

Osman bowed his head. He thought for a long time. Then he looked
up at them.

"I won't tell her," he said at last. "Why should I want to say here?
There are other villages . . ."

Before dawn the next day, he set out for the sheep pen which
Stumpy Veli had indicated.

"I don't know . . ." He hesitated at the door. "I don't know . . ." Then 270
he called out softly, "Fadik? Fadik, girl . . ."

There was no answer. Trembling with hope and fear, he stepped in,
then stopped aghast. Fadik was lying there on the dirt floor with only a
few tatters left to cover her naked body. Her huge eyes were fixed va-
cantly on the branches that roofed the pen.

He stood frozen, his eyes filling with tears. Then he bent his large
body over her.

"Fadik," he whispered, "are you all right?"

Her answering moan shook him to the core. He slipped off his shirt
and helped her into it. Then he noticed The Tick who had shrunk back
into a corner, trying to make himself invisible. Osman moved on him
threateningly.

"Uncle Osman," cried The Tick shaking with fear, "I didn't do it. It 275
was Halil. He said he'd buy me a pair of shoes . . . And Fadik would
have died if I hadn't been here . . ."

Osman turned away, heaved Fadik onto his back swiftly, and threw
himself out of the pen.

The mountain peaks were pale and the sun was about to rise. A few
white clouds floated in the sky and a cool breeze caressed his face. The
earth was wet with dew.

The Tick was scurrying off toward the village.

"Brother," Osman called after him, "go to the Mistress and tell her I
thank her for all she's done for me, but I have to go. Tell her to forgive
me . . ."

He set out in the opposite direction with Fadik on his back. He 280
walked without a break until the sun was up the height of two minarets.

Then he lowered Fadik to the ground and sat down opposite her. They looked at each other for a long while without speaking.

"Tell me," said Osman. "Where shall we go now? I don't know . . ." Fadik moaned.

The air smelled of spring and the earth steamed under the sun.

EXPLORATIONS

1. In what ways is "A Dirty Story" an appropriate title for Yashar Kemal's narrative? What people or factors does Kemal blame for Fadik's fate? What remedies, if any, does he recommend?

2. Reread the opening scene of "A Dirty Story" (paras. 1–11). What concept of women's role is presented here? Who holds this concept? How do we as readers learn it? How would the story's impact change if Kemal had written this scene as an expository paragraph from the author's point of view?

3. The third scene in "A Dirty Story" (paras. 56–86) takes place among the village women. How do they interpret the situation between Fadik, Huru, and the local youths? How do their comments about Omarja's dog and Velo's donkey suggest that the situation is not really as the women depict it? What do you think is actually going on between Fadik, the youths, Osman, and Huru at this point in the story? What other clues in this scene help you to guess what is happening?

CONNECTIONS

1. Like Jan Goodwin's "Muslims, the First Feminists" (p. 371), Kemal's "A Dirty Story" examines sex roles and stereotypes. What aspects of women's and men's social roles in the poor, rural Turkish village of Chukurova match the rules and practices Goodwin describes? What aspects do not match? What factors do you think account for the differences?

2. According to Kemal, by what qualities are men in this culture judged as successful or unsuccessful by other men? By women? How does women's concept of their own social role differ from men's concept? How are the male and female roles in this story similar to those in Curtis Sittenfeld's "Your Life as a Girl" (p. 319)? How do you explain these similarities?

3. In "Woman as Other" (p. 341) Simone de Beauvoir gives several reasons why women collaborate with men's perception and treatment of them as Other. What evidence of those reasons can you find in "A Dirty Story"? Why do you think the women of Chukurova show so little inclination to protect or even stand up for Fadik?

ELABORATIONS

1. Kemal avoids editorializing in "A Dirty Story"; he follows the time-honored writers' rule of "*show* rather than *tell*." For example, woven into his narrative is a vivid description of his native Anatolia. Go through "A Dirty Story" and pick out passages about its setting. Then write an imaginary travel article for a magazine in which you describe this region of Turkey as it would appear to a Western visitor.

2. Kemal also applies a strategy of "show rather than tell" to his characters' weaknesses. How would the story's impact change if he stated their faults and mistakes explicitly? Think of a dramatic incident in your experience in which one person or group caused harm to another without acknowledging that they were behaving badly. An example might be schoolmates bullying a weakling, an older sibling teasing a younger, or an employer or landlord discriminating on the basis of race or sex. Write a narrative essay about the incident in which you let the characters' actions speak for them, as Kemal does.

PART FIVE

MYTH AND MAGIC

OBSERVATIONS

Albert Einstein, John Updike, Joyce Carol Oates,
Martin Luther King Jr.,
Marcellina U. Okehie-Offoha,
Fadia Faqir, Celestine Bohlen, William J. Bennett,
Leslie Marmon Silko, Mara Freeman, Derek Walcott,
Pablo Neruda

▼ ▼ ▼

Ursula K. LeGuin, *Myth and Archetype in Science Fiction*
(UNITED STATES)

Gary Engle, *What Makes Superman So Darned American?*
(UNITED STATES)

Joseph Bruchac, *Digging into Your Heart* (UNITED STATES)

Eudora Welty, *Fairy Tale of the Natchez Trace* (UNITED STATES)

Toni Morrison, *From Beloved* (UNITED STATES)

Barry Bearak, *Caste Hate, and Murder, Outlast Indian Reforms*
(INDIA)

Nikos Kazantzakis, *The Gentleman* (GREECE/GREAT BRITAIN)

Chinua Achebe, *The Writer and His Community* (NIGERIA)

Isabel Allende, *Clarisa* (CHILE)

Gabriel García Márquez, *Dreams for Hire* (COLOMBIA/CUBA)

OBSERVATIONS

The fairest thing we can experience is the mysterious. It is the fundamental emotion which stands at the cradle of true art and true science. He who knows it not and can no longer wonder, no longer feel amazement, is as good as dead, a snuffed-out candle. It was the experience of mystery — even if mixed with fear — that engendered religion. A knowledge of the existence of something we cannot penetrate, of the manifestations of the profoundest reason and the most radiant beauty, which are only accessible to our reason in their most elementary forms — it is this knowledge and this emotion that constitute the truly religious attitude; in this sense, and in this alone, I am a deeply religious man.

– ALBERT EINSTEIN
The World As I See It, 1956

▼ ▼ ▼

The word *spirituality* comes, by way of "spirit," from the Latin verb for the act of breathing, *spirare*. Spirit, then, is the principle of life within us, our invisible essence. A parallel derivation took a rather different turn in French, becoming the noun *esprit*, which came to signify the mind, the rarefied human gift of understanding. In English the word remains brainless, and it has diminished over the decreasingly metaphysical decades to a semi-comic ghost, as when we say "evil spirits," which are not to be confused with spirits of alcohol or turpentine. The concept of spirituality retains connotations of the volatile, the impalpable, the immaterial, the dispensable. . . . Pressed, I would define spirituality as the shadow of light humanity casts as it moves through the darkness of everything that can be explained. I think of Buddha's smile and Einstein's halo of hair. I think of birthday parties. I think of common politeness, and the breathtaking attempt to imagine what someone else is feeling. I think of spirit lamps.

– JOHN UPDIKE
Odd Jobs: Essays and Criticism, 1991

▼ ▼ ▼

Once, when we were living in London, and I was very sick, I had a mystical vision. That is, I "had" a "mystical vision" — the heart sinks: such pretension — or something resembling one. A fever-dream, let's call it. It impressed me enormously and impresses me still, though I've long since lost the capacity to see it with my mind's eye, or even, I

411

suppose, to believe in it. There is a statute of limitations on "mystical visions" as on romantic love.

I was very sick, and I imagined my life as a thread, a thread of breath, or heartbeat, or pulse, or light, yes it was light, radiant light, I was burning with fever and I ascended to that plane of serenity that might be mistaken for (or *is*, in fact) Nirvana, where I had a waking dream of uncanny lucidity —

My body is a tall column of light and heat.

My body is not "I" but "it."

My body is not one but many.

My body, which "I" inhabit, is inhabited as well by other creatures, unknown to me, imperceptible — the smallest of them mere sparks of light.

My body, which I perceive as substance, is in fact an organization of infinitely complex, overlapping, imbricated structures, radiant light their manifestation, the "body" a tall column of light and blood-heat, a temporary agreement among atoms, like a high-rise building with numberless rooms, corridors, corners, elevator shafts, windows. . . . In this fantastical structure the "I" is deluded as to its sovereignty, let alone its autonomy in the (outside) world; the most astonishing secret is that the "I" doesn't exist! — but it behaves as if it does, as if it were one and not many.

In any case, without the "I" the tall column of light and heat would die, and the microscopic life-particles would die with it . . . will die with it. The "I," which doesn't exist, is everything.

— JOYCE CAROL OATES
"Against Nature," 1986

▼ ▼ ▼

In a sense, the history of man is the story of the struggle between good and evil. All of the great religions have recognized a tension at the very core of the universe. Hinduism, for instance, calls this tension a conflict between illusion and reality; Zoroastrianism, a conflict between the god of light and the god of darkness; and traditional Judaism and Christianity, a conflict between God and Satan. Each realizes that in the midst of the upward thrust of goodness there is the downward pull of evil.

— MARTIN LUTHER KING JR.
Strength to Love, 1963

▼ ▼ ▼

[Nigeria's] traditional Igbo religion centers on worship of the gods of their forefathers and veneration of the land (Ala). The belief that the dead hover about in invisible form, looking at the actions of men, directing, assisting, punishing, and rewarding their deeds, and the belief that newborn babies are reincarnations of the dead are cardinal beliefs of the religion.

Inasmuch as tubers and seeds must decay to yield plants, traditional Igbo religious worshipers believe that relatives must die to enable new births. They believe that as seeds can be aided artificially to grow better, the dying may regret the bad things she or he did in life and reincarnate into a better being or may die unrepentant and reincarnate basically into the same being, but nevertheless produce another generation. . . .

The traditional religion of the Igbo is similar to other African religions as described by [John S.] Mbiti:

> African Religion has no scriptures or holy books. It is written in the history, the hearts and experiences of the people. It is very pragmatic and realistic. It is applied to a situation as the need arises. [Mbiti, *Introduction to African Religion*]

> — MARCELLINA U. OKEHIE-OFFOHA
> "The Igbo"
> *Ethnic and Cultural Diversity
> in Nigeria* (with Matthew N. O. Sadiku), 1995

▼ ▼ ▼

Since I was a little girl, I have puzzled over some of the teachings of the Koran. In adolescence, a number of questions came to mind. Why are some of the references to women an incitement to violence against them? Who are the seven *houris* promised to each true Muslim in paradise? Who are the women slaves or prisoners of war men can keep as courtesans? Do I have a place in the Muslim paradise? If the 7, 10, 46,000 *houris* — the number of *houris* given to each man vary according to the interpretation — promised to true Muslim men, are not Muslim women, then who are they? If they are not women believers then I have no place in Muslim paradise.

What is this Islam that promises paradise to the true Muslim? There are many "Islams" in the Muslim world based on different interpretations and applications of the Koran and Hadith. . . . However, in the Islamic world today, and among Islamic minorities in the West, there is what Salman Rushdie has described as "Already Existing Islam," with "granite, heartless certainties," stifling Muslim societies. Between us and Allah stand the self-appointed clerics who claim to be the sole defenders of the Islamic faith, and who use "holier than thou" techniques to politicize Islam beyond recognition.

. . . But if there is no place for me in the Muslim paradise of others, then I have my own vision of that paradise: the Islam of eleventh-century Andalucía, or how I imagine it to have been. Imagination is respected by this Islam, which was the Arab bearer of art and science to medieval Europe. Translators of Greek and Persian books were not stabbed, but rather given gold equal in weight to the books they had translated. The Islam of Andalucía, sure of its identity, was open to other cultures and influences. This was an Islam committed to the pursuit of knowledge and literacy with all their consequences. Burning books was alien to it.

> — FADIA FAQIR
> *New Statesman and Society*, 1992

▼ ▼ ▼

In the nearly two weeks since the Vatican inaugurated its own electronic hookup, more than a million people have logged on to http://www.vatican.va/ — a new computer address that promises to be the next bully pulpit for a Pope who has already established himself as a television star and best-selling author. . . . "I don't know if this is a prayer line or not, but I figure this is the closest I'll get to the Vatican and to asking the Pope to say a prayer for my father-in-law," said an American named Richard. Another said that knowing the Pope was on the Internet gave him "a feeling of being close to God." . . . To date, the Vatican has received 1,200 personal messages from seventy-one countries, many from the United States, most of them addressed to the Pope himself. Dr. Joaquín Navarro-Valls, chief spokesman for the Vatican, said the Pope had seen only a sampling and would send out a single standard reply, offering his greetings and promising his prayers. . . . But the message traffic has already been an eye-opener for the Vatican. "It has been a little bit revealing of the difference between what we think people think about religious matters, and what they really think," Dr. Navarro-Valls said. "We can theorize and conceptualize, but this way, we see what really preoccupies them."

> — CELESTINE BOHLEN
> "Pope John Paul @ Vatican:
> How Many Angels Can Dance . . . ?"
> *New York Times*, 1996

▼ ▼ ▼

The vast majority of Americans share a respect for certain fundamental traits of character: honesty, compassion, courage, and perseverance. These are virtues. But because children are not born with this knowledge, they need to learn what these virtues are. We can help them gain a grasp and appreciation of these traits by giving children material to read about them. We can invite our students to discern the moral dimensions of stories, of historical events, of famous lives. There are many wonderful stories of virtue and vice with which our children should be familiar. . . .

First, these stories, unlike courses in "moral reasoning," give children some specific reference points. Our literature and history are a rich quarry of moral literacy. . . .

Second, these stories and others like them are fascinating to children. . . . Nothing in recent years, on television or anywhere else, has improved on a good story that begins "Once upon a time. . . ."

Third, these stories help anchor our children in their culture, its history and traditions. Moorings and anchors come in handy in life; moral anchors and moorings have never been more necessary.

Fourth, in teaching these stories we engage in an act of renewal. We welcome our children to a common world, a world of shared ideals, to the community of moral persons. In that common world we invite them to the continuing task of preserving the principles, the ideals, and the notions of goodness and greatness we hold dear.

– WILLIAM J. BENNETT
The Book of Virtues, 1993

▼ ▼ ▼

A lot of people think of storytelling as something that is done at bedtime — that it is something that is done for small children. When I use the term *storytelling*, I include a far wider range of telling activity. I also do not limit storytelling to simply old stories, but to again go back to the original view of creation, which sees that it is all part of a whole; we do not differentiate or fragment stories and experiences. In the beginning, Tséitsínako, Thought Woman, thought of all these things, and all of these things are held together as one holds many things together in a single thought. . . .

The storytelling always includes the audience and the listeners, and, in fact, a great deal of the story is believed to be inside the listener, and the storyteller's role is to draw the story out of the listeners. This kind of shared experience grows out of a strong community base. The storytelling goes on and continues from generation to generation.

The Origin story functions basically as a maker of our identity — with the story we know who we are. We are the Lagunas. This is where we came from. We came this way. We came by this place. And so from the time you are very young, you hear these stories, so that when you go out into the wider world, when one asks who you are, or where you came from, you immediately know: We are the people who came down from the north. We are the people of these stories. It continues down into clans so that you are not just talking about Laguna Pueblo people, you are talking about your own clan. Within the clans there are stories which identify the clan.

In the Creation story, Antelope says that he will help knock a hole in the earth so that the people can come up, out into the next world. Antelope tries and tries, and he uses his hooves and is unable to break through; and it is then that Badger says, "Let me help you." And Badger very patiently uses his claws and digs a way through, bringing the people into the world. When the Badger clan people think of themselves, or when the Antelope people think of themselves, it is as people who are of *this* story, and this is *our* place, and we fit into the very beginning when the people first came, before we began our journey south.

– LESLIE MARMON SILKO
"Language and Literature from a Pueblo
Indian Perspective," 1979

▼ ▼ ▼

From ancient times, it was the custom in each Irish village to start the Celtic New Year on November 1 with storytelling every night until May brought the summer back. Only in the dark of evening could tales be spun — it was unlucky to tell stories during the day. The "magic casements" could be flung open only at night; it was dangerous for fantastic Otherworldly goings-on to invade the normalcy of day.

. . . For centuries, many of these fireside tales were the property of the Celtic aristocracy, recited in hall or battle-camp by men of the highest rank, known as *filidh*. These were members of a learned order within the privileged class, guardians of an oral-based culture and living repositories of its history and mythology. They underwent at least twelve years of intensive training in developing memory and concentration, and learned literally hundreds of stories and verses, histories, and genealogies. A *fili*'s repertoire had to include tales of Destructions, Cattle Raids, Courtships, Battles, Deaths, Feasts, Adventures in the Otherworld, Elopements, and Visions. He was a composer, too, who had mastered the art of crafting verse in intricate metrical forms.

Such a long education was rewarded well: On graduating, a *fili* wore a cloak of crimson and yellow feathers, and carried a golden rod. Each year he received twenty-one cows, food for himself and twenty attendants. He could keep six horses and two dogs, and was granted immunity from arrest for any crime save treason or murder.

> – MARA FREEMAN
> "Word of Skill"
> *Parabola*, 1995

▼ ▼ ▼

The function of literature is sacramental in the sense that when we go to a book that is a work of art, to a book of poems that we admire, we go privately; we don't go collectively. We go in quiet, we go in silence, and we go in respect that may turn into awe and certainly may reconfirm beliefs. . . . The value of an individual reading a particular work of art, I think, is a wider thing, eventually, than something that evaporates and is evanescent like a football game or a quiz show. That's part of our consumption of stuff — you know, it's part of our digestion. It's not to be taken any more seriously than, say, a sandwich is to be taken seriously. On the other hand, if we transform that sandwich into a communion wafer . . . Without being pompous and overreligious, that is exactly the kind of feeling you may have reading a great poem: that you have taken a wafer and something has happened within you.

> – DEREK WALCOTT
> *The Georgia Review*, 1995

▼ ▼ ▼

. . . What a great language I have, it's a fine language we inherited from the fierce conquistadors . . . They strode over the giant cordilleras, over the rugged Americas, hunting for potatoes, sausages, beans, black tobacco, gold, corn, fried eggs, with a voracious appetite not found in the world since then . . . They swallowed up everything, religions, pyramids, tribes, idolatries just like the ones they brought along in their huge sacks . . . Wherever they went, they razed the land . . . But words fell like pebbles out of the boots of the barbarians, out of their beards, their helmets, their horseshoes, luminous words that were left glittering here . . . our language. We came up losers . . . We came up winners . . . They carried off the gold and left us the gold . . . They carried everything off and left us everything . . . They left us words.

> – PABLO NERUDA
> "Lost in the City"
> *Memoirs*, 1976

EXPLORATIONS

1. Albert Einstein links religion to "the experience of mystery . . . A knowledge of the existence of something we cannot penetrate"; Martin Luther King Jr. notes the conflict between opposites at the heart of religion. How do these two ideas appear in the Igbo religion as Marcellina U. Okehie-Offoha describes it? How do they appear in John Updike's definition of spirituality? In Derek Walcott's comments on the sacramental aspect of literature?

2. King writes, "In the midst of the upward thrust of goodness there is the downward pull of evil." What concepts of good and evil can you identify in Fadia Faqir's examination of Islam? In William J. Bennett's discussion of virtue? In Pablo Neruda's lines about the Spanish conquistadors in America?

3. Compare Bennett's, Leslie Marmon Silko's, and Mara Freeman's Observations about the functions of storytelling. What shared views appear in these selections? How does the role of the storyteller differ for Bennett's "majority of Americans," Silko's Lagunas, and Freeman's Celts?

URSULA K. LeGUIN

Myth and Archetype in Science Fiction

Ursula K. LeGuin (pronounced luh-*gwin*) comes naturally to writing socially conscious science fiction: Her father was an anthropologist, her mother an author. She was born Ursula Kroeber in Berkeley, California, in 1929; she married historian Charles A. LeGuin in 1953. In between she graduated from Radcliffe College, got her master's degree in romance literatures of the Middle Ages and Renaissance at Columbia University, and won a Fulbright fellowship. She taught French, had three children, and in 1961 published her first short story, "An die Musik," in the *Western Humanities Review.* Her first novel, *Rocannon's World,* came out in 1966. Two years later she published the first volume in her Earthsea trilogy, *A Wizard of Earthsea,* which won the Boston Globe–Horn Book Award and several other honors. By the early 1970s LeGuin had become one of the foremost science fiction–fantasy authors; she has won five Hugos and four Nebulas, among other awards. Her work is not limited to that genre, however, but includes poetry, essays, and children's books as well as a variety of short and long fiction. "Myth and Archetype in Science Fiction" first appeared in *Parabola* in 1976. LeGuin lives in Portland, Oregon.

"Science fiction is the mythology of the modern world." It's a good slogan, and a useful one when you're faced with people ignorant and contemptuous of science fiction, for it makes them stop and think. But like all slogans it's a half-truth, and when used carelessly, as a whole truth, can cause all kinds of confusion.

Where care must be taken is with that complex word, "mythology." What is a myth?

"Myth is an attempt to explain, in rational terms, facts not yet rationally understood." That is the definition provided by the reductive, scientistic mentality of the first half of the twentieth century, and still accepted by many. According to this definition, the god Apollo "is merely" an inadequate effort made by primitive minds to explain and systematize the nature and behavior of the Sun. As soon as the Sun is rationally understood to be a ball of fire much larger than the Earth, and its behavior has been described by a system of scientific laws, the old mythological pseudoexplanation is left empty. The fiery horses and the golden chariot vanish, the god is dethroned, and his exploits remain only a pretty tale for children. According to this view, the advance of science is a progressive draining dry of the content of mythology.[1] And, insofar as the content of myth is rational and the function of myth is explanatory, this definition is suitable. However, the rational and explanatory is only one function of the myth. Myth is an expression of one of the several ways the human being, body/psyche, perceives, understands, and relates to the world. Like science, it is a product of a basic human mode of apprehension. To pretend that it can be replaced by abstract or quantitative cognition is to assert that the human being is, potentially or ideally, a creature of pure reason, a disembodied Mind. It might, indeed, be nice if we were all little bubbles of pure reason floating on the stream of time; but we aren't. We are rational beings, but we are also sensual, emotional, appetitive, ethical beings, driven by needs and reaching out for satisfactions which the intellect alone cannot provide. Where these other modes of being and doing are inadequate, the intellect should prevail. Where the intellect fails, and must always fail, unless we become disembodied bubbles, then one of the other modes must take over. The myth, mythological insight, is one of these. Supremely effective in its area of function, it needs no replacement. Only the schizoid arrogance of modern scientism pretends that it ought to be replaced, and that pretension is pretty easily deflated. For example, does our scientific understanding of the nature and behavior of the Sun explain (let alone explain away) Apollo's remarkable sex life, or his role as the god of music and of the divine harmony? No, it has nothing whatever to do with all that; it has nothing to do with sex, or music, or harmony, or divinity; nor, *as science,* did it ever pretend to — only scientism made the claim. Apollo is not the Sun, and never was. The Sun, in fact, "is merely" one of the names of Apollo.

Reductionism cuts both ways, after all.

So long, then, as we don't claim either that the science in science   5
fiction replaces the "old, false" mythologies, or that the fiction in science fiction is a mere attempt to explain what science hasn't yet got around to explaining, we can use the slogan. Science fiction is the mythology of the modern world — or one of its mythologies — even though it is a highly intellectual form of art, and mythology is a nonintellectual mode of apprehension. For science fiction does use the myth-making faculty to apprehend the world we live in, a world profoundly

---

[1]This schema is reproduced in Freudian psychology, where the myth or symbol is considered to be a disguise, and the raising into consciousness of unconscious contents leads to a progressive emptying or draining dry of the unconscious: in contrast to the schema followed by Jung and others, where the emphasis is on the irreducibility of symbol, and the compensatory, mutually creative relationship between the conscious and the unconscious.

shaped and changed by science and technology; and its originality is that it uses the mythmaking faculty on new material.

But there's another catch to look out for. The presence of mythic material in a story does not mean that the mythmaking faculty is being used.

Here is a science fiction story: its plot is modeled directly upon that of an ancient myth, or there are characters in it modeled upon certain gods or heroes of legend. Is it, therefore, a myth? Not necessarily; in fact, probably not. No mythmaking is involved: just theft.

Theft is an integral function of a healthy literature. It's much easier to steal a good plot from some old book than to invent one. Anyhow, after you've sweated to invent an original plot, it very often turns out to be a perfect parallel to one of the old stories (more on this curious fact later). And since there are beautiful and powerful stories all through world legendry, and since stories need retelling from generation to generation, why not steal them? I'm certainly not the one to condemn the practice; parts of my first novel were lifted wholesale from the Norse mythos (Brisingamen, Freya's necklace, and episodes in the life of Odin). My version isn't a patch on the original, of course, but I think I did the gods of Asgard no harm, and they did my book some good. This sort of pilfering goes on all the time, and produces many pleasant works of art, though it does not lead to any truly new creations or cognitions.

There is a more self-conscious form of thievery which is both more destructive and more self-destructive. In many college English courses the words "myth" and "symbol" are given a tremendous charge of significance. You just ain't no good unless you can see a symbol hiding, like a scared gerbil, under every page. And in many creative writing courses the little beasts multiply, the place swarms with them. What does this Mean? What does that Symbolize? What is the Underlying Mythos? Kids come lurching out of such courses with a brain full of gerbils. And they sit down and write a lot of empty pomposity, under the impression that that's how Melville did it.

Even when they begin to realize that art is not something produced   10 for critics, but for other human beings, some of them retain the overintellectualizing bent. They still do not realize that a symbol is not a sign of something known, but an indicator of something not known and not expressible otherwise than symbolically. They mistake symbol (living meaning) for allegory (dead equivalence). So they use mythology in an arrogant fashion, rationalizing it, condescending to it. They take plots and characters from it, not in the healthily furtive fashion of the literary sneakthief, but in a posturing, showy way. Such use of myth does real disservice to the original, by trivializing it, and no good at all to the story. The shallowness of its origin is often betrayed either by an elaborate vocabulary and ostentatiously cryptic style, or by a kind of jocose, chatty discomfort in the tone. Watch me up here on Olympus, you peasants, being fresh with Aphrodite. Look at me juggling symbols, folks! We sophisticates, we know how to handle these old archetypes.

But Zeus always gets 'em. ZAP!

So far I have been talking as if all mythologies the writer might use were dead — that is, not believed in with some degree of emotion, other than aesthetic appreciation, by the writer and his community. Of course this is far from being the case. It's easy to get fresh with Aphrodite. Who believes in some old Greek goddess, anyhow? But there are living mythologies, after all. Consider the Virgin Mary; or the State.

For an example of the use of science fiction of a living religious mythos one may turn to the work of Cordwainer Smith, whose Christian beliefs are evident, I think, all through his work, in such motifs as the savior, the martyr, rebirth, the "underpeople." Whether or not one is a Christian, one may admire wholeheartedly the strength and passion given the works by the author's living belief. In general, however, I think the critics' search for Christian themes in science fiction is sterile and misleading. For the majority of science-fiction writers, the themes of Christianity are dead signs, not living symbols, and those who use them do so all too often in order to get an easy emotional charge without working for it. They take a free ride on the crucifix, just as many now cash in cynically on the current occultist fad. The difference between this sort of thing and the genuine, naive mysticism of an Arthur Clarke, struggling to express his own, living symbol of rebirth, is all the difference in the world.

Beyond and beneath the great living mythologies of religion and power there is another region into which science fiction enters. I would call it the area of the Submyth: by which I mean those images, figures, and motifs which have no religious or moral resonance and no intellectual or aesthetic value, but which are vigorously alive and powerful, so that they cannot be dismissed as mere stereotypes. They are shared by all of us; they are genuinely collective. Superman is a submyth. His father was Nietzsche and his mother was a funnybook, and he is alive and well in the mind of every ten-year-old — and millions of others. Other science-fictional submyths are the blond heroes of sword and sorcery, with their unusual weapons; insane or self-deifying computers; mad scientists; benevolent dictators; detectives who find out who done it; capitalists who buy and sell galaxies; brave starship captains and/or troopers;

evil aliens; good aliens; and every pointy-breasted brainless young woman who was ever rescued from monsters, lectured to, patronized, or, in recent years, raped, by one of the aforementioned heroes.

It hurts to call these creatures mythological. It is a noble word, and 15 they are so grotty. But they are alive, in books, magazines, pictures, movies, advertising, and our own minds. Their roots are the roots of myth, are in our unconscious — that vast dim region of the psyche and perhaps beyond the psyche, which Jung called "collective" because it is similar in all of us, just as our bodies are basically similar. Their vigor comes from there, and so they cannot be dismissed as unimportant. Not when they can help motivate a world movement such as fascism! — But neither can they furnish materials useful to art. They have the vitality of the collective unconscious, but nothing else, no ethical, aesthetic, or intellectual value. They have no element of the true myth except its emotive, irrational "thereness." The artist who deliberately submits his work to them has forfeited the right to call his work science fiction; he's just a pop cultist cashing in.

True myth may serve for thousands of years as an inexhaustible source of intellectual speculation, religious joy, ethical inquiry, and artistic renewal. The real mystery is not destroyed by reason. The fake one is. You look at it and it vanishes. You look at the Blond Hero — really look — and he turns into a gerbil. But you look at Apollo, and he looks back at you.

The poet Rilke looked at a statue of Apollo about fifty years ago, and Apollo spoke to him. "You must change your life," he said.

When the genuine myth rises into consciousness, that is always its message. You must change your life.

The way of art, after all, is neither to cut adrift from the emotions, the senses, the body, etc., and sail off into the void of pure meaning, nor to blind the mind's eye and wallow in irrational, amoral meaninglessness — but to keep open the tenuous, difficult, essential connections between the two extremes. To connect. To connect idea with value, sensation with intuition, cortex with cerebellum.

The true myth is precisely one of these connections. 20

Like any artist, the science fiction writer is trying to make and use such a connection or bridge between the conscious and the unconscious — so that his readers can make the journey too. If the only tool he uses is the intellect, he will produce only lifeless copies or parodies of the archetypes that live in his own deeper mind and in the great works of art and mythology. If he abandons intellect, he's likely to submerge his own personality and talent in a stew of mindless submyths, themselves coarse, feeble parodies of their archetypal origins. The only way to the truly collective, to the image that is alive and meaningful in all of us, seems to be through the truly personal. Not the impersonality of pure reason; not the impersonality of "the masses"; but the irreducibly personal — the self. To reach the others, the artist goes into himself. Using reason, he deliberately enters the irrational. The farther he goes into himself, the closer he comes to the other.

If this seems a paradox it is only because our culture overvalues abstraction and extraversion. Pain, for instance, can work the same way. Nothing is more personal, more unshareable, than pain; the worst thing about suffering is that you suffer alone. Yet those who have not suffered, or will not admit that they suffer, are those who are cut off in cold isolation from their fellow men. Pain, the loneliest experience, gives rise to sympathy, to love: the bridge between self and other, the means of communion. So with art. The artist who goes into himself most deeply — and it is a painful journey — is the artist who touches us most closely, speaks to us most clearly.

Of all the great psychologists, Jung best explains this process by stressing the existence, not of an isolated "id," but of a "collective unconscious." He reminds us that the region of the mind/body that lies beyond the narrow, brightly lit domain of consciousness is very much the same in all of us. This does not imply a devaluing of consciousness or of reason. The achievement of individual consciousness, which Jung calls "differentiation," is to him a great achievement, civilization's highest achievement, the hope of our future. But the tree grows only from deep roots.

So it would seem that true myth arises only in the process of connecting the conscious and the unconscious realms. I won't find a living archetype in my bookcase or my television set. I will find it only in myself: in that core of individuality lying in the heart of the common darkness. Only the individual can get up and go to the window of his house, and draw back the curtains, and look out into the dark.

Sometimes it takes considerable courage to do that. When you open 25 the curtains you don't know what may be out there in the night. Maybe starlight; maybe dragons; maybe the secret police. Maybe the grace of God; maybe the horror of death. They're all there. For all of us.

The writer who draws not upon the works and thoughts of others, but upon his own thoughts and his own deep being, will inevitably hit upon common material. The more original his work, the more imperiously *recognizable* it will be. "Yes, of course!" says the reader, recognizing himself, his dreams, his nightmares. The characters, figures, images, motifs, plots, events of the story may be obvious parallels, even seemingly reproductions, of the material of myth and legend. There will be — openly in fantasy, covertly in naturalism — dragons, heroes, quests, objects of power, voyages at night and under sea, and so forth. In narrative, as in painting, certain familiar patterns will become visible.

This again is no paradox, if Jung is right, and we all have the same kind of dragons in our psyche, just as we all have the same kind of heart and lungs in our body. It does imply that nobody can invent an archetype by taking thought, any more than he can invent a new organ in his body. But this is no loss: rather a gain. It means that we can communicate, that alienation isn't the final human condition, since there is a vast common ground on which we can meet, not only rationally, but aesthetically, intuitively, emotionally.

A dragon, not a dragon cleverly copied or mass-produced, but a creature of evil who crawls up, threatening and inexplicable, out of the artist's own unconscious, is alive: terribly alive. It frightens little children, and the artist, and the rest of us. It frightens us because it is part of us, and the artist forces us to admit it. We have met the enemy, as Pogo remarked, and he is us.

"What do you mean? There aren't any dragons in my living room, dragons are extinct, dragons aren't real. . . ."

"Look out of the window. . . . Look into the mirror. . . ." 30

The artist who works from the center of his own being will find archetypal images and release them into consciousness. The first science-fiction writer to do so was Mary Shelley. She let Frankenstein's monster loose. Nobody has been able to shut him out again, either. There he is, sitting in the corner of our lovely modern glass and plastic living room, right on the tubular steel contour chair, big as life and twice as ugly. Edgar Rice Burroughs did it, though with infinitely less power and originality — Tarzan is a true myth-figure, though not a particularly relevant one to modern ethical/emotional dilemmas, as Frankenstein's monster is. Čapek did it, largely by *naming* something (a very important aspect of archetypizing): "Robots," he called them. They have walked among us ever since. Tolkien did it; he found a ring, a ring which we keep trying to lose. . . .

Scholars can have great fun, and can strengthen the effect of such figures, by showing their relationship to other manifestations of the archetype in myth, legend, dogma, and art.[2] These linkages can be highly

---

[2]Note that a manifestation is all we ever get; the archetype itself is beyond the reach of reason, art, or even madness. It is not a thing, an object, but is rather, Jung guessed, a psychic modality, a function, comparable to a function/limitation such as the visual range of the human eye, which, by limiting our perception of electromagnetic vibrations to a certain range, enables us to see. The archetypes "do not in any sense represent things as they are in themselves, but rather the forms in which things can be perceived and conceived." They are "*a priori* structural forms of the stuff of consciousness" (Jung: *Memories, Dreams, Reflections*, p. 347).

illuminating. Frankenstein's monster is related to the Golem; to Jesus; to Prometheus. Tarzan is a direct descendant of the Wolfchild/Noble Savage on one side, and every child's fantasy of the Orphan-of-High-Estate on the other. The robot may be seen as the modern ego's fear of the body, after the crippling division of "mind" and "body," "ghost" and "machine," enforced by post-Renaissance mechanistic thought. In "The Time Machine" there is one of the great visions of the End, an archetype of eschatology comparable to any religious vision of the day of judgment. In "Nightfall" there is the fundamental opposition of dark and light, playing on the fear of darkness that we share with our cousins the great apes. Through Philip K. Dick's work one can follow an exploration of the ancient themes of identity and alienation, and the sense of the fragmentation of the ego. In Stanislaw Lem's works there seems to be a similarly complex and subtle exploration of the archetypal Other, the alien.

Such myths, symbols, images do not disappear under the scrutiny of the intellect, nor does an ethical, or aesthetic, or even religious examination of them make them shrink and vanish. On the contrary: the more you look, the more there they are. And the more you think, the more they mean.

On this level, science fiction deserves the title of a modern mythology.

Most science fiction doesn't, of course, and never will. There are   35
never very many artists around. No doubt we'll continue most of the time to get rewarmed leftovers from Babylon and Northrop Frye served up by earnest snobs, and hordes of brawny Gerbilmen ground out by hacks. But there will be mythmakers, too. Even now — who knows? — the next Mary Shelley may be lying quietly in her tower-top room, just waiting for a thunderstorm.

·

EXPLORATIONS

1. What is the first definition Ursula LeGuin gives of *myth*? Whose definition is it? What definition of her own does she offer in response? How would her definition's impact be different if she had started her essay with it?

2. According to LeGuin, what does a true myth force us to do? In what way or ways does she believe science fiction can serve as "the mythology of the modern world"?

3. What does LeGuin say about the role of intellect in science fiction? What are her reasons for giving it the place she does?

CONNECTIONS

1. Compare LeGuin's comments on mythology with Albert Einstein's Observation on religion (p. 411). How do you think each of these writers would summarize the value of the god Apollo (see LeGuin's paras. 3–4 and 16–17) to the cultures in which he was worshiped?

2. How would the "reductive, scientistic mentality" LeGuin refers to (para. 3) interpret the Laguna Pueblo creation myth told by Leslie Marmon Silko (p. 415)? How would LeGuin interpret this myth?

3. What are the parallels between LeGuin's assessment of myths and submyths in contemporary science fiction and Derek Walcott's Observation on "an individual reading a particular work of art" (p. 417)?

ELABORATIONS

1. "You just ain't no good unless you can see a symbol hiding, like a scared gerbil, under every page" (para. 9). How does LeGuin use this simile throughout the rest of her essay? Is the gerbil a symbol? What other similes, analogies, or symbols does she rely on, and for what purposes? Write an essay about LeGuin's use of representation — an image standing for or calling up something else — in "Myth and Archetype in Science Fiction."

2. What is an archetype? What is its role in mythology? On the basis of LeGuin's essay (including her footnotes) and any additional research you care to do, write a definition essay clarifying this concept and giving examples.

GARY ENGLE

What Makes Superman
So Darned American?

Gary Engle is an associate professor of English at Cleveland State University in Ohio. Born in 1947, he received his B.A. from Northwestern University and his Ph.D. (also in English) from the University of Chicago. A writer of journalism, fiction, and nonfiction, he is a frequent contributor to *Cleveland Magazine*. Engle coauthored with Dennis Dooley the 1987 book *Superman at 50: The Persistence of a Legend*. He has served on the editorial board for several books, including the *Encyclopedia of American Humorists*. He lives in Cleveland.

When I was young I spent a lot of time arguing with myself about who would win in a fight between John Wayne and Superman. On days when I wore my cowboy hat and cap guns, I knew the Duke would win because of his pronounced superiority in the all-important matter of swagger. There were days, though, when a frayed army blanket tied cape-fashion around my neck signaled a young man's need to believe there could be no end to the potency of his being. Then the Man of Steel was the odds-on favorite to knock the Duke for a cosmic loop. My greatest childhood problem was that the question could never be resolved because no such battle could ever take place. I mean, how would a fight start between the only two Americans who never started anything, who always fought only to defend their rights and the American way?

Now that I'm older and able to look with reason on the mysteries of childhood, I've finally resolved the dilemma. John Wayne was the best older brother any kid could ever hope to have, but he was no Superman.

Superman is *the* great American hero. We are a nation rich with legendary figures. But among the Davy Crocketts and Paul Bunyans and Mike Finks and Pecos Bills and all the rest who speak for various regional identities in the pantheon of American folklore, only Superman achieves truly mythic stature, interweaving a pattern of beliefs, literary conventions, and cultural traditions of the American people more powerfully and more accessibly than any other cultural symbol of the twentieth century, perhaps of any period in our history.

The core of the American myth in *Superman* consists of a few basic facts that remain unchanged throughout the infinitely varied ways in which the myth is told — facts with which everyone is familiar, however marginal their knowledge of the story. Superman is an orphan rocketed to Earth when his native planet Krypton explodes; he lands near Smallville and is adopted by Jonathan and Martha Kent, who inculcate in him their American middle-class ethic; as an adult he migrates to Metropolis where he defends America — no, the world! no, the Universe! — from all evil and harm while playing a romantic game in which, as Clark Kent, he hopelessly pursues Lois Lane, who hopelessly pursues Superman, who remains aloof until such time as Lois proves worthy of him by falling in love with his feigned identity as a weakling. That's it. Every narrative thread in the mythology, each one of the thousands of plots in the fifty-year stream of comics and films and TV shows, all the tales involving the demigods of the Superman pantheon — Superboy, Supergirl, even Krypto the Superdog — every single one reinforces by never contradicting this basic set of facts. That's the myth, and that's where one looks to understand America.

It is impossible to imagine Superman being as popular as he is and speaking as deeply to the American character were he not an immigrant and an orphan. Immigration, of course, is the overwhelming fact in American history. Except for the Indians, all Americans have an immediate sense of their origins elsewhere. No nation on Earth has so deeply embedded in its social consciousness the imagery of passage from one social identity to another: the Mayflower of the New England separatists, the slave ships from Africa and the subsequent underground railroads toward freedom in the North, the sailing ships and steamers running shuttles across two oceans in the nineteenth century, the freedom airlifts in the twentieth. Somehow the picture just isn't complete without Superman's rocketship.

Like the peoples of the nation whose values he defends, Superman is an alien, but not just any alien. He's the consummate and totally uncompromised alien, an immigrant whose visible difference from the norm is underscored by his decision to wear a costume of bold primary colors so tight as to be his very skin. Moreover, Superman the alien is real. He stands out among the hosts of comic book characters (Batman is a good example) for whom the superhero role is like a mask assumed when needed, a costume worn over their real identities as normal Americans. Superman's powers — strength, mobility, x-ray vision, and the like — are the comic-book equivalents of ethnic characteristics, and they protect and preserve the vitality of the foster community in which he lives in the same way that immigrant ethnicity has sustained

5

American culture linguistically, artistically, economically, politically, and spiritually. The myth of Superman asserts with total confidence and a childlike innocence the value of the immigrant in American culture.

From this nation's beginnings Americans have looked for ways of coming to terms with the immigrant experience. This is why, for example, so much of American literature and popular culture deals with the theme of dislocation, generally focused in characters devoted or doomed to constant physical movement. Daniel Boone became an American legend in part as a result of apocryphal stories that he moved every time his neighbors got close enough for him to see the smoke of their cabin fires. James Fenimore Cooper's Natty Bumppo spent the five long novels of the Leatherstocking saga drifting ever westward, like the pioneers who were his spiritual offspring, from the Mohawk valley of upstate New York to the Great Plains where he died. Huck Finn sailed through the moral heart of America on a raft. Melville's Ishmael, Wister's Virginian, Shane, Gatsby, the entire Lost Generation, Steinbeck's Okies, Little Orphan Annie, a thousand fiddlefooted cowboy heroes of dime novels and films and television — all in motion, searching for the American dream or stubbornly refusing to give up their innocence by growing old, all symptomatic of a national sense of rootlessness stemming from an identity founded on the experience of immigration.

Individual mobility is an integral part of America's dreamwork. Is it any wonder, then, that our greatest hero can take to the air at will? Superman's ability to fly does more than place him in a tradition of mythic figures going back to the Greek messenger god Hermes or Zetes the flying Argonaut. It makes him an exemplar in the American dream. Take away a young man's wheels and you take away his manhood. Jack Kerouac and Charles Kurault go on the road; William Least Heat Moon looks for himself in a van exploring the veins of America in its system of blue highways; legions of gray-haired retirees turn Air Stream trailers and Winnebagos into proof positive that you can, in the end, take it with you. On a human scale, the American need to keep moving suggests a neurotic aimlessness under the surface of adventure. But take the human restraints off, let Superman fly unencumbered when and wherever he will, and the meaning of mobility in the American consciousness begins to reveal itself. Superman's incredible speed allows him to be as close to everywhere at once as it is physically possible to be. Displacement is, therefore, impossible. His sense of self is not dispersed by his life's migration but rather enhanced by all the universe that he is able to occupy. What American, whether an immigrant in spirit or in fact, could resist the appeal of one with such an ironclad immunity to the anxiety of dislocation?

In America, physical dislocation serves as a symbol of social and psychological movement. When our immigrant ancestors arrived on America's shores they hit the ground running, some to homestead on the Great Plains, others to claw their way up the socioeconomic ladder in coastal ghettos. Upward mobility, westward migration, Sunbelt relocation — the wisdom in America is that people don't, can't, mustn't end up where they begin. This belief has the moral force of religious doctrine. Thus the American identity is ordered around the psychological experience of forsaking or losing the past for the opportunity of reinventing oneself in the future. This makes the orphan a potent symbol of the American character. Orphans aren't merely free to reinvent themselves. They are obliged to do so.

When Superman reinvents himself, he becomes the bumbling Clark   10
Kent, a figure as immobile as Superman is mobile, as weak as his alter ego is strong. Over the years commentators have been fond of stressing how Clark Kent provides an illusory image of wimpiness onto which children can project their insecurities about their own potential (and, hopefully, equally illusory) weaknesses. But I think the role of Clark Kent is far more complex than that.

During my childhood, Kent contributed nothing to my love for the Man of Steel. If left to contemplate him for too long, I found myself changing from cape back into cowboy hat and guns. John Wayne, at least, was no sissy that I could ever see. Of course, in all the Westerns that the Duke came to stand for in my mind, there were elements that left me as confused as the paradox between Kent and Superman. For example, I could never seem to figure out why cowboys so often fell in love when there were obviously better options: horses to ride, guns to shoot, outlaws to chase, and savages to kill. Even on the days when I became John Wayne, I could fall victim to a never-articulated anxiety about the potential for poor judgment in my cowboy heroes. Then, I generally drifted back into a worship of Superman. With him, at least, the mysterious communion of opposites was honest and on the surface of things.

What disturbed me as a child is what I now think makes the myth of Superman so appealing to an immigrant sensibility. The shape-shifting between Clark Kent and Superman is the means by which this mid-twentieth-century, urban story — like the pastoral, nineteenth-century Western before it — addresses in dramatic terms the theme of cultural assimilation.

At its most basic level, the Western was an imaginative record of the American experience of westward migration and settlement. By bringing the forces of civilization and savagery together on a mythical frontier, the Western addressed the problem of conflict between apparently mutually exclusive identities and explored options for negotiating between them. In terms that a boy could comprehend, the myth explored the dilemma of assimilation — marry the school marm and start wearing Eastern clothes or saddle up and drift further westward with the boys.

The Western was never a myth of stark moral simplicity. Pioneers fled civilization by migrating west, but their purpose in the wilderness was to rebuild civilization. So civilization was both good and bad, what Americans fled from and journeyed toward. A similar moral ambiguity rested at the heart of the wilderness. It was an Eden in which innocence could be achieved through spiritual rebirth, but it was also the anarchic force that most directly threatened the civilized values America wanted to impose on the frontier. So the dilemma arose: In negotiating between civilization and the wilderness, between the old order and the new, between the identity the pioneers carried with them from wherever they came and the identity they sought to invent, Americans faced an impossible choice. Either they pushed into the New World wilderness and forsook the ideals that motivated them or they clung to their origins and polluted Eden.

The myth of the Western responded to this dilemma by inventing   15
the idea of the frontier in which civilized ideals embodied in the institutions of family, church, law, and education are revitalized by the virtues of savagery: independence, self-reliance, personal honor, sympathy with nature, and ethical uses of violence. In effect, the mythical frontier represented an attempt to embody the perfect degree of assimilation in which both the old and new identities came together, if not in a single self-image, then at least in idealized relationships, like the symbolic marriage of reformed cowboy and displaced school marm that ended Owen Wister's prototypical *The Virginian*, or the mystical masculine bonding between representatives of an ascendant and a vanishing America — Natty Bumppo and Chingachgook, the Lone Ranger and Tonto. On the Western frontier, both the old and new identities equally mattered.

As powerful a myth as the Western was, however, there were certain limits to its ability to speak directly to an increasingly common twentieth-century immigrant sensibility. First, it was pastoral. Its imagery of dusty frontier towns and breathtaking mountainous desolation spoke most affectingly to those who conceived of the American dream in terms of the nineteenth-century immigrant experience of rural settlement. As the twentieth century wore on, more immigrants were, like Superman, moving from rural or small-town backgrounds to metropolitan environments. Moreover, the Western was historical, often elegiacally so. Underlying the air of celebration in even the most epic and romantic of Westerns — the films of John Ford, say, in which John Wayne stood tall for all that any good American boy could ever want to be — was an awareness that the frontier was less a place than a state of mind represented in historic terms by a fleeting moment glimpsed imperfectly in the rapid wave of westward migration and settlement. Implicitly, then, whatever balance of past and future identities the frontier could offer was itself tenuous or illusory.

Twentieth-century immigrants, particularly the Eastern European Jews who came to America after 1880 and who settled in the industrial and mercantile centers of the Northeast — cities like Cleveland where Jerry Siegel and Joe Shuster grew up and created Superman — could be entertained by the Western, but they developed a separate literary tradition that addressed the theme of assimilation in terms closer to their personal experience. In this tradition issues were clear-cut. Clinging to an Old World identity meant isolation in ghettos, confrontation with a prejudiced mainstream culture; second-class social status, and impoverishment. On the other hand, forsaking the past in favor of total absorption into the mainstream, while it could result in socioeconomic progress, meant a loss of the religious, linguistic, even culinary traditions that provided a foundation for psychological well-being. Such loss was particularly tragic for the Jews because of the fundamental role played by history in Jewish culture.

Writers who worked in this tradition — Abraham Cahan, Daniel Fuchs, Henry Roth, and Delmore Schwarz, among others — generally found little reason to view the experience of assimilation with joy or optimism. Typical of the tradition was Cahan's early novel *Yekl*, on which Joan Micklin Silver's film *Hester Street* was based. A young married couple, Jake and Gitl, clash over his need to be absorbed as quickly as possible into the American mainstream and her obsessive preservation of their Russian-Jewish heritage. In symbolic terms, their confrontation is as simple as their choice of headgear — a derby for him, a babushka for her. That the story ends with their divorce, even in the context of their gradual movement toward mutual understanding of one another's point of view, suggests the divisive nature of the pressures at work in the immigrant communities.

Where the pressures were perhaps most keenly felt was in the schools. Educational theory of the period stressed the benefits of rapid assimilation. In the first decades of this century, for example, New York schools flatly rejected bilingual education — a common response to the plight of non-English-speaking immigrants even today — and there were conscientious efforts to indoctrinate the children of immigrants with American values, often at the expense of traditions within the ethnic community. What resulted was a generational rift in which children were openly embarrassed by and even contemptuous of their parents' values, setting a pattern in American life in which second-generation immigrants migrate psychologically if not physically from their parents, leaving it up to the third generation and beyond to rediscover their ethnic roots.

Under such circumstances, finding a believable and inspiring bal-   20
ance between the old identity and the new, like that implicit in the myth of the frontier, was next to impossible. The images and characters that did emerge from the immigrant communities were often comic. Seen over and over in the fiction and popular theater of the day was the figure of the *yiddische Yankee*, a jingoistic optimist who spoke heavily accented American slang, talked baseball like an addict without understanding the game, and dressed like a Broadway dandy on a budget — in short, one who didn't understand America well enough to distinguish between image and substance and who paid for the mistake by becoming the butt of a style of comedy bordering on pathos. So engrained was this stereotype in popular culture that it echoes today in TV situation comedy.

Throughout American popular culture between 1880 and the Second World War the story was the same. Oxlike Swedish farmers, German brewers, Jewish merchants, corrupt Irish ward heelers, Italian gangsters — there was a parade of images that reflected in terms often comic, sometimes tragic, the humiliation, pain, and cultural insecurity of people in a state of transition. Even in the comics, a medium intimately connected with immigrant culture, there simply was no image that presented a blending of identities in the assimilation process in a way that stressed pride, self-confidence, integrity, and psychological well-being. None, that is, until Superman.

The brilliant stroke in the conception of Superman — the sine qua non that makes the whole myth work — is the fact that he has two identities. The myth simply wouldn't work without Clark Kent, mild-mannered newspaper reporter and later, as the myth evolved, bland TV newsman. Adopting the white-bread image of a wimp is first and foremost a moral act for the Man of Steel. He does it to protect his parents from nefarious sorts who might use them to gain an edge over the powerful alien. Moreover, Kent adds to Superman's powers the moral guidance of a Smallville upbringing. It is Jonathan Kent, fans remember, who instructs the alien that his powers must always be used for good. Thus does the myth add a mainstream white Anglo-Saxon Protestant ingredient to the American stew. Clark Kent is the clearest stereotype of a self-effacing, hesitant, doubting, middle-class weakling ever invented. He is the epitome of visible invisibility, someone whose extraordinary ordinariness makes him disappear in a crowd. In a phrase, he is the consummate figure of total cultural assimilation, and significantly, he is not real. Implicit in this is the notion that mainstream cultural norms, however useful, are illusions.

Though a disguise, Kent is necessary for the myth to work. This uniquely American hero has two identities, one based on where he comes from in life's journey, one on where he is going. One is real, one an illusion, and both are necessary for the myth of balance in the assimilation process to be complete. Superman's powers make the hero capable of saving humanity; Kent's total immersion in the American heartland makes him want to do it. The result is an improvement on the Western: an optimistic myth of assimilation but with an urban, technocratic setting.

One must never underestimate the importance to a myth of the most minute elements which do not change over time and by which we recognize the story. Take Superman's cape, for example. When Joe Shuster inked the first Superman stories, in the early thirties when he was still a student at Cleveland's Glenville High School, Superman was strictly beefcake in tights, looking more like a circus acrobat than the ultimate Man of Steel. By June of 1938 when *Action Comics* no. 1 was issued, the image had been altered to include a cape, ostensibly to make flight easier to render in the pictures. But it wasn't the cape of Victorian melodrama and adventure fiction, the kind worn with a clasp around the neck. In fact, one is hard-pressed to find any precedent in popular culture for the kind of cape Superman wears. His emerges in a seamless line from either side of the front yoke of his tunic. It is a veritable growth from behind his pectorals and hangs, when he stands at ease, in a line that doesn't so much drape his shoulders as stand apart from them and echo their curve, like an angel's wings.

In light of this graphic detail, it seems hardly coincidental that Superman's real, Kryptonic name is Kal-El, an apparent neologism by George Lowther, the author who novelized the comic strip in 1942. In Hebrew, *el* can be both root and affix. As a root, it is the masculine singular word for God. Angels in Hebrew mythology are called *benei Elohim* (literally, sons of the Gods), or *Elyonim* (higher beings). As an affix, *el* is most often translated as "of God," as in the plenitude of Old   25

Testament given names: Ishma-el, Dani-el, Ezeki-el, Samu-el, etc. It is also a common form for named angels in most Semitic mythologies: Israf-el, Aza-el, Uri-el, Yo-el, Rapha-el, Gabri-el and — the one perhaps most like Superman — Micha-el, the warrior angel and Satan's principal adversary.

The morpheme *Kal* bears a linguistic relation to two Hebrew roots. The first, *kal*, means "with lightness" or "swiftness" (faster than a speeding bullet in Hebrew?). It also bears a connection to the root *hal*, where *h* is the guttural *ch* of *chutzpah*. *Hal* translates roughly as "everything" or "all." *Kal-el*, then, can be read as "all that is God," or perhaps more in the spirit of the myth of Superman, "all that God is." And while we're at it, *Kent* is a form of the Hebrew *kana*. In its *k-n-t* form, the word appears in the Bible, meaning "I have found a son."

I'm suggesting that Superman raises the American immigrant experience to the level of religious myth. And why not? He's not just some immigrant from across the waters like all our ancestors, but a real alien, an extraterrestrial, a visitor from heaven if you will, which fact lends an element of the supernatural to the myth. America has no national religious icons nor any pilgrimage shrines. The idea of a patron saint is ludicrous in a nation whose Founding Fathers wrote into the founding documents the fundamental if not eternal separation of church and state. America, though, is pretty much as religious as other industrialized countries. It's just that our tradition of religious diversity precludes the nation's religious character from being embodied in objects or persons recognizably religious, for such are immediately identified by their attachment to specific sectarian traditions and thus contradict the eclecticism of the American religious spirit.

In America, cultural icons that manage to tap the national religious spirit are of necessity secular on the surface and sufficiently generalized to incorporate the diversity of American religious traditions. Superman doesn't have to be seen as an angel to be appreciated, but in the absence of a tradition of national religious iconography, he can serve as a safe, nonsectarian focus for essentially religious sentiments, particularly among the young.

In the last analysis, Superman is like nothing so much as an American boy's fantasy of a messiah. He is the male, heroic match for the Statue of Liberty, come like an immigrant from heaven to deliver humankind by sacrificing himself in the service of others. He protects the weak and defends truth and justice and all the other moral virtues inherent in the Judeo-Christian tradition, remaining ever vigilant and ever chaste. What purer or stronger vision could there possibly be for a child? Now that I put my mind to it, I see that John Wayne never had a chance.

EXPLORATIONS

1. What is the thesis of "What Makes Superman So Darned American?" Where and how is that thesis presented? What definition of "American" is Engle using in this essay? Where and how is that definition presented?

2. "Except for the Indians, all Americans have an immediate sense of their origins elsewhere" (para. 5). On what evidence does Engle base this statement? What conclusions does he base on this statement? How would the impact of his conclusions change if he used additional kinds of evidence?

3. What is the impact of "darned" in Engle's title? How would you respond differently to his essay without that word?

CONNECTIONS

1. According to Engle, "Superman achieves truly mythic stature." Would Ursula K. LeGuin agree? Why or why not? Cite specific evidence from "Myth and Archetype in Science Fiction" (p. 419).

2. Compare Engle's discussion of myth and identity (see especially para. 15) with LeGuin's (see especially paras. 17–18). What ideas are expressed by both writers? On what points do they differ?

3. "Superman's powers — strength, mobility, x-ray vision, and the like — are the comic-book equivalents of ethnic characteristics" (para. 6). Look at other selections in this book where ethnic characteristics are discussed, such as Danzy Senna's "The Mulatto Millennium" (p. 18) and Amy Tan's "Two Kinds" (p. 24). Compare Superman's powers with the ethnic characteristics mentioned by these writers. In what ways are the two sets of qualities equivalent? In what ways are they different?

EXPLORATIONS

1. Are you now, or have you ever been, a Superman fan? Do you agree with Engle's analysis of the Man of Steel's appeal? If so, write an essay showing how your own experience supports his thesis. If not, write your own analysis of the reasons why Americans, or people in general, like Superman.

2. "From this nation's beginnings Americans have looked for ways of coming

to terms with the immigrant experience. This is why, for example, so much of American literature and popular culture deals with the theme of dislocation, generally focused in characters devoted or doomed to constant physical movement" (para. 7). Based on your experience with literature and popular culture (from this country and others), is this an accurate statement of cause and effect? Does most American literature and popular culture deal with the theme of dislocation? Does it relate that theme to the immigrant experience? Is dislocation and physical movement a uniquely American preoccupation? Write an essay supporting or opposing Engle's statement, comparing enough examples from literature and popular culture to answer some or all of these questions.

JOSEPH BRUCHAC

Digging into Your Heart

Not until adulthood did Joseph Bruchac III learn that the grandfather who reared him in the Adirondack foothills of New York State was an Abenaki Indian. Today Bruchac is a member of the Abenaki Nation, carrying the name Gahnegohheyoh ("the good mind"). He was born in 1942 in Saratoga Springs, New York. At Cornell University he was active in civil rights and the antiwar movement; after receiving his master's degree from Syracuse University in 1966, he went to Ghana, West Africa, "to teach — but more than that to be taught." Returning to the United States in 1969, he did graduate work at the State University of New York at Albany while teaching creative writing and African and black literatures at Skidmore College. He also started editing and publishing the *Greenfield Review* in Greenfield Center, New York, where he now lives. Bruchac's first book of poetry, *Indian Mountain and Other Poems*, appeared in 1971. The next year he began teaching creative writing at Comstock Prison; in 1975 he received his Ph.D. from Union Graduate School. A winner of numerous grants, fellowships, and writing awards, Bruchac has contributed poems, essays, and stories to hundreds of periodicals and dozens of collections. His writing about Native American traditions draws on firsthand experience as well as formal and informal research. Among his many books are the award-winning children's book *Thirteen Moons on Turtle's Back*; the novels *Dawn Land* (1993) and *Long River* (1995); and the essay collection *Roots of Survival* (1999). "Digging into Your Heart" first appeared in the Winter 1994 issue of *Parabola*.

A traditional Wabanaki story tells of four men who make a difficult journey to visit Gluskap, the powerful ancient being who did many things to make the earth a better place for his human "grandchildren" before he retired to an island shrouded in a magical mist created by the tobacco smoke from his pipe.

Each of the men has a wish and Gluskap grants those wishes. He gives each one a pouch and tells them not to open them until they are within their own lodges. Three of those wishes, however, are selfish ones and bring about ironic consequences. Not only that, the first three men are so eager to get their heart's desire that they each open their pouches before they reach their homes. The man who wishes to be taller than all others becomes a tree; the one who wishes never to die becomes a stone; the one who wishes to have more possessions than anyone else receives so many things that they sink his canoe, and he is drowned. Only the fourth man, who wishes to be able to help his people, waits until he is in his lodge before looking in his pouch. It is empty, but when he opens it, good thoughts come into his mind and he finds within his own heart that which was formerly hidden from him. In one version of the story, he discovers the knowledge needed to be a better hunter, in another he finds the knowledge needed to show his people the right ways to live.

This story, like a Seneca story about Handsome Lake, teaches about the power of wishes and actions: to desire things which benefit only yourself will eventually result in your own downfall; to wish something which will bring good to your people will produce good results for everyone. In June of 1800, at a time when the Seneca people had lost most of their land and were deep in despair, on the verge of losing everything else, the prophet Handsome Lake was given a vision by three messengers as he lay in an alcoholic coma. The vision was intended to guide him and his people back from the brink of destruction. As the messengers took him along the sky road of the Milky Way, pointing out the evils which his people must avoid, one of the sights he was shown illustrated the results of such wrong desires:

> Now they said to him
> "We will pause here
> in order for you to see."
>
> And as he watched,
> he saw a large woman
> sitting there.
> She was grasping frantically
> at all the things
> within her reach
> and because of her great size
> she could not stand.
> That was what he saw.
>
> Then they asked him
> "What did you see?"
>
> He answered
> "It is hard to say.
> I saw a woman of great size,
> snatching at all that was about her.
> It seemed she could not rise."

Then the messengers answered,
"It is true.
What you saw was the evil of greed,
She cannot stand
and will remain thus forever.

Thus it will always be with those
who think more of the things of earth
than of this new world above.
They cannot stand upon the heaven road."

The story of the four wishes also illustrates the virtue of patience and the necessity of following the instructions of elders. As a result, the man who waits receives what he desires — something not material, but knowledge, found by looking into his heart. There is a word in the Cree language which describes the place that knowledge and stories come from — *achimoona,* "the sacred place within." The Micmac people speak of the "great man inside," a spiritual being within each person's heart who will provide good guidance if heeded.

Although more than 400 very different Native cultures and lan- 5 guages are found within the North American continent, the lessons of that Wabanaki story seem to hold true for all Native traditions. Father Claude Chauchetiere, who was a priest at the Mohawk mission of Kah-nawake (near present-day Montreal), wrote the following (which was collected in the *Jesuit Relations* and later published in 1981 in the *Narrative of the Mission of Sault St. Louis, 1667–1685*):

We see in these savages the fine roots of human nature which are en-tirely corrupted in civilized nations . . . Living in common, without dis-putes, content with little, guiltless of avarice . . .

The context which this interpretation of the Wabanaki story of the four wishes creates helps us see into the heart of the Mohegan elder Gladys Tantaquidgeon's tale of frustrated treasure seekers:
Sometime around 1900, Burrill Fielding [Gladys' uncle] had the same dream three nights in a row — a sure sign that the dream was going to come true. In it, he found himself walking at midnight in the old Shantup burying ground near the river. Each time he came to a stand of three white birches near a flat rock. In the dream, he knew that was the place to dig. Finally, after the third time he had the dream, he asked Henry Dolbeare, another Mohegan, to go with him that night to the spot he had seen. They took their shovels with them and, sure

enough, they found the stand of birches and the flat rock. It was close to midnight. They started to dig, neither one of them saying a word, because to speak when you were digging for a treasure would make that treasure go away. The bright light of a full moon shone down on them as they dug, and soon Fielding's shovel struck a wooden, hollow-sounding object. Just at that moment, something big and black jumped down into the hole between them. Both men let out a yell, dropped their shovels and ran away as fast as they could. When Fielding finally got up the courage to come back — several days later in the middle of the day — he found the shovels resting on the rock and the hole they had dug was filled in.

"Uncle Burrill," Gladys Tantaquidgeon said, "never went digging at midnight again!"

There are, of course, many elements in this story which appear to come directly from Western folklore. The themes of buried treasures and murdered men whose ghosts become supernatural guardians are familiar ones in both European-American and European traditions. As William S. Simmons points out in *Spirit of the New England Tribes, Indian History and Folklore, 1620–1984*:

> The treasure story is a category of folk narrative that is widespread and particularly well represented in historic American, West European, Caribbean, and Latin American oral traditions. The stories are not indigenous to the New England Indians, and none were recorded among them until the twentieth century . . .
>
> The Euro-American treasure legend usually involves pirates who bury their ill-gotten wealth and kill one of their crew, whose ghost guards the chest or kettle filled with gold.

The coast of Connecticut where the Mohegan people live was a familiar place for such notorious pirates as Captain Kidd, and many sites, including one particular area up the Thames River close to the present-day Mohegan community, have been said to be places where he buried his treasure. For centuries now people have looked for that treasure. Poe's famous story, "The Gold Bug," is one of the best-known literary treatments of that theme and takes place in roughly the same landscape.

But the Mohegan story of Captain Kidd's treasure, though it may seem familiar, has a different slant. The point of Poe's tale is the figuring out of a mystery: Wealth comes to the treasure seekers as a result of their intellectual puzzle-solving — and their defiling of a pirate grave. In the Mohegan tale, the knowledge of the treasure's location is arrived at through purely supernatural means — a dream vision. And just when the two Mohegan men are about to uncover the treasure, it is taken away from them under equally mystical circumstances.

Another tale of pirate treasure is told by the Wampanoag people. Written down in 1934 by Mrs. Frederick Gardner, herself a Mashpee Wampanoag, it tells the story of Hannah Screecham, a Wampanoag woman who befriended the pirates and helped them in the burial of their treasure and the accompanying murder of the sailors who would guard those gold-filled graves. But then, when Hannah went to dig up some of that treasure for herself, she was strangled by the ghosts of the murdered men.

The messages held in a story of seeking pirate treasure may be quite different when the tale is told as part of the traditions of a Native American people, even when that story is told in a way which seems completely in line with European-American traditions. It is not just the *how* of the story's telling, it is also the *why*.

Bearing in mind what happened in the traditional story of the four wishes, in the more modern tales of failed quests for buried pirate treasure we can understand that desire for personal, selfish gain dooms the seeker to, at best, failure and, at worst, destruction. But there is another message which is held in these stories, one that is so much a part of the consciousness of all Native peoples of North and South America that we sometimes forget that European Americans do not share or understand this point of view, this feeling which Native peoples have about "buried treasure," about gold and graves.

In contrast to the tradition in pirate legends of burying someone else   15
with your gold — gold which you plan to dig up and use at a later time (the eighteenth-century equivalent of an IRA?) — the Native traditions of the Americas frequently included interring material possessions as "grave goods" to go in spirit with the deceased person into the next life. The idea of digging up those grave goods was an abomination, whether they were gold ornaments to wear, or baskets filled with corn to feed the spirit. Yet the thoughtless digging up of such graves by less-than-professional "archaeologists," "pot-hunters," and fortune seekers continues to this day. Wampanoag traditions indicate that when the ill-prepared Pilgrims of the Plymouth Colony arrived in Massachusetts, the Native people watched them for some time before deciding whether or not to approach them. One of the Wampanoags, Squanto (who was clearly a man of a forgiving nature, having just made his way back to Massachusetts after being taken some years before to Europe as a slave

by another group of Englishmen), finally made the fateful decision to assist them, although many of the others urged him not to do so. They had observed the Pilgrims digging up Indian graves to obtain the baskets of corn buried there as food for the dead, something even a starving Native would never have done.

Throughout the Americas, there are still stories told of lost Indian gold, from the Seven Cities of Cibola in the American Southwest to the South American tale of El Dorado — the lake where a fabled "chief" would coat his body with gold and then wash it off in the waters as a sacrifice. Even the Adirondack mountains of New York State have one such tale. It is said (in a story which seems to have originated with Jed Rossman, a tall-tale teller who worked for years at Adirondack Loj in the heart of the High Peaks) that there is a hidden cave filled with Indian treasure on the side of Mount Colden. That cave can only be seen when standing on another peak at midnight under a full moon in the month of August. But the ghost of a giant Indian guards the treasure in that cave, which was brought there by Kahnawake Mohawk and St. Francis Abenaki Indians on their way back north after a raid in 1690 on Schenectady.

Whether such stories hold a grain of truth or not, they illustrate the popular mindset concerning "Indian treasures": It does not matter if those treasures are grave goods or sacrifices to the spirits. Quite simply, that hidden wealth, placed by Native people to rest forever in the breast of the earth, is there for the taking. And, until quite recently, much of the archaeological community felt the same about the wealth of knowledge to be uncovered in Native graves — it was there for the taking. Although it has long been illegal to dig up the graves of non-Natives, finding and exhuming Native remains was standard practice throughout the last four centuries and in a number of American states is still legal. As Dean R. Snow notes in his book *The Archaeology of North America:*

> For a long time American archaeology has involved Europeans or their descendants as scholars and American Indians as subjects. Fortunately, this situation has begun to change as some Indians have become archaeologists and some non-Indian sites have become the subject of excavation . . .
>
> Unfortunately, people calling themselves archaeologists have angered both Indians and legitimate archaeologists by looting burials and other sites for fun and profit. Even professional archaeologists have sometimes contributed to the misunderstanding by showing less sensitivity toward Indian burial sites than they would toward their own.

The repatriation to Native peoples of the remains of their ancestors who were dug up by "scientific researchers" is a very new phenomenon. Some Native communities, like my own Abenaki people, believe that bad luck has come to both white and Indian communities as a result of those ancestors not being placed back to rest. Yet even those enlightened non-Native people who have agreed to return human remains still find it hard to understand that the "grave goods" are also supposed to be returned so that the journey to the spirit world can be continued in the proper way. I recall a meeting in the 1980s (which the Abenaki Nation has on videotape) in which several hours were spent trying to explain that point to a group of people from the University of Vermont who were unable to understand why the return of the bones alone was not enough. Thus, we may also hear Gladys Tantaquidgeon's story of the failed treasure hunt — and such legends as that of Hannah Screecham — as teaching tales and a response to that long-standing European passion for grave robbing. The dead, and whatever has been sent with them to the next world, must be left in peace. Those who do not heed that injunction will find themselves confronted by guardians from the spirit world. No one, Indian or non-Indian, should disturb Indian graves, and Native people should not fall into the trap of the avaricious thinking which sometimes seems to characterize European cultures.

The 1990s have brought a further irony to the locale of that first story I told: Where European Americans once sought out Captain Kidd's buried millions, crowds now flock to Indian-run casinos all over the United States. Because of current federal laws which recognize the "sovereign" status of Native lands, gambling operations are legal on Indian reservations and hundreds of casinos have been constructed and are bringing new wealth to Native communities — among them are the Mashantucket Pequots and the Mohegans. With that new wealth — and all of the dangers of corruption brought by such sudden riches — flowing into those previously impoverished Native communities, the tale of the four wishes and the stories of search for pirate treasure may take on new meaning for Native communities. Understanding that meaning may help them make the right wishes, help them remember that the only place to dig for the true treasure is in your heart.

EXPLORATIONS

1. What is the message of the first two Native American stories Joseph Bruchac tells? What is the message of the next two stories? What third, more practical message does Bruchac convey in the last third of his essay by connecting those first two messages?

2. What advice does Bruchac give (directly or indirectly) to Native American readers of "Digging into Your Heart"? What details in the essay seem meant to appeal particularly to those readers?

3. What advice does Bruchac give (directly or indirectly) to European-American readers of "Digging into Your Heart"? What details in the essay seem meant to appeal particularly to those readers?

CONNECTIONS

1. What role do the stories in Bruchac's essay play in the cultures they come from? How is their role similar to and different from the role that Superman stories (comic books, TV episodes, movies) play in the culture they come from? What features of Superman, as described by Gary Engle in "What Makes Superman So Darned American?" (p. 428), are shared by characters in Bruchac's American Indian Stories?

2. Reread Leslie Marmon Silko's explanation of storytelling among the Laguna (p. 415). Which of her points are applied in the Native American stories Bruchac tells? Which of her points are applied in Bruchac's essay itself?

3. Which of William J. Bennett's reasons for telling stories (p. 415) do you think Bruchac would agree with, and why? How and why do you think Bruchac would disagree with Bennett?

ELABORATIONS

1. Would Ursula LeGuin ("Myth and Archetype in Science Fiction," p. 419) consider any of the stories Bruchac tells to be myths? If so, which one(s), and why? If not, why not? Using the essays by Bruchac, LeGuin, and Engle as resources, as well as the Observations by Silko, Bennett, and others, write a definition or classification essay about mythology in the United States.

2. What stories did your parents or other family members tell or read to you as a child that have influenced your sense of who you are, what your heritage is, how to behave, or all of these? Has the effect of these stories on you been positive, negative, or both? Write an essay answering these questions.

EUDORA WELTY

Fairy Tale of the Natchez Trace

Among the novelist, essayist, critic, and short-story writer Eudora
Welty's recent awards was the Legion of Honor, France's highest distinction. Her first award was a Guggenheim fellowship in 1942; others
include the O. Henry Award (in 1942, 1943, and 1968); the William
Dean Howells Medal of the American Academy of Arts and Letters
(1955, for *The Ponder Heart*), the National Institute of Arts and Letters
Gold Medal for fiction writing (1972); the Pulitzer Prize in fiction
(1973, for *The Optimist's Daughter*); the National Medal for Literature
(1980); the Presidential Medal of Freedom (1980); the American Book
Award (1981, for *The Collected Stories of Eudora Welty*, and 1984, for
One Writer's Beginnings); and the National Medal of Arts (1987).

Welty was born in 1909 in Jackson, the capital of Mississippi; she
still lives in a house her father built there in 1925. She attended the
Mississippi State College for Women but completed her B.A. degree at
the University of Wisconsin in 1929. Urged toward a more practical career than writing, she spent a year studying advertising at the Columbia
University Graduate School of Business. In New York City the Harlem
Renaissance was in full swing; Welty went dancing at Harlem jazz
clubs, saw plays, and every Sunday visited the Metropolitan Museum of
Art. Her father's death brought Welty home in 1931. She worked for
local newspapers and a radio station, then traveled around Mississippi
reporting, interviewing, and photographing for the Works Progress Administration (WPA). Although her photographs were not published
until much later (*One Time, One Place: Mississippi in the Depression:
A Snapshot Album*, 1971), she wove her observations into short stories
which began appearing in print in the mid-1930s. Following her first
story collection (*A Curtain of Green*, 1941) came her critically acclaimed novella *The Robber Bridegroom* (1942). Welty explains that
book's origins in "Fairy Tale of the Natchez Trace," a talk she gave to
the Mississippi Historical Society and published in *The Eye of the Story*
(1978). In the essay she mentions that southern Mississippi belonged to
Spain 200 years ago, having been claimed by Hernando de Soto and
held (despite counterclaims from France, Britain, and the United
States) until 1810. She describes the Natchez Trace, two miles from the
Mississippi River, as "that old buffalo trail where travelers passed along
and were set upon by the bandits and the Indians and torn apart by the
wild animals."

The Robber Bridegroom, my second book, was my first novel — or novella — and different from the fiction I'd done before or was yet to do in exactly this respect: It did not spring from the present-day world, from life I could see around me, from human activities I might run into every day. My fictional characters are always imaginary — but the characters of *The Robber Bridegroom* are peculiarly so.

The novel is set in the Natchez country of the late eighteenth century, in the declining days of Spanish rule. It opens like this:

> It was the close of day when a boat touched Rodney's Landing on the Mississippi River, and Clement Musgrove, an innocent planter, with a bag of gold and many presents, disembarked. He had made the voyage from New Orleans in safety, his tobacco had been sold for a fair price to the King's men. In Rodney he had a horse stabled against his return, and he meant to spend the night there at an inn, for the way home through the wilderness was beset with dangers.
>
> As his foot touched shore, the sun sank into the river the color of blood, and at once a wind sprang up and covered the sky with black, yellow, and green clouds the size of whales, which moved across the face of the moon. The river was covered with foam, and against the landing the boats strained in the waves and strained again. River and bluff gave off alike a leaf-green light, and from the water's edge the red torches lining the Landing-under-the-Hill and climbing the bluff to the town stirred and blew to the left and right. There were sounds of rushing and flying, from the flourish of carriages hurrying through the streets after dark, from the bellowing throats of the flatboatmen, and from the wilderness itself, which lifted and drew itself in the wind, and pressed its savage breath even closer to the little galleries of Rodney, and caused a bell to turn over in one of the steeples, and shook the fort and dropped a tree over the racetrack.
>
> Holding his bag of gold in his hand, Clement made for the first inn he saw under the hill. It was all lighted up and full of the sounds of singing.[1]

In the first sentence, there is one word in particular that may have signaled to the reader the kind of story that this is *not*. It is the word "innocent." Used to describe Clement Musgrove's character — and the only description allotted to him — "innocent" has nothing to do with the historical point of view; and it shines like a cautionary blinker to what lies on the road ahead.

In *The Robber Bridegroom*, the elements of wilderness and pioneer settlements, flatboats and river trade, the Natchez Trace and all its life,

---

[1]All excerpts are from Welty's *The Robber Bridegroom*; see headnote. — ED.

including the Indians and the bandits, are all to come together. The story is laid in an actual place, traces of which still exist, and in historical times — which, all of you need no reminding, have been well recorded. And you historians and scholars would be the first to recognize that this is not a *historical* historical novel.

The Robber Bridegroom does not fit anywhere that I know of into that pattern, which conventionally tends to be grand and to run to length. Nor was fitting into the pattern ever its aim. It *is* a story laid in and around Rodney just before 1798 — but you had better now meet all the characters.

Clement Musgrove, on this opening night at the Rodney inn, draws two strangers for bedfellows, which was not uncommon. However, the two strangers *are*. Here speaks one of them:

> "I'm an alligator!" yelled the flatboatman, and began to flail his mighty arms through the air. "I'm a he-bull and a he-rattlesnake and a he-alligator all in one! I've beat up so many flatboatmen and thrown them in the river I haven't kept a count since the Flood, and I'm a lover of women like you'll never see again . . . I can outrun, out-hop, out-jump, throw down, drag out, and lick any man in the country! . . . I can pick up a grown man by the neck in each hand and hold him out at arm's length, and often do, too . . . I eat a whole cow at one time, and follow her up with a live sheep if it's Sunday . . . I only laugh at the Indians, and I can carry a dozen oxen on my back at one time, and as for pigs, I tie them in a bunch and hang them to my belt!"

As you have recognized, the innocent planter has for one bedfellow Mike Fink, the legendary folk hero. And for the other? We see a young man: "brawny and six feet tall, dressed up like a New Orleans dandy, with his short coat knotted about him capewise . . . His heavy yellow locks hung over his forehead and down to his shoulders . . . When he removed his cloak, there was a little dirk hid in the knot."

And so it's a night of wondering who will succeed in robbing or murdering whom, but Jamie Lockhart establishes himself as the hero to the innocent planter by saving his life, and to us as a bandit at the same time. "We shall surely meet again," says Jamie to Clement as they part. It's surer than history! Knotting the sleeves of his coat about his shoulders, Jamie takes up a Raven in his fingers, which speaks boding words:

> "Turn back, my bonny,
> Turn away home."

Jamie Lockhart's Raven — though I have let him avail himself of it from the possession of Mike Fink — has really got here from the same place Jamie did: the fairy tale. The Robber Bridegroom, the double character of the title, owes his existence on the one side to history — the history of the Natchez Trace outlaws — and on the other side to the Brothers Grimm.

It is not only the character of our hero that partakes of the fairy tale. Mike Fink, in his bragging just now, might have been speaking the words of Jack the Giant Killer. And here is the planter Clement Musgrove telling Jamie the story of his wife Salome:

> "There on the land which the King of Spain granted to me," said Clement, "I built a little hut to begin with. But when my first tobacco was sold on the market, Salome, my new wife, entreated me in the night to build a better house, like the nearest settler's, and so I did . . .
>
> "'Clement,' Salome would say, 'I want a gig to drive in to Rodney.' 'Let us wait another year,' said I. 'Nonsense!' So there would be a gig. Next, 'Clement, I want a row of silver dishes to stand on the shelf.' 'But my dear wife, how can we be sure of the food to go in them?' And the merchants, you know, have us at their mercy. Nevertheless, my next purchase off the Liverpool ship was not a new wrought-iron plow, but the silver dishes. And it did seem that whatever I asked of the land I planted on, I would be given, when she told me to ask, and there was no limit to its favors."
>
> "How is your fortune now?" asked Jamie, leaning forward on his two elbows.
>
> "Well, before long a little gallery with four posts appeared across the front of my house, and we were sitting there in the evening; and new slaves sent out with axes were felling more trees, and indigo and tobacco were growing nearer and nearer to the river there under the black shadow of the forest. Then in one of the years she made me try cotton, and my fortune was made."

You'll be reminded of a story in Grimm, "The Fisherman and His 10 Wife." The Fisherman, because he kindly returned to the sea a magic Flounder he'd caught, is offered his wish; and his wife sends him to the Flounder again and again to have a new wish granted: From living in a pot, she wants to rise to be owner of a cottage, then owner of a castle, then king, then emperor, then pope, and then the Lord Almighty — at which the Flounder loses his patience.

> "Next year," said Salome, and she shaded her eagle eye with her eagle claw, and scanned the lands from east to west, "we must cut down more of the forest, and stretch away the fields until we grow twice as much of

everything. Twice as much indigo, twice as much cotton, twice as much tobacco. For the land is there for the taking, and I say, if it can be taken, take it."

"To encompass so much as that is greedy," said Clement. "It would take too much of time and the heart's energy."

"All the same, you must add it on," said Salome. "If we have this much, we can have more."

"Are you not satisfied already?" asked her husband.

"Satisfied!" cried Salome. "Never, until we have got rid of this house which is little better than a Kentuckian's cabin, with its puncheon floor, and can live in a mansion at least five stories high, with an observatory of the river on top of that, with twenty-two Corinthian columns to hold up the roof."

"My poor wife, you are ahead of yourself," said Clement.

(The reason she's ahead of herself, as you will know, is that she's describing Windsor Castle, out from Port Gibson, which did not get built until 1861.)

I think it's become clear that it was by no accident that I made our local history and the legend and the fairy tale into working equivalents in the story I came to write. It was my firm intention to bind them together. And the intention further directed that beyond the innocent planter, the greedy second wife, the adventurous robber, the story needed its beautiful maiden. Of these, as we know, there were plenty in that part of the world: They were known as "the Rodney heiresses." Rosamond is beautiful and young and unwed, with a devoted father and a wicked stepmother, and she is also an heiress. We see her first leaning from her window to sing a lovesick ballad out to the waiting air, "truly a beautiful golden-haired girl, locked in the room by her stepmother for singing, and still singing on." And Rosamond ".did not mean to tell anything but the truth, but when she opened her mouth in answer to a question, the lies would simply fall out like diamonds and pearls." So she has every fairy-tale property. Diamonds and pearls normally fall from the lips of fairy-tale maidens because they can speak nothing but what is truthful and pure — otherwise, the result is snakes and toads — but Rosamond is a romantic girl, not a wicked one, and the lies she's given to telling are simply a Rodney girl's daydreams, not intended to do any harm: perfectly good pearls.

In several other ways her fairy-tale character has ironic modifications. Jamie Lockhart and Rosamond meet for the first time when he, now as the robber with his face disguised in berry juice, rides up to her in the woods to rob her of her fine clothes: Clement's present from New

Orleans, a wonderful gown with a long train, is what she's wearing out
to pick herbs.

When he has the gown —

> Then she stood in front of Jamie in her cotton petticoats, two deep,
> and he said, "Off with the smocks, girl, and be quick . . . Now off with
> the rest."
> "God help me," said Rosamond, who had sometimes imagined such a
> thing happening, and knew what to say. "Were you born of woman? For
> the sake of your poor mother, who may be dead in her grave, like mine, I
> pray you to leave me with my underbody."

Jamie will do no such thing, and —

> Rosamond, who had imagined such things happening in the world,
> and what she would do if they did, readily reached up and pulled the
> pins out of her hair, and down fell the long golden locks, almost to the
> ground, but not quite, for she was very young yet."

Jamie, as he gathered up the gold hairpins from France, asks politely —

> "Which would you rather? Shall I kill you with my little dirk, to save
> your name, or will you go home naked?"
> "Why, sir, life is sweet," said Rosamond, looking straight at him
> through the two curtains of her hair, "and before I would die on the
> point of your sword, I would go home naked any day."

The fairy-tale daughter, as we see, is also the child of her times, a [15]
straightforward little pioneer herself.

Jamie has to come a second time in order to steal Rosamond herself.
He sweeps her up as she carries in the milk from the barn and gallops
away with her on his horse. "So smoothly did they travel that not a
single drop was spilled." As I read somewhere in the history books, "It
was the habit of the day for heiresses to disappear."

And so the circle is joined: Jamie Lockhart the New Orleans dandy is
besought by Clement Musgrove to find his lost daughter Rosamond,
and Jamie Lockhart the bandit is already her enamored kidnapper. And
neither lover knows who the other is.

The title of the novel is the title of the fairy tale; and it may be appropriate at this point to recall the original story of the Robber Bridegroom
to mind.

In Grimm, a maiden becomes engaged to a man, and preceding her
wedding day goes to his house to surprise him with a visit. There, no

one seems to be at home. Only a bird speaks to her. This bird says — he's more explicit than my Raven — "Turn back, turn back, young maiden dear, 'Tis a murderer's house you enter here." On she goes. An old old woman kept prisoner deep in the lower part of the house gives the maiden the further news that her bridegroom and his gang are cannibals and make a habit of eating young girls like her. The bride-to-be hides behind a cask to await the robbers' return, and just as my Rosamond at length will do, she sees, in place of herself, another young girl dragged in to be their victim. Grimm relates: "They gave her wine to drink, three glasses full, one glass of white wine, one glass of red, and a glass of yellow, and with this her heart burst in twain." (Rosamond is given only her stepmother's poisonous insinuations.) Thereupon the robbers "cut her beautiful body in pieces and strewed salt thereon." The little finger flies out and falls into the maiden's bosom. And so with Rosamond. Only, in my story it is not Jamie's own self whom Rosamond sees perform this act of monstrosity — it's his terrible, and real-life, counterpart, the Little Harpe — who might have done it.

Nothing has stopped the maiden yet, in the very sinister tale of Grimm's, and after this revelation she goes right ahead with the wedding. And then afterward, at the feast, she has her turn: She tells the bridegroom the whole story of her visit to the house and what she saw, saying disingenuously at every stage, "My darling, I only dreamt this," until she reaches the part about the finger. "It fell in my bosom," she says, " — and here it is!" She holds it up for all present to see, and the wedding guests hold the bridegroom fast and "deliver him over to justice."   20

Whereas all that Rosamond is frightened into doing, after what she sees in the robbers' house, is making a direct investigation on her own. After she and Jamie are in bed and he falls asleep, she washes off those berry stains.

Jamie's berry stains, the disguise in which he carries on his work, in which he kidnaps Rosamond, and in which he has continued to keep his identity secret from her after she joins him in the robbers' house (he never lets her see his face unwashed) are conventional in Mississippi history (the bandit Mason blacked his face as a disguise) and still more widely in song and story. Bandits, adventurers, lovers, and gods have the disguise in common. But girls always fall for taking it off. Psyche, in the fable, held a candle over Cupid's sleeping face — a god who only came in the dark — then let a drop of hot wax fall, and up he jumped, away he flew. Rosamond tries a mixture — her witch of a stepmother gives her the recipe, which concludes with a recipe's magic words, "It can't fail" — and she makes her version of the classic mistake.

In my novel, Jamie rises out of his bed, waked up by having his face washed.

> "Good-bye," he said. "For you did not trust me, and did not love me, for you wanted only to know who I am. Now I cannot stay in the house with you."
>
> And going straight to the window, he climbed out through it and in another moment was gone.
>
> Then Rosamond tried to follow and climbed out after him, but she fell in the dust.
>
> At the same moment, she felt the stirring within her that sent her a fresh piece of news.
>
> And finally a cloud went over the moon, and all was dark night.

Actually, the fairy tale exceeds my story in horror. But even so, it isn't so much worse than what really went on during those frontier times, is it? History tells us worse things than fairy tales do. People were scalped. Babies had their brains dashed out against tree trunks or were thrown into boiling oil when the Indians made their captures. Slavery was the order on the plantations. The Natchez Trace outlaws eviscerated their victims and rolled their bodies downhill, filled with stones, into the Mississippi River. War, bloodshed, massacre were all part of the times. In my story, I transposed these horrors — along with the felicities that also prevailed — into the element I thought suited both just as well, or better — the fairy tale. The line between history and fairy tale is not always clear, as *The Robber Bridegroom* along the way points out. And it was not from the two elements taken alone but from their interplay that my story, as I hope, takes on its own headlong life.

In the strivings and carryings-on of the day, there was also, you must   25
agree, an element of comedy. Every period has its parodists and clowns. In *The Robber Bridegroom*, Goat and his mother and flock of sisters are the clowns — folk clowns. They go scrambling about at the heels of the purposeful, and live by making sly bargains and asking "What's in it for me?" — cashing in on other people's troubles. (You could almost accuse me of unearthing some of the collateral forerunners of the family Snopes.)

Goat, who has through mutual attraction become the familiar of Rosamond's wicked stepmother, is out to do her bidding one day when he comes upon a certain robber sitting out in front of his cave, and salutes him. This robber —

> blinked his eyes and smiled, for nothing pleased him on a fine day like a lack of brains. "Come here," he said, "I will give you work to do."

"Gladly," replied Goat, "but I am already working for another, a very rich lady who wants me to see that her stepdaughter is well kidnapped by a bandit. But I don't see why a young fellow like me could not take care of two commissions at once."

"That is the way to talk," said the Little Harpe. "You will come up in the world."

For of course, you will have had in mind the real-life bandits of the day, and here is the sample. The historical Little Harpe is hiding out correctly here, very close to Rodney. He is in possession — again correctly — of the head of his brother, the Big Harpe, which he keeps in a trunk. He can always turn it in and claim the reward on it — it's like money in the savings bank.

The Little Harpe is in the novel right along with Jamie Lockhart; a side story develops in clownish parallel to Jamie and Rosamond's story: a ludicrous affair of hapless kidnapping and mistaken identity between the Little Harpe and Goat's oldest sister with a sack over her head.

For while Jamie Lockhart leads a double life by hero's necessity, clearly this isn't the only aspect of duality in the novel. Crucial, or comical, scenes of mistaken identity take place more or less regularly as the story unwinds. There's a doubleness in respect to identity that runs in a strong thread through all the wild happenings — indeed, this thread is their connection, and everything that happens hangs upon it. I spun that thread out of the times. Life was so full, so excessively charged with energy in those days, when nothing seemed impossible in the Natchez country, that leading one life hardly provided scope enough for it all. In the doubleness there was narrative truth that I felt the times themselves had justified.

Of the story's climax, it's sufficient to say that all the elements are caught up in one whirl together, in which identities and disguises and counterdisguises, stratagems and plans and deceits and betrayals and gestures heroic and desperate all at one time come into play. 30

I think I've proved my claim that mine was not a *historical* historical novel. *The Robber Bridegroom*, from the start, took another direction: Instead of burying itself deep in historical fact, it flew up, like a cuckoo, and alighted in the borrowed nest of fantasy.

Fantasy, like any other form of fiction, must have its validity. Fantasy is no good unless the seed it springs up from is a truth, a truth about human beings. The validity of my novel has to lie in the human motivations apparent alike in the history of a time and in the timeless fairy tale. In whatever form these emerge, they speak out of the same aspirations — to love, to conquer, to outwit and overcome the enemy, to reach the goal in view. And, in the end, to find out what we all wish to find out, exactly who we are and who the other fellow is, and what we are doing here all together.

Subservient to the needs of the fantasy, the characters may take on an exaggerated size. But to whatever scale they are drawn, they are each and every one human beings at the core. Even Little Harpe. When Jamie puts an end to him after a terrible battle that lasts all night, "the Little Harpe, with a wound in his heart, heaved a deep sigh and a tear came out of his eye, for he hated to give up his life as badly as the harmless deer in the wood."

In correct historical detail, the end of the Little Harpe was having his own head stuck on a pole. My reading tells me that the heads of Little Harpe and one of his partners, brought in for reward, were mounted on poles at the north and south ends of the town of Old Greenville where the Natchez Trace went by — I can't recall if it's certain who was responsible. Naturally, in *The Robber Bridegroom*, the Robber Bridegroom himself alone is responsible. It's necessary that Jamie Lockhart kill his evil counterpart, the Little Harpe, for the sake of Jamie Lockhart's future and that of his love, Rosamond; for as the novel ends — and this is the only ending possible — the hero is to be a robber no longer.

But of course, the Robber Bridegroom's pursuit of a double life was 35 (like his subsequent renunciation of it) by hero's necessity. On the one occasion when Rosamond manages to leave the robbers' house for a visit home, Clement, her father, says to her:

> "If being a bandit were his breadth and scope, I should find him and kill him for sure. But since in addition he loves my daughter, he must be not one man but two, and I should be afraid of killing the second. For all things are double, and this should keep us from taking liberties with the outside world, and acting too quickly to finish things off . . . And perhaps after the riding and robbing and burning and assault is over with this man you love, he will step out of it all like a beastly skin, and surprise you with his gentleness. For this reason, I will wait and see; but it breaks my heart not to have seen with my own eyes what door you are walking into and what your life has turned out to be.

Clement, for his good prophecy, gets his wish. Several years later (enough for the steamboat to have been invented), on a trip to the New Orleans market, he goes walking about, and this is the way the novel ends:

New Orleans was the most marvelous city in the Spanish country or anywhere else on the river. Beauty and vice and every delight possible to the soul and body stood hospitably, and usually together, in every doorway and beneath every palmetto by day and lighted torch by night. A shutter opened, and a flower bloomed. The very atmosphere was nothing but aerial spice, the very walls were sugar cane, the very clouds hung as golden as bananas in the sky. But Clement Musgrove was a man who could have walked the streets of Baghdad without sending a second glance overhead at the Magic Carpet, or heard the tambourines of the angels in Paradise without dancing a step, or had his choice of the fruits of the Garden of Eden without making up his mind. For he was an innocent of the wilderness, and a planter of Rodney's Landing, and this was his good.

So, holding a bag of money in his hand, he went to the docks to depart . . . And as he was putting his foot on the gangplank, he felt a touch at his sleeve, and there stood his daughter Rosamond, more beautiful than ever, and dressed in a beautiful, rich, white gown.

Then how they embraced, for they had thought each other dead and gone.

"Father!" she said. "Look, this wonderful place is my home now, and I am happy again!"

And before the boat could leave, she told him that Jamie Lockhart was now no longer a bandit but a gentleman of the world in New Orleans, respected by all that knew him, a rich merchant in fact. All his wild ways had been shed like a skin, and he could not be kinder to her than he was. They were the parents of beautiful twins, one of whom was named Clementine, and they lived in a beautiful house of marble and cypress wood on the shores of Lake Pontchartrain, with a hundred slaves, and often went boating with other merchants and their wives, the ladies reclining under a blue silk canopy; and they sailed sometimes out on the ocean to look at the pirates' galleons. They had all they wanted in the world, and now that she had found her father still alive, everything was well. Of course, she said at the end, she did sometimes miss the house in the wood, and even the rough-and-tumble of their old life when he used to scorn her for her curiosity. But the city was splendid, she said; it was the place to live.

"Is all this true, Rosamond, or is it a lie?" said Clement.

"It is the truth," she said, and they held the boat while she took him to see for himself, and it was all true but the blue canopy.

Then the yellow-haired Jamie ran and took him by the hand, and for the first time thanked him for his daughter. And as for him, the outward transfer from bandit to merchant had been almost too easy to count it a change at all, and he was enjoying all the same success he had ever had. But now, in his heart Jamie knew that he was a hero and had always been one, only with the power to look both ways and to see a thing from all sides.

Then Rosamond prepared her father a little box lunch with her own hands. She asked him to come and stay with them, but he would not.

"Good-bye," they told each other. "God bless you."

So I present them all — the characters of *The Robber Bridegroom* — to you historians in order that you may claim them. They're fanciful, overcharged with high spirits, perhaps, and running out of bounds when advisable or necessary, some of them demented — but they are legitimate. For they're children of their time, and fathered, rather proudly, by its spirit. If I carried out well enough my strongest intentions, fantasy does not take precedence over that spirit, but serves the better to show it forth. It partakes, in a direct way possible to fantasy alone, of the mood and tempo and drive of those challenging times, in the wild and romantic beauty of that place.

Some of the novel's reviewers called it a dream. I think it more accurate to call it an awakening to a dear native land and its own story of early life, made and offered by a novelist's imagination in exuberance and joy.

EXPLORATIONS

1. Early in "Fairy Tale of the Natchez Trace," Eudora Welty calls attention to the word "innocent" (para. 3). What other words and phrases in her first quoted passage from *The Robber Bridegroom* (para. 2) foreshadow trouble ahead?

2. Welty identifies some aspects of *The Robber Bridegroom* as coming from local history. What other countries or cultures besides the Natchez area does she mention as sources?

3. What historic reasons does Welty give for the dualities in *The Robber Bridegroom*? What are the dramatic advantages of this doubleness?

CONNECTIONS

1. In paragraphs 9–10, Welty quotes a disagreement between Clement Musgrove and his wife Salome. What would Joseph Bruchac (p. 439) say about the message behind Salome's ambitions in this fairy tale?

2. How do Welty's comments about fantasy compare with Ursula LeGuin's (p. 419)? What do these two writers see as the value of fantasy? What positions do they take on using elements of existing stories or myths in contemporary fiction? Do Welty's and LeGuin's views generally agree or conflict?

3. Reread William J. Bennett's (p. 415) and Leslie Marmon Silko's (p. 415) Observations about the purposes of storytelling. Which of the purposes they mention are evidently important to Welty?

ELABORATIONS

1. According to Welty, the validity of a fairy tale comes from the validity of its human motivations: "to love, to conquer, to outwit and overcome the enemy, to reach the goal in view" (para. 32). Choose a story you enjoyed reading in this book. Using "Fairy Tale of the Natchez Trace" as a model, write a brief literary analysis of it, showing where and how it includes these motivations.

2. In *The Robber Bridegroom*, Welty weaves threads of various myths, local legends, and facts into a fairy tale. "History tells us worse things than fairy tales do," she reminds us. "People were scalped. Babies had their brains dashed out against tree trunks . . ." (para. 24). What violent, tragic, or glorious events are part of your community's history? With local facts and legends for a starting point, write your own short fairy tale.

TONI MORRISON

From Beloved

The first African American to receive the Nobel Prize for literature, Toni Morrison was born Chloe Anthony Wofford in Lorain, Ohio, in 1931. Growing up during the Depression and World War II, she started working at age twelve but still managed to graduate from high school with honors. She received her bachelor's degree from Howard University in 1953 and her master's from Cornell University in 1955. After teaching at Texas Southern University she returned to Howard, where she met and married Jamaican architect Harold Morrison. Her efforts to juggle marriage, an academic career, writing, and motherhood ended in divorce in 1964. Moving to New York with her two sons, Morrison became an editor for Random House. For twenty years she worked on both sides of the publishing fence: Her novel *The Bluest Eye* appeared in 1969, followed by *Sula* in 1973 and the even more successful *Song of Solomon* in 1977. Meanwhile, she periodically lectured and taught at such universities as Cambridge, Harvard, and Princeton (where she is the Robert F. Goheen Professor of Humanities). Her most recent novel is *Paradise* (1998).

Morrison's novel *Beloved* (1987), from which the following chapter comes, won the Pulitzer Prize for fiction and the Robert F. Kennedy Award. A decade later, Oprah Winfrey produced and starred in a film version with a script cowritten by Morrison. *Beloved* also paved the way for the author's 1993 Nobel Prize for literature, which followed her publication in 1992 of the novel *Jazz*, the essay collection *Playing in the Dark: Whiteness and the Literary Imagination*, and the edited volume *Race-ing Justice, En-Gendering Power*. "Myth . . . has enormous effect on my own imagination," Morrison commented at a 1995 panel discussion in Atlanta. "I am perhaps enchanted still by enchantment and by what used to be called superstition and magic. But those words are very small for what . . . I'm looking for, which is just a way in which to describe and recreate the enhanced life, life as in an upper register that comes from one's very close association with the world that we already inhabit."

124 was spiteful. Full of a baby's venom. The women in the house knew it and so did the children. For years each put up with the spite in his own way, but by 1873 Sethe and her daughter Denver were its only victims. The grandmother, Baby Suggs, was dead, and the sons,

Howard and Buglar, had run away by the time they were thirteen years old — as soon as merely looking in a mirror shattered it (that was the signal for Buglar); as soon as two tiny handprints appeared in the cake (that was it for Howard). Neither boy waited to see more; another kettleful of chickpeas smoking in a heap on the floor; soda crackers crumbled and strewn in a line next to the doorsill. Nor did they wait for one of the relief periods: the weeks, months even, when nothing was disturbed. No. Each one fled at once — the moment the house committed what was for him the one insult not to be borne or witnessed a second time. Within two months, in the dead of winter, leaving their grandmother, Baby Suggs; Sethe, their mother; and their little sister, Denver, all by themselves in the gray and white house on Bluestone Road. It didn't have a number then, because Cincinnati didn't stretch that far. In fact, Ohio had been calling itself a state only seventy years when first one brother and then the next stuffed quilt packing into his hat, snatched up his shoes, and crept away from the lively spite the house had for them.

Baby Suggs didn't even raise her head. From her sickbed she heard them go but that wasn't the reason she lay still. It was a wonder to her that her grandsons had taken so long to realize that every house wasn't like the one on Bluestone Road. Suspended between the nastiness of life and the meanness of the dead, she couldn't get interested in leaving life or living it, let alone the fright of two creeping-off boys. Her past had been like her present — intolerable — and since she knew death was anything but forgetfulness, she used the little energy left her for pondering color.

"Bring a little lavender in, if you got any. Pink, if you don't."

And Sethe would oblige her with anything from fabric to her own tongue. Winter in Ohio was especially rough if you had an appetite for color. Sky provided the only drama, and counting on a Cincinnati horizon for life's principal joy was reckless indeed. So Sethe and the girl Denver did what they could, and what the house permitted, for her. Together they waged a perfunctory battle against the outrageous behavior of that place, against turned-over slop jars, smacks on the behind, and gusts of sour air. For they understood the source of the outrage as well as they knew the source of light.

Baby Suggs died shortly after the brothers left, with no interest whatsoever in their leave-taking or hers, and right afterward Sethe and Denver decided to end the persecution by calling forth the ghost that tried them so. Perhaps a conversation, they thought, an exchange of views or something would help. So they held hands and said, "Come on. Come on. You may as well just come on." 5

The sideboard took a step forward but nothing else did.

"Grandma Baby must be stopping it," said Denver. She was ten and still mad at Baby Suggs for dying.

Sethe opened her eyes. "I doubt that," she said.

"Then why don't it come?"

"You forgetting how little it is," said her mother. "She wasn't even   10 two years old when she died. Too little to understand. Too little to talk much even."

"Maybe she don't want to understand," said Denver.

"Maybe. But if she'd only come, I could make it clear to her." Sethe released her daughter's hand and together they pushed the sideboard back against the wall. Outside a driver whipped his horse into the gallop local people felt necessary when they passed 124.

"For a baby she throws a powerful spell," said Denver.

"No more powerful than the way I loved her," Sethe answered and there it was again. The welcoming cool of unchiseled headstones; the one she selected to lean against on tiptoe, her knees wide open as any grave. Pink as a fingernail it was, and sprinkled with glittering chips. Ten minutes, he said. You got ten minutes I'll do it for free.

Ten minutes for seven letters. With another ten could she have got-   15 ten "Dearly" too? She had not thought to ask him and it bothered her still that it might have been possible — that for twenty minutes, a half hour, say, she could have had the whole thing, every word she heard the preacher say at the funeral (and all there was to say, surely) engraved on her baby's headstone: Dearly Beloved. But what she got, settled for, was the one word that mattered. She thought it would be enough, rutting among the headstones with the engraver, his young son looking on, the anger in his face so old; the appetite in it quite new. That should certainly be enough. Enough to answer one more preacher, one more abolitionist and a town full of disgust.

Counting on the stillness of her own soul, she had forgotten the other one: the soul of her baby girl. Who would have thought that a little old baby could harbor so much rage? Rutting among the stones under the eyes of the engraver's son was not enough. Not only did she have to live out her years in a house palsied by the baby's fury at having its throat cut, but those ten minutes she spent pressed up against dawn-colored stone studded with star chips, her knees wide open as the grave, were longer than life, more alive, more pulsating than the baby blood that soaked her fingers like oil.

"We could move," she suggested once to her mother-in-law.

"What'd be the point?" asked Baby Suggs. "Not a house in the country ain't packed to its rafters with some dead Negro's grief. We lucky this ghost is a baby. My husband's spirit was to come back in here? or yours?

Don't talk to me. You lucky. You got three left. Three pulling at your skirts and just one raising hell from the other side. Be thankful, why don't you? I had eight. Every one of them gone away from me. Four taken, four chased, and all, I expect, worrying somebody's house into evil." Baby Suggs rubbed her eyebrows. "My first-born. All I can remember of her is how she loved the burned bottom of bread. Can you beat that? Eight children and that's all I remember."

"That's all you let yourself remember," Sethe had told her, but she was down to one herself — one alive, that is — the boys chased off by the dead one, and her memory of Buglar was fading fast. Howard at least had a head shape nobody could forget. As for the rest, she worked hard to remember as close to nothing as was safe. Unfortunately her brain was devious. She might be hurrying across a field, running practically, to get to the pump quickly and rinse the chamomile sap from her legs. Nothing else would be in her mind. The picture of the men coming to nurse her was as lifeless as the nerves in her back where the skin buckled like a washboard. Nor was there the faintest scent of ink or the cherry gum and oak bark from which it was made. Nothing. Just the breeze cooling her face as she rushed toward water. And then sopping the chamomile away with pump water and rags, her mind fixed on getting every last bit of sap off — on her carelessness in taking a shortcut across the field just to save a half mile, and not noticing how high the weeds had grown until the itching was all the way to her knees. Then something. The plash of water, the sight of her shoes and stockings awry on the path where she had flung them; or Here Boy lapping in the puddle near her feet, and suddenly there was Sweet Home rolling, rolling, rolling out before her eyes, and although there was not a leaf on that farm that did not make her want to scream, it rolled itself out before her in shameless beauty. It never looked as terrible as it was and it made her wonder if hell was a pretty place too. Fire and brimstone all right, but hidden in lacy groves. Boys hanging from the most beautiful sycamores in the world. It shamed her — remembering the wonderful soughing trees rather than the boys. Try as she might to make it otherwise, the sycamores beat out the children every time and she could not forgive her memory for that.

When the last of the chamomile was gone, she went around to the front of the house, collecting her shoes and stockings on the way. As if to punish her further for her terrible memory, sitting on the porch not forty feet away was Paul D, the last of the Sweet Home men. And although she could never mistake his face for another's, she said, "Is that you?"

"What's left." He stood up and smiled. "How you been, girl, besides barefoot?"

When she laughed it came out loose and young. "Messed up my legs back yonder. Chamomile."

He made a face as though tasting a teaspoon of something bitter. "I don't want to even hear 'bout it. Always did hate that stuff."

Sethe balled up her stockings and jammed them into her pocket. "Come on in."

"Porch is fine, Sethe. Cool out here." He sat back down and looked   25
at the meadow on the other side of the road, knowing the eagerness he felt would be in his eyes.

"Eighteen years," she said softly.

"Eighteen," he repeated. "And I swear I been walking every one of em. Mind if I join you?" He nodded toward her feet and began unlacing his shoes.

"You want to soak them? Let me get you a basin of water." She moved closer to him to enter the house.

"No, uh uh. Can't baby feet. A whole lot more tramping they got to do."

"You can't leave right away, Paul D. You got to stay awhile."   30

"Well, long enough to see Baby Suggs, anyway. Where is she?"

"Dead."

"Aw no. When?"

"Eight years now. Almost nine."

"Was it hard? I hope she didn't die hard."   35

Sethe shook her head. "Soft as cream. Being alive was the hard part. Sorry you missed her though. Is that what you came by for?"

"That's some of what I came for. The rest is you. But if all the truth be known, I go anywhere these days. Anywhere they let me sit down."

"You looking good."

"Devil's confusion. He lets me look good long as I feel bad." He looked at her and the word "bad" took on another meaning.

Sethe smiled. This is the way they were — had been. All of the Sweet   40
Home men, before and after Halle, treated her to a mild brotherly flirtation, so subtle you had to scratch for it.

Except for a heap more hair and some waiting in his eyes, he looked the way he had in Kentucky. Peachstone skin; straight-backed. For a man with an immobile face it was amazing how ready it was to smile, or blaze or be sorry with you. As though all you had to do was get his attention and right away he produced the feeling you were feeling. With less than a blink, his face seemed to change — underneath it lay the activity.

"I wouldn't have to ask about him, would I? You'd tell me if there was anything to tell, wouldn't you?" Sethe looked down at her feet and saw again the sycamores.

"I'd tell you. Sure I'd tell you. I don't know any more now than I did then." Except for the churn, he thought, and you don't need to know that. "You must think he's still alive."

"No. I think he's dead. It's not being sure that keeps him alive."

"What did Baby Suggs think?"   45

"Same, but to listen to her, all her children is dead. Claimed she felt each one go the very day and hour."

"When she say Halle went?"

"Eighteen fifty-five. The day my baby was born."

"You had that baby, didn't you? Never thought you'd make it." He chuckled. "Running off pregnant."

"Had to. Couldn't be no waiting." She lowered her head and   50 thought, as he did, how unlikely it was that she had made it. And if it hadn't been for that girl looking for velvet, she never would have.

"All by yourself too." He was proud of her and annoyed by her. Proud she had done it; annoyed that she had not needed Halle or him in the doing.

"Almost by myself. Not all by myself. A whitegirl helped me."

"Then she helped herself too, God bless her."

"You could stay the night, Paul D."

"You don't sound too steady in the offer."   55

Sethe glanced beyond his shoulder toward the closed door. "Oh it's truly meant. I just hope you'll pardon my house. Come on in. Talk to Denver while I cook you something."

Paul D tied his shoes together, hung them over his shoulder and fol-lowed her through the door straight into a pool of red and undulating light that locked him where he stood.

"You got company?" he whispered, frowning.

"Off and on," said Sethe.

"Good God." He backed out the door onto the porch. "What kind of   60 evil you got in here?"

"It's not evil, just sad. Come on. Just step through."

He looked at her then, closely. Closer than he had when she first rounded the house on wet and shining legs, holding her shoes and stockings up in one hand, her skirts in the other. Halle's girl — the one with iron eyes and backbone to match. He had never seen her hair in Kentucky. And though her face was eighteen years older than when last he saw her, it was softer now. Because of her hair. A face too still for comfort; irises the same color as her skin, which, in that still face, used to make him think of a mask with mercifully punched-out eyes. Halle's woman. Pregnant every year including the year she sat by the fire telling him she was going to run. Her three children she had already packed into a wagonload of others in a caravan of Negroes crossing the river. They were to be left with Halle's mother near Cincinnati. Even in that tiny shack, leaning so close to the fire you could smell the heat in her dress, her eyes did not pick up a flicker of light. They were like two wells into which he had trouble gazing. Even punched out they needed to be covered, lidded, marked with some sign to warn folks of what that emptiness held. So he looked instead at the fire while she told him, because her husband was not there for the telling. Mr. Garner was dead and his wife had a lump in her neck the size of a sweet potato and unable to speak to anyone. She leaned as close to the fire as her pregnant belly allowed and told him, Paul D, the last of the Sweet Home men.

There had been six of them who belonged to the farm, Sethe the only female. Mrs. Garner, crying like a baby, had sold his brother to pay off the debts that surfaced the minute she was widowed. Then school-teacher arrived to put things in order. But what he did broke three more Sweet Home men and punched the glittering iron out of Sethe's eyes, leaving two open wells that did not reflect firelight.

Now the iron was back but the face, softened by hair, made him trust her enough to step inside her door smack into a pool of pulsing red light.

She was right. It was sad. Walking through it, a wave of grief soaked 65
him so thoroughly he wanted to cry. It seemed a long way to the normal light surrounding the table, but he made it — dry-eyed and lucky.

"You said she died soft. Soft as cream," he reminded her.

"That's not Baby Suggs," she said.

"Who then?"

"My daughter. The one I sent ahead with the boys."

"She didn't live?"   70

"No. The one I was carrying when I run away is all I got left. Boys gone too. Both of em walked off just before Baby Suggs died."

Paul D looked at the spot where the grief had soaked him. The red was gone but a kind of weeping clung to the air where it had been.

Probably best, he thought. If a Negro got legs he ought to use them. Sit down too long, somebody will figure out a way to tie them up. Still . . . if her boys were gone . . .

"No man? You here by yourself?"

"Me and Denver," she said.   75

"That all right by you?"

"That's all right by me."

She saw his skepticism and went on. "I cook at a restaurant in town. And I sew a little on the sly."

Paul D smiled then, remembering the bedding dress. Sethe was thirteen when she came to Sweet Home and already iron-eyed. She was a timely present for Mrs. Garner who had lost Baby Suggs to her husband's high principles. The five Sweet Home men looked at the new girl and decided to let her be. They were young and so sick with the absence of women they had taken to calves. Yet they let the iron-eyed girl be, so she could choose in spite of the fact that each one would have beaten the others to mush to have her. It took her a year to choose — a long, tough year of thrashing on pallets eaten up with dreams of her. A year of yearning, when rape seemed the solitary gift of life. The restraint they had exercised possible only because they were Sweet Home men — the ones Mr. Garner bragged about while other farmers shook their heads in warning at the phrase.

"Y'all got boys," he told them. "Young boys, old boys, picky boys,   80 stroppin boys. Now at Sweet Home, my niggers is men every one of em. Bought em thataway, raised em thataway. Men every one."

"Beg to differ, Garner. Ain't no nigger men."

"Not if you scared, they ain't." Garner's smile was wide. "But if you a man yourself, you'll want your niggers to be men too."

"I wouldn't have no nigger men round my wife."

It was the reaction Garner loved and waited for. "Neither would I," he said. "Neither would I," and there was always a pause before the neighbor, or stranger, or peddler, or brother-in-law or whoever it was got the meaning. Then a fierce argument, sometimes a fight, and Garner came home bruised and pleased, having demonstrated one more time what a real Kentuckian was: one tough enough and smart enough to make and call his own niggers men.

And so they were: Paul D Garner, Paul F Garner, Paul A Garner,   85 Halle Suggs and Sixo, the wild man. All in their twenties, minus women, fucking cows, dreaming of rape, thrashing on pallets, rubbing their thighs and waiting for the new girl — the one who took Baby Suggs' place after Halle bought her with five years of Sundays. Maybe that was why she chose him. A twenty-year-old man so in love with his mother he gave up five years of Sabbaths just to see her sit down for a change was a serious recommendation.

She waited a year. And the Sweet Home men abused cows while they waited with her. She chose Halle and for their first bedding she sewed herself a dress on the sly.

"Won't you stay on awhile? Can't nobody catch up on eighteen years in a day."

Out of the dimness of the room in which they sat, a white staircase climbed toward the blue-and-white wallpaper of the second floor. Paul

D could see just the beginning of the paper; discreet flecks of yellow sprinkled among a blizzard of snowdrops all backed by blue. The luminous white of the railing and steps kept him glancing toward it. Every sense he had told him the air above the stairwell was charmed and very thin. But the girl who walked down out of that air was round and brown with the face of an alert doll.

Paul D looked at the girl and then at Sethe who smiled saying, "Here she is my Denver. This is Paul D, honey, from Sweet Home."

"Good morning, Mr. D."   90

"Garner, baby. Paul D Garner."

"Yes sir."

"Glad to get a look at you. Last time I saw your mama, you were pushing out the front of her dress."

"Still is," Sethe smiled, "provided she can get in it."

Denver stood on the bottom step and was suddenly hot and shy. 95 It had been a long time since anybody (good-willed whitewoman, preacher, speaker, or newspaperman) sat at their table, their sympathetic voices called liar by the revulsion in their eyes. For twelve years, long before Grandma Baby died, there had been no visitors of any sort and certainly no friends. No coloredpeople. Certainly no hazelnut man with too long hair and no notebook, no charcoal, no oranges, no questions. Someone her mother wanted to talk to and would even consider talking to while barefoot. Looking, in fact acting, like a girl instead of the quiet, queenly woman Denver had known all her life. The one who never looked away, who when a man got stomped to death by a mare right in front of Sawyer's restaurant did not look away; and when a sow began eating her own litter did not look away then either. And when the baby's spirit picked up Here Boy and slammed him into the wall hard enough to break two of his legs and dislocate his eye, so hard he went into convulsions and chewed up his tongue, still her mother had not looked away. She had taken a hammer, knocked the dog unconscious, wiped away the blood and saliva, pushed his eye back in his head and set his leg bones. He recovered, mute and off-balance, more because of his untrustworthy eye than his bent legs, and winter, summer, drizzle or dry, nothing could persuade him to enter the house again.

Now here was this woman with the presence of mind to repair a dog gone savage with pain rocking her crossed ankles and looking away from her own daughter's body. As though the size of it was more than vision could bear. And neither she nor he had on shoes. Hot, shy, now Denver was lonely. All that leaving: first her brothers, then her grandmother — serious losses since there were no children willing to circle her in a game or hang by their knees from her porch railing. None of that had mattered as long as her mother did not look away as she was doing now, making Denver long, downright *long*, for a sign of spite from the baby ghost.

"She's a fine-looking young lady," said Paul D. "Fine-looking. Got her daddy's sweet face."

"You know my father?"

"Knew him. Knew him well."

"Did he, Ma'am?" Denver fought an urge to realign her affection.   100

"Of course he knew your daddy. I told you, he's from Sweet Home."

Denver sat down on the bottom step. There was nowhere else gracefully to go. They were a twosome, saying "Your daddy" and "Sweet Home" in a way that made it clear both belonged to them and not to her. That her own father's absence was not hers. Once the absence had belonged to Grandma Baby — a son, deeply mourned because he was the one who had bought her out of there. Then it was her mother's absent husband. Now it was this hazelnut stranger's absent friend. Only those who knew him ("knew him well") could claim his absence for themselves. Just as only those who lived in Sweet Home could remember it, whisper it and glance sideways at one another while they did. Again she wished for the baby ghost   its anger thrilling her now where it used to wear her out. Wear her out.

"We have a ghost in here," she said, and it worked. They were not a twosome anymore. Her mother left off swinging her feet and being girlish. Memory of Sweet Home dropped away from the eyes of the man she was being girlish for. He looked quickly up the lightning-white stairs behind her.

"So I hear," he said. "But sad, your mama said. Not evil."

"No sir," said Denver, "not evil. But not sad either."   105

"What then?"

"Rebuked. Lonely and rebuked."

"Is that right?" Paul D turned to Sethe.

"I don't know about lonely," said Denver's mother. "Mad, maybe, but I don't see how it could be lonely spending every minute with us like it does."

"Must be something you got it wants."   110

Sethe shrugged. "It's just a baby."

"My sister," said Denver. "She died in this house."

Paul D scratched the hair under his jaw. "Reminds me of that headless bride back behind Sweet Home. Remember that, Sethe? Used to roam them woods regular."

"How could I forget? Worrisome . . ."

"How come everybody run off from Sweet Home can't stop talking 115
about it? Look like if it was so sweet you would have stayed."

"Girl, who you talking to?"

Paul D laughed. "True, true. She's right, Sethe. It wasn't sweet and it
sure wasn't home." He shook his head.

"But it's where we were," said Sethe. "All together. Comes back
whether we want it to or not." She shivered a little. A light ripple of skin
on her arm, which she caressed back into sleep. "Denver," she said,
"start up that stove. Can't have a friend stop by and don't feed him."

"Don't go to any trouble on my account," Paul D said.

"Bread ain't trouble. The rest I brought back from where I work. 120
Least I can do, cooking from dawn to noon, is bring dinner home. You
got any objections to pike?"

"If he don't object to me I don't object to him."

At it again, thought Denver. Her back to them, she jostled the
kindlin and almost lost the fire. "Why don't you spend the night, Mr.
Garner? You and Ma'am can talk about Sweet Home all night long."

Sethe took two swift steps to the stove, but before she could yank
Denver's collar, the girl leaned forward and began to cry.

"What is the matter with you? I never knew you to behave this way."

"Leave her be," said Paul D. "I'm a stranger to her."   125

"That's just it. She got no cause to act up with a stranger. Oh baby,
what is it? Did something happen?"

But Denver was shaking now and sobbing so she could not speak.
The tears she had not shed for nine years wetting her far too womanly
breasts.

"I can't no more. I can't no more."

"Can't what? What can't you?"

"I can't live here. I don't know where to go or what to do, but I can't 130
live here. Nobody speaks to us. Nobody comes by. Boys don't like me.
Girls don't either."

"Honey, honey."

"What's she talking 'bout nobody speaks to you?" asked Paul D.

"It's the house. People don't — "

"It's not! It's not the house. It's us! And it's you!"

"Denver!"   135

"Leave off, Sethe. It's hard for a young girl living in a haunted house.
That can't be easy."

"It's easier than some other things."

"Think, Sethe. I'm a grown man with nothing new left to see or do
and I'm telling you it ain't easy. Maybe you all ought to move. Who
owns this house?"

Over Denver's shoulder Sethe shot Paul D a look of snow. "What you care?"

"They won't let you leave?"   140

"No."

"Sethe."

"No moving. No leaving. It's all right the way it is."

"You going to tell me it's all right with this child half out of her mind?"

Something in the house braced, and in the listening quiet that fol-   145
lowed Sethe spoke.

"I got a tree on my back and a haint in my house, and nothing in between but the daughter I am holding in my arms. No more running —
from nothing. I will never run from another thing on this earth. I took
one journey and I paid for the ticket, but let me tell you something,
Paul D Garner: it cost too much! Do you hear me? It cost too much.
Now sit down and eat with us or leave us be."

Paul D fished in his vest for a little pouch of tobacco — concentrat-
ing on its contents and the knot of its string while Sethe led Denver into
the keeping room that opened off the large room he was sitting in. He
had no smoking papers, so he fiddled with the pouch and listened
through the open door to Sethe quieting her daughter. When she came
back she avoided his look and went straight to a small table next to the
stove. Her back was to him and he could see all the hair he wanted
without the distraction of her face.

"What tree on your back?"

"Huh." Sethe put a bowl on the table and reached under it for flour.

"What tree on your back? Is something growing on your back? I   150
don't see nothing growing on your back."

"It's there all the same."

"Who told you that?"

"Whitegirl. That's what she called it. I've never seen it and never
will. But that's what she said it looked like. A chokecherry tree. Trunk,
branches, and even leaves. Tiny little chokecherry leaves. But that was
eighteen years ago. Could have cherries now for all I know."

Sethe took a little spit from the tip of her tongue with her forefinger.
Quickly, lightly she touched the stove. Then she trailed her fingers
through the flour, parting, separating small hills and ridges of it, looking
for mites. Finding none, she poured soda and salt into the crease of her
folded hand and tossed both into the flour. Then she reached into a can
and scooped half a handful of lard. Deftly she squeezed the flour
through it, then with her left hand sprinkling water, she formed the
dough.

"I had milk," she said. "I was pregnant with Denver but I had milk 155 for my baby girl. I hadn't stopped nursing her when I sent her on ahead with Howard and Buglar."

Now she rolled the dough out with a wooden pin. "Anybody could smell me long before he saw me. And when he saw me he'd see the drops of it on the front of my dress. Nothing I could do about that. All I knew was I had to get my milk to my baby girl. Nobody was going to nurse her like me. Nobody was going to get it to her fast enough, or take it away when she had enough and didn't know it. Nobody knew that she couldn't pass her air if you held her up on your shoulder, only if she was lying on my knees. Nobody knew that but me and nobody had her milk but me. I told that to the women in the wagon. Told them to put sugar water in cloth to suck from so when I got there in a few days she wouldn't have forgot me. The milk would be there and I would be there with it."

"Men don't know nothing much," said Paul D, tucking his pouch back into his vest pocket, "but they do know a suckling can't be away from its mother for long."

"Then they know what it's like to send your children off when your breasts are full."

"We was talking 'bout a tree, Sethe."

"After I left you, those boys came in and took my milk. That's what 160 they came in there for. Held me down and took it. I told Mrs. Garner on em. She had that lump and couldn't speak but her eyes rolled out tears. Them boys found out I told on em. Schoolteacher made one open up my back, and when it closed it made a tree. It grows there still."

"They used cowhide on you?"

"And they took my milk."

"They beat you and you was pregnant?"

"And they took my milk!"

The fat white circles of dough lined the pan in rows. Once more 165 Sethe touched a wet forefinger to the stove. She opened the oven door and slid the pan of biscuits in. As she raised up from the heat she felt Paul D behind her and his hands under her breasts. She straightened up and knew, but could not feel, that his cheek was pressing into the branches of her chokecherry tree.

Not even trying, he had become the kind of man who could walk into a house and make the women cry. Because with him, in his presence, they could. There was something blessed in his manner. Women saw him and wanted to weep — to tell him that their chest hurt and their knees did too. Strong women and wise saw him and told him things they only told each other: that way past the Change of Life, desire in them had suddenly become enormous, greedy, more savage than when they were fifteen, and that it embarrassed them and made them sad; that secretly they longed to die — to be quit of it — that sleep was more precious to them than any waking day. Young girls sidled up to him to confess or describe how well-dressed the visitations were that had followed them straight from their dreams. Therefore, although he did not understand why this was so, he was not surprised when Denver dripped tears into the stovefire. Nor, fifteen minutes later, after telling him about her stolen milk, her mother wept as well. Behind her, bending down, his body an arc of kindness, he held her breasts in the palms of his hands. He rubbed his cheek on her back and learned that way her sorrow, the roots of it; its wide trunk and intricate branches. Raising his fingers to the hooks of her dress, he knew without seeing them or hearing any sigh that the tears were coming fast. And when the top of her dress was around her hips and he saw the sculpture her back had become, like the decorative work of an ironsmith too passionate for display, he could think but not say, "Aw, Lord, girl." And he would tolerate no peace until he had touched every ridge and leaf of it with his mouth, none of which Sethe could feel because her back skin had been dead for years. What she knew was that the responsibility for her breasts, at last, was in somebody else's hands.

Would there be a little space, she wondered, a little time, some way to hold off eventfulness, to push busyness into the corners of the room and just stand there a minute or two, naked from shoulder blade to waist, relieved of the weight of her breasts, smelling the stolen milk again and the pleasure of baking bread? Maybe this one time she could stop dead still in the middle of a cooking meal — not even leave the stove — and feel the hurt her back ought to. Trust things and remember things because the last of the Sweet Home men was there to catch her if she sank?

The stove didn't shudder as it adjusted to its heat. Denver wasn't stirring in the next room. The pulse of red light hadn't come on and Paul D had not trembled since 1856 and then for eighty-three days in a row. Locked up and chained down, his hands shook so bad he couldn't smoke or even scratch properly. Now he was trembling again but in the legs this time. It took him a while to realize that his legs were not shaking because of worry, but because the floorboards were and the grinding, shoving floor was only part of it. The house itself was pitching. Sethe slid to the floor and struggled to get back into her dress. While down on all fours, as though she were holding her house down on the ground, Denver burst from the keeping room, terror in her eyes, a vague smile on her lips.

"God damn it! Hush up!" Paul D was shouting, falling, reaching for anchor. "Leave the place alone! Get the hell out!" A table rushed toward him and he grabbed its leg. Somehow he managed to stand at an angle and, holding the table by two legs, he bashed it about, wrecking everything, screaming back at the screaming house. "You want to fight, come on! God damn it! She got enough without you. She got enough!"

The quaking slowed to an occasional lurch, but Paul D did not stop   170 whipping the table around until everything was rock quiet. Sweating and breathing hard, he leaned against the wall in the space the sideboard left. Sethe was still crouched next to the stove, clutching her salvaged shoes to her chest. The three of them, Sethe, Denver, and Paul D, breathed to the same beat, like one tired person. Another breathing was just as tired.

It was gone. Denver wandered through the silence to the stove. She ashed over the fire and pulled the pan of biscuits from the oven. The jelly cupboard was on its back, its contents lying in a heap in the corner of the bottom shelf. She took out a jar, and, looking around for a plate, found half of one by the door. These things she carried out to the porch steps, where she sat down.

The two of them had gone up there. Stepping lightly, easy-footed, they had climbed the white stairs, leaving her down below. She pried the wire from the top of the jar and then the lid. Under it was cloth and under that a thin cake of wax. She removed it all and coaxed the jelly onto one half of the half a plate. She took a biscuit and pulled off its black top. Smoke curled from the soft white insides.

She missed her brothers. Buglar and Howard would be twenty-two and twenty-three now. Although they had been polite to her during the quiet time and gave her the whole top of the bed, she remembered how it was before: the pleasure they had sitting clustered on the white stairs — she between the knees of Howard or Buglar — while they made up die-witch! stories with proven ways of killing her dead. And Baby Suggs telling her things in the keeping room. She smelled like bark in the day and leaves at night, and Denver would not sleep in her old room after her brothers ran away.

Now her mother was upstairs with the man who had gotten rid of the only other company she had. Denver dipped a bit of bread into the jelly. Slowly, methodically, miserably she ate it.

EXPLORATIONS

1. In this opening chapter to her novel *Beloved,* much of Toni Morrison's exposition is indirect. Who are the three living characters in the present, and how are they related to each other? Who is Halle, and how is he related to each of them?

2. "Now at Sweet Home, my niggers is men every one of em," Mr. Garner brags. "Bought em thataway, raised em thataway" (para. 80). How are these statements contradictory? What is the impact of that contradiction on the men he refers to?

3. How would the opening to this story change if Morrison used the word "haunted" instead of "spiteful" in her first sentence? What point is she making about the ghost's significance? How does the choice of "spiteful" rather than "haunted" relate to Denver's later statements, "It's not the house. It's us! And it's you!" (para. 134)?

CONNECTIONS

1. In "Fairy Tale of the Natchez Trace" (p. 447), Eudora Welty points out that the word "innocent" early in her novel *The Robber Bridegroom* "shines like a cautionary blinker to what lies on the road ahead" (para. 6). What cautionary blinker appears in the second sentence of *Beloved?* Why does it stand out as unusual? What horror does it warn us about?

2. Like Joseph Bruchac's "Digging into Your Heart" (p. 439), *Beloved* contains different messages for different audiences. What do you think are Morrison's intended audiences, and what messages are they likely to draw from this chapter? What specific aspects of *Beloved* seem meant to appeal to each audience?

3. "When the Antelope people think of themselves," writes Leslie Marmon Silko, "it is as people who are of *this* story, and this is *our* place, and we fit into the very beginning when the people first came . . ." (p. 415). In what ways do these ideas apply to Morrison's story?

ELABORATIONS

1. In "Fairy Tale of the Natchez Trace," Welty describes mixing local history with other historical facts and legends to create *The Robber Bridegroom.* With Welty's essay as a model, write a short literary analysis of this chapter from *Beloved* showing how Toni Morrison has used a similar strategy to combine her own set of ingredients into a different kind of story.

2. Choose some aspect of Morrison's opening chapter that interests you — for instance, the impact of slavery in the United States, how plantations operated in Kentucky, the history of Cincinnati, the pros and cons of living in an extended family, the effects of a baby's death on a family, or the role of ghost stories in American folklore. Find out more about it and write an expository essay based on your discoveries.

BARRY BEARAK

Caste Hate, and Murder, Outlast Indian Reforms

Barry Bearak became a co-bureau chief for the *New York Times* New Delhi bureau in India in August 1998. "Caste Hate, and Murder, Outlast Indian Reforms" appeared in the *Times* a month later. Bearak joined the *Times* as a reporter on its metropolitan desk in March 1997 after working as a roving national correspondent for the *Los Angeles Times* since 1982. His 1995 *L.A. Times* series "The Waning Power of Workers," about the United Auto Workers strike against Caterpillar Inc., won him the James Aronson Award for Social Justice Journalism. From 1976 to 1982, he was a general assignment reporter for the *Miami Herald*. Born in Chicago in 1949, Bearak graduated from Knox College in Galesburg, Illinois, with a degree in political science. He received his M.S. degree in journalism from the University of Illinois in 1974. He is married to Celia Dugger, who is a co-bureau chief for New Delhi; they have two children.

MEERUT, India — When Srichand, among the least touchable of untouchables, was killed on September 2, he was doing the humiliating work of his subcaste, the balmikis, going from house to house with a broom, a scoop, and a bowl, carrying away the "night soil" from the dry toilets in people's houses.

Srichand had been chosen for death by a gang of jatavs, another untouchable subcaste that is a few notches above the balmikis in India's ancient pecking order. Days before, a balmiki boy had left the city with a jatav girl, a departure that the balmikis took to be teenage love and the jatavs considered a spiteful kidnapping.

While the spark for this strife was a disputed romance, the kindling lay in the caste-based tensions of India, where a half century of well-intended efforts to erase the lines of prejudice have in some ways made caste more important than ever.

The constitution of 1950 nominally abolished the notion of untouchability. At the same time, it expanded a system of "reservations," first applied in India by the British, that guarantees untouchables 15 percent of all seats in Parliament. This reservation system, which came to include state elected offices and government jobs, shook the rigid scaffolding of caste hierarchy. Untouchables, now more commonly called *dalits* or the scheduled castes, increasingly resented being shunned. They demanded their rights and, numbering 150 million — more than a sixth of India's population — became voters that political parties could not ignore.

Untouchables, however, are not a unified multitude. Divided and   5 subdivided into hundreds of social stations, some have accrued the spoils that come with political horsetrading — such as jobs and better schools. And some have not. Here in Meerut, a city of 1.5 million in the northern state of Uttar Pradesh, the more-numerous jatavs — descendants of cobblers — have begun to develop political muscle and advance economically. Left behind are the balmikis, who have grown ever more resentful and now look for their own political alliances.

"Up until now, the jatavs have gotten most of the reserved seats, and this must change," said Prem Nath Dhingra, a balmiki activist. "We demand 50 percent, and there are political parties encouraging us. It threatens the jatavs that we raise our voices."

Bhagwat Pura is a neighborhood of narrow alleyways where the noise of smoke-belching trucks gives way to the squeal of handcarts. Amid the cement hovels, some jatavs still live side by side with balmikis, and it was from here on August 27 that the boy disappeared with the girl. Rumors quickly began to stoke animosity, and taunting from both sides overheated into stoning and looting. Even after the police found the girl unharmed in a nearby town five days later, the trouble went on.

On September 2, forty-five-year-old Srichand — who used but that single name — began his work day at 4 A.M., going off to his city job, sweeping excrement into sewers. It paid him $71 a month. He had two sons and four daughters. For them, he wanted education, and they all remain in no-tuition state schools. On the morning he died, his eldest daughter, Seema, who has completed college, warned him not to go into the tense streets. "My father told me, 'We work daily so that we make money daily so that we eat daily,'" she recalled.

Around 10 A.M., he came home to join his wife, Uma. Side by side, they made the rounds each day to forty houses, collecting night soil. This earned them another $14 a month.

They had just come from a Muslim house when the jatavs leaped   10 from hiding. "First, they started beating him and then they dragged him into an alley," she said. "My husband told me, 'They'll kill you, so run.' And I ran."

She stopped when she heard gun shots. Hurrying back, she found her husband bleeding from wounds made by bullets and a knife. "I saw no more," she said. "I fainted."

Legends of Inequality Rooted in Scriptures

Indian civilization, so rich with wonderment and greatness, has been marred by the proposition that all men are created unequal. Ancient Hindu scriptures tell of how the gods created the world and the social order within it by sacrificing a primeval man, Purusha. From his face came the priestly elite Brahmans, his arms the warrior Kshatriya, his thighs the merchant Vaishyas, his feet the servile, hapless Shudras. Beneath them all were those whom nature had ordained to be unclean — people destined to do filthy work. The jatavs are an offshoot of such pariahs, a subcaste scorned because of their traditional work as cobblers, which requires the handling of dead flesh. Names for subcastes have varied, and sometimes the hierarchical order has differed as well, but the result has always been the same, a ranking of human worth.

In modern India, caste has not disappeared, only changed. "The ritual side of caste — the eating separately, the maintaining of ritual distances, may have broken down — but the politics of caste has become extremely important," said Andre Beteille, a sociologist at the Delhi School of Economics. "Different castes unite into coalitions, and the coalitions are always shifting."

Most untouchables are now agricultural laborers, no longer doing the polluted work associated with their kind. In the minds of many others, however, that change means nothing. The stigma is indelible, coursing from one generation to the next. The most vilified remain the balmikis. There are roughly 4 million of them, and 500,000 still carry night soil, according to Bind eshwar Pathak, a Brahman who has won international honors for trying to free balmikis from inherited shame.

That effort at liberation is complicated not only by age-old biases, 15 but also by India's immense poverty. Some 700 million people, primarily villagers, still defecate outside, Pathak said. Among the urban poor, dry latrines continue to be common. "We do the work a mother does for her children, but we are not looked upon as mothers but as scum," said Suresh Richpal, a balmiki. "Our children go to school, but teachers have it in mind: He is the son of a scavenger. He is worthless."

Richpal was Srichand's cousin. "Why is he dead?" he asked. "The jatavs wanted to teach the balmikis a lesson."

Assumptions about Age: Consent or Abduction?

The boy goes by the single name Amit, and by all accounts he is nineteen. The girl is Renu Rani and she is variously said to be twenty, nineteen, seventeen, or fifteen. Whether he eloped with her or abducted her is hard to know for sure. Amit is in jail and Renu Rami is in Punjab, 200 miles away, secreted with relatives. But while the truth is elusive, looking for it provided a lesson in the combustible mix of caste prejudice and murderous assumptions.

Amit's house in Bhagwat Pura was empty, but friends of the family quickly gathered at the sight of strangers. They spoke of a love affair. "Both families knew of their feelings, and at times the girl was beaten by her parents, but the girl said, 'No, no, no, I will go away with this boy, I love this boy,'" said Ravi Mehrol, nineteen, one of Amit's friends. Amit's uncle lives near Renu, he said, and Amit had met her at the uncle's house a year ago. Neither were minors. He is nineteen years and three months old. She is nineteen years and six months.

This version, with small variations, is what most balmikis believe. Srichand's grieving family repeated much of it as they sat in a park near the city commissioner's office, where they had come to demand justice and were awaiting an audience. "The girl made a statement at the police station," said Srichand's daughter Seemar. "She said, 'It is not that the boy ran away with me, but that I ran away with the boy.'"

Because of skirmishes in the streets, Srichand was denied a funeral 20 procession, his body taken directly from a hospital to the funeral pyre. The injustice of it angered Seema. "Our troubles with the jatavs are all caused by a misunderstanding," she said. "And for this my father has died."

A Money Dispute Takes On Old Biases, Then Violence

Renu Rani's home is behind her parents' tiny grocery. Her mother said the family has lived there for twenty years, though, some months back, they decided to move, to get away from the balmikis, and that is where the roots of the conflict begin. A balmiki family had given them a down payment for their house and store, but then had failed to pay the balance. Renu's family believed it was their right to keep the initial money — and that infuriated the balmikis.

"I took my daughter to the Friday market, and four balmiki boys snatched her away," said Prem Wati, forty-five. "They had their faces covered and put a gun to her head. They shouted that the same would happen to other jatav girls, so our community is very upset." One of those boys was indeed Amit, Mrs. Wati said, but there had never been any romance going on. Her daughter was only fifteen. Someone ran off to retrieve a two-year-old photograph. "This is Renu," said her brother Amar, pointing to a rather mature-looking girl.

This conversation, occurring in an open courtyard, had drawn a small crowd. People egged on Mrs. Wati when she declared, "Balmikis are beneath us, and we cannot tolerate it when they run off with our girls." A woman beside her added: "Balmikis clear away the excrement. We are not going to do this job."

But hadn't the jatavs themselves long suffered from caste degradation — and didn't they want it to die away?

An older man standing near the open window of the grocery answered earnestly: "Discrimination against us may end. But discrimination against the balmiki is right and it must go on."   25

Sitting at an old wooden desk in a well-pressed uniform, Police Superintendent Dhom Singh Tomar said the investigation had gone well. Six of the seven jatav men who had killed Srichand were in custody and had confessed. As for Amit, he was being charged with kidnapping and statutory rape.

"The official statement of the girl is that she was lured away," the superintendent said. "As for anything she said to us unofficially, that is no longer important."

A physician had examined the girl. While he had found her to be "a sexually active female," Tomar reported, it was also the doctor's opinion that she was only fifteen or sixteen. "So she is a minor, and the matter of her consent is irrelevant," he said, ready now to put things to rest. Srichand's murder had not been a terribly urgent matter, but the disturbances in the streets had required police manpower and he wanted it stopped. "You must understand that these people are illiterate and poor, and for them talk is cheap," the superintendent said.

By birth, Tomar is a jat, a peasant subcaste that ranks far above the jatavs and balmikis, for whom he has little patience. "These people drink through the night," he said disdainfully. "Generally, you cannot expect them to behave in a civilized way."

EXPLORATIONS

1. Who killed Srichand and why? What idea did his murderers have about him that most Westerners would regard as based on mythology rather than fact?

2. According to Barry Bearak, what is the origin of the Indian caste system? What factors have weakened it over time? What factors have kept it going?

3. What story do Amit's family and friends tell to explain his involvement with Renu? What story do Renu's family and friends tell to explain her involvement with Amit? Why are the two stories so different?

CONNECTIONS

1. Where in Toni Morrison's excerpt from *Beloved* (p. 460) do we see parallels with the caste hatred Bearak reports in Meerut, India? What beliefs in each case lead to what tragic results?

2. Ursula LeGuin (p. 419) presents a "reductive, scientistic" definition of myth as "an attempt to explain, in rational terms, facts not yet rationally understood" (para. 3). In what sense does this definition apply to the Indian caste system? When that system began, what facts not yet rationally understood did it attempt to explain? What explanation did it offer? What alternative explanation do contemporary rationalists propose instead?

3. Jan Goodwin writes: "It is ironic that the most outstanding contradiction regarding the inequities suffered by Muslim women is that Mohammad, the founder of Islam, was among the world's greatest reformers on behalf of women" ("Muslims, the First Feminists," p. 371, para. 3). What ironic contradiction does Bearak's essay show among Hindus, whose religion asserts that all life is sacred?

ELABORATIONS

1. In the half century since India became independent from Great Britain, Bearak writes, "efforts to erase the lines of prejudice have in some ways made caste more important than ever" (para. 3). Reread the Observation by Bharati Mukherjee on page 3 and the headnote on India on page 86. In what sense is Bearak's statement true of the decades when Britons ran India as well as the decades since independence? Do some additional research; choose an aspect of India, British rule, and the caste system that interests you; and write a cause-and-effect or argumentative essay on the impact of prejudice, tradition, and power discrepancies between groups.

2. Barry Bearak is a journalist from the United States reporting on caste hate and murder in India. What might a journalist from India have to say about hate and violence in the United States? Take an incident from either Morrison's excerpt from *Beloved* or contemporary U.S. news reports. Using Bearak's essay as a model, write about that incident as a non-American journalist might interpret it.

NIKOS KAZANTZAKIS

The Gentleman

A novelist, poet, essayist, playwright, travel writer, and translator, Nikos Kazantzakis is best known in the United States for his novel *Zorba the Greek* (1952; *Bios kai politeia tou Alexi Zorba,* 1946), which also became a motion picture (1964) and Broadway musical (1968). Kazantzakis was born into a peasant farming family on the island of Crete in 1883. In 1897 the Cretans revolted against Turkish rule, and the family fled to the Greek island of Naxos. At a monastery there Kazantzakis studied languages and Western philosophy, as well as the Christian preoccupation with the mystery of existence. In 1906 he earned a law degree from the University of Athens, published his first novella, and moved to France. He continued to travel, write, and study; later he also worked for the Greek government. Kazantzakis wrote in the spoken (demotic) form of Greek rather than the customary literary form. He was nearly excommunicated from the Greek Orthodox Church for portraying it unfavorably in his novel *The Greek Passion* (*Ho Christos xanastavronetai,* 1954). A series of controversial novels culminated in *The Last Temptation of Christ* (1960; *Ho teleftaios peirasmos,* 1955; motion picture, 1988). When Kazantzakis died from leukemia in Germany in 1957, the Church refused him a burial Mass in Greece, so he was buried where he was born, in Iraklion, Crete. "The Gentleman" comes from his book *England,* published in 1965.

Iraklion is named for the hero Hercules. In the web of Greek history and mythology, his twelve labors included mastering a Cretan bull terrorizing the court of King Minos. Minos's palace — built around 1600 B.C. — also housed the labyrinth devised by Daedalus and Icarus to hide the monstrous Minotaur. Excavated in this century, it contained lavish frescoes, pottery, jewelry, the earliest form of written Greek, and indoor plumbing. The Athenian prince Theseus overthrew Minos, winning Crete for his father, King Aegeus (namesake of the Aegean Sea). Over the next thousand years Athens became a hub of Mediterranean civilization, the birthplace of democracy, theater, and Western philosophy. Rome conquered Greece between 150 and 100 B.C. In the mid-1400s the Turks took over; and in 1827 Greece won independence. George I became king in 1863 and reigned for fifty-seven years, during which Crete and other Aegean islands shifted from Turkish back to Greek control. The monarchy was replaced by a republic in 1923, followed by a series of military dictatorships, another brief monarchy, a briefer republic, and finally, in 1967, a civilian government. In 1981 Greece joined the European Union.

The Indian hero Yudhistra fought and conquered all men. And when he died, he went to heaven. All his friends had abandoned him. There was only one companion still faithful to him: his dog — faithful even unto death.

The gates of heaven opened, and God came out. "Enter, Yudhistra," He bade him. "Here is your home."

"I will not enter without my dog!" Yudhistra exclaimed.

"Dogs are not allowed to enter heaven!" God answered, knitting his eyebrows.

"Then I'll go away!" said Yudhistra, and he turned his back on   5
heaven.

This Yudhistra might have been a Japanese samurai or an English gentleman. Heroism and tenderness, a perfectly polite demonstration of force. "The good warrior," the old samurai used to say, "can never be crude." Faith, gallantry, kindness. Never to betray a friend, be it only a dog — even in order to enter the eternal kingdom!

The ancient Greeks had created their own human prototype: the *kalos kagathos*. A harmony of body and soul. "A coordinated training of all the senses." The perfect human being is neither the great but withered wise man, nor the inhuman ascetic, nor the disfigured athlete. Balance — here lies the Greek secret of perfection.

The Romans created the proud *civis Romanus* — order, discipline, coarsely integrated power, bereft of flexibility and grace. Responsibility — the intrepid Roman citizen felt the entire Empire resting on his own shoulders!

The Italian Renaissance created the flexible, delightful, charming sinner, *Il cortegiano*, free of any strict morals. Life was a short-lived feast where the unknown host had laid rich banquets for us, bidding us to eat and drink, and setting us next to fair ladies and telling us: "Kiss them! Only eat and kiss with grace and nobility, like aristocrats!"

Spain created the fierce *hidalgo*, who saw the honor of the whole vis-   10
ible and invisible world dangling on the tip of his own sword. Life was no feast. For the men it was a military encampment and for the women a nunnery. God, King, Honor — the three great values; but above all honor.

France created the *honnête homme*, exuding social finesse and grace. Life was a compromise and a coexistence. Social conscience must set the pace for individual conscience. Virtues and vices must be measured so as not to annoy anyone. And indeed, if possible, they must be agreeable for human intercourse. Man was a social animal, decked out in wigs and laces.

And England created the Gentleman.

The ingredients of the gentleman changed according to each epoch. If we follow the various meanings of the gentleman from the fourteenth century on, we can see, as in a small faithful mirror, the characteristic ideal of the developed English mentality.

In the Middle Ages the gentleman was the noble knight with his coat of arms and his sword. His sword was double-edged, for he was duty-bound to strike the rich man who tormented and wronged the poor man as well as the strong man who oppressed the weak man. The gentleman was in the service of a militant God. He went to the Crusades as hero and saint.

In England, however, the gentleman never attained the ecstatic whim- 15 sicality of a Don Quixote. Here the gentleman was a rational person, practical, bereft of great imagination. His manners were simple and his attire modest. He saw human beings clearly as human beings and windmills as windmills. He never confused cloud and stone, desire and reality. He was hero and saint — but in the current human proportions.

In time, the military facets of the gentleman atrophied and his everyday social virtues multiplied. He had begun to crystallize and survive in English society as a rich, peace-loving bourgeois, no longer as a feudal warrior. It was no longer indispensable for a nobleman to have a coat of arms and a sword in order to be called a gentleman. Good manners sufficed, as well as self-respect and respect for other people and the refusal to stoop to falsehood or any base act.

Old-fashioned chivalry blended with the new humanism. There was a slight translation of values, and with them the human model changed. But as always happens with English institutions, the new reality did not absolutely reject tradition, and the new gentleman preserved many of his old characteristics: his faithfulness and devotion to his ruler, the King; his profound way of life based on personal honor; respect for women; a fine but simple manner of dressing; and the determined cultivation and care of his own body.

Henceforth, nobleman and gentleman were no longer synonymous. You might be a prince, yet not be a gentleman. The former was a chance circumstance, a gift that came by birth. The latter was a personal feat, your own triumph alone. Once a mother begged King James II to make her worthless son a gentleman, and the King answered: "I could make your son a baron or a marquess, but not even Almighty God could make him a gentleman."

From the middle of the sixteenth century on, the word "gentleman" had already begun to mirror the new social ideals. A scribbler of the period made bold to remark: "The unworthy son of a prince is no gentleman. The worthy son of a peasant is a gentleman."

But the wheel kept rolling. Time passed. The ideal human type   20
changed. Puritanism descended on England. Now the indispensable
ingredients of the gentleman became dour honesty, ascetic morality, a
frowning manner, hair shaven to the roots, dark, somber clothes, a
Bible in the pocket. "Merry England" became sulky, and the gentleman with her.

Once again, time passed, and the appearance of the land changed
with it. The Stuarts reascended the throne. The face of England grew
lighter and more pleasant. Once again the English people could let
their virtues smile. Once more, they treated the body lovingly, bathed
and dressed it in brightly colored clothes and plumes and ruffles and
laces. Discreetly, without creating any scandal, they allowed their bodies to enjoy large or small transgressions of morality.

In the nineteenth century, during the austere Victorian era, the
meaning of "gentleman" assumed the stable form it still has to this very
day. The ideal was constantly becoming more democratic, without losing its aristocratic essence. Now the gentleman became the person who
harmoniously cultivated his own personal and social idiosyncrasies,
who controlled his passions, who never spoke about himself or slan-
dered others — the master of his own nerves, the "captain of his own
soul."

He kept all the virtues of the preceding types of gentleman, but with
more flexibility and discretion. He promised less than he had decided
to do. He never flaunted his passions in any obvious way and had perfect control over them, both the good ones and the bad ones. To a high
degree, he possessed that great English virtue, self-control.

In his everyday life he was cordial and hospitable, but never familiar.
And he spent his money as generously and regally as he could, because
avarice (and even economy) were characteristics he thought unworthy
of the gentleman.

> Whoever is well born or by nature inclining to the good,
> Even if his mother be an Ethiopian, is a noble man!

Here the word "noble," as Menander used it, is translated in English as
"gentleman."

"How can we define the gentleman?" I once asked one of the most   25
perfect gentlemen of contemporary England, Sir Sidney Waterloo.

"The gentleman," he answered me, "is he who feels himself at ease
in the presence of everyone and everything, and who makes everyone
and everything else feel at ease in his presence."

A correct definition, but how could it possibly include the whole indescribable atmosphere — the invisible, quivering tilting of the scale between ego-worship and nobility, between sensitivity and psychological control, between passion and discipline — out of which the gentleman is molded?

We catch an inkling of him from uncalculated, apparently insignificant details: a movement of the hand, a tone of voice, a kind of gait, a style of dressing, eating, amusement; . . . the cold invincible intensity with which he loves the countryside, sports, women, horses, the *Times*.

In a Latin schoolbook from the tenth century, we read the following dialogue:

> "Did they whip you today?"
> "No, for I behaved well."
> "Whom of your schoolmates did they whip?"
> "Why do you ask? I can't betray them!"

This little English boy of the tenth century was a gentleman!   30

EXPLORATIONS

1. What are the different techniques Nikos Kazantzakis uses to define a gentleman? At what point does he state a definition? What are the effects of his taking such a roundabout approach?

2. Do you think Kazantzakis approves of the gentleman? Why or why not? On what specific evidence do you base your answer?

3. What is the impact of Kazantzakis's starting "The Gentleman" with a story about a mythical hero? How would your reaction to his essay change if his opening story were about a real person instead? If his first examples were English instead of Indian and Japanese?

CONNECTIONS

1. What characteristic of "gentlemanhood" both begins and ends Kazantzakis's essay? What does that suggest about the significance of this characteristic in defining a gentleman? What role does this characteristic play in the caste system as Barry Bearak describes it in "Caste Hate, and Murder, Outlast Indian Reform" (p. 477)?

2. What qualities do the English gentleman and his non-English counterparts share with the legendary American Indian heroes in Joseph Bruchac's "Digging into Your Heart" (p. 439)? Which national archetypes in

Kazantzakis's essay most closely resemble the tribal archetypes in Bruchac's?

3. What qualities do the gentleman and his counterparts share with Superman, as Gary Engle depicts him in "What Makes Superman So Darned American?" (p. 428)? Why would Superman be, or not be, a good example of the American version of the gentleman?

ELABORATIONS

1. What socioeconomic position was held by the various nationalities of gentleman Kazantzakis describes (paras. 1–12)? What benefits, and what costs, did these men impose on their societies? What were their responsibilities? Their privileges? What social, economic, military, or other advantages and disadvantages does a culture stand to gain from encouraging its male members to strive to be gentlemen (or its female members to be ladies)? Using "The Gentleman," other selections in this book, and any other resources you wish, write an essay analyzing the impact of a society's creating such an ideal class.

2. If you were going to add a paragraph to "The Gentleman" about America's contribution, whom would it feature and why? The cowboy? The private eye? The Hollywood actor? The high-tech enterpreneur? The Jedi knight? Write a short essay defining the American version, or versions over time, of the gentleman.

CHINUA ACHEBE

The Writer and His Community

One of the foremost contemporary African writers, Albert Chinualu-
mogu Achebe was born in the Igbo (or Ibo) village of Ogidi, Nigeria, in
1930. His father was a teacher for the Church Missionary Society who
screened the family from the tribal beliefs and festivities around them.
Achebe attended a government-run secondary school modeled on those
in England, where the Igbo storytelling tradition interwove with Dickens,
Swift, and Shakespeare. After studying at University College in Ibadan,
he graduated from London University in 1953. He vowed to become a
writer, shortened his name, and published several stories before going to
work for the Nigerian Broadcasting Company as a producer and later as a
director. In 1959 Achebe's first novel appeared: *Things Fall Apart*, which
has sold more than 2 million copies in forty-five languages. The book depicts an Igbo village in the late 1880s, just before Nigeria became a
British colony. His next novel, *No Longer at Ease*, examines the clash between an Igbo upbringing and a Western education and lifestyle; it appeared in 1960, the year Nigeria became an independent entity within
the British Commonwealth. Achebe turned to writing essays and poetry
and joined the University of Nigeria, Nsukka, as a senior research fellow
in 1966. The following year Eastern Nigeria, his tribal homeland, proclaimed itself the Republic of Biafra. Civil war followed, with casualties
of over a million — including many Biafrans (mostly Igbos) who starved
despite international relief efforts. In 1970 the secessionists capitulated.
Achebe, who had been active on Biafra's side, began editing *Okike: An
African Journal of New Writing* the next year. Since then he has taught at
the Universities of Massachusetts and Connecticut; published essays, poetry, stories, and children's literature; and won dozens of international
awards and honorary degrees. His long-awaited fifth novel, *Anthills of the
Savannah*, appeared in 1987. He lives in Nsukka, where he is a professor
emeritus at the university and continues to accept worldwide invitations
as a visiting writer and lecturer. "The Writer and His Community" was
Achebe's 1984 Regent's Lecture at the University of California at Los Angeles, reprinted in his 1989 book *Hopes and Impediments*.

For more information on Nigeria, see page 158.

One of the most critical consequences of the transition from oral traditions to written forms of literature is the emergence of individual au-
thorship.

The story told by the fireside does not belong to the storyteller once he has let it out of his mouth. But the story composed by his spiritual descendant, the writer in his study, "belongs" to its composer.

This shift is facilitated by the simple fact that, whereas a story that is told has no physical form or solidity, a book has; it is a commodity and can be handled and moved about. But I want to suggest that the physical form of a book cannot by itself adequately account for the emergent notion of proprietorship. At best it facilitates the will to ownership which is already present. This will is rooted in the praxis of individualism in its social and economic dimensions.

Part of my artistic and intellectual inheritance is derived from a cultural tradition in which it was possible for artists to create objects of art which were solid enough and yet make no attempt to claim, and sometimes even go to great lengths to deny, personal ownership of what they have created. I am referring to the tradition of *mbari* art in some parts of Igboland.

Mbari is an artistic "spectacular" demanded of the community by   5
one or other of its primary divinities, usually the Earth goddess. To execute this "command performance" the community is represented by a small group of its members selected and secluded for months or even years for the sole purpose of erecting a befitting "home of images" filled to overflowing with sculptures and paintings in homage to the presiding god or goddess.

These representatives (called *ndimgbe*; sing.: *onyemgbe*), chosen to re-enact, as it were, the miracle of creation in its extravagant profusion, are always careful to disclaim all credit for making, which rightly belongs to gods; or even for initiating homage for what is made, which is the prerogative of the community. *Ndimgbe* are no more than vessels in which the gods place their gifts of creativity to mankind and in which the community afterwards make their token return of sacrifice and thanksgiving. As soon as their work is done behind the fence of their seclusion and they re-emerge into secular life, *ndimgbe* set about putting as much distance as possible between themselves and their recently executed works of art.

As Herbert Cole tells us in his study of this profound phenomenon:

> A former *onyemgbe* fears that he might slip up and say, "Look, I did this figure." If he [says] that, he has killed himself. The god that owns that work will kill him.

This may sound strange and exotic to some ears, but I believe that it dramatizes a profoundly important aspect of the truth about art without which our understanding must remain seriously limited.

I am suggesting that what is at issue here is the principle which has come to be known as individualism and which has dominated the life and the psychology of the West in its modern history. The virtues of individualism are held to be universally beneficial but particularly so to the artist. John Plamenatz in his introduction to *Man and Society* separates the artist from the scholar in these words: "The artist ploughs his own furrow, the scholar, even in the privacy of his study, cultivates a common field."

It has been said that the American Ralph Waldo Emerson was perhaps the first to use the word "individualism" in the English language, rather approvingly, as a definition for the way of life which upholds the primacy of the individual. His definition was imbued with typically American optimistic faith. Emerson's contemporary, the Frenchman Alexis de Tocqueville, was far less enthusiastic. In his book *Democracy in America* he used "individualism" pejoratively — as a threat to society. As it turned out, however, it was the vision defined by Emerson that carried the day not just in America but in the Western world generally, from where it has made and continues to make serious inroads into the lives of other peoples. 10

The phenomenal success of the West in the mastery of the natural world is one of the dominant facts of modern history. It is only natural to attribute this dazzling achievement to the ruling values of the West, and also to hold these values up to the rest of the world not just as values but as the *right* values. By and large the rest of the world has been increasingly inclined to be persuaded. But from time to time, in life as in literature, voices of doubt have also been heard.

In a crucial passage in the novel *Ambiguous Adventure*, by the Senegalese Muslim writer Cheikh Hamidou Kane, the hero, an African student of philosophy in Paris, is asked by his dinner host how the history of Western thought strikes an African. And his reply — in my view one of the highlights of that fine novel — is as follows:

> It seems to me that this history has undergone an accident which has shifted it and, finally, drawn it away from its plan. Do you understand me? Socrates's scheme of thinking does not seem to me, at bottom, different from that of Saint Augustine though there was Christ between them. The plan is the same, as far as Pascal. It is still the plan of all the thought which is not occidental . . . I do not know. But don't you feel as if the philosophical plan were already no longer the same with Descartes as with Pascal? It is not the mystery which has changed but the questions which are asked of it and the revelations which are expected from it. Descartes is more niggardly in his quest. If, thanks to this and also to his

method, he obtains a greater number of responses, what he reports also
concerns us less and is of little help to us.

It may be thought overbold, if not downright impertinent, for anyone, but more particularly for an African student, to describe Descartes,
the very father of modern Western philosophy, as the cause of a gigantic
philosophical accident. But there are undoubtedly good grounds for the
proposition advanced here that if they should return to the world today
Socrates — or his student Plato, whom we know better — and Augustine
might find African communalism more congenial than Western individualism. *The Republic,* "conjured out of the ruins of fourth-century
Athens," was after all a grand design for the *ordering* of men in society;
and *The City of God* a Christian reordering of society after the destruction of the Roman Empire by pagans. In other words, philosophy for
Plato and Augustine, historically equidistant from Christ, was concerned with architectural designs for a better world.

Descartes, on the other hand, would probably become an American
citizen if he should return. He had rejected the traditional contemplative ideal of philosophy and put in its place a new experimental ra-
tionalism and a mechanistic view of the physical world. He regarded
science as a means of acquiring mastery over nature for the benefit of
mankind and led the way himself with experiments in optics and physiology. But — and this perhaps more than all else makes him a true modern, Western man — he made the foundation of his philosophical edifice, including the existence of God, contingent on his own first person
singular! *Cogito ergo sum.* I think therefore I am!

Perhaps it is the triumphant, breathtaking egocentrism of that decla-   15
ration that occasionally troubles the non-Western mind, conscious as it
must be of hierarchies above self; and so leads it to the brazen thought
of a Western ontological accident.

But troubled though he may be, non-Western man is also, in spite of
himself, dazzled by the technological marvels created by the West; by
its ability to provide better than anybody else for man's material needs.
And so we find him going out to meet the West in a bid to find out the
secret of its astonishing success or, if that proves too rigorous, then simply to taste its fruits.

The philosophical dialogue between the West and Africa has rarely
been better presented than in *Ambiguous Adventure.* In the first part of
the story the proud rulers of the Diallobe people — bearers of the cres-
cent of Islam in the West African savannah for close upon a thousand
years — are suffering the traumatic anguish of defeat by French imperial
arms, and pondering what the future course of their life should be.

Should they send their children to the new French school or not? After a long and anguished debate they finally opt for the school but not on the admission that their own institutions are in any way inferior to those of the French, nor on the aspiration that they should become like the French in due course, but rather on the tactical grounds only that they must learn from their new masters "the art of conquering without being in the right."

The trouble with their decision, however, is that the children, these "wanderers on delicate feet" as the poet Senghor might have called them, these infant magi launched into an ambiguous journey with an ambivalent mandate to *experience* but not to *become,* are doomed from the start to distress and failure.

The hero of the novel, the deliverer-to-be and paragon of the new generation, returns from France a total spiritual wreck, his once vibrant sense of community hopelessly shattered. Summoned to assume the mantle of leadership, his tortured soul begs to be excused, to be left alone. "What have their problems to do with me?" he asks. "I am only myself. I have only me." Poor fellow; the West has got him!

Western literature played a central role in promoting the ideal of in- 20 dividual autonomy. As Lionel Trilling pointed out, this literature has, in the last 150 years, held "an intense and adverse imagination of the culture in which it has its being." It promoted the view of society and of culture as a prisonhouse from which the individual must escape in order to find space and fulfillment.

But fulfillment is not, as people often think, uncluttered space or an absence of controls, obligations, painstaking exertion. No! It is actually a presence — a powerful demanding presence limiting the space in which the self can roam uninhibited; it is an aspiration by the self to achieve spiritual congruence with the other.

When people speak glibly of fulfillment they often mean self-gratification, which is easy, short-lived and self-centered. Like drugs, it has to be experienced frequently, preferably in increasing doses.

Fulfillment is other-centered, a giving or subduing of the self, perhaps to somebody, perhaps to a cause; in any event to something external to it. Those who have experienced fulfillment all attest to the reality of this otherness. For religious people the soul of man aspires to God for fulfillment. St. Augustine, Bishop of Hippo in North Africa and one of the greatest fathers of the early Christian Church, understood this very well, having led a life of self-centered pleasure in his youth. He found fulfillment and left his great prayer in testimony: "For thyself hast thou made us, O God, and our heart is restless until it rests in Thee." Artists, scientists, and scholars may find fulfillment in their creative work, humanitarians in their service. But even more important, ordinary men and women have found fulfillment in their closeness to others — to children, to parents, to wife or husband, to lover — and in social work of all kinds.

The French anthropologist O. Manoni wrote as follows about the Merina of Malagasy:

> We do not find in him that disharmony almost amounting to conflict between the social being and the inner personality which is so frequently met with among the civilized.

We must note in passing, but not be diverted by, Manoni's typically 25 occidentalist notion of civilization. The valuable part of his observation is that there is "disharmony almost amounting to conflict between the social being and the inner personality" in Western culture and, we may add, increasingly among its newly "civilized" and "civilizing" surrogates.

It was widely believed that this psychological disharmony, if not exactly desirable, was the inevitable price to be paid for the enormous advances made by the West in material wealth, in technology, in medicine, etc. Consequently the possibility that non-Western values might have insights to contribute to the process of modernization around the world was hardly even considered — until Japan.

In the area of literature, I recall that we have sometimes been informed by the West and its local zealots that the African novels we write are not novels at all because they do not quite fit the specifications of that literary form which came into being at a particular time in specific response to the new spirit of individual freedom set off by the decay of feudal Europe and the rise of capitalism. This form, we were told, was designed to explore individual rather than social predicaments.

As it happens, the novel, even in its home of origin, has not behaved very well; it has always resisted the straitjacket. What is more, being a robust art form, it has traveled indefatigably and picked up all kinds of strange habits!

Not so long ago the Czech writer Milan Kundera was reported as follows:

> The novel is an investigation into human existence . . . [It] proclaims no truth, no morality . . . That is a job for others: leaders of political parties, presidents, terrorists, priests, revolutionaries, and editorial writers. The novel came about at the beginning of modern times when man was discovering how hard it is to get at the truth and how relative human affairs really are.

I must confess I do like some things in that statement, not least his   30
juxtaposition of presidents and terrorists, for when a president pursues a
terrorist the two become quite indistinguishable! Nevertheless, I consider Kundera's position too Eurocentric, too dogmatic, and therefore
erroneous. If the novel came about in particular ways and circumstances, must it remain forever in the mold of its origin? If Europe discovered relativity in human affairs rather late, does it follow that everybody else did? And finally, can anyone seriously suggest that the novel
proclaims no morality?

In the introduction to his book *Ninety-nine Novels — the Best in English Since 1939* the British novelist Anthony Burgess states — correctly
in my opinion — that "the novel is what the symphony or painting or
sculpture is not — namely a form steeped in morality." Needless to say,
Burgess is not talking about what he himself calls black-and-white,
Sunday-sermon, conventional morality. "Rather," he says, "a novel will
question convention and suggest to us that the making of moral judgments is difficult. This can be called the higher morality."

And yet we cannot simply dismiss the desperate plea of Milan Kundera, an artist speaking out of the experience of an authoritarian state
that arrogates to itself powers to define truth and morality for the writer.
No! We must recognize his special exigencies or, as he himself says,
"how relative human affairs really are." Or, as Burgess says, "that the
making of moral judgments is difficult."

We may have been talking about individualism as if it was invented
in the West or even by one American, Emerson. In fact, individualism
must be, has to be, as old as human society itself. From whatever time
humans began to move around in groups the dialogue between
Manoni's polarities of "social being" and "inner personality" or, more
simply, between the individual and the community must also have
been called into being. It is inconceivable that it shouldn't. The question then is not whether this dialectic has always existed but rather how
particular peoples resolved it at particular times.

One of mankind's oldest written records, the Old Testament, has
a fine and dramatic moment when the prophet Ezekiel proposes to
his people a shift in dealing with the old paradox. "The soul that sin-
neth, it shall die," he says, superseding in that bold declaration the
teaching that when fathers eat sour grapes their children's teeth are set
on edge.

Some years ago, John Updike after he had finished reading my *Arrow*   35
of God wrote me a letter in which he made some interesting observations. I'd like to quote a paragraph from that letter because it has an interesting bearing on what I have been trying to say:

The final developments of *Arrow of God* proved unexpected and, as I think about them, beautifully resonant, tragic, and theological. That Ezeulu, whom we had seen stand up so invincibly to both Nwaka and Clarke, should be so suddenly vanquished by his own god Ulu and by something harsh and vengeful within himself, and his defeat in a page or two be the fulcrum of a Christian lever upon his people, is an ending few Western novelists would have contrived; having created a hero they would not let him crumble, nor are they, by and large, as truthful as you in their witness to the cruel reality of process.

Of course a Westerner would be most reluctant to destroy "in a page or two" the very angel and paragon of creation — the individual hero. If indeed he has to be destroyed, it must be done expansively with detailed explanations and justifications, not to talk of lamentations. And he must be given as final tribute the limelight in which to speak a grand, valedictory soliloquy!

The non-Westerner does not as a rule have those obligations because in his traditional scheme and hierarchy the human hero does not loom so large. Even when, like Ezeulu, he is leader and priest, he is still in a very real sense subordinate to his community. But even more important, he is subject to the sway of nonhuman forces in the universe, call them God, Fate, Chance, or what you will. I call them sometimes the Powers of Event, the repositories of causes and wisdoms that are as yet, and perhaps will always be, inaccessible to us.

To powers inhabiting that order of reality the human hero counts for little. If they should desire his fall they will not be obliged to make a long-winded case or present explanations.

Does this mean then that among these people, the Igbo to take one example, the individual counts for nothing? Paradoxical as it may sound the answer is an emphatic "No." The Igbo are second to none in their respect of the individual personality. For whereas many cultures are content to demonstrate the value and importance of each man and woman by reference to the common fatherhood of God, the Igbo postulate an unprecedented uniqueness for the individual by making him or her the sole creation and purpose of a unique god-agent, *chi*. No two persons, not even blood brothers, are created and accompanied by the same *chi*.

And yet the Igbo people as we have seen immediately set about bal- 40 ancing this extraordinary specialness, this unsurpassed individuality, by setting limits to its expression. The first limit is the democratic one, which subordinates the person to the group in practical, social matters. And the other is a moral taboo on excess, which sets a limit to personal ambition, surrounding it with powerful cautionary tales.

I began by describing — all too briefly — an aspect of the question of the "ownership" of art among a major Igbo group. I will end by quoting what an American anthropologist, Simon Ottenberg, reported about another group. He is describing an Afikpo carver at work on ritual masks:

> Sometimes his friends or other secret society members hear him working in the bush, so they come and sit with him and watch him carve. They give him advice telling him how to carve, even if they themselves do not know how. He is not offended by their suggestions. . . . I felt myself that he rather enjoyed the company.

Clearly, this artist and his people are in very close communion. They do not all have to agree on how to make the best mask. But they are all interested in the process of making and the final outcome. The resulting art is important because it is at the center of the life of the people and so can fulfill some of that need that first led man to make art: the need to afford himself through his imagination an alternative handle on reality.

There is always a grave danger of oversimplification in any effort to identify differences between systems such as I have attempted here between "The West and the Rest of Us," to borrow the catchy title of Chinweizu's remarkable book. I hope that while drawing attention to peculiarities which, in my view, are real enough at this point in time I have not fallen, nor led my indulgent reader, into the trap of seeing the differences as absolute rather than relative. But to be completely sure let me restate that the testimony of John Updike and certainly of Anthony Burgess does not encourage the notion of an absolute dichotomy between the West and ourselves on the issues I have been dealing with.

And I should like to go further and call to testimony a very distinguished witness indeed — J. B. Priestley — who wrote in a famous essay, "Literature and Western Man," as follows:

> Characters in a society make the novel . . . Society itself becomes more and more important to the serious novelist, and indeed turns into a character itself, perhaps the chief character.

Priestley could be speaking here more about the fictional use a novelist might make of his society rather than the real-life relationship between them. But in either case the level of understanding of, and even identification with, society he implicitly demands of the writer is a far cry from the adversary relationship generally assumed and promoted in the West.

The final point I wish to address myself to is the crucial one of identity. Who is my community? The *mbari* and the Afikpo examples I referred to were clearly appropriate to the rather small, reasonably stable and self-contained societies to which they belonged. In the very different, wide-open, multicultural, and highly volatile condition known as modern Nigeria, for example, can a writer even begin to know who his community is let alone devise strategies for relating to it?

If I write novels in a country in which most citizens are illiterate, who then is my community? If I write in English in a country in which English may still be called a foreign language, or in any case is spoken only by a minority, what use is my writing?

These are clearly grave issues. And it is not surprising that very many thoughtful people have exercised their minds in seeking acceptable answers. Neither is it surprising that less serious people should be handy with an assortment of instant and painless cures.

To the question of writing at all we have sometimes been counseled to forget it, or rather the writing of books. What is required, we are told, is plays and films. Books are out of date! The book is dead, long live television! One question which is not even raised let alone considered is: Who will write the drama and film scripts when the generation that can read and write has been used up?

On language we are given equally simplistic prescriptions. Abolish   50
the use of English! But after its abolition we remain seriously divided on what to put in its place. One proffered solution gives up Nigeria with its 200-odd languages as a bad case and travels all the way to East Africa to borrow Swahili; just as in the past a kingdom caught in a succession bind sometimes solved its problem by going to another kingdom to hire an underemployed prince!

I will not proceed with these fancy answers to deeply profound problems. To those colleagues who might be tempted into a hasty switch of genres I will say this: Consider a hypothetical case. A master singer arrives to perform in a large auditorium and finds at the last moment that three-quarters of his audience are totally deaf. His sponsors then put the proposition to him that he should dance instead because even the deaf can *see* a dancer. Now, although our performer may have the voice of an angel his feet are as heavy as concrete. So what should he do? Should he proceed to sing beautifully to only a quarter or less of the auditorium or dance atrociously to a full house?

I guess it is clear where my stand would be! The singer should sing well even if it is merely to himself, rather than dance badly for the whole world. This is, of course, putting the case in its utmost extremity; but it becomes necessary to do it in defense of both art and good sense in the face of what I see as a new onslaught of barbaric simple-mindedness.

Fortunately, in real life, we are not in danger of these bizarre extremes unless we consciously work our way into them. I can see no situation in which I will be presented with a Draconic choice between reading books and watching movies; or between English and Igbo. For me, no either/or; I insist on both. Which, you might say, makes my life rather difficult and even a little untidy. But I prefer it that way.

Despite the daunting problems of identity that beset our contemporary society, we can see in the horizon the beginnings of a new relationship between artist and community which will not flourish like the mango-trick in the twinkling of an eye but will rather, in the hard and bitter manner of David Diop's young tree, grow patiently and obstinately to the ultimate victory of liberty and fruition.

EXPLORATIONS

1. According to Chinua Achebe, why do the *ndimgbe* refuse to claim credit for the works of art they make? What do you think would be the benefits of this policy for their community? For an individual *onyemgbe*?

2. Why does Cheikh Hamidou Kane "describe Descartes, the very father of modern Western philosophy, as the cause of a gigantic philosophical accident" (para. 13)? Does Achebe agree? What are the reasons for his position?

3. What is the thesis of Achebe's essay? What kinds of evidence does he use to support his argument? How are his sources appropriate for the audience who originally heard his essay in the form of a lecture?

CONNECTIONS

1. "The principle which has come to be known as individualism . . . has dominated the life and the psychology of the West in its modern history" (para. 9). After reading "The Gentleman" (p. 483), do you think Nikos Kazantzakis would agree? What evidence in that essay supports Achebe's statement? What evidence suggests the gentleman is not necessarily an individualist?

2. Compare Achebe's comments on storytelling, ownership, and individualism with those by Joseph Bruchac in "Digging into Your Heart" (p. 439) and Leslie Marmon Silko (p. 415). By Achebe's criteria, are the American Indian societies described by Bruchac and Silko closer to the Western or non-Western tradition? How can you tell?

3. Beginning in paragraph 17, Achebe describes the novel *Ambiguous Adventure*, in which an African student goes to Paris and then returns to his homeland "a total spiritual wreck, his once vibrant sense of community hopelessly shattered" (para. 19). Compare James Baldwin's chronicle of an African American's encounter with Paris in "The New Lost Generation" (p. 263).What role does community play for Baldwin at home and abroad? What are the main similarities and differences between his experience and the student's as Achebe summarizes it?

ELABORATIONS

1. Reread Achebe's comments on *mbari* art (paras. 4–7). Contrast writer Derek Walcott's Observation on page 417. What rituals in the United States, if any, foster a sense of both community and spirituality? What are the functions of art in those rituals? Write an essay in which you either classify the ways art encourages Americans' connections with each other and the mysterious (see Albert Einstein's Observation on p. 411) or examine one ritual and analyze the contribution art and artists make to it.

2. Is Superman an individualist? Is he a gentleman? Is his contribution to American culture positive, negative, mixed, or neutral? Using "The Writer and His Community," "The Gentleman" (p. 483), and Gary Engle's "What Makes Superman So Darned American?" (p. 428) as resources, write an essay evaluating Superman as you think Achebe and Kazantzakis would regard him.

ISABEL ALLENDE

Clarisa

Isabel Allende (pronounced ah-*yen*-day) was born in 1942 in Lima, Peru, where her father was stationed as a Chilean diplomat. The family traveled extensively: Allende discovered *The Thousand and One Nights* at age twelve in Beirut, Lebanon. Back home in Chile's capital city of Santiago, she got a job with the Food and Agriculture Organization (FAO) of the United Nations. Allende became a journalist when she had to fill television time for the FAO. After a fellowship to study radio and television in Belgium, she worked in Chilean television and wrote plays and a magazine column. In 1970 her uncle, Dr. Salvador Allende Gossens, became president — the first Marxist-Leninist freely elected by a non-Communist country. Three years later he was ousted and killed in a U.S.-backed coup led by Augusto Pinochet Ugarte, who launched a brutally repressive right-wing dictatorship. Isabel Allende and her family fled to Venezuela, where she began writing fiction. "To lose Chile and all of my past because of the military coup and being forced into exile pushed me to write *The House of the Spirits* (1985; *La casa de los espiritus*, 1982). The loss of political innocence, when I became aware of the disappeared, the tortured, the dead, the brutal repression throughout Latin America, impelled me to write *Of Love and Shadows* (1987; *De amor y de sombra*, 1984). *The Infinite Plan* (1993; *El Plan Infinito*) was inspired by the love of my present husband." So Allende told an interviewer in 1994 at her home in California, where she continues to create award-winning books. "Clarisa," translated by Margaret Sayers Peden, comes from *The Stories of Eva Luna* (1991; *Cuentos de Eva Luna*, 1989), a book of tales spun Scheherezade-fashion by the heroine of Allende's novel *Eva Luna* (1987, 1988).

Chile is a long strip of seacoast that runs from Peru and Bolivia to South America's southern tip. The Andes Mountains divide it on the east from Argentina. Spain took northern Chile from the native Incas in the mid-1500s; the southern Araucanian Indians held out for another three centuries. Chile won independence in the early 1800s under José de San Martín and Bernardo O'Higgins, who became its first dictator. A constitution adopted in 1925 brought democracy, which lasted until the overthrow of President Allende. Under a new constitution in 1980, dictator Pinochet became president for an eight-year term. At its end he was forced to hold a plebiscite which rejected his bid to stay in power; in 1990 he finally stepped down. His elected successors have sought to balance the need to investigate and punish past brutalities with the need for national reconciliation, as well as to continue strengthening

501

Chile's economy. As we go to press, Chilean authorities are contesting Pinochet's 1998 arrest at a London medical clinic on an extradition warrant from Spain for his involvement in the murders of Spanish citizens in Chile in 1973.

Clarisa was born before the city had electricity, she lived to see the television coverage of the first astronaut levitating on the moon, and she died of amazement when the Pope came for a visit and was met in the streets by homosexuals dressed up as nuns. She had spent her childhood among pots of ferns and corridors lighted by oil lamps. Days went by slowly in those times. Clarisa never adjusted to the fits and starts of today's time; she always seemed to have been captured in the sepia tints of a nineteenth-century portrait. I suppose that once she had had a virginal waist, a graceful bearing, and a profile worthy of a medallion, but by the time I met her she was already a rather bizarre old woman with shoulders rounded into two gentle humps and with white hair coiled around a sebaceous cyst the size of a pigeon egg crowning her noble head. She had a profound, shrewd gaze that could penetrate the most hidden evil and return unscathed. Over the course of a long lifetime she had come to be considered a saint, and after she died many people placed her photograph on the family altar along with other venerable images to ask her aid in minor difficulties, even though her reputation for being a miracle worker is not recognized by the Vatican and undoubtedly never will be. Her miraculous works are unpredictable: She does not heal the blind, like Santa Lucia, or find husbands for spinsters, like St. Anthony, but they say she helps a person through a hangover, or problems with the draft, or a siege of loneliness. Her wonders are humble and improbable, but as necessary as the spectacular marvels worked by cathedral saints.

I met Clarisa when I was an adolescent working as a servant in the house of La Señora, a lady of the night, as Clarisa called women of her occupation. Even then she was distilled almost to pure spirit; I thought at any minute she might rise from the floor and fly out the window. She had the hands of a healer, and people who could not pay a doctor, or were disillusioned with traditional science, waited in line for her to relieve their pain or console them in their bad fortune. My *patrona* used to call her to come lay her hands on her back. In the process, Clarisa would rummage about in La Señora's soul with the hope of turning her life around and leading her along the paths of righteousness — paths my employer was in no hurry to travel, since that direction would have unalterably affected her commercial enterprise. Clarisa would apply the curative warmth of the palms of her hands for ten or fifteen minutes, depending on the intensity of the pain, and then accept a glass of fruit juice as payment for her services. Sitting face to face in the kitchen, the two women would have their chat about human and divine topics, my *patrona* more on the human side and Clarisa more on the divine, never straining tolerance nor abusing good manners. Later, when I found a different job, I lost sight of Clarisa until we met once again some twenty years later and reestablished a friendship that has lasted to this day, overcoming the many obstacles that lay in our way, including death, which has put a slight crimp in the ease of our communications.

Even in the times when age had slowed her former missionary zeal, Clarisa persevered steadfastly in her good works, sometimes even against the will of the beneficiaries — as in the case of the pimps on Calle República, who had to bear the mortification of the public harangues that good lady delivered in her unwavering determination to redeem them. Clarisa gave everything she owned to the needy. As a rule she had only the clothes on her back, and toward the end of her life it was difficult to find a person any poorer than she. Charity had become a two-way street, and you seldom could tell who was giving and who was receiving.

She lived in an old run-down three-story house; some rooms were empty but some she rented as a storehouse for a saloon, so that the rancid stench of cheap liquor always hung in the air. She had never moved from the dwelling she had inherited from her parents because it reminded her of an aristocratic past, and also because for more than forty years her husband had buried himself alive in a room at the back of the patio. He had been a judge in a remote province, an office he had carried out with dignity until the birth of his second child, when disillusion robbed him of the will to accept his fate, and like a mole he had taken refuge in the malodorous cave of his room. He emerged only rarely, a scurrying shadow, and opened the door only to hand out his chamber pot and collect the food his wife left for him every day. He communicated with her by means of notes written in his perfect calligraphy and by knocks on the door — two for yes and three for no. Through the walls of his room you could hear asthmatic hacking and an occasional longshoreman's curse intended for whom, no one ever knew.

"Poor man, I pray that God will soon call him to His side, and he will take his place in the heavenly choir," Clarisa would sigh without a suspicion of irony. The opportune passing of her husband, however, was one grace Divine Providence never granted, for he has survived to the present day. He must be a hundred by now, unless he has already died and the coughs and the curses we hear are only echoes from the past.

Clarisa married him because he was the first person to ask her, and also because her parents thought that a judge would be the best possible match. She left the sober comfort of her paternal hearth and reconciled herself to the avarice and vulgarity of her husband with no thought of a better fate. The only time she was ever heard to utter a nostalgic comment about the refinements of her past was in regard to a grand piano that had enchanted her as a little girl. That is how we learned of her love for music and much later, when she was an old woman, a group of us who were her friends gave her a modest piano. It had been sixty years since she had been anywhere near a keyboard, but she sat down on the piano stool and played, by memory and without hesitation, a Chopin nocturne.

A year or so after the marriage to the judge, she gave birth to an albino daughter, who as soon as she began to walk accompanied her mother to church. The tiny creature was so dazzled by the pageantry of the liturgy that she began pulling down drapes to "play bishop," and soon the only game that interested her was imitating the ecclesiastical ritual, chanting in a Latin of her own invention. She was hopelessly retarded; her only words were spoken in an unknown tongue, she drooled incessantly, and she suffered uncontrollable attacks during which she had to be tied like a circus animal to prevent her from chewing the furniture and attacking guests. With puberty, however, she grew more tractable, and helped her mother around the house. The second child was born into the world totally devoid of curiosity and bearing gentle Asian features; the only skill he ever mastered was riding a bicycle, but it was of little benefit to him since his mother never dared let him out of the house. He spent his life pedaling in the patio on a stationary bicycle mounted on a music stand.

Her children's abnormality never affected Clarisa's unalterable optimism. She considered them pure souls immune to evil, and all her relations with them were marked by affection. Her greatest concern was to save them from earthly suffering, and she often asked herself who would look after them when she was gone. The father, in contrast, never spoke of them, and used the pretext of his retarded children to wallow in shame, abandon his career, his friends, even fresh air, and entomb himself in his room, copying newspapers with monklike patience in a series of stenographic notebooks. Meanwhile, his wife spent the last cent of her dowry, and her inheritance, and took on all kinds of jobs to support the family. In her own poverty, she never turned her back to the poverty of others, and even in the most difficult periods of her life she continued her works of mercy.

Clarisa had a boundless understanding of human weaknesses. One night when she was sitting in her room sewing, her white head bent over her work, she heard unusual noises in the house. She got up to see what they might be, but got no farther than the doorway, where she ran into a man who held a knife to her throat and threatened, "Quiet, you whore, or I'll slash your throat."

"This isn't the place you want, son. The ladies of the night are across   10
the street, there where you hear the music."

"Don't try to be funny, this is a robbery."

"What did you say?" Clarisa smiled, incredulous. "And what are you going to steal from me?"

"Sit down in that chair. I'm going to tie you up."

"I won't do it, son. I'm old enough to be your mother. Where's your respect?"

"Sit *down,* I said!"   15

"And don't shout, you'll frighten my husband, and he's not at all well. By the way, put that knife down, you might hurt someone," said Clarisa.

"Listen, lady, I came here to rob you," the flustered robber muttered.

"Well, there's not going to be any robbery. I will not let you commit a sin. I'll *give* you some money of my own will. You won't be taking it from me, is that clear? I'm giving it to you." She went to her purse and took out all the money for the rest of the week. "That's all I have. We're quite poor, as you see. Come into the kitchen, now, and I'll set the kettle to boil."

The man put away his knife and followed her, money in hand. Clarisa brewed tea for both of them, served the last cookies in the house, and invited him to sit with her in the living room.

"Wherever did you get the notion to rob a poor old woman like me?"   20
The thief told her he had been watching her for days; he knew that she lived alone and thought there must be something of value in that big old house. It was his first crime, he said; he had four children, he was out of a job, and he could not go home another night with empty hands. Clarisa pointed out that he was taking too great a risk, that he might not only be arrested but was putting his immortal soul in danger — although in truth she doubted that God would punish him with hell, the worst might be a while in purgatory, as long, of course, as he repented and did not do it again. She offered to add him to her list of wards and promised she would not bring charges against him. As they

said good-bye, they kissed each other on the cheek. For the next ten years, until Clarisa died, she received a small gift at Christmastime through the mail.

Not all Clarisa's dealings were with the indigent; she also knew people of note, women of breeding, wealthy businessmen, bankers, and public figures, whom she visited seeking aid for the needy, with never a thought for how she might be received. One day she presented herself in the office of Congressman Diego Cienfuegos, known for his incendiary speeches and for being one of the few incorruptible politicians in the nation, which did not prevent his rising to the rank of Minister and earning a place in history books as the intellectual father of an important peace treaty. In those days Clarisa was still young, and rather timid, but she already had the unflagging determination that characterized her old age. She went to the Congressman to ask him to use his influence to procure a new modern refrigerator for the Teresian Sisters. The man stared at her in amazement, questioning why he should aid his ideological enemies.

"Because in their dining room the Little Sisters feed a hundred children a day a free meal, and almost all of them are children of the Communists and evangelicals who vote for you," Clarisa replied mildly.

That was the beginning of a discreet friendship that was to cost the politician many sleepless nights and many donations. With the same irrefutable logic, Clarisa obtained scholarships for young atheists from the Jesuits, used clothing for neighborhood prostitutes from the League of Catholic Dames, musical instruments for a Hebrew choir from the German Institute, and funds for alcohol rehabilitation programs from viniculturists.

Neither the husband interred in the mausoleum of his room nor the debilitating hours of her daily labors prevented Clarisa's becoming pregnant again. The midwife advised her that in all probability she would give birth to another abnormal child, but Clarisa mollified her with the argument that God maintains a certain equilibrium in the universe, and just as He creates some things twisted, He creates others straight; for every virtue there is a sin, for every joy an affliction, for every evil a good, and on and on, for as the wheel of life turns through the centuries, everything evens out. The pendulum swings back and forth with inexorable precision, she said.

Clarisa passed her pregnancy in leisure, and in the proper time gave birth to her third child. The baby was born at home with the help of the midwife and in the agreeable company of the two inoffensive and smiling retarded children who passed the hours at their games, one spouting gibberish in her bishop's robe and the other pedaling nowhere on his stationary bicycle. With this birth the scales tipped in the direction needed to preserve the harmony of Creation, and a grateful mother offered her breast to a strong boy with wise eyes and firm hands. Fourteen months later Clarisa gave birth to a second son with the same characteristics.

"These two boys will grow up healthy and help me take care of their brother and sister," she said with conviction, faithful to her theory of compensation; and that is how it was, the younger children grew straight as reeds and were gifted with kindness and goodness.

Somehow Clarisa managed to support the four children without any help from her husband and without injuring her family pride by accepting charity for herself. Few were aware of her financial straits. With the same tenacity with which she spent late nights sewing rag dolls and baking wedding cakes to sell, she battled the deterioration of her house when the walls began to sweat a greenish mist. She instilled in the two younger children her principles of good humor and generosity with such splendid results that in the following years they were always beside her caring for their older siblings, until the day the retarded brother and sister accidentally locked themselves in the bathroom and a leaking gas pipe transported them gently to a better world.

When the Pope made his visit, Clarisa was not quite eighty, although it was difficult to calculate her exact age; she had added years out of vanity, simply to hear people say how well preserved she was for the ninety-five years she claimed. She had more than enough spirit, but her body was failing; she could barely totter through the streets, where in any case she lost her way, she had no appetite, and finally was eating only flowers and honey. Her spirit was detaching itself from her body at the same pace her wings germinated, but the preparations for the papal visit rekindled her enthusiasm for the adventures of this earth. She was not content to watch the spectacle on television because she had a deep distrust of that apparatus. She was convinced that even the astronaut on the moon was a sham filmed in some Hollywood studio, the same kind of lies they practiced in those stories where the protagonists love or die and then a week later reappear with the same faces but a new destiny. Clarisa wanted to see the pontiff with her own eyes, not on a screen where some actor was costumed in the Pope's robes. That was how I found myself accompanying her to cheer the Pope as he rode through the streets. After a couple of hours fighting the throngs of faithful and vendors of candles and T-shirts and religious prints and plastic saints, we caught sight of the Holy Father, magnificent in his portable glass cage, a white porpoise in an aquarium. Clarisa fell to her knees, in danger of being crushed by fanatics and the Pope's police escort. Just at the instant when the Pope was but a stone's throw away, a rare spectacle surged from a side street: a group of men in nun's habits, their faces garishly painted, waving posters in favor of abortion, divorce, sodomy, and the right of women to the priesthood. Clarisa dug through her purse with a trembling hand, found her eyeglasses, and set them on her nose to assure herself she was not suffering a hallucination.

She paled. "It's time to go, daughter. I've already seen too much."   30

She was so undone that to distract her I offered to buy her a hair from the Pope's head, but she did not want it without a guarantee of authenticity. According to a socialist newspaperman, there were enough capillary relics offered for sale to stuff a couple of pillows.

"I'm an old woman, and I no longer understand the world, daughter. We'd best go home."

She was exhausted when she reached the house, with the din of the bells and cheering still ringing in her temples. I went to the kitchen to prepare some soup for the judge and heat water to brew her a cup of chamomile tea, in hopes it would have a calming effect. As I waited for the tea, Clarisa, with a melancholy face, put everything in order and served her last plate of food to her husband. She set the tray on the floor and for the first time in forty years knocked on his door.

"How many times have I told you not to bother me," the judge protested in a reedy voice.

"I'm sorry, dear, I just wanted to tell you that I'm going to die."   35
"When?"
"On Friday."
"Very well." The door did not open.

Clarisa called her sons to tell them about her imminent death, and then took to her bed. Her bedroom was a large dark room with pieces of heavy carved mahogany furniture that would never become antiques because somewhere along the way they had broken down. On her dresser sat a crystal urn containing an astoundingly realistic wax Baby Jesus, rosy as an infant fresh from its bath.

"I'd like for you to have the Baby, Eva. I know you'll take care of   40
Him."

"You're not going to die. Don't frighten me this way."

"You need to keep Him in the shade, if the sun strikes Him, He'll melt. He's lasted almost a century, and will last another if you protect Him from the heat."

I combed her meringue hair high on her head, tied it with a ribbon, and then sat down to accompany her through this crisis, not knowing exactly what it was. The moment was totally free of sentimentality, as if in fact she was not dying but suffering from a slight cold.

"We should call a priest now, don't you think, child?"

"But Clarisa, what sins can you have?"

"Life is long, and there's more than enough time for evil, God willing."

"But you'll go straight to heaven — that is, if heaven exists."

"Of course it exists, but it's not certain they'll let me in. They're very strict there," she murmured. And after a long pause, she added, "When I think over my trespasses, there was one that was very grave . . ."

I shivered, terrified that this old woman with the aureole of a saint was going to tell me that she had intentionally dispatched her retarded children to facilitate divine justice, or that she did not believe in God and had devoted herself to doing good in this world only because the scales had assigned her the role of compensating for the evil of others, an evil that was unimportant anyway since everything is part of the same infinite process. But Clarisa confessed nothing so dramatic to me. She turned toward the window and told me, blushing, that she had not fulfilled her conjugal duties.

"What does that mean?" I asked.

"Well, I mean I did not satisfy my husband's carnal desires, you understand?"

"No."

"If you refuse your husband your body, and he falls into the temptation of seeking solace with another woman, you bear that moral responsibility."

"I see. The judge fornicates, and the sin is yours."

"No, no. I think it would be both our sins. . . . I would have to look it up."

"And the husband has the same obligation to his wife?"

"What?"

"I mean, if you had had another man, would your husband share the blame?"

"Wherever did you get an idea like that, child!" She stared at me in disbelief.

"Don't worry, because if your worst sin was that you slighted the judge, I'm sure God will see the joke."

"I don't think God is very amused by such things."

"But Clarisa, to doubt divine perfection *would* be a great sin."

She seemed in such good health that I could not imagine her dying, but I supposed that, unlike us simple mortals, saints have the power to die unafraid and in full control of their faculties. Her reputation was so solid that many claimed to have seen a circle of light around her head and to have heard celestial music in her presence, and so I was not

surprised when I undressed her to put on her nightgown to find two inflamed bumps on her shoulders, as if her pair of great angel wings were
about to erupt.

The rumor of Clarisa's coming death spread rapidly. Her children
and I had to marshal an unending line of people who came to seek her
intervention in heaven for various favors, or simply to say good-bye.
Many expected that at the last moment a significant miracle would
occur, such as, the odor of rancid bottles that pervaded the house would
be transformed into the perfume of camellias, or beams of consolation
would shine forth from her body. Among the visitors was her friend the
robber, who had not mended his ways but instead become a true professional. He sat beside the dying woman's bed and recounted his es-
capades without a hint of repentance.

"Things are going really well. I rob only upper-class homes now. I   65
steal from the rich, and that's no sin. I've never had to use violence, and
I work clean, like a true gentleman," he boasted.

"I will have to pray a long time for you, my son."

"Pray on, Grandmother. It won't do me any harm."

La Señora came, too, distressed to be saying good-bye to her beloved
friend, and bringing a flower crown and almond-paste sweets as her
contribution to the death vigil. My former *patrona* did not know me,
but I had no trouble recognizing her despite her girth, her wig, and the
outrageous plastic shoes printed with gold stars. To offset the thief, she
came to tell Clarisa that her advice had fallen upon fertile ground, and
that she was now a respectable Christian.

"Tell Saint Peter that, so he'll take my name from his black book,"
was her plea.

"What a terrible disappointment for all these good people if instead   70
of going to heaven I end up in the cauldrons of hell," Clarisa said after I
was finally able to close the door and let her rest for a while.

"If that happens, no one down here is going to know, Clarisa."

"Thank heavens for that!"

From early dawn on Friday a crowd gathered outside in the street,
and only her two sons' vigilance prevented the faithful from carrying off
relics, from strips of paper off the walls to articles of the saint's meager
wardrobe. Clarisa was failing before our eyes and, for the first time, she
showed signs of taking her own death seriously. About ten that morning, a blue automobile with Congressional plates stopped before the
house. The chauffeur helped an old man climb from the back seat; the
crowds recognized him immediately. It was *don* Diego Cienfuegos,
whom decades of public service had made a national hero. Clarisa's
sons came out to greet him, and accompanied him in his laborious as-

cent to the second floor. When Clarisa saw him in the doorway, she became quite animated; the color returned to her cheeks and the shine to her eyes.

"Please, clear everyone out of the room and leave us alone," she whispered in my ear.

Twenty minutes later the door opened and *don* Diego Cienfuegos   75
departed, feet dragging, eyes teary, bowed and crippled, but smiling. Clarisa's sons, who were waiting in the hall, again took his arms to steady him, and seeing them there together I confirmed something that had crossed my mind before. The three men had the same bearing, the same profile, the same deliberate assurance, the same wise eyes and firm hands.

I waited until they were downstairs, and went back to my friend's room. As I arranged her pillows, I saw that she, like her visitor, was weeping with a certain rejoicing.

"*Don* Diego was your grave sin, wasn't he?" I murmured.

"That wasn't a sin, child, just a little boost to help God balance out the scales of destiny. You see how well it worked out, because my two weak children had two strong brothers to look after them."

Clarisa died that night, without suffering. Cancer, the doctor diagnosed, when he saw the buds of her wings; saintliness, proclaimed the throngs bearing candles and flowers; astonishment, say I, because I was with her when the Pope came to visit.

EXPLORATIONS

1. A skilled writer sets out to work immediately creating a story's world. How does the first paragraph of "Clarisa" transport us into the world where the story takes place? How does that world differ from ours? What facts in Clarisa's world (as Isabel Allende develops it throughout her story) are superstitions in ours? What facts in our world are superstitions in Clarisa's?

2. In paragraph 2 the narrator says that her friendship with Clarisa "has lasted to this day, overcoming the many obstacles that lay in our way, including death, which has put a slight crimp in the ease of our communications." What other statements by the narrator of "Clarisa" refer to improbabilities as realities? How do these statements affect the story's impact?

3. When Clarisa is pregnant with her third child, what is her stated reason for believing the baby will be normal? What is her unstated reason? Why is it appropriate that her husband sired the children he did, "one spouting gibberish in her bishop's robe and the other pedaling nowhere on his stationary bicycle" (para. 26)?

CONNECTIONS

1. Reread Chinua Achebe's comments on fulfillment in "The Writer and His Community" (p. 489, paras. 20–23). Which definition of fulfillment would Clarisa endorse? How can you tell?

2. In *Beloved* (p. 460), what evidence indicates whether we as readers are meant to believe in the ghost in Sethe's house? Aside from location and other external trappings, how is the world of *Beloved* similar to and different from that of "Clarisa"? What strategies does Toni Morrison use to place us in her characters' world that are similar to Allende's strategies?

3. Compare Martin Luther King Jr.'s Observation on page 412 with Clarisa's argument in paragraph 25. What ideas appear in both selections? How do these two commentators apparently differ in their attitudes toward evil?

ELABORATIONS

1. Allende writes in the tradition called magic realism, treating phenomena such as ghosts and miracles as matter-of-factly as any other events. Find out more about magic realism, particularly in Latin American literature. Write an essay defining the term and showing how "Clarisa" exemplifies it.

2. Reread Allende's description of the Pope's visit in paragraph 29. What improbable details does she treat realistically? What real (albeit fictional) details does she distort so that they seem bizarre and unreal? What techniques does she use to accomplish these reversals? Describe some event you have attended or experienced, using similar techniques to distort and reverse reality.

GABRIEL GARCÍA MÁRQUEZ

Dreams for Hire

"It bothers me that the people of the United States have appropriated the word *America* as if *they* were the only Americans," Gabriel García Márquez told an interviewer shortly before he won the 1982 Nobel Prize for literature. A devotee of North American fiction, García Márquez was for a time prevented from entering the United States because he had worked for the Cuban news agency in New York in 1961. His old friendship with Fidel Castro, he says, is based on a shared love of literature and fish recipes. Born in the Caribbean coastal village of Aracataca, Colombia, in 1928, García Márquez grew up listening to his grandfather's tales of war and politics and his grandmother's stories of the supernatural. Out of this mix came the imaginary town of Macondo (named for a nearby banana plantation), the setting for much of his fiction. García Márquez studied at the Universidad Nacional in Bogotá, Colombia's capital; he left to be a journalist, traveling to other parts of South America, the United States, and Europe, and began writing short stories. Recognition came with his 1961 novella *El coronel no tiene quien le escriba* (*No One Writes to the Colonel*, 1968), during the flowering of Latin American literature referred to as "El Boom." But it was *Cien años de soledad* (1967; *One Hundred Years of Solitude*, 1970), which sold many million copies in more than thirty languages, that made him famous. García Márquez's fusion of naturalism and fantasy has given him a central place in the genre known as magic realism. Among his other novels are *Crónica de una muerte anunciada* (1981; *Chronicle of a Death Foretold*, 1982), which prompted the Nobel Prize; *El amor en los tiempos de cólera* (1985; *Love in the Time of Cholera*, 1988); and *El Otoño del patriarca* (1975; *The Autumn of the Patriarch*, 1991), which is in the works as a motion picture directed by Sean Penn and starring Marlon Brando. In 1999 García Márquez returned to journalism when he became the owner and editor of *Cambio*, a weekly newsmagazine. "Dreams for Hire," translated from the Spanish by Nick Caistor, appeared in the Autumn 1992 volume of *Granta*.

Central and South America meet on the Panama-Colombia border. Colombia thus is the only South American country with both a Caribbean and a Pacific coast. The national language is Spanish, and 97 percent of Colombians are Roman Catholic. Ethnically a majority are mestizos (mixed Spanish and Indian). Like Panama, Venezuela, and Ecuador, Colombia was ruled by Spain from the 1500s until Simón Bolívar led the region to independence (1819–1824) and became its first president. (Venezuela and Ecuador broke away ten years later;

Panama followed in 1903.) Although Colombia is one of the continent's longest-lived democracies, its history has been turbulent. Struggles for power between Liberal and Conservative parties often have erupted into literal battles and coups d'état, including the nationwide War of a Thousand Days (1899–1902); the 1928 "banana massacre" of striking United Fruit Company workers by government troops (depicted in *One Hundred Years of Solitude*); and *la violencia* ("the violence"), a decade of rioting and civil war following a 1948 political assassination. Today, strife between Colombia's government and its drug cartels exacerbates the country's economic and social problems.

Cuba comprises one large and several small islands 135 miles off Florida's southern tip. Christopher Columbus claimed it for Spain in 1492; its native Arawak Indians soon died off from enslavement, slaughter, and disease. After the Spanish-American War, Spain freed Cuba (1899) and the United States occupied it, withdrawing its troops in 1902 but remaining a force in the economy. In 1958 Fidel Castro and a guerrilla army, including Argentine physician Ernesto "Che" Guevara, overthrew dictator Fulgencio Batista. Allying with the Soviet Union, Castro nationalized foreign-owned businesses and instituted many Soviet-style changes. The United States responded with a trade embargo which, coupled with the breakup of the Soviet Union in 1991 and the collapse of the Communist Bloc in Europe, has hamstrung Cuba's economy.

At nine o'clock in the morning, while we were having breakfast on the terrace of the Hotel Riviera in Havana, a terrifying wave appeared out of nowhere — the day was sunny and calm — and came crashing upon us. It lifted the cars that had been passing along the sea front, as well as several others that had been parked nearby, and tossed them into the air, smashing one into the side of our hotel. It was like an explosion of dynamite, spreading panic up and down the twenty floors of our building and transforming the lobby into a pile of broken glass, where many of the hotel guests were hurled through the air like the furniture. Several were wounded in the hail of glass shards. It must have been a tidal wave of monumental size: The hotel is protected from the sea by a wall and the wide two-way avenue that passes before it, but the wave had erupted with such force that it obliterated the glass lobby.

Cuban volunteers, with the help of the local fire brigade, set to sweeping up the damage, and in less than six hours, after closing off the hotel's sea front entrance and opening up an alternative, everything was back to normal. Throughout the morning no one paid any attention to the car that had been smashed against the wall of the hotel, believing it had been among the vehicles parked along the avenue. But by the time it was eventually removed by a crane, the body of a woman was discovered inside, moored to the driving seat by her seat belt. The blow had been so great that there wasn't a bone in her body which was left unbroken. Her face was messy and unrecognizable, her ankle boots had burst at the seams, her clothes were in tatters. But there was a ring, still worn on her finger, which remained intact: It was made in the shape of a serpent and had emeralds for eyes. The police established that she was the housekeeper for the new Portuguese ambassador and his wife. In fact she had arrived with them only fifteen days before and had that morning left for the market in their new car. Her name meant nothing to me when I read about the incident in the papers, but I was intrigued by that ring, made in the shape of a serpent with emeralds for its eyes. I was, unfortunately, unable to find out on which finger the ring had been worn.

It was an essential detail: I feared that this woman might be someone I knew and whom I would never forget, even though I never learned her real name. She, too, had a ring made in the shape of a serpent, with emeralds for its eyes, but she always wore it on the first finger of her right hand, which was unusual, especially then. I had met her forty-six years ago in Vienna, eating sausages and boiled potatoes and drinking beer straight from the barrel, in a tavern frequented by Latin American students. I had arrived from Rome that morning, and I still recall that first impression made by her ample opera-singer's bosom, the drooping fox tails gathered around the collar of her coat, and that Egyptian ring made in the shape of a serpent. She spoke a rudimentary Spanish, in a breathless shopkeeper's accent, and I assumed that she must be Austrian, the only one at that long wooden table. I was wrong: She had been born in Colombia and between the wars had traveled to Austria to study music and singing. When I met her she must have been around thirty, and she had begun aging before her time. Even so, she was magical; and, also, among the most fearsome people I've ever met.

At that time — the late forties — Vienna was nothing more than an ancient imperial city that history had reduced to a remote provincial capital, located between the two irreconcilable worlds left by the Second World War, a paradise for the black market and international espionage. I couldn't imagine surroundings better suited to my fugitive compatriot, who went on eating in the students' tavern on the corner only out of nostalgia for her roots, because she had more than enough money to buy the whole place, its diners included. She never told us her real name; we always referred to her by the German tongue twister that the Latin American students in Vienna had invented for her: Frau Frida. No sooner had

we been introduced than I committed the fortuitous imprudence of asking her how she came to find herself in a part of the world so distant and
different from the windy heights of the Quindio region in Colombia. She
replied matter-of-factly, "I hire myself out to dream."

That was her profession. She was the third of eleven children of a   5
prosperous shopkeeper from the old region of Caldas, and by the time
she learned to speak, she had established the habit of telling all her
dreams before breakfast, when, she said, her powers of premonition
were at their most pure. At the age of seven, she dreamt that one of her
brothers had been swept away by a raging torrent. The mother, simply
out of a nervous superstitiousness, refused to allow her son to do what
he most enjoyed, swimming in the local gorge. But Frau Frida had already developed her own system of interpreting her prophecies.

"What the dream means," she explained, "is not that he is going to
drown, but that he mustn't eat sweets."

The interpretation amounted to a terrible punishment, especially for
a five-year-old boy who could not imagine life without his Sunday
treats. But the mother, convinced of her daughter's divinatory powers,
ensured that her injunction was adhered to. Unfortunately, following a
moment's inattention, the son choked on a gob-stopper that he had
been eating in secret, and it proved impossible to save him.

Frau Frida had never thought that it would be possible to earn a living from her talent until life took her by the scruff of the neck and, during a harsh Viennese winter, she rang the bell of the first house where
she wanted to live, and, when asked what she could do, offered the simple reply: "I dream." After only a brief explanation, the lady of the
house took her on, at a wage that was little more than pocket money,
but with a decent room and three meals a day. Above all, there was a
breakfast, the time when the members of the family sat down to learn
their immediate destinies: the father, a sophisticated *rentier*;[1] the
mother, a jolly woman with a passion for Romantic chamber music;
and the two children, aged eleven and nine. All of them were religious
and therefore susceptible to archaic superstitions, and they were delighted to welcome Frau Frida into their home, on the sole condition
that every day she revealed the family's destiny through her dreams.

She did well, especially during the war years that followed, when reality was more sinister than any nightmare. At the breakfast table every
morning, she alone decided what each member of the family was to do
that day, and how it was to be done, until eventually her prognostica-

---

[1]Someone of independent means. — ED.

tions became the house's sole voice of authority. Her domination of the family was absolute: Even the slightest sigh was made on her orders. The father had died just prior to my stay in Vienna, and he had had the good grace to leave Frau Frida a part of his fortune, again on the condition that she continued dreaming for the family until she was unable to dream any more.

I spent a month in Vienna, living the frugal life of a student while waiting for money which never arrived. The unexpected and generous visits that Frau Frida paid to our tavern were like fiestas in our otherwise penurious regime. One night, the powerful smell of beer about us, she whispered something in my ear with such conviction that I found it impossible to ignore.

"I came here specially to tell you that last night I saw you in my dreams," she said. "You must leave Vienna at once and not come back here for at least five years."

Such was her conviction that I was put, that same night, on the last train for Rome. I was so shaken that I have since come to believe that I survived a disaster I never encountered. To this day I have not set foot in Vienna again.

Before the incident in Havana I met up with Frau Frida once more, in Barcelona, in an encounter so unexpected that it seemed to me especially mysterious. It was the day that Pablo Neruda set foot on Spanish soil for the first time since the [Spanish] Civil War, during a stopover on a long sea journey to Valparaiso in Chile.[2] He spent the morning with us, big game hunting in the antiquarian bookshops, buying eventually a faded book with torn covers for which he paid what must have been the equivalent of two months' salary for the Chilean consulate in Rangoon. He lumbered along like a rheumatic elephant, showing a childlike interest in the internal workings of every object he came across. The world always appeared to him as a giant clockwork toy.

I have never known anyone who approximated so closely the received idea of a Renaissance Pope — that mixture of gluttony and refinement — who even against his will, would dominate and preside over any table. Matilde, his wife, wrapped him in a bib which looked more like an apron from a barbershop than a napkin from a restaurant, but it was the only way to prevent him from being bathed in sauces. That day Neruda ate three lobsters in their entirety, dismembering them with the precision of a surgeon, while concurrently devouring everyone else's

10

---

[2]See page 417. Neruda was living in Spain when the war broke out, after working at the Chilean consulate in Rangoon, Burma; later he frequently returned to Spain. — ED.

dishes with his eyes, until he was unable to resist picking from each plate, with a relish and an appetite that everyone found contagious: clams from Galicia, barnacle geese from Cantabria, prawns from Alicante, swordfish from the Costa Brava. All the while he was talking, just like the French, about other culinary delights, especially the prehistoric shellfish of Chile that were his heart's favorite. And then suddenly he stopped eating, pricked up his ears like the antennae of a lobster, and whispered to me: "There's someone behind me who keeps staring at me."

I looked over his shoulder. It was true. Behind him, three tables   15
back, a woman, unabashed in an old-fashioned felt hat and a purple scarf, was slowly chewing her food with her eyes fixed on Neruda. I recognized her at once. She was older and bigger, but it was her, with the ring made in the form of a serpent on her first finger.

She had traveled from Naples on the same boat as the Nerudas, but they had not met on board. We asked her to join us for coffee, and I invited her to talk about her dreams, if only to entertain the poet. But the poet would have none of it, declaring outright that he did not believe in the divination of dreams.

"Only poetry is clairvoyant," he said.

After lunch, and the inevitable walk along the Ramblas, I deliberately fell in with Frau Frida so that we could renew our acquaintance without the others hearing. She told me that she had sold her properties in Austria and, having retired to Porto, in Portugal, was now living in a house that she described as a fake castle perched on a cliff from where she could see the whole Atlantic as far as America. It was clear, although she didn't say as much explicitly, that, from one dream to another, she had ended up in possession of the entire fortune of her once unlikely Viennese employers. Even so, I remained unimpressed, only because I had always thought that her dreams were no more than a contrivance to make ends meet. I told her as much.

She laughed her mocking laugh. "You're as shameless as ever," she said. The rest of our group had now stopped to wait for Neruda who was speaking in Chilean slang to the parrots in the bird market. When we renewed our conversation, Frau Frida had changed the subject.

"By the way," she said, "you can go back to Vienna if you like."   20

I then realized that thirteen years had passed since we first met.

"Even if your dreams aren't true, I will never return," I told her, "just in case."

At three o'clock we parted in order to accompany Neruda to his sacred siesta, which he took at our house, following a number of solemn preparatory rituals that, for some reason, reminded me of the Japanese tea ceremony. Windows had to be opened, others closed — an exact temperature was essential — and only a certain kind of light from only a certain direction could be tolerated. And then: an absolute silence. Neruda fell asleep at once, waking ten minutes later, like children do, when we expected it least. He appeared in the living room, refreshed, the monogram of the pillow case impressed on his cheek.

"I dreamt of that woman who dreams," he said.

Matilde asked him to tell us about the dream.   25

"I dreamt she was dreaming of me," he said.

"That sounds like Borges," I said.

He looked at me, crestfallen. "Has he already written it?"

"If he hasn't, he's bound to write it one day," I said. "It'll be one of his labyrinths."

As soon as Neruda was back on board ship at six that afternoon, he   30
said his farewells to us, went to sit at an out-of-the-way table, and began writing verses with the same pen of green ink that he had been using to draw flowers, fish, and birds in the dedications he signed in his own books. With the first announcement to disembark, we sought out Frau Frida and found her finally on the tourist deck just as we were about to give up. She, too, had just woken from a siesta.

"I dreamt of your poet," she told us.

Astonished, I asked her to tell me about the dream.

"I dreamt he was dreaming about me," she said, and my look of disbelief confused her. "What do you expect? Sometimes among all the dreams there has to be one that bears no relation to real life."

I never saw or thought about her again until I heard about the ring made in the form of a serpent on the finger of the woman who died in the sea disaster at the Hotel Riviera. I could not resist asking the Portuguese ambassador about it when we met up a few months later at a diplomatic reception.

The ambassador spoke of her with enthusiasm and tremendous ad-   35
miration. "You can't imagine how extraordinary she was," he said. "You would have been unable to resist wanting to write a story about her." And he continued in the same spirit, on and on, with some occasional, surprising details, but without an end in sight.

"Tell me then," I said finally, interrupting him, "what exactly did she do?"

"Nothing," he replied, with a shrug of resignation. "She was a dreamer."

EXPLORATIONS

1. In what ways does Gabriel García Márquez express skepticism of Frau Frida's dreams? In what ways does he express credulity? How does the poet Pablo Neruda react to her, and why?

2. In what ways do the structure, content, and style of "Dreams for Hire" make it seem more like a short story than an essay? What aspects of the piece remind us that it is a factual account?

3. In what ways is the last sentence of "Dreams for Hire" ambiguous? How would the narrative's impact change if the Portuguese ambassador explicitly answered the questions García Márquez has raised?

CONNECTIONS

1. García Márquez writes of the Viennese family who first employed Frau Frida: "All of them were religious and therefore susceptible to archaic superstitions" (para. 8). What evidence of this connection between religion and superstition appears in Isabelle Allende's "Clarisa" (p. 501)? What evidence in each of these two selections indicates the writer's attitude toward religious and superstitious beliefs?

2. Although "Dreams for Hire" resembles Allende's short story "Clarisa" in its structure, technique, and use of magic realism, it is a nonfictional essay. How do you think Chinua Achebe would explain García Márquez's use of tools normally associated with fiction to tell a "true" story?

3. What similar reactions to dream revelations are expressed by García Márquez and by Joyce Carol Oates (p. 411)? Which writer places more importance on explaining — finding rational reasons for — the seeming power of dreams? What are some likely reasons for that contrast?

ELABORATIONS

1. To analyze the art of García Márquez is a task beyond the most ambitious critic; but we can learn a lot about writing by studying his craft. For instance, how does he use the literary device of a quest to create purpose, momentum, and suspense in this essay? Whose quest is it, and what is its object? What incidents begin and end it? What adventures along the way maintain our curiosity? Write an essay analyzing García Márquez's use of a quest as his central thread in "Dreams for Hire."

2. Have your dreams ever come true? Have you learned anything from dreams about yourself or your relationships with other people? What are your beliefs about the nature and purposes of dreams? Write an essay defining or classifying dreams or narrating an experience involving a powerful dream.

PART SIX

PEOPLE AND POWER

OBSERVATIONS

Haunani-Kay Trask, Vine Deloria Jr. and Clifford M. Lytle,
Nader Mousavizadeh, Serge Schmemann,
Elaine Ruth Fletcher, Roger Cohen, Frank Langfitt,
Susan Sontag, Thomas L. Friedman,
Saul Bellow, Ted Koppel, Octavio Paz

▼ ▼ ▼

Neil Postman, *Future Shlock* (UNITED STATES)

Jianying Zha, *Yearnings* (CHINA)

Masha Gessen, *The Day After Technology* (RUSSIA)

Amos Oz, *Between Word and Picture* (ISRAEL/GERMANY)

Elaine Salinas, *Still Grieving over the Loss of the Land*
(UNITED STATES)

Esther Dyson, *Cyberspace: If You Don't Love It, Leave It*
(UNITED STATES)

Henry Louis Gates Jr. and Cornel West, *The Talented Tenth*
(UNITED STATES)

Nelson Mandela, *Black Man in a White Court* (SOUTH AFRICA)

Grace Paley, *Six Days: Some Rememberings* (UNITED STATES)

Fay Weldon, *Down the Clinical Disco* (GREAT BRITAIN)

OBSERVATIONS

From the earliest days of Western contact my people told their guests that *no one* owned the land. The land — like the air and the sea — was for all to use and share as their birthright. Our chiefs were *stewards* of the land; they could not own or privately possess the land any more than they could sell it.

But the *haole* insisted on characterizing our chiefs as feudal land-lords and our people as serfs. Thus, a European term which described a European practice founded on the European concept of private prop-erty — feudalism — was imposed upon a people halfway around the world from Europe and vastly different from her in every conceivable way. . . . Land tenure changes instituted by Americans and in line with current Western notions of private property were then made to appear beneficial to the Hawaiians. But in practice, such changes benefited the *haole*, who alienated the people from the land, taking it for themselves.

— HAUNANI-KAY TRASK
"From a Native Daughter"
*The American Indian and
the Problem of History*, 1987

▼ ▼ ▼

The most profound and persistent element that distinguishes Indian ways of governing from European-American forms is the very simple fact that non-Indians have tended to write down and record all the prin-ciples and procedures that they believe essential to the formation and operation of a government. The Indians, on the other hand, benefiting from a religious, cultural, social, and economic homogeneity in their tribal societies, have not found it necessary to formalize their political institutions by describing them in a document. In addition, at least with the American experience, citizenship has been a means by which di-verse peoples were brought into a relatively homogeneous social whole, and in order to ensure good citizenship, the principles of government have been taught so that newcomers to society can adapt themselves to the rules and regulations under which everyone has agreed to live. Within an Indian tribal society, on the other hand, the simple fact of being born establishes both citizenship and, as the individual grows, a homogeneity of purpose and outlook. Customs, rituals, and traditions are a natural part of life, and individuals grow into an acceptance of them, eliminating the need for formal articulation of the rules of Indian tribal society.

> – Vine Deloria Jr. and Clifford M. Lytle
> *The Native Within: The Past and Future of American Indian Sovereignty*, 1984

▼ ▼ ▼

This New Year's Eve in Denmark, as on every New Year's Eve that I can recall, one ritual of respect was re-enacted, one moment of reflection allowed before the revelries and the all-too-ritualized cheers of new beginnings could start. We had all gathered, about twenty or so old friends at a house in the country, surrounded by the snows of Denmark's first white Christmas in over ten years. Though none of us is exceedingly royalist, we had dropped everything in order to crowd around the television at precisely 6 P.M. for the Queen's New Year's address. It struck me, with my Americanized sensibilities (I have lived here for the past seven years but grew up in Denmark), as a remarkable moment in the life of a modern nation: The entire waking population tuning in, not for entertainment or pleasure or shock, but to be addressed by the monarch. . . .

What does it mean, though, that all of Denmark halts to hear the Queen's words? It doesn't mean that Danes are observing a royal tradition for the sake of tradition, but that they are renewing a tradition year after year, of their own free will. And, more importantly, it means that the Queen and the royal household have grasped a central irony of the constitutional monarchy. An institution as fundamentally undemocratic and unmeritocratic as royal authority can only be sustained, in the modern age, by the most fundamentally democratic and meritocratic conditions of individual ability and achievement. That is to say, only by winning over the people through dignity and charisma and exemplary behavior — by winning their approval — can a monarch earn what he or she in other times was born to: their allegiance.

> – Nader Mousavizadeh
> "Copenhagen Diarist: The Royal We"
> *The New Republic*, 1996

▼ ▼ ▼

Measured against its own ambitions, the Union of Soviet Socialist Republics died a monumental failure. It had promised no less than the creation of a "new Soviet man," selflessly devoted to the common good, and ended up all but crushing the initiative and spirit of the people. It had proclaimed a new humanitarian ideology and in its name butchered 10 million of its own. It had envisioned a planned economy

in which nothing was left to chance and created an elephantine bureaucracy that finally smothered it. It had promised peace and freedom,
and created the world's most militarized and ruthless police state. It had
promised a people's culture and created an anticulture in which medi-
ocrity was glorified and talent mercilessly suppressed.

In the end, promising a new life, it created a society that was unspeakably bleak — polluted, chronically short of everything, stripped of initiative
and spirituality. While the bulk of the nation stood in line or guzzled rotgut
vodka, the Communist elite raised corruption to new heights: the likes of
Leonid Brezhnev and his cronies pinned endless medals on one another
and surrounded themselves with fancy cars, vast hunting estates, armies of
sycophants, and secret hospitals filled with the latest Western technology.

Yet the Soviet Union had also been an indisputable superpower, a
state and a nation that achieved epic feats in science, warfare, culture.
Perhaps all this was achieved despite Communism rather than because
of it. Yet by some combination of coercion and inspiration, the system
unleashed a potent national energy that made possible the rapid indus-
trialization of the 1930s, the defeat of Nazi Germany in the 1940s, the
launching of the first Sputnik in the 1950s, and the creation of a nuclear arsenal in the 1960s and 1970s. Even as the state collapsed, two
cosmonauts circled the globe.

It is easy now, gazing over the ruins of the Soviet empire, to list the fatal
illusions of the Marxist system. Yet the irresistible utopian dream fired
generations of reformers, revolutionaries, and radicals here and abroad,
helping to spread Soviet influence to the far corners of the globe. Until
recently, rare was the third-world leader who did not espouse some vari-
ant or other of Marxist doctrine, who did not make regular pilgrimages to
Moscow or join in the ritual denunciations of the "imperialists." It was a
monumental failure, but it had been a grand dream, and an experiment
on a scale the world had never known before.

> — SERGE SCHMEMANN
> *Echoes of a Native Land:*
> *Two Centuries of a Russian Village,* 1997

▼ ▼ ▼

After a slump that saw increasing numbers of young Israelis avoiding
the draft, Israel's army is reshaping its image to make itself relevant to a
generation far more affluent, more sophisticated, and more career-
oriented than earlier ranks of soldiers.

For the first time, the once-secretive army has gone public, opening
a Web site where prospective draftees can get answers to basic questions
about army life. New draftees are being asked to cite job preferences

during their three years of obligatory service — two for women — and about half are placed in their first choice of unit. . . .

"There is no doubt that the meaning of the army in the eyes of Israel's founders fifty years ago, in a country that was created out of 600,000 Jews on the ashes of the Holocaust, is different than what we have now," said Ariel Kapon, [a] senior figure in the army's personnel branch. "Then, there was an existential threat to the state — and the willingness of people to contribute was very great, both because of the Holocaust and because Israel was a state in the making. Today, in my opinion, despite the threat of missiles, there is no longer an existential threat, and like all other cultures in the world, Israelis are looking for self-realization," he continued. "We have to know how to use that — to go from the 'us' to the 'we' for the needs of the army."

> – ELAINE RUTH FLETCHER
> *San Francisco Examiner*, 1998

▼ ▼ ▼

The fight to be the leading newspaper of the city with ambitions to be Europe's new capital is ferocious, so executives at the *Berliner Morgenpost* thought long and hard to dream up a new advertising slogan.

What they came up with was: "Simply the Best."

Not *"Einfach besser,"* German for the same idea, but "Simply the Best," as in Tina Turner's popular song.

"Our target group was young people," said Rolf Buer, the paper's marketing manager, "and this slogan was young, fresh, simple, and sure to get people talking. German words are just too long."

. . . Language, of course, is a paramount expression of identity, and German identity has been a delicate issue ever since Hitler perverted the notion with disastrous consequences for those he considered un-German.

Not for nothing have many Germans embraced the idea of being "Europeans" or "cosmopolitans" or "citizens of the world." And of course the language of such world citizens is English.

"I don't like to think in terms of national borders," said Ulrich Veigel, head of the Bates advertising agency in Germany. "I live in Germany, and was born here, but I'm a citizen of the world, and that is the way we should all think."

> – ROGER COHEN
> *New York Times*, 1998

▼ ▼ ▼

Members of China's neighborhood committees used to be known as "KGB with tiny feet" — nosy elderly women who padded about in tightly bound shoes spying on local residents for the Communist Party.

During the tumultuous Cultural Revolution (1966–1976), they helped expose and punish "Capitalist Roaders," people who strayed from Communist ideology.

More than two decades later, many neighborhood committee members themselves are Capitalist Roaders. Instead of pouring out mind-numbing propaganda and trying to keep China faithful to Mao Zedong's Communist vision, they now provide much-needed social services and oversee a network of community-related businesses.

"In the past, we were more involved in ideological work," says Tong Meirong, 71, who heads a neighborhood committee in southeast Beijing about a mile from the city's Temple of Heaven Park. Now, she says cheerfully, "as we increase our businesses, we make more profit."

The evolution of the neighborhood committee from a snoop network to an increasing role as social service provider and entrepreneur mirrors some of the changes sweeping across this nation of 1.2 billion people. In the 1950s, the government established the committees to serve as thought police, maintaining social order, settling arguments, and disseminating the Communist Party line.

Zhang Yundeng, a 62-year-old retired lumber-factory worker, recalls how the committee that Tong now runs once forced perceived enemies of the state to stand with their heads bowed for half an hour and confess their "crimes." After Mao's death in 1976, the Great Helmsman's ideology faded, and a very different ethic emerged: making money.

— FRANK LANGFITT
Baltimore Sun, 1998

▼ ▼ ▼

For a long time almost all influential foreign scholarship and thinking about China started from the assumption that China was an essentially collectivist society with no indigenous tradition of individual rights. Hence, sinologists argued, we shouldn't expect a real movement for democracy and for individual rights as these are understood in the West to emerge in China. This double-standard thinking about China reflects the general decline of universalist moral and political standards — of Enlightenment values — in the past generation. There is an increasing reluctance to apply a single standard of political justice, of freedom, and of individual rights and of democracy. The usual justifications for this reluctance are that it is "colonialist" (the label used by people on the left) or "Eurocentric" (the label used both by multiculturalist academics and by businessmen, who talk admiringly of authoritarian "Confucian cultures") to expect or to want non-European peoples to have "our" values. My own view is that it is precisely the

527

reluctance to apply these standards — as if "we" in the European and the neo-European countries need them, but the Chinese and the peoples of Africa don't — that is colonialist and condescending.

– Susan Sontag
New York Review of Books, 1996

▼ ▼ ▼

Like one of the great sea powers of old, Microsoft today controls access to the modern lanes of communication. Microsoft operating systems run 85 percent of the world's personal computers. Microsoft doesn't need Washington to open doors for it because foreign governments are begging Microsoft to come in and translate Windows 95 into their languages, so they can get on the information highway. . . . China has the greatest potential, not just because it has 1.2 billion people but because its birth control policies restricting every family to one child mean there are often two sets of grandparents and two parents — that is, six adults — saving to buy a computer and software for each kid.

[Redmond, WA, executive Steve] Ballmer says Japan is just now taking off for Microsoft products, while Israel is so far advanced it has one of the few Microsoft development centers outside Redmond. But Microsoft's hottest market in the Middle East is Saudi Arabia. Iran and Egypt are nil, but India and Brazil are booming. The one European democracy that is slipping is France. Says Mr. Ballmer: "I don't want to say [France] has fallen behind," but "the penetration of PCs relative to population was quite high in France. That's not true anymore." . . .

While Microsoft is a coldblooded economic giant, its technology, along with that of its competitors, can foster democracy in ways G.M. never could. Its software is making it possible for individuals to communicate horizontally, through the Internet, across international boundaries, and to create groups and information pools that are outside all government authority. To take full advantage of that software, societies have to become more open, deregulated, and interactive. Says Mr. Ballmer: "Once you let people on the Internet, the control aspects are reasonably out the window."

– Thomas L. Friedman
New York Times, 1995

▼ ▼ ▼

There is simply too much to think about. It is hopeless — too many kinds of special preparation are required. In electronics, in economics, in social analysis, in history, in psychology, in international politics, most of us are, given the oceanic proliferating complexity of things, paralyzed by the very suggestion that we assume responsibility for so much. This is what makes packaged opinion so attractive.

It is here that the representatives of knowledge come in — the pundits, the anchormen, the specialist guests of talk shows. What used to be called an exchange of views has become "dialogue," and "dialogue" has been invested with a certain sanctity. Actually, it bears no resemblance to any form of real communication.

> – SAUL BELLOW
> "There Is Simply Too Much
> to Think About"
> *It All Adds Up*, 1994

▼ ▼ ▼

Let us give a name to that sandwich that my colleagues and I produce on television. Let us call it, for want of a better name, McThought. Just as the McDonald's hamburger has a vast distribution, so, too, does the McThought that is disseminated on television. Just as an increasingly large share of our population in this country is deriving its physical sustenance from McDonald's hamburgers, so, too, I fear, that an ever increasing number of people in this country are drawing their intellectual sustenance from television.

> – TED KOPPEL
> *Georgia Review*, 1995

▼ ▼ ▼

Literature has always been the product of a small group of writers and a small group of readers. I think the great difference between the past and modern times is not the *number* of people who read good books — these people have always been the minority   but the *kind* of people. In the time of Dante, the clerics and politicians, the directors of society, read poetry. In the Renaissance, you may recall, all the kings used to write poetry, some bad, some good, but poetry was popular in the upper class. With democracy, something changed, and the first one to notice this was Tocqueville, who saw very clearly that in the United States something new had appeared: the masses. The daily food for the masses became the newspapers, television, and other things.

It's useful to have television; it is useful to have newspapers; it is also useful to have good books. The problem is finding the right readers.

> – OCTAVIO PAZ
> *Georgia Review*, 1995

EXPLORATIONS

1. Judging from the Observations by Haunani-Kay Trask (p. 523) and Vine
   Deloria Jr. and Clifford M. Lytle (p. 523), what did early Hawaiian culture
   have in common with American Indian cultures? How did the cultural
   characteristics noted by Deloria and Lytle facilitate the process described by
   Trask?

2. Nader Mousavizadeh (p. 524) comments on the new tactics for maintaining
   power (or at least influence) of the Danish monarchy, which formerly could
   take its power for granted. Which other Observations show formerly powerful political and social institutions facing a similar challenge? What new
   tactics has each institution adopted to keep its grip on its constituency?

3. "Once you let people on the Internet, the control aspects are reasonably out
   the window" (p. 528). What does Microsoft executive Steve Ballmer
   (quoted by Thomas L. Friedman) mean by this? What evidence in other
   Observations in this section supports Ballmer's statement? What factors besides the Internet have played a role in the change he is referring to?

NEIL POSTMAN

Future Shlock

The social critic, writer, educator, and communications theorist Neil Postman started young. "When I went to Dodgers' games with my father and brothers," he told an interviewer, "I would come home and immediately write up the game as if I were a sportswriter for the *Daily News*." Born in Brooklyn, New York, Postman received his B.S. degree in 1953 from the State University of New York at Fredonia and his Ed.D. in 1958 from Columbia University. His early work focused on language and education. With such books as *Teaching as a Subversive Activity* (1969) and *The Soft Revolution: A Student Handbook for Turning Schools Around* (1971), both coauthored with Charles Weingartner, he became known as an advocate of radical education reform. For ten years he was editor of *Et Cetera*, the journal of general semantics. As television has played an increasingly central role in American culture, Postman has critically analyzed its impact not only on what information is available but on how we receive and understand information. Many of his numerous articles and books, including the internationally acclaimed *Amusing Ourselves to Death* (1986) and *How to Watch TV News* (with TV newsman Steve Powers, 1992), explore these issues. "Future Shlock" comes from his 1988 book *Conscientious Objections: Stirring Up Trouble About Language, Technology, and Education*. A former elementary and high school teacher, Postman returned to his old preoccupations with the award-winning *The End of Education: Redefining the Value of Schools* (1995). Other recent books include *Post-Intellectualism and the Decline of Democracy*, with Donald N. Wood (1997), and *Marshall McLuhan: The Medium and the Messenger*, with Philip Marchand (1998). Postman chairs the Department of Culture and Communications at New York University's School of Education; he also serves on the editorial board of *The Nation* magazine. He lives in Flushing, New York.

Sometime about the middle of 1963, my colleague Charles Weingartner and I delivered in tandem an address to the National Council of Teachers of English. In that address we used the phrase future shock *as a way of describing the social paralysis induced by rapid technological change. To my knowledge, Weingartner and I were the first people ever to use it in a public forum. Of course, neither Weingartner nor I had the brains to write a book called* Future Shock, *and all due credit must go to Alvin Toffler for having recognized a good phrase when one came along.*

I mention this here not to lament lost royalties but to explain why I now feel entitled to subvert the phrase. Having been among the first to trouble the public about future shock, I may be permitted to be among the first to trouble the public about future shlock.

Future shlock is the name I give to a cultural condition characterized by the rapid erosion of collective intelligence. Future shlock is the aftermath of future shock. Whereas future shock results in confused, indecisive, and psychically uprooted people, future shlock produces a massive class of mediocre people.

Human intelligence is among the most fragile things in nature. It doesn't take much to distract it, suppress it, or even annihilate it. In this century, we have had some lethal examples of how easily and quickly intelligence can be defeated by any one of its several nemeses: ignorance, superstition, moral fervor, cruelty, cowardice, neglect. In the late 1920s, for example, Germany was, by any measure, the most literate, cultured nation in the world. Its legendary seats of learning attracted scholars from every corner. Its philosophers, social critics, and scientists were of the first rank; its humane traditions an inspiration to less favored nations. But by the mid-1930s — that is, in less than ten years — this cathedral of human reason had been transformed into a cesspool of barbaric irrationality. Many of the most intelligent products of German culture were forced to flee — for example, Einstein, Freud, Karl Jaspers, Thomas Mann, and Stefan Zweig. Even worse, those who remained were either forced to submit their minds to the sovereignty of primitive superstition, or — worse still — willingly did so: Konrad Lorenz, Werner Heisenberg, Martin Heidegger, Gerhardt Hauptmann. On May 10, 1933, a huge bonfire was kindled in Berlin and the books of Marcel Proust, André Gide, Émile Zola, Jack London, Upton Sinclair, and a hundred others were committed to the flames, amid shouts of idiot delight. By 1936, Joseph Paul Goebbels, Germany's minister of propaganda, was issuing a proclamation which began with the following words: "Because this year has not brought an improvement in art criticism, I forbid once and for all the continuance of art criticism in its past form, effective as of today." By 1936, there was no one left in Germany who had the brains or courage to object.

Exactly why the Germans banished intelligence is a vast and largely unanswered question. I have never been persuaded that the desperate economic depression that afflicted Germany in the 1920s adequately explains what happened. To quote Aristotle: "Men do not become tyrants in order to keep warm." Neither do they become stupid — at least not *that* stupid. But the matter need not trouble us here. I offer the German case only as the most striking example of the fragility of human intelligence. My focus here is the United States in our own time, and I wish to worry you about the rapid erosion of our own intelligence. If you are confident that such a thing cannot happen, your confidence is misplaced, I believe, but it is understandable.

After all, the United States is one of the few countries in the world founded by intellectuals — men of wide learning, of extraordinary rhetorical powers, of deep faith in reason. And although we have had our moods of anti-intellectualism, few people have been more generous in support of intelligence and learning than Americans. It was the United States that initiated the experiment in mass education that is, even today, the envy of the world. It was America's churches that laid the foundation of our admirable system of higher education; it was the Land-Grant Act of 1862 that made possible our great state universities; and it is to America that scholars and writers have fled when freedom of the intellect became impossible in their own nations. This is why the great historian of American civilization Henry Steele Commager called America "the Empire of Reason." But Commager was referring to the United States of the eighteenth and nineteenth centuries. What term he would use for America today, I cannot say. Yet he has observed, as others have, a change, a precipitous decline in our valuation of intelligence, in our uses of language, in the disciplines of logic and reason, in our capacity to attend to complexity. Perhaps he would agree with me that the Empire of Reason is, in fact, gone, and that the most apt term for America today is the Empire of Shlock.

In any case, this is what I wish to call to your notice: the frightening displacement of serious, intelligent public discourse in American culture by the imagery and triviality of what may be called show business. I do not see the decline of intelligent discourse in America leading to the barbarisms that flourished in Germany, of course. No scholars, I believe, will ever need to flee America. There will be no bonfires to burn books. And I cannot imagine any proclamations forbidding once and for all art criticism, or any other kind of criticism. But this is not a cause for complacency, let alone celebration. A culture does not have to force scholars to flee to render them impotent. A culture does not have to burn books to assure that they will not be read. And a culture does not need a minister of propaganda issuing proclamations to silence criticism. There are other ways to achieve stupidity, and it appears that, as in so many other things, there is a distinctly American way.

To explain what I am getting at, I find it helpful to refer to two films, 5 which taken together embody the main lines of my argument. The first film is of recent vintage and is called *The Gods Must Be Crazy*. It is about a tribal people who live in the Kalahari Desert plains of southern Africa, and what happens to their culture when it is invaded by an empty Coca-Cola bottle tossed from the window of a small plane passing overhead. The bottle lands in the middle of the village and is construed by these gentle people to be a gift from the gods, for they not only have never seen a bottle before but have never seen glass either. The people are almost immediately charmed by the gift, and not only because of its novelty. The bottle, it turns out, has multiple uses, chief among them the intriguing music it makes when one blows into it.

But gradually a change takes place in the tribe. The bottle becomes an irresistible preoccupation. Looking at it, holding it, thinking of things to do with it displace other activities once thought essential. But more than this, the Coke bottle is the only thing these people have ever seen of which there is only one of its kind. And so those who do not have it try to get it from the one who does. And the one who does refuses to give it up. Jealousy, greed, and even violence enter the scene, and come very close to destroying the harmony that has characterized their culture for a thousand years. The people begin to love their bottle more than they love themselves, and are saved only when the leader of the tribe, convinced that the gods must be crazy, returns the bottle to the gods by throwing it off the top of a mountain.

The film is great fun and it is also wise, mainly because it is about a subject as relevant to people in Chicago or Los Angeles or New York as it is to those of the Kalahari Desert. It raises two questions of extreme importance to our situation: How does a culture change when new technologies are introduced to it? And is it always desirable for a culture to accommodate itself to the demands of new technologies? The leader of the Kalahari tribe is forced to confront these questions in a way that Americans have refused to do. And because his vision is not obstructed by a belief in what Americans call "technological progress," he is able with minimal discomfort to decide that the songs of the Coke bottle are not so alluring that they are worth admitting envy, egotism, and greed to a serene culture.

The second film relevant to my argument was made in 1967. It is Mel Brooks's first film, *The Producers*. *The Producers* is a rather raucous comedy that has at its center a painful joke: An unscrupulous theatrical producer has figured out that it is relatively easy to turn a buck by producing a play that fails. All one has to do is induce dozens of backers to invest in the play by promising them exorbitant percentages of its profits. When the play fails, there being no profits to disperse, the producer walks away with thousands of dollars that can never be claimed. Of course, the central problem he must solve is to make sure that his play is a disastrous failure. And so he hits upon an excellent idea: He will take the most tragic and grotesque story of our century — the rise of Adolf Hitler — and make it into a musical.

Because the producer is only a crook and not a fool, he assumes that the stupidity of making a musical on this theme will be immediately grasped by audiences and that they will leave the theater in dumbfounded rage. So he calls his play *Springtime for Hitler*, which is also the name of its most important song. The song begins with the words:

> Springtime for Hitler and Germany;
> Winter for Poland and France.

The melody is catchy, and when the song is sung it is accompanied   10 by a happy chorus line. (One must understand, of course, that *Springtime for Hitler* is no spoof of Hitler, as was, for example, Charlie Chaplin's *The Great Dictator*. The play is instead a kind of denial of Hitler in song and dance; as if to say, it was all in fun.)

The ending of the movie is predictable. The audience loves the play and leaves the theater humming *Springtime for Hitler*. The musical becomes a great hit. The producer ends up in jail, his joke having turned back on him. But Brooks's point is that the joke is on us. Although the film was made years before a movie actor became president of the United States, Brooks was making a kind of prophecy about that — namely, that the producers of American culture will increasingly turn our history, politics, religion, commerce, and education into forms of entertainment, and that we will become as a result a trivial people, incapable of coping with complexity, ambiguity, uncertainty, perhaps even reality. We will become, in a phrase, a people amused into stupidity.

For those readers who are not inclined to take Mel Brooks as seriously as I do, let me remind you that the prophecy I attribute here to Brooks was, in fact, made many years before by a more formidable social critic than he. I refer to Aldous Huxley, who wrote *Brave New World* at the time that the modern monuments to intellectual stupidity were taking shape: Nazism in Germany, Fascism in Italy, Communism in Russia. But Huxley was not concerned in his book with such naked and crude forms of intellectual suicide. He saw beyond them, and mostly, I must add, he saw America. To be more specific, he foresaw that the greatest threat to the intelligence and humane creativity of our culture would not come from Big Brother and ministries of propaganda, or gulags and concentration camps. He prophesied, if I may put it this way, that there is tyranny lurking in a Coca-Cola bottle; that we could be ruined not by what we fear and hate but by what we welcome and love, by what we construe to be a gift from the gods.

And in case anyone missed his point in 1932, Huxley wrote *Brave New World Revisited* twenty years later. By then, George Orwell's *1984* had been published, and it was inevitable that Huxley would compare Orwell's book with his own. The difference, he said, is that in Orwell's book people are controlled by inflicting pain. In *Brave New World*, they are controlled by inflicting pleasure.

The Coke bottle that has fallen in our midst is a corporation of dazzling technologies whose forms turn all serious public business into a kind of *Springtime for Hitler* musical. Television is the principal instrument of this disaster, in part because it is the medium Americans most dearly love, and in part because it has become the command center of our culture. Americans turn to television not only for their light entertainment but for their news, their weather, their politics, their religion, their history — all of which may be said to be their serious entertainment. The light entertainment is not the problem. The least dangerous things on television are its junk. What I am talking about is television's preemption of our culture's most serious business. It would be merely banal to say that television presents us with entertaining subject matter. It is quite another thing to say that on television all subject matter is presented as entertaining. And that is how television brings ruin to any intelligent understanding of public affairs.

Political campaigns, for example, are now conducted largely in the   15
form of television commercials. Candidates forgo precision, complexity, substance — in some cases, language itself — for the arts of show business: music, imagery, celebrities, theatrics. Indeed, political figures have become so good at this, and so accustomed to it, that they do television commercials even when they are not campaigning. . . . Even worse, political figures appear on variety shows, soap operas, and sitcoms. George McGovern, Ralph Nader, Ed Koch, and Jesse Jackson have all hosted *Saturday Night Live*. Henry Kissinger and former president Gerald Ford have done cameo roles on *Dynasty*. [Former Massachusetts officials] Tip O'Neill and Governor Michael Dukakis have appeared on *Cheers*. Richard Nixon did a short stint on *Laugh-In*. The late senator from Illinois, Everett Dirksen, was on *What's My Line?*, a prophetic question if ever there was one. What *is* the line of these people? Or, more precisely, *where* is the line that one ought to be able to draw between politics and entertainment? I would suggest that television has annihilated it. . . .

But politics is only one arena in which serious language has been displaced by the arts of show business. We have all seen how religion is packaged on television, as a kind of Las Vegas stage show, devoid of ritual, sacrality, and tradition. Today's electronic preachers are in no way like America's evangelicals of the past. Men like Jonathan Edwards, Charles Finney, and George Whiteside were preachers of theological depth, authentic learning, and great expository power. Electronic preachers such as Jimmy Swaggart, Jim Bakker, and Jerry Falwell are merely performers who exploit television's visual power and their own charisma for the greater glory of themselves.

We have also seen *Sesame Street* and other educational shows in which the demands of entertainment take precedence over the rigors of learning. And we well know how American businessmen, working under the assumption that potential customers require amusement rather than facts, use music, dance, comedy, cartoons, and celebrities to sell their products.

Even our daily news, which for most Americans means television news, is packaged as a kind of show, featuring handsome news readers, exciting music, and dynamic film footage. Most especially, film footage. When there is no film footage, there is no story. Stranger still, commercials may appear anywhere in a news story — before, after, or in the middle. This reduces all events to trivialities, sources of public entertainment and little more. After all, how serious can a bombing in Lebanon be if it is shown to us prefaced by a happy United Airlines commercial and summarized by a Calvin Klein jeans commercial? Indeed, television newscasters have added to our grammar a new part of speech — what may be called the "Now . . . this" conjunction, a conjunction that does not connect two things but disconnects them. When newscasters say, "Now . . . this," they mean to indicate that what you have just heard or seen has no relevance to what you are about to hear or see. There is no murder so brutal, no political blunder so costly, no bombing so devastating that it cannot be erased from our minds by a newscaster saying, "Now . . . this." He means that you have thought long enough on the matter (let us say, for forty seconds) and you must now give your attention to a commercial. Such a situation is not "the news." It is merely a daily version of *Springtime for Hitler*, and in my opinion accounts for the fact that Americans are among the most ill-informed people in the world. To be sure, we know *of* many things; but we know *about* very little.

To provide some verification of this, I conducted a survey a few years back on the subject of the Iranian hostage crisis. I chose this subject because it was alluded to on television *every day for more than a year.* I did not ask my subjects for their opinions about the hostage situation. I am not interested in opinion polls; I am interested in knowledge polls. The questions I asked were simple and did not require deep knowledge. For example, Where is Iran? What language do the Iranians speak? Where did the Shah come from? What religion do the Iranians practice, and what are its basic tenets? What does *Ayatollah* mean? I found that almost everybody knew practically nothing about Iran. And those who did know something said they had learned it from *Newsweek* or *Time* or the *New York Times.* Television, in other words, is not the great information machine. It is the great disinformation machine. A most nerve-racking confirmation of this came some time ago during an interview with the producer and the writer of the TV mini-series "Peter the Great." Defending the historical inaccuracies in the drama — which included a fabricated meeting between Peter and Sir Isaac Newton — the producer said that no one would watch a dry, historically faithful biography. The writer added that it is better for audiences to learn something that is untrue, if it is entertaining, than not to learn anything at all. And just to put some icing on the cake, the actor who played Peter, Maximilian Schell, remarked that he does not believe in historical truth and therefore sees no reason to pursue it.

I do not mean to say that the trivialization of American public discourse is all accomplished on television. Rather, television is the paradigm for all our attempts at public communication. It conditions our minds to apprehend the world through fragmented pictures and forces other media to orient themselves in that direction. You know the standard question we put to people who have difficulty understanding even simple language: We ask them impatiently, "Do I have to draw a picture for you?" Well, it appears that, like it or not, our culture will draw pictures for us, will explain the world to us in pictures. As a medium for conducting public business, language has receded in importance; it has been moved to the periphery of culture and has been replaced at the center by the entertaining visual image. 20

Please understand that I am making no criticism of the visual arts in general. That criticism is made by God, not by me. You will remember that in His Second Commandment, God explicitly states that "Thou shalt not make unto thee any graven image, nor any likeness of anything that is in Heaven above, or that is in the earth beneath, or the waters beneath the earth." I have always felt that God was taking a rather extreme position on this, as is His way. As for myself, I am arguing from the standpoint of a symbolic relativist. Forms of communication are neither good nor bad in themselves. They become good or bad depending on their relationship to other symbols and on the functions they are made to serve within a social order. When a culture becomes overloaded with pictures; when logic and rhetoric lose their binding authority; when historical truth becomes irrelevant; when the spoken or written word is distrusted or makes demands on our attention that we are incapable of giving; when our politics, history, education, religion, public information, and commerce are expressed largely in visual imagery rather than words, then a culture is in serious jeopardy.

Neither do I make a complaint against entertainment. As an old song has it, life is not a highway strewn with flowers. The sight of a few blossoms here and there may make our journey a trifle more endurable. But in America, the least amusing people are our professional entertainers. In our present situation, our preachers, entrepreneurs, politicians, teachers, and journalists are committed to entertaining us through media that do not lend themselves to serious, complex discourse. But these producers of our culture are not to be blamed. They, like the rest of us, believe in the supremacy of technological progress. It has never occurred to us that the gods might be crazy. And even if it did, there is no mountaintop from which we can return what is dangerous to us.

We would do well to keep in mind that there are two ways in which the spirit of a culture may be degraded. In the first — the Orwellian — culture becomes a prison. This was the way of the Nazis, and it appears to be the way of the Russians.[1] In the second — the Huxleyan — culture becomes a burlesque. This appears to be the way of the Americans. What Huxley teaches is that in the Age of Advanced Technology, spiritual devastation is more likely to come from an enemy with a smiling countenance than from one whose face exudes suspicion and hate. In the Huxleyan prophecy, Big Brother does not watch us, by his choice; we watch him, by ours. When a culture becomes distracted by trivia; when political and social life are redefined as a perpetual round of entertainments; when public conversation becomes a form of baby talk; when a people become, in short, an audience and their public business a vaudeville act, then — Huxley argued — a nation finds itself at risk and culture-death is a clear possibility. I agree.

---

[1]That is, the Soviet Union. — ED.

EXPLORATIONS

1. What is Neil Postman's greatest concern about technological progress? What specific technology or technologies does his essay indict? Do his fears apply equally to all technological advances? Why or why not?

2. At what points does Postman address the reader directly? What is the effect of these shifts into the second person ("you")? What is the effect of his frequent use of the first person singular ("I")? The first person plural ("we")?

3. In what ways does Postman use entertainment to make his case? Is his essay a contradiction of his own argument? Why or why not?

CONNECTIONS

1. Postman infers this warning from Mel Brooks's film *The Producers:* "that the producers of American culture will increasingly turn our history, politics, religion, commerce, and education into forms of entertainment, and that we will become as a result a trivial people, incapable of coping with complexity, ambiguity, uncertainty, perhaps even reality" (para. 11). Which writers of the Observations on pages 523–529 evidently share this concern? Which ones seem not to be worried about it, and why?

2. "How does a culture change when new technologies are introduced to it? And is it always desirable for a culture to accommodate itself to the demands of new technologies?" (para. 7) According to Postman, these questions raised by the movie *The Gods Must Be Crazy* are "as relevant to people in Chicago or Los Angeles or New York as . . . to those of the Kalahari Desert" (para. 7). Reread Sven Birkerts's Observation on page 212. How does Birkerts answer Postman's first question as it applies to our own culture? What does he say about Postman's second question?

3. "No scholars, I believe, will ever need to flee America. . . . [But] a culture does not have to force scholars to flee to render them impotent" (para. 4). What development in American culture is Postman condemning? Judging from "The New Lost Generation" (p. 263), would James Baldwin agree? What do you think Baldwin would add to Postman's argument?

ELABORATIONS

1. Postman makes his case by encouraging the reader to draw conclusions from evidence; sometimes he does not state his point directly. Go through "Future Shlock" and identify the thesis of each paragraph. Then write a brief essay incorporating these thesis statements into a shorter and more explicit version of Postman's argument.

2. Postman wrote "Future Shlock" during Ronald Reagan's presidency. Has the evolution of American culture since then confirmed or contradicted his diagnosis? Write an update of "Future Shlock" using more recent evidence to argue for or against Postman's position.

JIANYING ZHA

Yearnings

"Born and raised in Beijing, I grew up in the chaotic years of the Cultural Revolution, and was among the first lucky batch to obtain a college education right afterward," writes Jianying Zha. "I arrived on the campus of Beijing University straight from a year of 'reeducation' farm labor with the peasants." After Chairman Mao Zedong became head of the People's Republic of China, his victorious Communist party began restructuring China's economy on the Soviet model: Private property was turned over to collectives, and central planning replaced markets. The Party's goals were ambitious, its tactics drastic, and its impact often tragic. The Hundred Flowers Movement toward openness in the mid-1950s was followed by the repressive Anti-Rightist Movement, in which many of those who had spoken out were expelled and punished. During the Great Leap Forward, launched in 1958, hundreds of millions of people were put to work on large industrial projects and over 40 million starved to death. In 1966 the decade-long Cultural Revolution began, glorifying workers, peasants, and soldiers and purging "bourgeois" intellectuals and officials — including Deng Xiaoping, who would become Mao's successor. During this period every family had to include a peasant, and many young people were sent away from their homes to labor on remote collective farms.

Zha continues: "In 1981, I came to America at the age of twenty-one, and after five and a half years of graduate school in South Carolina and New York, I went back to China in 1987 with a dissertation grant and hopes of reconnecting with my roots. In the following two years of living there, I started a moderately successful career writing Chinese fiction, and became increasingly involved in China's lively cultural trends and intellectual circles. By the time the students arrived in Tiananmen, I was coediting an elite Beijing magazine with a group of high-profile Chinese writers and working at a temporary job at the *New York Times*'s Beijing bureau." Tiananmen Square is the central plaza in China's capital city of Beijing. In the spring of 1989, Chinese students gathered there to demand faster-paced and wider-ranging reforms from Deng Xiaoping's Communist government. In June the army dispersed them, killing hundreds — perhaps thousands — of unarmed protesters.

"Tiananmen brought all that to a halt. After witnessing the June 4th massacre, I returned to the United States. Since then, my working life has been spent in both China and America. Since 1990, my job as a China program coordinator at an independent research center in Chicago [the Center for Transcultural Studies] has enabled me to visit China regularly. I have been able to stay in my mother's apartment in

542

Beijing for weeks, sometimes months, in order to conduct research and interviews. In the past two years, I've been writing a regular column of commentary on Beijing for a leading Hong Kong monthly. I am married to a Chinese-American and have made a home in Chicago while writing in both Chinese and English."

These biographical notes come from the introduction to Zha's book *China Pop: How Soap Operas, Tabloids, and Bestsellers are Transforming a Culture* (1995). "Yearnings" is excerpted from the book's chapter by that name.

Chinese civilization dates back some 5,000 years. The writing system used there today was created around 2,200 years ago, three centuries after Confucius laid some of the philosophical foundations of Chinese society. Unlike most of the world's other cultures, China's was unified early enough — thanks partly to strong emperors — to pass from generation to generation for centuries. Mongolian invaders led by Genghis Khan and his grandson Kublai Khan ruled China from 1276 to 1368. The next unwelcome barbarians were traders from Portugal, Britain, and elsewhere in Europe 100 years later. When China tried to stop the British from bringing in opium from India, Britain launched the Opium Wars. Defeated, China lost territory to Japan as well. But outsiders had brought ideas as well as drugs, weapons, and demands; and nationalists began allying to expel the interlopers. In 1911 Sun Yat-sen rallied other generals and proclaimed a republic. A decade later, a tiny group in Shanghai launched the Chinese Communist Party.

At first the Communists allied with Chiang Kai-shek's Kuomintang (KMT) nationalists, but in 1927 the KMT slaughtered thousands of Communist leaders. Mao Zedong began organizing a peasant army which traveled for over a year to evade the KMT — his famous Long March. The two parties joined again to repel the Japanese in the 1940s but split after World War II. In 1949 the victorious Maoists forced the U.S.-backed KMT into exile on Taiwan.

After Mao's death in 1976, Premier Deng Xiaoping recognized the country's need for intellectuals as well as for workers, peasants, and soldiers. He took steps to open China to the outside world, countering Mao's dogmatic socialism with remarks like "Black cat, white cat — it's a good cat if it catches mice." Living and working conditions remained harsh by Western standards. Still, progress toward greater political freedom and a more market-driven economy gave China the reputation of a model for Communist reform until the Tiananmen Square massacre in 1989. Deng's government fended off Western reprisal by continuing to loosen restrictions on free enterprise and trade while insisting on Chinese sovereignty. Jiang Zemin, who succeeded Deng after his death in 1997, has continued these policies.

A note on names: People's names in China normally are in reverse order from those in the West, with family name first and given name second. Jianying Zha, publishing in English, has switched her name from Chinese to English format, which we preserve here.

Teacher Bei is a buxom, sixty-three-year-old retired elementary school teacher who lives in a prefabricated apartment in the east side of Beijing. I call her "Teacher Bei," instead of "Aunt Bei" as Chinese normally call somebody her age, because of a warning from the friend who introduced us: It is very important, he said, to make her feel that she belongs to the educated class and is someone with culture. Teacher Bei was so pleased by our visit and got to talking so much that she skipped her nap and made a big pot of tea. She made us a delicious lunch in her spotless, drab living room, but she herself only nibbled. "I haven't had such a good time since *Yearning*," she admitted.

She says she has always been prone to depression. She has a history of breakdowns — the first one when she was twenty-five and married off against her will. Maybe this is why she always finds the gloom of Beijing's harsh winters so difficult. Last year, though, she didn't mind the winter because *Yearning* was on television just about every night. Two stations were showing it on different evenings, and she watched them both. "A good show gets better the second time," she says. She would shop, clean, wash, cook, and do what she could for herself and her husband (which was not that much at all), then get ready for the evening. She has two sons, both married, living away. They only drop by once in a while. "They are good children, as filial and respectful as anybody's, but they're always busy and have their own families to worry about now," Teacher Bei tells me stoically, not wanting to complain about what is obvious in her old age: the boredom, the emptiness, the marriage that never would have lasted were it not for the children.

Her husband, old Tang, is a railway engineer, half deaf from an accident but still working part-time. They have long lived in separate rooms; nowadays they hardly talk to each other. But in the months when *Yearning* was on, their household was almost conjugal. Every evening at 6:30, Tang would arrive from work and find dinner ready on a tray and his wife settled into a puffy lounge chair in front of the television, ready for *Yearning*. He would join her, sitting doggedly through the show, his eyes fixed on the screen even though half of the dialogue was lost on him. "It was bliss," Teacher Bei admits, sounding wistful. "Why can't they make a show like that more often? I guess it must be hard to come up with a story so complicated and gripping."

Yearning was a fifty-part Chinese television serial, in a genre that the Chinese television people call "indoor drama" because it is mostly shot with studio-made indoor scenes. The Chinese title, *Kewang*, literally means "a desire like thirst." Desire is a central theme of the show, which covers the lives of two Beijing families during the years of the Cultural Revolution and the eighties reforms. In normal times, according to normal social customs in China, they are not the kind of families who would care much to mix or socialize with one another: The Lius are simple workers living in a traditional courtyard house, whereas the Wangs are sophisticated intellectuals living in a modern apartment. However, the Cultural Revolution struck a heavy blow to the Wang family's fortunes, creating a chance for their son, a forlorn, sappy, soft young man of the type the Chinese call a "Little White Face," to meet the daughter of the Liu family. Of course, they get married, not out of love so much as a desire for the qualities of the opposite class: he for the simplicities of a heart of gold, she for the charm of being "cultured." From there on, despite the omnipresent Chairman Mao portraits on the walls of both homes, the Cultural Revolution and larger political events remain a blurry, underexamined background. Instead, the show focuses on daily family life and various romantic relationships.

At the heart of the story is Huifang, daughter of the Liu family, whose saintly presence quietly dominates and holds the moral high ground above the clatter of worldly events. Also central to the drama is a little girl whom the Liu family accidentally picks up: Huifang raises her through all manner of hardship, only to find out that she is the baby abandoned by the Wang family. Huifang is forever patient, kind, and giving — what Americans would call a goody-goody — yet she has the worst luck in the world. By the end of the show, she is divorced from her ungrateful husband, hit by a car, paralyzed and bedridden, and has to give back the adopted daughter so dear to her. In the true spirit of a long, drawn-out melodrama, *Yearning* entices its viewers with a fairly convoluted plot, conveniently linked by unlikely twists and turns, a good dose of tearjerking scenes, and a large gallery of characters from a broad spectrum of life.

There was little advertising for *Yearning* when it first aired in Nanjing in November 1990. The first few episodes attracted little attention, but by the end of the month just about anybody who cared anything about what's happening in China knew that the country was in for a "*Yearning* craze." By January 1991, all the major television stations had picked up the show. The number of stations quickly climbed to over 100, and the reception rate was unusually high. In the greater Beijing area, for instance, the rating was 27 percent, surpassing all previous foreign hits. In Yanshan, an oil and chemical industrial town with a population of over 100,000, the audience share was a stunning 98 percent.

Thousands of letters and phone calls flooded the stations daily. Demands were made with a good deal of fervor: People wanted *Yearning* on their television every night, and as many episodes as possible. Those who missed the earlier portion begged for a replay. Startled networks responded quickly. The time slot for the show increased, and reruns began even before the first run had ended — which helped to fan the flames and give the show more publicity. In some heavily populated cities such as Nanjing and Wuhan, the streets were deserted whenever *Yearning* was on. A department store in Hubei province broke its sales record: Over 1,500 television sets were sold while *Yearning* was on the air. In Wuhan, a scheduled power cut occurred in the middle of one episode; instead of sitting in the dark or going to bed as they had always done, an angry crowd surrounded the power plant and put so much pressure on the mayor that he ordered the power back on immediately.

People talked about *Yearning* everywhere — in the crowded commuter buses, on the streets, in the factories, offices, stores, and at family dinner tables. You could hear people humming the show's theme music in the narrow, deep lanes of Beijing and Nanjing. The audio track was packaged quickly into eighteen cassette versions, all of which sold like hotcakes. By the time the crew took its promotion tour for the show around the country, the main actors were already household names and the crew was mobbed by huge crowds everywhere. In some instances, the crew's arrival caused monumental traffic jams, de facto strikes, and work stoppages.

According to one report, the crew received such a spectacular welcome in Nanjing that the only other comparable turnout in the history of the city was when Chairman Mao first visited there decades ago. Fans waved banners and posters, some wept openly in front of the main actress, who had become, for them, a symbol of the virtuous victim; some even threatened to beat up the main actor, the embodiment of the selfish villain. Male viewers said that they yearned for a wife like Huifang; female viewers said that she was like a lovely sister to them. Everybody said that *Yearning* had brought out the best in them and made them understand better what it meant to be Chinese and how deeply rooted they all were in the Chinese values of family and human relations — and how all of this made them yearn for *Yearning* every night.

The press also jumped in. All sorts of stories about the series were   10
rushed into print in every possible form: behind-the-scenes reports, on-the-spot interviews, profiles, special columns, analytical essays, letters from the audience, statements from the writers and actors. For months, the promotions raged on fantastically, heating up a public already gripped by the show. Amid the flood of literature on *Yearning*, a 300-

page book topped all others: From collecting the pieces to editing, laying it out, printing, and binding, the entire book was processed in sixteen days. And how could a title like *The Shock Waves of Yearning*, with a glossy cover photo of the demurely smiling star, fail to stop the heart of a *Yearning* fan browsing at a bookstall?

Such excitement had not stirred in China since Tiananmen.

By the time Teacher Bei was watching *Yearning* for the second time (it was soon to be shown a third time, and she along with many others would watch it a third time), a certain standing member of the Politburo was also watching it at home. On January 8, 1991, this Politburo member, Comrade Li Ruihuan — who had risen from his first job as a carpenter to become overseer of national ideology — met with the *Yearning* crew. It was in a reception room inside Zhongnanhai, the Chinese Communist Party headquarters, nuzzled against the red walls of the Forbidden Palace.

Li Ruihuan was clearly in a very good mood. He congratulated the crew on its success and called it "a worthy model for our literary and artistic workers." It is a lesson for us, he said, that a television drama depicting ordinary life could elicit such a warm *and* positive response from society. It tells us that an artistic work must entertain first, or it is useless to talk about educating people with it. The influence we exert must be subtle, imperceptible, and the people should be influenced without being conscious of it. In order to make the socialist principles and moral virtues acceptable to the broad masses, we must learn to use the forms that the masses favor. What he meant by socialist principles and moral virtues was "new types of human relations" — honesty, tolerance, harmony, and mutual help among the people. These, he said, were precisely what *Yearning* had portrayed so well.

On the following day, all the major Chinese newspapers reported Li's remarks on the front page.

Li Ruihuan had been assigned the job of ideology control right after the massacre at Tiananmen. It was an important promotion because, in the Chinese Communist Party's brutal history of power struggles, ideology was deployed like the army: Both were used as weapons of control and intensely fought over. Intellectuals, writers, and artists were watchful, for here was the new boss of the political campaigns and the ideological policies that had the power to advance or destroy their careers, to still their pens, even to rob them of their livelihoods. The promotion of Li Ruihuan, the well-liked mayor of Tianjin with a reputation of being a down-to-earth, no-nonsense man on economic matters, was itself a significant political signal.

The mechanism of control in these areas is extremely complex. The centralized party structure has its people in every small office, building itself up level by level all the way to the central party committee. But in the last ten years, it has been weakened from both within and without: Independent research associations, political and artistic salons, and joint ventures that crisscross institutions and countries had grown and provided the Chinese with something like an alternative, parallel structure. Still, nobody seemed to doubt that Li, at the top rung of the party structure, would be a most valuable player in the game. He was called into a Beijing fraught with tension, where the victorious but nervous hard-liners were trying to reclaim as many controlling posts as possible after the crackdown at Tiananmen.

Li surprised everyone with his first move. With energy, spunk, and a good deal of charisma, he launched a campaign against pornography. He went everywhere, and everywhere he went he talked about "sweeping out the pornographic literature and trade poisoning our society." His speeches were filled with a conviction that pornography was the chief evil of bourgeois liberalism and the chief object of his rectification campaign. He vowed to stamp out pornography and called on every leader to join him in this important battle. Other issues tended to sound abstract or muddled in Li's speeches — obscured by the heated antipornography rhetoric. The hard-liners didn't know what to say about this, since pornography was definitely a disease of Western liberalism and bourgeois decadence, and antipornography was surely a politically correct line. The intellectuals smiled knowingly and relaxed a little. Seasoned by decades of party campaigns, Chinese intellectuals, especially those above thirty-five, possess a keen political consciousness: They can read between the lines of a party document or a party leader's speech — which to an outsider or novice in Chinese politics may seem like dull, standard party lines worded in dull, standard party jargon — and detect at a glance signs of a new political shift. Even at private gatherings, discussing and speculating on the latest party policies is a perverse fixation among elder, educated Chinese. As for the ideologically minded cadres at various levels, the correct interpretation and response to signals and messages from above is an automatic reflex. Some intellectuals began to find Li quite appealing, for a politician; some even worried that his style might be a bit too flamboyant, too bold, that such a style would backfire all too easily, that he wouldn't last very long — there had been plenty of instances like this in the history of Chinese Communist Party politics.

Others who saw in the former carpenter a born statesman, shrewd and crafty in the games of politics, liked to cite a widely known story about Li Ruihuan's actions during the critical period of the students' movement in 1989. The students of Tianjin, a big city only two hours away from Beijing by train, had been agitated by the hunger strike on Tiananmen Square and wanted to join forces. Many other cities were already swept up by local student demonstrations. Li Ruihuan, then mayor of Tianjin, quietly offered free train fares to those who wanted to go to Beijing. With the stream of students flowing to Beijing — to rock someone else's boat — and his conciliatory speeches about the importance of keeping up Tianjin's economic production, Li managed to preserve peace in his own territory. There were also other rumors about Li's personal friendship with Deng, for whom Li had made home furniture with his own hands. This is playing politics Chinese style: With clever maneuvers and personal ties, you can go far, sometimes very far, in China's political arena.

Whatever Li Ruihuan's political prospects might be, he was a powerful figure and his words carried a formidable weight among the intelligentsia. Thus, the fact that Li Ruihuan had so graced *Yearning* with his warm endorsement seemed to indicate that the top leadership was well disposed toward the show. The large number of party VIPs accompanying Li to the Zhongnanhai reception included even leaders from the Beijing municipal party committee, a notoriously conservative bastion much hated for its active role in cracking down on the students at Tiananmen. Among them was Li Tieying, the education chief in the Politburo, whose image had been tarnished among educated Chinese because he took a firm stance alongside the hard-liners when the students went on their hunger strike. Li Tieying, as the papers reported the following day, used the occasion to talk about the need for "an in-depth campaign against cynicism about our country." Of course, he himself was hardly exempt from the charge of cynicism, after an embarrassing incident on television a few days after the Tiananmen massacre. It was one of those public political performances for politics: Li Tieying had been conducting a group of school children through a famous propaganda song, "Socialism Is Good," but the camera, fixing on his face, revealed that the conductor himself couldn't sing the song. His vaguely moving lips didn't match the words: A sinister ritual had been turned into a laughable farce.

Despite all the standard propaganda lines, however, the general tone 20 of the reception was clearly conciliatory, for Li Ruihuan's was the dominant voice. Li's remarks, highlighted in some papers by boldface print, were punctuated by telltale words like "harmony," "unity," "tolerance," and "prosperity." He kept saying things like: "Under socialism, everybody shares the same fundamental interests." Any Chinese with a degree of political sensitivity could see what was going on: Li was using *Yearning* to push his moderate line, to imply the need for political relief. While the hard-liners had been drumming about deepening the campaign of repression, using phrases like "live-or-die ideological struggles" to describe the post-Tiananmen situation, here was Li Ruihuan saying, basically, "Comrades, let's look at the bright side of the picture, let's focus on positive values."

When *Yearning* was first televised, some of China's writers and intellectuals tuned in too. At least here was something watchable, some of it even enjoyable. True, the story slowed down and the lines got repetitive, but the plot was absorbing enough, the tone not too didactic, and there was even some decent acting. The Wang family — and the intellectuals in general — didn't come out too well, but there was no need to take it so seriously. After all, it was only a soap opera. Their innocent enjoyment didn't last too long, though, because it soon became clear that *Yearning* was not being seen as simple lighthearted entertainment. Apart from the enthusiasm of the general public, officials from every level were following Li Ruihuan's cue and showering praises on the show. "They were wrapping the show up in a royal robe," a writer later told me. There was no question that the series was being exploited by a wide spectrum of officials, all of them lauding an aspect of the show to justify their particular approach to politics, or to illustrate their own theory of the Chinese national character.

The person who led the cheers within the literary community was a Mongolian by the name of Marlaqinfu, author of several undistinguished novels in the fifties and at the time party chief of the Chinese Writers Association. He dashed off an essay gloating over the public enthusiasm for *Yearning* as if it had been his personal victory. The show's success was living proof, declared Marlaqinfu, of how socialist realism is still vital in China and, what was more, how literature and art prosper after bourgeois influences have been cleaned away.

This kind of touting, so obviously opportunistic, was nevertheless joined by some other writers' more earnest, heartfelt appreciation of *Yearning*. These were the writers who, in the initial thaw after the Cultural Revolution, had won fame overnight, when a newly liberated literature assumed the prodigious role of moral spokesman for a people long silenced, and when writers became celebrities on the basis of a single "taboo-breaking," "truth-telling" story. Most of their works, though serious and courageous, had no style to speak of, let alone any breathtaking technique; they practiced a tiresome realism lacking the sophistication and depth that marked the great works of classical Chinese fiction and European realism. In the ensuing years, several waves of younger writers exploded onto the scene, dazzling the reader with their stylistic and narrative energy. They spearheaded an avant-garde movement infatuated with style, especially the styles of Western modernism. Their drive for new styles so overwhelmed literary circles that, suddenly, all previous writings seemed unimaginative, outdated, and irrelevant. In the meantime, nurtured by economic reform, commercial publishing was booming. It wasn't much of a fight: The majority of readers didn't have to be won over by sensational reportage and easy, entertaining materials — they rejoiced in them. Snubbed by elite critics and dropped by the general public, a great number of "outdated," "serious" writers, their memory of yesterday's glory still fresh, either had gone on producing works that were thoroughly ignored, or had stopped writing completely.

It was not surprising, then, that *Yearning*'s phenomenal success should excite them. As they saw it, here was a work done in a manner of good old realism, a show that depicted unambiguous, solid characters, gave them authentic, down-to-earth dialogue, followed an absorbing plot, and involved the audience emotionally with the dramatic fate of the characters. And it worked! The audience laughed and cried with it! What could be more precious, more satisfying to a writer than such a vital reaction? Chen Jiangong, a Beijing writer whose fiction was rather popular in the early eighties and who has been suffering a creative block since then, sounded almost grateful in a rave review of *Yearning*: In his view, the series owed its success to the good literary quality of its script — and by "good literary quality" he meant the solid creation of lifelike characters, from which Chinese writers had strayed. He was voicing the frustrations of an entire generation of writers for whom the popularity of *Yearning* had stirred the hope that perhaps their writing careers were not over yet.

Those who considered themselves members of the literary avant- 25 garde, on the other hand, regarded *Yearning* with unreserved disgust. In their eyes, everything about the show was offensive — its official status of "model product" and "campaign fruit," its crude, derogatory portrayal of the intellectuals, its vulgar, melodramatic style, and its celebration, in the service of party politics, of old Chinese values such as self-sacrifice and endurance (versus modern, Western values such as individualism and initiative). Beyond their antagonism toward the government — and they would have found whatever the current regime promoted repulsive, even if it were promoted by a moderate politician such as Li Ruihuan — the contempt for mass culture ran quite deep in the minds of these elite and elitist intellectuals. Most of them never bothered to watch *Yearning*; it was enough to condemn the show by its reputation, and for its success.

Yet in their sneer one could easily detect a certain embarrassment. After all, *Yearning* had been a great showcase for the state: The Chinese people may have followed the students and the elite intellectuals to Tiananmen Square, but now these same people were suddenly re-united with the government. Their love of *Yearning* stood in jarring contrast to their indifference toward the avant-garde scene, which by this time was suffering a rapid, cheerless deterioration: Works continued to be published, but the movement had lost its steam, and nobody seemed to care. Another disconcerting thing about the series was that one of its seven script writers, Wang Shuo, happened to be a young novelist who was not only tremendously popular among urban youths and common folk in Beijing but also respected, if grudgingly, by many elite critics. Puzzled by this man's role in *Yearning*, one such critic could not refrain from telling me that Wang Shuo was merely "playing" with television, earning a few easy bucks, and that he could not be responsible for such a gross product. "What about Zheng Wanlong?" I asked — about another widely acclaimed writer who was involved in developing the script. The critic's face fell. He was not at all ready to absolve Zheng the way he tried to excuse Wang. Frowning, he said coldly: "Oh, *he* sold out. I have no respect for writers like that. It's unforgivable." . . .

Zheng Wanlong now says that the whole thing was absurd. "What do you think my friends in exile would think of me getting mixed up in a model TV serial?" he asked me from behind the shroud of thick smoke from four hours of his chain-smoking. A fortyish, dark-skinned man, Zheng never went to college and had been a model factory worker and a low-level party bureaucrat until his fiction began to win critical acclaim ten years ago. A number of the critics who praised his fiction live in exile now. Since I knew some of them, and knew what they would say, I hesitated. He said, "Wouldn't they say that I have totally degenerated?" Without waiting for my reply, he shrugged and said: "Well, all my life, throughout my writing career, I have never degenerated. Let me taste just once what it feels like to degenerate."

In fact, the success of *Yearning* has transformed not only Zheng's image among his intellectual friends but, even more miraculously, his political fate. It was widely suspected that Zheng had something to do with organizing demonstrations and petitions in May 1989 — even that he had held up huge banners on the front lines. Serious trouble was in store for him. After the military crackdown on June 4, 1989, the Party moved on to a pervasive campaign of "facts verification." Every party member, especially in Beijing, was required to report his or her own activities during the democracy movement — whether one had gone to the Square, marched or signed any petitions, whether one had been sympathetic toward the movement, and what one thinks of it now, if one's "level of thinking and understanding" has improved after studying Deng's speeches and party documents regarding the "counterrevolutionary rebellion," and so on. This process of "facts verification" is normally referred to in Chinese conversation as *jiang qing chu*, "making things clear"; but when an investigation deals with a million people on the streets, and thousands daily on the world's largest square, there is really no way to make things clear at all. Many people simply denied that they had done anything in May and June — and, anyway, they said, now they were taking the "correct stance" alongside the Party. In most such cases, so long as nobody came up with hard proof to the contrary, that was the end of it.

A friend of mine, a college teacher who had marched, designed humorous posters, and written slogans, flatly denied everything he had done. "You see, I was lying, and they probably knew I was lying, but they didn't mind my lies," he told me glibly, with no trace of shame or guilt on his face. "It saved me some trouble, and it saved them some work, so both sides are happy, and both sides are cynical. Thirty years ago the party wanted us to believe in it, now the party just wants us to *say* that we believe in it. And, what's more, so long as they need us intellectuals to do some work, they'd rather close one eye and pretend that things weren't really that bad."

Zheng, however, could not disentangle himself quite so easily. What with certain complications about his signature on a certain petition, and his status as a prominent writer and vice editor in chief of a large publishing house, it was not so easy to "close one eye" to him. So when things didn't become "clear," a special task force was formed, its task being to interrogate him daily. Members of this task force consisted of various political work cadres from the security and personnel divisions of Zheng's publishing house; among the perks they received was a car put at their disposal. The investigation went on for almost a year. For months, Zheng had to answer meticulous questions about everything — for instance, where had he been on a certain hour of a certain day, with whom, for how long, by what type of vehicle he had gotten there, and what he did there, what he saw, and so on and so forth. "That's when you find how inadequate your own memory is and how much they know about you," Zheng now says, smiling. "Well, they know much

30

more than you think. For example, I said that on a certain morning around 9:00 I had left home by bicycle. One of them would be taking this down in his notebook, while the other checked *his* notebook and frowned: 'Are you sure about this?' He would say this looking into my eyes. 'According to our record here, you left at 8:15 that morning by bus.' That's the sort of thing that puts you in a cold sweat and makes your head throb, trying to recall every fucking little detail." In order not to complicate the situation and get more people entangled, Zheng simply stopped visiting or receiving friends. He also stopped writing letters and making phone calls. "Now I know what it means to be a hermit in a big city," he said, shaking his head, and laughed cheerfully.

Zheng can laugh, though, because his year of bad luck has turned into a new round of celebrity with *Yearning*. When his name appeared as a group of official censors screened the working copy, one of them asked if this Zheng was the writer from the publishing house; when this was confirmed, the official looked thoughtful for a moment, but the screening went on without further questions. From that moment on, the investigation of Zheng fizzled out. Since then, journalists have been flocking to Zheng's apartment and interrogating him about his role in the series. Because of *Yearning*, anything he says has news value and will find its way into a deliciously gossipy story; reporters reverently quote casual remarks he makes about writing, not because they care about his views on such things, but because of the fan club–like curiosity the show has inspired. One Beijing writer told me when I arrived there, "For a whole year Zheng was a criminal hiding in his hole; now he's once more a *xiang bo bo*" — a piece of sweet bread, which in Beijing slang refers to somebody who is hotly pursued. Zheng, though, says, "It's absurd," shaking his head, visibly pleased and a bit dazed by the turn of things for him. "First I felt like a hunted dog — then all of a sudden the search light switched, but I'm still a hunted dog!"

EXPLORATIONS

1. Why do the Chinese people say they liked *Yearning* so much? What other reasons does Jianying Zha suggest for the show's popularity?

2. Which parts of the political endorsement *Yearning* received (paras. 12–14) might a TV show in the United States receive from a high official? What parts are distinctly Chinese? How do the Chinese apparently see the role of television differently from Americans?

3. Zha writes that the comments on *Yearning* by Li Ruihuan, China's overseer of national ideology, "carried a formidable weight among the intelligentsia"

(para. 19). Why? Who are the intelligentsia, according to Zha? How does Li's approval of the show potentially affect them?

CONNECTIONS

1. In what ways does the impact of *Yearning* on China resemble the impact of the Coke bottle on the tribe in *The Gods Must Be Crazy*, as Neil Postman describes it in "Future Shlock" (p. 531)?

2. In "Future Shlock," what threats does Postman suggest television poses to American society? Which of these threats are also a danger to Chinese society, as characterized by Zha and by the Observations on pages 523–29, and which ones are not? What are the reasons for the difference?

3. Compare Frank Langfitt's Observation on page 526 with Zha's account of the Communist Party's investigation of Zheng Wanlong (paras. 27–31). How have things changed in China between the beginning of the 1990s (Langfitt) and the end (Zha)? How have things stayed the same?

ELABORATIONS

1. Reread Thomas L. Friedman's Observation (p. 528) on the impact of the Internet on China and on political control in general. Use the Internet or your library or both to do some research on the political situation in China since Tiananmen Square. Write an essay about the ways technology has influenced the policies of Deng Xiaoping's successor, Jiang Zemin. Consider some or all of the following questions: Has worldwide communication changed how much control China's government can exert over its people? Does China's desire for state-of-the-art technology from the West affect its human-rights policies? Its treatment of its "intelligentsia"? What new television shows have captivated the Chinese people since *Yearning*, and what approach is Jiang's government taking toward television and its creators?

2. When you are investigated by the Communist Party, says the writer Zheng Wanlong, "That's when you find out how inadequate your own memory is and how much they know about you" (para. 30). Reread Zheng's account of his investigation. Then imagine you are being watched and interrogated as Zheng was. Choose a day about a week ago; write down everything you did that day, and what time you did it, from memory. Afterward, check as many details as you can against other sources. How close is your memory to the facts? Write an essay in the form of an interrogation (dialogue) or an interrogator's report (exposition) based on your findings.

MASHA GESSEN

The Day After Technology

The journalist, author, translator, and editor Masha Gessen was born in Russia — then part of the Soviet Union — in 1967. Fleeing anti-Semitism, her family emigrated to the United States when she was fourteen. After working as a writer and editor on magazines including *The Advocate* and *Outweek*, she returned to Moscow in 1994, following the collapse of the Soviet Union in 1991. She found a country in political, social, and economic turmoil, as the centralized Communist systems were disintegrating without a stable new structure to replace them. Gessen writes regularly about Russia for *The New Republic* and *The New Statesman* in the United States and is a contributing editor for *Lingua Franca*. She also is a staff writer for the Russian magazine *Itogi*, a columnist for the English-language daily newspaper the *Moscow Times*, and a political columnist for the journal *Matador*. Her book *Dead Again: The Russian Intelligentsia After Communism* was published in 1997. She also has edited and translated *Half a Revolution: Contemporary Fiction by Russian Women* (1995), translated the upcoming book *In the Here and There*, and was a contributing editor to *Long Road to Freedom: The Advocate History of the Gay and Lesbian Movement*. The following essay comes from the March 1996 issue of the online magazine *Wired*.

From its creation in 1922, the Union of Soviet Socialist Republics (USSR), or Soviet Union, was the world's largest country. Its twelve member republics were forcibly united after the Russian Revolution toppled that nation's hereditary czar in 1917, and the Bolshevik Revolution swept Nikolai Lenin into power. For most of the twentieth century, Lenin and his successor, Josef Stalin, shaped the Soviet Union to fit their Communist ideal of a centrally run society and economy. Although the idea was for the workers (instead of capitalist profiteers) to own the means of production, the result was inefficiently run enterprises that often turned out second-rate goods. In the late 1980s President Mikhail Gorbachev announced new policies of perestroika (restructuring) and glasnost (openness). His efforts at reform led to the breakup of the Communist Party and soon afterward the Soviet Union itself. Russia, its biggest member republic, is now the world's largest country, still struggling with the difficult transition to new political, social, economic, and even (for the first time in decades) religious structures.

Technology is the future. Everyone knows that. Or knew it. Certainly, everyone in what used to be the Soviet Union did. Schools, party leaders, and banners on every street corner proclaimed the promise of electrified, technologized Communist bliss. Its much-sung harbingers included electric light bulbs, tractors on every collective farm, but most of all, "the peaceful atom" — nuclear power.

On April 26, 1986, the future ground to a halt. One of the Soviet nuclear-power reactors malfunctioned, blew apart, then burned in the single worst nuclear disaster in human history. Since that day, all of Europe has measured its health by its distance from Chernobyl. "The entire country is falling out Chernobyl-like," a prominent Soviet writer recorded in his journal four months after the catastrophe. "Matter is disintegrating uncontrollably, and spiritual substance is dissipating." He meant that no matter what the authorities did to stem the leaks of radiation and information, the country grew sick with the devastating news stripping it of its faith and its future.

The man who brings me into the disaster area, a youthful police major who oversees the region's security, is angry, like a man whose faith has been ripped away. "The peaceful atom wipes towns off the face of the earth," he growls, stopping the car on a burned-out patch. "Make sure you write about that."

He has brought me to the area immediately surrounding the reactor. It's the "Estrangement Zone": an area supposed to be dead, deserted, a vast memorial to the catastrophe. But the land refuses to lie in silent testimony. Instead, it has become a haven for all those whose future has been taken away — by the Chernobyl disaster or by war, age, illness, or their own demons.

People started trickling back almost as soon as they were evacuated.   5
One old woman stayed with friends at the border of the zone and snuck in every day for a year to tend to her garden; the soldiers guarding the zone finally let her move back to stay. Slowly the area started to come to life — a new and different life, a life conscious of its opposite, a life of refugees and survivors. Alongside villagers returning to their homes came new people fleeing death or cruelty or uncertainty. They have run from civilization to a place where civilization has fled. Most of them will tell you they lead futureless lives; tomorrow — the day after radiation — is thousands of years away, which, in human terms, is never. But these are people who don't need a future so much as they need a present that's better than the past. Confined in time and space, they are remaking life in the absence of the beliefs and conveniences that might prop it up. Their rewards are the barren freedom

that follows disaster and the eerie peace left in the wake of the peaceful atom.

The Chernobyl nuclear-power plant sits right by the border of Ukraine and Belarus, two former Soviet republics. After the explosion, radioactive particles covered the immediate area; winds carried radiation clouds to more distant parts of Ukraine, Belarus, Russia, the Baltics, and other parts of Europe. The worst of it fell on Belarus, one of the smallest and poorest of the former republics. Of its total area of 80,200 square miles, almost 10,000 square miles (about the size of Maryland) have been contaminated. In the Gomel region in southern Belarus, which includes the area just around the reactor, approximately 800 square miles (nearly the size of Rhode Island) have been turned into what officials call simply the Zone.

The year following the disaster, officials moved people out of 212 villages to apartments in "clean" parts of Belarus. Then, in 1990, they suddenly discovered a radiation "stain" almost 100 miles north of the reactor, and another 46 villages were evacuated. Altogether, according to the Belarus Ministry of Internal Affairs, 15,804 families — 37,231 people — left their homes behind.

That left 14,923 homes abandoned. Mostly, these were wooden village houses built tens or hundreds of years ago. They did not look dangerous — not like the reactor. They looked like lived-in homes with windows low to the ground, fruit trees growing up around them, picket fences out front, and elaborate roofed gates traditional to the area. They did not look left — no boarded-up windows or double-locked gates or fruit trees wrapped for the winter — they looked forgotten.

Something had to be done with these vacated towns. At first, teams of police and relief workers, sent here from all over the Soviet Union, tried to hide every remnant of life gone awry: They buried thousands of head of cattle, two trains full of contaminated meat, equipment, vehicles, whole villages. The reactor itself was encased in a white concrete housing known as "the sarcophagus." Relief teams raced looters who snuck in to steal people's abandoned belongings and use materials from houses to build radioactive structures elsewhere. At first, workers erected signposts or crosses to mark the spots where homes had vanished, now dismantled and hidden underground. Then they stopped. The unmarked burial sites today are overgrown with grass five feet high; only fruit trees linked in circles around empty patches indicate there were houses there once.

Then the relief teams stopped burying altogether: They ran out of money or energy or, perhaps, faith, because the line between life and   10 death — the buryable and the unburyable — grew fuzzy. Those who were doing the digging started dying and had to be buried along with their tools, while the land they were covering up started itself coming to life. Authorities put up a ring of barbed wire around the reactor, placed thirteen checkpoints along the borders of the Zone, and left the place to invent its own life on the ruins.

A couple in their fifties, their son, and his wife and year-old daughter live in the village of Bartolomeyevka in the house where they have always lived — dark, wooden, and filled with the smell of burning wood and dried apples. Cows have staked out the house across the street; they probably like it for its large dark-red gate and comfortable, well-worn yard. One of the cows likes to lie by the gate, with its enormous black-and-white head draped over the threshold. A rusty-colored chicken leans over to peck flies out of the cow's ears. A reddish-brown horse is just going out for a walk when my photographer friend and I arrive. The horse acknowledges our presence (or maybe the presence of flies) with a wave of his luxurious tail and wanders off down the street. The dogs — small, nameless, bowlegged specimens of indeterminate heritage — are catching some rays on the pavement: Cars don't come down this country road more than once a week, thanks to the police checkpoints.

In 1990, after the stain was discovered, interior ministry soldiers came to take an inventory of Bartolomeyevka and the neighboring villages, painting numbers on every house and every shed on every street, canceling out civilization's street addresses. Police came to dig up lampposts, disconnecting electrical, radio, and television cables. Then 6,200 people left for new city apartments, and only a handful of mostly old people — none in some villages, half a dozen in others — refused to move. The elders in this house — they introduce themselves only as Baba Anya (Grandma Anya) and Ded Ivan (Grandpa Ivan) — saw their son, Sasha, a tractor driver, leave with his wife for the small city of Svetlogorsk only to return about a year later, after the young people were laid off from their jobs.

Now life is simple, simpler even than it ever was — which is not to say that it's easy. Baba and Ded reinvent living off the land: They grow potatoes and squash, wheat and rye, apples and even grapes. They sometimes hitch a ride to the nearest populated town, about fifteen kilometers away, to get bread; for the most part, though, they use a flail — a length of heavy chain tied to a stick for threshing — and make their own. Before the accident, bread was baked at factories and sold at stores. But in a time long ago, before mills, and certainly before motors, peasants used to lay ripe wheat out on a piece of hard, compressed soil and beat it with a flail to separate the grain from the chaff. Now, Baba and Ded have discovered, blacktop pavement makes a better surface. Sasha and friends who come from their new "clean" towns all over Belarus go fishing in a nearby river, though fish, according to scientists studying the area, collect the greatest amount of radiation, along with mushrooms and blueberries. Their boots — a motley collection of about twenty misshapen pairs — dry on the fence of the cows' house.

In the city, life is impossible, Baba and Ded know: just ask their son, or any of the friends who've moved and now complain of misery. But here life is simple, if hard. The supposed harm — radiation — has no look or taste or smell, while the benefits — the fruits of familiar labor — look and taste and smell like plenitude. To me, the vegetables even seem bigger and more colorful than elsewhere, just as the sun here seems brighter and the air drier, though all that, probably, is an illusion, spawned by fear and the absence of people.

"Here, take some apples," Baba Anya offers, in keeping with the local 15 tradition of giving gifts to guests. My friend and I demur, but Baba forms a catch with the bottom of her apron and frantically fills it with apples and grapes. "They came and checked, and the apples are clean," she says. We back up into the house in a panic. "Thank you, but we're afraid," my friend musters even as Baba Anya fills his camera bag with fruit. Only after we had disposed of the gifts do I learn that, for some reason, apples in the Zone do keep coming up radiation-free. No one knows why.

"Look," Baba Anya says, standing on a piece of wooden planking to show me the luxuriously colorful garden extending for more than 100 yards behind the house. "Everything grows in radiation," she exclaims, her worn angular face suddenly animated. "Pumpkins and beets and potatoes and wheat and apples and grapes. Everything grows and blooms in radiation."

If Ded Ivan and Baba Anya's preference for an off-the-land lifestyle is instinctive and heartfelt, former mathematics teacher Arkady Nabokin's is highly rational and meticulously articulated. Nabokin lives in a neighboring village, where only two homes at either end of one street are occupied; between them, about twenty houses are silently sinking into the ground. Nabokin, an eighty-four-year-old widower, explains his philosophy of life and work as he shepherds his thirty cows.

Why would one man need thirty cows? "I am conducting a study," Nabokin explains importantly. "I am researching the problem of raising productivity among cattle growers. You see, you say now that machines should do the work. But no. Divide the number of machines by the number of head of cattle, and you see that I have greater productivity than a machine. Furthermore, I have no concept of per-head cost: I pay nothing to anyone. Mechanized farmers cut the grass with machines and pay for the fuel, the cost of which keeps growing. Then they must transport and warehouse the straw, and they pay for that, too. They transport manure. I don't have any of that. Therefore, my product is competitive with anyone's, including the Americans'."

During his lifetime, which spans the Soviet Union's industrial revolution, Nabokin has collected excessive amounts of data and opinions. He was born on a small farm just outside the Zone, on the other side of a level, straight-edged evergreen forest planted by local authorities on scientific recommendation. Nabokin stands erect and fragile, contemptuously stretching a bony arm in the direction of an asphalt factory blowing black smoke where the family's farm used to stand. "Stalin's goal was to build a military-industrial machine, so he destroyed all that," he says, indicating that the black smoke is the symbol of industrial violence. Rather than labor on a collective farm — which he sees as an industrialist plot against true farming — Nabokin worked as a schoolteacher for forty years. Only the collapse of the collective farm system, which coincided with the depopulation of this area, allowed him finally to launch his study into small farming. The potential of man unencumbered by machine, he says, is unlimited.

"I don't plan to stop at this number of cows," he declares. "I must 20 continue the exploration." He brushes off with utter disdain the idea of moving like the rest of his neighbors. "The scientists who tell us to leave are amateurs," he teaches. "Look, those who were at Chernobyl during the fire are dead. Whereas being here, I feel wonderful. I challenge you to find a man my age in America who keeps this many cows. Moving would be harmful to my health: the change in climate, the psychological stress."

In Nabokin's garden my Geiger counter stops at 173 microrads, or more than ten times the acceptable level of environmental radiation. Still, scientists who study the area agree that he is right: A person his age is better off exposing himself to the dangers of radiation than to the stress of uprooting. This may be the only idea that meets with agreement among virtually all scholars of the area.

Researchers of the Chernobyl disaster fall into two distinct schools: those who share the government-approved position that the contaminated lands should be "rehabilitated" — that is, resettled — and the mavericks who obsessively collect proof of the high-school-level-physics axiom that radiation produces mutation. The state-funded Institute of

Radiation Medicine continues the work started by officials sent to the area ten years ago to tell residents that they were in no danger and even stood to benefit from "low doses of radiation." (Post-Soviet scientists have since admitted they knowingly broadcast lies to stem spreading panic. So now their goal is different: to bring back to life some of the best land in impoverished Belarus.)

Anatoly Skriabin, a laboratory head and former director of the Gomel branch of the Institute of Radiation Medicine, has been covering the ill effects of nuclear disasters his entire professional life. Before coming to Gomel — the largest town in southern Belarus, which is fully populated, though much of the surrounding area is in the Zone — he was posted to an area in Siberia devastated in the 1950s by nuclear weapons tests and radioactive waste-disposal accidents. Over the last few years, as the facts of what was called the Kyshtym Tragedy have come to light, some scientists have claimed its scope exceeds every catastrophe before or since, including Chernobyl. Yet, Skriabin points out, "people have been living there just fine." In fact, he says, they've had fewer illnesses than their Chernobyl-affected counterparts, because they have not been overwhelmed with information about the harm of radiation. The institute's working hypothesis is that all the new illnesses in the Zone are psychosomatic. "They are told, 'You and your children are doomed,'" Skriabin explains in the tone of the Good Doctor, which corresponds neatly with his gray hair and white lab coat. "Then a hub forms in the brain, and it affects all systems, including the immune system."

On the opposite end of the radiation-hysteria spectrum are rumors, validated by numerous media reports, of hideous mutations in the Zone: crocodile-headed pigs, eight-legged calves, and the like. Oddly, the root of both interpretations of what has happened to this land is probably the same: Each offers a sort of comfort. Reality, it appears, is more insidious: Illnesses of all sorts are on the rise in the Zone, including thyroid cancer among children (400 cases in the last four years, up from next to zero), immune-system disorders (up 875 percent since 1986), tuberculosis, and diabetes. Women give birth not to monsters but to weak, slow-to-develop children; men in their thirties suffer strokes. Instead of showing itself in frightening disfigurements, the danger lurks everywhere: in the soil, the water, the food. It hits at random: Of three tractor drivers working contaminated land, one dies while two remain healthy.

Grigory Goncharenko brings the concept of random danger down to   25
the level of the lab, the Molecular Genetics Laboratory, at the Forest

Institute in Gomel, which he heads up. "At my lab I have about ten scientists," says Goncharenko. And with a circular nod of the head, he presents his youthful team: half a dozen bespectacled, bearded nerds and a couple of pale, long-haired young women, one of whom is busy making Turkish coffee in a large glass retort on a hot plate. "At the time of the accident, they were all young, and most of them had no children. So now they want to know, what are their chances of having mutant babies?" The nerds smile politely and nod.

Goncharenko is not talking about purple frog babies or similar nightmares of the irradiated imagination. He means what he calls "the usual stuff": Down's syndrome, urinary-tract abnormalities that lead to retardation, inborn autoimmune disorders. "To figure this out, I would have to take sperm from each of my boys, eggs from each of my girls, isolate the DNA, and analyze gene mutation so that then I can say, 'OK, you have a one-in-ten chance of having a mutant baby.'" Barring that — and the technical level of the lab does bar the complicated procedures required to carry out such a study — Goncharenko and his boys and girls have been studying evergreens, whose susceptibility to radiation happens to match that of humans nearly perfectly. They collect samples of evergreen seeds in the Zone, isolate thirty genes from their DNA, and — over and over again — keep finding some genes knocked out entirely, others disfigured beyond recognition.

Of course, they could have learned that much from a high-school textbook. But, because officials kept saying that the accident would have no influence on future generations, Goncharenko rushed to Moscow as soon as the lab got its first results. There, he was ridiculed for proving what every scientist learned as a kid. "They told me, 'Of course we know this,'" he recalls. "'But it's classified information.'"

Goncharenko continues to tell me about his work after we leave the lab and walk around Gomel. Or, not walk around exactly, but in circles and zigzags, with the esteemed scientist occasionally grabbing me by the sleeve to pull me in a new direction. "They still monitor the intelligentsia here," he explains in a stage whisper. "There is a young man with an umbrella behind us." There are a lot of young men with umbrellas around us, because it's been raining all day. Still, every time Goncharenko spots a male with an umbrella, we lurch onto a bus or into an archway.

Perhaps because I am female or maybe because I am thoroughly soaked, Goncharenko trusts me with the story of his life. In the late 1970s, he was harassed by the KGB for minor transgressions: signing a letter in support of a dissident scientist, reading *samizdat* literature. He was terrified. To be allowed to defend his first dissertation, he had to write letters renouncing all dissident affiliations. Then he ran away from the large city where he was living and settled in quiet, backward Gomel. Even now, lauded with virtually every honor in his field, including his recent election to the U.S. National Academy of Sciences, Goncharenko remains in this woefully underequipped lab, prisoner to his fear of the world. Like everyone else I meet here, he has made a clear-cut deal: to flee his demons and to do his life's work in a place where the very presence of an elusive peril offers peace.

In a sense he is not much different from Vladimir Kondakov, a   30
thirty-eight-year-old resident of the Zone. Kondakov has a blond beard and hair that reaches down just past his ear on one side and to the bottom of his chin on the other. He wears a sort of wraparound shirt, and an indeterminate-color suit whose fly is held together by a safety pin, and otherwise looks like the kind of man who could be sitting in a puddle of his own piss in the underground of any city in the world. Instead, he has been living in the Zone since 1989. How did he get here? "Generally speaking," Kondakov answers in his educated, almost bureaucratic-sounding way, "I entered."

There was once a time when Kondakov lived in Ukraine and worked as a welder. He had some family, though this part of the story gets tricky for him: "Well, in other words, that's a different world that bears no relevance," he recalls. "At first, I possessed cash. Then it became more difficult to get work, and money ran out. Additionally, I had no residence. And generally speaking, I had seen it on television, this disaster. So I came here. Here everything had been conducted on an emergency basis, which is to say, urgently, so a portion of the groceries had been abandoned here. Therefore, I would pick them up and partake. I would examine the hermetic seal, then the expiration date, and then the taste qualities. In most cases, it was apparent that the product was suitable for consumption."

At first Kondakov was regularly detained by police, who would take away his documents. But as police became scarce and he went farther into the Zone, he was left alone. Eventually, though, he ran out of food and last year resurfaced on the Belarussian side, on the territory of the Radiation Ecology Preserve, where 700 workers prevent forest fires and monitor the effects of contamination. His new home is a lonely white-brick structure on the side of a road. Kondakov is now considered a "laborer," which, to him, means that he lives in the house and gets food delivered once a day — a magnanimous gesture on the part of preserve suppliers who pass his house on their daily route.

Kondakov's droning description of the workings of the preserve sheds much light on why life didn't work out for him in the outside world.

What do the people in the preserve do? "Oh, they work," he explains importantly. And he? "My responsibilities range from the jurisprudential, such as writing an application to the director expressing my desire for employment, to the humanitarian, meaning having contacts with the bosses. And here you have to watch out, because not everything is spoken and some signals are communicated on the biological level in the form of endo-messages." In other words, it's hard for Kondakov to tell what other people want from him.

Fortunately, here they don't want much, which — as Kondakov can explain in hours of run-on educatese — makes the Zone a kinder place than the civilized world.

The civilized world on this part of the planet has grown only more   35
chaotic and cruel during the last ten years. Hundreds — possibly thousands — of people have fled from it and come here, to the quiet and predictable Zone. In the wake of the worst that technological culture has wrought, they've taken up ownership of the remnants and given new meaning to the notion of adaptation.

In the village of Strelichevo alone, eighty-four refugee families from various conflict areas in the former Soviet Union have settled into homes left by Belarussians who fled the danger of radiation. Strelichevo is in the part of the Zone that was not buried or forcibly depopulated; it is wedged between the preserve and the populated rest of the world, which means it enjoys some of the conveniences of civilization, such as electricity. Residents here were told they could leave if they wanted to and that they would be given housing. They trickled out, disabling the local farm and wine factory, a quaint turn-of-the-century architectural ensemble that looks like a monastery or a tiny white fortress. Eventually, the head of the local administration placed newspaper ads inviting working people to come to the emptied Strelichevo, where he had jobs, apartments, and services for them. They came — and only after they arrived did many of them learn what had driven out the former residents.

But these refugees had seen the face of death, and they opted for danger that was invisible. Tamara Yefimova, a forty-seven-year-old woman with dark eyes and skin that give her away as a stranger to this land of fair blonds, came with her husband, three children, and five grandchildren from Tadzhikistan, a former Soviet republic ravaged by civil war over the last four years. An ethnic Russian, she says she lost her ability to sleep in 1991, when enraged mobs traveled the streets of her city beating and stoning Russians to death.

In 1992, she sent her daughter and small grandchild to Belarus. Soon most of the family followed, moving into a small apartment and taking menial jobs. In Tadzhikistan, she remembers, "I had a good job, a good salary, a five-room apartment with hot water and a telephone. Then it all vanished in a single instant, like a mirage." Now a laborer at the local vegetable farm, she learned to use a shovel and a pitchfork to dig into soil where the Geiger counter comes in at 58 microrads — about the cutoff point for possibly safe background radiation.

"I didn't know much about this radiation thing at first," she admits, flashing a smile that's half gold and half omissions. "I just knew that that thing blew up and there is — what do they call it? — background radiation. Maybe it's affecting us — I don't know. I can't feel it. At least I can sleep at night."

The old idols of Soviet technology — the tractor on every collective   40
farm, the peaceful atom — promised many things: prosperity through efficiency, justice through plenitude. But they did not promise quiet and the coveted state of being left alone.

Tulgovichi is a village like any other: low houses — similar in structure but each adapted to its owner's needs — hug a road that follows a nonlinear rural logic. Far into the depopulated Zone, Tulgovichi has not been looted like other settlements — though all but three of about one hundred families have left. It is the quietest village on earth. Even the power lines no longer buzz; their posts are capped by storks' nests, which throw soft, irregular shadows on the dust-covered pavement.

Arkady Akulenko sits sideways on the cart as he rides down the road, to return not half an hour later walking beside the cart, now loaded with the biggest pumpkins atop the biggest zucchinis that have ever grown anywhere. He'll need help lifting some, which, he estimates, weigh upward of forty pounds. Some newspaper accounts claim it's the radiation that makes vegetables grow big and beautiful in the Zone; locals say they've always been like this. In fact, according to sixty-one-year-old Akulenko, the only difference between now and before radiation is that there are fewer people, more freedom, and a lot more wild boars — "plain herds of them."

Akulenko and his wife, Olga, used to work at the village collective farm. She milked cows, he drove a combine harvester. As the farm packed up and left, they stayed. "I don't know," shrugs Akulenko. "Some people can just up and leave this land; we couldn't." They bought a cow and a horse from the disassembling collective and learned to live off the land. The preserve helped them put up a small mill on the old farm grounds.

We set off in the direction in which they point us to look for the mill. The old collective farm is rows of identical gray-brick buildings, doors — rusted garage doors, peeling barn doors — gaping black. In its deserted industrial-age sameness, the abandoned farm brings to mind the remains of Nazi concentration camps just across the border in Poland.

The comparison is not as bizarre as it may seem. To local peasants, 45 the decades of forced collective farming — and the willy-nilly mechanization that came with it — meant, first and foremost, prison. "It was nothing but serfdom," explains the didactic cow-herding Arkady Nabokin, who survived the birth and death of this Soviet institution. Until the 1960s, collective-farm workers had no right to move off the land, to have cash, or to keep identification documents of their own. Even after these rules were loosened, peasants were constrained by the ways of living and working prescribed from above. It took the worst nuclear accident in history for rural living once again to mean freedom.

After the peaceful atom, there is a different kind of peace. History once again is short because tomorrow is out of reach. The world once again is small. Every wild boar, every cow, and every person has staked out a small piece of this limited world, its own slice of freedom to redeem. The Teacher pursues his study in an abandoned forest; the Mad Scientist retreats to his remote makeshift lab to escape his fears; the Refugee makes home and hearth in a small city-style apartment; and the Village Idiot finds his own house on a stretch of emptiness. And in this time — the time after fear of the future and the alienation it may force — freedom is measured in silence, in separateness, in solitude.

EXPLORATIONS

1. Why is this essay called "The Day After Technology"?
2. Why were the villages Masha Gessen visits evacuated, and by whom? What was supposed to be accomplished by their evacuation? What reasons does Gessen give for the failure of this plan?
3. What are the disadvantages of living in the Zone irradiated by the Chernobyl explosion? According to the returned evacuees, what are the advantages? Which arguments on each side do you think are the most and least convincing?

CONNECTIONS

1. "The old idols of Soviet technology — the tractor on every collective farm, the peaceful atom — promised many things: prosperity through efficiency, justice through plenitude. But they did not promise quiet and the coveted state of being left alone" (para. 40). What evidence in Jianying Zha's "Yearnings" (p. 542) suggests that Chinese Communism forced a similar trade-off on its citizens? Which characters in "Yearnings" seem to favor "prosperity through efficiency"? Which characters prefer "quiet and the coveted state of being left alone"?

2. Compare "The Day After Technology" with Neil Postman's "Future Shlock" (p. 531). What role does television play in the Zone? What are the reasons why it is not more important? What are the effects of its not being as central as it is to the Americans in "Future Shlock" or the Chinese in "Yearnings"?

3. What ideas about Soviet Communism appear in both Gessen's essay and Serge Schmemann's Observation on page 524? On what points do you think these two writers would disagree?

EXPLORATIONS

1. "The Teacher pursues his study in an abandoned forest; the Mad Scientist retreats to his remote makeshift lab to escape his fears; the Refugee makes home and hearth in a small city-style apartment; and the Village Idiot finds his own house on a stretch of emptiness" (para. 46). Everyone who left the Zone was evacuated for the same reason, but everyone who returned had reasons of his or her own. Write an essay examining those reasons. First, summarize why each of Gessen's characters says he or she came to live in the Zone. Then compare and contrast those statements with what you think are the real reasons each person is able to live there successfully.

2. What are the top priorities of the scientists who appear in Gessen's essay? What are the top priorities of the nonscientists? How and why do these two groups disagree over who should have decision-making power? What techniques does Gessen use to dramatize their differences without creating heroes and villains? Think of one or more groups of people with different priorities from yours who have decision-making power in your life. Do you trust them to act in your best interest? Why or why not? If not, what do you do about it? Write an essay contrasting your differences, using Gessen's essay as a model if you wish.

AMOS OZ

Between Word and Picture

Born Amos Klausner in Jerusalem in 1939, Amos Oz belongs to the
first generation of Israeli writers who are *sabras* (native born). His grandfather had fled anti-Semitism in Russia and Poland to help build an
ideal Jewish state in Palestine. In 1952, as the fledgling state of Israel
struggled to accommodate over a million refugees, Oz's mother committed suicide. Her son cast off his father's scholarly right-wing Zionism
to become a peasant-soldier on Kibbutz Hulda, midway between
Jerusalem (then half in Israel and half in Jordan) and Tel Aviv to the
north. There Oz took his new last name, which means "strength" in Hebrew; worked in the cotton fields; studied socialism; and eventually was
sent to Hebrew University in Jerusalem for his bachelor's degree. On his
return he adopted the routine he followed until recently: teaching in
the high school, doing assigned chores, spending time with his wife and
three children, and writing stories and novels involving kibbutz life and
ideals. Oz left Kibbutz Hulda for fellowships at Oxford and Hebrew
Universities and a lecture tour of U.S. campuses and to fight in the
Sinai Desert and Golan Heights in the 1967 and 1973 wars. The recipi-
ent of several international literary awards, he is a leader of Israel's
Peace Now movement. Among his recent books are the novels *To Know
a Woman* (1991) and *Fima* (1993) and the essay collection *Israel, Palestine, and Peace* (1995). "Between Word and Picture" comes from *The
Slopes of Lebanon* (1989; *Mi-mordot ha-Levanon*, 1987), translated by
Maurie Goldberg-Bartura.

Israel consists of roughly 8,000 square miles of land on the eastern
Mediterranean coast, only a fifth of which is arable. Archaeological evidence documents a Hebrew kingdom in this region (known as Palestine) going back to about 1000 B.C., the era of the biblical House of
David. Jews here always have been surrounded by Arabs: Israel currently
is bounded on the north by Lebanon, on the east by Jordan, and on the
southwest by Egypt. After World War I, victorious Britain and France
divided up the Middle Eastern remnants of Turkey's Ottoman Empire.
France was to control Syria and Lebanon, while Britain continued to
dominate Egypt, Iraq, the newly created Transjordan, and Palestine
(the southeastern Mediterranean coast). Their plans to make these territories independent were hampered in Palestine by the struggle for dominance between its Arab and Jewish populations. With World War II
and the Nazi slaughter of Jews (and others) known as the Holocaust,
the need for an official Jewish homeland became urgent. Claude

Lanzmann's 1985 film *Shoah*, discussed by Oz in this essay, documents
that extermination campaign. After Nazi Germany's defeat, Britain
turned Palestine over to the United Nations, which in 1948 voted to create the state of Israel. The angry Arabs denied Israel's right to exist. Tensions flared in 1967 into the Six-Day War (see para. 1), which ended
with Israel not only intact but in control of the rest of Palestine, previously managed by Syria, Jordan, and Egypt. A new attack on Israel by
Syria and Egypt in 1973 brought the United States into the picture as a
mediator. An Arab summit conference the next year recognized the
Palestine Liberation Organization (PLO) under Yasir Arafat as the sole
legitimate representative of the Palestinian people — that is, the Arab
Palestinians living in the West Bank and Gaza Strip, now occupied by
Israel. In 1993 Israel and the PLO officially recognized each other's le-
gitimacy and agreed that Israel would cede control of the Gaza Strip
and the West Bank town of Jericho to the Palestinians. Progress toward
peace has been slowed by violence and reprisals, particularly the 1996
assassination of Israeli Prime Minister Yitzhak Rabin of the leftist Labor
Party. His successor, Benjamin Netanyahu of the more conservative
Likud Party, took a harder line and resumed the controversial policy of
building new Israeli settlements in the West Bank. Netanyahu lost re-
election in 1999 to Labor candidate Ehud Barak, who as we go to press
promises to renew Rabin's quest for peace.

From a moving car the camera captures the smokestacks of the Ruhr
Valley, the industrial heart of Germany both then and now. Huge con-
glomerates, industrial parks, conveyor belts, enormous cranes — steel,
concrete, and smoke. Against the backdrop of these passing scenes, the
narrator reads a German document dated June 5, 1942 (exactly twenty-
five years later, the Six-Day War was to break out in Israel). This document is a technical blueprint for making alterations and improvements
in the gassing trucks, on the basis of accumulated experience. "Ninety-
seven thousand Jews have been processed in the trucks to date, but
minor operating defects have been discovered and we recommend the
following improvements. It would be desirable in future to install electric lights, shielded by a steel grill, in the ceiling of the truck. For it is
dark in the car when the doors are closed, and when the exhaust gas begins to be piped in, the result has been panic and loud screams, which
made the work of the drivers more difficult and may attract undesirable
attention. We also recommend the installation of properly graduated
drains in the floor of the truck, because those who are being asphyxiated discharge bodily wastes during the course of the procedure, which
lasts approximately fifteen to twenty-five minutes. The cleanup between

operations consumes unnecessary time. In addition, it is desirable to make the car shorter — although we are aware of the concern expressed by the engineers regarding the increased pressure on the front axle. There is no need for concern about overweight on the front axles of the trucks, for the merchandise, without exception, is pushed together during the journey and, for understandable psychological reasons, pressed to the locked doors at the rear end, so that the weight will nevertheless be well distributed on both axles. In order to save time, the above improvements should be made only when the trucks are otherwise out of service due to periodic overhauls."

You pause and reflect on the style of this document. Was Hannah Arendt right, after all, when she said that the greatest murder in all history was carried out by little gray people who knew not what they did? Is this not the language of bureaucratic nothingness, of a petty technocrat coping with a task to the best of his petty ability?

Or was Mr. Sammler, in Saul Bellow's novel, right when he rebuked Hannah Arendt, saying that every man knows what murder is and that the grayness is just a cover?

Distortion of language is what paved the way for this murder. Generations before the birth of Hitler, mass murderers already knew that you must first corrupt the words before you can corrupt those who use these words, so that they may be capable of murder in the guise of purification, cleaning, and healing. One who calls his enemy an "animal," "parasite," "louse," "beast of prey," or "germ" trains hearts for murder.

The German dictionary of destruction — "solution," "final solution," "training for productive work," "resettlement," "treatment," "special treatment," even the most explicit term used, "*Vernichtung*" (annihilation) — still calls to mind mice or termites, not human beings.   5

The Jewish dictionary of shudders — "Holocaust," "sheep to the slaughter," "raging foe," "oppressor," "Amalek," "the Nazi beast," and even, and always in the same breath, "Holocaust and heroism" — all these words attempt to bypass, to soften, to prettify, to console, or to place everything into one known familiar historic pattern: "Pharaoh," "wicked," "Haman," "Cossacks," "pogroms," "anti-Semites."

Therefore, when we wake up each morning, we should check the words in the newspaper as well as the words in our own mouths. We must treat words like hand grenades.

The murderer Franz Suchomel, who has a heart condition, responded to [filmmaker Claude] Lanzmann's entreaties and sang for him (and for the hidden camera and tape recorder) the anthem of the unit that carried out the murders. It was a hymn to duty, praise for those who obeyed even when obedience was difficult and frightening, even when there was no prospect of glory. Lanzmann also persuaded Simon Srebnik, "the Chelmno nightingale," to sing some of the songs from those days. Suchomel's voice, in contrast to Srebnik's, is cracked. He doesn't sing well. The melody sounds ludicrously out of tune, and the murderer heartily apologizes for it: "We are laughing now, but it's not right. Please, don't laugh at me. There's nothing to laugh at. All this is very sad. Not funny at all." (Neither of them had laughed.)

And afterward, pointer in hand, as though delivering a lecture, he elucidates, "for history's sake," how it was done, using an enlarged map of the Treblinka camp. "Treblinka was not large at all. Maybe five hundred meters at its widest point. And . . . eighteen thousand — that's an exaggeration. Absolutely. We never reached eighteen thousand a day. On the busiest days, when they worked all night, maybe twelve or fifteen thousand went through. Not more. In each transport there were between thirty and fifty cars. They would divide them into groups of ten to twelve cars and take each group in to the platform inside the camp. The others waited their turn inside the cars. Lithuanian and Ukrainian guards sat on the roof of the cars. Bloodhounds, that's what they were. I tell you, they were the worst!

"In every shift there were three to five Germans, another ten Ukraini-   10
ans and Lithuanians, and maybe twenty Jews. The Red Commando processed the clothes that the people took off."

Lanzmann: "How much time elapsed between the unloading, the undressing, and the liquidation?"

Suchomel: "Women — one hour. The whole train — two hours. Within two hours it was all finished. You couldn't wait long. It was cold as hell. Fifteen or twenty degrees below zero, sometimes. Those poor things were even colder. They were naked."

The "tunnel," or the "tube," was a path covered over with barbed wire, camouflaged with pine branches. Special details of Jews would bring fresh branches from the woods each morning. According to Suchomel, the Jews called this tube *Himmelweg* — "the path to heaven." According to one Jewish witness, some Germans called the tube by the same name. So we have a little copyright dispute here.

"The men," says Suchomel, "had to be beaten hard so they would walk into the tube. But women were not beaten."

"Why?" asks Lanzmann.   15

Suchomel looks at him with total incomprehension.

"Why weren't the women beaten?"

Astonishment spreads across the aging Nazi's face. He is silent. His features express shock. How can a civilized person ask such a question?

How could anyone have such ugly thoughts? Finally, he breaks his silence and says, "I don't know. I never went near there — near the women, that is. Lithuanians and Ukrainians were there. You couldn't get close. They were naked. Besides, they relieved themselves right then and there. Out of fear of death. *Todesangst.* It is perfectly natural, from a scientific point of view. For example, my own mother, who died in her own bed, while she was dying, got up and did it at the foot of the bed." Suchomel gestures with his hands, illustrating a little heap. And then there comes a strange, amazing moment of manly kinship between Lanzmann and Suchomel, a kinship deriving from the fact that both of them are cultured people who know that it isn't nice to use vulgar language and that there are limits established by universal good taste, limits that must not be transgressed. It is simply not done. Lanzmann accompanies his next question with an up-and-down motion of both hands, without words (meaning, did the women do it standing up?). Suchomel answers Lanzmann with a nod of his head and the same movement of his hands (meaning, yes, standing up). A moment later he corrects himself, "No. No. Not standing up. Why standing up? No. No. They could . . . squat."

These things, and others like them, can be captured only by a camera: the embarrassment, the silences, and the body language. The film gives full expression to several cinematic possibilities. There are dozens of minutes of silence, of unanswered questions, of unsolicited answers, of embarrassment, squirming, and evasiveness, of stammering and play-acting, hand and body gestures, mimicry and laughter. Yes, laughter, too, and trembling lips and open weeping.

And there are many minutes of freight trains standing, moving, stopping, by night with frightening headlights, by day, and at dusk. The camera ignores many of the generally accepted rules of "cinematic syntax," such as orderly modulations, deleting background noises, editing out various stutters, shortening "empty" minutes, and giving special attention to "quality" or "uniformity." On the other hand, most of the ten hours are hours of face-to-face talks or silence or contorted faces. It seems that the victims, the murderers, and the witnesses, along with the interviewer, all suffer from "verbal insufficiency." No language is adequate (although the characters in the film use any of six or seven languages). But the language of the film is the language of photographed silence; the language of pursed lips and gaping, speechless mouths; the language of never-ending freight trains, and the language of snowscapes of barren fields. The dark green language of the Polish winter and the clear dazzling blue summer language of the Tel Aviv seashore. The language of the skyscrapers of New York and the alleyways of Corfu; and more trains moving through the twilight and past station signs and Polish villages and the lake at Lausanne, the industrial plants of Germany, and an Israeli barbershop in the town of Holon; trains in the rain and in the sun, at night and during the day. It is impossible to imagine any way other than film by which this creation could have been produced.

Franz Suchomel's finale: "Children, the old, and the sick were taken directly to the infirmary in the woods. There was a big white flag with a big red cross on it. They went willingly. They believed they would be taken care of there. Suddenly they saw the ditch. It was full of burning corpses. They were ordered to undress and to sit on a sort of ramp. Here [he indicates the spot on the map of Treblinka]. That is where they each got a bullet in the back of the head. There was always a fire burning in the ditch. They would throw in wood, papers; they'd spill gasoline, rags; they'd throw in garbage and, of course, the people. People burn very well."

The murderers and the witnesses, Poles and Germans alike, use, almost exclusively, one grammatical form: the third person plural. Sometimes they use the passive voice: "were taken," "were beaten," "were transported," "were unloaded," "were treated."

Most of the Jews in the film also use the same grammatical forms. But not all of them, and not always. Some say "we" and "I." Not one of the Nazis in the film ever says "we took them," or even "we told them," or at least "they told us to transport them." The words "I" and "we" are uttered by the Germans only in tandem with the words "didn't know" or "didn't see."

Rudolf Vrba and Filip Müller, two Jews who had "worked" in Auschwitz and survived, describe the death factory in detail and sometimes in technical language. When the Jews were removed from the boxcars, a "preliminary sorting" was done. The dead — including those who pretended to be dead — were thrown by the Jewish *Sonderkommando* people into trucks and cremated in the ovens. Others, after the infamous "selection" of those able to work, were chased by whip lashes into the disrobing rooms. They were told they were going to have a shower and be disinfected. The disrobing rooms were adjacent to the gas chambers, where up to three thousand people could be asphyxiated at one time. Four crematoria were kept going almost around the clock to turn the bodies into ashes.

In the words of Rudolf Vrba, the disrobing rooms were like an "international information center." On the walls were signs in several languages. There were special hooks on which to hang clothes. There were also several wooden benches for the convenience of the "clients." The signs said, "Cleanliness Is Good," "Wash!," "Cleanliness Is Health," "Head Lice Can Kill!" The purpose of the signs, of course, was to keep up the illusion and extend the deception until the very last minute. The gas itself arrived at Auschwitz in tanker trucks marked with the symbol of the International Red Cross and the word "Disinfectant."

Thus, the inventor of this scheme of deception, of murder in the guise of a hygienic procedure, had no banal mind. We don't know whose idea it all was. But it undeniably contains a spark of originality. It seems that other means of deception could have been devised. For instance, the Jews could have been told that they were going to be taken to a registration office, or to some employment bureau, or to a lecture hall, as part of their "retraining." From among all these and other possibilities, the unknown "poet" chose the metaphor of hygiene: "shower," "soap," "cleanliness," "delousing," "disinfection." So he had the wisdom of infinite cunning, extraordinary psychological subtlety, and a finely tuned sensitivity, to choose the most effective nuances. He chose to employ European values common to both the murderers and their victims, to exploit some universal urge for cleanliness, to touch upon a point on which the Jews, like every minority, were exceptionally sensitive, because of the age-old accusation leveled by racists at victims of racism: You are hated because you are dirty, because you stink, because you are carriers of disease. Take a bath, and then you can be worthy of us, of being accepted by us, even in our living rooms. There was infinite cunning behind the seductive German offer that was made to the Jews at the threshold of the "showers": "Enter as a (dirty) Jew, emerge as a (clean) human being."

Besides, after days in a boxcar, everyone would yearn for a bath, and truly need one. Therefore, they could imagine they saw a clear logic, a sanitary justification — for the good of all concerned — in the idea of showers and disinfection. Result: They marched in almost willingly, maybe they even marched in gladly.

Millions of human beings arrived in this fashion — quiet, naked, deceived, and hoping for the best — at the gas chambers. "The gas," Filip Müller relates, "was introduced in the form of crystals. The lights were turned off. A fierce battle broke out in the dark. The strong climbed on top of the weak. Driven by the blind instinct of self-preservation, they surged toward the doors — and toward the ceiling. Parents stepped on their children. They tore each other to pieces with their fingernails. When the doors were opened and the gas was pumped out, and we had to enter and remove them fast, we found them all twisted, trampled, covered with blood, urine, and feces. . . ."

Intimidation, attrition, deception — these were not by-products of the plot of destruction, but, rather, crucial components of its effectiveness. A single woman carrying a child and bursting into hysterical screams, thus stirring panic in the crowd, was enough to slow down the entire "procedure." It was imperative to bring them into the asphyxiation chamber in a quiet, submissive state. Starved, thirsty, exhausted, half-crazed from the horrors of the terrible journey, the dogs, the floodlights, the shouts, the blows, and the gunfire, they arrived at the platforms begging for water and, perhaps with their last bit of strength, grateful for the "offer" of a shower. "There was no point in warning them," Müller says. "Why turn their last moments into horror? To deprive them of vain hope? How would it have helped them to know that in a few minutes they would be dead? Once, a *Sonderkommando* member met a woman here whom he knew well. He whispered to her that she and all the other passengers in the transport would soon be turned into ashes. The woman ran like a maniac to warn the other women. They didn't believe her. They told her she'd gone out of her mind. They refused to listen. She screamed and raked herself with her fingernails. Maybe she really had gone mad from shock and despair. And how did it all end? Everyone went to the gas chamber — except for this one woman. The Germans subjected the woman to hellish tortures until she broke down and pointed out the *Sonderkommando* man who had revealed the truth to her. They threw him, live, into the oven. That's why we didn't tell them."

"I didn't know a thing," says Walter Steier, a former Nazi party member who was director-general of the Reich Railroad Authority for the eastern areas. "I was glued to my desk day and night. I never went outdoors. I did not see the transports. Department 33 was in charge of the *Sonderzüge* [special trains] and supplied trains and schedules at the request of the Gestapo in Berlin. At group fares. Yes, I had some idea that many of these special trains went to Treblinka and Auschwitz. But how was I to know what they were carrying? Or what was going to happen to the cargo there? This was not my department. Yes, there were all kinds of rumors. Rumors always circulate in wartime. They said they were transporting Jews or criminals or that sort of people, in these trains. Of course it was better not to talk about it. I knew nothing. *Ach nein! Ach, Gott im Himmel, nein.*"

EXPLORATIONS

1. What are the central arguments in "Between Word and Picture"? What audience do you think Amos Oz is addressing? What is he trying to persuade his readers to believe or to do?

2. "Distortion of language is what paved the way for this murder . . . . One who calls his enemy an 'animal,' 'parasite,' 'louse,' 'beast of prey,' or 'germ' trains hearts for murder" (para. 4). What does Oz mean by "distortion of language"? What other words and phrases in the document he quotes in paragraph 1 illustrate such distortion?

3. A question commonly asked about the Holocaust is, "How could a civilized people like the Germans do such a thing?" How do the Germans in this essay answer that question? How does Oz answer it?

CONNECTIONS

1. "Technology is the future. Everyone knows that," Masha Gessen writes in "The Day After Technology" (p. 556). In what sense do these sentences express the view of the Germans in "Between Word and Picture"? What are the fatal flaws in the Russians' dream of the technological future? What are the fatal flaws in the Germans' dream of the technological future?

2. "Exactly why the Germans banished intelligence is a vast and largely unanswered question," Neil Postman states in "Future Shlock" (p. 531, para. 2). What answers does Oz propose or cite in "Between Word and Picture"? After reading both essays, what answers do you favor?

3. Oz fought in two Israeli wars; now he is a passionate advocate for peace. Compare his essay with the Observation by Elaine Ruth Fletcher (p. 525). What does Ariel Kapon mean by, "The meaning of the army in the eyes of Israel's founders fifty years ago . . . is different than what we have now"? Reread the headnote to this selection. How do changes in the Israeli Army and Israel's situation parallel the changes in Oz's stance?

ELABORATIONS

1. Reread paragraphs 8–11 in "Future Shlock" (p. 531). Based on that essay and "Between Word and Picture" — as well as Mel Brooks's film *The Producers*, if you have seen it — write an essay explaining in more detail why Postman concludes, "Brooks's point is that the joke is on us."

2. "No language is adequate," writes Oz. "It is impossible to imagine any way other than film by which this creation could have been produced" (para. 20). Yet Oz's essay is an attempt to render the film, or some threads of it,

into language. Write an argumentative essay explaining why this is a valuable undertaking — what you got out of "Between Word and Picture" that justifies Oz's attempt. Or, choose another medium for which no language is adequate (jazz, for instance), and write an essay modeled on Oz's, rendering it into words.

ELAINE SALINAS

Still Grieving over the Loss of the Land

Elaine Salinas, a member of the White Earth Ojibway/Chippewa tribe, describes her life and family history in this essay. "Ojibway" or "Ojibwa" and "Chippewa" are alternate forms of the same name, spelled as it was heard on the United States or Canadian side of the border. Salinas was born in 1949 on the White Earth Reservation in Minnesota; she now lives on the Oneida Reservation near Green Bay, Wisconsin. She works as a scout and steward with the Annenberg Rural Challenge for the states of Minnesota, Wisconsin, and Michigan and for Native American sites across the country; she is also a core planning team member for the Wisconsin Rural Challenge. Salinas graduated from Moorhead State University and holds a master's degree in education administration from the University of Minnesota. An educator with over twenty-five years of experience in K–12 and adult education in public and alternative schools, she has served as a legislative advocate in Minnesota for education policy reforms. "Still Grieving over the Loss of the Land" is an interview of Salinas by Jane B. Katz, included in Katz's 1995 book *Messengers of the Wind: Native American Women Tell Their Life Stories*. In the opening paragraphs, Katz introduces Salinas.

They call themselves the Anishinabe, "the original people." The elders of Minnesota's White Earth Reservation remember the days when their small cabins were set deep in tall stands of birch and scrub oak trees. They fished, hunted, logged with horses, and harvested wild rice. Despite treaties decreeing that the land would be theirs "in perpetuity," they witnessed a land grab of massive proportions. Today only an estimated 6 percent of the 830,000 acres originally promised to them is in Ojibway hands, the reservation's leading product seems to be not lumber but poverty, and tribal members are in negotiations with the state, federal government, and private corporations to reclaim the land. Through gaming and other enterprises, the tribe seeks to improve its economic status, and reassert its sovereignty.

Uprooted from her childhood home at White Earth, Elaine Salinas experienced the dislocation that afflicted her generation, then went to work helping other Native Americans put the pieces of their lives back together. We met in her office at the Urban Coalition in St. Paul, where she works for increased educational opportunities for people of color. Elaine Salinas has served on the Governor's Task Force on Prejudice and Violence. Her

lobbying efforts have resulted in passage of legislation calling for the teach-
ing of Indian languages and culture in the public schools. Tall and lithe
with brown shoulder-length hair, she's warm and outspoken.

I was born in 1949 on the White Earth Reservation, a member of the Pembina Band. When I was seven, my family moved to Wahpeton, North Dakota. My parents went to work at the Wahpeton Indian School, a Bureau of Indian Affairs boarding school. My father was a carpenter, my mother worked in the dormitories. Because I was the child of staff, I could not attend that school, but we lived on the campus so I saw what went on.

Since the late 1800s, Indian boarding schools have existed in various parts of the country. Initially the thinking was that if you left Indian children on reservations, they'd remain "savages," so representatives of the Bureau of Indian Affairs virtually kidnaped children from tribes all over the country and bussed them to military-style boarding schools to "civilize" them.

I'd stand in front of the school at the beginning of the year and watch the buses arrive: children from six to eighteen looked lonely and scared. School personnel herded them like cattle into showers and treated them for lice. The youngsters slept in large, cold dormitory rooms. At night, I heard little children and even older ones crying for their parents.

Some of the children spoke their Native languages; some did not. But all had been isolated from families and traditions. In this period, they were not allowed to speak their languages or practice their ceremonies at the school.

The system was dehumanizing. If a girl disobeyed a rule she'd have   5
to wear a long, green dress as a signal to others that she had misbehaved, or she'd have her beautiful long hair cut short. A boy who disobeyed had to scrub the basement floor with toothbrushes; if he was defiant, he was sprayed with a fire hose. If he tried to run away, the police would track him down, the school superintendent would pick him up and make him run beside the car.

The most severe punishment I witnessed was "the hot line." An eighteen-year-old boy had been allowed to attend a movie downtown and had come back late. The staff made the male students form two lines and gave them belts; the boy had to run the gauntlet and be whipped by his peers. That created a lot of hostility within the student body, which I think is what the staff intended. There was a divide-and-conquer mentality.

I witnessed a gradual reduction in abusive practices at the school and eventually, they were outlawed. But I was becoming aware of a policy of cultural genocide implemented in the boarding schools.

I attended a Catholic elementary school. I had to defend myself against racial slurs. I played the system, I did what I had to do to win approval from the nuns. But I always reserved a part of myself. In high school, the prejudice of the white students was more subtle. By then, I hated school, but I knew I could not fail — that would hurt my parents. My grandfather spoke several languages. My grandmother was the first Indian teacher in Minnesota and wrote music.

After graduating from college, I got a job as community services director for a school on my reservation. Returning to White Earth cured my sense of separation, and it brought back memories of what it was like growing up there. We used to live in a house on a little dirt road running through the village. Nearby were aunts, uncles, and grandparents. A whole gang of us kids hung around together. We hardly had any toys, but the outdoors was there for us. We'd ice-skate and play ball, we'd invent stories and games. We'd collect live frogs, and dare each other to bite off their legs — we were awful kids. [Laughs.]

I had a Raggedy Ann doll that I loved. Once, my dad was leaving 10 town in his old pickup truck to work on a construction job. I ran to him to say good-bye, and when he was gone, I realized I'd lost my doll. It hurt, because I had only one doll.

As part of my job, I visited elderly people in their homes. Some of them didn't speak English, and I didn't know Ojibway, but we communicated. Grandma Ellis, a ninety-eight-year-old woman, was out chopping wood in the middle of winter. She lived to be a hundred and four. Fred Weaver made kinnikinnick out of red willow, and he told marvelous stories.

I found out that in the nineteenth century, White Earth had been a thriving town with a hotel and a number of stores. Ojibway worked in the fur trade and the logging industry. My grandfather owned a livery stable. The Allotment Act passed in 1887 divided tribal land into small plots. Indians were supposed to become farmers, "productive citizens." They had been used to moving with the seasons in search of wild game, fish, and rice, sharing what nature provided. The idea of dividing the land into individual plots and planting seeds was totally alien to them. People sold acreage just to buy food for their families. In desperation, they accepted the low prices whites offered for the land. A lot of land was also lost through illegal tax forfeitures. That's how we lost most of the White Earth Reservation.

When the Relocation Act was passed in 1956, the government told the Indians, "You move off the reservations, come to the city, we'll find you a job." But the people weren't trained for the few jobs open to them. They crowded together in small, overpriced flats. To this day,

many Indians don't like living in places where there is so much conges-
tion and traffic, where the pace is so much faster than on the reservation. Those who have settled in the city have sometimes had to relin-
quish close ties to family and community, and a chance to practice
their religion on ancestral land. A lot of Indians feel like foreigners in
the city. They are still grieving over the loss of the land.

Relocation was hardest on the men. Historically, the man was the
provider. Indians who had some status within their tribe as religious
leaders, chiefs, hunters, and warriors came to the city to find themselves
viewed by the larger society as extinct. When you're faced with racism
and unemployment, how do you express your anger and frustration? Do
you strike out at the community's business leaders? That wouldn't be
tolerated. A man's anger often surfaces as self-destructive behavior and
violence against others.

There were so many losses for the women. There were cases in   15
South Dakota where contaminated water caused abortions and prema-
ture births. A number of Indian women were sterilized — it happened
in hospitals across the country. Children were taken away from their
mothers. Collectively, we lost so much.

There's a theory that Indian people have never been allowed to go
through a grieving period for the world we lost. So, this theory goes, the
problem is depression, which often leads to chemical dependency.
Every Indian is touched by that. I have it in my family. Studies show
that many hard-core street alcoholics were brought up as traditional Indians. They could not adjust to the loss of land and culture. I think Indian people need to find a way to live in the world as it is, and still remain Indian.

Life in the Indian community has changed. Today most of our Indian parents are single women, and for them, the job of supporting and
holding the family together is overwhelming. In tribal communities,
women's lives were difficult; they often did backbreaking labor. But you
had a group of people who operated in sync with each other toward a
common goal. Today, there are so many forces undermining what we
do, it's amazing we survive at all.

Walk down Franklin Avenue, the hub of our community, and you'll
see people without homes or medical care lining up for free meals. The
poor become poorer as the rich become richer, and there's anger. Recently, an Indian boy was killed in the crossfire between rival gangs. A
baby caught in the middle of a fight was hit by a chair and killed. These
are innocent victims! But in our communities, it's old news. It's as if the
community is turning on itself.

The police often turn their backs on violence in our community, or they perpetrate it. When they don't respond to calls for help, Indians feel that as long as we're killing each other, the police don't care. Hate crimes are on the rise. We have mobilized to protect ourselves. The American Indian Movement patrol has had some success in dealing with crime, but it's hard to get Indians to believe that they can make a difference. There's a sense that what you do won't change anything.

It's hard for young people to feel good about themselves in a hostile   20
environment. Look at what happened to the Cherokee after they were removed from their homeland and brought to Oklahoma. Within a span of about forty years, they became "civilized" by every definition the white man had. I mean, they became literate in English, they had a newspaper, they made tremendous economic gains, but still they were not accepted. The Cherokee experience suggests that education is not "the great equalizer."

Inherent in this country is a real sense of white supremacy. You can go to college and get a doctorate, but if you're a minority, especially if you're a woman, you have to prove yourself all the time.

Sure, education can help to change this negative climate. But when white people talk about education, they're talking about more math, more science — they want their kids to graduate and fit into the cogs white people have created, so they will serve this market-based economy. Fewer kids fit that mold today. More and more of them come from low-income backgrounds where the market economy has never worked. You have families on AFDC for generations, so the public school system becomes less and less relevant.

Indians today are obtaining college degrees and becoming social workers, architects, computer programmers, managers of businesses, so there are more role models. Still, in our community as a whole, life has not improved significantly. We have the highest rate of poverty, unemployment, infant mortality, diabetes, alcoholism, and suicide of any group in the country.

What hope is there? We are looking at traditional programs that worked within tribal societies. People in the mental health field are using the "talking circle" for healing. Our Indian-run school programs work for many of our kids because in them, being Indian is an asset. We are trying to convince those who have the resources that they should be investing money in our communities, but there are often issues about who "owns" the program.

I think that young people are our hope. Tribal societies nurtured the   25
young, and prepared them for adult roles. As children aged, their

responsibilities within the family and tribe increased. We need to give our young men a voice in decision making, we need to build their self-esteem and leadership skills. Another thing we can do is to reconnect young people with elders who transmit an appreciation of life; kids often find them more accepting, less judgmental than their parents. To join the young and the old — that is a healthy alliance.

I talk to schoolchildren about careers. I urge them to develop their skills so they will have choices. I talk to my son about using his strength to give back to the people. In order for Indian people to survive, we all have to contribute.

I don't value money or position. What really matters is that Native people will continue to be distinguishable as a people by virtue of our sovereignty, our value system, our worldview, and our respect for un-born generations. They are our future, our hope.

EXPLORATIONS

1. What is the meaning of this essay's title? Who is still grieving over the loss of what land? How and why did they lose it? What impact has the loss had on them?

2. What evidence does Elaine Salinas offer for her belief that "education is not 'the great equalizer'" (para. 20)? Why does she nevertheless believe education is essential?

3. How would you react differently to "Still Grieving over the Loss of the Land" if it were structured as an expository essay instead of an interview? What are the advantages and disadvantages of the interview form?

CONNECTIONS

1. Compare Salinas's recollections with Amos Oz's description of the Holocaust (p. 569). In what ways were children at the Wahpeton Indian School in the 1950s treated like Jews in Germany a decade earlier? What were the Nazis' goals for the Jews? What were the goals of the U.S. government's Bureau of Indian Affairs for the Native Americans? How did the differences in their goals affect their treatment of those over whom they had power?

2. What resemblances do you notice between the history of White Earth (see especially paras. 12–13) and that of the villagers in the radiation zone around Chernobyl, as Masha Gessen describes them in "The Day After Technology" (p. 556)? Why does each group leave their land? Why does each group come back?

3. What common ideas appear in this essay and Joseph Bruchac's "Digging into Your Heart" (p. 439)? What explanation does Salinas offer for the alcohol abuse she says is common among Indians (para. 16)? What story in Bruchac's essay suggests that Indians may have a positive reason for dependence on alcohol?

ELABORATIONS

1. In "African Literature: What Tradition?" (p. 73), Es'kia Mphahlele recalls what it was like to be an African in a European educational system. In "A View from Canada" (p. 79), Margaret Atwood recalls what it was like to be a Canadian in a British educational system. Write an essay comparing Salinas's experience as an Indian in the United States with either of theirs, or both.

2. Reread Salinas's description of the Wahpeton Indian School (paras. 1–7). Were you ever sent away from your family to a school, camp, or other place where you felt isolated and alienated? Write an essay about your experience.

ESTHER DYSON

Cyberspace:If You Don't Love It, Leave It

Esther Dyson is chairman of EDventure Holdings, "a small but diversified company focused on emerging information technology worldwide, and on the emerging computer markets of Central and Eastern Europe." Among EDventure's many enterprises are the monthly newsletter *Release 1.0*, with Dyson as editor, and two annual conferences, *PC* (Platforms for Communication) *Forum* and *High-Tech Forum*. Born in 1951, Dyson graduated from Harvard University in 1972 with a B.A. in economics. While in Cambridge she worked on the *Harvard Crimson*; in 1974 she became a reporter for *Forbes* magazine. With what she had learned about business she got a job as a securities analyst and spent the next five years learning the dynamics of the computer and software businesses. Dyson currently sits on the boards of numerous software, consulting, and public service organizations and has investments in many of them. Her articles have appeared in the *New York Times*, *Wired*, *Forbes*, *Brill's Content*, and Russia's *CompuTerra* magazine, among others. Fluent in Russian, she is a founding member of the Russian Software Market Association and is listed in Russia's *Who's Who in the Computer Market* as Number 23 of the most influential people in Russia's computer industry. *Fortune* magazine recently named her one of the most powerful women in American business. She lives in New York City. "Cyberspace: If You Don't Love It, Leave It" first appeared in the *New York Times Magazine* on July 6, 1995.

Something in the American psyche loves new frontiers. We hanker after wide open spaces; we like to explore; we like to make rules instead of follow them. But in this age of political correctness and other intrusions on our national cult of independence, it's hard to find a place where you can go and be yourself without worrying about the neighbors.

There is such a place: cyberspace. Lost in the furor over porn on the Net is the exhilarating sense of freedom that this new frontier once promised — and still does in some quarters. Formerly a playground for computer nerds and techies, cyberspace now embraces every conceivable constituency: schoolchildren, flirtatious singles, Hungarian Americans, accountants — along with pederasts and porn fans. Can they all get along? Or will our fear of kids surfing for cyberporn behind their bedroom doors provoke a crackdown?

The first order of business is to grasp what cyberspace *is*. It might help to leave behind metaphors of highways and frontiers and to think instead of real estate. Real estate, remember, is an intellectual, legal, artificial environment constructed *on top of* land. Real estate recognizes the difference between parkland and shopping mall, between red-light zone and school district, between church, state, and drugstore.

In the same way, you could think of cyberspace as a giant and unbounded world of virtual real estate. Some property is privately owned and rented out; other property is common land; some places are suitable for children, and others are best avoided by all but the kinkiest citizens. Unfortunately, it's those places that are now capturing the popular imagination: places that offer bomb-making instructions, pornography, advice on how to procure stolen credit cards. They make cyberspace sound like a nasty place. Good citizens jump to a conclusion: better regulate it. . . .

Regardless of how many laws or lawsuits are launched, regulation   5 won't work.

Aside from being unconstitutional, using censorship to counter indecency and other troubling "speech" fundamentally misinterprets the nature of cyberspace. Cyberspace isn't a frontier where wicked people can grab unsuspecting children, nor is it a giant television system that can beam offensive messages at unwilling viewers. In this kind of real estate, users have to *choose* where they visit, what they see, what they do. It's optional, and it's much easier to bypass a place on the Net than it is to avoid walking past an unsavory block of stores on the way to your local 7-Eleven.

Put plainly, cyberspace is a voluntary destination — in reality, many destinations. You don't just get "onto the Net"; you have to go someplace in particular. That means that people can choose where to go and what to see. Yes, community standards should be enforced, but those standards should be set by cyberspace communities themselves, not by the courts or by politicians in Washington. What we need isn't government control over all these electronic communities: We need self-rule.

What makes cyberspace so alluring is precisely the way in which it's *different* from shopping malls, television, highways, and other terrestrial jurisdictions. But let's define the territory:

First, there are private E-mail conversations, akin to the conversations you have over the telephone or voice mail. These are private and consensual and require no regulation at all.

Second, there are information and entertainment services, where   10
people can download anything from legal texts and lists of "great new
restaurants" to game software or dirty pictures. These places are like
bookstores, malls, and movie houses — places where you go to buy
something. The customer needs to request an item or sign up for a sub-
scription; stuff (especially pornography) is not sent out to people who
don't ask for it. Some of these services are free or included as part of a
broad service like CompuServe or America Online; others charge and
may bill their customers directly.

Third, there are "real" communities — groups of people who communicate among themselves. In real-estate terms, they're like bars or
restaurants or bathhouses. Each active participant contributes to a general conversation, generally through posted messages. Other participants may simply listen or watch. Some are supervised by a moderator;
others are more like bulletin boards — anyone is free to post anything.
Many of these services started out unmoderated but are now imposing
rules to keep out unwanted advertising, extraneous discussions, or increasingly rude participants. Without a moderator, the decibel level
often gets too high.

Ultimately, it's the rules that determine the success of such places.
Some of the rules are determined by the supplier of content; some of
the rules concern prices and membership fees. The rules may be
simple: "Only high-quality content about oil-industry liability and pollution legislation: $120 an hour." Or: "This forum is unmoderated, and
restricted to information about copyright issues. People who insist on
posting advertising or unrelated material will be asked to desist (and
may eventually be barred)." Or: "Only children 8 to 12, on school-
related topics and only clean words. The moderator will decide what's
acceptable."

Cyberspace communities evolve just the way terrestrial communities
do: People with like-minded interests band together. Every cyberspace
community has its own character. Overall, the communities on Compu-
Serve tend to be more techy or professional; those on America Online, affluent young singles; Prodigy, family oriented. Then there are indepen-
dents like Echo, a hip, downtown New York service, or Women's Wire,
targeted to women who want to avoid the male culture prevalent elsewhere on the Net. There's SurfWatch, a new program allowing access
only to locations deemed suitable for children. On the Internet itself,
there are lots of passionate noncommercial discussion groups on topics
ranging from Hungarian politics (Hungary-Online) to copyright law.

And yes, there are also porn-oriented services, where people share
dirty pictures and communicate with one another about all kinds of

practices, often anonymously. Whether these services encourage the fantasies they depict is subject to debate — the same debate that has raged about pornography in other media. But the point is that no one is forcing this stuff on anybody.

What's unique about cyberspace is that it liberates us from the 15 tyranny of government, where everyone lives by the rule of the majority. In a democracy, minority groups and minority preferences tend to get squeezed out, whether they are minorities of race and culture or minorities of individual taste. Cyberspace allows communities of any size and kind to flourish; in cyberspace, communities are chosen by the users, not forced on them by accidents of geography. This freedom gives the rules that preside in cyberspace a moral authority that rules in terrestrial environments don't have. Most people are stuck in the country of their birth, but if you don't like the rules of a cyberspace community, you can just sign off. Love it or leave it. Likewise, if parents don't like the rules of a given cyberspace community, they can restrict their children's access to it.

What's likely to happen in cyberspace is the formation of new communities, free of the constraints that cause conflict on earth. Instead of a global village, which is a nice dream but impossible to manage, we'll have invented another world of self-contained communities that cater to their own members' inclinations without interfering with anyone else's. The possibility of a real market-style evolution of governance is at hand. In cyberspace, we'll be able to test and evolve rules governing what needs to be governed — intellectual property, content and access control, rules about privacy and free speech. Some communities will allow anyone in; others will restrict access to members who qualify on one basis or another. Those communities that prove self-sustaining will prosper (and perhaps grow and split into subsets with ever more particular interests and identities). Those that can't survive — either because people lose interest or get scared off — will simply wither away.

In the near future, explorers in cyberspace will need to get better at defining and identifying their communities. They will need to put in place — and accept — their own local governments, just as the owners of expensive real estate often prefer to have their own security guards rather than call in the police. But they will rarely need help from any terrestrial government.

Of course, terrestrial governments may not agree. What to do, for instance, about pornography? The answer is labeling — not banning — questionable material. In order to avoid censorship and lower the political temperature, it makes sense for cyberspace participants themselves to agree on a scheme for questionable items, so that people or auto-matic filters can avoid them. In other words, posting pornography in "alt.sex.bestiality" would be O.K.; it's easy enough for software manu-facturers to build an automatic filter that would prevent you — or your child — from ever seeing that item on a menu. (It's as if all the items were wrapped, with labels on the wrapper.) Someone who posted the same material under the title "Kid-Fun" could be sued for mislabeling.

Without a lot of fanfare, private enterprises and local groups are al-ready producing a variety of labeling and ranking services, along with kid-oriented sites like Kidlink, EdWeb, and Kids' Space. People differ in their tastes and values and can find services or reviewers on the Net that suit them in the same way they select books and magazines. Or they can wander freely if they prefer, making up their own itinerary.

In the end, our society needs to grow up. Growing up means under-   20
standing that there are no perfect answers, no all-purpose solutions, no government-sanctioned safe havens. We haven't created a perfect soci-ety on earth and we won't have one in cyberspace either. But at least we can have individual choice — and individual responsibility.

EXPLORATIONS

1. In the 1960s and 1970s, supporters of the U.S. government's war in Vietnam responded to antiwar protests with the slogan "America: Love It or Leave It." How does the title of this essay express its thesis? What allusion does Esther Dyson make within her essay to the earlier slogan?

2. What actions (and inactions) is Dyson advocating in this essay? What audi-ence is she addressing? What power does that audience have to implement her recommendations?

3. What argument do you think Dyson is responding to in this essay? How can you tell? What points does she concede to her opponent? Do her conces-sions strengthen or weaken her position? Why?

CONNECTIONS

1. What ideas about community appear in both this essay and Elaine Salinas's "Still Grieving over the Loss of the Land" (p. 579)? What ideas about the federal government appear in both essays?

2. "In this age of political correctness and other intrusions on our national cult of independence, it's hard to find a place where you can go and be yourself without worrying about the neighbors" (para. 1). In what sense could Masha

Gessen apply this statement to her interviewees in "The Day After Technology" (p. 556)? Do you think Dyson would side with the villagers in that essay or with the technology fans? What evidence supports your answer?

3. Do any of Neil Postman's objections to television in "Future Shlock" (p. 531) apply to cyberspace? If not, why not? If so, which ones?

ELABORATIONS

1. Postman asks: "How does a culture change when new technologies are introduced to it? And is it always desirable for a culture to accommodate itself to the demands of new technologies?" (p. 531, para. 7). In his Observation on page 212, Sven Birkerts asks: "We talk up a storm when it comes to policy issues — who should have jurisdiction, what rates may be charged. . . . But why do we hear so few people asking whether we might not *ourselves* be changing, and whether the changes are necessarily for the good?" Having read "Cyberspace: If You Don't Love It, Leave It," write an essay examining these questions in relation to cyberspace.

2. Do you agree or disagree with Dyson's argument? How and how much do you think the Internet should be regulated or censored? Write an argumentative essay stating more specifically than Dyson does what the pros and cons would be of a stronger system of regulation, or recommending how such a system could beneficially be set up.

HENRY LOUIS GATES JR.
and CORNEL WEST

The Talented Tenth

Henry Louis "Skip" Gates Jr. is a professor of English, chair of Afro-American studies, and director of the W. E. B. Du Bois Institute for Afro-American Research at Harvard University. Born in Piedmont, West Virginia, in 1950, he spent a year at Potomac State College before transferring to Yale University. After graduating summa cum laude with a degree in history, he worked as a London correspondent for *Time* magazine and received his M.A. and Ph.D. in English from Cambridge University. He taught at Yale, Cornell, and Duke Universities before moving to Harvard, where Cornel West also teaches. Gates continues to write essays, features, and criticism for such publications as *Harper's*, *The New Yorker*, *The Village Voice*, and the *New York Times Book Review*. A member of numerous committees and professional associations, including the Council on Foreign Relations and the American Civil Liberties Union National Advisory Council, he holds honorary degrees from several American universities. He received a MacArthur Fellowship in 1981. Gates's books include *The Signifying Monkey: Towards a Theory of African-American Literary Criticism* (1988), which won an American Book Award; *Loose Canons: Notes on the Culture Wars* (1992); and *Thirteen Ways of Looking at a Black Man* (1997).

The scholar, theologian, and activist Cornel West was born in Tulsa, Oklahoma, in 1953. His family moved around before settling in Sacramento, California. The Baptist church, in which his grandfather had been a preacher, taught him early lessons about faith and commitment; from the nearby Black Panthers he learned the value of community-based political action. At the age of eight, West read a biography of Theodore Roosevelt — a fellow asthmatic — and decided he too would go to Harvard University. He graduated from Harvard magna cum laude at twenty. After receiving his M.A. in 1975 and his Ph.D. in 1980 from Princeton University, he joined Princeton's faculty, where he became professor of religion and director of Afro-American studies in 1988. West's books include *Post-Analytic Philosophy* (1985), *Prophetic Fragments* (1988), and *Race Matters* (1993), a best-seller which inspired profiles of West in both *Time* and *Newsweek*. He is currently professor of Afro-American studies and the philosophy of religion at Harvard University. With department chair Henry Louis Gates Jr., West recently finished writing *The Future of the Race*; "The Talented Tenth" comes from the introduction. He lives near Boston with his wife, Elleni, a social worker from Addis Ababa, Ethiopia, and their son, Clifton.

> The Negro race, like all races, is going to be saved by its exceptional men. The problem of education, then, among Negroes must first of all deal with the Talented Tenth; it is the problem of developing the Best of this race that they may guide the Mass away from the contamination and death of the Worst, in their own and other races. Now the training of men is a difficult and intricate task. Its technique is a matter for educational experts, but its object is for the vision of seers. If we make money the object of man-training, we shall develop money-makers but not necessarily men; if we make technical skill the object of education, we may possess artisans but not, in nature, men. Men we shall have only as we make manhood the object of the work of the schools — intelligence, broad sympathy, knowledge of the world that was and is, and of the relation of men to it — this is the curriculum of that Higher Education which must underlie true life. On this foundation we may build bread winning, skill of hand and quickness of brain, with never a fear lest the child and man mistake the means of living for the object of life.
>
> —W. E. B. Du Bois

Twenty-five years ago, historically white male institutions of higher learning — such as Yale and Harvard — opened their doors to blacks and women in unprecedented numbers, a direct result of so-called "affirmative action" lobbying for the diversification of America's middle classes. Harvard and Yale, where we were undergraduates, were both quite self-conscious about their new admissions policies. At Yale, for example, Kingman Brewster, addressing the entering class in September of 1969 in a speech crafted more for the benefit of the "old Blue" alumni and the press than of those students seated in Woolsey Hall, welcomed each as one of that year's "1,000 male leaders." Pointing rather awkwardly to the "250 women" sitting in the audience, he promised that, despite their presence, Yale would never abandon its commitment to what at the turn of the century Du Bois had called America's "exceptional men."

If Yale went coed in 1969, never before had it seen more color in its classes: of the Class of 1973, ninety-six students, or 7.9 percent, were black, compared with eighteen students, or 1.8 percent, of the Class of

1968. Often "first-generation Ivy," and sometimes first-generation college, these students congregated in the pre-med and pre-law curricula, in search of security in the soon-to-be-integrated professional circles, especially the law, medicine, journalism, and business. But while they sought to enter the traditional professions — the academy, curiously enough, was not a popular option — a remarkably large percentage sought knowledge about their cultural and their ethnic heritages in the newly established programs in Afro-American Studies.

It is one of the dramatic — and, we believe, defining — facts of our generation that the birth of Afro-American Studies and the influx of a "critical" number of black students coincided on the campuses of America's historically white research colleges and universities. The agitation of black students, of course, had led to the creation of African-American Studies as an academic field in 1969, both at Harvard and Yale and throughout the country. Many of us took at least one Afro-American Studies course per term, as much to bolster the enrollment of these fledgling programs as to help retrace an invisible scaffolding that we felt undergirded us as citizens and as intellectuals. We were seeking to read and understand the canonical texts of the black tradition, which, we hoped, would enable us to tap into a vast black cultural "unconscious."

No less than three times that year — the year that culminated in strikes all across America's college campuses, called to protest the Vietnam war — Gates was a student in classes assigned to read Harold Cruse's *The Crisis of the Negro Intellectual* and Du Bois's "The Talented Tenth." These were the two signal works in the black tradition meant to help us find our way through the abyss of integration.

"The Talented Tenth" was held up as a model for the social, political, and ethical role of the members of what we might call a "crossover" generation, those of us who, as a result of the great civil rights movement, were able to integrate historically white educational and professional institutions. Cornel West and Henry Louis Gates Jr., in other words, were trained at Harvard and Yale, respectively, only as a result of the pressure of affirmative action to end these schools' racist quotas, which had barely been disturbed for over a century. (Harvard graduated its first black American only in 1870, 234 years after it was founded.) Had it not been for affirmative action, we, like so many of our ancestors, familial and fraternal, would have met at one of the superb historically black colleges or universities, such as Spelman or Talladega, Howard or Morehouse, Fisk or Lincoln, and not in the Ivy League. It is no accident that 25 years later, we are colleagues on the faculty of one of these very institutions.

More than a quarter of a century later, since that dreadful day in 1968 when Dr. King was so brutally murdered, the size of the black middle class — again, primarily because of affirmative action — has quadrupled, doubling in the 1980s alone. Simultaneously — and paradoxically — the size of the black underclass has grown disproportionately as well: in 1995, 45 percent of all black children are born at, or beneath, the poverty line. Economists have shown that fully one-third of the members of the African American community are *worse off* economically today than they were the day that King was killed. *If it is the best of times for the black middle class — the heirs of Du Bois's "Talented Tenth" — it is the worst of times for an equally large segment of our community.*

That American society has failed to protect the basic, ostensibly inalienable rights of its people — equal access to education, adequate housing, affordable medical care, and equal economic opportunity — equal access, indeed, to hope itself — and that the leadership of the African American community has a special responsibility to attend to these rights, to analyze the peculiar compounding effect of race, gender, and class, and to design, promote, lobby, and agitate for bold and imaginative remedies to conditions of inequality and injustice — these are [our] underlying premises. . . . We decided to begin to address these complex issues by rereading the essay that sought to define the "ethical content" of our "ethnic identities," as Cornel West has put it — the moral responsibilities of black leadership.

Precisely now, so near to the turn of the century, when the right wing of the Republican Party and a slim majority of the Supreme Court would seem to be hell bent on dismantling the very legal principles that led to the integration of women and people of color into the larger American middle class to an unprecedented degree — programs that indirectly result in the presence of a black person such as Mr. Justice Clarence Thomas on that very Court, for example — and when pseudoscientific arguments such as those put forth in Charles Murray and Richard J. Herrnstein's *The Bell Curve* seek to use the sanction of "scientific" or "objective" inquiry to justify the dissolution of compensatory education and entitlement programs, we both feel that it is urgent to make this argument now, to generate even deeper reflection on the nature of the society in which we live, the sort of country that we want to inhabit, and want our children's children to inhabit, in the century to come. And we would like to contribute in our small way to the creation of innovative policies that we hope will emerge from discussions such as these.

Race differences and class differentials have been ground together in this country in a crucible of misery and squalor, in such a way that few of us know where one stops and the other begins. But we do know that the causes of poverty within the black community are both *structural* and *behavioral*, as the sociological studies of William J. Wilson have amply demonstrated, and we would be foolish to deny this. A household in which its occupants cannot sustain themselves economically cannot possibly harbor hope or optimism, or stimulate eager participation in the full prerogatives of citizenship. One of our tasks, it seems to us, is to lobby for those social programs that have made a demonstrable difference in the lives of those sufficiently motivated to seize these expanded opportunities, and to reinforce those programs that reignite motivation in the face of despair.

More important, however, we have to demand a structural change in   10 this country, the equivalent of a Marshall Plan for our cities, as the National Urban League has called for repeatedly. We have to take people off welfare, train them for occupations relevant to the highly technological economy of the twenty-first century, and put them to work. Joblessness, as Wilson has shown, is the central cause of our country's so-called racial crisis. The figure in the carpet of America's racial crisis, we are arguing, is economic scarcity and unequal opportunity.

And while we favor a wide array of economic incentives to generate new investment in inner cities, youth apprenticeships with corporations, expanded tax credits for earned income, and tenant ownership of inner-city property, we believe that we must face the reality that economic prosperity and corporate investment will not come easily to our inner cities and we should most probably begin to think about moving black inner-city workers to sites where new jobs are being created, rather than merely holding our breath waiting for new factories or industries to crop up miraculously in the inner city.

That said, we strongly support Urban League President Hugh Price's proposals to develop the economic health of black neighborhoods in America's cities:

> Promoting economic development means that all of our children must understand and become comfortable with entrepreneurship. Too many of them have an unrealistic sense of the way things work or just don't know what their possibilities are. We must help them understand that they can earn a decent and honorable living through operating very small businesses. . . .
>
> Many cities are experiencing economic revivals. They are doing so by emphasizing what I call "quality of life" industries. They are building stadiums, museums, and aquariums downtown. They are restoring downtown restaurant, entertainment, and residential districts. Some are even building unsubsidized single-family housing within walking distance of

downtown. Our entrepreneurs should be in the middle of all that action. We need investment banks to assure access to capital for these enterprises. That is why the idea of an investment trust that the Leadership Summit is developing is intriguing.

It is only by confronting the twin realities of white racism, on the one hand, and our own failures to seize initiative and break the cycle of poverty, on the other, that we, the remnants of the Talented Tenth, will be able to assume a renewed leadership role for, and within, the black community. We must stand boldly against *any* manifestation of anti-black racism, whatever form it might take. On this matter, there can be *no* compromise. But to continue to repeat the same old stale formulas, to blame "the man" for oppressing us all, in exactly the same ways; to scapegoat Koreans, Jews, women, or even black immigrants for the failure of African Americans to seize local entrepreneurial opportunities, is to neglect our duty as leaders of our own community.

Not to demand that each member of the black community accept individual responsibility for her or his behavior — whether that behavior assumes the form of black-on-black homicide, violations by gang members against the sanctity of the church, unprotected sexual activity, gangster rap lyrics, misogyny and homophobia — is to function merely as ethnic cheerleaders selling woof tickets from the campus or the suburbs, rather than saying the difficult things that may be unpopular with our fellows. Being a leader does not necessarily mean being loved; loving one's community means daring to risk estrangement and alienation from that very community, in the short run, in order to break the cycle of poverty, despair, and hopelessness that we are in, over the long run. For what is at stake is nothing less than the survival of our country, *and* the African American people.

Just as we must continue to fight so that more people of color are admitted to the student bodies and hired on the faculty and staff of our colleges and universities, and integrated into every phase of America's social and commercial life, we must fight to see that Congress and the President enact a comprehensive jobs bill. And finally, to help bridge the painful gap between those of us on campus and those of us left behind on the streets, we call upon the African American Studies departments in this country to institutionalize sophomore and junior year summer internships for public service and community development, in cooperation with organizations such as the black church, the Children's Defense Fund, the National Urban League, the NAACP, PUSH, etc., so that we can begin to combat teenage pregnancies, black-on-black crime, and the spread of AIDS from drug abuse and unprotected

sexual relations, and help counter the despair, nihilism, and hopelessness that so starkly afflict our communities. Working together with
other scholars, politicians, and activists who have developed these programs, we can begin to close the economic gap that divides the black
community in two.

Dr. King did not die so that *half* of us would "make it," and *half* of us
perish, forever tarnishing two centuries of struggle and agitation for our
equal rights. We, the members of Du Bois's Talented Tenth, must accept our historical responsibility and live King's credo that none of us is
free until each of us is free. And that all of us are brothers and sisters, in
spirit — white and black, brown, red, and yellow, rich and poor black,
Protestant and Catholic, Gentile, Jew, and Muslim, gay and straight —
even if — to paraphrase Du Bois — we are not brothers- or sisters-in-law.

EXPLORATIONS

1. What is the thesis of "The Talented Tenth"? What statements by W. E. B.
   Du Bois (p. 593) could serve as a thesis statement for Henry Louis Gates Jr.
   and Cornel West's essay? What are the effects of Gates and West's focusing
   on Du Bois as they do?

2. What audience are Gates and West addressing? How can you tell? What actions and beliefs do they want that audience to adopt?

3. What arguments do Gates and West rebut in this essay? What clues suggest
   whose arguments these are?

CONNECTIONS

1. How would you describe the language in "The Talented Tenth"? What
   "voice" have the authors chosen, and how does it affect your reaction to
   their argument? Compare the language in Esther Dyson's "Cyberspace: If
   You Don't Love It, Leave It" (p. 586). What "voice" has she chosen, and
   how does it affect your reaction to her argument?

2. What common problems besetting the Americans they speak for are cited
   by Gates and West in this essay and Elaine Salinas in "Still Grieving over
   the Loss of the Land" (p. 579)? What proposed solutions, or approaches to
   solutions, appear in both essays? How do Gates and West's diagnoses and
   recommendations differ from Salinas's?

3. "Now the training of men is a difficult and intricate task." Du Bois's epi-
   graph to this essay was written almost a century ago, just two generations
   after the Civil War. Recall the plantation owner in Toni Morrison's excerpt

from *Beloved* (p. 460) bragging that his male slaves were men (paras. 80–84). What did he mean? What does Du Bois mean when he applies that term to their grandsons?

ELABORATIONS

1. According to Salinas (p. 579), "Inherent in this country is a real sense of white supremacy. You can go to college and get a doctorate, but if you're a minority, especially if you're a woman, you have to prove yourself all the time" (para. 21). After reading their essay, do you think Gates and West would agree? How are the historic and present positions of American Indians and African Americans similar and different? Do both groups now face essentially the same problems? Are the same solutions appropriate for both? Draw on these essays, others in this book, and additional research, if you wish, to write an essay answering these questions.

2. At the beginning of the twentieth century Du Bois wrote of the danger of "mistak[ing] the means of living for the object of life" (p. 593). At the end of the century, have we managed to avoid that mistake? Reread his recommendations for "man-training." Are they good guidelines for American educa tion in general? Why or why not? Write an essay applying Du Bois's advice to this country's present, past, and future.

NELSON MANDELA

Black Man in a White Court

In February 1990 the world celebrated Nelson Mandela's release from a South African prison after twenty-seven years. In April 1994 it celebrated his election as his country's first black president. Nelson Rolihlahla Mandela was born in 1918 to one of the royal families of the Transkei, the eldest son of a Tembu chief. He ran away to Johannesburg to escape an arranged tribal marriage; there he studied arts by correspondence and law at the University of Witwatersrand. With his law partner, Oliver Tambo, Mandela became active in the then-illegal African National Congress (ANC), whose mission Tambo has described as "the African struggle against the most powerful adversary in Africa: a highly industrialized, well-armed State manned by a fanatical group of White men determined to defend their privilege and their prejudice, and aided by the complicity of American, British, West German, and Japanese investment in the most profitable system of oppression on the continent."

When an all-white referendum voted to declare South Africa a Nationalist Republic in 1961 (see p. 73), Mandela called a general strike to dramatize black opposition. He left his home, family, and office to live as a political outlaw, nicknamed "the Black Pimpernel." In 1962 he was betrayed by an informer, arrested, tried, and sentenced to three years in prison for leading the strike and for leaving the country illegally. "Black Man in a White Court" is an excerpt from his trial, reprinted in his book *No Easy Walk to Freedom* (1965). From his cell Mandela became a defendant in the notorious Rivonia Trial, accused of sabotage and conspiracy to overthrow the government by force. He and six codefendants were sentenced to life in prison.

The growing worldwide human rights movement increased international pressure on the South African government, which made such concessions as allowing Asians and Coloreds (but not blacks) to vote and repealing laws banning interracial marriage. The slow pace and limited scope of change fueled protest inside and outside South Africa, some of it violent. After President P. W. Botha was replaced by the more liberal F. W. De Klerk, De Klerk met with Mandela in prison, unbanned the ANC and the Communist Party, desegregated beaches, limited detention without trial, lifted restrictions on the media, dismantled the repressive state security management system, and released seven other jailed ANC leaders before freeing Mandela. The two men began negotiating immediately for full political rights for black South Africans. In 1993 Mandela and De Klerk won the Nobel Peace Prize.

The following year Mandela won the presidency in South Africa's first election open to all races. De Klerk served in the new government for two years before resigning. Progress toward economic and social justice has been expectedly slow. Among the new government's efforts to foster national unity was the Truth and Reconciliation Commission, led by Bishop Desmond Tutu: Those who had committed crimes during apartheid were encouraged to make a public confession, and the victims or their families to testify. In 1999 Mandela's deputy president, Thabo Mbeki, was elected to succeed him.

For more background on South Africa, see page 73.

"Black Man in a White Court" First Court Statement, 1962

Extracts from the court record of the trial of Mandela held in the Old Synagogue court, Pretoria, from October 15 to November 7, 1962. Mandela was accused on two counts, that of inciting persons to strike illegally (during the 1961 stay-at-home) and that of leaving the country without a valid passport. He conducted his own defense.

Mandela: Your Worship, before I plead to the charge, there are one or two points I would like to raise.

Firstly, Your Worship will recall that this matter was postponed last Monday at my request until today, to enable counsel to make the arrangements to be available here today.[1] Although counsel is now available, after consultation with him and my attorneys, I have elected to conduct my own defense. Some time during the progress of these proceedings, I hope to be able to indicate that this case is a trial of the aspirations of the African people, and because of that I thought it proper to conduct my own defense. Nevertheless, I have decided to retain the services of counsel, who will be here throughout these proceedings, and I also would like my attorney to be available in the course of these proceedings as well, but subject to that I will conduct my own defense.

The second point I would like to raise is an application which is addressed to Your Worship. Now at the outset, I want to make it perfectly clear that the remarks I am going to make are not addressed to Your Worship in his personal capacity, nor are they intended to reflect upon

---

[1]Mandela had applied for a remand, because the trial had two and a half months previously been scheduled to take place in the Johannesburg Regional Court, where Mandela had arranged for his defense by advocate Joe Slovo. During the weekend before it opened, however, it was suddenly switched to Pretoria — and Slovo was restricted by a government banning order to the magisterial district of Johannesburg.

the integrity of the court. I hold Your Worship in high esteem and I do not for one single moment doubt your sense of fairness and justice. I must also mention that nothing I am going to raise in this application is intended to reflect against the prosecutor in his personal capacity.

The point I wish to raise in my argument is based not on personal considerations, but on important questions that go beyond the scope of this present trial. I might also mention that in the course of this application I am frequently going to refer to the white man and the white people. I want at once to make it clear that I am no racialist, and I detest racialism, because I regard it as a barbaric thing, whether it comes from a black man or from a white man. The terminology that I am going to employ will be compelled on me by the nature of the application I am making.

I want to apply for Your Worship's recusal[2] from this case. I challenge the right of this court to hear my case on two grounds.   5

Firstly, I challenge it because I fear that I will not be given a fair and proper trial. Secondly, I consider myself neither legally nor morally bound to obey laws made by a parliament in which I have no representation.

In a political trial such as this one, which involves a clash of the aspirations of the African people and those of whites, the country's courts, as presently constituted, cannot be impartial and fair.

In such cases, whites are interested parties. To have a white judicial officer presiding, however high his esteem, and however strong his sense of fairness and justice, is to make whites judges in their own case.

It is improper and against the elementary principles of justice to entrust whites with cases involving the denial by them of basic human rights to the African people.

What sort of justice is this that enables the aggrieved to sit in judg-   10 ment over those against whom they have laid a charge?

A judiciary controlled entirely by whites and enforcing laws enacted by a white parliament in which Africans have no representation — laws which in most cases are passed in the face of unanimous opposition from Africans —

Magistrate: I am wondering whether I shouldn't interfere with you at this stage, Mr. Mandela. Aren't we going beyond the scope of the proceedings? After all is said and done, there is only one court today and that is the white man's court. There is no other court. What purpose

---

[2]Withdrawal from the case on grounds of prejudice.

does it serve you to make an application when there is only one court, as you know yourself? What court do you wish to be tried by?

Mandela: Well, Your Worship, firstly I would like Your Worship to bear in mind that in a series of cases our courts have laid it down that the right of a litigant to ask for a recusal of a judicial officer is an extremely important right, which must be given full protection by the court, as long as that right is exercised honestly. Now I honestly have apprehensions, as I am going to demonstrate just now, that this unfair discrimination throughout my life has been responsible for very grave injustices, and I am going to contend that that race discrimination which outside this court has been responsible for all my troubles, I fear in this court is going to do me the same injustice. Now Your Worship may disagree with that, but Your Worship is perfectly entitled, in fact, obliged to listen to me and because of that I feel that Your Worship —

Magistrate: I would like to listen, but I would like you to give me the grounds for your application for me to recuse myself.

Mandela: Well, these are the grounds, I am developing them, sir. If   15
Your Worship will give me time —

Magistrate: I don't wish to go out of the scope of the proceedings.

Mandela: — Of the scope of the application. I am within the scope of the application, because I am putting forward grounds which in my opinion are likely not to give me a fair and proper trial.

Magistrate: Anyway proceed.

Mandela: As Your Worship pleases. I was developing the point that a judiciary controlled entirely by whites and enforcing laws enacted by a white parliament in which we have no representation, laws which in most cases are passed in the face of unanimous opposition from Africans, cannot be regarded as an impartial tribunal in a political trial where an African stands as an accused.

The Universal Declaration of Human Rights provides that all men   20
are equal before the law, and are entitled without any discrimination to equal protection of the law. In May 1951, Dr. D. F. Malan, then prime minister, told the Union parliament that this provision of the declaration applies in this country. Similar statements have been made on numerous occasions in the past by prominent whites in this country, including judges and magistrates. But the real truth is that there is in fact no equality before the law whatsoever as far as our people are concerned, and statements to the contrary are definitely incorrect and misleading.

It is true that an African who is charged in a court of law enjoys, on the surface, the same rights and privileges as an accused who is white insofar as the conduct of his trial is concerned. He is governed by the same rules of procedure and evidence as apply to a white accused. But it would be grossly inaccurate to conclude from this fact that an African consequently enjoys equality before the law.

In its proper meaning equality before the law means the right to participate in the making of the laws by which one is governed, a constitution which guarantees democratic rights to all sections of the population, the right to approach the court for protection or relief in the case of the violation of rights guaranteed in the constitution, and the right to take part in the administration of justice as judges, magistrates, attorneys-general, law advisers, and similar positions.

In the absence of these safeguards the phrase "equality before the law," insofar as it is intended to apply to us, is meaningless and misleading. All the rights and privileges to which I have referred are monopolized by whites, and we enjoy none of them.

The white man makes all the laws, he drags us before his courts and accuses us, and he sits in judgment over us.

It is fit and proper to raise the question sharply, What is this rigid   25
color bar in the administration of justice? Why is it that in this courtroom I face a white magistrate, am confronted by a white prosecutor, and escorted into the dock by a white orderly? Can anyone honestly and seriously suggest that in this type of atmosphere the scales of justice are evenly balanced?

Why is it that no African in the history of this country has ever had the honor of being tried by his own kith and kin, by his own flesh and blood?

I will tell Your Worship why: The real purpose of this rigid color bar is to ensure that the justice dispersed by the courts should conform to the policy of the country, however much that policy might be in conflict with the norms of justice accepted in judiciaries throughout the civilized world.

I feel oppressed by the atmosphere of white domination that lurks all around in this courtroom. Somehow this atmosphere calls to mind the inhuman injustices caused to my people outside this courtroom by this same white domination.

It reminds me that I am voteless because there is a parliament in this country that is white-controlled. I am without land because the white minority has taken a lion's share of my country and forced me to occupy poverty-stricken reserves, overpopulated and overstocked. We are ravaged by starvation and disease . . .

Magistrate: What has that got to do with the case, Mr. Mandela?   30

Mandela: With the last point, sir, it hangs together, if Your Worship will give me the chance to develop it.

Magistrate: You have been developing it for quite a while now, and I feel you are going beyond the scope of your application.

Mandela: Your Worship, this to me is an extremely important ground which the court must consider.

Magistrate: I fully realize your position, Mr. Mandela, but you must confine yourself to the application and not go beyond it. I don't want to know about starvation. That in my view has got nothing to do with the case at the present moment.

Mandela: Well, Your Worship has already raised the point that here   35
in this country there is only a white court. What is the point of all this? Now if I can demonstrate to Your Worship that outside this courtroom race discrimination has been used in such a way as to deprive me of my rights, not to treat me fairly, certainly this is a relevant fact from which to infer that wherever race discrimination is practiced, this will be the same result, and this is the only reason why I am using this point.

Magistrate: I am afraid that I will have to interrupt you, and you will have to confine yourself to the reasons, the real reasons for asking me to recuse myself.

Mandela: Your Worship, the next point which I want to make is this: I raise the question, how can I be expected to believe that this same racial discrimination which has been the cause of so much injustice and suffering right through the years should now operate here to give me a fair and open trial? Is there no danger that an African accused may regard the courts not as impartial tribunals, dispensing justice without fear or favor, but as instruments used by the white man to punish those amongst us who clamor for deliverance from the fiery furnace of white rule? I have grave fears that this system of justice may enable the guilty to drag the innocent before the courts. It enables the unjust to prosecute and demand vengeance against the just. It may tend to lower the standards of fairness and justice applied in the country's courts by white judicial officers to black litigants. This is the first ground for this application: that I will not receive a fair and proper trial.

The second ground of my objection is that I consider myself neither morally nor legally obliged to obey laws made by a parliament in which I am not represented.

That the will of the people is the basis of the authority of government is a principle universally acknowledged as sacred throughout the civilized world, and constitutes the basic foundations of freedom and justice. It is understandable why citizens, who have the vote as well as the right to direct representation in the country's governing bodies, should be morally and legally bound by the laws governing the country.

It should be equally understandable why we, as Africans, should 40 adopt the attitude that we are neither morally nor legally bound to obey laws which we have not made, nor can we be expected to have confidence in courts which enforce such laws.

I am aware that in many cases of this nature in the past, South African courts have upheld the right of the African people to work for democratic changes. Some of our judicial officers have even openly criticized the policy which refuses to acknowledge that all men are born free and equal, and fearlessly condemned the denial of opportunities to our people.

But such exceptions exist in spite of, not because of, the grotesque system of justice that has been built up in this country. These exceptions furnish yet another proof that even among the country's whites there are honest men whose sense of fairness and justice revolts against the cruelty perpetrated by their own white brothers to our people.

The existence of genuine democratic values among some of the country's whites in the judiciary, however slender they may be, is welcomed by me. But I have no illusions about the significance of this fact, healthy a sign as it might be. Such honest and upright whites are few and they have certainly not succeeded in convincing the vast majority of the rest of the white population that white supremacy leads to dangers and disaster.

However, it would be a hopeless commandant who relied for his victories on the few soldiers in the enemy camp who sympathize with his cause. A competent general pins his faith on the superior striking power he commands and on the justness of his cause which he must pursue uncompromisingly to the bitter end.

I hate race discrimination most intensely and in all its manifesta- 45 tions. I have fought it all during my life; I fight it now, and will do so until the end of my days. Even though I now happen to be tried by one whose opinion I hold in high esteem, I detest most violently the setup that surrounds me here. It makes me feel that I am a black man in a white man's court. This should not be. I should feel perfectly at ease and at home with the assurance that I am being tried by a fellow South African who does not regard me as an inferior, entitled to a special type of justice.

This is not the type of atmosphere most conducive to feelings of security and confidence in the impartiality of a court.

The court might reply to this part of my argument by assuring me that it will try my case fairly and without fear or favor, that in deciding whether or not I am guilty of the offense charged by the state, the court will not be influenced by the color of my skin or by any other improper motive.

That might well be so. But such a reply would completely miss the point of my argument.

As already indicated, my objection is not directed to Your Worship in his personal capacity, nor is it intended to reflect upon the integrity of the court. My objection is based upon the fact that our courts, as presently constituted, create grave doubts in the minds of an African accused, whether he will receive a fair and proper trial.

This doubt springs from objective facts relating to the practice of unfair discrimination against the black man in the constitution of the country's courts. Such doubts cannot be allayed by mere verbal assurances from a presiding officer, however sincere such assurances might be. There is only one way, and one way only, of allaying such doubts, namely, by removing unfair discrimination in judicial appointments. This is my first difficulty.

I have yet another difficulty about similar assurances Your Worship might give. Broadly speaking, Africans and whites in this country have no common standard of fairness, morality, and ethics, and it would be very difficult to determine on my part what standard of fairness and justice Your Worship has in mind.

In their relationship with us, South African whites regard it as fair and just to pursue policies which have outraged the conscience of mankind and of honest and upright men throughout the civilized world. They suppress our aspirations, bar our way to freedom, and deny us opportunities to promote our moral and material progress, to secure ourselves from fear and want. All the good things of life are reserved for the white folk and we blacks are expected to be content to nourish our bodies with such pieces of food as drop from the tables of men with white skins. This is the white man's standard of justice and fairness. Herein lies his conception of ethics. Whatever he himself may say in his defense, the white man's moral standards in this country must be judged by the extent to which he has condemned the vast majority of its inhabitants to serfdom and inferiority.

We, on the other hand, regard the struggle against color discrimination and for the pursuit of freedom and happiness as the highest aspiration of all men. Through bitter experience, we have learned to regard the white man as a harsh and merciless type of human being whose contempt for our rights, and whose utter indifference to the promotion of our welfare, makes his assurances to us absolutely meaningless and hypocritical.

I have the hope and confidence that Your Worship will not hear this objection lightly nor regard it as frivolous. I have decided to speak frankly and honestly because the injustice I have referred to contains the seeds of an extremely dangerous situation for our country and I make no threat when I say that unless these wrongs are remedied without delay, we might well find that even plain talk before the country's courts is too timid a method to draw the attention of the country to our political demands.

Finally, I need only to say that the courts have said that the possibil- 55
ity of bias and not actual bias is all that needs be proved to ground an application of this nature. In this application I have merely referred to certain objective facts, from which I submit that the possibility be inferred that I will not receive a fair and proper trial.

Magistrate: Mr. Prosecutor, have you anything to say?

Prosecutor: Very briefly, Your Worship, I just wish to point out that there are certain legal grounds upon which an accused person is entitled to apply for the recusal of a judicial officer from the case in which he is to be tried. I submit that the accused's application is not based on one of those principles, and I ask the court to reject it.

Magistrate: [to Mandela] Your application is dismissed. Will you now plead to your charges?

Mandela: I plead *not guilty* to both charges, to all the charges.

EXPLORATIONS

1. What application is Nelson Mandela making to the court in this argument? What two grounds does he give for his application? What appears to be the true purpose of his application? Is he successful? Why or why not?

2. Does the court seriously consider Mandela's application? What statements by Mandela and by the judge are the basis for your answer?

3. In what ways does Mandela emphasize that, as a lawyer, he is part of the same elite group as the judge and prosecutor? How does his stressing that point strengthen the impact of his speech?

CONNECTIONS

1. What ideas on racial inequity expressed by Mandela about South Africa are also expressed by Henry Louis Gates Jr. and Cornel West about the United States in "The Talented Tenth" (p. 592)? What statements by Mandela could be applied to racial injustice in the United States?

2. What points about white domination made by Mandela are also made by Elaine Salinas (p. 579)? In what ways does the situation of blacks in South Africa more closely resemble that of Indians than African Americans in the United States?

3. Like Nadine Gordimer in "Where Do Whites Fit In?" (p. 284), Mandela refers to *Africans* and *whites* in paragraphs 7–11 and elsewhere rather than to *black South Africans* and *white South Africans*. What is the effect of this usage? What comments in Mandela's paragraphs 2, 7, and 45 illuminate his choice of words?

ELABORATIONS

1. Look closely at the transcript and background notes for "Black Man in a White Court." In what sense has the white South African government stacked the deck so that Mandela cannot win? How does Mandela use this stacked deck to set up a situation in which he cannot lose? Write a classification essay analyzing the various political agendas and strategies represented in this trial, and identifying winners and losers.

2. What statements about men and women in Simone de Beauvoir's "Woman as Other" (p. 341) express points made about white and black South Africans in "Black Man in a White Court"? Based on Beauvoir's discussion of the "Other," Mandela's transcript, and other relevant selections in this book, write an essay analyzing the causes and effects of racism.

GRACE PALEY

Six Days: Some Rememberings

Poet and short-story writer Grace Paley was born in New York City's borough of the Bronx in 1922. She studied at Hunter College and New York University. Married twice and the mother of two children, Paley has described herself as "a typist, a housewife, and a writer" as well as "a somewhat combative pacifist and cooperative anarchist." She has taught at Columbia and Syracuse Universities, Dartmouth and Sarah Lawrence Colleges, and the City College of New York. The winner of several writing awards, Paley also has been a faculty member and writer in residence at numerous writers' workshops, including the Fine Arts Work Center in Provincetown, Massachusetts; the Prague Summer Writers' Workshop; and Art Workshop International in Assisi, Italy. Many of the stories in her collections, which include *The Little Disturbances of Man* (1959), *Enormous Changes at the Last Minute* (1974), and *Later the Same Day* (1985), reflect her experience as a female Jewish New Yorker. Paley told an interviewer for *Threepenny Review* in 1996, "You don't have to love your cultural roots, but you have to recognize them in some way. They are the sounds that were always in your ear." Her poetry appears in the prose and poetry collection *Long Walks and Intimate Talks* (1991) and in *New and Collected Poems* (1992). In 1989, Governor Mario Cuomo declared Paley the first official New York State Writer. Her book *The Collected Stories* (1994) was nominated for the National Book Award and Pulitzer Prize. Her most recent book, *Just As I Thought* (1998), is her first nonfiction collection. "Six Days: Some Rememberings" first appeared in the *Alaska Quarterly Review* (1995).

I was in jail. I had been sentenced to six days in the Women's House of Detention, a fourteen-story prison right in the middle of Greenwich Village, my own neighborhood. This happened during the American War in Vietnam, I have forgotten which important year of the famous sixties. The civil disobedience for which I was paying a small penalty probably consisted of sitting down to impede or slow some military parade.

I was surprised at the sentence. Others had been given two days or dismissed. I think the judge was particularly angry with me. After all, I was not a kid. He thought I was old enough to know better, a forty-five-year-old woman, a mother and teacher. I ought to be too busy to waste time on causes I couldn't possibly understand.

I was herded with about twenty other women, about 90 percent black and Puerto Rican, into the bullpen, an odd name for a women's holding facility. There, through someone else's lawyer, I received a note from home, telling me that since I'd chosen to spend the first week of July in jail, my son would probably not go to summer camp, because I had neglected to raise the money I'd promised. I read this note and burst into tears, real running-down-the-cheek tears. It was true: Thinking about other people's grown boys, I had betrayed my little son. The summer, starting that day, July 1, stood up before me day after day, the steaming city streets, the after-work crowded city pool.

I guess I attracted some attention. You — you white girl you — you never been arrested before? A black woman about a head taller than I put her arm on my shoulder. — It ain't so bad. What's your time sugar? I gotta do three years. You huh?

Six days.

Six days? What the fuck for?   5

I explained, sniffling, embarrassed.

You got six days for sitting down in front of a horse? Cop on the horse? Horse step on you? Jesus in hell, cops gettin crazier and stupider and meaner. Maybe we get you out.

No, no, I said. I wasn't crying because of that. I didn't want her to think I was scared. I wasn't. She paid no attention. Shoving a couple of women aside — Don't stand in front of me, bitch. Move over. What you looking at? — she took hold of the bars of our cage, commenced to bang on them, shook them mightily, screaming — Hear me now, you motherfuckers, you grotty pigs, get this housewife out of here! She returned to comfort me — Six days in this low-down hole for sitting in front of a horse!

Before we were distributed among our cells, we were dressed in a   10
kind of nurse's aide scrub uniform, blue or green, a little too large or a little too small. We had had to submit to a physical in which all our hiding places were investigated for drugs. These examinations were not too difficult, mostly because a young woman named Andrea Dworkin had fought them, refused a grosser, more painful examination some months earlier. She had been arrested protesting the war in front of the U.S. Mission to the UN. I had been there too, but I don't think I was arrested that day. She was mocked for that determined struggle at the Women's House, as she had been for other braveries, but according to the women I questioned, certain humiliating, perhaps sadistic customs had ended — for that period at least.

My cellmate was a beautiful young woman, twenty-three years old, a prostitute who'd never been arrested before. She was nervous, but she had been given the name of an important long-termer. She explained in a businesslike way that she *was* beautiful, and would need protection. She'd be O.K. once she found that woman. In the two days we spent together, she tried *not* to talk to the other women on our cell block. She said they were mostly street whores and addicts. She would never be on the street. Her man wouldn't allow it anyway.

I slept well for some reason, probably the hard mattress. I don't seem to mind where I am. Also I must tell you, I could look out the window at the end of our corridor and see my children or their friends, on their way to music lessons or Greenwich House pottery. Looking slantwise I could see right into Sutter's Bakery, then on the corner of Tenth Street. These were my neighbors at coffee and cake.

Sometimes the cell block was open, but not our twelve cells. Other times the reverse. Visitors came by: They were prisoners, detainees not yet sentenced. They seemed to have a strolling freedom, though several, unsentenced, unable to make bail, had been there for months. One woman peering into the cells stopped when she saw me. Grace! Hi! I knew her from the neighborhood, maybe the park, couldn't really remember her name.

What are you in for? I asked.

Oh nothing — well a stupid drug bust. I don't even use — oh well forget it. I've been here six weeks. They keep putting the trial off. Are you O.K.?

Then I complained. I had planned not to complain about anything while living among people who'd be here in these clanging cells a long time; it didn't seem right. But I said, I don't have anything to read and they took away my pen and I don't have paper.

Oh you'll get all that eventually, she said. Keep asking.

Well they have all my hairpins. I'm a mess.

No no she said, you're O.K. You look nice.

(A couple of years later, the war continuing, I was arrested in Washington. My hair was still quite long. I wore it in a kind of bun on top of my head. My hairpins gone, my hair straggled wildly every which way. Muriel Rukeyser, arrested that day along with about thirty other women, made the same generous sisterly remark. No no Grace, love you with your hair down, you really ought to always wear it this way.)

The very next morning, my friend brought me *The Collected Writings of William Carlos Williams.* — These O.K.?

God! O.K. — Yes!

My trial is coming up tomorrow, she said. I think I'm getting off with time already done. Overdone. See you around?

That afternoon, my cellmate came for her things — I'm moving to the fourth floor. Working in the kitchen. Couldn't be better. We were sitting outside our cells, she wanted me to know something. She'd already told me, but said it again. — I still can't believe it. This creep, this guy, this cop, he waits he just waits till he's fucked and fine, pulls his pants up, pays me, and arrests me. It's not legal. It's not. My man's so mad, he'd like to kill *me*, but he's not that kind of — he's not a criminal type, *my* man. She never said the word pimp. Maybe no one did. Maybe that was our word.

I had made friends with some of the women in the cells across the aisle. How can I say "made friends." I just sat and spoke when spoken to, I was at school. I answered questions — simple ones. Why would I do such a fool thing on purpose? How old were my children? My man any good? Then, you live around the corner? That was a good idea, Evelyn said, to have a prison in your own neighborhood, so you could keep in touch, yelling out the window. As in fact we were able to do right here and now, calling and being called from Sixth Avenue, by mothers, children, boyfriends.

About the children: One woman took me aside. Her daughter was brilliant, she was in Hunter High School, had taken a test. No she hardly ever saw her, but she wasn't a whore — it was the drugs. Her daughter was ashamed, the grandmother, the father's mother made the child ashamed. When she got out in six months it would be different. This made Evelyn and Rita, right across from my cell, laugh. Different, I swear. Different. Laughing. But she *could* make it, I said. Then they really laughed. Their first laugh was a bare giggle compared to these convulsive roars. Change her ways? That dumb bitch Ha!!

Another woman, Helen, the only other white woman on the cell block, wanted to talk to me. She wanted me to know that she was not only white but Jewish. She came from Brighton Beach. Her father, he should rest in peace, thank God, was dead. Her arms were covered with puncture marks almost like sleeve patterns. But she needed to talk to me, because I was Jewish (I'd been asked by Rita and Evelyn — was I Irish? No, Jewish. Oh, they answered). She walked me to the barred window that looked down on West Tenth Street. She said, How come you so friends with those black whores? You don't hardly talk to me. I said I liked them, but I liked her too. She said, If you knew them for true, you wouldn't like them. They nothing but street whores. You know, once I was friends with them. We done a lot of things together, I knew them fifteen years Evy and Rita maybe twenty, I been in the streets with them, side by side, Amsterdam, Lenox, West Harlem; in bad weather we covered each other. Then one day along come

Malcolm X and they don't know me no more, they ain't talking to me. You too white. I ain't all that white. Twenty years. They ain't talking.

My friend Myrt called one day, that is called from the street, called — Grace Grace. I heard and ran to the window. A policeman, the regular beat cop, was addressing her. She looked up, then walked away before I could yell my answer. Later on she told me that he'd said, I don't think Grace would appreciate you calling her name out like that.

What a mistake! For years, going to the park with my children, or simply walking down Sixth Avenue on a summer night past the Women's House, we would often have to thread our way through whole families calling up — bellowing, screaming to the third, seventh, tenth floor, to figures, shadows behind bars and screened windows — How you feeling? Here's Glena. She got big. Mami mami you like my dress? We gettin you out baby. New lawyer come by.

And the replies, among which I was privileged to live for a few days —   30
shouted down. — You lookin beautiful. What he say? Fuck you James. I got a chance? Bye bye. Come next week.

Then the guards, the heavy clanking of cell doors. Keys. Night.

I still had no pen or paper despite the great history of prison literature. I was suffering a kind of frustration, a sickness in the way claustrophobia is a sickness — this paper-and-penlessness was a terrible pain in the area of my heart, a nausea. I was surprised.

In the evening, at lights out (a little like the army or on good days a strict, unpleasant camp), women called softly from their cells. Rita hey Rita sing that song — Come on sister sing. A few more importunings and then Rita in the cell diagonal to mine would begin with a ballad. A song about two women and a man. It was familiar to everyone but me. The two women were prison sweethearts. The man was her outside lover. One woman, the singer, was being paroled. The ballad told her sorrow about having been parted from him when she was sentenced, now she would leave her loved woman after three years. There were about twenty stanzas of joy and grief.

Well, I was so angry not to have pen and paper to get some of it down that I lost it all — all but the sorrowful plot. Of course she had this long song in her head, and in the next few nights she sang and chanted others, sometimes with a small chorus.

Which is how I finally understood that I didn't lack pen and paper   35
but my own memorizing mind. It had been given away with a hundred poems, called rote learning, old-fashioned, backward, an enemy of creative thinking, a great human gift, disowned.

Now there's a garden where the Women's House of Detention once stood. A green place, safely fenced in, with protected daffodils and tulips; roses bloom in it too, sometimes into November.

The big women's warehouse and its barred blind windows have been removed from Greenwich Village's affluent throat. I was sorry when it happened; the bricks came roaring down, great trucks carried them away.

I have always agreed with Rita and Evelyn that if there are prisons, they ought to be in the neighborhood, near a subway — not way out in distant suburbs, where families have to take cars, buses, ferries, trains, and the population that considers itself innocent forgets, denies, chooses to never know that there is a whole huge country of the bad and the unlucky and the self-hurters, a country with a population greater than that of many nations in our world.

EXPLORATIONS

1. What is Grace Paley's attitude toward being in jail? What are the effects of her not describing her feelings explicitly? What cues in "Six Days: Some Rememberings" reveal her reactions to the experience?

2. How do Paley's choices not to use quotation marks and not to identify speakers in the usual way suit the setting of her narrative? What other stylistic choices does she make that are appropriate to this memoir, and why are they appropriate?

3. "That was a good idea, Evelyn said, to have a prison in your own neighborhood, so you could keep in touch, yelling out the window" (para. 25). What are some likely reasons why this prison later was moved out of Paley's Greenwich Village neighborhood in downtown New York City? Why was Paley "sorry when it happened" (para. 37)?

CONNECTIONS

1. "The population that considers itself innocent forgets, denies, chooses to never know that there is a whole huge country of the bad and the unlucky and the self-hurters, a country with a population greater than that of many nations in our world" (para. 38). How does this statement of Paley's about prisoners in New York City help to explain why apartheid could be enforced for so long in South Africa (see "Black Man in a White Court," p. 600), and

how Nazi Germany could slaughter millions of Jews (see "Between Word and Picture," p. 569)?

2. Vine Deloria Jr. and Clifford M. Lytle note that non-Indians tend to write down all the principles and procedures of their government, while Indians have not found this necessary (p. 523). How is this non-Indian habit echoed in Paley's essay? After comparing Paley's and Deloria and Lytle's comments, what advantages can you see in an oral tradition that relies on memory, and what advantages can you see in a record-keeping tradition?

3. Salman Rushdie writes in "Imaginary Homelands" about the partial and fragmentary nature of memory (p. 86). How does Paley alert us from the start of her essay that her memory of her six days in the Women's House of Detention is fragmented in the way Rushdie describes?

ELABORATIONS

1. Simone de Beauvoir in "Woman as Other" (p. 341) and Amos Oz in "Between Word and Picture" (p. 569) write about some of the ways one person may decide that another person does not deserve to be treated as a fellow human being. How does being sent to jail change someone's standing and deserts? Are the annoyances Paley describes in "Six Days: Some Rememberings" reasonable ways for prison employees to treat prisoners? For prisoners to treat each other? If so, why? If not, why not? Use these three selections and others in this book, as well as outside references if you wish, to write an essay on "prisoners as other."

2. A number of internationally known writers have been jailed for political reasons, including some represented in this book: Paley, Wole Soyinka in Nigeria, and Nelson Mandela in South Africa, for instance. Choose two such writers from different countries and write an essay comparing and contrasting their experiences: the governmental policies that sent them to prison, their situation while serving time, the impact of their clash with the government on their work and vice versa.

FAY WELDON

Down the Clinical Disco

Fay Weldon was born Franklin Birkinshaw in 1931 in Worcester-shire, England. Her family moved to New Zealand soon afterward; her father, a physician, and her mother, a writer, divorced a few years later. Weldon spent most of her youth among women, attending the Girls' High School in Christchurch, and then a convent school in London, where she lived with her mother, sister, and grandmother. She received her master's degree in economics and psychology from St. Andrews University at age twenty. Weldon married a schoolmaster twenty-five years older than she, had a son, divorced, and began writing novels. For money she worked in the Foreign Office, then as a market researcher for the *Daily Mirror*, and then as an advertising copywriter. In 1960 she married Ron Weldon, with whom she had three more sons. Her first novel was published in 1967: *The Fat Woman's Joke* (U.S. title, *And the Wife Ran Away*, 1968). Continuing to write fiction, she also branched into television scripts, plays, radio plays, and nonfiction. Weldon is best known in the United States for her novel *The Life and Loves of a She-Devil* (1983), which was made into an award-winning television serial by the British Broadcasting Company (1986) and a motion picture, *She-Devil*, starring Meryl Streep and Roseanne (1989). Weldon was the first woman ever to head the prestigious Booker Prize panel (1983). She is currently a contributing editor for *Allure* magazine. Her most recent books are *Big Girls Don't Cry* (1998) and *A Hard Time to Be a Father* (1999). She lives in Shepton Mallet, Somerset, and keeps a house in London. "Down the Clinical Disco" comes from her short story collection *Moon Over Minneapolis* (1991).

The United Kingdom of Great Britain and Northern Ireland is a constitutional monarchy currently headed by Queen Elizabeth II and run by a prime minister and a parliament comprising the House of Lords (traditionally, but no longer, hereditary) and House of Commons (elected). Although the United Kingdom is slightly smaller than Oregon, it has commanded an empire that at various times included Australia and parts of Europe, North America, Asia, Africa, and Antarctica. The present United Kingdom consists of England, Scotland, and Wales on the island of Great Britain, and the six Irish counties that make up Northern Ireland (see p. 136); among its dominions are the Channel Islands, the Isle of Man, Gibraltar, the British West Indies, Bermuda, the Falklands, and several other South Atlantic islands. Geologically, Britain was part of the European continent until about 6000 B.C. The

Romans conquered it in A.D. 43; after they withdrew in 410, Jutes, Angles, and Saxons raided and invaded from what are now Scandinavia and Germany. The Norman Conquest of 1066 subjugated England to France and blended its Anglo-Saxon language with French to produce English. England and France vied for power over the next several centuries, with Scotland in and out of the fray. Henry VIII split off the Church of England from the Roman Catholic Church in 1534; his daughter Elizabeth I saw England established as a world naval power. She was succeeded by James VI of Scotland, who as James I of England united the two countries in 1603. The age of exploration and empire followed, peaking in the 1800s under Queen Victoria. In the twentieth century, independence movements have reversed British expansion: In 1999, Scotland elected its own legislature, and negotiations are under way for a compromise between separatists and loyalists in Northern Ireland. Meanwhile, the rise of air power has made Britain's legendary sea power less critical. The United Kingdom was a founding member of NATO and the Common Market and is a cornerstone of the European Union.

You never know where you'll meet your own true love. I met mine down the clinical disco. That's him over there, the thin guy with the jeans, the navy jumper,[1] and the red woolly cap. He looks pretty much like anyone else, don't you think? That's hard work on his part, not to mention mine, but we got there in the end. Do you want a drink? Gin? Tonic? Fine. I'll just have an orange juice. I don't drink. Got to be careful. You never know who's watching. They're everywhere. Sorry, forget I said that. Even a joke can be paranoia. Do you like my hair? That's a golden gloss rinse. Not my style really; I have this scar down my cheek: See, if I turn to the light? A good short crop is what suits me best, always has been: I suppose I've got what you'd call a strong face. Oops, sorry, dear, didn't mean to spill your gin; it's the heels. I do my best but I can never quite manage stilettos. But it's an ill wind; anyone watching would think I'm ever so slightly tipsy, and that's normal, isn't it. It is not absolutely A-okay not to drink alcohol. On the obsessive side. *Darling, of course there are people watching.*

Let me tell you about the clinical disco while Eddie finishes his game of darts. He hates darts but darts are what men do in pubs, okay? The clinical disco is what they have once a month at Broadmoor. (Yes, that place. Broadmoor. The secure hospital for the criminally insane.) You didn't know they had women there? They do. One woman to every

---

[1]Sweater. — ED.

nine men. They often don't look all that like women when they go in but they sure as hell look like them when (and if, if, if, if, if, if) they go out.

How did I get to be in there? You really want to know? I'd been having this crummy time at home and this crummy time at work. I was pregnant and married to this guy I loved, God knows why, in retrospect, but I did, only he fancied my mother, and he got her pregnant too — while I was out at work — did you know women can get pregnant at fifty? He didn't, she didn't, I didn't — but she was! My mum said he only married me to be near her anyway and I was the one who ought to have an abortion. So I did. It went wrong and messed me up inside, so I couldn't have babies, and my mum said what did it matter, I was a lesbian anyway, just look at me. I got the scar in a road accident, in case you're wondering. And I thought what the hell, who wants a man, who wants a mother, and walked out on them. And I was working at the Royal Opera House for this man who was a real pain, and you know how these places get: The dramas and the rows and the overwork and the underpay and the show must go on though you're dropping dead. Dropping dead babies. No, I'm not crying. What do you think I am, a depressive? I'm as normal as the next person.

What I did was set fire to the office. Just an impulse. I was having these terrible pains and he made me work late. He said it was my fault Der Rosenkavalier's wig didn't fit; he said I'd make his opera house a laughingstock: The wig slipped and the *New York Times* noticed and jeered. But it wasn't my fault about the wig: Wardrobe had put the message through to props, not administration. And I sat in front of the VDU[2] — the union is against them, they cause infertility in women but what employer's going to worry about a thing like that — they'd prefer everyone childless any day — and thought about my husband and my mum, five months pregnant, and lit a cigarette. I'd given up smoking for a whole year but this business at home had made me start again. Have you ever had an abortion at five months? No? Not many have.

How's your drink? How's Eddie getting on with the darts? Started an-   5
other game? That's A-okay, that's fine by me, that's normal.

So what were we saying, Linda? Oh yes, arson. That's what they called it. I just moved my cigarette lighter under the curtains and they went up, whoosh, and they caught some kind of soundproof ceiling infill they use these days instead of plaster. Up it all went. Whoosh again. Four hundred pounds' worth of damage. Or so they said. If you ask me, they were glad of the excuse to redecorate.

---

[2]Video display unit; a computer monitor. — ED.

Like a fool, instead of lying and just saying it was an accident, I said I'd done it on purpose, I was glad I had, opera was a waste of public funds, and working late a waste of my life. That was before I got to court. The solicitor[3] laddie warned me off. He said arson was no laughing matter, they came down very hard on arson. I thought a fine, perhaps; he said no, prison. Years not months.

You know my mum didn't even come to the hearing? She had a baby girl. I thought there might be something wrong with it, my mum being so old, but there wasn't. Perhaps the father being so young made up for it.

There was a barrister chappie. He said look you've been upset, you are upset, all this business at home. The thing for you to do is plead insane; we'll get you sent to Broadmoor, it's the best place in the country for psychiatric care, they'll have you right in the head in no time. Otherwise it's Holloway, and that's all strip cells and major tranquilizers, and not so much of a short sharp shock as a long sharp shock. Years, it could be, arson.

So that's what I did, I pleaded insane, and got an indefinite sentence,   10
which meant into Broadmoor until such time as I was cured and safe to be let out into the world again. I never was unsafe. You know what one of those famous opera singers said when she heard what I'd done? "Good for Philly," she said. "Best thing that could possibly happen: the whole place razed to the ground." Only of course it wasn't razed to the ground, there was just one room already in need of redecoration slightly blackened. When did I realize I'd made a mistake? The minute I saw Broadmoor: a great black pile; the second I got into this reception room. There were three women nurses in there, standing around a bath of hot water; great hefty women, and male nurses too, and they were talking and laughing. Well, not exactly laughing, but an Inside equivalent; a sort of heavy grunting ha-ha-ha they manage, halfway between sex and hate. They didn't even look at me as I came in. I was terrified, you can imagine. One of them said "strip" over her shoulder and I just stood there not believing it. So she barked "strip" again, so I took off a cardigan and my shoes, and then one of them just ripped everything off me and pushed my legs apart and yanked out a Tampax — sorry about this, Linda — and threw it in a bin and dunked me in the bath without even seeing me. Do you know what's worse than being naked and seen by strangers, including men strangers? It's being naked and unseen, because you don't even count as a woman. Why men? In case the women

---

[3]Solicitor: a consulting lawyer. A barrister (para. 9) is a courtroom lawyer. — ED.

patients are uncontrollable. The bath was dirty. So were the nurses. I asked for a sanitary towel but no one replied. I don't know if they were being cruel: I don't think they thought that what came out of my mouth were words. Well I was mad, wasn't I? That's why I was there. I was mad because I was a patient, I was wicked because I was prisoner; they were sane because they were nurses and good because they could go home after work.

Linda, is that guy over there in the suit watching? No? You're sure?

They didn't go far, mind you, most of them. They lived, breathed, slept The Hospital. Whole families of nurses live in houses at the foot of the great Broadmoor wall. They intermarry. Complain about one and you find you're talking to the cousin, aunt, lover, or best friend of the complainee. You learn to shut up; you learn to smile. I was a tea bag for the whole of one day and I never stopped smiling from dawn to dusk. That's right, I was a tea bag. Nurse Kelly put a wooden frame around my shoulders and hung a piece of gauze front and back and said, "You be a tea bag all day," so I was. How we all laughed. Why did he want me to be a tea bag? It was his little joke. They get bored, you see. They look to the patients for entertainment.

Treatment? Linda, I saw one psychiatrist six times and I was there three years. The men do better. They have rehabilitation programs, Ping-Pong, carpentry, and we all get videos. Only the men get to choose the video and they always choose blue films. They have to choose them to show they're normal, and the women have to choose not to see them to show the same. You have to be normal to get out. Sister[4] in the ward fills in the report cards. She's the one who decides whether or not you're sane enough to go before the Parole Committee. The trouble is, she's not so sane herself. She's more institutionalized than the patients.

Eddie, come and join us! How was your game? You won? Better not do that too often. You don't want to be seen as an overachiever. This is Linda, I'm telling her how we met. At the clinical disco. Shall we do a little dance, just the pair of us, in the middle of everything and everyone, just to celebrate being out? No, you're right, that would be just plain mad. Eddie and I love each other, Linda, we met at the clinical disco, down Broadmoor way. Who knows, the doctor may have been wrong about me not having babies; stranger things happen. My mum ran out on my ex, leaving him to look after the baby; he came to visit me in Broadmoor once and asked me to go back to him, but I wouldn't. Sister put me back for that: A proper woman wants to go back to her

---

[4]Head nurse. — ED.

husband, even though he's her little sister's father. And after he'd gone I cried. You must never cry in Broadmoor. It means you're depressed; and that's the worst madness of all. The staff all love it in there, and think you're really crazy if you don't. I guess they get kind of offended if you cry. So it's on with the lipstick and smile, smile, smile, though everyone around you is ballooning with largactyl and barking like the dogs they think they are.

I tell you something, Linda, these places are madhouses. Never,   15 never plead the balance of your mind is disturbed in court: Get a prison sentence and relax, and wait for time to pass and one day you'll be free. Once you're in a secure hospital, you may never get out at all, and they fill the women up with so many tranquilizers, you may never be fit to. The drugs give you brain damage. But I reckon I'm all right; my hands tremble a bit, and my mouth twitches sometimes, but it's not too bad. And I'm still *me*, aren't I. Eddie's fine — they don't give men so much, sometimes none at all. Only you never know what's in the tea. But you can't be seen not drinking it, because that's paranoia.

Eddie says I should sue the barrister, with his fine talk of therapy and treatment in Broadmoor, but I reckon I won't. Once you've been in you're never safe. They can pop you back inside if you cause any trouble at all, and they're the ones who decide what trouble is. So we keep our mouths shut and our noses clean, we ex-inmates of Broadmoor.

Are you sure that man's not watching? Is there something wrong with us? Eddie? You're not wearing your earring, are you? Turn your head. No, that's all right. We look just like everyone else. Don't we? Is my lipstick smudged? Christ, I hate wearing it. It makes my eyes look small.

At the clinical disco! They hold them at Broadmoor every month. Lots of the men in there are sex offenders, rapists, mass murderers, torturers, child abusers, flashers. The staff like to see how they're getting on, how they react to the opposite sex, and on the morning of the disco Sister turns up and says "you go" and "you" and "you" and of course you can't say no, no matter how scared you are. Because you're supposed to want to dance. And the male staff gee up the men — hey, look at those titties! Wouldn't you like to look up *that* skirt — and stand by looking forward to the trouble, a bit of living porno, better than a blue film any day. And they gee up the women too: Wow, there's a handsome hunk of male; and you have to act interested, because that's normal: If they think you're a lezzie you never get out. And the men have to act interested, but not too interested. Eddie and I met at the clinical disco, acting just gently interested. Eddie felt up my titties, and I rubbed myself against him and the staff watched and all of a sudden he said "Hey, I mean really," and I said "Hi," and he said "Sorry about this, keep smiling," and I said, "Ditto, what are you in for?" and he said "I got a job as a woman teacher. Six little girls framed me. But I love teaching, not little girls. There was just no job for a man," and I believed him; nobody else ever had. And I told him about my mum and my ex, and he seemed to understand. Didn't you, Eddie! That's love, you see. Love at first sight. You're just on the other person's side, and if you can find someone else like that about you, everything falls into place. We were both out in three months. It didn't matter for once if I wore lipstick, it didn't matter to him if he had to watch blue films: You stop thinking that acting sane is driving you mad: You don't have not to cry because you stop wanting to cry: The barking and howling and screeching stop worrying you; I guess when you're in love you're just happy so they have to turn you out; because your being happy shows them up. If you're happy, what does sane or insane mean, what are their lives all about? They can't bear to see it.

Linda, it's been great meeting you. Eddie and I are off home now. I've talked too much. Sorry. When we're our side of our front door I scrub off the makeup and get into jeans and he gets into drag, and we're ourselves, and we just hope no one comes knocking on the door to say, hey that's not normal, back to Broadmoor, but I reckon love's a talisman. If we hold on to that we'll be okay.

EXPLORATIONS

1. Who is the narrator of this story? To whom is she speaking? Where does the story take place?

2. Why does the story's narrator believe she has to act normal? Who defines and enforces normality? What are the criteria?

3. What characters in "Down the Clinical Disco" behave abnormally — that is, dysfunctionally — and in what ways? What social and political institutions encourage their behavior?

CONNECTIONS

1. What parallels can you find between the experience of Fay Weldon's English narrator in Broadmoor and Grace Paley's experience in a New York prison in "Six Days: Some Rememberings" (p. 610)? What are some notable differences?

2. Compare Weldon's narrator's attitude toward incarceration — and the social system that incarcerated her — with Nelson Mandela's attitude in *Black*

Man in a White Court (p. 600). How are they alike? How are they different? Why are they different? Who is better equipped for life after being released, and why?

3. How is "Down the Clinical Disco" similar in form and theme to T. Coraghessan Boyle's "Achates McNeil" (p. 245)? To whom is the narrator of each story speaking? In what ways does each narrator's speaking style suit her or his identity?

ELABORATIONS

1. "Down the Clinical Disco" is full of institutions and individuals that fail to carry out their assigned functions. Write a comparison-contrast essay examining these contradictions — for instance, the official purpose of the clinical disco at Broadmoor versus the role it actually plays for patients and staff. What point is conveyed by these contradictions?

2. Look closely at the techniques Weldon uses to tell her story in the form of a monologue. How does she change scenes and time frames? What is the effect of the questions at the beginning of some paragraphs? What other functions are served by the invisible character, Linda? Choose an incident in your life, such as a clash with authority, and write about it in the same monologue form Weldon uses.

Liliana Heker, "The Stolen Party," from *Other Fires: Short Fiction by Latin American Women*, edited and translated by Alberto Manguel. Copyright © 1982 by Liliana Heker. Translation copyright © 1986 by Alberto Manguel. Reprinted by permission of the author and Clarkson N. Potter, a division of Crown Publishers, Inc.

Kazuo Ischiguro, "A Family Supper" (first published in *Quarter Magazine* in 1980 and then in the Penguin anthology entitled *Firebird 2* in 1982). Copyright © 1980 Kazuo Ishiguro. Reproduced by permission of the author c/o Rogers, Coleridge & White, Ltd., 20 Powis Mews, London W11 1JN.

Lisa Jones, "Grave Matters at Monticello," from *The Village Voice* (online), December 30, 1998–January 5, 1999. Copyright © V.V. Publishing Corporation. Reprinted by permission of *The Village Voice.*

Nikos Kazantzakis, "The Gentleman," from *England: A Travel Journal* by Nikos Kazantzakis. Copyright © 1965 by Simon & Schuster, Inc. Original Greek Language edition entitled ΑΓΓΛΙΑ. Copyright © renewed 1981 by Helen N. Kazantzakis. Reprinted by permission of Dr. Patroclos Stavrou, Kazantzakis Publications, Athens.

Sam Keen, "Man and WOMAN," from *Fire in the Belly* by Sam Keen. Copyright © 1991 by Sam Keen. Used by permission of Bantam Books, a division of Random House, Inc.

Yashar Kemal, "A Dirty Story," from *Anatolian Tales*. Reprinted by permission of the publisher, Collins Harvill.

Barbara Kingsolver, "Stone Soup," from *High Tide in Tucson* by Barbara Kingsolver. Copyright © 1995 by Barbara Kingsolver. Reprinted by permission of HarperCollins Publishers, Inc.

Ursula K. LeGuin, "Myth and Archetype in Science Fiction." First appeared in *Parabola I, 4*. Copyright © 1976 by Ursula K. Le Guin. Reprinted by permission of the author and the author's agent.

Sophronia Liu, "So Tsi-fai." Originally appeared in *Hurricane Alice*, Vol. 2, No. 4 (Fall 1986). Copyright © 1986 by Sophronia Liu. Reprinted by permission of the author.

Nelson Mandela, "Black Man in a White Court," from *Mandela: No Easy Walk To Freedom*. Reprinted with permission of Heinemann Publishers (Oxford), a division of Reed Educational and Professional publishing.

Frank McCourt, "Limerick Homecoming" (editor's title), excerpted with the permission of Scribner, a Division of Simon & Schuster, Inc., from *Angela's Ashes: A Memoir* by Frank McCourt. Copyright © 1996 by Frank McCourt.

Rigoberta Menchú, "Birth Ceremonies," from *I, Rigoberta Menchú: An Indian Woman in Guatemala*, edited by Elisabeth Burgos-Debray, translated by Ann Wright. Copyright © 1984 by Verso. Reprinted by permission of Verso Books.

Alberto Moravia, "The Chase" (originally titled "Una Cosa e una Cosa"), from *Command and I Will Obey* by Alberto Moravia. English translation copyright © 1967 by Gruppo Editoriale Fabbri, Bompiani, Sonzogno, Etas Spa. Reprinted by permission.

John David Morley, "Acquiring a Japanese Family," from *Pictures from the Water Trade: Adventures of a Westerner in Japan* (Boston: Atlantic Monthly Press, 1985). Copyright © 1985 by John David Morley. Reprinted by permission of the author.

Toni Morrison, excerpt from *Beloved* by Toni Morrison. Reprinted by permission of International Creative Management, Inc. Copyright © 1987 by Toni Morrison.

Ezekiel Mphahlele, "African Literature: What Tradition?" from *Voices in the Whirlwind* by Ezekiel Mphahlele. Copyright © 1976 by Ezekiel Mphahlele. Reprinted by permission of Farrar, Straus and Giroux, LLC.

Susan Orlean, "Quniceañera," from *Saturday Night* by Susan Orlean. Copyright © 1990 by Susan Orlean. Reprinted by permission of Alfred A. Knopf, Inc.

Amos Oz, "Between Word and Picture," from *The Slopes of Lebanon* by Amos Oz. Copyright © 1987 by Amos Oz and Am Oved Publishers, Ltd., Tel Aviv. English translation copyright © 1989 by Harcourt, Inc., reprinted by permission of Harcourt, Inc.

Camille Paglia, "Woman and Nature," from *Woman and Nature* by Camille Paglia. Copyright © 1990 by Yale University Press. Reprinted by permission.

Grace Paley, "Six Days: Some Rememberings," from *Best American Essays 1995*. Originally published in *Alaska Quarterly Review*. Copyright © 1973 by Harcourt Brace & Company. Reprinted by permission of the publishers.

Octavio Paz, "The Art of the Fiesta" (editor's title; excerpted from "The Day of the Dead"), from *The Labyrinth of Solitude*, translated by Lysander Kemp. Copyright © 1961 by Grove Press, Inc. Reprinted by permission of Grove/Atlantic, Inc.

Walker Percy, "A Short Quiz" (originally titled "A Preliminary Short Quiz"), from *Lost in the Cosmos: The Last Self-Help Book* by Walker Percy. Copyright © 1983 by Walker Percy. Reprinted by permission of Farrar, Straus and Giroux, LLC.

Neil Postman, "Future Schlock," from *Conscientious Objections* by Neil Postman. Copyright © 1988 by Neil Postman. Reprinted by permission of Alfred A. Knopf, Inc.

Robert Reich, "The Three Jobs of the Future," from *The Work of Nations* by Robert Reich. Copyright © 1991 by Robert Reich. Reprinted by permission of Alfred A. Knopf, Inc.

Richard Rodriguez, "Europe Once Gripped America's Imagination — Now It's the Other Way Around," from *Cronica* (online magazine) April 1998. Copyright © 1998 by Richard Rodriguez. Reprinted by permission of Georges Borchardt, Inc.

Salman Rushdie, "Imaginary Homelands," from *Imaginary Homelands* by Salman Rushdie. Copyright © 1982 by Salman Rushdie. Used by permission of Viking Penguin, a division of Penguin Putnam Inc. and Aitken, Stone & Wylie Ltd.

Elaine Salinas, "Still Grieving over the Loss of the Land," from *Messengers of the Wind*, edited by Jane Katz. Copyright © 1995 by Jane Katz. Reprinted by permission of Ballantine Books, a Division of Random House Inc.

Danzy Senna, reprint of "The Mulatto Millennium," from *Half and Half* by Claudine O'Hearn. Copyright © 1998 by Danzy Senna. Reprinted by permission of Pantheon Books, a division of Random House, Inc.

Marjorie Shostak, "Nisa's Marriage." Reprinted by permission of the publisher from *Nisa: The Life and Words of a !Kung Woman* by Marjorie Shostak. Cambridge, Mass: Harvard University Press. Copyright © 1981 by Marjorie Shostak.

Curtis Sittenfeld, "Your Life As a Girl," from *Ms. Magazine*, July/August 1993. Reprinted by permission of Ms. Magazine. Copyright © 1993 by Curtis Sittenfeld.

Wole Soyinka, "Nigerian Childhood," from *Ake: The Years of Childhood* by Wole Soyinka. Copyright © 1981 by Wole Soyinka. Reprinted by permission of Random House, Inc.

Alessandra Stanley, "The New Europeans: Multi-tlingual, Cosmopolitan, Borderless," from *The New York Times*, December 24, 1998. Copyright © 1998 by The New York Times. Reprinted by permission.

Amy Tan, "Two Kinds," from *The Joy Luck Club* by Amy Tan. Copyright © 1989 by Amy Tan. Used by permission of Putnam Berkley, a division of Penguin Putnam Inc.

Deborah Tannen, "How Male and Female Students Use Language Differently" (originally titled "Teachers' Classroom Strategies Should Recognize That Men and Women Use Language Differently"), from *The Chronicle of Higher Education*, June 19, 1991. Copyright © 1991 by Deborah Tannen. Reprinted by permission.

John Updike, "The Disposable Rocket," from *More Matters* by John Updike. Copyright © 1999 by John Updike. Reprinted by permission of Alfred A. Knopf, Inc.

Fay Weldon, "Down the Clinical Disco," from *Moon Over Minneapolis and Other Stories* by Fay Weldon. Copyright © 1991 by Fay Weldon. Used by permission of Viking Penguin, a division of Penguin Putnam Inc.

GEOGRAPHICAL INDEX

Africa

Botswana: Nisa's Marriage (Shostak), 363
Nigeria: Nigerian Childhood (Soyinka), 158; The Writer and His Community (Achebe), 489
South Africa: African Literature: What Tradition? (Mphahlele), 73; Black Man in a White Court (Mandela), 600; Where Do Whites Fit In? (Gordimer), 284

Asia

China: Yearnings (Zha), 542
Hong Kong: So Tsi-fai (Liu), 231
India: Caste Hate, and Murder, Outlast Indian Reforms (Bearak), 477; Imaginary Homelands (Rushdie), 86
Japan: Acquiring a Japanese Family (Morley), 185; A Family Supper (Ishiguro), 197
Russia: The Day After Technology (Gessen), 556

Australia

One Man's Mutilation Is Another Man's Beautification (Greer), 55

Europe

Europe Once Gripped America's Imagination—Now It's the Other Way Around (Rodriguez), 273; The New Europeans: Multilingual, Cosmopolitan, Borderless (Stanley), 277
France: The New Lost Generation (Baldwin), 263; Woman as Other (de Beauvoir), 341
Germany: Between Word and Picture (Oz), 569
Great Britain: Down the Clinical Disco (Weldon), 617; The Gentleman (Kazantzakis), 483; Imaginary Homelands (Rushdie), 86
Greece: The Gentleman (Kazantzakis), 483
Ireland: Limerick Homecoming (McCourt), 136
Italy: The Chase (Moravia), 349

RHETORICAL INDEX

The following definitions are designed to help you distinguish rhetorical strategies used by authors in this book. *Rhetorical strategies* are tactics and ways of writing that make a work more successful. Many authors use more than one strategy in a single piece. For example, an essay designed to persuade you of a particular point ("Argument and Persuasion") may also provide a series of examples ("Example and Illustration") or tell a story ("Narration") in the process of supporting that point. The rhetorical index identifies selections that rely *heavily* on each of the techniques; you will find many other pieces in the book that use the techniques more sporadically. Because fiction as well as nonfiction incorporates these strategies, short stories and essays are both listed as examples.

Analogy

An essay that relies on analogy develops its primary point through an extended metaphor or comparison. Unlike a straightforward comparison, an analogy does not necessarily link two things that are similar. Instead, it explores something that is familiar as a way of clarifying something that is less familiar, or more complex, abstract, or technical. The writer explains the association between the two and demonstrates how the information under discussion stands for or is similar to the larger, more complicated issues.

Gary Engle, "What Makes Superman So Darned American?," 428
Lisa Jones, "Grave Matters at Monticello," 168
Alberto Moravia, "The Chase," 349 (fiction)
Salman Rushdie, "Imaginary Homelands," 86

Argument and Persuasion

Argumentative essays strive to support a primary claim or thesis statement. Persuasive essays make a specific argument by attempting to convince a potentially hostile reader that a particular point of view about a given issue is correct; often, they try to change a reader's mind. A good argumentative essay considers opposing positions on the topic, provides evidence and examples to support its claims, and draws conclusions based on logical reasoning.

Joseph Bruchac, "Digging into Your Heart," 439
Esther Dyson, "Cyberspace: If You Don't Love It, Leave It," 586
Jan Goodwin, "Muslims, the First Feminists," 371
Nadine Gordimer, "Where Do Whites Fit In?," 284
Paul Harrison, "The Westernization of the World," 66

Cause and Effect

Cause-and-effect essays seek to explain why something happened, or what the consequences of its happening were, or both. They may be in the form of investigative reports, which aim to find out what caused an existing condition. Or they may require the author to suggest potential future effects of that condition. Essays arguing for changes in policies, procedures, attitudes, goals, or interpretations often present a cause-and-effect situation as evidence for why such change is necessary.

Classification

A classification essay offers a method (or schema) for organizing something specific. It outlines categories and provides definitions or descriptions of items that fit into those categories. A strong classification essay justifies why the categories it identifies are accurate and discusses examples in detail.

Comparison and Contrast

A comparison-and-contrast essay focuses on the major similarities and differences between two or more things, which may require a definition or description of these things. A sophisticated comparison-and-contrast essay not only identifies how things are alike and unalike but also articulates what is significant about these similarities and differences and draws conclusions or forwards an argument.

Margaret Atwood, "A View from Canada," 79
James Baldwin, "The New Lost Generation," 263
Simone de Beauvoir, "Woman as Other," 341
Gary Engle, "What Makes Superman So Darned American?," 428
John David Morley, "Acquiring a Japanese Family," 185
Richard Rodriguez, "Europe Once Gripped America's Imagination—Now It's the Other Way Around," 273
Salman Rushdie, "Imaginary Homelands," 86

Definition

The primary purpose of a definition essay is to clarify a specific concept. It relies on narration or example, and its main objective is to show how a term has shifted in meaning or how and why the same term can be interpreted differently. Sometimes, definition is not the entire focus of an essay but is used to support an argument that may require detailed background information.

Simone de Beauvoir, "Woman as Other," 341
Esther Dyson, "Cyberspace: If You Don't Love It, Leave It," 586
Nikos Kazantzakis, "The Gentleman," 483
Ursula K. LeGuin, "Myth and Archetype in Science Fiction," 419
Alberto Moravia, "The Chase," 349 (fiction)
Susan Orlean, "Quinceañera," 36
Neil Postman, "Future Shlock," 531
Alessandra Stanley, "The New Europeans: Multilingual, Cosmopolitan, Borderless," 277
Amy Tan, "Two Kinds," 24 (fiction)

Description

A descriptive essay provides rich details to make a point about a situation. Unlike a definition essay, it is not designed to define a concept but to explore a particular cultural moment, experience, or perspective. A descriptive essay will often answer these questions: Who? What? Why? When? Where? How?

Margaret Atwood, "A View from Canada," 79
Barry Bearak, "Caste Hate, and Murder, Outlast Indian Reforms," 477
Masha Gessen, "The Day After Technology," 556
Rigoberta Menchú, "Birth Ceremonies," 146
Susan Orlean, "Quinceañera," 36
Amos Oz, "Between Word and Picture," 569
Octavio Paz, "The Art of the Fiesta," 48
Wole Soyinka, "Nigerian Childhood," 158
Jianying Zha, "Yearnings," 542

Example and Illustration

Essays that use example and illustration spend a significant amount of time supporting their claims with evidence. Examples and illustrations may take the form of brief stories, first-hand accounts, statistics, lists, comparisons, quotations from other written works, excerpts from speeches or interviews, and descriptions of objects, places, or people. To be effective, essays that use this strategy must provide enough examples to lend credibility to their claims, while also explaining *how* and *why* those examples support their claims.

Exposition

Expository writing attempts to provide information, explain difficult concepts, or interpret and explain the meaning of events. The term *exposition* generally refers to the writing of essays as opposed to fiction or other genres. In this book, essays that rely on exposition combine elements of description and interpretation to convey information about a specific subject. The essays do not necessarily make an argument, yet they are different from descriptive essays because they also offer some evaluation of the matter under discussion.

Interview

Essays based on interviews are not always filled with quotations, even though interviewers use tape recorders and take notes as they talk with people. Authors may make generalizations based on information provided by their sources, or they may write in a narrative style, allowing the information to unfold like a story. No matter what the format, good interview-based essays clearly identify their sources and offer some way of assessing the reliability of those sources.

Irony

Essays and short stories that use irony imply one meaning by presenting an often extended portrait of its opposite. Sometimes, an explicit statement of an author's position on a matter is framed by a context that reveals that he or she actually holds a different position. Or an author may provide information that shows how characters in an essay face consequences that are opposite to those they intended by their actions. Irony should not be confused with sarcasm, which often depends on a speaker's tone of voice and is generally a brief comment such as "Nice outfit!"

Narration

Narration is story telling, and narrative essays rely on the same techniques used in fiction: character development, a carefully structured plot, and attention to details of setting. In a narrative essay, events unfold chronologically, whereas in a descriptive essay, details about a situation may be given intermittently, but a story is not created out of those details. Rather, a narrative essay uses a story to make a specific point or to support an argument.

Process Analysis

A process-analysis essay examines the process by which something occurs, breaks the process down into its component steps, and analyzes those steps. Its many purposes include improving the process or its outcomes; determining what caused the outcomes of a particular process; charting how the process has changed over time; defining the process so it can be replicated or avoided; illuminating a tradition; and discovering the relationship between a part of the process and its social or individual consequences. Process-analysis essays may cover topics in science, social science, history, culture, politics, and religion — any realm in which humans have tried to regulate the process by which something happens.

INDEX OF
AUTHORS AND TITLES

UNITED KINGDOM
OF GREAT BRITAIN
AND
NORTHERN IRELAND

IRELAND

GERMANY

FRANCE

ITALY

Mediterranean
Sea

TUNISIA

GREECE

CRETE

TURKEY

SYRIA

ISRAEL

IRAQ

IRAN

AFGHANISTAN

PAKISTAN

RUSSIA

CHINA

INDIA

EGYPT

SAUDI
ARABIA

NIGERIA

Gulf of
Guinea

ATLANTIC

OCEAN

INDIAN OCEAN

BOTSWANA

SOUTH
AFRICA

In the interest of visual clarity and simplicity, only
countries covered in this book are labeled on
the map.